Plymouth University
Charles Seale-Hayne Library
Subject to status this item may be renewed
via your Primo account

http://primo.plymouth.ac.uk
Tel: (01752) 588588

THE INTEGRITY OF CRIMINAL PROCESS

Criminal proceedings, it is often now said, ought to be conducted with integrity. But what, exactly, does it mean for criminal process to have, or to lack, 'integrity'? Is integrity in this sense merely an aspirational normative ideal, with possibly diffuse influence on conceptions of professional responsibility? Or is it also a juridical concept with robust institutional purchase and enforceable practical consequences in criminal litigation? The 16 new essays contained in this collection, written by prominent legal scholars and criminologists from Australia, Hong Kong, the UK and the USA, engage systematically with—and seek to generate further debate about—the theoretical and practical significance of 'integrity' at all stages of the criminal process. Reflecting the flexibility and scope of a putative 'integrity principle', the essays range widely over many of the most hotly contested issues in contemporary criminal justice theory, policy and practice, including: the ethics of police investigations, charging practice and discretionary enforcement; prosecutorial independence, policy and operational decision-making; plea bargaining; the perils of witness coaching and accomplice testimony; expert evidence; doctrines of admissibility and abuse of process; lay participation in criminal adjudication; the role of remorse in criminal trials; the ethics of appellate judgment writing; innocence projects; and state compensation for miscarriages of justice.

The Integrity of Criminal Process

From Theory into Practice

Edited by
Jill Hunter
Paul Roberts
Simon NM Young
and
David Dixon

·H A R T·
PUBLISHING
OXFORD AND PORTLAND, OREGON
2016

Hart Publishing
An imprint of Bloomsbury Publishing Plc

Hart Publishing Ltd
Kemp House
Chawley Park
Cumnor Hill
Oxford OX2 9PH
UK

Bloomsbury Publishing Plc
50 Bedford Square
London
WC1B 3DP
UK

www.hartpub.co.uk
www.bloomsbury.com

Published in North America (US and Canada) by
Hart Publishing
c/o International Specialized Book Services
920 NE 58th Avenue, Suite 300
Portland, OR 97213-3786
USA

www.isbs.com

**HART PUBLISHING, the Hart/Stag logo, BLOOMSBURY and the
Diana logo are trademarks of Bloomsbury Publishing Plc**

First published 2016

© The Editors

British Library Cataloguing-in-Publication Data
A catalogue record for this book is available from the British Library.

ISBN: HB: 978-1-84946-594-6
ePDF: 978-1-78225-571-0
ePub: 978-1-78225-572-7

Library of Congress Cataloging-in-Publication Data

Names: Hunter, Jill B., editor. | Roberts, Paul, 1968– editor. | Young, Simon N. M., editor. | Dixon, David,
1954 June 21– editor. | University of Hong Kong. Faculty of Law, sponsoring body. | University of New South Wales.
Faculty of Law, sponsoring body. | University of Nottingham. School of Law, sponsoring body.

Title: The integrity of criminal process : from theory into practice / edited by Jill Hunter, Paul Roberts,
Simon NM Young, and David Dixon.

Description: Oxford ; Portland, Oregon : Hart Publishing Ltd, an imprint of Bloomsbury Publishing Plc, 2016. | Includes
papers presented at linked workshops "Conduct Unbecoming: Realising Integrity in Criminal Justice" at the
University of Hong Kong Faculty of Law's Centre for Comparative and Public Law in December 2012, and "Realising
Integrity in Criminal Justice" at the University of New South Wales Faculty of Law, Sydney, in April 2013."—ECIP
Acknowledgements. | Includes bibliographical references and index.

Identifiers: LCCN 2016015043 (print) | LCCN 2016015642 (ebook) | ISBN 9781849465946
(hardback : alk. paper) | ISBN 9781782255727 (Epub)

Subjects: LCSH: Criminal justice, Administration of—Congresses.

Classification: LCC K5001.A6 I58 2016 (print) | LCC K5001.A6 (ebook) | DDC 345/.05—dc23

LC record available at https://lccn.loc.gov/2016015043

Typeset by Compuscript Ltd, Shannon
Printed and bound in Great Britain by
CPI Group (UK) Ltd, Croydon CR0 4YY

ACKNOWLEDGEMENTS

The 16 original essays and substantive, contextualising Introduction published in this volume are the latest harvest from a fruitful research collaboration between legal scholars from the universities of New South Wales, Nottingham and Hong Kong. Each essay began life as a presentation or arose from discussion at one or both of two linked workshops held in Sydney and Hong Kong. The first workshop, *Conduct Unbecoming: Realising Integrity in Criminal Justice*, was hosted by the University of Hong Kong Faculty of Law's Centre for Comparative and Public Law in December 2012. We are grateful to Sharron Fast and Flora Leung for taking care of organisational arrangements. The second workshop, *Realising Integrity in Criminal Justice*, took place at the University of New South Wales Faculty of Law, Sydney, in April 2013, where Sandra Cepeda kept proceedings running smoothly. We gratefully acknowledge generous financial and administrative support for the project from the law schools at HKU and UNSW.

Participants contributed a range of perspectives and a wealth of collective experience to the two workshops, which were structured to prioritise discussion, particularly across disciplinary and jurisdictional boundaries. Draft papers were circulated in advance so that the workshops could dispense with detailed presentations and focus on commentary, constructive criticism and debate. Two meetings allowed time for reflection and the development of ideas and arguments, and further facilitated rigorous intellectual engagement. Each written-up draft chapter was subjected to extensive editorial review and revision. This methodology was designed to produce, not only individual essays of the highest quality, but also collective coherence across the volume as a whole, with multiple points of cross-referencing and intersection around the core theme of integrity in criminal process. Readers must judge for themselves whether the result vindicates the ambition.

We want to record our sincere thanks to all of our contributors, not only for their scholarship and collegiality, but also for their patience, cooperation and diligence in rolling with the punches of the editorial process. With unfailing good humour, they have collaborated in our practical demonstration that nothing worthwhile is quick or painless.

Richard Hart was very receptive to this project from the outset, and when Hart Publishing changed hands, Bill Asquith was equally enthusiastic. We have been ably assisted by Tom Adams, Mel Hamill, Annie Mirza, Emma Platt and Rachel Turner in the book's production and marketing, and Bryony Matthews provided first-rate copyediting. We are grateful to all at Hart for their unstinting support and professionalism.

JH, Birchgrove   St Andrew's Day 2015
PR, Beeston
SNMY, Pokfulam
DD, Clovelly

CONTENTS

LIST OF CONTRIBUTORS

Susan A Bandes, Centennial Distinguished Professor, DePaul University College of Law

Peter Chau, Assistant Professor, University of Hong Kong, Faculty of Law

Nicholas Cowdery AM QC, Visiting Professorial Fellow, University of New South Wales and University of Wollongong; Adjunct Professor, University of Sydney and Charles Sturt University; formerly Director of Public Prosecutions, New South Wales

David Dixon, Dean and Professor, University of New South Wales, Faculty of Law

Gary Edmond, Professor, Director of the Expertise, Evidence & Law Program, University of New South Wales, School of Law; Research Professor (Fractional), Northumbria Law School; Visiting Professorial Fellow, University of Wollongong, School of Law

Jeremy Gans, Professor, Melbourne Law School

Carolyn Hoyle, Professor of Criminology and Director of the Centre for Criminology, University of Oxford

Jill Hunter, Professor, University of New South Wales, Faculty of Law

John Jackson, Professor of Comparative Criminal Law and Procedure, University of Nottingham

Michael I Jackson, Associate Professor, University of Hong Kong, Faculty of Law

Mike McConville, Founding Dean and Emeritus Professor, Chinese University of Hong Kong, Faculty of Law

Luke Marsh, Assistant Professor, Chinese University of Hong Kong, Faculty of Law

Paul Roberts, Professor of Criminal Jurisprudence, University of Nottingham; Adjunct Professor, University of New South Wales, Faculty of Law; Adjunct Professor of Law, China University of Political Science and Law, Beijing

Julie Stubbs, Professor, University of New South Wales, Faculty of Law

Charles D Weisselberg, Shannon Cecil Turner Professor of Law and Associate Dean, University of California, Berkeley, School of Law

Amanda Whitfort, Associate Professor, University of Hong Kong, Faculty of Law

Simon NM Young, Professor and Associate Dean (Research), University of Hong Kong, Faculty of Law

TABLE OF CASES

Australia

Canada

Court of Justice of the European Union

European Court of Human Rights

Hong Kong

Ireland (Republic of)

New Zealand

Solomon Islands

South Africa

United States of America

TABLE OF LEGISLATION

Statutory Instruments (also see Table of Codes, etc below)

Australia

Canada

Hong Kong

TABLE OF CODES, GUIDELINES AND PROFESSIONAL STANDARDS

Canada

Hong Kong

New Zealand

United States of America

International

TABLE OF INTERNATIONAL
INSTRUMENTS

Introduction: Re-examining Criminal Process Through the Lens of Integrity

PAUL ROBERTS, JILL HUNTER, SIMON NM YOUNG AND DAVID DIXON

1. Methodological Integrity

This book explores the relationship between integrity and criminal process. By 'criminal process' we mean, roughly speaking, the institutions, procedures and practices constituting official responses to suspected criminal wrongdoing, encompassing criminal investigations, prosecutions, trials, appeals and extraordinary post-conviction procedures. We do not extend our analysis to 'the penal system' and the treatment of convicted offenders, largely on pragmatic rather than theoretical grounds. The book's central thesis is that 'integrity' offers a powerful conceptual lens through which the criminal process in its entirety, or selected phases or aspects of it, can be viewed and critically re-examined. Our general approach could in principle be extended to penality[1] at large, but we had to stop somewhere to keep the volume within reasonable bounds, and adjudication marks a natural temporal break-point, distinguishing the participation of suspects, victims, witnesses and the accused in the investigative process and at trial from the treatment of convicted offenders in the penal system.[2]

This study is properly characterised as exploratory for at least two, mutually reinforcing reasons. First, as a themed collection of essays by 17 authors, each with their own theoretical preferences and perspectives, the analyses, discussions and arguments presented in the following chapters are necessarily somewhat open-ended, idiosyncratic and disputatious. More fundamentally, however, the juxtaposition between integrity and criminal process is relatively novel and unexamined. To the best of our knowledge, this is the first work to attempt anything like a systematic exploration. With this in mind, our primary objective in breaking new conceptual ground is to stimulate further discussion and critical reflection,

---

[1] Garland's handy neologism encapsulating 'the whole of the penal complex, including its laws, sanctions, institutions, and practices and its discourses, symbols, rituals, and performances'. See D Garland, 'Penality and the Penal State' (2013) 51 *Criminology* 475; D Garland, *Punishment and Modern Society* (Oxford, Clarendon Press, 1990).

[2] The natural break between criminal process and the penal system is institutionally reinforced in common law jurisdictions, inasmuch as common law courts do not supervise the imposition of punishment (beyond generic powers of judicial review applicable to all administrative exercises of public power) in the direct way that, for example, German courts do. See M Bohlander, *Principles of German Criminal Procedure* (Oxford, Hart Publishing, 2012) ch 7.

rather than purporting to supply the last word on the topic—as preposterous as that would be, given the complexity and richness of our subject-matter. The pluralistic, open-ended, productively argumentative format of an edited collection is eminently well suited to these programmatic objectives.

Our methodology is also pluralistic in a second, more theoretical sense. Surveying existing disciplinary literatures, and trying to begin without too many theoretical stipulations or preconceptions, there are many different ways and means in which one could conceivably attempt to conceptualise, analyse and debate criminal process. Some approaches are purely descriptive, empirical or more broadly factual, whilst others adopt avowedly normative, idealistic,[3] moral or political perspectives. Many accounts blend descriptive and normative elements with varying levels of clarity and illumination (not all of them are optimally explicit about which element of their account is which). Criminal process is often conceptualised holistically in terms of one or more comprehensive 'models'. Herbert Packer's 'due process' and 'crime control' dyad is perhaps the most celebrated and influential process model in the Anglo-American literature,[4] but there are many other alternatives and variations.[5] Process modelling is continuously updated to accommodate significant developments in criminal justice policy and practice, as we see, for example, in the fairly recent emergence of a 'human rights model' of criminal process—a conceptualisation that would never have occurred to criminal law theorists of Packer's vintage. Comparative perspectives introduce further layers of complexity and sophistication in conceptual modelling. In substantive law (including criminal law), comparative lawyers routinely distinguish 'common law' from civilian or Romanist jurisprudence, concepts and approaches, treating jurisdiction and institutional history as their touchstones.[6] In criminal procedure, the more familiar contrast is between 'adversarial' and 'inquisitorial' systems.[7] Each of these primary comparative vectors can be manipulated and worked up into more sophisticated theories, for example by populating the globe with multiple 'families of law'[8] or by combining

---

[3] See RA Duff, 'Retributive Punishment—Ideals and Actualities' (1991) 25 *Israel Law Review* 422.

[4] HL Packer, 'Two Models of the Criminal Process' (1964) 113 *University of Pennsylvania Law Review* 1; HL Packer, *The Limits of the Criminal Sanction* (Palo Alto CA, Stanford University Press, 1969).

[5] Prominently including MR Damaška, *The Faces of Justice and State Authority* (New Haven CT, Yale University Press, 1986). See further, P Roberts, 'Faces of Justice Adrift? Damaška's Comparative Method and the Future of Common Law Evidence' in J Jackson, M Langer and P Tillers (eds), *Crime, Procedure and Evidence in a Comparative and International Context* (Oxford, Hart Publishing, 2008); A Ashworth and M Redmayne, *The Criminal Process*, 4th edn (Oxford, Oxford University Press, 2010) chs 1–3; A Sanders, R Young and M Burton, *Criminal Justice*, 4th edn (Oxford, Oxford University Press, 2010) ch 1; N Lacey, 'Making Sense of Criminal Justice' in N Lacey (ed), *A Reader on Criminal Justice* (Oxford, Oxford University Press, 1994).

[6] LE Chiesa, 'Comparative Criminal Law' in MD Dubber and T Hörnle (eds), *The Oxford Handbook of Criminal Law* (Oxford, Oxford University Press, 2014).

[7] M Langer, 'The Long Shadow of the Adversarial and Inquisitorial Categories' in Dubber and Hörnle, ibid; S Field, 'Fair Trials and Procedural Traditions in Europe' (2009) 29 *Oxford Journal of Legal Studies* 365; J McEwan, 'Ritual, Fairness and Truth: The Adversarial and Inquisitorial Models of Criminal Trial' in A Duff, L Farmer, S Marshall and V Tadros (eds), *The Trial on Trial Volume I: Truth and Due Process* (Oxford, Hart Publishing, 2004). For imaginative metaphorical extensions, see E Grande, 'Dances of Criminal Justice: Thoughts on Systemic Differences and the Search for the Truth'; and R Lempert, 'Anglo-American and Continental Systems: Marsupials and Mammals of the Law', both in Jackson et al (eds), above n 5; WT Pizzi, 'Soccer, Football and Trial Systems' (1995) 1 *Columbia Journal of European Law* 369.

[8] HP Glenn, 'Comparative Legal Families and Comparative Legal Traditions' in M Reimann and R Zimmermann (eds), *The Oxford Handbook of Comparative Law* (Oxford, Oxford University Press, 2006); K Zweigert and H Kötz, *An Introduction to Comparative Law*, 3rd edn, T Weir trans (Oxford, Oxford University Press, 1998) Part I.

adversarial and inquisitorial elements with other political, socio-economic or cultural factors into a galaxy of procedural hybrids.[9] The advent of international criminal proceedings and the pervasive contemporary influences of globalisation and legal cosmopolitanism on domestic criminal proceedings present further challenges, and opportunities for insight, in theoretical modelling.

Many of these models of criminal process have demonstrated their heuristic value through longevity and myriad insightful applications, and most of them have *something* interesting to say about some aspect of criminal process, be it ever so local and temporally circumscribed. Models, to some extent, come in and go out of fashion with the times. Crucially, there is no reason to think that any single model must enjoy a unique or exclusive claim to wisdom and insight. Indeed, most—if not all—of the familiar models of criminal process tend to emphasise certain features of interest whilst downplaying or ignoring, and thus potentially obscuring, other significant features of criminal proceedings. For example, it might simultaneously be true (for any specified criminal justice process) that police stop and search is discriminatory as a practice *and* that defendants generally receive fair trials irrespective of ethnicity; or again, that criminal process is systematically class-biased *and* that working-class offenders generally receive their just deserts. To build up a lifelike portrait of this complex reality, in all its light and shade, will almost certainly require a range of theoretical models and methodological techniques rather than a single reductive pen-and-ink sketch.

It is in this methodologically pluralistic spirit that this book promotes 'integrity' as a timely, significant and powerfully illuminating, but as yet still largely untapped, conceptual resource for investigating and evaluating criminal process. The timeliness of 'integrity' derives from its increasing popularity with police, prosecution agencies, regulatory bodies and common law courts; and this institutional anchorage underscores its significance. 'Integrity' is not merely a scholar's or external critic's explanatory concept: it is also embedded in practitioners' discourses and has jurisprudential significance in positive law. Finally, the power of illumination we ascribe to 'integrity' is attributable to a combination of its resonance with extant legal categories and prevailing practices and its potential contributions to normative projects of critical jurisprudence and law reform. Integrity, in short, contributes an additional high-powered lens to the existing kaleidoscope of theoretical perspectives on criminal process.

The following chapters supply the proof of the pudding for this sweeping theoretical claim (or less ambitiously, will test our primary methodological hypothesis), by reconsidering afresh perennial topics and issues in the light of criminal process integrity. The essays are loosely organised according to the sequential logic of common law criminal

---

[9] See eg J Jackson and S Summers, *The Internationalisation of Criminal Evidence* (Cambridge, Cambridge University Press, 2012); JJ Capowski, 'China's Evidentiary and Procedural Reforms, the Federal Rules of Evidence, and the Harmonization of Civil and Common Law' (2012) 47 *Texas International Law Journal* 455; B Yin and P Duff, 'Criminal Procedure in Contemporary China: Socialist, Civilian or Traditional?' (2010) 59 *International and Comparative Law Quarterly* 1099; P Roberts, 'Comparative Criminal Justice Goes Global' (2008) 28 *Oxford Journal of Legal Studies* 369; M Delmas-Marty, 'Reflections on the "Hybridisation" of Criminal Procedure' in Jackson et al (eds), above n 5; JD Jackson, 'The Effect of Human Rights on Criminal Evidentiary Processes: Towards Convergence, Divergence or Realignment?' (2005) 68 *Modern Law Review* 737; M McConville and C Mirsky, 'Guilty Plea Courts: A Social Disciplinary Model of Criminal Justice' (1995) 42 *Social Problems* 216; M King, *The Framework of Criminal Justice* (London, Croom Helm, 1981) ch 2.

proceedings, starting with the initial phases of criminal investigation, interrogation of suspects and charging practice, prosecutorial discretion, pre-trial case preparation (including interviewing witnesses and instructing experts), plea-bargaining, trial procedure and evidence, verdict and judgment, and concluding with appeals and post-conviction remedies for miscarriages of justice. But the progression of ideas in the following pages is not entirely linear or confined within an (idealised) structural model of criminal process. Different strands of the theme of integrity are woven throughout each chapter's topical discussion, building up into a series of thematically related case studies in the integrity of criminal process. In bringing together discussions of Australian, British, Hong Kong and US criminal process, this volume should also be regarded as an extension of previous work and a further exemplar of 'common law comparativism'.[10]

The tasks for this Introduction are, first, to supply a little more institutional context through a potted survey of recent 'integrity jurisprudence', and secondly, to offer, by way of initial orientation for explorers of unfamiliar territory, a working conceptual elucidation and taxonomy of integrity in criminal process, emphasising its dual character as (explanatory) theoretical heuristic and (normative) juristic ideal.

2. Integrity Jurisprudence

Integrity is not an entirely novel jurisprudential concept. Numerous nineteenth-century English cases invoke 'integrity' in relation to personal or professional honesty,[11] good character[12] or witness credibility.[13] Intriguingly, one also finds early reported references to the 'justice and integrity' of courts and judges,[14] the integrity of schemes of criminal penalties,[15] and 'principles which do form part of the law, and which it is of the highest importance to maintain in their integrity'.[16] References to 'integrity' in primary English legislation can be traced back, at least, to 1843.[17] Further afield, judicial references to the integrity of legal proceedings appear as early as 1825 in Tasmania, within two decades of the founding of the grim Hobart penal colony. A little later we find a circuit judge extolling the importance of 'integrity' to jurymen at Bathurst Circuit Court, west of the Sydney penal colony.[18] Nonetheless, integrity-talk appears to have increased dramatically in recent

---

[10] P Roberts and J Hunter (eds), *Criminal Evidence and Human Rights* (Oxford, Hart Publishing, 2012).

[11] For example, *Hunter v Walters* (1870) LR 11 Eq 292, 293 ('Ralph Walters was a person in whose integrity the highest confidence was placed by his clients'); *Speight v Gaunt* (1883) 9 AC 1, 6 (HL) ('The respondent had no reason to distrust either the professional capacity, or the solvency, or the integrity of Richard Ernest Cooke').

[12] For example, *Guardians of Halifax Union v Wheelwright* (1875) LR 10 Ex 183, 193 ('A confidence might be well placed in the integrity and character of some persons, which would not belong to *any* person entrusted with money').

[13] For example, *Wright v Sanderson* (1884) 9 PD 149, 156 (CA) ('In the present case (as in others of the same kind) there is neither any suspicion of fraud nor any ground for calling in question the integrity of the witnesses').

[14] *R v Almon* (1765) Wilm 243, 256–57; 97 ER 94, 100; cited by Wills J in *R v Davies* [1906] 1 KB 32, 40 (DC).

[15] *Jenks v Turpin* (1884) 13 QBD 505, 521 (DC).

[16] *R v Cox and Railton* (1884) 14 QBD 153, 166 (CCR) (Grove J).

[17] Public Notaries Act 1843, s 4 (concerning 'testimonials, certificates, or proofs as to the character, integrity, ability, and competency of any person who shall hereafter apply for admission or re-admission as a public notary').

[18] *Speech to Jury (2)* [1841] NSWSupC 94; *R v Davidson* [1841] NSWSupC 43. And see *In re Tyler; R v Rossi* [1829] NSWSupC 25, (1828) NSW Sel Cas (Dowling) 568.

years, both in volume and significance. It is striking, for example, that whereas Winfield's two 1921 volumes on abuse of legal procedure contained just one incidental mention of 'integrity',[19] Andrew Choo's contemporary reconsideration of the topic founds the courts' inherent jurisdiction to stay criminal proceedings for abuse of process on a 'principle of legitimacy' cashed out in terms of 'protecting the moral integrity of the adjudicative process'.[20] Integrity's burgeoning jurisprudential significance is amply confirmed by rough quantitative snapshots from basic Westlaw searches.[21] These data indicate that juridical discourses of integrity, at least in English and UK jurisprudence, are a predominantly late twentieth-century phenomenon, displaying exponential increases since about 1980.

There is both more, and less, than semantics in the current popularity of juridical integrity. To some extent, 'integrity' might be invoked as a proxy, synonym or placeholder for other, familiar procedural values such as 'fairness', 'due process', 'natural justice' or 'judicial legitimacy', the relative prominence of which has varied over time and between jurisdictions, partly—of course—as a reflection of the locally applicable doctrinal law. *Pace* Bentham's dogmatic insistence on factual rectitude, modern courts have always known that, '[t]ruth, like all other good things, may be loved unwisely—may be pursued too keenly—may cost too much',[22] so that trade-offs must be made in adjudication between truth-finding and other normative considerations. One might say, adopting a broad view, that the judicial concern with procedural integrity begins with such trade-offs, whether or not the explicit terminology of 'integrity' is employed. Judicial decisions to admit, or exclude, improperly obtained evidence are one familiar context in which zero-sum conflicts between procedural values routinely arise in criminal trials. Despite some widely cited dicta extolling procedural fairness,[23] English law during the twentieth century was largely characterised by a preference for admissibility over 'integrity'-inspired exclusion whenever evidential reliability could reasonably be assumed. (This also accounts for the partial exception of confession evidence, which could be excluded at common law when admissions were 'involuntary' and thus presumptively unreliable.)[24] Courts in Scotland,[25] the Republic of Ireland,[26]

---

[19] PH Winfield, *History of Conspiracy and Abuse of Legal Procedures* (Cambridge, Cambridge University Press, 1921) 171 (noting that if the practice of parties paying jurors were to become a 'common occurrence ... it would have an evil effect on the integrity of jurors in general').

[20] AL-T Choo, *Abuse of Process and Judicial Stays of Criminal Proceedings*, 2nd edn (Oxford, Oxford University Press, 2008) 16. Also see P Roberts and A Zuckerman, *Criminal Evidence*, 2nd edn (Oxford, Oxford University Press, 2010) 22.

[21] A free-text word search for 'integrity' of the entire Westlaw UK database conducted on 8 January 2015 produced 8,655 'hits' for case law and another 1,097 for legislation. A total of 2,508 of these hits are categorised as relating to Criminal Law. Restricting the search parameters to pre-1 January 2000 mentions reduces the corresponding hits to 2,802 (case law), 269 (legislation) and 436 (crime). For the period up to 1 January 1980, hits further decrease to 1,400 (case law), 24 (legislation) and 122 (crime). For the entire century 1850–1950, the corresponding hits are 621 (case law), 2 (legislation) and 49 (crime); which is significantly fewer in all categories than for *the last two years* 1 January 2013 to 1 January 2015 (case law = 966; legislation = 251; crime = 341).

[22] *Pearse v Pearse* (1846) 1 De G & Sm 12, 28–29; 63 ER 950, 957.

[23] Notably including *R v Christie* [1914] AC 545 (HL); *Kuruma v R* [1955] AC 197, 204 (PC) (Lord Goddard CJ); and *R v Sang* [1980] AC 402 (HL).

[24] *Ibrahim v R* [1914] AC 599, 609–10 (PC); P Mirfield, *Confessions* (London, Sweet & Maxwell, 1985).

[25] *Lawrie v Muir* 1950 SLT 37; critically contextualised by P Duff, 'Irregularly Obtained Real Evidence: The Scottish Solution?' (2004) 8 *International Journal of Evidence and Proof* 77.

[26] *People v O'Brien* [1965] IR 142. Generally, see J Jackson, 'Human Rights, Constitutional Law and Exclusionary Safeguards in Ireland' in Roberts and Hunter (eds), above n 10.

Australia,[27] Canada[28] and the US federal jurisdiction[29] have arguably been more receptive than English judges to arguments for rights- or values-based evidentiary exclusion, at least until recently. Differences in these broader institutional frameworks will necessarily condition the extent to which any linguistic turn to 'integrity' represents a substantial shift in judicial attitudes and criminal procedure law, rather than merely a change of nomenclature, in particular jurisdictions.

Even more closely than its natural affinity with evidentiary exclusion, judicial integrity-talk is bound up with permanent stays of proceedings on the grounds of abuse of process. Although a tribunal's inherent jurisdiction to control abuses of its own process is a generic power, deriving from the core idea of a judicial proceeding under the rule of law,[30] its development within common law *criminal* process has been particularly striking over the last several decades. In a 1991 forced rendition case, the South African Court of Appeal intervened to prevent an abuse of process 'so as to protect and promote the dignity and integrity of the judicial system'.[31] This judgment was cited by Lord Bridge several years later in what has become a leading authority on granting stays for abuse of process in several common law jurisdictions, *R v Horseferry Road Magistrates Court, ex parte Bennett*.[32] Albeit without propounding the concept of 'integrity' per se, *Bennett* famously declared that serious procedural irregularities might require legal proceedings to be stayed irrespective of their substantive merits, on the principled basis that 'the judiciary accept a responsibility for the maintenance of the rule of law that embraces a willingness to oversee executive action and to refuse to countenance behaviour that threatens either basic human rights or the rule of law'.[33] Two and half years later, Lord Steyn explicitly adopted the language of 'integrity' in considering the impact of alleged police entrapment on procedural propriety. '[T]he issue', his Lordship stated, 'is whether, despite the fact that a fair trial was possible, the judge ought to have stayed the criminal proceedings on broader considerations of the integrity of the criminal justice system'.[34]

---

[27]   *R v Ireland* (1970) 126 CLR 321, 335; [1970] HCA 21 (Barwick CJ); *Driscoll v R* [1977] HCA 43; (1977) 137 CLR 517 (exclusion of a disputed unsigned confession); *Bunning v Cross* (1978) 141 CLR 54; [1978] HCA 22, [29] (Stephen and Aickin JJ). The common law was subsequently superseded by the Australian uniform Evidence Acts, s 138; see K Mellifont, *Fruit of the Poisoned Tree: Evidence Derived from Illegally or Improperly Obtained Evidence* (Annandale NSW, Federation Press, 2010).

[28]   *Collins v R* [2007] 1 SCR 350, (1987) 38 DLR (4th) 508, applying s 24(2) of the Constitution Act 1982. The Canadian Supreme Court subsequently disavowed *Collins*, holding that '[t]he phrase "bring the administration of justice into disrepute" must be understood in the long-term sense of maintaining the integrity of, and public confidence in, the justice system': *R v Grant* [2009] 2 SCR 353, [68]. See further, Young, Chapter 1 in this volume.

[29]   *Weeks v US*, 232 US 383 (1914); *Mapp v Ohio*, 367 US 643 (1961). The scope, and even the very existence, of the constitutional exclusionary rule have remained controversial in the USA. For a range of views, see eg RM Bloom and DH Fentin, '"A More Majestic Conception": The Importance of Judicial Integrity in Preserving the Exclusionary Rule' (2010) 13 *University of Pennsylvania Journal of Constitutional Law* 47; TE Pettys, 'The Immoral Application of Exclusionary Rules' [2008] *Wisconsin Law Review* 463; G Calabresi, 'The Exclusionary Rule' (2003) 26 *Harvard Journal of Law and Public Policy* 111.

[30]   *Connelly v DPP* [1964] AC 1254 (HL); *Mills v Cooper* [1967] 2 QB 459, 467 (DC).

[31]   *S v Ebrahim* 1991 (2) SA 553, 582 (CA).

[32]   *R v Horseferry Road Magistrates' Court, ex parte Bennett* [1994] 1 AC 42 (HL).

[33]   Ibid 62 (Lord Griffiths). Cf Lord Oliver's reassertion, in dissent, of the traditional view that pre-trial abuses, 'whatever the degree of outrage or affront they may occasion', should be addressed through collateral civil or criminal law remedies rather than being 'thought to justify the assumption by a criminal court of a jurisdiction to terminate a properly instituted criminal process which it is its duty to try': ibid 73.

[34]   *R v Latif* [1996] 2 Cr App R 92, 101 (HL).

Since these pioneering decisions of the mid 1990s judicial references to 'the integrity' of the criminal process have become commonplace. English appellate courts were soon expatiating on 'the integrity of police operations and public confidence in them';[35] 'the integrity of police evidence';[36] 'the integrity of the discovery process';[37] 'the integrity of an individual juror, and thus of the jury as a whole';[38] and 'confidence in the integrity of the sentencing or tariff-fixing process'.[39] In the unreported but publicly high-profile appeals in *R v Hickey* (1997)—the case popularly known as the 'Bridgewater Four'—Roch LJ declared that 'the integrity of the criminal process is the most important consideration for courts which have to hear appeals against conviction'.[40] More recent case law is peppered with generalised references to 'the integrity of the trial process',[41] 'the integrity of the adminis-tration of justice',[42] 'the integrity of the criminal trial',[43] and 'the integrity of the criminal justice system'.[44] Integrity-talk likewise features in judgments of the Scottish High Court of Justiciary[45] and the Northern Ireland Court of Appeal.[46] In *Warren*, a case in which the police had employed tracking and listening devices without first obtaining the necessary permissions for their use outside the jurisdiction, the Privy Council endorsed Choo's 'useful summary' of relevant jurisprudential principles, making the definitive issue 'whether the continuation of the proceedings would compromise the moral integrity of the criminal justice system to an unacceptable degree'.[47] Lord Kerr emphasised that '[t]he focus should always be on whether the stay is required in order to safeguard the integrity of the criminal justice system'.[48] In *Maxwell*,[49] where the question before the courts was whether, follow-ing a successful appeal against conviction, a retrial could properly proceed in the light of revelations of serious misconduct and criminality by investigating officers, the UK Supreme Court mentions 'integrity' no fewer than 21 times. By a narrow three to two majority, the prosecution was allowed to proceed, but only on the basis of untainted evidence. Dissent-ing on the facts, Lord Collins stated emphatically that 'the interests of justice demand the application of the integrity principle'.[50]

Increasing judicial resort to the language of 'integrity' can also be observed across the wider Commonwealth. An early Canadian example is *Rothman*,[51] where Justice Estey,

---

[35] *R v Donald* [1997] 2 Cr App R (S) 272, 275 (CA).

[36] *R v Edwards (Maxine)* [1996] 2 Cr App R 345, 349 (CA).

[37] *Taylor v Serious Fraud Office* [1998] EMLR 463, 478 (CA).

[38] *R v Comerford* [1998] 1 WLR 191, 195. Also see *R v Thorpe* [1996] 1 Cr App R 269 (CA).

[39] *R v Home Secretary ex parte Hindley* [1998] QB 751, 770 (DC).

[40] Quoted approvingly in *R v Davis (Michael George)* [2001] 1 Cr App R 8, [53] (CA).

[41] *R v Farooqi* [2014] 1 Cr App R 8, [2013] EWCA Crim 1649, [102]; *R v Connors* [2013] EWCA Crim 368, [33].

[42] *R v C* [2014] EWCA Crim 343, [6].

[43] *In re ITN* [2014] 1 WLR 199, [2013] EWCA Crim 773, [10].

[44] *R v Clayton* [2014] 1 WLR 3994, [2014] EWCA Crim 103, [10].

[45] For example, *Barclay v Richardson* [2012] HCHAC 168 (integrity of investigations and prosecutions); *Toal v HM Advocate* [2012] HCJAC 123 (integrity of a jury's verdict); *Telford v HM Advocate* [2012] HCJAC 88 (integrity of the court); *Starrs v Ruxton* 2000 JC 208, [2000] HRLR 191.

[46] For example, *R v McConville* [2014] NICA 41; *R v McKeown* [2004] NICA 41.

[47] *Warren v A-G for Jersey* [2012] 1 AC 22, [2011] UKPC 10, [24]–[25]. Lord Dyson added that 'an infinite variety of cases can arise and how the discretion should be exercised will depend on the particular circumstances of the case'.

[48] Ibid [83].

[49] *R v Maxwell* [2011] 1 WLR 1837, [2010] UKSC 48.

[50] Ibid [115].

[51] *R v Rothman* [1981] 1 SCR 640.

in dissent, linked the concept of integrity to the common law evidentiary rule excluding involuntary confessions from criminal trials. The 'basic reason for the rule', Justice Estey asserted, 'is a concern for the integrity of the criminal justice system', considering that the 'support and respect of the community for that system can only be maintained if persons in authority conduct themselves in a way that does not bring the administration of justice into disrepute'.[52] Since *Rothman*, integrity has been expansively woven into the Supreme Court of Canada's jurisprudence on constitutional rights and freedoms. It is now settled Canadian law that prosecutorial discretion can be reviewed where state officials' conduct is 'egregious and seriously compromises trial fairness and/or the integrity of the justice system'.[53] Recent cases expressly link 'the integrity' of criminal proceedings to, for example, access to pre-trial custodial legal advice,[54] the special responsibilities of prosecuting Crown Attorneys as 'ministers of justice',[55] procedural rules governing witness testimony,[56] the evils of jury tampering,[57] and the finality of adjudication.[58] The Supreme Court of Canada has stated that '[t]he integrity of our legal system depends in large measure on the integrity of those charged with its administration and enforcement'.[59] It has also—not unproblematically[60]— opined that '[t]he decision to exclude evidence always represents a balance between the interests of truth on one side and the integrity of the judicial system on the other'.[61]

References to integrity in the jurisprudence of the High Court of Australia follow a similar pattern and trajectory, with dissenting judgments playing a pioneering role. In a 1979 case in which the trial court had refused to grant an adjournment to an unrepresented defendant, Justice Murphy was a lone voice in finding a substantial miscarriage of justice, on the basis that '[c]ourts should not allow the integrity of the judicial process to be undermined by the financial exigencies of legal aid schemes'.[62] In another dissent in *Lowe* a few years later, Justice Mason warned that 'inconsistency in punishment, because it is regarded as a badge of unfairness and unequal treatment under the law, is calculated to lead to an erosion of public confidence in the integrity of the administration of justice'.[63] Later, the integrity motif begins to surface and play a more significant role in majority opinions, doubtless reinforced by the courts' parallel development of a fair trial jurisprudence rooted

---

[52] Ibid 658.

[53] *R v Anderson* [2014] 2 SCR 167, [50]; *R v Nixon* [2011] 2 SCR 566, [38], [64].

[54] *R v Sinclair* [2010] 2 SCR 310, [167]: '[I]t is also in society's interest that constitutional rights be respected at the pre-trial stage, as doing so ensures the integrity of the criminal process from start to finish'. See further, C Boyle and E Cunliffe, 'Right to Counsel During Custodial Interrogation in Canada: Not Keeping Up with the Common Law Joneses' in Roberts and Hunter (eds), above n 10.

[55] *R v Regan* [2002] 1 SCR 297, [151]: 'It is clear that Crown Attorneys perform an essential "Minister of Justice" role at all stages of their work. Their role in considering or carrying forward a prosecution is of the highest importance for the integrity of our criminal justice system …'

[56] *R v NS* [2012] 3 SCR 726, [78].

[57] *R v Yumnu* [2012] 3 SCR 777, [38]: 'The mere thought of the Crown and the police "checking out" potential jurors carries with it the spectre of jury tampering and the evils associated with it. Care must be taken to guard against this. The integrity of our criminal justice system hangs in the balance.'

[58] *R v Sipos* [2014] SCC 47, [30]; *R v Hay* [2013] 3 SCR 394 [64] ('finality and order—values essential to the integrity of the criminal process').

[59] *R v Beaudry* [2007] 1 SCR 190, [113].

[60] Because institutional integrity and truth-finding are not *necessarily* opposed.

[61] *R v Buhay* [2003] 1 SCR 631, [73].

[62] *R v McInnis* (1979) 143 CLR 575, [26].

[63] *Lowe v R* (1984) 154 CLR 606, 611–12.

in normative principles.[64] For example, in *Moti*, where the majority found that the defendant's illegal deportation to Australia amounted to an abuse of process, the court emphasised 'the trust reposed constitutionally in the courts to protect the integrity and fairness of their processes'.[65] In *Smith v Western Australia*, the High Court recently averred that 'the first duty of the courts [is] to preserve the integrity of the system of criminal justice which they administer'. Serious allegations of juror misconduct were matters of prime judicial responsibility, because '[t]he institutional integrity of the system of justice is at stake in a way that is not the case where the issue is solely one between the parties'.[66]

Similar references to the integrity of criminal process also feature in the jurisprudence of the New Zealand Supreme Court, which was established in 2004. In *Hansen*, for example, that Court observed that 'the presumption of innocence helps command the confidence of the general public in the integrity of the administration of the criminal law'.[67] More recently, in *Siemer v Solicitor-General*,[68] the New Zealand Supreme Court noted the conceptual and normative connections between institutional integrity and the (human) right to a fair trial, whilst in *Wilson*[69] the Court was confronted with a catalogue of police impropriety (a falsely sworn search warrant, followed by a bogus prosecution and an attempt to implicate the Chief Judge of the District Court in an elaborate police ruse) which, the appellant submitted, would 'undermine the integrity of the justice system'[70] unless the proceedings were stayed. Although the appellant's convictions were quashed without any order for a re-trial, only Elias CJ concluded that the 'irremediably tainted' proceedings should have been stayed[71]—an indication of the malleability and indeterminacy of appeals to 'integrity', which is another of this book's recurring themes.

Hong Kong courts have been debating similar issues in recent years, and likewise employing integrity-based arguments and concepts. In relation to the discretionary exclusion of unconstitutionally obtained evidence, the Hong Kong courts are charged with 'ensuring that the integrity of the judicial system is not compromised'.[72] In an earlier case, the Hong Kong Court of Final Appeal noted the legitimate 'public expectation that persons charged

---

[64] See eg *Dietrich v R* (1992) 177 CLR 292. Gaudron J, for example, affirmed that '[t]he requirement of fairness is not only independent, it is intrinsic and inherent ... Thus, every judge in every criminal trial has all powers necessary or expedient to prevent unfairness in the trial': ibid 363–64.

[65] *R v Moti* (2011) 245 CLR 456, [57].

[66] *Smith v Western Australia* [2014] HCA 3; (2014) 250 CLR 473, [45], [52]. See J Spigelman, 'Institutional Integrity and Public Law: An Address to the Judges of Hong Kong' (2014) 44 *Hong Kong Law Journal* 779.

[67] *R v Hansen* [2007] NZSC 7, [2007] 3 NZLR 1, [198].

[68] *Siemer v Solicitor-General* [2013] NZSC 68, [156]: 'The right to a fair trial is not only a fundamental right of an individual facing criminal proceedings; it is also essential to the administration of criminal justice and the integrity of the courts'.

[69] *Wilson v R* [2015] NZSC 189.

[70] Ibid [3]. Proceedings against the appellant's co-accused had already been stayed, on a finding by the trial judge that 'what the police did here is a fundamental and serious abuse of the court's processes': ibid [140]. These rulings were not challenged on appeal.

[71] 'The present case does not give rise to concern about fair trial. Rather, it is one where it is said that to hold a trial at all would be an affront to justice because the process is irremediably tainted by the undercover police operation which led to the charges. ... The salutary jurisdiction to stay proceedings is properly deployed only when the integrity of the criminal justice system would be compromised. ... What happened was inconsistent with minimum standards of criminal justice. To allow the trial to continue before a tribunal compromised in this way is a serious affront to the criminal justice system which required the exceptional course [of granting a stay]': ibid [124], [128], [153] (Elias CJ, concurring on disposal but dissenting in part from the majority's reasoning).

[72] *HKSAR v Muhammad Riaz Khan* (2012) 15 HKCFAR 232, [18].

with serious criminal offences will be brought to trial', but immediately added that, '[o]n the other hand, the Court must have regard to preserving the integrity of the criminal justice system'.[73]

We do not purport to offer a comprehensive or systematic survey of increasing judicial resort to the concept of integrity in recent decades across the common law world. A great deal more might conceivably be said concerning ostensible patterns of usage and significance, their geographical spread, cross-jurisdictional influences, and noteworthy fluctuations—including shortfalls—in the currency of integrity. In Chapter 1 of this volume, Simon Young extends this preliminary exposition of integrity jurisprudence, drawing out its broader constitutional implications and significance for human rights, accountability, legitimacy and public confidence in the administration of criminal justice. Many further examples and illustrations of juridical integrity will be encountered in the following pages, embedded within contributors' discussions of particular criminal process issues, debates and developments. For now, by way of introduction, it is enough to have demonstrated that 'integrity jurisprudence' is a real, trans-jurisdictional phenomenon, which evidently merits careful scholarly scrutiny and critical evaluation.

3. Juridical Integrity

Further discussion might profitably begin with some semantic and conceptual clarification. The *Oxford English Dictionary*[74] defines 'integrity' as, '[t]he condition of having no part or element taken away or wanting; undivided or unbroken state; material wholeness, completeness, entirety … The condition of not being marred or violated; unimpaired or uncorrupted condition; original perfect state; soundness'. And specifically in relation to moral integrity, '[s]oundness of moral principle; the character of uncorrupted virtue, esp. in relation to truth and fair dealing; uprightness, honesty, sincerity'. Its Latin etymology anchors the concept of integrity in that which is whole and wholesome, unsullied, pristine.

As a normative value, integrity conveys the impression of being almost unequivocally laudable, right and good. Whereas most virtues (Aristotle taught us)[75] tend to become vices when practised to excess, it is difficult to see how somebody could have *too much* integrity. Of course, there can always be competing considerations of prudence (think of Thomas More having too much integrity for his own—self-interested—good) or competing values potentially outweighing integrity in particular contexts, in the way that justice ought sometimes to be tempered by mercy.[76] But it is not easy to think of obvious analogues for integrity of, say, over-generosity or foolish bravery or brutal honesty, where the tipping point

---

[73] *HKSAR v Lee Ming Tee* (2003) 6 HKCFAR 336, [187]. For detailed discussion, see Whitfort, Chapter 10 in this volume.

[74] (Oxford, Oxford University Press, 2015), www.oed.com/.

[75] 'Virtue … is a mean between two vices, that which depends on excess and that which depends on defect … the vices respectively fall short of or exceed what is right in both passions and actions': Aristotle, *The Nicomachean Ethics*, trans D Ross (Oxford, Oxford University Press, 1998) 39.

[76] See eg JG Murphy, *Getting Even: Forgiveness and its Limits* (New York, Oxford University Press, 2005); EL Muller, 'The Virtue of Mercy in Criminal Sentencing' (1993) 24 *Seton Hall Law Review* 288.

to excess is internal to the value itself. (Fanatical integrity, perhaps?) Integrity is linked to authenticity, reliability, constancy, fair dealing and sound judgement. A person of integrity treats others in accordance with her deepest enduring convictions about how people ought to be treated; she is true to her values and true to herself. The sycophant and the gadfly as much as the hypocrite lack integrity. A person of integrity may be vulnerable to certain kinds of suasion or blackmail, but she is not easily corruptible. To say that everybody can be coerced or bullied if you can locate and exploit their human weaknesses is not the same as saying that 'every man has his price'.

It may be possible to characterise moral rigidity as an excess of integrity, as where 'the man of principle' is actually an insufferable holier-than-thou prig. That might be a fair criticism of those who ostentatiously stand on their honour and seek to inflate every contestable issue into a matter of principle. But it is not obvious why such a character flaw or its associated lapses of judgement should be regarded as symptoms of too much, rather than betraying too little, integrity. To be sure, to err is human, and to make a mistake—including a mistake about the requirements of morality—is not per se to lack integrity. But a prig is not merely in error. Utilitarians have been known to dismiss moral integrity as a kind of narcissistic vanity elevating personal conscience over the dictates of collective morality, but this objection arises from a thoroughgoing agent-neutrality with disturbing normative implications which few but card-carrying utilitarians are prepared to countenance.[77]

Part of the particular appeal of integrity is attributable to what might be described as its essentially 'procedural' character. Integrity can be distinguished from 'substantive' virtues like generosity, loyalty, honesty, or bravery, inasmuch as integrity is concerned with the way in which we relate to, think about, schedule, prioritise, and act on and through our other (substantive) values, whatever they happen to be. It follows that a person of integrity is not necessarily a good person. Bigots and brutal dictators are not necessarily lacking in personal integrity, whatever their other serious moral failings. So integrity shares this much with familiar juristic procedural values like 'natural justice' and 'due process': although they are plausibly regarded as intrinsic values in their own right, forming an irreducibly constitutive part of comprehensive accounts of justice, procedural values promote good outcomes only in conjunction with other, substantive values requiring independent normative justification.

Viewed in this way, there is an instructive parallel between integrity as a moral virtue and the second-order, superintending role played by practical reasonableness in theories of moral deliberation and practical action.[78] Like practical reason, integrity is integrative with regard to our other values, both at the moment of deliberation or action and also, crucially, over time. Integrity has nothing to do with tunnel vision or bloody-mindedness. A person

---

[77] See further, B Williams, *Moral Luck* (Cambridge, Cambridge University Press, 1981) ch 3; J Raz, *The Morality of Freedom* (Oxford, Clarendon Press, 1986) Part IV.

[78] '[T]he good of practical reasonableness has been explained as inner integrity and outer authenticity: authenticity in that one's actions carry out one's own choice that one made in line with one's own deliberations; integrity, in that one's emotions—passions—and sensibilities are integrated with one's reasons, judgments and choices': J Finnis, *Reason in Action* (Oxford, Oxford University Press, 2011) 14. See further, C Rovane, 'Rationality and Persons' in AR Mele and P Rawling (eds), *The Oxford Handbook of Rationality* (Oxford, Oxford University Press, 2004); J Raz, *Engaging Reason* (Oxford, Oxford University Press, 1999); N MacCormick, 'Contemporary Legal Philosophy: The Rediscovery of Practical Reason' (1983) 10 *Journal of Law and Society* 1; J Finnis, *Natural Law and Natural Rights* (Oxford, Clarendon Press, 1980) ch V.

of integrity may well change her mind in response to new experiences or other pertinent information, even in relation to matters of fundamental moral significance to her. But a person of integrity does not blow hot and cold or mindlessly follow fashion. Just as a court should arrive at the same decision on the basis of the same evidence tomorrow or in a year's time as it does today (assuming no material change in the law), the person of integrity can be relied upon to embrace an enduring commitment to her convictions and practical judgements. Having made her bed, she lies in it without compunction or regret. The person of integrity is 'for all seasons', durable in any weather without losing her essential moral bearings or casting off her character-defining commitments before the prevailing winds of short-term pragmatism or social convention. Indeed, keeping faith with our past moral commitments and taking responsibility for our decisions and their future consequences is, in significant measure, what it means to be a *person* and to be *the same* person over time. We are experientially fully ourselves—we 'keep it together', colloquially speaking— only when we are able to sustain both psychological and normative integration across space and time.[79] Institutions claiming political authority—including policing, courts and legal systems—can analogously be thought of as having, or lacking, an integrated character and normative coherence over time.

It is tempting to think that substantive values are always, *ceteris paribus*, more important than 'mere' procedural considerations. But the simple equation of the procedural with the relatively less important is fallacious.[80] Procedural concepts and values like 'fair trial' or the presumption of innocence, for example, have far greater institutional purchase and symbolic resonance than many rules of substantive criminal law. And so it is that integrity is not merely a personal virtue of moral action. It is also an *institutional* virtue with especial significance for public institutions concerned with fair process and just outcomes. People might fervently wish—investing, perhaps, in hope over experience—for a world in which politicians behaved with integrity, but they positively demand this from their courts and judges and, more generally, from institutions administering justice and from the law itself. Law without integrity is capriciousness in robes, naked power without legitimacy.[81] One might even argue, echoing Dworkin, that 'integrity' should replace 'justice-as-fairness' in Rawls' celebrated account of the first virtue of public institutions.[82] Dworkin championed integrity as 'a distinct political ideal'[83] providing the best interpretation of our existing practices of legislation and adjudication, 'best' in the two-fold sense that law-as-integrity aspires both to describe institutional practices accurately *and* simultaneously to supply their best normative justification. Dworkin's methodological turn to interpretivism[84] was

---

[79] See D Parfit, *Reasons and Persons* (Oxford, Clarendon Press, 1984) Part 3. Cf J Gray, *Straw Dogs* (London, Granta, 2002) 73, 76 (contending that '[w]e act in the belief that we are all of one piece, but we are able to cope with things only because we are a succession of fragments. We cannot shake off the sense that we are enduring selves, and yet we know we are not … We are hardwired for the illusion of self.')

[80] For one contextual elucidation of this argument, see P Roberts, 'The Priority of Procedure and the Neglect of Evidence and Proof: Facing Facts in International Criminal Law' (2015) 13 *Journal of International Criminal Justice* 479.

[81] Or as Augustine more eloquently put it in his *City of God* (one-and-a-half millennia before a similar thought appealed to Karl Marx), *Remota itaque iustitia, quid sunt regna nisi magna latrocinia?*

[82] 'Justice is the first virtue of social institutions, as truth is of systems of thought': J Rawls, *A Theory of Justice* rvsd edn (Oxford, Oxford University Press, 1999) 3.

[83] R Dworkin, *Law's Empire* (London, Fontana, 1986) 404.

[84] Ibid ch 2.

intended to break the sterile impasse between 'legal positivist' and 'natural law' arguments in contemporary Anglo-American jurisprudence by transcending hackneyed contrasts between law as found and law as made,[85] between law as it is and law as it ought to be.[86] Dworkin insisted that:

> Law's empire is defined by attitude, not territory or power or process ... It is an interpretive, self-reflective attitude addressed to politics in the broadest sense ... [T]he imperatives of integrity always challenge today's law with the possibilities of tomorrow's... every decision in a hard case is a vote for one of law's dreams.[87]

Setting aside for present purposes points of exegetical dispute and general debates about Dworkin's philosophy of law (which tend to elicit rather polarised reactions),[88] the concept of integrity as a fundamental procedural value of law, legality and legal process seems both analytically illuminating and normatively appealing. Particularly as developed by Gerald Postema in his resonant evocation of 'justice in workclothes',[89] integrity might be viewed as a fundamental value not only for legislators or appellate court judges deciding 'hard cases', but also as a primary normative resource, and commitment, informing the everyday conduct and decision-making of police detectives, prosecutors, defence lawyers, trial counsel, and first instance judges in criminal proceedings. Integrity, in other words, should be regarded as integral to legal professional ethics, informal occupational practices (especially those involving 'discretionary' decision-making), administrative rules and orders, codes of practice, and similar variations on the theme of 'soft-law' regulation or institutionalised 'working rules'[90] materially affecting the conduct and influencing the outcomes of criminal investigations, prosecutions and trials. Or as Chief Justice Brennan of the Australian High Court once put it:

> Integrity is the fidelity to legal duty ... It is the faithful adherence of the courts to the laws enacted by the Parliament, however undesirable the courts may think them to be, which is the guarantee of public confidence in the integrity of the judicial process and the protection of the courts' repute as the administrator of criminal justice.[91]

---

[85] '[L]aw as integrity rejects as unhelpful the ancient question whether judges find or invent law; we understand legal reasoning, it suggests, only by seeing the sense in which they do both and neither': ibid 225.

[86] 'Interpretivism ... denies that law and morals are wholly independent systems. It argues that law includes not only the specific rules enacted in accordance with the community's accepted practices but also the principles that provide the best moral justification for those enacted rules ... We must therefore do our best, within the constraints of interpretation, to make our country's fundamental law what our sense of justice would approve, not because we must sometimes compromise law with morality, but because that is exactly what the law, properly understood, itself requires': R Dworkin, *Justice For Hedgehogs* (Cambridge MA, Harvard University Press, 2011) 402, 415.

[87] Dworkin, above n 83, 413, 410.

[88] Dworkin seems like a man who, encountering jurisprudential trench warfare between positivists and naturalists, decided to set up camp in No Man's Land. He consequently attracted unfriendly fire from all directions, but also a small band of loyal lieutenants and disciples: generally, see S Guest, *Ronald Dworkin*, 3rd edn (Redwood City CA, Stanford University Press, 2013).

[89] GJ Postema, 'Integrity: Justice in Workclothes' (1997) 82 *Iowa Law Review* 821.

[90] See eg A Sanders and R Young, 'From Suspect to Trial' in M Maguire, R Morgan and R Reiner (eds), *The Oxford Handbook of Criminology*, 5th edn (Oxford, Oxford University Press, 2012); M Stroshine, G Alpert and R Dunham, 'The Influence of "Working Rules" on Police Suspicion and Discretionary Decision Making' (2008) 11 *Police Quarterly* 315; K Hawkins, *Law as Last Resort* (Oxford, Oxford University Press, 2003); D Dixon, *Law in Policing: Legal Regulation and Police Practices* (Oxford, Oxford University Press, 1997); J Goldstein, 'Police Discretion Not to Invoke the Criminal Process: Low-Visibility Decisions in the Administration of Justice' (1960) 69 *Yale Law Journal* 543.

[91] *R v Nicholas* (1998) 193 CLR 173, [37].

4. Integrity and Criminal Process

Our preliminary efforts at definition and conceptual elucidation have established an intimate connection between integrity, as a primary institutional virtue, and theories of law, constitutional government under the rule of law, procedural justice, judicial responsibility and professional ethics. These relatively abstract connections are given more concrete, institutionalised, tangible form in the following pages. Each of this volume's essays might be thought of as a practical test bed for integrity's theoretical and methodological virtues in the context of criminal proceedings; or perhaps, as a collection of practice pieces embroidering justice's workclothes. Simon Young, in Chapter 1, further explores the conceptual parameters, historical development and doctrinal substance of integrity jurisprudence from a more overtly Public Law perspective. Young urges us to see that '[r]ecognising criminal courts as public law courts, and their integrity as a prime consideration of public policy and political morality',[92] opens up a broader range of public interest factors and remedial possibilities in the administration of criminal justice. The relationship between Public Law and Criminal Law features prominently in several other essays in the volume, especially those concerned with the powers, responsibilities and democratic accountability of public prosecutors. This is one, relatively localised manifestation of the book's appetite for interdisciplinarity which, in other contributions, embraces socio-legal research, policy studies, feminism, cognitive science, epistemology, narrative, ethics and political theory.

To suggest a more structured analytical framework, and by way of potted preview of the essays themselves, the remainder of this Introduction identifies four principal strands or facets of the complex relationship between integrity and criminal process, which together constitute the volume's unifying threads. There are also, of course, unresolved tensions, unanswered questions, and plenty of scope for sceptical appraisals of appeals to the 'integrity' of criminal process, in theory or in practice. The language of integrity, in professional discourses or policy pronouncements, must not become fatuous rhetoric or, worse, an ideological smokescreen cloaking its absence in reality.

(a) Integrity as Fidelity to Advertised Normative Standards

The most straightforward question that we might pose about the 'integrity' of criminal process is to ask whether, in practice, it lives up to its advertised principles and policies. Is there a seamless progression, or rather a disconcerting gap, between criminal process's normative ideals and policy commitments and their institutionalised practical realities? Implicit in this question is the need to specify the criminal process's authentic normative ideals; and this is likely to be a controversial, and possibly convoluted, undertaking.[93] Any complex set of institutionalised human practices will fail to live up to its idealised

---

[92] p 51, below.

[93] For elucidation and illustrations, see P Roberts (ed), *Theoretical Foundations of Criminal Trial Procedure* (Farnham, Ashgate, 2014) Part II; A Duff, L Farmer, S Marshall and V Tadros, *The Trial on Trial Volume Three: Towards a Normative Theory of the Criminal Trial* (Oxford, Hart Publishing, 2007); HL Ho, *A Philosophy of Evidence Law: Justice in the Search for Truth* (Oxford, Oxford University Press, 2008).

self-conception on occasion, just as wrongful conviction of the innocent is an occupational hazard of operating *any* criminal justice process. Isolated instances of human frailty should not be taken to constitute collective lapses of integrity (though they might well demonstrate failures of integrity on the part of the particular individuals concerned). However, *repeated* or *systematic* failures to live up to advertised standards raise justified suspicions of complacency, if not flagrant hypocrisy, suggesting that criminal process has no real intention of practicing what it preaches. Default in gross might properly be characterised as a failure of institutional integrity.

Julie Stubbs, in Chapter 2, poses this question in relation to the apparent failures of policing, over many years and across multiple legal jurisdictions, successfully to implement effective strategies to combat so-called 'domestic' violence. Feminist activism, criminological research data and official statistics accumulated over many decades converge on the conclusion that female victims of intimate violence are 'over-policed and under-protected' by criminal law.[94] However, as Stubbs' comparative survey shows, the issues are complex. 'Pro-arrest' and 'no-drop' policies designed to improve enforcement come in several varieties, and they can fail or even backfire for various reasons. An interesting recent development is the novel use in domestic litigation of international human rights standards as a source of positive obligations on states to protect everyone, in equality, from lethal threats and serious harm.[95] Albeit an imaginative way of testing the sincerity of official policy commitments to tackling domestic violence, in court these arguments predictably run up against the common law's traditional deference to operational discretion in policing.[96] A more fundamental objection is that more intensive state surveillance and extensive intervention, especially in the form of aggressive policing and criminal law enforcement, do not necessarily empower victims *or* treat suspects and offenders fairly. Stubbs calls for thoroughgoing reconsideration of how a polity might respond with integrity to the challenges and contradictions of domestic violence policing. This would seemingly require a victim-centred and holistic perspective, in which criminal law enforcement is only one strand of an integrated approach, buttressed by an intelligent division of institutional labour and effective inter-agency partnerships.

David Dixon's critical discussion of police interrogation tactics, in Chapter 3, exposes another potential gap between operational practice and the law's own advertised normative requirements—which in the two notorious murder cases he analyses in detail led to the inadmissibility of confessions procured in breach of the Police and Criminal Evidence Act (PACE) 1984.[97] It is unnecessary to develop a sophisticated conceptual analysis to grasp the elementary point that police investigators sometimes break the procedural rules designed to regulate their conduct. The more interesting proposition emerging from Dixon's discussion

---

[94] Symposium, 'Overpoliced and Underprotected: Women, Race, and Criminalization' (2012) 59(6) *UCLA Law Review* 1418; A Natapoff, 'Underenforcement' (2006) 75 *Fordham Law Review* 1715.

[95] Generally, see L Lazarus, 'Positive Obligations and Criminal Justice: Duties to Protect or Coerce?' in L Zedner and JV Roberts (eds), *Principles and Values in Criminal Law and Criminal Justice* (Oxford, Oxford University Press, 2012); A Mowbray, *The Development of Positive Obligations under the European Convention on Human Rights by the European Court of Human Rights* (Oxford, Hart Publishing, 2004).

[96] *Van Colle v Chief Constable of Hertfordshire Police* [2009] 1 AC 225, [2008] UKHL 50; *Town of Castle Rock v Gonzales*, 545 US 748, 125 S Ct 2796 (2005).

[97] See Roberts and Zuckerman, above n 20, ch 12.3; DJ Birch, 'The Pace Hots Up: Confessions and Confusions under the 1984 Act' [1989] *Criminal Law Review* 95.

is that the rules themselves may be uncertain or contested. For example, the highly controversial 'Reid Technique' for interviewing criminal suspects widely embraced in the USA, and which seems to pervade police officers' questioning in some of the interview excerpts reproduced by Dixon in Chapter 3, is evidently in tension with English law's demands for non-oppressive interrogations and reliable confessions.[98] But this theory of interrogation, directly or indirectly, reinforced British detectives in their existing investigative practices, which they believed to be lawful and legitimate; until the courts said otherwise.[99] In such instances of normative ambiguity, competing claims to authority or conflicting loyalties, integrity serves as a prescriptive standard, or reasoning methodology, for reordering priorities and adjudicating 'hard cases' where there is something to be said on both sides of an argument. Similar normative ambiguities and operational dilemmas arise, for example, in relation to prosecutors' pre-trial interviews with witnesses (explored by Paul Roberts in Chapter 7), immunised accomplice testimony (reconsidered by Michael Jackson in Chapter 8) and the duties of prosecutors in adducing expert evidence (vigorously asserted by Gary Edmond in Chapter 9). Each chapter offers further illustrations of practical contexts in which integrity might afford criminal practitioners, policymakers and theorists greater direction and insight into their respective legal and ethical duties and practical objectives.

Contextual failures of integrity, in policy implementation or adherence to procedural law, might sometimes plausibly be regarded as sporadic and localised. They do not necessarily undermine the legitimacy of the entire adjudicative system. This is, however, precisely the dystopian scenario entertained by Mike McConville and Luke Marsh in Chapter 4. Their contribution to this volume develops an astonishing parallel between the indefensible practices of industrialised factory farming and a morally bankrupt criminal process corrupted by its addiction to pressurised guilty pleas. The analogy encompasses both process and product, to serve up (in either case) a distinctly unappetising dish. The implications are radical. Yet recent reforms of English criminal procedure, introduced against a backdrop of fiscal austerity, tend to reinforce rather than contradict their position.[100]

Writing from the perspective of a very experienced senior prosecutor, Nicholas Cowdery in Chapter 5 denies neither the inherent risks of accepting guilty pleas nor the institutional constraints and practical frustrations of criminal justice administration. He nonetheless maintains that pleas of guilty attracting sentencing discounts can in principle achieve just outcomes, at least where they are the product of a structured legal process (such as that in operation in New South Wales) rooted in prosecutorial independence, informed decision-making and appropriate consultation with interested parties. Justice through negotiation, on this fairly orthodox common law view,[101] is not a contradiction in terms. Cowdery rightly insists on disaggregating the nebulous—and somewhat emotive—term 'plea bargaining'[102] into the discreet institutional practices through which negotiated

---

[98]   PACE 1984, s 76(2).

[99]   *R v Paris, Abdullahi and Miller* (1993) 97 Cr App R 99 (CA). Cf *R v Foster* [2003] EWCA Crim 178.

[100]   M McConville and L Marsh, 'Adversarialism Goes West: Case Management in Criminal Courts' (2015) 19 *International Journal of Evidence and Proof* 172; J McEwan, 'From Adversarialism to Managerialism: Criminal Justice in Transition' (2011) 31 *Legal Studies* 519; A Edwards, 'The Other Leveson Report—The Review of Efficiency in Criminal Proceedings' [2015] *Criminal Law Review* 399; L Marsh, 'Leveson's Narrow Pursuit of Justice: Efficiency and Outcomes in the Criminal Process' (2016) 45 *Common Law World Review* 51.

[101]   For a civilian counterblast, see T Weigend, 'The Decay of the Inquisitorial Ideal: Plea Bargaining Invades German Criminal Procedure' in Jackson et al (eds), above n 5.

[102]   Cf N Vamos, 'Please Don't Call it "Plea Bargaining"' [2009] *Criminal Law Review* 617.

outcomes are actually secured in particular legal systems. Negotiations may focus on a range of variables (charges, facts, pleas) and be facilitated by widely differing procedures and incentives. Differentiated models of negotiated justice invite nuanced appraisal. Whilst the most plausible theoretical defences of guilty pleas tend to provide only qualified defences of existing institutional practices,[103] Cowdery takes 'the actuality of criminal proceedings, in which compromise is an embedded fact of life',[104] as his baseline assumption.

How might integrity inform these perennial debates? One of several methodologically instructive contrasts between these two chapters concerns the question of scale. McConville and Marsh address the 'guilty plea system' as a whole, whereas Cowdery is ultimately concerned with outcomes in particular cases (in a particular Australian state jurisdiction). Even on the pessimistic assumption that negotiated justice suffers from serious integrity deficits, where does that leave conscientious practitioners in individual cases? Should they resign or defect in protest? Or strive to secure just outcomes within the scope of their professional discretion? It would not follow from the fact that a justice system is broadly fair and legitimate that it always achieves just outcomes in every case. Conversely, particular guilty plea agreements might appropriately serve the ends of justice even in an adjudicative system ultimately lacking integrity. So it seems that, for our heuristic purposes, we should conceive integrity as a relative and scalar virtue of particular practical contexts, rather than only an all-or-nothing attribute of entire criminal processes (though it could be that as well). Systems, institutions, organisations, policies, practices and actors may exhibit more, or less, integrity at particular points in time. Integrity ideals, moreover, should inspire improvement without mocking feasibility,[105] not least because in the domain of criminal justice choosing not to act or decide means abandoning victims of injustice to their fate. As the essays by McConville and Marsh and Cowdery both demonstrate in their different ways, intelligent normative appraisal of negotiated justice must be critical,[106] informed, realistic and jurisdiction-specific; conducted, in other words, with intellectual integrity.

(b) Institutional and Remedial Integrity as Normative Coherence

A second interpretation of 'the integrity principle' employs the integrity-as-wholeness trope to consider whether a particular aspect of criminal process, or the administration of criminal justice viewed in its entirety, achieves an integrated holistic integrity. One might apply this analysis to the principal agencies of criminal proceedings—police, prosecution, judiciary, etc—or to particular aspects of their policy, function or practice. We might then ask, for example, whether the policing of domestic violence (discussed by Stubbs in Chapter 2) or interrogation policy and practice (Dixon's topic in Chapter 3) are coherent with the general values and policies of the police organisation. Or in relation to prosecutorial practice, we might try to assess the normative coherence of plea negotiation (Cowdery in Chapter 5), charging policy (Gans in Chapter 6), pre-trial witness interviewing (Roberts in Chapter 7),

---

[103] See eg R Lippke, *The Ethics of Plea Bargaining* (Oxford, Oxford University Press, 2011).
[104] p 121, below.
[105] Cf P Pettit, 'Is Criminal Justice Politically Feasible?' (2002) 5 *Buffalo Criminal Law Review* 427.
[106] By which we mean open-minded, imaginative, courageous and unscandalised, rather than (expressly *not*) committed to any ideological programme.

immunising accomplices (M Jackson in Chapter 8) or adducing expert witness testimony (Edmond in Chapter 9) with the advertised policies, standards and professional ethics of the organs of state prosecution. Criminal justice institutions and officials may lack integrity, not only in the first sense of failing to live up to advertised standards (hypocrisy), but alternatively (or also) in failing to present a unified and integrated normative vision across their various departments, functions and activities (incoherence).

The internal normative coherence of particular criminal process agencies, divisions or departments should be a matter of concern to policymakers and senior administrators within those agencies or departments. Coherence at this microscopic or 'local' level also equips researchers and scholars focusing on policing, prosecutions or the judiciary, etc with a critical standard for evaluating prevailing practices in each particular organisational setting. The heuristic potential of integrity is greatly amplified, however, when we consider the extent of normative coherence between different parts of the criminal process or in terms of the process as a whole. As with organs in the body or components of an engine, procedural integrity might be assessed piecemeal (examining each organ or component part separately), comparatively (considering two or more items together as a coherent package), or holistically, in terms of the overall health of the organism or the proper functioning of the machine.

Joanna Shapland once memorably characterised criminal proceedings as a sort of feudal economy, with each organ or agency jealously protecting its own jurisdiction and prerogatives largely in members' self-interest, leaving the disenfranchised peasants—complainants and witnesses—to fend for themselves.[107] Although the role and status of victims in criminal proceedings has improved somewhat in the ensuing three decades,[108] promoting effective inter-agency cooperation to achieve comprehensive criminal justice goals remains a central, and somewhat elusive, objective of criminal justice policymaking (as Stubbs also observes in relation to domestic violence policing in Chapter 2). To what extent, then, does procedural integrity as normative coherence presuppose effective collaboration and coordination between independent agencies and organisations in the criminal process neighbourhood?

The institutional integrity of criminal process is a complex idea. It implies neither frictionless normative coherence nor perfect institutional harmony on a day-to-day basis. Particularly within an adversarial procedural system premised on vigorous defence, excessively cosy relationships between criminal practitioners might themselves be a form of corruption betraying a lack of institutional integrity.[109] Even in less avowedly adversarial procedural systems, however, relationships between professionals representing different parts of the process should be characterised by mutual respect for each other's functionally

---

[107] J Shapland, 'Fiefs and Peasants: Accomplishing Change for Victims in the Criminal Justice System' in M Maguire and J Pointing (eds), *Victims of Crime: A New Deal?* (Buckingham, Open University Press, 1988).

[108] C Hoyle, 'Victims, the Criminal Process, and Restorative Justice' in M Maguire, R Morgan and R Reiner (eds), *The Oxford Handbook of Criminology*, 5th edn (Oxford, Oxford University Press, 2012); M Hall, 'Victims in the Criminal Justice Process' in A Hucklesby and A Wahidin (eds), *Criminal Justice*, 2nd edn (Oxford, Oxford University Press, 2013).

[109] Not a new worry: see AS Blumberg, 'The Practice of Law as Confidence Game: Organizational Cooptation of a Profession' (1967) 1(2) *Law & Society Review* 15; D Sudnow, 'Normal Crimes: Sociological Features of the Penal Code in a Public Defender Office' (1965) 12 *Social Problems* 255.

differentiated roles rather than jovial collegiality, lest over-familiarity should breed a collusive contempt for distinct professional roles and responsibilities.[110] Further complications arise from the *hierarchical* nature of some of these relationships. The Public Law principles elucidated by Young in Chapter 1 underpin the legitimacy of judicial review of administrative action as a concrete institutional expression of the Rule of Law. The principle of judicial review itself, albeit open to competing interpretations and varying degrees of intensity,[111] is unexceptional in liberal political theory. But this still leaves plenty of scope for jurisdictional competition and vigorous debate at the level of practice.

The question of the proper scope of judicial review of criminal prosecutions is posed by Cowdery in Chapter 5. The starting point for any legal system respecting the accusatorial principle (that is, the functional separation of adjudication from prosecution, in contrast to the all-purpose medieval inquisitor or modern coroner) must be that prosecutors prosecute allegations of criminality and courts judge them; that notwithstanding the hierarchical seniority of the judiciary, the prosecutor is—as the Scots and civilians say—'master of the instance'.[112] Of course, it does not follow from possession of an authentic original jurisdiction that prosecutorial decision-making involves completely unreviewable exercises of discretion. Cowdery shows, for example, that plea and charge negotiations in New South Wales are regulated by a principled set of standards and accompanied by procedural duties (including duties to consult with victims and police) which courts sometimes enforce, in the name of integrity. This discussion is extended in Chapter 6 through Jeremy Gans' detailed critical analysis of Australian and other common law authorities specifying the legitimate scope of judicial review of prosecutors' charging decisions. The topic is arcane, but not without intermittent media and public interest.[113] The leading Australian authority is *Maxwell*,[114] to which Gans administers a forensic hammering. The Australian High Court in *Maxwell* expressly invoked the 'integrity of the judicial process'[115] as its motivation for restricting judicial interventions into prosecutors' charging decisions. Gans is unimpressed: partly because the Court seemed to have judicial self-interest at heart, but mainly because— as Gans' extended analysis demonstrates—common law courts, whatever they might *say*, routinely employ a variety of doctrinal categories and strategies to constrain prosecutorial discretion, at least where the facts are capable of satisfying a range of overlapping offence definitions. Here, appeals to 'integrity' strike the discordant tone of empty judicial rhetoric.

Comprehensive conceptions of normative coherence imply what we might characterise as 'remedial integrity'. Injustice unremedied—justice delayed *indefinitely*—is a fortiori justice denied. In the service of integrity, criminal process should make appropriate institutional

---

[110] It is sometimes said that investigating judges, police and prosecutors in continental systems may become too friendly and end up working hand-in-glove: see eg J Hodgson, *French Criminal Justice* (Oxford, Hart Publishing, 2005) ch 7.

[111] *Anisminic v Foreign Compensation Commission* [1969] 2 AC 147 (HL); cf *Marbury v Madison*, 1 Cranch 137, 5 US 137 (1803) (holding that 'a law repugnant to the constitution is void').

[112] See eg *Jude v HM Advocate* [2011] UKSC 55, 2012 SLT 75, [17]. In private prosecutions, the complainant (Scots 'complainer') is master: *HM Advocate v Caldwell* 2010 SLT 1023, [2010] HCJAC 12, [12].

[113] A high-profile decision not to pursue charges of child sex abuse recently prompted (misguided) calls for the DPP's resignation, for example: see R Greenslade, 'Most Newspapers call on Alison Saunders to resign as DPP', *The Guardian*, 30 June 2015 (blogpost); S O'Neill, 'Janner to be prosecuted amid calls for law chief's resignation', *The Times*, 29 June 2015.

[114] *Maxwell v R* (1996) 184 CLR 501.

[115] Ibid 534.

provision for correcting the errors which are a foreseeable, and in aggregate unavoidable, consequence of human fallibility in the administration of justice. An obvious example is the provision for defence appeals against conviction or sentence, today widely recognised as integral to the fundamental right to fair trial,[116] albeit a relatively recent innovation in the historical evolution of criminal adjudication.[117] Remedial integrity must balance flexibility, rigour and accuracy in decision-making against the cost and finality of authoritative verdicts and judgments. It would hardly serve the ends of justice to allow appeals against appeals against appeals, and onwards to infinite regress.[118] Nor can collateral challenges or 'satellite litigation' be permitted to spiral out of control and gobble up resources that could more profitably be devoted to other, more deserving causes.[119] When criminal justice budgets are fixed, and indeed shrinking, remedial integrity is a zero-sum game.

Remedial integrity poses the question of the extent to which different parts of the criminal process may be held accountable for the errors or misbehaviour of other parts of the process, and for correcting their mistakes. One might think that responsibility is limited to direct institutional failings; that agencies and officials are accountable only for their own (mis)conduct without also having to answer vicariously for others' misdeeds. On this view, for example, the notion of a 'fair trial' refers only to what takes place in the courtroom, leaving alleged official improprieties or failings at earlier—or later—stages of criminal proceedings to be addressed through alternative procedural mechanisms and remedies.[120] Alternatively, one might regard criminal proceedings as a single continuous process for which the state is ultimately responsible, notwithstanding liberal constitutional doctrines insisting on the separation of powers. This is the view encouraged by integrity as normative coherence. It suggests, for example, that gross impropriety in criminal investigations may so taint what comes later in the process that it is simply impossible, normatively speaking, for just punishment to be imposed on a guilty offender. The state, through its miscreant agents, has effectively forfeited its legitimate authority to judge and punish. The recent progress of integrity as an influential jurisprudential principle in many common law systems is chiefly attributable to a major shift in judicial thinking, from the first model of criminal adjudication in which balkanised institutional fiefdoms are allowed to proclaim 'we are not our brother's keeper', to the second model of collective institutional responsibility for the morality of criminal proceedings.[121] The jurisprudential scaffolding for remedial integrity in criminal trials has mainly been supplied through developments of two traditional common law procedural mechanisms: the first, a rejuvenated doctrine of abuse of process, is described by Amanda Whitfort in Chapter 10; the second, evidentiary exclusion of improperly obtained evidence, is Peter Chau's topic in Chapter 11.

---

[116] See eg ICCPR Article 14(5); S Trechsel with SJ Summers, *Human Rights in Criminal Proceedings* (Oxford, Oxford University Press, 2005) ch 14.

[117] R Pattenden, *English Criminal Appeals 1844–1994* (Oxford, Oxford University Press, 1996).

[118] R Nobles and D Schiff, 'The Right to Appeal and Workable Systems of Justice' (2002) 65 *Modern Law Review* 676.

[119] See eg *R v DPP ex parte Kebilene* [2000] 2 AC 326 (HL).

[120] As expressed, for example, in the juridical aphorism *male captus, bene detentus*: see *United States v Alvarez-Machain*, 504 US 655 (1992); P Michell, 'English-Speaking Justice: Evolving Responses to Transnational Forcible Abduction after *Alvarez-Machain*' (1996) 29 *Cornell International Law Journal* 383.

[121] In particular, see *R v Horseferry Road Magistrates' Court, ex parte Bennett* [1994] 1 AC 42 (HL); *Teixeira de Castro v Portugal* (1998) 28 EHRR 101; Roberts and Zuckerman, above n 20, 176–78.

Whitfort surveys recent abuse of process jurisprudence in Hong Kong, Australia and the UK, drawing out several key points of continuity and comparison. Arguments over abuse of process have taken place in high profile cases, and produced a fair amount of dissonance between appellate courts' judgments and first instance rulings. Judicial decision-making in this context seems especially unpredictable and uncertain, even with regard to its underpinning rationales (for example, is disciplining the police ever a legitimate objective for a judge considering whether to impose a stay?) and operative legal tests. Whitfort helpfully draws together the main precepts that can be extracted from this evolving Commonwealth jurisprudence, but it is hard not to see in this 'principled guidance' a collection of rather disparate, open-ended, frequently rhetorical[122] and completely indeterminate prescriptions lacking any strong internal coherence and ripe for judicial manipulation in concrete cases. Perhaps the jurisprudence is still underdeveloped at this stage; possibly, the psychological imperative of convicting serious offenders even where 'the constable has blundered' (or worse) will inevitably win out in the vast majority of disputes whatever the formal procedural rule is supposed to be. The need for general principles to be flexible enough to accommodate subtle variations in the material facts and circumstances of individual cases is also an important, sometimes overlooked or under-appreciated, constraint on the specification of procedural norms.[123]

Chau, in the following chapter, revisits the underlying rationales for excluding improperly obtained evidence from criminal trials. More specifically, Chau is concerned with *non-consequentialist* rationales for exclusion, ie those that seek to justify exclusion on intrinsic rather than instrumental (typically epistemic) grounds. The evidence should be excluded, when it should, not because it is (probably) unreliable and may therefore lead to a factually incorrect determination, but *for some other (non-consequentialist) reason*. Judicially articulated rationales for exclusion embrace, and sometimes blend together, consequentialist and non-consequentialist (deontological) thinking. The motivation might be, for example, deterrence of future official misconduct, vindicating rights and remedying their breaches, serving the internal logic of procedural due process (or some aspect of it), or upholding the moral integrity of the proceedings and thereby preserving the legitimacy of trial verdicts. Although this is fairly well charted territory for Evidence scholars,[124] Chau moves the debate forward in two significant respects. First, his terse recapitulation and juxtaposition of familiar arguments opens up established rationalisations to closer critical examination. Secondly, Chau draws attention to the relatively untapped potential of the idea of unjust enrichment as a source of non-consequentialist reasons for excluding improperly obtained evidence. His chapter presents an outline sketch of the 'no profit principle' as a rival or supplement to integrity-based exclusionary rationales. It is an imaginative proposal worthy of further elucidation and critical scrutiny.

---

[122] *Moti v R* (2011) 245 CLR 456, [86] (Heydon J dissenting).

[123] The complexity theme is developed in P Roberts, 'Excluding Evidence as Protecting Constitutional or Human Rights?' in L Zedner and JV Roberts (eds), *Principles and Values in Criminal Law and Criminal Justice: Essays in Honour of Andrew Ashworth* (Oxford, Oxford University Press, 2012).

[124] See eg P Mirfield, *Silence, Confessions and Improperly Obtained Evidence* (Oxford, Clarendon Press, 1997); S Sharpe, *Judicial Discretion and Criminal Investigation* (London, Sweet & Maxwell, 1998); R Pattenden, *Judicial Discretion and Criminal Litigation*, 2nd edn (Oxford, Clarendon Press, 1990) ch 7.

What are the temporal limits of remedial integrity? Bitter experience of miscarriages of justice in recent decades—the latest chapters in a very long story[125]—indicates why criminal verdicts cannot always be final even after the normal appeals process has run its course. In the book's concluding pair of essays, Charles Weisselberg and Carolyn Hoyle canvass issues bearing on the integrity of post-conviction procedures for dealing with alleged miscarriages of justice. Weisselberg, in Chapter 15, is concerned with the perils of emphasising 'actual innocence' in appeals against conviction. Of course it is not disputed that criminal proceedings should strive to protect the innocent from wrongful conviction. However, the extensive information marshalled by Weisselberg describing the activities of Innocence Projects, state commissions of inquiry and wider debates around miscarriages of justice and law reform in the USA[126] highlights the risks associated with treating 'actual innocence' as the sole or predominant criterion for reviewing and, where necessary, remedying institutional failings. Over-concentration on factual innocence can lead to an excessively outcome-orientated instrumentalisation of criminal adjudication, which fails to address flawed or faulty official practices (treating the symptoms rather than the underlying causes) and marginalises process values of the type emphasised, for example, by Whitfort and Chau. It risks, in other words, systemic normative incoherence. Weisselberg explores these themes particularly in relation to unreliable confessions and the (disputed) practical significance of the US Supreme Court's iconic ruling in *Miranda v Arizona*.[127]

In Chapter 16, Hoyle investigates persistent shortcomings in arrangements for providing state compensation to victims of miscarriages of justice. This is a topic with cosmopolitan resonance,[128] which has also generated policy discussion and recent case law in England and Wales.[129] By way of context, Hoyle reviews institutional developments stretching back to the creation of the Court of Criminal Appeal in 1907, but focussing more particularly on the work of the Criminal Cases Review Commission since 1997.[130] She notes the formal distinction between 'not guilty' verdicts or quashed convictions following a successful appeal and positive declarations of *innocence*, and describes a handful of rare instances in which appellate courts went beyond their strictly legal remit and actually apologised to victims of miscarriages of justice. The problem, as Hoyle observes, with such doubtless well-motivated but selective and very infrequent departures from the Court of Appeal's formal jurisdiction, is that there is a danger of creating *de facto* a two tier system of acquittals: 'first

---

[125]   See eg RC Huff and M Killias (eds), *Wrongful Convictions and Miscarriages of Justice: Causes and Remedies in North American and European Criminal Justice Systems* (New York, Routledge, 2013); BL Garrett, *Convicting the Innocent: Where Criminal Prosecutions Go Wrong* (Cambridge MA, Harvard University Press, 2012); R Nobles and D Schiff, *Understanding Miscarriages of Justice* (Oxford, Oxford University Press, 2000); J Rozenburg, 'Miscarriages of Justice' in E Stockdale and S Casale (eds), *Criminal Justice Under Stress* (London, Blackstone Press, 1992); K Carrington, M Dyer, R Hogg, J Bargen and A Lohrey (eds), *Travesty! Miscarriages of Justice* (Leichhardt NSW, Pluto Press, 1991); B Woffinden, *Miscarriages of Justice* (London, Hodder & Stoughton, 1987); L Kennedy, *Ten Rillington Place* (London, Gollancz, 1961); Pattenden, above n 117, ch 1.

[126]   For UK debates, in addition to Hoyle, Chapter 16 in this volume, see M Naughton (ed), *The Criminal Cases Review Commission: Hope for the Innocent?* (Basingstoke, Palgrave, 2010); S Roberts and L Weathered, 'Assisting the Factually Innocent: The Contradictions and Compatibility of Innocence Projects and the Criminal Cases Review Commission' (2009) 29 *Oxford Journal of Legal Studies* 43; H Quirk, 'Identifying Miscarriages of Justice: Why Innocence in the UK is Not the Answer' (2007) 70 *Modern Law Review* 759.

[127]   384 US 436 (1966).

[128]   Cf International Covenant on Civil and Political Rights, Art 14(6).

[129]   See, in particular, *R (Adams) v Secretary of State for Justice* [2012] 1 AC 48, [2011] UKSC 18.

[130]   The CCRC was created by the Criminal Appeal Act 1995, and became operational in 1997.

class' acquittals of the truly innocent, and decidedly inferior acquittals of individuals who (to exaggerate only slightly) 'might well have been guilty but were given the benefit of the doubt or got off on a technicality'.

Applications for state compensation by those claiming to be victims of miscarriages of justice have crystallised this issue, because English courts and policymakers have always resisted the idea that compensation should be paid automatically to anybody whose conviction is finally quashed on appeal. What was formally an entirely discretionary *ex gratia* compensation scheme was subsequently placed on a statutory footing, and recent litigation has centred on the meaning of the statutory test for establishing eligibility for compensation. Hoyle retells the tale in detail. She is hostile to an 'actual innocence' standard, partly for the principled reasons advanced by Weisselberg in the preceding chapter, but also on pragmatic grounds. Whilst factual innocence may be difficult to ascertain reliably at the best of times, the Court of Appeal is a particularly unsuitable venue for attempting such determinations. The practical constraints, normative legal framework and forensic strategies of criminal appeals preclude, or at least strongly discourage, the presentation of evidence capable of proving actual innocence. Appellants rarely need to provide such information to succeed in their appeals. In this procedural environment 'actual innocence' would operate as an uncertain and quite possibly capricious standard. It would fail to meet threshold requirements of rationality in adjudication,[131] and therefore lack integrity in the sense of cohering with an integrated scheme of basic values. Hoyle also canvasses a more local (and controversial) potential source of normative incoherence: are *de facto* second class ('*not* actually innocent') acquittals compatible with the presumption of innocence? Not on her account.

Without any pretence to comprehensiveness, the contributors to this volume range widely over the terrain of criminal investigations, prosecutions, trials, appeals and post-conviction remedies. We claim, and hope in the following pages to have demonstrated through numerous examples, that it is illuminating to consider whether existing law and practice in relation to any particular criminal process institution, phase, stage or functional operation is coherent, and at least in that sense has 'integrity', in its own terms and viewed holistically, as a constituent part of the administration of criminal justice. A police force that routinely accepted bribes to drop criminal charges whilst planting incriminating evidence on unforthcoming suspects would obviously lack integrity. But so, too, would charging practices that systematically failed to reflect the gravity of criminal wrongdoing, or a plea bargaining system incompatible with the presumption of innocence, or procedures for assessing demeanour at trial that resulted in discriminatory or unfair punishments being meted out to offenders. These aberrations do not necessarily involve departures from advertised policies or legal standards or exhibit the crasser forms of hypocrisy mentioned in the previous subsection. Rather, they suffer from a more profound normative incoherence, in being ultimately incompatible with a defensible conception of criminal justice. More localised incoherence is seen where a particular institutional policy, process or norm is self-defeating in its own terms. Anticipating John Jackson's argument in Chapter 12, it

---

[131] See W Twining, 'The Rationalist Tradition of Evidence Scholarship' in E Campbell and L Waller (eds), *Well and Truly Tried* (Sydney, The Law Book Company, 1982); LL Fuller, 'The Forms and Limits of Adjudication' (1978) 92 *Harvard Law Review* 353; M Damaška, 'Rational and Irrational Proof Revisited' (1997) 5 *Cardozo Journal of International and Comparative Law* 25.

would be irrational, for example, to insist on unreasoned jury verdicts in the name of pre-serving public confidence in criminal adjudication, if the failure to provide reasons came to be regarded as incompatible with the right to a fair trial and itself a source of widespread public criticism and dissatisfaction. The traditional practice would have shrivelled into a hollow husk, devoid of institutional integrity.

Promoting an ideal of integrity as 'normative coherence' does not deny the pervasiveness of competition between norms or the practical inevitability of jurisprudential loose ends and moral remainders. *Perfect* normative coherence is a Platonic chimera. Nor are we falling into the category error of thinking that questions of normative evaluation can be answered *purely* through methodological innovation or conceptual refinements. Value conflicts are an inherent, routine and—in gross[132]—irremediable feature of criminal proceedings. Whether we are thinking about the tension between securing fair trials for the accused and appropri-ate concern and respect for victims and witnesses, or calculating the costs to truth-finding of excluding improperly obtained evidence, or calibrating the delicate balance between finality in adjudication and correcting miscarriages of justice, 'integrity' offers a heuristic for managing normative complexity rather than a whitewash for concealing its existence. In the following pages the reader will find many more illustrations of institutional moral dilemmas and tragic choices, where the righteous path of integrity may be circuitous, over-grown and difficult to discern and abide.

(c) Epistemological Integrity: Evidence, Proof and Legal Narratives

It is a minimum requirement for any plausible and normatively attractive conception of criminal adjudication that it should take fact-finding seriously; that it should strive, in other words, to convict the guilty but acquit the innocent. On traditional accounts, moreo-ver, it is not acceptable to pursue more convictions of the guilty by creating disproportion-ately greater risks of wrongfully convicting the innocent.[133] Orthodoxy in this regard has not gone unchallenged.[134] However this *normative* balance might be struck, the rationality of proof and accurate fact-finding always ultimately rests on the integrity of the processes by which evidence is generated, collected, preserved, interpreted, packaged, presented, tested, challenged and, finally, evaluated by the fact-finder (and possibly re-evaluated dur-ing appeals and post-conviction procedures). The integrity of evidence is a third prominent theme of this book, reflecting—and more broadly contextualising—professional legal dis-course around preserving 'the continuity of evidence'[135] and fidelity to truth in litigation.[136]

---

[132] That is to say, some *particular* value conflicts may be remediable, but value conflicts *tout court* are not.

[133] The traditional criminal standard of proof 'beyond reasonable doubt' is a keystone of the principled asym-metry of criminal adjudication: Roberts and Zuckerman, above n 20, ch 6.3. Also see eg A Volokh, '*n* Guilty Men' (1997) 146 *University of Pennsylvania Law Review* 173; S Sheppard, 'The Metamorphoses of Reasonable Doubt: How Changes in the Burden of Proof have Weakened the Presumption of Innocence' (2003) 78 *Notre Dame Law Review* 1165.

[134] Notably by L Laudan, *Truth, Error and Criminal Law: An Essay in Legal Epistemology* (Cambridge, Cambridge University Press, 2006).

[135] See eg *R (Byrne) v DPP* [2003] EWHC 397 Admin; *Paterson v DPP* [1990] RTR 329; *R v M* [2001] EWCA Crim 2850, [15].

[136] M Damaška, 'Truth in Adjudication' (1998) 49 *Hastings Law Journal* 289; S Haack, 'Of Truth, in Science and in Law' (2008) 73 *Brooklyn Law Review* 985.

As before, it is easy to think of instances where the evidential process *lacks* integrity, including cases of deliberate tampering or perjury, and extending to cultured 'testilying'[137] in all its shades and manifestations. However, as the essays in this volume show, preserving and authenticating the integrity of evidence-generating processes can be a subtle and multifaceted endeavour, demanding expertise and professional judgement. Judicial 'evidence' is properly conceptualised as a 'constructed' entity, in the sense of being an intentional product of human decision making, interactions and institutionalised processes. Whether we are thinking about police interrogation strategies (Dixon), or prosecutors interviewing complainants or other potential prosecution witnesses (Roberts) or negotiating with erstwhile accomplices to secure their testimonial cooperation (M Jackson), or the processes and practical routines for generating expert evidence (Edmond)—in each of these practical contexts, as well as in many others, evidence is a crafted artefact of its institutionalised production. Whether it is a *carefully* crafted product—and, indeed, what this nicely ambiguous phrase might mean and entail in practice—are contingent matters to be investigated, both at the aggregated level of routine procedures and with regard to particular cases.

Conceding the sociological truth of evidence 'construction' opens the way to nuanced (normative and descriptive) inquiries concerning the epistemological integrity of judicial evidence and proof. Are particular procedures, processes or practices truth-conducive, or alternatively, liable to frustrate forensic truth-finding? This is often a disputed question. Coercive police interrogation poses obvious risks of false confession, but aren't arrest, detention and interrogation *inherently* coercive? If so, why not disqualify *all* extrajudicial confessions as automatically inadmissible at trial? It is already settled practice in many common law jurisdictions for prosecutors to interview key witnesses as a routine aspect of thorough trial preparation.[138] But if evidence is produced through interactions, is there not a risk that rehearsing a witness's evidence will *change* it? At what point does legitimate witness preparation become illegitimate 'coaching'? Paul Roberts explores these issues in Chapter 7, in the light of significant developments in English law and practice following the introduction of 'pre-trial witness interviews' (PTWI).[139] And it goes without saying that doing deals with accomplices is an ethical minefield. Supping with the devil requires a long spoon. We should ask whether prosecutors' metaphorical cutlery is long enough to preserve the integrity of fact-finding, despite inviting courts to rely on the testimony of witnesses with such obvious incentives to lie, and who often possess insider-knowledge enabling them to do so effectively.[140] Michael Jackson revisits these epistemic challenges and assesses institutional responses to them, from a Hong Kong perspective, in Chapter 8.

---

[137] A redolent neologism reputedly coined by the New York Police Department to categorise testimonial lies about the manner in which evidence was procured in order to circumvent the Fourth Amendment exclusionary rule. See J Simon-Kerr, 'Systemic Lying' (2015) 56 *William and Mary Law Review* 2175.

[138] See eg JS Applegate, 'Witness Preparation' (1989) 68 *Texas Law Review* 277; SV Vasiliev, 'From Liberal Extremity to Safe Mainstream? The Comparative Controversies of Witness Preparation in the United States' (2011) 9 *International Commentary on Evidence*, Article 5

[139] P Roberts and C Saunders, 'Introducing Pre-Trial Witness Interviews—A Flexible New Fixture in the Crown Prosecutor's Toolkit' [2008] *Criminal Law Review* 831.

[140] This worry is reflected in the common law's long-standing suspicion of accomplice testimony and witnesses with 'a purpose of their own to serve in giving evidence': *R v Beck* [1982] 1 WLR 461, 466; *R v Spencer* [1987] AC 128 (HL).

Expert evidence introduces further epistemological complexities, which are tackled by Gary Edmond in Chapter 9. Law and Science can be conceptualised as *alternative* systems of practical epistemic authority, which can often be combined successfully (think about the power of DNA evidence or modern forensic medicine in contemporary criminal proceedings) but also sometimes compete in forensically problematic ways.[141] Judicial reliance on science, through the medium of expert evidence, has a very long and somewhat chequered history in the common law.[142] Edmond takes up the story of recent critical examinations of forensic science and forensic medicine, which have exposed the quite startling extent to which routine forensic procedures lack secure foundations in rigorous scientific method.[143] More worryingly still, the traditional tools of adversarial trial, cross-examination and defence counter-expertise have patently failed to expose flaws and fallibilities in prosecution evidence, leading to miscarriages of justice.[144] Having identified the true extent of the epistemological challenge for criminal adjudication presented by modern forensic science and forensic medical evidence, Edmond's essay draws out further institutional implications for the professional responsibilities of prosecutors, defence lawyers and courts.

In addition to considering the epistemological integrity of evidence and proof, we can also interrogate the integrity of broader criminal process narratives from an epistemological perspective. Symbolically and literally, criminal process tells culturally resonant 'stories' about crime and punishment. But are these *true* stories, or only convenient, media-friendly or fictionalised accounts, singing to the tune of powerful social interests rather than factual verisimilitude? For example, what kind of story do the no-drop policies discussed by Stubbs in Chapter 2 relate about domestic violence? The charging policies and plea negotiations examined by McConville and Marsh (Chapter 4), Cowdery (Chapter 5) and Gans (Chapter 6) play a vital role in framing the offence to be tried, ensuring (or not) that the punishment fits the crime in the event of a conviction. Whether or not narratives of crime and punishment generated by high volume guilty pleas retain epistemological integrity goes to the heart of disputes between critics and defenders of plea-bargaining. Are those pleading guilty *actually* guilty of *the offence charged*? To the extent that guilty pleas may be facilitated—or possibly dictated—by suspects' custodial confessions, the factual distortions potentially introduced by deficient police interrogation techniques, such as those criticised by Dixon in Chapter 3, are all the more troubling in this regard. Later in the progress of contested proceedings, judicial rulings on procedural submissions or the admissibility of evidence, such as those considered by Whitfort (Chapter 10) and Chau (Chapter 11), tell

---

[141] For discussion, see P Roberts, 'Renegotiating Forensic Cultures: Between Law, Science and Criminal Justice' (2013) 44 *Studies in the History and Philosophy of Biological and Biomedical Sciences* 47; S Haack, 'Irreconcilable Differences? The Troubled Marriage of Science and Law' (2009) 72 *Law and Contemporary Problems* 1; AKY Wonder, 'Science and Law, A Marriage of Opposites' (1989) 29 *Journal of the Forensic Science Society* 75; CAG Jones, *Expert Witnesses: Science, Medicine and the Practice of Law* (Oxford, Oxford University Press, 1994).

[142] Generally, see P Roberts (ed), *Expert Evidence and Scientific Proof in Criminal Trials* (Farnham, Ashgate, 2014).

[143] See in particular, National Research Council, *Strengthening Forensic Science in the United States: A Path Forward* (Washington DC, National Academies Press, 2009).

[144] BL Garrett and PJ Neufeld, 'Invalid Forensic Science Testimony and Wrongful Convictions' (2009) 95 *Virginia Law Review* 1; E Beecher-Monas, 'Reality Bites: The Illusion of Science in Bite-Mark Evidence' (2009) 30 *Cardozo Law Review* 1369; SA Cole, 'The Prevalence and Potential Causes of Wrongful Conviction by Fingerprint Evidence' (2006) 37 *Golden Gate University Law Review* 39.

their own stories about the values embedded in criminal adjudication, revealing judicial priorities when those values conflict or threaten the efficacy of criminal prosecutions.

A contested trial might be thought of as a kind of tournament of narratives, often vying against each other but sometimes proceeding in parallel or even in collaboration, for official recognition and authentication. A trial verdict is a narrative whose epistemic integrity is warranted by official endorsement. This legitimising relationship is contingent but, ideally, mutually reinforcing: the truth of the verdict is guaranteed by the integrity of the trial process, just as the integrity of the trial process is confirmed by the truth of its particularised verdicts. Conversely, the currency of criminal proceedings lacking integrity is false verdicts and miscarriages of justice. Although institutional details are partly a function of procedural tradition and will necessarily (and often harmlessly) vary across time and space, the manner in which verdicts and judgments are delivered and their detailed content will always be significant variables under the lens of epistemological integrity.

In Chapter 12, John Jackson revisits the question whether, in the modern era of human rights law, a growing expectation that important public decision-making should be explicitly reasoned and justified should be extended to impose associated obligations on the criminal trial jury. After all, formulating and publicising reasons for important decisions are widely regarded as minimal criteria of rationality and prime judicial responsibilities. Yet juries deliberate in secret and give no reasons to justify their determinations.[145] This has generally been seen as an important guarantor of finality in verdicts, even by those with impeccable rationalist credentials.[146] As Jackson describes, however, modern realities—both technological and juridical—seemingly call into question the extent to which tried-and-tested procedural approaches will be sufficient to sustain the legitimacy and public acceptability of unreasoned verdicts. Procedural innovation may be required to enable juries to live up to contemporary demands, underpinned by European human rights law,[147] for transparency, rationality, fairness and accountability in their deliberations and verdicts. The implications for the integrity of criminal adjudication could hardly be more profound. Are juries on the traditional common law model *capable* of meeting novel expectations for a more 'judicial' style of decision-making? Which procedural changes are necessary, and how are they to be designed and implemented? Supposing that Jackson is right about the current direction of travel, will the model of criminal adjudication that emerges constitute a sensible and necessary development of our existing (and always evolving) procedural traditions, or a decisive break with the past heralding a new kind of 'jury verdict' for the twenty-first century?

In Chapter 13, Susan Bandes embarks upon a different kind of epistemological inquiry. Her topic is the role of remorse in criminal adjudication. This sounds like a normative issue for sentencing and punishment, and some of the material Bandes considers does indeed relate to the sentencing phases of US criminal trials, including death penalty hearings determined by juries. However, the methodological foundations of Bandes' discussion, which draws extensively on behavioural science and psychological research, are more

---

[145] HL Ho, 'The Judicial Duty to Give Reasons' (2000) 20 *Legal Studies* 42; JD Jackson, 'Making Juries Accountable' (2002) 50 *American Journal of Comparative Law* 477.

[146] JC Smith, 'Is Ignorance Bliss? Could Jury Trial Survive Investigation?' (1998) 38 *Medicine, Science and the Law* 98.

[147] Cf P Roberts, 'Does Article 6 of the European Convention on Human Rights Require Reasoned Verdicts in Criminal Trials?' (2011) 11 *Human Rights Law Review* 213.

generic and far-reaching. By posing the question whether 'remorse' in the juridically relevant sense actually exists as a tangible practical emotion, Bandes opens up issues that are at once both conceptual and epistemological. How does one know when a convicted offender is (genuinely) remorseful? Since contrition in the courtroom must invariably be inferred from demeanour—with or without accompanying words of apology—infusing remorse with legal significance is vulnerable to similar behavioural science criticisms as can be made of orthodox legal rationales for inviting jurors to infer veracity and reliability, or their opposites, from witnesses' testimonial demeanour.[148] This is especially problematic, as Bandes notes, where stereotypical or culturally blinkered expectations are liable to reinforce prejudice or unfair discrimination. But even where these particular concerns do not arise, legal procedures should be astute to ensure that findings of remorsefulness (or its absence) are epistemically well warranted; *and* that fact-finders' informal judgements of remorselessness (or other inappropriate or forensically damaging emotions) do not seep into verdicts and contaminate the integrity of criminal trials.

Having reviewed the relevant cognitive science literature, Bandes is sceptical about the robustness of evaluations of remorse in criminal trials, and this in turn leads her to recommend curtailing the influence of such shaky assessments on decision making in criminal adjudication, insofar as this is practically feasible. Normative arguments about the salience of remorse for questions of legal culpability, sentencing or punishment are idle, or in bad faith, unless 'remorse' can be defined and reliably identified, in the context of criminal prosecutions and trials, with epistemological integrity. This pattern of argumentation, underpinned by research in the cognitive and behavioural sciences, might be extended to challenge the epistemic integrity of legal fact-finding in relation to other emotions or practical attitudes associated with standards of criminal responsibility or criteria of aggravation or mitigation at sentencing. It also implies an interdisciplinary research programme for scholars with relevant skills and interests.[149]

Jill Hunter, in Chapter 14, likewise draws upon literatures outside the law to develop a counter-narrative to legal orthodoxy. The focus now shifts from first instance trials to appellate court judgments. In contrast to jury verdicts, which are the paradigmatic form of legal decision-making for Jackson and Bandes in the preceding two chapters, criminal appeals *do*, at least ostensibly, provide detailed rationalisations for their conclusions. Hunter's critical deconstruction of one judgment of the High Court of Australia[150] grapples with multiple, intersecting narratives of contemporary doctrinal analysis, historical jurisprudence, and gender inequality, implicitly inviting further reflection on the range of audiences to which legal judgments—especially those delivered by constitutional or apex courts—might conceivably be addressed. Like Gans in Chapter 6, Hunter's discussion proceeds from what

---

[148] See OG Wellborn III, 'Demeanor' (1991) 76 *Cornell Law Review* 1075; JA Blumenthal, 'A Wipe of the Hands, A Lick of the Lips: The Validity of Demeanor Evidence in Assessing Witness Credibility' (1993) 72 *Nebraska Law Review* 1157.

[149] Generally, see eg DW Vick, 'Interdisciplinarity and the Discipline of Law' (2004) 31 *Journal of Law and Society* 163; C Menkel-Meadow, 'Taking Law and __ Really Seriously: Before, During and After "The Law"' (2007) 60 *Vanderbilt Law Review* 555; J McEwan, *The Verdict of the Court: Passing Judgment in Law and Psychology* (Oxford, Hart Publishing, 2003). But for words of methodological caution, see R Bagshaw, 'Behavioural Science Data in Evidence Teaching and Scholarship' in P Roberts and M Redmayne (eds), *Innovations in Evidence and Proof* (Oxford, Hart Publishing, 2007).

[150] *PGA v R* (2012) 245 CLR 355, [2012] HCA 21.

might initially appear to be a fairly technical doctrinal question, in the context of allegations of 'historic' sexual offending: was it a crime in 1963 for a man in South Australia to rape his wife? The majority of the High Court concluded it was, and Hunter does not directly contest the legitimacy of that conclusion. Her critique of the majority judgments centres on the *arguments* and *information* deployed to reach it, and the symbolic messages the judgment conveys to multiple audiences.

Specifically, Hunter argues that the High Court majority's resort to formalistic common law reasoning effectively airbrushes the true narrative of married women's lack of protection from sexual violence, in both substantive criminal law and prosecutorial practice (echoing a theme developed by Stubbs in Chapter 2); and that the Court was indefensibly recalcitrant to being better informed by readily available social scientific data indicating the realities of women's inequality before the law, extending far beyond the definitions of sexual offences and more recently in time than 1963. Just as the fairness of trials cannot be reduced to the accuracy of verdicts, Hunter's critical discussion demonstrates that the integrity of appellate judgment-writing is not simply a question of reaching the 'right' result. There are (even) bigger themes lurking here, pertaining to technology, democracy and the place of law in society. Within living memory, appellate court judgments were the preserve of dusty library bookshelves and technical interpretations by the legal priesthood. In the internet age, the pronouncements of appeal (especially apex) courts are now part of the law's immediately accessible public profile. This novel kind of exposure to 'the laity' inevitably brings with it new demands and expectations of judgment-writing with integrity, which courts cannot ignore if public confidence in the judiciary is to be maintained.

Provision for appeals and exceptional post-conviction review reflects the level of a particular legal system's commitment not only to correcting apparent factual errors, but also its willingness to contemplate fallibility in the first place and to facilitate proactive remedial measures in an effort to set the record straight. However, as Weisselberg shows in Chapter 15, focussing on unvarnished 'actual innocence' is not unproblematic for the administration of criminal justice, even if considered in purely epistemic terms. One reason for caution is that, by implicitly appearing to condone official illegality in order to uphold convictions of the guilty, truth-finding in future proceedings may be compromised (for example, because investigative practices eroding evidential reliability become routinised and unchallenged), even if factual accuracy is not undermined in the instant case. Further exploring the normative gap between 'acquittal' and 'innocence', in the volume's final chapter, Hoyle elucidates the narrative implications of denying monetary compensation to those whose convictions have been quashed following long sentences of imprisonment. How are we supposed to read the official truth of these cases, in which the prisoner is released and the conviction expunged, yet the courts still refuse to award compensation or even to issue an official apology?

Thinking about criminal process in terms of its epistemological integrity demands no less sophistication than trying to assess its adherence to advertised policy or prescriptive standards, modelling institutional coherence, or evaluating conformity with more comprehensive procedural ideals. 'Finding the truth' is far from a simple, reductive idea.[151]

---

[151] See eg RP Burns, *A Theory of the Trial* (Princeton NJ, Princeton University Press, 1999) (elucidating a non-empiricist conception of legal fact-finding); AAS Zuckerman, 'Law, Fact or Justice?' (1986) 66 *Boston University Law Review* 487.

Even at the granular level of individual pieces of evidence, the notion of evidential integrity is complex (though it can certainly be compromised in entirely prosaic ways),[152] owing to the inherently constructed nature of judicial evidence and proof, the meshing of empirical and normative considerations, and the variety of institutional and social contexts in which facts are investigated, presented, disputed, evaluated and pronounced. When the analytical lens is widened to accommodate the plurality of competing and contested criminal process narratives, the adaptable concept of epistemological integrity can be deployed to illuminate the darker recesses of legal storytelling in, and about, proof, truth and fact-finding in criminal adjudication.

(d) Personal and Professional Integrity

In one tangible sense, the integrity of criminal process always comes down to the integrity of the professionals who operate it. Institutions, processes and procedures are not self-actuating, but rather represent an aggregation of human decision-making and concerted activity. Our fourth conception of criminal process integrity, as the personal and professional integrity of the men and women involved in the administration of criminal justice, might, then, just as easily have been our analytical point of departure.

The choices of individual police officers,[153] prosecutors[154] or even judges[155] to take bribes, plant evidence or otherwise deliberately subvert the proper administration of justice are obvious failings of personal and professional integrity, which by extension also threaten the integrity of criminal process at large. Partly owing to the special responsibilities with which officials are entrusted, their wrongdoing may be difficult to detect or prove. This calls for robust institutional mechanisms for monitoring, deterring and exposing official corruption and other wrongdoing. It also demands effective institutional checks and balances, not only in terms of intelligent institutional design (addressed, in particular, by M Jackson in Chapter 8), but also in the sense that individual practitioners must rise to the challenge of

---

[152] Physical contamination of forensic samples is one constant risk. For a striking illustration, see J Gans, 'Ozymandias on Trial: Wrongs and Rights in DNA Cases' in Roberts and Hunter (eds), above n 10.

[153] Official policing policy in relation to corruption, and more broadly, increasingly invokes the ideal (or rhetoric) of 'integrity'. See eg HMIC, *Police Integrity and Corruption Force Reports* (2014), www.justiceinspec-torates.gov.uk/hmic/publications/police-integrity-corruption-force/ (accessed 7 January 2016); Police Integrity Commission, *Annual Report 2014–15* (Sydney, NSW PIC, 2015), www.pic.nsw.gov.au/Report.aspx?ReportId=165 (accessed 7 January 2016) (including discussion of 'integrity hazards'); Office of Police Integrity, *Talking about Integrity: A Guide for Police Managers* (Melbourne, OPI Victoria, 2009), www.ibac.vic.gov.au/docs/default-source/guidelines/talking-about-integrity--a-guide-for-police-managers--apr-2009.pdf?sfvrsn=6 (accessed 7 January 2016); National Institute of Justice, 'Police Integrity', www.nij.gov/topics/law-enforcement/legitimacy/pages/integrity.aspx (accessed 7 January 2016) (linking integrity to accountability, equal treatment, public accessibility, audit, and education of personnel); US Department of Justice, *Police Integrity—Public Service with Honor*, NCJ 163811 (Washington DC, Department of Justice, 2007); HMIC, *Police Integrity: England, Wales and Northern Ireland—Securing and Maintaining Public Confidence* (London, HMIC, 1999).

[154] *Ramanauskas v Lithuania* (2010) 51 EHRR 11.

[155] The UN Basic Principles on the Independence of the Judiciary, endorsed by GA Res 40/32 (29 November 1985) and GA Res 40/146 (13 December 1985), provide in paragraph [2] that judges 'shall decide matters before them impartially, on the basis of facts and in accordance with the law, without any restrictions, improper influences, inducements, pressures, threats or interferences, direct or indirect, from any quarter or for any reason'. Paragraph [10] further mandates that: 'Persons selected for judicial office shall be individuals of integrity and ability with appropriate training or qualifications in law.'

discharging their designated institutional responsibilities skilfully and courageously. This applies, perforce, to the judicial responsibility to review the legality of all administrative action, a cornerstone of the rule of law in common law jurisdictions, as restated in general terms by Young in Chapter 1 and applied to judicial supervision of prosecutorial discretion by Cowdery (Chapter 5) and Gans (Chapter 6). Judicial willingness to visit illegality in the conduct of criminal investigations and prosecution with appropriate sanctions, including evidentiary exclusion, is another significant factor in this discussion, explored by Whitfort (Chapter 10) and Chau (Chapter 11), amongst others, in this volume.

This is not to say that institutional failings can always be laid wholly or directly at the door of individual miscreants. The conduct of criminal proceedings involves coordinated collective action. Individual practitioners operate within a framework of law, organisational policies and embedded routines and practices, which properly structure and constrain their individual preferences and judgements. Frontline practitioners may bear little personal responsibility for faithfully implementing their organisation's policies in accordance with its published objectives and priorities[156] (though the same cannot necessarily be said for organisational leaders and their senior managers). Tensions between personal conviction and fidelity to professional duty may induce conflicts of loyalty, complicating the notion of acting with personal *and* professional integrity. This is a subplot of Hunter's critical discussion of judicial law-making in Chapter 14. Whistleblowers may be obliged to betray their friends and comrades in order to expose official wrongdoing. As Dixon cautions in Chapter 3, 'integrity' is not necessarily to be celebrated if it refers only to a self-defensive 'blue wall of silence' or, in broader terms, an impoverished criminal process committed to protecting 'its own' from external criticism and defending the existing social order at almost any cost.

It nonetheless remains an undeniable feature of criminal process that frontline officials retain significant spheres of personal operational discretion to exercise, as they deem fit, on a day-to-day basis. This is notoriously true of routine street policing, as ethnographers continually rediscover.[157] In this volume, with its topical inclination towards litigated cases, it is prosecutorial discretion that looms particularly large, especially in the essays by Cowdery, Gans, Roberts and M Jackson (Chapters 5 to 8). Edmond, in Chapter 9, introduces the further complicating factor of expert witnesses' professional ethical responsibilities.[158] An important methodological moral to be drawn from these discussions concerns the under-appreciated theoretical significance of codes of professional ethics, alongside other 'soft

---

[156] Assuming the 'normal' functioning of a broadly legitimate criminal process. Whether, for example, a judge in a racist legal system should resign or use their position to promote equality raises altogether different (existential) questions of personal and professional integrity: cf D Dyzenhaus, *Judging the Judges, Judging Ourselves* (Oxford, Hart Publishing, 1998). On related questions of the integrity of positive law, see D Fraser, *Law after Auschwitz: Towards a Jurisprudence of the Holocaust* (Durham NC, Carolina Academic Press, 2005).

[157] See eg CG Gerstein and JJ Prescott, 'Process Costs and Police Discretion' (2015) 128 *Harvard Law Review Forum* 268, 271–72 ('substantive law is mostly irrelevant to the matter of police discretion', referring specifically to minor public order offending); S Portillo and DS Rudes, 'Construction of Justice at the Street Level' (2014) 10 *Annual Review of Law and Social Science* 321; DA Harris, 'The Stories, the Statistics, and the Law: Why "Driving While Black" Matters' (1999) 84 *Minnesota Law Review* 265, 269, 319 (concluding that 'officers are free, for all practical purposes, to act on the assumption that being black increases the probability that an individual is a criminal', such that '"[d]riving while black" has begun to threaten the integrity of the entire process'). Generally, see D Dixon, *Law in Policing* (Oxford, Oxford University Press, 1997); R Reiner (ed), *Policing II* (Aldershot, Dartmouth, 1996).

[158] Also see J Sanders, 'Expert Witness Ethics' (2007) 76 *Fordham Law Review* 1539.

law' instruments, for the conduct and supervision of criminal proceedings. Whilst primary legislation and appellate case law tend to dominate academic discussion and legal education, legal practitioners are often more directly concerned with codes of practice, internal guidelines, 'working rules' and local cultures of practice as normative resources structuring and guiding their discretionary decision-making.[159]

Professional legal ethics are too often assimilated to a list of mandatory directives for rote-learning by practitioners. Ethical practice should instead be conceptualised, and taught to practitioners, as a complex interface between abstract normative requirements and their concrete, contextualised applications, which professionals are obliged to negotiate for themselves under the aegis of integrity.[160] Ethical legal practice is functionally differentiated, the more so in an adversarial procedural system.[161] The duties of the prosecutor, as representative of the public interest and conscripted 'minister of justice' (see Cowdery in Chapter 5), are not coterminous with zealous representation of the accused, as Edmond (Chapter 9) also argues. Although none of our contributors affords systematic consideration to the ethics of criminal defence, the professional duties of defence lawyers crop up in relation to custodial police interviews with suspects (Dixon), negotiated pleas (McConville and Marsh), and adversarial challenges to expert evidence (Edmond). Concepts of professional integrity are further complicated by the appearance of criminal justice professionals embedded in alternative systems of practical authority and ethical responsibility. One thinks here of the forensic pathologist answerable to the dictates of medical ethics, as well as, more generally, of any expert witness committed to upholding scientific standards of validity, objectivity and non-partisanship. The integrity of criminal proceedings as a whole rests on the possibility of keeping potentially conflicting professional loyalties in productive tension, without allowing any one occupational group to dominate or to disrupt the normative equilibrium, but also without leaving any 'dead zones' in the coverage of professional responsibility. Circumstances of overlapping ethical duty can paradoxically conduce to ethical *irresponsibility*, as where everybody assumes (or too easily allows themselves to believe) that proactively managing the integrity of the process is ultimately 'somebody else's business' whilst systemic failures in the meantime are 'not my fault'.

Critical discussion of personal integrity in criminal process is not exhausted by professionals' ethical obligations. Indeed, one might think that officials are really only the supporting cast. The primary actors in criminal proceedings are laypeople, in the guise of suspects, offenders, complainants, victims and witnesses. Do we expect even criminal defendants to play their designated role with integrity? In a sense, we do. After all, accused who elect to testify in their own defence take an oath (or affirm) to tell the truth under

---

[159] In addition to citations at nn 90 and 157, above, see eg D Dixon 'The Normative Structure of Policing' in D Dixon (ed), *A Culture of Corruption* (Sydney, Hawkins Press, 1999); Pattenden, above n 124; MR Damaška, 'Structures of Authority and Comparative Criminal Procedure' (1975) 84 *Yale Law Journal* 480.

[160] See further, AT Kronman, 'Living in the Law' (1987) 54 *University of Chicago Law Review* 835; WH Simon, 'Ethics, Professionalism, and Meaningful Work' (1997) 26 *Hofstra Law Review* 445.

[161] See eg WH Simon 'The Ethics of Criminal Defense' (1993) 91 *Michigan Law Review* 1703. But cf TL Shaffer, 'The Unique, Novel, and Unsound Adversary Ethic' (1988) 41 *Vanderbilt Law Review* 697; AW Alschuler, 'How to Win the Trial of the Century: The Ethics of Lord Brougham and the OJ Simpson Defense Team' (1998) 29 *McGeorge Law Review* 291; HS Drinker, 'Some Remarks on Mr Curtis' "The Ethics of Advocacy"' (1952) 4 *Stanford Law Review* 349.

sanction of perjury,[162] theoretical though the threat of prosecution for advancing a lying defence may be in most cases.[163] Even those who remain mute in the dock are expected to play their part, by entering a valid plea and standing their trial without disrupting the proceedings.[164] These are admittedly rather minimalist standards of ethical propriety, and perhaps there is not a great deal more to be said about criminal defendants' integrity per se. Like lay witnesses of fact more generally, who are also often reluctant and sometimes unwilling conscripts in criminal proceedings, the duties of citizenship (at least as liberals generally conceive them) may be largely confined to turning up to court, speaking when spoken to, and telling the truth as the witness believes it. The fact that common law criminal trial procedure seems to have grown out of a pervasive distrust of witnesses[165] tends to betray an institutionalised lack of confidence that even these minimalist reciprocal duties of citizenship will be discharged with integrity.

Is the position of complainants and victims any different in this regard to that of bystander witnesses? The prevailing view, bolstered by human rights law and several decades of victim-centred policy-making,[166] is that it is, or at any rate ought to be. What, then, would integrity require of victims' participation in criminal proceedings, over and above every witness' duty to tell the truth? This is difficult terrain. One might reasonably expect enhanced rights of victim participation to be balanced by additional responsibilities. On the other hand, victims of crime are often emotionally vulnerable and are at risk of secondary victimisation through insensitive official processing. Perhaps the system itself should underwrite the integrity of their participation, at the same time as meeting their needs for support and information. Here, we can do no more than pose the question for further reflection and discussion.

Jurors are likewise conscripts to criminal proceedings, but in other respects represent a special case. Jurors are laypeople, but they also partly constitute the judicial tribunal and serve as the embodiment of the community in microcosm. The jury's special, indeed *sacred*, responsibility of judgment echoes down the centuries.[167] It is plausible to think that the jury's pivotal role in a matter of such pre-eminent public importance as determining liability to criminal conviction and punishment might impose special responsibilities, even though jury service is mandatory for those selected. John Jackson pursues this line of

---

[162] Intriguingly, this appears to be a cultural peculiarity of common law jurisdictions. Defendants do not testify under oath in civilian jurisdictions. See G van Kessel, 'European Perspectives on the Accused as a Source of Testimonial Evidence' (1998) 100 *West Virginia Law Review* 799; JK Walker, 'A Comparative Discussion of the Privilege Against Self-Incrimination' (1993) 14 *New York Law School Journal of International and Comparative Law* 1.

[163] Not in all cases: see eg *R v Miell* [2008] 1 WLR 627, [2007] EWCA Crim 3130; *DPP v Humphrys* [1977] AC 1 (HL).

[164] Disruptive accused are liable to be sent out of court, and may be held in contempt: see eg *R v McGrath* [2013] EWCA Crim 1261, [2014] Crim LR 144; *R v Gough* [2015] EWCA Crim 1079 (accused who 'held a sincere and deep belief in the philosophical approach to living life naked' and 'sought to live his life following his own reason and with integrity' was convicted *in absentia*, having insisted on appearing naked in court). Trials *in absentia* pose further challenges to the integrity of adversarial criminal adjudication: cf *R v Gee* [2012] SASCFC 86.

[165] EJ Imwinkelried, 'The Worst Evidence Principle: The Best Hypothesis as to the Logical Structure of Evidence Law' (1992) 46 *University of Miami Law Review* 1069.

[166] K Starmer, 'Human Rights, Victims and the Prosecution of Crime in the 21st Century' [2014] *Criminal Law Review* 777; J Doak, *Victims' Rights, Human Rights and Criminal Justice* (Oxford, Hart Publishing, 2008); JD Jackson, 'Justice for All: Putting Victims at the Heart of Criminal Justice?' (2003) 30 *Journal of Law and Society* 309.

[167] JQ Whitman, *The Origins of Reasonable Doubt: Theological Roots of the Criminal Trial* (New Haven, Yale University Press, 2008).

argument in Chapter 12, to reach conclusions challenging conventional wisdom. Criminal juries deliberate and decide collectively, but *individual* conscience plays an important role in the common law theory of jury trial, especially in North America where unanimous verdicts are still the norm and the 'hold out' juror is something of a cultural icon.[168] Juries cannot be described as bearing 'professional' responsibility for their conduct in criminal trial proceedings, but the role of juror in a criminal case certainly does bring with it institutionally-defined as well as personal ethical responsibilities. For example, juries are required to deliberate in secret, and in England and Wales it is a contempt of court punishable by imprisonment to betray the secrets of the juryroom, even after proceedings are concluded.[169] Still, ought implies can. Any existing or putative obligation on jurors to deliberate in a particular fashion, or to report the process or outcome of their deliberations in a particular way (with or without published 'reasons'), must be consistent with the (bounded) cognitive competence of human beings and the psychological dynamics of group decision-making. Personal and professional integrity is only a meaningful practical ideal whilst it remains on a human scale. It would be fatuous to criticise juries, or any other criminal process actors or agencies, for failing to live up to a supererogatory standard of integrity modelled on sainthood or superhuman cognition.

5. Promoting Integrity

The purpose of this book is to kick-start a methodologically sophisticated conversation about the 'integrity' of criminal process, and to make significant contributions towards its development across a range of familiar, and some less familiar, topics and issues. As befits an exploratory study of this nature, we make no pretentions to comprehensiveness, nor do we offer any firm conclusions in drawing this Introduction to a close. Having elucidated the concept of integrity and sketched out a preliminary taxonomy of criminal process applications, it is high time that we allowed the individual contributors to speak for themselves.

Some of the following chapters are primarily critically descriptive and diagnostic of shortcomings in contemporary criminal process. Others attempt to draw more programmatic lessons from deficient policies or practices, offering concrete proposals for procedural reforms calculated to promote integrity in criminal adjudication. Numerous pressure points, obscurities and blemishes in the evolving jurisprudence of integrity are identified along the way, informed by comparative legal scholarship. Integrity provides a methodologically well-appointed meeting place for vigorous, pluralistic debate encompassing a rich diversity of theoretical approaches and perspectives. Severally, and in collective synergy, the essays comprising this collection demonstrate both the heuristic value and the normative potential of refocusing criminal process through the lens of integrity.

---

[168] An icon with complex cultural resonances, to be sure: see J Abramson, 'Anger at Angry Jurors' (2007) 82 *Chicago-Kent Law Review* 591.

[169] PR Ferguson, 'The Criminal Jury in England and Scotland: the Confidentiality Principle and the Investigation of Impropriety' (2006) 10 *International Journal of Evidence and Proof* 180; K Quinn, 'Jury Bias and the European Convention on Human Rights: A Well-Kept Secret?' [2004] *Criminal Law Review* 998.

1

A Public Law Conception of Integrity in the Criminal Process

SIMON NM YOUNG*

Introduction

Integrity has become a prominent theme in current discourse on the criminal process. It is referred to in cases involving police or prosecutorial misconduct. Courts increasingly make reference to integrity as a ground for ordering relief against and for the government. Integrity lies at the heart of the entrapment and abuse of process doctrines. What more can be expected of the integrity principle will depend on a proper understanding of its scope and meaning. The principle is said to be 'an influential but also a puzzling principle of criminal justice'.[1] What is the relationship between integrity and human rights? And what is its relationship to notions such as public confidence in the administration of justice, disrepute, accountability and legitimacy? Does it mean anything more than having minimum standards of conduct (and if so, when and in what context), and again is this anything different from a rights-based approach to criminal process? Does it refer to having coherence in the system and if so, coherent by what underlying premises?

This chapter further explores the principle of integrity with reference to the views expressed by courts and scholars. It assesses whether the principle has relevance outside the stay of proceedings and exclusion of evidence cases, as a general and defining element of criminal process. I begin the chapter by reflecting critically on existing literature and case law on integrity theory which fit schematically around six characteristics. In the second half of the chapter, I construct a new way of thinking about integrity from an institutional perspective that may help to explain what courts and public officials do in practice. The new approach brings together ideas about judicial review, abuse of process and prosecutorial discretion. I argue that public law and judicial review concepts can be used to understand the stay and exclusion cases. From this survey of the landscape comes a broadly encompassing institutional approach to integrity in criminal process that springs from the concept of overriding public interest.

* I thank Paul Roberts, Jill Hunter, David Dixon, Daniel Yip, Peter Chau, Amanda Whitfort and Michael Jackson for their helpful comments on and assistance with this chapter.
[1] A Duff, L Farmer, S Marshall and V Tadros, *The Trial on Trial: Volume 3 Towards a Normative Theory of the Criminal Trial* (Oxford, Hart Publishing, 2007) 256.

1. Reflections on Integrity Theory Literature

(a) Integrity of 'The System', Rather than of the Individual or Office

Most writings refer to the principle of integrity in relation to the criminal justice system as a whole.[2] This is consistent with how common law courts have used the principle.[3] However, there is a need to explain why pre-trial misconduct by police might matter for the judge in his or her conduct of the trial. If the judge and police are conceived as being part of a single system (which they no doubt are) then for the judge to ignore or appear to condone the police misconduct puts the system in a self-contradiction.[4] Andrew Ashworth suggests that in this situation the judge excludes the evidence or stays the proceedings to achieve coherence and maintain the moral authority of the system.[5] Antony Duff et al refer to 'integrity as integration' in the sense that 'the normative validity of the trial rests on the validity of the state's conduct pre-trial'.[6]

But it might be said that the notion of integrity 'of the system' was a fiction invented in response to the separation thesis (so powerfully articulated in *R v Sang*) prior to the rise of domestic human rights law, as we now know it.[7] This approach is supported by the view that the abuse of process doctrine developed from reactionary judicial thinking that assumes a greater role than *Sang* allows for upholding the rule of law. Court-enforced 'respect for the rule of law' is a practical means to achieve coherence in a legal system founded on the rule of law.[8] One wonders whether resort to the integrity principle would have been necessary had human rights law been established earlier.[9] Once fundamental rights, both pre-trial and trial rights, can be directly invoked in the criminal trial proper, the judge must necessarily pay attention to the pre-trial conduct of other agencies, irrespective of the integrity principle.

Rarely is the integrity principle defined from the standpoint of an individual's character or integrity, or the integrity of a particular office—which is probably more in line with the ordinary usage of the word integrity. Ashworth provides an exception. He describes two varieties of the principle, the first concerns the integrity of the system and coherence, and the second is the 'principle of judicial integrity', compromised where the judge acts 'on

---

[2] A Ashworth, 'Exploring the integrity principle in evidence and procedure' in P Mirfield and R Smith (eds), *Essays for Colin Tapper* (Oxford, Oxford University Press, 2003) 107, 108; P Roberts and A Zuckerman, *Criminal Evidence*, 2nd edn (Oxford, Oxford University Press, 2010) 189, referring to 'the integrity of the administration of criminal justice'.

[3] For example, *R v Maxwell* [2011] 2 Cr App R 31, [13] (UKSC) referring to the 'integrity of the criminal justice system'; *R v Hart* [2014] 2 SCR 544, [87] ('to preserve the integrity of the justice system').

[4] Ashworth, above n 2, 108.

[5] Ibid.

[6] Duff et al, above n 1, 236.

[7] *R v Sang* [1980] AC 402 (HL). But see earlier development of an integrity-based public policy ground for exclusion in Australia: *R v Ireland* (1970) 126 CLR 321 (HC); *Bunning v Cross* (1978) 141 CLR 54 (HC), discussed in K Mellifont, *Fruit of the Poisonous Tree: Evidence derived from illegally or improperly obtained evidence* (Sydney, Federation Press, 2010) 135–39.

[8] See eg *R v Horseferry Road Magistrates' Court, ex parte Bennett* [1994] 1 AC 42, 67 (Lord Bridge).

[9] But note how in Canada complementary rights and integrity doctrines have developed to protect fundamental interests and guard against false confessions, prejudicial evidence and police misconduct, see *R v Hart* [2014] 2 SCR 544, [68]–[80].

the evidential and procedural results of a violation of a fundamental right' and thereby becomes complicit in the violation.[10] Ashworth treats the two variations of the principle as having much in common, but does not explore the second variation in greater depth or beyond the judicial office.[11] In contrast, a 1993 Ontario report on pre-trial criminal matters conceives the integrity of the each of the main participants in the criminal trial process as being essential to the functioning of the justice system.[12] 'Judicial integrity' is also described as the original reason for the US Supreme Court to adopt the exclusionary rule for federal criminal proceedings in its 1914 decision, *Weeks v United States*.[13]

(b) Close Association with Rights Thesis

Ashworth confines his analysis of the integrity principle to breaches of fundamental rights and does not explore whether the principle could be engaged outside of rights discourse or ever be used to justify restrictions on rights.[14] Others have noted the more expansive potential of the integrity principle, as being able to explain responses to misconduct short of rights violations.[15]

Rarely is it contemplated that the integrity principle could be invoked to limit rights or otherwise work against the interests of a defendant or suspect. As Duff et al note 'when it applies it frustrates, or at least tends to frustrate, conviction', and since '[s]omething very significant is thus lost', they argue to keep the application of the principle narrow.[16] But it is not implausible to speak of restricting a person's rights or opportunities in order to protect the integrity of the legal system, especially when threatened with possible abuse, for example, collateral challenges that disrupt trial proceedings.[17] Another illustration, from Canadian bail law, is what is known as the tertiary ground for denying bail where 'necessary in order to maintain confidence in the administration of justice, having regard to all the circumstances'.[18] A bare majority of the Supreme Court justices held that the power did not infringe the right 'not to be denied reasonable bail except for just cause' under section 11(e) of the Charter of Rights and Freedoms.[19] The majority recognised the issue as being closely

---

[10] Ashworth, above n 2, 108.

[11] Ibid.

[12] *Report of the Attorney General's Advisory Committee on Charge Screening, Disclosure, and Resolution Discussions*, chaired by Hon G Arthur Martin (Toronto, Ontario Ministry of the Attorney General, 1993) ('Martin Committee Report') 26: 'The need for all participants in the early stages of the criminal justice process to act with uncompromising integrity cannot be overstated … [W]ithout integrity, no system of justice, no matter how ingeniously designed and lavishly funded, can function.'

[13] RM Bloom and DH Fentin, '"A More Majestic Conception": The Importance of Judicial Integrity in Preserving the Exclusionary Rule' (2010) 13 *University of Pennsylvania Journal of Constitutional Law* 47, 50 (tracing the history from *Weeks v United States*, 232 US 383 (1914)).

[14] Ashworth, above n 2, 108.

[15] See Duff et al, above n 1, 235 ('The rights thesis plays a role in the integrity thesis, but it does not exhaust the integrity principle'); Roberts and Zuckerman, above n 2, 189 ('certain official conduct—eg forms of race, class, or gender bias—may harm the integrity of criminal proceedings without actually breaching any identifiable rights').

[16] Duff et al, above n 1, 241.

[17] For example, *Yeung Ka Sing, Carson v Secretary for Justice*, unreported, HCAL59/2013, 26 March 2013, CFI (HK); *Salahuddin Amin v Director General of the Security Service [MI5]* [2013] EWHC 1579 (QB).

[18] Criminal Code, RSC 1985, c C-46, s 515(10)(c).

[19] *R v Hall* [2002] 3 SCR 309. More recently see *R v St-Cloud*, 2015 SCC 27, [78] (making the connection with s 24(2) of the Charter of Rights and Freedoms).

related to judicial integrity: 'public confidence and the integrity of the rule of law are inextricably intertwined'.[20]

(c) Narrow Focus on Judicial Power to Stay or Exclude

Academic discussion of the integrity principle tends to relate almost exclusively to the power of the court to exclude improperly obtained evidence or to stay proceedings for abuse of process. Thus reference is made to 'judicial' integrity[21] and sometimes to prosecutorial integrity.[22] But to be a defining element of the criminal process, integrity should have something to say more generally and specifically about the other actors in the criminal process. Consider, for example, the lay jury. What, if anything, does the integrity principle have to say about the role of the jury and the implications of jury misconduct?[23] Writings on the conduct of non-judicial actors tend to be from the perspective of ethics,[24] professional standards and even civility.[25]

(d) No Consensus on the Significance of Public Confidence

Peter Mirfield helpfully identifies three forms of the integrity principle: (1) court-centred integrity where the judge applies 'its own standards of propriety and decency'; (2) public conduct integrity where 'attention is directed to the likely reaction of the general public, rather than to the court's own standards'; and (3) public attitude integrity where 'the court must seek to gauge how the public will respond in its attitude to the criminal legal system'.[26] The latter looks to the court's assessment of public confidence in the system. Mirfield uses these three forms as descriptive tools without favouring any one over the others.[27] Ashworth, by contrast, is highly critical of the 'public attitude' of integrity, primarily because public attitude (in the form of public opinion) may favour positions contrary to fundamental rights.[28] It would also be antithetical to the rule of law for courts to be swayed by popular opinion in all situations.

However, Canadian Charter law has managed to apply a public confidence approach to integrity in its test for excluding unconstitutionally obtained evidence.[29] From its earliest

---

[20] *R v Hall* [2002] 3 SCR 309, [27]. See also in this volume Chapters 3 (Stubbs) and 14 (Hunter) on integrity from a victim perspective.

[21] Mellifont, above n 7, 20; Ashworth, above n 2, 108.

[22] See early cases *Connelly v DPP* [1964] AC 1254, 1354–35 (HL); *DPP v Humphrys* [1977] AC 1, 34, 41 (HL).

[23] See Chapter 12 (J Jackson) in this volume.

[24] D Callahan, 'Applied Ethics in Criminal Justice' (1982) 1 *Criminal Justice Ethics* 2; C Banks, *Criminal Justice Ethics*, 3rd edn (Thousand Oaks CA, Sage, 2013); A Ashworth and M Redmayne, *The Criminal Process*, 4th edn (Oxford, Oxford University Press, 2010) ch 3.

[25] G Trotter, 'Integrity and Honour in Criminal Litigation: Hollow Aspirations or Enforceable Standards?', paper for 6th Colloquium on the Legal Profession, March 2006, Law Society of Upper Canada, Toronto, Ontario.

[26] P Mirfield, *Silence, Confessions and Improperly Obtained Evidence* (Oxford, Oxford University Press, 1997) 24.

[27] Ibid.

[28] Ashworth, above n 2, 111.

[29] Section 24(2) of the Charter of Rights and Freedoms provides that where 'a court concludes that evidence was obtained in a manner that infringed or denied any rights or freedoms guaranteed by this Charter, the evidence shall be excluded if it is established, having regard to all the circumstances, the admission of it in the proceedings would bring the administration of justice into disrepute'.

case on the issue, the Supreme Court recognised that ascertaining the repute of the system from public opinion polls was objectionable.[30] The matter was to be assessed by the court objectively and from a long-term perspective.[31] In its current position on exclusion, the Supreme Court has articulated a test that blends non-epistemic considerations (seriousness of Charter infringing conduct and impact on defendant's rights) with more epistemic concerns (importance of having a trial on the merits).[32] The Hong Kong Court of Final Appeal has articulated a similar balancing test that aims to ensure 'the administration of justice is not brought into disrepute', 'public conscience is not affronted' and 'the integrity of the judicial system is not compromised'.[33] It was held that unconstitutionally obtained evidence could be admitted if 'its reception (i) is conducive to a fair trial, (ii) is reconcilable with the respect due to the right or rights concerned [and] (iii) appears unlikely to encourage any future breaches of that, those or other rights'.[34]

A growing number of scholars have noted the importance of public confidence in discussing the principle of integrity. Paul Roberts and Adrian Zuckerman argue that the moral legitimacy of a system of law requires that there be public confidence in and respect for the system.[35] If judges 'routinely winked at rights violations ... criminal proceedings would be tainted by the appearance of double standards, and the public would probably quickly lose respect for a system of law'.[36] Ian Dennis goes as far as asserting that the 'aims of the law of evidence are ultimately referable to an overall objective of promoting legitimacy of decision in adjudication'.[37] Such legitimacy depends on 'integrity', which 'signifies an aspiration that an adjudicative decision should as far as possible be factually accurate and also consistent with other fundamental moral and political values embedded in the legal system'.[38] Australian writers have also noted the judicial integrity principle serving 'to preserve public confidence in the justice system'[39] and protect 'the integrity of the judicial institution'.[40]

---

[30] *R v Collins* [1987] SCR 265, 281–82.

[31] Ibid.

[32] *R v Grant* [2009] 2 SCR 353, [71].

[33] *HKSAR v Muhammad Riaz Khan* (2012) 15 HKCFAR 232, [18], following *R v Looseley* [2001] 1 WLR 2060, [25], [36], [71] (HL).

[34] Ibid [20]. It awaits to be seen how each of these factors will be interpreted and applied, but there appears to be a strong emphasis on protecting rights and deterring future breaches. See A Pun, 'The Admissibility of Evidence Obtained in Breach of Constitutional Rights in Hong Kong' (2013) 14 *Asia-Pacific Journal on Human Rights and the Law* 67.

[35] Roberts and Zuckerman, above n 2, 188.

[36] Ibid.

[37] I Dennis, *The Law of Evidence*, 4th edn (London, Sweet & Maxwell, 2010) 49. Similarly see P Duff, 'Admissibility of Improperly Obtained Physical Evidence in the Scottish Criminal Trial: The Search for Principle' (2004) 8 *Edinburgh Law Review* 152, 171–76.

[38] Dennis, above n 37, 50. More recently, see L Hoyano, 'What is Balanced on the Scales of Justice? In Search of the Essence of the Right to a Fair Trial' [2014] *Criminal Law Review* 4, 5 (focusing on the 'integrity of the verdict, unclouded by nebulous "balancing"').

[39] Mellifont, above n 7, 20, 189, citing from McHugh J in *Ridgeway v R* (1995) 184 CLR 19, 83 (HC), referring to 'ensuring that public confidence in the justice system is not undermined by the perception that the courts of law condone or encourage unlawful or improper conduct on the part of those who have the duty to enforce the law', originating from *R v Ireland* (1970) 126 CLR 321 (HC). See also *R v Nicholas* (1998) 193 CLR 173 (HC); *Lee v R* [2014] HCA 20, [51].

[40] B Selway, 'Principle, Public Policy and Unfairness—Exclusion of Evidence on Discretionary Grounds' (2002) 23 *Adelaide Law Review* 1, 11.

A full account of the integrity principle must reckon with the increasing regard paid by courts and scholars to public confidence in the system. Even before the rise of domestic human rights law, courts referred to public confidence in shaping criminal law doctrine. Lord Reid in the famous strict liability case of *Sweet v Parsley* noted in his construction of the legislation how 'every manifestly unjust conviction made known to the public' tended to undermine 'public confidence in the justice of the law and of its administration'.[41]

(e) Difficulty Explaining what Courts do in Practice

Rights-based accounts of the integrity principle struggle to explain courts' discretionary exclusion and stay determinations. As Roberts and Zuckerman 'frankly' note, such decisions are 'too complex, circumstantial, and uncertain to be reduced to any simple, algorithmic, all-purpose rule'.[42] Ashworth's coherence theory taken to its logical limits demands prima facie exclusion for all evidence obtained in breach of fundamental rights and any exception to this rule is seen as a 'compromise' between two extreme positions.[43] Even the approaches of Duff et al, namely, integrity as integration and integrity as moral standing, have difficulty explaining the admission of evidence in cases of more than a merely technical breach.[44]

Public confidence based accounts of integrity provide more plausible explanations for decisions to exclude and admit evidence or to stay or not stay a proceeding. Typically, a balancing exercise is involved. Under the Canadian approach, a stay will be refused, (i) if there is no risk that any prejudice to a fair trial or the integrity of the justice system will be 'manifested, perpetuated or aggravated through the conduct of the trial or by its outcome'; (ii) some alternative remedy exists capable of redressing the prejudice; or (iii) society's interest in having a 'final decision on the merits' outweighs the 'interests in favour of granting a stay'.[45] Where evidence is not excluded under section 24(2) of the Canadian Charter, it is because the court is not convinced that admitting the evidence would bring the administration of justice into disrepute. By the test developed by the Supreme Court, this typically means that 'society's interest in the adjudication of the case on its merits' is strong when compared to the risk that admitting the evidence would 'send the message [that] the justice system condones serious state misconduct [or] individual rights count for little'.[46]

(f) Abstract and Absolutist Theorising, Stripped of Historical Context

Theorising about the integrity principle tends to proceed in the abstract, without admitting the possibility that the principle might mean different things in different times and

---

[41] *Sweet v Parsley* [1970] AC 132, 150 (HL).

[42] Roberts and Zuckerman, above n 2, 190; developed and affirmed in P Roberts, 'Excluding Evidence as Protecting Constitutional or Human Rights?' in L Zedner and JV Roberts (eds), *Principles and Values in Criminal Law and Criminal Justice: Essays in Honour of Andrew Ashworth* (Oxford, Oxford University Press, 2012) 171, 188–90.

[43] Ashworth, above n 2, 118. Even Ireland has now moved away from its absolute exclusionary rule, see *DPP v JC* [2015] IESC 31, though only by a 4:3 majority.

[44] Duff et al, above n 1, 241.

[45] *R v Babos*, 2014 SCC 16, [32].

[46] *R v Grant* [2009] 2 SCR 353, [71].

contexts. Normative conceptions of the principle try to operate on the basis of universals, for example, a legal system, the administration of criminal justice, the rule of law. But 'integrity' has a richer meaning that evolves over time and circumstances, depending on the attitude of the polity towards its public officials and leaders. Public confidence-based evaluations of integrity evolve, not with the day-to-day shifts of public opinion, but on the basis of objective judicial assessments of public attitudes towards the legal system. Legal doctrine in this area is also sensitive to broader implications for law enforcement, the administration of justice and society at large. The evolution of the Canadian section 24(2) Charter test is a case in point. For many years, the Supreme Court's original approach set down in its 1987 decision of *R v Collins* used a trial fairness criterion that effectively excluded almost all 'conscriptive evidence' obtained in breach of a Charter right.[47] This approach held sway until the late 1990s when a shift in judicial opinion began to take root as a result of prosecutorial initiatives to change the law.[48] The Supreme Court eventually responded to these diffuse pressures in 2009, by finessing its position on trial fairness and developing the current approach to section 24(2).[49]

In recent years, there has also been more attention paid globally to the integrity of public officials and greater expectations in terms of their accountability.[50] It is part of a trend towards identifying and recognising new international standards to combat the impact of bribery and corruption upon the justice system.[51] Each State party to the United Nations Convention against Corruption is expected to promote 'integrity, honesty and responsibility among its public officials, in accordance with the fundamental principles of its legal system'.[52] The Arab Spring in 2011 and other political developments presaging greater democracy, transparency and public accountability all point to higher expectations of public officials. Might these new developments also be relevant to the shaping of an integrity principle that has wider application in criminal justice systems?

This review of integrity theory literature, developing themes canvassed in this volume's Introduction, reveals a gap between the theory and application of the integrity principle. Of the different theoretical approaches to integrity, ensuring the moral legitimacy of adjudication and decisions by courts best explains why common law courts have invoked the integrity principle.

---

[47] *R v Collins* [1987] SCR 265. Conscriptive evidence was defined in *R v Stillman* [1997] 1 SCR 607, [80] as evidence obtained when 'an accused, in violation of his Charter rights, is compelled to incriminate himself at the behest of the state by means of a statement, the use of the body or the production of bodily samples'.

[48] Only a minority of the justices in *R v Stillman* [1997] 1 SCR 607 was prepared to rethink the exclusion test.

[49] *R v Grant* [2009] 2 SCR 353, applied most recently in *R v Taylor*, 2014 SCC 50.

[50] See eg the 'Seven Principles of Public Life', 'integrity' being the second principle, established by the UK's Committee on Standards in Public Life in 1995, see Lord Nolan, *Standards in Public Life: First Report of the Committee on Standards in Public Life* (London, HMSO, 1995), www.public-standards.gov.uk (accessed 7 January 2016). More recently, see the College of Policing's *Code of Ethics*, laid before the UK Parliament in July 2014, which has 'honesty and integrity' as the first professional standard.

[51] See eg J Horder and P Alldridge (eds), *Modern Bribery Laws: Comparative Perspectives* (Cambridge, Cambridge University Press, 2013).

[52] United Nations Convention against Corruption, adopted by UNGA 31 October 2003, entry into force 14 December 2005, UN Doc A/58/422, Arts 8(1) and 11.

2. Institutional Aspects of the Integrity Principle

The aim of this section is to examine institutional manifestations of the integrity principle, rather than viewing it from a purely abstract or theoretical perspective. It is not the intention here to explore or defend any particular underlying theoretical rationale for the integrity principle. Instead, the aim is to conceptualise an institutional approach that can shine new light on the application of the principle.

(a) Public Officials and Public Expectations

In setting out the institutional approach, one begins by considering public expectations of government officials, such as police officers and prosecutors, who discharge public duties and exercise powers for the public benefit. Where individuals' conduct falls below expectations such shortcomings could affect public confidence, both in individuals and also in the institutions they represent. While precise expectations may vary, the public will generally expect officials to discharge their official duties with honesty and integrity and always in the public interest. The 'Seven Principles of Public Life', established in 1995 by the UK Committee on Standards in Public Life, are instructive.[53] They are part of a global trend to declare and accept international standards in the conduct of public officials, especially in the context of anti-corruption.[54] The Seven Principles apply to all public office holders in the UK, and have been influential in shaping codes of conduct and regulating government practices.

The first principle is that holders of public office 'should act solely in terms of the public interest'. The second principle, titled 'integrity', requires office-holders to avoid or declare conflicts of interests. The other principles are unsurprising: objectivity, accountability, openness, honesty and leadership. The leadership principle has relevance to thinking about the court and prosecutor relationship: 'Holders of public office should exhibit these principles in their own behaviour. They should actively promote and robustly support the principles and be willing to challenge poor behaviour wherever it occurs.'[55] A court that ignores police or prosecutorial misconduct would run up against this last principle.

In common law countries, there is also a socially entrenched expectation that the acts of public officials may be subject to challenge on public law grounds, and relief can be obtained either from courts or administrative tribunals.[56] The public expects officials to act lawfully, rationally, fairly, and with regard to legitimate expectations. Where there are failings in this regard, in the absence of administrative relief, the expectation is that an individual can obtain relief by judicial review from an independent judiciary.

---

[53] 'Seven Principles of Public Life', above n 50.

[54] E Armstrong, *Integrity, Transparency and Accountability in Public Administration: Recent Trends, Regional and International Developments and Emerging Issues* (New York, United Nations, 2005).

[55] Committee on Standards in Public Life, *Ethics in Practice: Promoting Ethical Conduct in Public Life* (London, July 2014) 3, www.public-standards.gov.uk.

[56] For example, the Queensland Crime and Misconduct Commission has an 'overriding responsibility to promote public confidence' in performing its misconduct function', see Crime and Misconduct Act 2001, s 34(d).

(b) Judicial Review of Prosecutorial Action

Historically, common law courts were loath to interfere with prosecutorial decision-making, even going so far as holding at one time that such decisions were not reviewable.[57] But in recent times the immunity of prosecutorial decisions has been eroded by courts. The trend has been towards recognising new bases upon which judicial review of such decisions may be brought.[58] The doctrine of separation of powers means, however, that courts cannot simply substitute their own decision for that of the independent prosecutor.

An important distinction should be drawn between extrinsic review of prosecutorial decisions by judicial review courts and intrinsic review of prosecutorial decisions by criminal trial courts. Extrinsic review tends to fragment criminal proceedings, leading to satellite litigation that delays the trial process. Intrinsic review proceeds within the trial by the trial court, thereby keeping issues within a single institutional (including appellate) process. Another difference is that intrinsic review will tend to be less deferential than extrinsic review, because of the trial court's anxiety to protect its own process and ensure fairness to the defendant. Thus intrinsic review should not necessarily be limited to the traditional grounds of judicial review. As guardian of its own process and the fairness of the trial, the trial judge should be more inclined to review prosecutorial action closely to ensure that the integrity of its own process is not compromised.

While courts have different views on the permissible extent of review over prosecutorial decisions, it is widely accepted that courts can stay proceedings on the ground of abuse of process. Andrew Choo traces the origins of the abuse of process doctrine in civil cases to the 1800s.[59] Though references to the doctrine in criminal cases have a shorter history, Choo states that in 'determining whether a criminal prosecution should be stayed, a court is effectively reviewing the exercise of prosecutorial discretion by the executive'.[60] It is the quintessential example of intrinsic review. The proliferation of abuse of process case law in numerous common law jurisdictions over the past three decades is well known.[61] Choo notes that the scope of the doctrine has now exceeded the limits suggested by the language of abuse or misuse of *process*.[62] Choo interprets the new jurisprudence by reference to a principle of legitimacy: 'a stay should be ordered where the principle of legitimacy would be compromised if the proceedings were permitted to continue'.[63] He elaborates, 'the principle of legitimacy would require a stay if there is a substantial danger of an innocent person being convicted if the proceedings were permitted to continue, and/or if the continuation of the proceedings would compromise the moral integrity of the criminal justice process'.[64]

---

[57] *The Queen, on the Prosecution of Gregory v Allen* (1862) 1 B & S 850; *R v Smythe* (1971) 3 CCC (2d) 97 (Ont CA); *Keung Siu Wah v Attorney General* [1990] 2 HKLR 238 (CA).

[58] *Corner House Research v Director of The Serious Fraud Office* [2009] 1 AC 756, [32] (HL); *R v Nixon* [2011] 2 SCR 566, [18]–[21]; *Re C* [2006] 4 HKC 582 (CA); *RV v Director of Immigration* [2008] 4 HKLRD 529 (CFI). See also Chapter 6 (Gans) in this volume.

[59] A Choo, *Abuse of Process and Judicial Stays of Criminal Proceedings*, 2nd edn (Oxford, Oxford University Press, 2008) 2–3.

[60] Ibid 5, 9.

[61] See eg D Young, M Summers and D Corker, *Abuse of Process of Process in Criminal Proceedings*, 3rd edn (West Sussex, Tottel Publishing, 2009).

[62] Choo, above n 59, 186.

[63] Ibid.

[64] Ibid.

There is commonality here with the abuse of process test developed and applied by the Canadian Supreme Court.[65]

Orders to stay a proceeding or exclude evidence directly address prosecutorial choices to proceed with a case or adduce evidence.[66] Relief is granted even if prosecutors are in no way complicit in the impugned misconduct. When prosecutors seek to advance their case at trial, either deliberately exploiting misconduct or knowingly taking advantage of it,[67] this is enough to trigger the trial court's jurisdiction to review the decisions to proceed or adduce evidence. Such orders to stay or exclude emulate the public law remedies of prohibition and certiorari.

(c) Public Interest Account of Integrity

Prosecutors are public officials who exercise discretionary powers within public law limits. Public interest is an explicit consideration that animates the decision-making of both the prosecution and courts. It is the express policy of common law prosecutorial agencies that the decision to prosecute is governed by both a sufficiency of evidence test and a public interest test.[68] Thus prosecutorial decisions must always be made in the public interest. It is said, 'nowadays the prosecutor embodies the protector of the human rights of the public, both victim and accused'.[69]

A generalised institutional account of integrity in criminal process brings together the two ideas of intrinsic review of prosecutorial discretion and the requirement that such discretion be exercised in the public interest. Building on Choo's conceptual taxonomy, applications for judicial stays may be characterised as intrinsic review of prosecutorial considerations of public interest. This reconceptualisation encompasses judicial stays and evidentiary exclusion, together with other pertinent public law remedies.

Decisions to stay or exclude should be understood as judicial review decisions protecting the court from being a forum for the unlawful or otherwise improper exercise of discretionary prosecutorial powers. The bounds of prosecutorial discretion are reached where there is an overriding public interest not to proceed with the prosecution or to adduce the evidence in question. Thus integrity in its institutional form seeks to ensure that public officials act in accordance with overriding public interest; and when courts invoke integrity in relation to prosecutorial discretion it is to protect judicial process from being tainted by a wrongful discharge of discretionary power.

Inherent in the notion of 'public interest' is the need to balance an array of considerations relevant to the nature of the determination and the circumstances of each case.

---

[65] See text accompanying n 45.

[66] *R v Looseley* [2001] 1 WLR 2060, [16] (HL): 'A prosecution founded on entrapment would be an abuse of process. The court will not permit the prosecutorial arm of the state to behave in this way.'

[67] *Ridgeway v R* (1995) 184 CLR 19, [17] (HC) referring to 'the obtaining of curial advantage'.

[68] Crown Prosecution Service, *The Code for Crown Prosecutors* (London, CPS, 2013) [4.1]–[4.12], www.cps.gov.uk/publications/code_for_crown_prosecutors/; Department of Justice, *Prosecution Code* (Hong Kong, 2013) [5.1]–[5.10], www.doj.gov.hk; Crown Law, *Solicitor-General's Prosecution Guidelines* (New Zealand, July 2013) [5.1]–[5.13], www.crownlaw.govt.nz; Public Prosecution Service of Canada, *The Federal Prosecution Service Deskbook* (Ottawa, 2005) ch 15, www.ppsc-sppc.gc.ca; Martin Committee Report, above n 12, 74–103.

[69] B Hancock and J Jackson, *Standards for Prosecutors: An Analysis of the United Kingdom National Prosecuting Agencies* (The Hague, International Association of Prosecutors, 2006) 17.

The notion itself can be said to express and reinforce democratic values.[70] Prosecutors are afforded a wide margin of appreciation on how that balancing should best be done. Policy statements addressing the decision to prosecute and decisions associated with prosecuting include a wide range of public interest considerations, reflecting both intrinsic and extrinsic policies[71] and duties owed to victims, witnesses, defendants and society in general.[72] Only an overriding public interest can justify judicial intervention. The need to find a public interest 'not' to continue the prosecution or 'not' to admit the evidence demonstrates where the onus lies and underlines the exceptional nature of the intervention.[73] Having considered all relevant public interest considerations, where an overriding public interest against proceeding or admitting the evidence is found, the court can legitimately intervene to keep discretionary powers in check.

The meaning of 'overriding public interest' is a pivotal element of this account. It needs to be explained why this approach is not simply one of gauging public confidence or moral legitimacy. Note, to begin with, that the term is not synonymous with balance of public interest or balance of convenience. The court is not rebalancing all public interest considerations, in the sense of second-guessing prosecutorial decision-making. That would violate the cardinal separation of powers principle. If there is sufficient evidence to proceed (for example, a reasonable prospect of conviction) there is already a public interest for the case to continue. Similarly, if evidence is relevant and admissible, the public interest in rational adjudication generally favours admitting the evidence at trial.[74]

Nor is the approach one of attempting to maximise public confidence in the system with each decision; such an approach too closely approximates public opinion polling which is obviously an objectionable standard. The word 'overriding' signifies the application of basic legal norms of such weight as to ground a public duty. What is the content of these norms? They are the same norms that govern the exercise of discretion and the review of such discretion in public law. First, in common law systems, there are the public law grounds of judicial review, for example, procedural fairness, relevant and irrelevant considerations, improper purpose, irrationality and so on. Secondly, there are statutory, and more significantly constitutional norms, especially those that relate to fundamental human rights. Thirdly, where domestic systems allow for it, there are international law norms that inform discretionary powers.

Two further points should be made about how the overriding public interest approach should be applied in practice. As the principle of integrity is most commonly invoked in the stay and exclusion cases, they can serve as a crucible for further exploration. First, the norm must be one against continuing the prosecution or adducing the evidence in question. Consider torture, for example. Torture is prohibited as a *jus cogens* international crime, but this is not the relevant norm for our purposes. The norm must be that evidence obtained by torture should not be admitted in evidence in a criminal prosecution.[75] In other words,

---

[70] M Feintuck, '*The Public Interest' in Regulation* (Oxford, Oxford University Press, 2004) 42–47, 247.

[71] Choo, above n 59, 17 refers to intrinsic policy as relating to 'the promotion of accurate fact-finding or truth' and extrinsic policy as relating to being '*external* to proof'.

[72] See policies mentioned in n 68, above.

[73] But under Australia's Evidence Act 1995, s 138(1), the burden lies on the prosecution to prove the 'desirability of admitting' improperly or illegally obtained evidence over its undesirability.

[74] There are jurisdiction-specific exceptions, such as the Australian provisions mentioned in n 73.

[75] *A v Secretary of State for the Home Department* [2006] 2 AC 221, [39] (HL). See also the Convention against Torture and Other Cruel, Inhuman or Degrading Treatment or Punishment, 1465 UNTS 85, UN Doc A/39/51, 197, Art 15.

the norm must be able to explain why the decisions to prosecute or adduce evidence are contrary to the public interest, even if the prosecution was innocent of any wrongdoing. Secondly, even where a relevant norm is engaged on a particular set of facts, it will not automatically trump all other relevant public interest considerations. The outcome will depend on how the norm is engaged and whether the particular public interest can be said to have 'overriding' importance or significance in the circumstances of a particular case. Take the example of evidence gathered, or a prosecution proceeding, in breach of a human rights norm. The circumstances in which evidence is obtained as a result of a rights breach can vary considerably in terms of both the seriousness of the rights violating conduct and the impact on interested parties. These considerations must be balanced together with the public interest factors favouring the admission of the evidence, such as the importance of having a trial on the merits (to borrow the language of the Canadian Supreme Court's test).

The concept of 'overriding public interest' already finds expression in legislation and legal doctrine in human rights and administrative law cases. In considering the legal standard of judicial impartiality, Lord Goff in *R v Gough* took note of 'an overriding public interest that there should be confidence in the integrity of the administration of justice' and that is why justice must be done and be seen to be done.[76] The concept is more typically invoked to mark a circumscribed exception to a right or interest, in order to underline the importance of that right or interest. It is employed in this way, for example, in animal and environmental protection legislation;[77] as an exception to the protection of confidential information;[78] as a limit on the disclosure or publication of information;[79] and, on occasion, as a defence to criminal liability.[80] Closer to the issue at hand, it is settled public law that only an 'overriding public interest' can justify the frustration of a person's legitimate expectation, procedural or substantive.[81] In *R v North and East Devon Health Authority, ex parte Coughlan*, Lord Woolf MR formulated the issue in terms of 'whether there is a sufficient overriding public interest to justify a departure from what has been previously promised'.[82] Moreover, '[w]hether there is an overriding public interest is a question for the court'.[83] By analogy, it requires an overriding public interest to stop a trial or exclude relevant prosecutorial evidence brought or adduced in the public interest.

The public interest account of integrity has explanatory power. It goes further than abstract statements of 'moral legitimacy' or 'integrity', requiring a specific articulation of

---

[76]   *R v Gough* [1993] AC 646, 659 (HL).

[77]   The Conservation of Habitats and Species Regulations 2010 (UK), reg 62; The Marine Strategy Regulations 2010 (UK), reg 15(2)(d); Offshore Petroleum Activities (Conservation of Habitats) Regulations 2001 (UK), reg 6; *Town Planning Board v Society for the Protection of the Harbour* (2004) 7 HKCFAR 1, [44].

[78]   *Re Inquiry under the Company Securities (Insider Dealing) Act 1985* [1988] AC 660, 702 (HL); *Attorney-General v Observer Ltd* [1990] 1 AC 109, 269 (HL); *Kingdom of Sweden v Commission of the European Communities* [2011] 2 AC 359, [6] (ECJ); *R v Secretary of State for Home Department ex parte Kingdom of Belgium* [2000] EWHC Admin 293 (QBD).

[79]   *R v National Post* [2010] 1 SCR 477, [26]; *R v Durette* [1994] 1 SCR 469; Government Information (Public Access) Act 2009 (NSW), s 3(1)(c).

[80]   See eg offences related to prison security in Offender Management Act 2007 (UK), ss 22–23; Prison Act (Northern Ireland) 1953, ss 34B and 34C.

[81]   *R v North and East Devon Health Authority, ex parte Coughlan* [2001] QB 213, [57] (CA); *Ng Siu Tung v Director of Immigration* (2002) 5 HKCFAR 1, [92], [363]–[364]; M Groves, 'Substantive Legitimate Expectations in Australian Administrative Law' (2008) 32 *Melbourne University Law Review* 470.

[82]   [2001] QB 213, [58].

[83]   Ibid [76].

the public interests engaged in a particular case and a justification for why a particular interest is of such overriding character to justify halting a case or excluding material evidence. It resonates with general public expectations that officials will act with integrity and be subject to judicial review where there are transgressions. There is no public investment in the separation thesis, which is clearly anachronistic. Its resurgence (of which there is no sign and little prospect) would significantly diminish confidence in the administration of criminal justice.

3. Illustrations of the Public Interest Account

A trial court must guard against improper use of its processes. If it finds that there is an overriding public interest for the case not to proceed or for the evidence to be excluded, it has a duty to intervene. For example, sufficiency of evidence is an overriding public interest consideration in the prosecution of criminal offences. If, after the prosecution's case in-chief has been presented, the trial court finds that the defendant has 'no case to answer', the defendant should be acquitted.

Case law has expounded on the concept of an overriding public interest justifying a permanent stay of criminal proceedings. Three recurrent scenarios may be mentioned, mindful that there are many more. First, there are cases concerning the fairness of trials, which engage the norm against unfair trials. Courts do not stay simply because the trial *might* conceivably be unfair. The test is more stringent, requiring either the impossibility of a fair trial or the likelihood of irreparable prejudice.[84] This high threshold reflects the requisite 'overriding' nature of the public interest. A second category comprises cases where the prosecution is brought for a fundamentally objectionable purpose, contrary to the norm that discretionary powers be exercised only for proper purposes. It is an overriding public interest that criminal trials not be used to prosecute state-created crime (the entrapment cases).[85] Equally objectionable is using the trial process to reprosecute a person who has already been convicted or acquitted of the same offence, unless there is compelling evidence of guilt or the first trial was fundamentally flawed (double jeopardy cases).[86] A third category of stay cases is where the court lacks jurisdiction over the person because illegal means have been used to bring the person before the court (illegal rendition cases).[87] The norm here would be the essential precondition of establishing lawful jurisdiction and custody over the defendant (essential where trial *in absentia* is not available).

Across all three categories of stay cases, the unifying thread is that there must be an overriding public interest for the prosecution to be discontinued.[88] Matters become more controversial where the misconduct, however serious, is not so directly related to the

---

[84] *HKSAR v Lee Ming Tee* (2001) 4 HKCFAR 133, 148; *R v O'Connor* [1995] 4 SCR 411, [82].

[85] *R v Mack* [1988] 2 SCR 903, [79]; *R v Looseley* [2001] WLR 2060, [19] (HL).

[86] *Connelly v DPP* [1964] AC 1254, 1359 (HL); *Yeung Chun Pong v Secretary for Justice* (2009) 12 HKCFAR 867, [21]; Law Commission, *Double Jeopardy and Prosecution Appeals*, Law Com No 267 (London, 2001) parts IV and V, www.lawcom.gov.uk/.

[87] *R v Horseferry Road Magistrates' Court, ex parte Bennett* [1994] 1 AC 42 (HL); Choo, above n 59, 113–23.

[88] Choo, ibid 186.

continuation of the prosecution that it prejudices the integrity or fairness of the trial. In these circumstances, it becomes more difficult to point to a controlling legal norm mandating a (presumptively evidentially sound) prosecution's abandonment. This difficulty is reflected in the concerns expressed by the Law Lords, in both *Warren v Attorney General of the Bailiwick of Jersey* and *R v Maxwell*, about cases in which prosecutions have been stayed owing to serious breaches of legal professional privilege by police officers deliberating recording confidential communications between lawyers and their clients.[89] The prosecution was not seeking to adduce the intercepted product as evidence, and the recordings themselves could not in those cases be said to have prejudiced the defence or unduly advantaged the prosecution. Thus the misconduct had no direct bearing on the continuation of the prosecution itself. This is an important point of distinction from the Hong Kong case, involving similar facts, where there was also an immunised prosecution witness who prepared a statement after the benefit of listening to the illegal recording, which was destroyed and not disclosed to the defence.[90] The prosecution had been unduly advantaged by the illegality and the defence irreparably disadvantaged.[91]

The Canadian case of *R v Carosella* presented similar difficulties.[92] In this case, a publicly funded sexual assault crisis centre deliberately destroyed the interview notes of the complainant's initial allegations, pursuant to the centre's victim-friendly policy to identify 'the cases that have police involvement and shred [notes] in advance to being served for the criminal proceedings'.[93] The complainant, not knowing the notes had been destroyed, consented to them being produced to the court and defence. A five to four majority in the Supreme Court of Canada upheld the trial judge's decision to stay the proceedings based on a violation of the defendant's right to make full answer and defence.[94] The stay was not based on a public interest that a publicly funded crisis centre should never have a policy to destroy interview notes, a policy intended to protect against re-victimisation.[95] Instead, the overriding public interest was against holding a trial in which the defendant's right to make full answer and defence had been deliberated impaired (that is, the inability of the defence to cross-examine the complainant on her first statement of the offence).[96] Thus, the case comes within the fair trial category of stays.

Unconditional stays terminate the prosecution. Less dramatically, excluding prosecutorial evidence might only weaken the prosecution's case or have no effect on the outcome of the trial. Given the varied consequences of exclusion, there is a wider array of public interest considerations at play in exclusion decisions. Courts in different jurisdictions have developed (and redeveloped) sophisticated doctrine to demonstrate and clarify the

---

[89] See *Warren v Attorney General of the Bailiwick of Jersey* [2012] 1 AC 22, [36] (PC); *R v Maxwell* [2011] 2 Cr App R 31, [28] and [96]–[98] (UKSC), criticising the decision in *R v Grant* [2006] QB 60 (CA). See Whitfort, Chapter 10 in this volume for further discussion.

[90] *HKSAR v Wong Hung Ki* [2011] 1 HKLRD 183 (CA), leave to the CFA refused (unreported, FAMC43/2010, 14 Sept 2010), but see reconsideration in *HKSAR v Ng Chun To Raymond* [2013] 5 HKC 390, [90]–[105] (CA). See further Whitfort, Chapter 10 in this volume.

[91] *HKSAR v Wong Hung Ki* [2011] 1 HKLRD 183, [95] (CA); *HKSAR v Shum Chiu* [2011] 2 HKLRD 746, [63] (CA).

[92] *R v Carosella* [1997] 1 SCR 80.

[93] Ibid [9].

[94] Ibid [57].

[95] Ibid [9].

[96] Ibid [53]–[56].

balancing process. The Supreme Court of Canada's decision in *R v Grant* identified 'three avenues of inquiry, each rooted in the public interests engaged by s. 24(2)'.[97] The first two avenues concern the seriousness of the Charter violation viewed from the perspective of, first, the infringing state conduct, and, second, the impact on the Charter-protected interests of the accused.[98] The third avenue of inquiry is 'society's interest in the adjudication of the case on its merits'.[99] None of the three considerations is meant to be 'overriding' in and of itself. The facts of each case would determine how strongly each is engaged, if at all. In practice, the court is assessing whether the first two considerations are engaged sufficiently strongly so as to override the third consideration. The facts of *Grant* illustrate circumstances where the first two factors did *not* override the third.[100] The police violated Grant's right to be free from arbitrary detention by briefly detaining him on the street, engaging him in conversation and discovering that he possessed a handgun. His right to be informed of his right to counsel was also denied. The issue was whether the handgun should have been excluded. The majority found the state conduct to be neither deliberate nor egregious. The officers had made an understandable mistake about the limits of their powers of lawful detention.[101] Though the impact on rights was significant, this consideration was not enough to outweigh the third consideration in this case, where the gun was highly reliable evidence and essential to the prosecution for firearms possession.

Another illustration comes from New Zealand, where the legislature codified an integrity-based power to exclude improperly obtained evidence after more than a decade of jurisprudence under the New Zealand Bill of Rights Act 1990.[102] Section 30 of the New Zealand Evidence Act 2006 confers a judicial power to exclude 'improperly obtained evidence' based on a balancing of listed public interest considerations.[103] Exclusion is mandatory if the court finds that exclusion of the evidence 'is proportionate to the impropriety', a determination to be made by 'means of a balancing process that gives appropriate weight to the impropriety but also takes proper account of the need for an effective and credible system of justice'.[104]

4. Beyond the Stay and Exclusion Cases

I have argued that procedural stays and evidentiary exclusion based on the integrity principle involve criminal trial courts invoking public law remedies to insulate their processes from unlawful or improper exercises of discretionary powers by prosecutors. Unlike traditional judicial review external to the criminal process, this form of judicial review is

---

[97] *R v Grant* [2009] 2 SCR 353, [71].
[98] Ibid [72]–[78].
[99] Ibid [79]–[86].
[100] Ibid [140].
[101] Ibid [133].
[102] See A Butler and P Butler, *The New Zealand Bill of Rights Act: A Commentary* (Wellington, LexisNexis, 2005) ch 29.
[103] Evidence Act 2006 (NZ), s 30(3). See *Omar Hamed v R* [2011] NZSC 101; but see Australia's Evidence Act 1995, s 138(3).
[104] Evidence Act 2006 (NZ), subss 30(2) and (4).

internal to criminal proceedings and more intensive. As an aspect of public law, the court's authority and legitimacy in ordering the stay or exclusion is grounded in basic public law assumptions about the role of courts in a democratic society, which in turn rest on liberal conceptions of the rule of law and the separation of powers in a balanced constitution.

Stays and exclusions are specific instances of the more general phenomenon of criminal courts granting public law relief following review of governmental action or inaction. A threshold precondition is that the criminal court is reviewing action implicating the integrity of its own process. In jurisdictions that have taken early interest in this exercise of curial integrity and those with a constitutional bill of rights, this expanded role of criminal courts is well known. Criminal trial courts in Canada, for example, are courts of competent jurisdiction to consider challenges to legislation and governmental action under the Charter of Rights and Freedoms. The same courts have jurisdiction to order a range of public law remedies, beyond stays and exclusion, where a violation of the Charter has been found. These remedies include declaratory relief (extending to substantive review of legislation), suspended declarations of invalidity, adjournments, disclosure and reduced sentences. In somewhat similar fashion, Hong Kong criminal courts have acquired a stronger public law role since 1991 when the Hong Kong Bill of Rights Ordinance was enacted.[105]

The public law role of criminal courts pays closer attention to the interests of victims and witnesses in the process. These interests are undoubtedly relevant to notions of integrity.[106] Such third parties can invoke the jurisdiction of the criminal court where it can be shown that there is an overriding public interest for the trial process to take an exceptional course in protection of their interests. Examples include addressing the rights of a female Muslim rape complainant to testify wearing her niqab out of respect for her religious freedom,[107] adjusting processes to accommodate the rights of witnesses, and refusing members of the public from viewing sensitive evidence out of respect for the privacy of victims and their family members.

While traditional judicial review of criminal proceedings has expanded in recent years, there has also been a trend in some superior courts to decline jurisdiction to avoid fragmenting and delaying criminal proceedings. In the UK, it has been held that there is a 'strong presumption against the Divisional Court entertaining a judicial review application where the complaint can be raised within the criminal trial and appeal process'.[108] The effect is that challenges of a public law type will be raised and dealt with by the criminal trial court, thereby giving greater prominence to its (public law) judicial review role.

Conclusion

The institutional account of integrity developed in this chapter prompts reconsideration of orthodox legal responses to official misconduct potentially tainting criminal proceedings.

---

[105] See SNM Young, 'Human Rights in Hong Kong Criminal Trials' in P Roberts and J Hunter (eds), *Criminal Evidence and Human Rights: Reimagining Common Law Procedural Traditions* (Oxford, Hart Publishing, 2012).

[106] See Chapters 2 (Stubbs) and 14 (Hunter) in this volume.

[107] See *R v NS* [2012] 3 SCR 726.

[108] *R v Director of Public Prosecutions, ex parte Kebilene* [2002] 2 AC 326, 370 (HL).

It is now broadly accepted in well-developed common law jurisdictions that it is no longer acceptable to ignore such conduct as irrelevant to criminal trial courts. The court's role is not cast as one focused solely upon establishing facts. Principles of integrity, as an intellectual justification and legal rationale for intrinsic judicial review, also serve the elementary public law principles of rule of law, separation of powers and executive accountability. Traditional judicial review courts do not claim, or enjoy, any monopoly over public law relief. Generally speaking, they have acknowledged the public law role of criminal courts.

With public law as its foundation, much of the mystical character of integrity is removed and greater clarity and specificity can be given to what courts mean when they act in the name of upholding 'integrity'. When courts act in this way, they are reviewing public powers or duties and giving effect to an overriding public interest. Granted that criminal courts are not free-standing public law tribunals, the pre-requisite to this special form of review is that the public power or duty in question implicates the court's process and if left unchecked could significantly diminish the legitimacy of that process.

Realising integrity in the criminal process requires that we first appreciate and clarify the public law function of criminal courts in exercising circumscribed powers of judicial review. For various reasons, we have yet to see the full potential of this role reflected either in legal theory or in prevailing judicial practice. While criminal courts and judges have laid important groundwork for this conclusion, they have not openly acknowledged its theoretical significance or practical implications, presumably because it ostensibly deviates from the trial court's traditional adjudicative function of determining guilt and innocence. Undoubtedly, entrenched conceptual and intellectual divisions separating the fields of administrative law, constitutional law and criminal law—and consequently estranging administrative and constitutional lawyers from criminal lawyers—have contributed to this tardy acknowledgement. Legal specialists tend to work in their own separate spheres and perceive interactions only in terms of traditional judicial review of criminal proceedings. The schism runs deeper and is probably traced to legal education's compartmentalisation of public law and criminal law. Recognising criminal courts as public law courts, and their integrity as a prime consideration of public policy and political morality, ultimately opens the door to new forms of procedural relief and the accommodation of a broader range of important public interest factors in the conduct and normative regulation of criminal proceedings.

2

Searching for Integrity in Domestic Violence Policing

JULIE STUBBS

Introduction

Police under-enforcement of law, what Slansky labels 'nonfeasance',[1] has received relatively little attention by policing scholars compared with over-enforcement and selective enforcement.[2] However, under-enforcement has for several decades been a key focus of criticisms of the policing of domestic violence. Under-enforcement in this context excludes victims, typically women, from the protection of the criminal justice system because it leaves them vulnerable to abuse and, in some cases, to lethal violence. While under-enforcement is rarely seen as related to police integrity, which is more often construed narrowly in terms of corruption and similar misconduct, more expansive definitions note that integrity 'encompasses fairness, probity, behaviour and equal treatment'.[3] These standards are related to 'how public confidence is secured and maintained'. Broadly construed, 'integrity means exercising powers and using discretion to the highest standards of competence, fairness and honesty'.[4] Thus, police under-enforcement of domestic violence legislation squarely raises concerns about police integrity, both in terms of the exercise of discretion by individual officers, and at the organisational level. Under-enforcement has the capacity to erode public confidence in policing.

Contemporary domestic violence laws and policies express both symbolic and instrumental purposes; they signal a commitment to public safety and may bolster police legitimacy, but these objectives are likely to be undermined when integrity is compromised such as through inadequate or unfair enforcement. Domestic violence laws commonly have a pro-active police response at their core. They aim to increase arrest rates, hold offenders accountable, reduce repeat offending and contribute to the safety of victims. In part, pro-arrest approaches developed in response to feminist advocacy and from widespread

---

[1] DA Slansky, *Democracy and the Police* (Stanford, Stanford University Press, 2008).
[2] A Natapoff, 'Underenforcement' (2006) 75 *Fordham Law Review* 1715, 1716–17; but see J Goldstein 'Police Discretion Not to Invoke the Criminal Process: Low Visibility Decisions in the Administration of Justice' (1960) 69 *Yale Law Journal* 543.
[3] Her Majesty's Inspectorate of Constabulary, *Police Integrity England, Wales and Northern Ireland: Securing and Maintaining Public Confidence* (London, HMIC, 1999) [1.5].
[4] Ibid [1.6].

criticism of police failure to enforce the law in domestic violence cases. In the US, for example, further pressure came from high-profile law suits against a number of police forces; *Thurman v City of Torrington*, in which the court found that failure to enforce the law constituted discrimination, has been especially influential.[5] In the attempt to redress nonfeasance regarding domestic violence incidents, many jurisdictions have gone further than merely encouraging arrest by adopting *mandatory* arrest laws and policies. Such approaches remain controversial. Debates about pro-arrest approaches to domestic violence policing, and especially mandatory arrest, justifiably have attracted a substantial literature. However, exclusive focus on the efficacy, or otherwise, of pro-arrest approaches elides the complexity of modern policing and the context within which pro-arrest laws and policies operate in any given jurisdiction and police organisation. Such a focus also does not fully capture contemporary developments that have been shaping the policing of domestic violence and the tensions that they entail, and is a poor fit with scholarship illuminating the complexity of domestic violence. Bringing questions about police integrity more to the fore may contribute to rethinking nonfeasance in more productive ways.

This chapter considers responses to police under-enforcement of domestic violence to identify a research agenda that moves beyond the narrow focus on the instrumental effects of pro-arrest approaches that pervades the literature. Section 1 provides an overview of pro-arrest policies in the policing of domestic violence in selected jurisdictions. Section 2 examines competing understandings of pro-arrest approaches and ongoing debates about pro-arrest laws and policies in the policing of domestic violence. Section 3 examines related developments in contemporary policing intended to redress police under-enforcement in domestic violence, and in doing so identifies several tensions that need to be acknowledged and subjected to closer examination. Finally, Section 4 examines how contemporary developments in domestic violence policing are shaped within a particular local context, namely Australia, and for one policing organisation—the New South Wales (NSW) Police Force. This case study illustrates the chapter's broader thesis, that pro-arrest policing sits within complex normative and institutional frameworks characterised by unresolved tensions, which may fruitfully be re-examined through the lens of integrity.

1. Pro-Arrest Approaches to Domestic Violence Policing

Developments in domestic violence policing internationally have been profoundly shaped by the US experience. Increased focus on police responses to domestic violence arising from feminist activism and litigation against police organisations in the late 1970s and 1980s

---

[5] *Thurman v City of Torrington* 595 F Supp 1521 (D Conn 1984), cited by Inter-American Commission on Human Rights (IACHR) Report No 80/11 (Case 12.626, Merits, Jessica Lenahan (Gonzales) et al, United States, July 21, 2011) [96], n 155 ('police refused to respond to woman's repeated requests for protection. Police watched as estranged husband stabbed and kicked victim in her neck, throat, and chest, paralyzing her from the neck down and causing permanent disfigurement') web.law.columbia.edu/sites/default/files/microsites/human-rights-institute/files/gonzales%20decision.pdf (accessed 28 October 2015). Earlier cases had been brought in Oakland California and New York City: *Bruno v Codd*, 396 NY S 2d 974 (Sup Ct Special Term 1977); *Scott v Hart*, No C-76-2395 (ND Cal Filed 28 Oct 1976). And see ES Buzawa, CG Buzawa and ED Stark, *Responding to Domestic Violence: The Integration of Criminal Justice and Human Services*, 4th edn (Thousand Oaks CA, Sage, 2012) 163–65.

was given added impetus by the results of the Minneapolis domestic violence experiment, which purported to demonstrate the deterrent effect of arrest.[6] The researchers actively promoted their findings and encouraged the adoption of pro-arrest approaches on the basis of their results. Notwithstanding methodological concerns about the original study, and the mixed results and debates about the implications of six replication studies,[7] from the mid 1980s increased criminalisation began to be adopted within the US and internationally through the enactment of new legislation, expanded definitions of domestic violence and the adoption of proactive policing policies, often in the form of mandatory arrest. That history is well known.[8]

Recent attention to the policing of domestic violence has been generated by competing concerns about pro-arrest laws and policies, especially regarding mandatory arrest. For some scholars and activists those laws and policies have had too little effect on police who continue to under-enforce the law in domestic violence cases. By contrast, others point to concerns that such approaches have produced substantial changes in enforcement practices with particularly harsh consequences for minority communities. Pro-arrest approaches to domestic violence in the US, Canada, England and Wales, Australia and New Zealand exemplify these global trends.

(a) North America

Mandatory arrest is common in US jurisdictions, and has subsequently been adopted in many other countries, including Canada.[9] It is conventional to distinguish truly mandatory arrest both from other types of pro-arrest laws or policies which formally retain some discretion (commonly referred to as 'preferred' or 'presumptive' arrest) as well as from unmodified discretionary arrest. In 2000, there were 22 states (plus the District of Columbia) with mandatory arrest laws, six with preferred arrest provisions and 22 with discretionary provisions.[10] However, this threefold classification masks considerable variation in coverage and application. For instance, 'may' arrest becomes 'shall' arrest under certain circumstances.[11] Operational practice is also shaped by local policies which may stipulate conditions or mandate arrest even when state law does not do so.[12] Thus, there is

---

[6] L Sherman and R Berk, 'The Specific Deterrent Effects of Arrest for Domestic Assault' (1984) 49 *American Sociological Review* 261.

[7] A Binder and JW Meeker, 'Experiments as Reforms' (1988) 16 *Journal of Criminal Justice* 347; C Maxwell, J Garner and J Fagan, *The Effects of Arrest on Intimate Partner Violence* (Washington DC, NIJ, US Department of Justice, 2001).

[8] Maxwell et al, ibid; Buzawa et al, above n 5, ch 6.

[9] Mandatory arrest and pro-arrest policies exist in various forms across Canada, dating from the 1980s and 1990s, sometimes in conjunction with specialist domestic violence courts or 'pro-charge' or 'no-drop' prosecution policies: see T Brown, *Charging and Prosecution Policies in Cases of Spousal Assault: A Synthesis of Research, Academic, and Judicial Responses* (Ottawa, Department of Justice, Canada, 2000); J Koshan and W Wiegers, 'Theorizing Civil Domestic Violence Legislation in the Context of Restructuring: A Tale of Two Provinces' (2007) 19 *Canadian Journal of Women and the Law* 145.

[10] D Hirschel, E Buzawa, A Pattavina, D Faggiani and M Reuland, *Final Report: Explaining the Prevalence, Context, and Consequences of Dual Arrest in Intimate Partner Cases* (Washington DC, US Department of Justice, 2007) 15, www.ncjrs.gov/pdffiles1/nij/grants/218355.pdf (accessed 28 October 2015).

[11] A Zeoli, A Norris and H Brenner, 'A Summary and Analysis of Warrantless Arrest Statutes for Domestic Violence in the United States' (2011) 26 *Journal of Interpersonal Violence* 2811.

[12] Hirschel et al, above n 10.

more complexity and variability in the US policing of domestic violence than is commonly acknowledged in the literature, calling into question some of the findings of studies that have sought to compare jurisdictions.[13]

Police failure to enforce the law in domestic violence matters and mandatory arrest provisions continues to be subject to considerable debate and legal challenge in the US. In 2005, in *Town of Castle Rock v Gonzales*,[14] the US Supreme Court found that police had discretion not to arrest if other options were statutorily available and that officers were not obligated to enforce protection orders.[15] While Castle Rock is in the state of Colorado which has a mandatory arrest law, the court held that a 'well-established tradition of police discretion has long co-existed with apparently mandatory arrest statutes', and that the 'deep-rooted nature of law-enforcement discretion, even in the presence of seemingly mandatory legislative commands', had been recognised by previous Supreme Court authority.[16] This case has attracted international attention and generated significant concern, both because it demonstrates ongoing police under-enforcement—in this case, with lethal consequences—and it is seen to undermine the promise of legal protection for battered women by asserting the primacy of police discretion. As discussed below, it also prompted activists to pursue a novel course of action, in bringing the matter before an international human rights tribunal.[17]

(b) England and Wales

Pro-arrest policies were introduced by police forces in England and Wales in the 1990s and given added impetus by the Domestic Violence, Crime and Victims Act 2004. Though influenced by US developments, arrest is not mandatory.[18] In England and Wales the development of pro-arrest stances occurred within a broader institutional reorganisation of policing. Notably, 'the drive for money, efficiency and effectiveness' in policing more

---

[13] Zeoli et al, above n 11, 2830.

[14] *Town of Castle Rock v Gonzales*, 545 US 748, 125 S Ct 2796 (2005).

[15] The children of Ms Lenahan (formerly Gonzales) were killed by their father, who was subsequently shot and killed by police. She had repeatedly sought police action to find and recover the children after they were taken by their father. The Supreme Court held that despite Colorado's mandatory arrest law and the express and mandatory terms of her restraining order, Jessica Lenahan had no personal entitlement to police enforcement of the order under the due process clause: IACHR Report No 80/11, above n 5, [39].

[16] Ibid [90]. See also *DeShaney v Winnebago County Department of Social Services*, 109 S Ct 998 (US Wis 1989) and *United States v Morrison*, 529 US 598 (2000), cited by the UN Special Rapporteur on Violence Against Women, at the conclusion of her fact finding mission to the US, as indicating that 'there is little in terms of actual legally binding federal provisions which provide substantive protection or prevention for acts of domestic violence against women': *Statement from Special Rapporteur on Violence Against Women, Its Causes, and Consequences* (8 February 2011) www.ohchr.org (accessed 28 October 2015). Commentators also point to subsequent Federal Court decisions that have found that police acted 'outside of their legal and discretionary authority': D Frantzen and C San Miguel, 'Mandatory Arrest—Police Response to Domestic Violence Victims' (2009) 32 *Policing: International Journal of Police Strategy and Management* 319.

[17] Z Fenton, '*Town of Castle Rock v Gonzales*: A Tale of State Enabled Violence' in E Schneider and S Wildman (eds), *Women and the Law Stories* (New York, Foundation Press/Thomson Reuters, 2011).

[18] M Hester, *Who Does What to Whom? Gender and Domestic Violence Perpetrators*, research commissioned by Northern Rock Foundation (2009) 1069, www.nr-foundation.org.uk/downloads/Who-Does-What-to-Whom.pdf (accessed 28 October 2015); B Stanko, 'Managing Performance in the Policing of Domestic Violence' (2008) 2 *Policing* 294, 296.

generally saw 'the recognition and acceptance of victims of crime as the consumers of criminal justice services'.[19] Developments in domestic violence policing have not been limited to presumptive arrest. From the mid 1990s, the Home Office encouraged collaborative approaches to domestic violence, inter-agency coordination at the local level and specialist domestic violence courts. Police forces in England and Wales have introduced specialist domestic violence units intended to offer support to victims, although attrition rates remain high[20] and there are inconsistencies in response.[21]

(c) Australia and New Zealand

All Australian jurisdictions have adopted domestic violence frameworks that emphasise coordination (or integration) between policy sectors with a focus on victim safety, improving criminal justice system responses, and enhancing support services—though details differ across the states and territories.[22] These frameworks pre-date the recently adopted *National Plan to Reduce Violence against Women and their Children*. In anticipation of the National Plan, the Australasian Police Commissioners adopted a policing strategy in 2008 'to prevent and reduce family violence' which, inter alia, endorses a coordinated approach, and aims to 'achieve more effective frontline policing responses ... enhance support for victims of family violence; [and] shift the focus from reaction to early intervention and prevention of family violence'.[23]

The proactive policing policies that have been adopted in the Australian Capital Territory (ACT), NSW, Queensland and Tasmania sit within this broader framework. Typically, preferred arrest policies in Australia have a presumption in favour of arrest where sufficient evidence exists.[24] For instance, in the ACT the preferred arrest approach, which does not have a legislative basis, exists together with a pro-prosecution policy in what is probably the most fully integrated family violence programme in Australia within which key justice agencies and community organisations work collaboratively.[25] The ACT is also one of only two Australian jurisdictions to have human rights legislation—the other is Victoria, where the relevant legislation states that family violence is a violation of human

---

[19] S Walklate, 'What is to be Done about Violence against Women?' (2008) 48 *British Journal of Criminology* 39, 41.

[20] Ibid 42.

[21] Stanko, above n 18, 295.

[22] S Murray and A Powell, *Domestic Violence, Australian Public Policy* (North Melbourne, Australian Scholarly Press, 2009) 43.

[23] *National Plan to Reduce Violence against Women and their Children* (including the first three-year Action Plan) (Canberra, Department of Families, Housing, Community Services and Indigenous Affairs, 2012), www.fahcsia.gov.au/sites/default/files/documents/05_2012/national_plan.pdf (accessed 28 October 2015); Australasian Policing Strategy for the Prevention and Reduction of Family Violence (2008) 4, www.police.nsw.gov.au/community_issues/domestic__and__family_violence/prevention_and_reduction_of_family_violence_-_an_australasian_policing_strategy (accessed 28 October 2015).

[24] R Braaf and C Sneddon, *Arresting Practices: Exploring Issues of Dual Arrest for Domestic Violence*, Australian Domestic & Family Violence Clearinghouse Stakeholder Paper No 3 (Sydney, 2007).

[25] R Holder, 'The Emperor's New Clothes: Court and Justice Initiatives to Address Family Violence' (2006) 16 *Journal of Judicial Administration* 30, 31; T Cussen and M Lyneham, *ACT Family Violence Intervention Program Review*, Technical and Background Paper Series No 52 (Canberra, Australian Institute of Criminology, 2012).

rights.[26] In these states, it is possible to bring a complaint against police under relevant human rights laws if they act in a way that is incompatible with a human right or fail to give proper consideration to a relevant human right when making a decision.[27] In Queensland, police may arrest without a warrant where there has been a breach of a domestic violence protection order,[28] while in NSW police who do not commence criminal proceedings for the breach of an apprehended violence order are required to record their reasons in writing.[29] It remains to be seen whether the Australasian Policing Strategy and the National Plan will prompt other Australian police forces to move towards preferred arrest policies.

New Zealand introduced mandatory arrest in some circumstances as early as 1987, via a directive of the Police Commissioner, and extended pro-arrest to a wider range of circumstances through a 1992 policy directive.[30] The pro-arrest approach in New Zealand was adopted as one part of an integrated model based on the well-known Duluth Abuse Intervention Project, which had been piloted in Hamilton, New Zealand. This model also included sentencing offenders to structured education programmes, enhanced advocacy and support for victims, greater coordination between community groups and state agencies, and enhanced monitoring of agency performance.[31] Since 2010 New Zealand police have had the power in family violence cases to make a Police Safety Order lasting up to five days, which requires the person bound by the order to leave the specified premises.[32] The police made 5,242 such orders in the first 12 months after it became available.[33]

2. Competing Understandings of Pro-Arrest Approaches to Domestic Violence

Pro-arrest approaches to domestic violence have both normative and instrumental dimensions. There is little agreement in the literature about their place within the broader domain of crime control, and profoundly different assessments of the instrumental effects

---

[26]   Family Violence Protection Act 2008 (Vic), Preamble.

[27]   Charter of Human Rights and Responsibilities Act 2006 (Vic), s 38; Human Rights Act 2004 (ACT), s 40b. See also CEDAW Committee, General Recommendation No 19: Violence against Women, UN Doc A/47/38 (1992) [7] (recognising that family or domestic violence violates such human rights as: the right to life; freedom from torture or cruel, inhuman or degrading treatment or punishment; equal protection according to humanitarian norms in time of international or internal armed conflict; liberty and security of person; equal protection under the law; equality in the family; the highest standard attainable of physical and mental health; and just and favourable conditions of work).

[28]   Police Powers and Responsibilities Act 2000 (Qld), s 365 (1) (j).

[29]   Crimes (Domestic and Personal Violence) Act 2007 (NSW), s 14(8). Pursuant to s 27(1) of this Act, NSW Police also have an obligation in some circumstances to apply for a provisional apprehended violence order to protect a victim of domestic violence. An amendment to the legislation which commenced in May 2014 now permits senior officers to make a provisional order: s 28A.

[30]   J Cross and G Newbold, 'Presumptive Arrest in Partner Assault: Use of Discretion and Problems of Compliance in the New Zealand Police' (2010) 43 *Australian and New Zealand Journal of Criminology* 51, 54; S Carswell, *Family Violence and the Pro-arrest Policy: A Literature Review* (Wellington, New Zealand Ministry of Justice, 2006).

[31]   Carswell, ibid [2.5.1].

[32]   Domestic Violence Act 1995 (NZ), Part 6A.

[33]   V Kingi, M Roguski and E Mossman, *Police Safety Orders Formative Evaluation Summary Report* (Wellington, Victoria University of Wellington Crime and Justice Research Centre, 2011) 1.

of pro-arrest approaches. While pro-arrest approaches are applauded by some as evidence that governments have begun to take domestic violence seriously,[34] others see them as undermining 'contemporary demands for increased professionalism and ethical policing' since officers may be required 'to act in ways contrary to their judgement'.[35] Some critics regard all forms of proactive policing as outgrowths of a resurgent punitive state under neo-liberalism.[36]

The normative value of police enforcement of domestic violence laws is widely acknowledged, but open to nuanced interpretations. Natapoff offers a useful analysis. She argues that '[d]omestic violence reform highlights the normative and distributional power of official under-enforcement'.[37] Under-enforcement 'sends official messages of dismissal and devaluation' of victims[38] and 'the authorization of male violence against them'.[39] Natapoff recognises that communities can be *under-* and simultaneously *over-*policed, and this is commonly experienced by minority communities.[40] Over-enforcement and under-enforcement are 'twin symptoms of a deeper democratic failure of the criminal justice system: its non-responsiveness to the needs of the poor, racial minorities, and the otherwise politically vulnerable'.[41] Social marginality and political vulnerability affect victims, suspects and offenders. Under-enforcement of domestic violence offences may occur in communities that are also vulnerable to over-policing and mass incarceration.[42] Not all forms of under-enforcement are 'bad', but under-enforcement is problematic when it 'reinforces and reinscribes existing group disadvantage'.[43] Thus, while '*fuller* enforcement' may be 'vital' in order to bring about a 'value reversal, in which the state steps in to protect female victims and revises traditional male violent prerogatives',[44] *full* enforcement may not be the best response to the problems of under-enforcement. Indeed, full enforcement may compromise values, such as fairness, which are vital to the integrity of criminal process. Natapoff proposes different forms of enforcement more aligned with remedying underlying social harms.[45] In similar fashion, Buzawa and colleagues acknowledge the normative shift afforded to domestic violence within the criminal justice system and the broader culture, such that 'partner violence has become the litmus test for the integrity of relationships',[46] but argue that it is time to replace the 'heady generalization' that 'arrest works'.[47]

---

[34]   B Meyersfeld, *Domestic Violence and International Law* (Oxford, Hart Publishing, 2010).

[35]   M Rowe, 'Rendering Visible the Invisible: Police Discretion, Professionalism and Decision-making' (2007) 17 *Policing and Society* 279, 293.

[36]   K Bumiller, *In an Abusive State: How Neoliberalism Appropriated the Feminist Movement against Sexual Violence* (Durham NC, Duke University Press, 2008).

[37]   Natapoff, above n 2, 1739.

[38]   Ibid 1749.

[39]   Ibid 1739.

[40]   Ibid 1718. And see US Department of Justice, *Investigation into the New Orleans Police Department* (2011), www.justice.gov/crt/about/spl/nopd.php (accessed 28 October 2015) (reporting systemic failures, including over-policing in terms of the misuse of force, stop and search and racial profiling, and under-enforcement of offences related to violence against women).

[41]   Natapoff, above n 2, 1719.

[42]   B Richie, *Arrested Justice: Black Women, Violence and America's Prison Nation* (New York, New York University Press, 2012).

[43]   Natapoff, above n 2, 1753.

[44]   Ibid 1739 (emphasis added).

[45]   Ibid 1775.

[46]   Buzawa et al, above n 5, 5.

[47]   Ibid 7.

(a) Empirical Research Demonstrates Uneven Impact

Although it is well established among policing scholars and some domestic violence researchers[48] that 'the capacity of the police to deal with criminality by detection and deterrence' is greatly exaggerated in police and popular culture,[49] the presumed deterrent effect of arrest continues to be influential in debates about policing domestic violence. Some proponents of pro-arrest emphasise other instrumental effects including heightened sensitivity to victims among officials and arrest as a gateway to support mechanisms.[50] There are contrasting accounts of the empirical realities of pro-arrest laws and policies and their likely beneficiaries. Some researchers have reported increased levels of arrest and prosecution, but differ in their overall evaluations of success, while others have detected little impact on police practices. Competing claims have been made about the consequences of such policies for victims generally, for women specifically, and for marginalised communities. Concerns include that victims' agency is undermined and that they are further disempowered when police act against their express wishes.[51] Further, women who are victims of domestic violence have themselves been subject to unfair treatment by police, including arrest or proceedings to seek domestic violence orders against them.[52] Some victims have become more vulnerable to other forms of punitive state intervention, by probation authorities, immigration officials and child protection services, amongst others.[53]

Research findings on the effects of pro-arrest policies on the prevalence of domestic violence and on police practices are mixed. Comparative research poses methodological challenges, due to jurisdictional differences in police powers and in the meaning of pro-arrest, the difficulty of isolating the effects of proactive policing from any co-existing pro-prosecution or 'no-drop' policies, and conceptual and terminological discrepancies. 'Arrest' is used imprecisely, and has come to serve as shorthand for greater police enforcement in general, including, in some studies, police action to seek or enforce domestic violence protection orders. According to US victimisation surveys, rates of non-fatal domestic violence declined over the period 1994 to 2012, but this mirrors violent crime rates overall. These findings reinforce the need to avoid simplistic assumptions that levels of offending are shaped by changes in law, policy or policing practices in any direct way.[54]

[48] Buzawa et al, above n 5.
[49] R Reiner, *The Politics of the Police*, 4th edn (Oxford, Oxford University Press, 2010) 244; P Manning, 'The Preventive Conceit: The Black Box in Market Context' in E Buzawa and C Buzawa (eds), *Do Arrests and Restraining Orders Work?* (Beverly Hills CA, Sage, 1996).
[50] E Stark, *Coercive Control: How Men Entrap Women in Personal Life* (New York, Oxford University Press, 2007) 65.
[51] C Hoyle and A Sanders, 'Police Response to Domestic Violence' (2000) 40 *British Journal of Criminology* 14. Cf PC Barata and F Schneider, 'Battered Women Add their Voices to the Debate about the Merits of Mandatory Arrest' (2004) 32 *Women's Studies Quarterly* 148.
[52] K Henning and L Feder, 'A Comparison of Men and Women Arrested for Domestic Violence' (2004) 19 *Journal of Family Violence* 69; C Simmons et al, 'A Comparison of Women versus Men Charged with Intimate Partner Violence' (2008) 23 *Violence and Victims* 571; M Hester, 'Portrayal of Women as Intimate Partner Domestic Violence Perpetrators' (2012) 18 *Violence Against Women* 1067; Hester, above n 18.
[53] K Bumiller, 'The Nexus of Domestic Violence Reform and Social Science: From Instrument of Social Change to Institutionalized Surveillance' (2010) 6 *Annual Review of Law and Social Science* 173, 177.
[54] J Truman and R Morgan, *Non-fatal Domestic Violence 2003–2012*, NCJ 244697 (Washington DC, US Bureau of Justice Statistics, 2014) 3.

Several US studies have found that arrests in domestic violence matters increased 'in many police departments' from around 7 to 15 per cent to 30 per cent or more following the adoption of mandatory or preferred arrests policies.[55] One major study examined data from 19 states and reported that the odds of arrest were much higher in mandatory arrest or preferred arrest states than in discretionary states.[56] Arrests were more likely for white offenders than for other racial groups, mandatory arrest 'helped provide more equal treatment of both black and white offenders',[57] and when all other factors were held constant, women and men were equally likely to be arrested.[58] While some researchers have noted a reduction in the proportion of minority men arrested for domestic violence and an increase in the willingness of African-American and Latina women to call the police for assistance,[59] others point to mandatory arrest as contributing to mass incarceration of African-American men, and making some African-American women, especially poor women and those 'outside the mainstream', more vulnerable to arrests.[60] Some studies have detected spill-over effects, whereby arrest rates for acquaintance *and* stranger relationships were both higher in states with mandatory or preferred arrest approaches.[61] These data suggest some basis for concern that the developments in the policing of domestic violence have been associated with, reflect and perhaps have legitimated, a more general shift towards punitive 'law and order' policing. Notably, researchers have found marked differences in outcomes between states in the US which do not simply reflect legislative differences, reinforcing the importance of local policies, implementation issues and factors specific to the parties, the offence, the policing organisation and the local context.[62]

Research conducted in other jurisdictions has reported pro-arrest policies exerting only modest impacts on policing practice. For instance, Hoyle and Sanders found in their study of an English police force, that 'the pro-arrest, pro-charge policy was not being fully implemented by officers', and that over the period 1993 to 1996 the arrest rate had not increased, although the charge rate had improved (a reminder that in some jurisdictions, pro-arrest does not necessarily mean pro-charge).[63] A recent review of domestic violence policing across the 43 county police forces in England and Wales found substantial variations in arrest rates for domestic violence offences, from 45 per cent to 90 per cent, and also identified other serious failings in 'core policing activities'.[64] A recent New Zealand

---

[55] Hirschel at al, above n 10, 7; W DeLeon-Granados et al, 'Arresting Developments: Trends in Female Arrests for Domestic Violence and Proposed Explanations' (2006) 12 *Violence Against Women* 355.

[56] 'In mandatory arrest states, with other factors held constant, the odds of arrest in intimate partner incidents increase by 97% compared to discretionary arrest states. In preferred arrest states the increase is even higher: about 177%', Hirschel et al, above n 10, 69.

[57] Ibid 81.

[58] Ibid.

[59] Stark, above n 50, 58 (citing studies in Duluth and New York City).

[60] Richie, above n 42, 83, 91–92.

[61] Hirschel et al, above n 10, 77–78.

[62] Buzawa et al, above n 5, 211–19.

[63] A Sanders, 'Victims in an Exclusionary Criminal Justice System' in C Hoyle and R Young (eds), *New Visions of Crime Victims* (Oxford, Hart Publishing, 2002) 211; Hoyle and Sanders, above n 51, 17.

[64] Her Majesty's Inspectorate of Constabulary, *Everyone's Business: Improving the Police Response to Domestic Abuse* (London, HMIC, 2014) 12, 17, www.hmic.gov.uk/wp-content/uploads/2014/04/improving-the-police-response-to-domestic-abuse.pdf (accessed 28 October 2015) (noting that '[u]nacceptable failings in core policing activities, investigating crime, preventing crime, bringing offenders to justice and keeping victims safe are the principal reasons').

study, reporting similarly uneven impact, noted that '[i]n most cases, research has shown that implementation of the policies has fallen short of expectations, with arrest rates that are surprisingly low'.[65] This study, based on police records, interviews and observations, found that about 20 per cent of cases resulted in arrests and this increased to 44 per cent of cases where there were injuries.[66] While police and their managers said that they supported the pro-arrest policy, 'the practical difficulties imposed by limiting arrest discretion, create an opportunity for police to "fudge" reports or to provide vague and incomplete information',[67] suggesting that police adaptations may mute or neutralise policy objectives.

(b) Dual Arrest and Negative Side Effects

Studies in the US and Canada,[68] and to a lesser extent in the UK,[69] have identified an increase in the arrest of women for domestic violence, commonly by way of dual arrest, as an unintended side effect of proactive approaches to policing domestic violence. According to Belknap and Melton, '[b]efore pro-arrest domestic violence policies, it was almost unheard of for women to be arrested for domestic violence'.[70] Researchers report that arrests for women and girls generally have risen, not just for domestic violence matters, but see these as 'collateral effects' of mandatory arrest policies.[71] Increases in arrests of women and girls for domestic violence and non-domestic violence offences may reflect broader shifts towards more punitive criminal justice practices and shifting cultural perspectives on gender relations, which in turn shape the context in which mandatory arrest provisions are given effect.

Estimates of the proportion of domestic violence matters that result in dual arrests and of increases in women's domestic violence-related arrests vary widely. One US study based on 19 states found an overall dual arrest rate of 1.3 per cent. While 'mandatory arrest laws produce higher rates of dual arrest in intimate partner and other domestic violence cases',[72]

---

[65] Cross and Newbold, above n 30.

[66] Ibid 70.

[67] Ibid.

[68] E Comack et al, *Mean Streets? The Social Locations, Gender Dynamics, and Patterns of Violent Crime in Winnipeg* (Ottawa, Canadian Centre for Policy Alternatives, 2000); S Dasgupta, 'A Framework for Understanding Women's Use of Nonlethal Violence in Intimate Heterosexual Relationships' (2002) 8 *Violence Against Women* 1364; D Hirschel and E Buzawa, 'Understanding the Context of Dual Arrest with Directions for Future Research' (2002) 8 *Violence Against Women* 1449; D Hirschel et al, 'Domestic Violence and Mandatory Arrest Laws: To What Extent do they Influence Police Arrest Decisions?' (2008) 98 *Journal of Criminal Law and Criminology* 255; A Lyon, 'Be Careful What You Wish For: An Examination of Arrest and Prosecution Patterns of Domestic Violence Cases in two Cities in Michigan' (1999) 5 *Michigan Journal of Gender and Law* 253; S Miller, 'The Paradox of Women Arrested for Domestic Violence' (2001) 7 *Violence Against Women* 1339; M Chesney-Lind, 'Criminalizing Victimization: The Unintended Consequences of Pro-arrest Policies for Girls and Women' (2002) 2 *Criminology & Public Policy* 81.

[69] Hester, above n 18.

[70] J Belknap and H Melton, *Are Heterosexual Men also Victims of Intimate Partner Violence?* (Harrisburg PA, National Resource Center on Domestic Violence, 2005) 7, www.vawnet.org/Assoc_Files_VAWnet/AR_MaleVictims.pdf (accessed 28 October 2015).

[71] Chesney-Lind, above n 68.

[72] Hirschel et al, above n 10, 82.

this was not the case for preferred arrest jurisdictions.[73] An earlier study in California (a pro-arrest jurisdiction) found that women's felony arrests increased from 5 per cent of all domestic violence arrests in 1987 to 18 per cent in 2000.[74] Durfee's analysis of 23 US states compared three policies: mandatory arrest, preferred arrest (which she labelled 'pro-arrest') and discretionary jurisdictions for cases that were 'situationally ambiguous', that is, where both intimate partners were said by police to have committed an offence against each other. Durfee hypothesised that mandatory arrest policies were likely to have greater impact on police decisions in these types of complex cases than in more straightforward cases with a clearly identifiable aggressor. She found a higher proportion of dual arrests in mandatory arrest jurisdictions, but even in those jurisdictions police took no action in 46 per cent of cases, a finding that is consistent with the previous research reviewed above. After controlling for type of offence and level of injury, Durfee concluded that mandatory arrest policies 'disproportionately affect women', in the sense that the odds of arrest for women were significantly higher than for men.[75]

Canadian research likewise found substantial increases in arrest for women for domestic violence following the introduction of a 'zero tolerance' policy in Winnipeg. Most domestic violence prosecutions of female accused arose from dual arrests, while only 10 per cent did so for men.[76] These findings are open to different interpretations,[77] but the discovery that dual arrests 'disproportionately end in dropped prosecutions' has fuelled concerns that the arrests were not justified in the first place.[78] Researchers repeatedly report significant differences in the characteristics of men and women arrested for domestic violence (as well as in the nature of the underlying incidents),[79] which challenges any complacent assumption that the increased arrest of women, or dual arrests, is an expression of equal treatment. These findings also expose the need for careful consideration of the construct 'equal treatment' as an element of integrity in policing; equal treatment by police may signify formal equality, but mask substantive inequality and thus constitute unfair treatment.

Some jurisdictions have responded to criticisms of dual arrest by introducing 'primary aggressor policies', which seek to assist police to identify who is the primary aggressor when attending domestic violence incidents in which conflicting accounts may be given by the parties. These policies typically require attending officers to consider factors such as any history of domestic violence, the nature of any injuries, the likelihood of future violence, and whether violence was in self-defence.[80] Winnipeg adopted a primary aggressor policy for police following a successful wrongful arrest suit by a woman who had been arrested at the same time as her abusive partner. Arrests of women subsequently declined from

---

[73] Ibid 83.

[74] DeLeon-Granados et al, above n 55, 359.

[75] '[I]n mandatory arrest states, after controlling for incident and individual characteristics, the odds of a female-only arrest is 1.47 times greater than the odds of a male-only arrest and 1.69 times greater than the odds of a dual arrest', A Durfee, 'Situational Ambiguity and Gendered Patterns of Arrest for Intimate Partner' (2012) 18 *Violence Against Women* 64, 75.

[76] Comack et al, above n 68, 20.

[77] See the review in Hirschel et al, above n 10.

[78] C Fraelich and J Ursel, 'Arresting Women: Pro-arrest Policies, Debates, and Developments' (2014) 29 *Journal of Family Violence* 507, 508.

[79] Henning and Feder, above n 52; Simmons et al, above n 52; Hester, above n 18; Hester, above n 52.

[80] Hirschel and Buzawa, above n 68.

18 per cent to 13 per cent of all arrests for intimate partner domestic violence, and dual arrests of women declined from 9 per cent to 3 per cent.[81] The apparent success of the primary aggressor policy in Winnipeg was buttressed by a long-standing family violence court and a network of criminal justice agencies and victim services focused on enhancing victim safety. However, research indicates that there is no uniform understanding of the term primary aggressor and that 'the passage of a primary aggressor law clearly does not negate the relationship between mandatory arrest laws and higher dual arrest rates'.[82] Hester's UK study found that, without an adequate understanding of the gender dynamics of domestic violence, police were unable to identify the primary aggressor.[83] Whether it is possible for the police to adopt a more nuanced approach in determining who needs protection in domestic violence settings, given the overriding emphasis of the criminal justice system on discrete incidents, has also been questioned.[84]

(c) Neo-liberalism, Punitive Populism and Domestic Violence Policing

While the increase in arrest rates for women and the inappropriate use of dual arrests have widely been seen as unintended consequences of proactive policing, some commentators have placed these developments in the context of larger shifts in criminal justice. Kristin Bumiller and Beth Richie have each offered compelling accounts of how progressive feminist programmes for dealing with violence against women have been reshaped and appropriated within neo-liberal and neo-conservative political contexts in ways that have done more to promote law enforcement than to promote women's autonomy and freedom, with particularly negative impacts on minorities.[85] These outcomes are 'cautionary tales for activists ... of counterproductive law reform and unintended consequences'.[86] However, when 'viewed in a historical and cultural context', Bumiller contends, 'it is clear that they are actually the "productive" and the "intended" consequences of state policies ... powerfully driven by social control priorities ... not to address women's systematic oppression'.[87]

These US commentaries demand much greater reflection on the ways in which proactive policing of domestic violence has proceeded in concert with law and order politics in other jurisdictions. However, one should not assume that neo-liberalism has a single referent or plays out uniformly in different local contexts. For instance, a study by Rosenberg which examined criminal justice responses to violence against women in two adjacent jurisdictions, the US state of Washington and the Canadian province of British Columbia, found key differences in experiences of neo-liberal governance that reinforce the necessity of paying attention to local context.[88]

---

[81] Fraelich and Ursel, above n 78, 511.

[82] Hirschel et al, above n 68, 296–97.

[83] Hester, above n 52, 1075.

[84] Hirschel and Buzawa, above n 68.

[85] Bumiller, above n 36; Richie, above n 42. See also M Kim, 'Challenging the Pursuit of Criminalisation in an Era of Mass Incarceration: The Limitations of Social Work Responses to Domestic Violence in the USA' (2012) *British Journal of Social Work* 1.

[86] Bumiller, above n 36, 12.

[87] Ibid 12–13.

[88] KE Rosenberg, *From Moderate Chastisement to Mandatory Arrest: Responses to Violence Against Women in Canada and the United States* (PhD Dissertation, University of Washington, ProQuest, 2008). Also see Koshan

3. Integrated Responses to Policing of Domestic Violence

Exclusive focus on pro-arrest law and policy hardly begins to capture the range or complexity of developments in contemporary domestic violence policing. The following representative illustrations of relevant developments in the field must suffice for present purposes.

(a) Multi-agency Partnerships

Contemporary research and thinking on good practice in response to domestic violence typically promotes police collaboration with other sectors and service providers who can offer victims support,[89] rather than narrowly focusing on police enforcement per se. Proactive policing is commonly promoted as a positive feature within an integrated approach. For instance, in the context of policing in England and Wales, Betsy Stanko has outlined a strategic performance management approach to domestic violence policing, intended to 'better orient criminal justice outcomes towards the safety of victims'.[90] It has three dimensions which aim to improve police responses and 'enrich an integrated approach to domestic violence': (1) police organisational reviews of lethal violence cases; (2) analysis of police data on victim contact, contexts of repeat victimisation and victim perspectives; and (3) working with NGOs and other partners to examine public demands for assistance with domestic violence and to assess the adequacy of services according to demography and location.[91]

As evidence of the value of integrating police responses across agencies, Stanko cites a scheme in Cardiff, Wales, which has focused on enhancing the safety of high-risk victims of domestic violence. Information concerning victims identified as high risk was shared between police and 15 other statutory agencies, NGOs and voluntary support agencies.[92] The scheme produced an improved understanding of the risks of domestic violence among police and participating agencies and resulted in additional support for victims. The level of repeat offending, as measured by official reports and victim interviews, was reduced substantially and in 60 per cent of cases there was no further reported violence during the follow-up period.

---

and Wiegers, above n 9, 177–78 (distinguishing between the effects on domestic violence policy of neo-liberalism in Saskatchewan, which maintained a more social democratic tradition—evident, for example, in funding of shelters—and neo-conservatism in Alberta).

[89] Hoyle and Sanders, above n 51; K Rollings and N Taylor, *Measuring Police Performance in Domestic and Family Violence*, Trends and Issues in Crime and Criminal Justice No 367 (Canberra, Australian Institute of Criminology, 2008); UN Commission on the Status of Women, *Report on the Fifty-seventh Session (4–15 March 2013)*, E/CN.6/2013/11, Agreed Conclusions, Part C, www.un.org/womenwatch/daw/csw/57sess.htm (accessed 28 October 2015).

[90] Stanko, above n 18, 296.

[91] Ibid 296–97.

[92] Ibid 300. For an evaluation, see A Robinson 'Reducing Repeat Victimization among High-risk Victims of Domestic Violence: The Benefits of A Coordinated Community Response in Cardiff, Wales' (2006) 12 *Violence Against Women* 761, 762. A similar scheme is currently being trialed in NSW.

(b) Procedural Justice and Human Rights

Much of the procedural justice literature has focused on fair treatment of suspects and offenders, and explored the relationship between police integrity and public confidence in policing from this perspective. Such analysis seeks to build legitimacy for policing as an institution and to promote compliance with the law.[93] This literature is beginning to influence ideas about good practice in domestic violence policing, prompting attention to the perspectives of victims of crime and their communities.[94] It has the potential to recognise both under-enforcement and over-enforcement as compromising police integrity. Research studies suggest that processes and not just case outcomes matter to victims. This work meshes with earlier research demonstrating that poor responses by police and other justice officials to domestic violence victims may discourage victims from seeking help in the future, thereby compromising victim safety and undermining trust in criminal justice.

International responses to violence against women also shape the policing of domestic violence in local contexts, sometimes in unanticipated ways. The UN Convention on the Elimination of All Forms of Discrimination against Women (CEDAW) emphasises that it is the responsibility of states to prosecute and punish perpetrators of domestic violence. In some countries this has resulted in the specific criminalisation of domestic violence offences or the application of criminal sanctions to the breach of civil orders.[95] Policing practices are being examined by human rights bodies against newly emerging standards.[96] For instance, the United Nations Human Rights Council has emphasised the need for states parties to exercise due diligence 'to prevent, investigate, prosecute and punish the perpetrators of violence against women and girl-children'.[97] Rulings of the European Court of Human Rights and the CEDAW Committee have held national governments responsible 'for failures to protect victims from imminent acts of domestic violence'.[98] Legislative and policy developments in the UK have been measured against the framework of the Council of Europe

---

[93] R Paternoster, R Brame, R Bachman and LW Sherman, 'Do Fair Procedures Matter? The Effect of Procedural Justice on Spouse Assault' (1997) 31 *Law & Society Review* 163. See also J Jackson, B Bradford, B Stanko and K Hohl, *Just Authority? Trust in the Police in England and Wales* (Abingdon, Routledge, 2013) ch 10.

[94] I Elliott, S Thomas and J Ogloff, 'Procedural Justice in Contacts with the Police: The Perspective of Victims of Crime' (2011) 13 *Police Practice and Research* 437. Cf LJ Hickman and SS Simpson, 'Fair Treatment or Preferred Outcome? The Impact of Police Behavior on Victim Reports of Domestic Violence Incidents' (2003) 37 *Law & Society Review* 607 (reporting that *both* procedural justice and just outcomes matter).

[95] For instance, breach of a non-molestation order was criminalised in England and Wales: Domestic Violence, Crime and Victims Act 2004, s 1.

[96] CEDAW Committee General Recommendation No 19, adopted in 1992, defines discrimination as including gender-based violence and makes it clear that States may be held accountable for the actions of private individuals if they fail to exercise due diligence in responding to violence against women: UN Doc HRI/GEN/1/Rev 9 (Vol II) (1992) Arts 1, 6 and 9. State responsibility to exercise due diligence was reaffirmed at the recent UN Commission on the Status of Women, above n 89, [9], [16].

[97] '[T]here is a broad international consensus over the use of the due diligence principle to interpret the content of State legal obligations towards the problem of violence against women; a consensus that extends to the problem of domestic violence … [T]he United Nations Human Rights Council, has underscored this year that States must exercise due diligence to prevent, investigate, prosecute and punish the perpetrators of violence against women and girl-children, and that the failure to do so "violates and impairs or nullifies the enjoyment of their human rights and fundamental freedoms".' IACHR Report 80/11, above n 5, [123]–[124] (quoting the UN Human Rights Council, *Accelerating Efforts to Eliminate All Forms of Violence Against Women: Ensuring Due Diligence in Prevention*, A/HRC/14/L 9/Rev 1, 16 June 2010).

[98] Ibid [132].

Blueprint to Combat Violence against Women, including Domestic Violence.[99] Even in the US, which has not ratified CEDAW, emerging human rights standards are beginning to influence policing policies.

International law and discourse endorses proactive law enforcement within a broader context of human rights and measures to promote equality,[100] challenging conventional constructions of domestic violence within criminal justice, which are commonly single-incident-based. It remains to be seen to what extent this human rights framework will shape proactive policing approaches to domestic violence. Some UK research, albeit not specific to domestic violence, affords limited grounds for optimism. Human rights provisions have been less successful in raising police awareness of rights, but instead have resulted in 'bureaucratic processes [being] used by officers to legitimize and justify their existing practices'.[101]

In 2011, the issues raised in *Town of Castle Rock v Gonzales* were considered by the Inter-American Commission on Human Rights (IACHR). This was the first case to be brought against the US government before an international human rights tribunal on behalf of a domestic violence survivor.[102] The tribunal 'found that the United States violated the human rights of Jessica Lenahan (formerly Gonzales) and her children', a holding that 'underscore[s] that the US is failing in its legal obligation to protect women and girls from domestic violence'.[103] The divergent approaches of the US Supreme Court and the IACHR in this litigation also demonstrate 'apparently conflicting national and international normative frameworks'.[104] While past practice indicates US reluctance to comply with the IACHR recommendations, activists and scholars have used the *Lenahan* decision to urge improvements in police practices concerning domestic violence and to reshape understandings of police integrity. For instance, they endorse 'refram[ing] the problem of police under-enforcement as misconduct' and they have influenced the development of US Department of Justice guidelines on 'discriminatory policing of domestic and sexual violence'.[105] Subsequent to *Lenahan*, the US Department of Justice conducted inquiries into police departments in New Orleans, Maricopa County Arizona, Missoula Minnesota and Puerto Rico, finding evidence of gender bias in the policing of crimes against women.[106]

---

[99] Task Force to Combat Violence against Women, including Domestic Violence (EG-TFV), *Final Activity Report* (Strasbourg, Council of Europe, 2008).

[100] See contributions to C Benninger-Bude (ed), *Due Diligence and Its Application to Protect Women from Violence* (Leiden, Martinus Nijhoff Publishers, 2008).

[101] K Bullock and P Johnson, 'The Impact of the Human Rights Act 1998 on Policing in England and Wales' (2012) 52 *British Journal of Criminology* 630.

[102] 'The petitioners claim that the US Supreme Court's decision in *Town of Castle Rock v Gonzales* leaves Jessica Lenahan and countless other domestic violence victims in the US without a judicial remedy by which to hold the police accountable for their failures to protect domestic violence victims and their children.' IACHR Report 80/11, above n 5, [40].

[103] American Civil Liberties Union (ACLU) media release, www.aclu.org/cases/jessica-gonzales-v-usa (accessed 28 October 2015).

[104] C Bettinger-Lopez, 'Introduction: *Jessica Lenahan (Gonzales) v United States*: Implementation, Litigation, and Mobilization Strategies' (2012) 21 *Journal of Gender, Social Policy & the Law* 207, 223.

[105] Ibid 225, 226.

[106] US Department of Justice, *Joint Statement of The Office of Community Oriented Policing Services, The Office for Victims of Crime, and The Office on Violence Against Women on Addressing Gender-Discrimination in Policing* (June 2013), blogs.justice.gov/ovw/archives/2406 (accessed 28 October 2015).

Yet there are some significant tensions arising from the application of human rights norms and discourses to policing. Constituting police as 'defenders of human rights' may be problematic.[107] Whilst '[d]omestic violence is an area of policing that indeed has been given immense prominence through human rights',[108] some commentators worry that there has been insufficient critical analysis of the incongruities between policing and law. Specifically, the nexus between human rights and policing has often served to legitimate policing and elides its inherently coercive nature. Human rights have conventionally been conceived as imposing limits on the coercive reach of criminal law and criminal justice. But what are the implications of human rights-based 'claims for the extension of criminal law' in the form of 'coercive duties on the state to criminalize, prevent, police and prosecute harmful acts'?[109] One illustration concerns 'zero tolerance' policing. This term has been deployed in public education campaigns around violence against women since the 1980s and is now routinely invoked in political discourse, human rights debate and official UN reports on domestic violence.[110] However, some commentators recognise and lament the manner in which it has been co-opted and used in other contexts, such as mandatory arrest, and in unintended ways.[111] For instance, it may rebound on women victims of domestic violence who are arrested for fighting back.[112] There is an extensive critical literature on the damaging effects of zero tolerance policing, especially for marginalised communities, suggesting that undue emphasis on zero tolerance in future developments of domestic violence policing would be unwise.[113]

4. Tensions in the Policing of Domestic Violence in New South Wales

The preceding discussion indicates that debates about police enforcement of domestic violence need to be informed by an examination of specific legal frameworks and local contexts, and with due regard to the complexities and tensions in policing policy and practice.

---

[107] J Hornberger, 'Human Rights and Policing: Exigency or Incongruence?' (2010) 6 *Annual Review of Law and Social Science* 259, 277.

[108] Ibid.

[109] L Lazarus, 'Positive Obligations and Criminal Justice: Duties to Protect or Coerce?' in L Zedner and JV Roberts (eds), *Principles and Values in Criminal Law and Criminal Justice: Essays in Honour of Andrew Ashworth* (Oxford, Oxford University Press, 2012) 135, 136.

[110] The recent UN Commission on the Status of Women, above n 89, Section B (ll), calls on States to promote zero tolerance of violence against women and girls.

[111] E Gillam and E Samson, 'The Zero Tolerance Campaigns' in J Hanmer and C Itzin (eds), *Home Truths about Domestic Violence: Feminist Influences on Policy and Practice—A Reader* (London, Routledge, 2000); E Comack and G Balfour, *The Power to Criminalize: Violence, Inequality and Law* (Halifax, Nova Scotia, Fernwood Publishing, 2004).

[112] D Coker, 'Transformative Justice: Anti-Subordination Processes in Cases of Domestic Violence' in H Strang and J Braithwaite (eds), *Restorative Justice and Family Violence* (Cambridge, Cambridge University Press, 2000).

[113] J Greene, 'Zero Tolerance: A Case Study of Police Policies and Practices in New York' (1999) 45 *Crime & Delinquency* 171; T Newburn and T Jones, 'Symbolizing Crime Control: Reflections on Zero Tolerance' (2007) 11 *Theoretical Criminology* 221; D Dixon 'Broken Windows, Zero Tolerance and the New York Miracle' (1998) 10 *Current Issues in Criminal Justice* 96; C Cunneen, 'Zero Tolerance Policing and the Experience of New York City' (1999) 10 *Current Issues in Criminal Justice* 299.

Contemporary domestic violence policing in NSW, where laws and practices differ in significant ways from other jurisdictions in which pro-arrest policies have been researched, exemplifies these complexities and tensions. For instance, NSW domestic violence legislation defines domestic relations broadly, so that domestic violence provisions extend to all those who live or have lived in the same household or residential facility, not just to intimates.[114] Prior to a recent amendment to the Law Enforcement (Powers and Responsibilities) Act 2002 (NSW),[115] arrest and prosecution was a last resort, to be used only where diversionary alternatives such as warnings, cautions, penalty notices or Court Attendance Notices were deemed inadequate. NSW is also distinctive in that police are the prosecuting authorities in the lower courts, where most domestic violence prosecutions take place. It is rare for cases in which charges have been laid not to proceed to court, although at court approximately 12 per cent of domestic violence-related cases are withdrawn or dismissed without a hearing.[116] This contrasts with practice in other jurisdictions. For instance, in many states in the US arrests do not necessarily result in charges and most arrests do not result in prosecution.[117]

The local context of policing in NSW and across Australia encompasses the distinctive experiences of indigenous people. Police were agents of colonisation, and the legacy of colonisation as well as current policing practices reinforce antipathy between indigenous people and the police. Some communities have experienced both under-policing and over-policing, in various forms. For instance, police have failed historically to protect Aboriginal women from domestic violence and racial abuse, but have over-policed Aboriginal women, men and their communities for offences committed in public places and especially those associated with alcohol.[118] There are self-policing initiatives in some indigenous communities, which operate independently of the formal police or sometimes in conjunction with them.[119]

(a) A Complex Institutional Framework

Domestic violence policing in NSW sits within a complex framework of national, state and organisational structures. The National Plan to Reduce Violence against Women and their Children and the Australasian Policing Strategy for the Prevention and Reduction of Family Violence ('the national policing strategy') operate at the federal level. Among the ten guiding principles of the national policing strategy, 'zero tolerance to perpetrators' is listed second.[120] Whilst there is no elaboration of what that might mean in practice, an action

---

[114] Crimes (Domestic and Personal Violence) Act 2007 (NSW), s 5.

[115] Amendments to the Law Enforcement (Powers and Responsibilities) Amendment (Arrest without Warrant) Act 2013, s 99, introduced in December 2013, widened the grounds for an arrest and removed the condition that an officer must *not* arrest unless it is for specified purposes. See V Sentas and R McMahon, 'Changes to Police Powers of Arrest in NSW' (2014) 3 *Current Issues in Criminal Justice* 785.

[116] L Rodwell and N Smith, *An Evaluation of the NSW Domestic Violence Intervention Court Model* (Sydney, NSW Bureau of Crime Statistics and Research, 2008) 28.

[117] M Martin, 'Double Your Trouble: Dual Arrests in Family Violence' (1997) 12 *Journal of Family Violence* 139.

[118] C Cunneen, *Conflict, Politics and Crime: Aboriginal Communities and the Police* (Sydney, Allen & Unwin, 2001) ch 7.

[119] H Blagg, *Crime, Aboriginality and the Decolonisation of Justice* (Annandale, NSW, Hawkins Press, 2008) ch 5.

[120] *National Plan to Reduce Violence against Women and their Children*, above n 23, 3.

plan to give effect to the National Plan explicitly promoted 'a zero tolerance approach to violence supported by stronger policing leading to arrest, consistent sentencing of perpetrators, and serious consequences for perpetrators if they breach orders'.[121] It is unclear how a shift away from reactive policing towards prevention might be consistent with zero tolerance. However, the action plan also acknowledged the limitations of punishment alone and emphasised the need for perpetrator interventions seeking to motivate behavioural change.[122] A second three-year plan subsequently adopted 'strengthening proactive policing' as one of its key strategies,[123] but there is little elucidation of practical implications.

At the state level, NSW has its own State Plan which requires police to reduce domestic violence, a Domestic and Family Violence Framework that, inter alia, mandates police use of a risk assessment tool in domestic violence cases,[124] and a Domestic Violence Justice Strategy that requires police to investigate domestic violence proactively and take legal action wherever possible, to gather evidence consistently, to refer victims to services and to engage in inter-agency risk management.[125] In addition, while NSW does not have generic human rights legislation, the objects clause of the Crimes (Domestic and Personal Violence) Act 2007 (NSW) specifically refers to CEDAW[126] and affirms that 'domestic violence is best addressed through a coordinated legal and social response of assistance and prevention of violence and, in certain cases, may be the subject of appropriate intervention by the court'.[127]

At the organisational level, the NSW Police Force is hardly unique in having generated a plethora of rules and codes of practice,[128] notwithstanding periodic attempts at rationalisation. A specific code of practice for domestic and family violence (the 'Domestic Violence Code') was adopted in 2009 on the recommendation of the NSW Ombudsman, following a critical review of the policing of domestic violence.[129] At that time there was no comprehensive framework to guide police and no standards against which to measure performance. The Domestic Violence Code aims to

promote the importance of early intervention, investigation and prosecution of criminal offences; recognise the significant value of specialist domestic violence service providers in the delivery of

---

[121] Department of Social Services, *National Implementation Plan for the First Action Plan 2010–2013: Building a Strong Foundation Safe and Free From Violence* (Canberra, Commonwealth of Australia, 2012) 30.

[122] *National Plan to Reduce Violence against Women and their Children*, above n 23, 29.

[123] Department of Social Services, *Moving Ahead: Second Action Plan 2013–2016 of the National Plan to Reduce Violence against Women and their Children 2010–2022* (Canberra, Commonwealth of Australia, 2014) 39, www.dss. gov.au/ (accessed 28 October 2015).

[124] *NSW 2021: A Plan to Make NSW Number One* (Sydney, NSW Government, 2011) 34, www.2021.nsw.gov.au/ sites/default/files/NSW2021_WEB%20VERSION.pdf (accessed 28 October 2015).

[125] *NSW Domestic Violence Justice Strategy, 2013–2017* (Sydney, NSW Department of Attorney General and Justice, 2012) 14–16, http://www.crimeprevention.nsw.gov.au/domesticviolence/home/domestic-violence-justice-strategy (accessed 18 February 2016).

[126] Section 9(1).

[127] Section 9(3)(g).

[128] D Dixon, 'The Normative Structure of Policing' in D Dixon (ed), *A Culture of Corruption* (Annandale NSW, Hawkins Press, 1999) 89–91.

[129] *Code of Practice for the NSW Police Force Response to Domestic and Family Violence* (Sydney, NSW Police Force, 2013) www.police.nsw.gov.au/__data/assets/pdf_file/0016/165202/domestic-and-family-violence-code-of-practice.pdf.pdf (accessed 28 October 2015) (Domestic Violence Code); NSW Ombudsman, *Domestic Violence: Improving Police Practice* (2006) 80, www.ombo.nsw.gov.au/news-and-publications/publications/reports/police/special-report-to-parliament-domestic-violence-improving-police-practice (accessed 28 October 2015).

integrated responses to break the cycle of domestic and family violence; and achieve good practice through an appropriate, consistent, transparent and accountable response to domestic and family violence.[130]

The Code describes the proactive approach of the NSW Police Force which 'requires police to not only respond to incidents of domestic and family violence and *give strongest consideration to arrest*; but to develop strategies to reduce repeat offender behaviour and manage repeat and high risk offenders'.[131] Other aspects of the Domestic Violence Code deal with the responsibilities of police officers appointed to Local Area Commands as Domestic Violence Liaison Officers to review and provide quality assurance of domestic violence complaints, victim assistance, and liaison with agencies and support services.[132] The Code is supplemented by detailed Standing Operating Procedures introduced in 2008, but it is a matter of concern that they are not publicly available, undermining their potential to promote accountability.[133]

The Domestic Violence Code is said to be consistent with the National Plan and with the principles of the strategy adopted by the Australasian Police Commissioners, including zero tolerance. However, the emphasis on arrest in the Domestic Violence Code stands in tension with the NSW Police's general Code of Practice for CRIME (Custody, Rights, Investigation, Management and Evidence: the 'CRIME code'), which requires that police 'always consider if there is an alternative to arrest'.[134] It also may be difficult to reconcile with the emphasis given to assistance and prevention in the CEDAW-derived objects clause of the Crimes (Domestic and Personal Violence) Act 2007 (NSW), mentioned above.

In 2009 the NSW Ombudsman identified a gap in the normative structure of domestic violence policing, but also found that frontline officers felt burdened by the legislative and administrative requirements of domestic violence policing. Since that time, the development of national, state and organisational frameworks and codes of practice have filled the gap, but they hardly convey a simple, unambiguous message about what is required of police. Tensions between these frameworks and codes seem to have gone largely unremarked. Moreover, greater attention needs to be devoted to other contextual factors that might shape the manner in which these frameworks and codes are interpreted and given effect by operational police and their supervisors.

(b) Dual Arrests in New South Wales

There has been little research on dual arrests in NSW or more generally across Australia.[135] A recent study of the ACT's integrated service delivery model concluded that dual arrest

---

[130]   Domestic Violence Code, above n 129, 10–11.

[131]   Ibid 12 (emphasis added).

[132]   Ibid 25.

[133]   Standing Committee on Social Issues, NSW Parliament, *Domestic Violence: Trends and Issues in NSW* (Sydney, NSW Parliament, 2012) 178–79.

[134]   'The CRIME Code' (Sydney, NSW Police Force, 2012) 13, www.police.nsw.gov.au/about_us/policies__ and__procedures/legislation_list/code_of_practice_for_crime (accessed 28 October 2015). This code has not been updated to take account of amendments to the Law Enforcement (Powers and Responsibilities) Act 2002 (NSW).

[135]   Ibid 8.

was not a problem experienced in that jurisdiction.[136] The NSW Domestic Violence Code 'discourages police from arresting and charging both parties', other than in exceptional circumstances. Police are required to consider any history of prior violence and other factors to determine 'the primary victim' and to seek the advice of a supervisor if uncertain.[137]

The number of women arrested for domestic violence-related assaults in NSW has increased over the period 2000 to 2010 (on average by 10 per cent per annum) to a greater extent than for men (on average by 1.9 per cent per annum).[138] Further research is needed to identify factors that may have contributed to this increase, but there is some evidence to suggest that it reflects changes in enforcement practices rather than any increase in domestic violence by women. For instance, victimisation surveys indicate that the prevalence of partner violence experienced by men or women has not changed during the period 2005 to 2012.[139] The trend towards increased arrests of women is not restricted to domestic violence, and the increases have been most apparent in offence categories that are particularly likely to be shaped by police enforcement practices.[140] In NSW there are, as yet, no data on dual arrests.[141] However, the legal and social services sectors continue to express concerns about police charging female domestic violence victims and proceeding against them for domestic violence orders, and these practices do not seem to be confined to dual arrest scenarios.[142]

Conclusion

It is striking that proactive policing laws and policies are characterised in markedly different ways across interdisciplinary literatures. Divergent depictions doubtless reflect, at least in part, different constructions of how proactive policing implicates moral and practical integrity in the administration of criminal justice.

Within international law and human rights discourse, proactive law enforcement is typically viewed as a response to under-enforcement, which reflects gender bias and is inconsistent with integrity. Proactive policing is seen as a positive indicator of a

---

[136] Holder, above n 25, 43.

[137] Domestic Violence Code, above n 129, 34.

[138] Standing Committee on Social Issues, above n 133, 18.

[139] National victimisation data indicate no change between 2005 and 2012: Australian Bureau of Statistics, *Personal Safety Survey 2012* (Canberra, ABS, 2013), Catalogue No 4906.0, Table 21. Survey data are not available on whether the proportion of men who reported partner violence to police changed over time, but the findings indicate that, for men who experienced partner violence in the preceding 12 months, 94% made no police report; whilst 80% of those experiencing partner violence at any time in the past had made no report: ibid, Tables 25 and 26.

[140] J Holmes, *Female Offending: Has There Been an Increase?* Issues Paper No 46 (Sydney, NSW Bureau of Crime Statistics and Research, 2010).

[141] But see J Wangmann, 'Gender and Intimate Partner Violence: A Case Study from NSW' (2010) 33 *University of New South Wales Law Journal* 945 (on cross-applications for domestic violence orders).

[142] Women's Legal Services NSW, *Women Defendants to AVOs: What is their Experience of the Justice System?* (Sydney, Women's Legal Services NSW, 2014), www.womenslegalnsw.asn.au/wlsnsw/wp-content/uploads/womendefAVOsreport.pdf (accessed 28 October 2015).

State's due diligence[143] and is routinely endorsed in the broader context of human rights implementation and associated measures to promote equality.[144] Researchers commonly focus on the intrinsic value of the State's due diligence, encompassing both symbolic and constitutive dimensions. Thus, for Dempsey (who develops her argument with respect to prosecution rather than arrest), State actors respond in ways that constitute characteristics of the State; effective action is that which is aligned with 'values that are relevant to the project of ending domestic violence'[145] to the extent that they help 'reconstitute the State's character as less patriarchal'.[146] On this view, States' international human rights obligations to take effective action against domestic violence do not necessitate limiting discretion, but rather more careful deployment of 'effective' discretion. Some scholars see human rights discourse and jurisprudence as having the potential to shift conceptions of good policing and police integrity, building on the positive legacy of the Gonzales/Lenahan litigation and drawing on equality principles.[147] It remains to be seen whether, and to what extent, human rights discourse and practice might inflect a more nuanced approach to the proactive policing of domestic violence. For example, human rights strategies might challenge single incident approaches to criminal law enforcement, which are ill-equipped to recognise the harm of domestic violence as linked to structural disadvantage, or those victims most in need of protection, for whom a more contextual understanding of the experience of domestic violence is needed.

Among criminal justice practitioners, by contrast, proactive policing has been interpreted narrowly, with a strong reliance on deterrence and a focus on removing police discretion. Practitioners and scholars who recognise the damaging effects of mandatory arrest, police over-enforcement and the harsh consequences of coercive policing on marginalised communities have convincingly exposed the (unintentionally) abusive side effects of these forms of proactive policing of domestic violence. Viewed in broader perspective, such approaches may be evidence of the resurgence of the punitive state under neo-liberalism and of the co-option of feminist advocacy to empower the state but not women.[148] These divergent disciplinary perspectives invite much more serious examination of the complexity of domestic violence policing and the threats to fairness and integrity wrought by both under- and over-enforcement.

Re-engaging with a more expansive definition of integrity, and with due regard to recent developments in conceptions of good policing, offers one avenue for opening up debate and scholarly inquiry about police responses to domestic violence. This chapter is a call to foster integrity in policing policy and practice beyond merely protecting the

---

[143] Meyersfeld, above n 34.

[144] See contributions to Benninger-Bude, above n 100.

[145] M Madden Dempsey, 'Toward a Feminist State: What does "Effective" Prosecution of Domestic Violence Mean?' (2007) 70 *Modern Law Review* 908, 916.

[146] Ibid 925. Dempsey does not argue in favour of limiting prosecutorial discretion, but instead for inflecting it with 'fine grained discretion' consistent with 'feminist practical reason' capable of distinguishing and responding differently to different forms of domestic violence. Ibid 931.

[147] Bettinger-Lopez, above n 104.

[148] Bumiller, above n 36; Kim, above n 85; DL Martin, 'Retribution Revisited: A Reconsideration of Feminist Criminal Law Reform Strategies' (1998) 36 *Osgoode Hall Law Journal* 151; L Snider, 'Toward Safer Societies: Punishment, Masculinities and Violence against Women' (1998) 38 *British Journal of Criminology* 1.

administration of criminal justice from official misconduct in the classical sense, that is, deliberate misfeasance breaching regulative standards. It is time for a new research agenda which engages more directly with the implications of different forms of under-enforcement and their uneven impact on vulnerable individuals and communities, focused on integrity at the organisational level, in professional decision-making and in exercising operational discretion. Scholarship needs to reconsider the meaning of 'good policing', taking proper account of research on procedural justice and critically examining the pre-conditions for inter-agency partnerships with effective police participation. The possibilities, albeit rife with tensions, that a human rights framework might offer in bringing new understandings of domestic violence and policing merit further careful consideration in a comprehensive re-examination of the normative complexities and practical challenges surveyed in this chapter.

3

Integrity, Interrogation and Criminal Injustice

DAVID DIXON

[W]hat matters is how the confession was obtained, not whether or not it may have been true … [T]he rationale of these provisions is that they are intended, among other things, to preserve the integrity of the Common Law principle, that no person is required or can be made to incriminate himself.

(Mitchell J, ruling on the voir dire in *R v Heron*, Leeds Crown Court, 1 November 1993)

Introduction: Two Murders, Two Flawed Investigations

This chapter explores the concept of integrity in criminal process through a close reading of the events surrounding two murder cases from the 1990s, which together had a significant impact on the conduct of criminal investigation in England and Wales. *R v Paris, Miller and Abdullahi*,[1] popularly known as the case of the 'Cardiff Three', became both a cause célèbre miscarriage of justice and a leading authority on the admissibility of confessions in English law. The second case is less well known, partly because the judgment was not formally reported. It concerns the unsuccessful prosecution of George Heron for the murder of Nikki Allan in 1992.

One way of telling the story of these cases is as a progressive strengthening of criminal justice integrity, due process values and professionalism in policing. This is an approach which, as will be shown below, has some validity. Progress in criminal justice reform should not be underestimated, not least because doing so threatens to undermine opposition to contemporary assaults on integrity, due process and professionalism in criminal investigation.[2] On a broader view, however, a more nuanced and less Whiggish history may be necessary, one which pays attention to the experiences and perceptions of individuals and communities affected by injustice and which helps us to understand the criminal process as opaque and often riddled with uncertainty and the concept of integrity as capable of conflicting interpretations.

---

[1] *R v Paris, Miller and Abdullahi* (1993) 97 Cr App R 99 (CA).
[2] D Dixon, 'Authorise and Regulate' in E Cape and R Young (eds), *Regulating Policing* (Oxford, Hart Publishing, 2008).

(a) The Murder of Lynette White and the Conviction of the Cardiff Three

Anthony Paris, Stephen Miller and Yusef Abdullahi were convicted of the murder of Lynette White in 1990.[3] (Two other defendants, John Actie and Ronald Actie, were acquitted.) Two years later, the Court of Appeal allowed their appeals and quashed all three convictions. The Court found that the key confession made by Stephen Miller, during what Lord Chief Justice Taylor described as a 'travesty of an interview',[4] had been obtained by oppression and should have been excluded from the trial.[5] The Court of Appeal was 'horrified' by the interrogation: 'Short of physical violence, it is hard to conceive of a more hostile and intimidating approach by officers to a suspect.'[6] The presence of legal advisors during the interviews had evidently not protected these suspects.

South Wales Police initially reacted angrily to the decision, making clear that their investigation was finished: as far as the police were concerned, those responsible for the murder had been caught and prosecuted.[7] The case was eventually re-opened, largely due to the persistence of an investigative journalist, Satish Sekar,[8] and in 2003 Jeffrey Gafoor was convicted of Lynette White's murder on the strength of new DNA evidence. Gafoor was one of the victim's sex work clients. He had acted alone and had no connection whatever to Miller, Paris or Abdullahi. With the innocence of the Cardiff Three positively established, South Wales Police found themselves embroiled in a decade of further controversy surrounding the investigation.

Gafoor had cut himself during the murder, leaving his blood (containing his DNA) at the scene. Heavily blood-stained with his own and his victim's blood, he was seen leaving the area by a witness whose description was used to produce a photofit image. When eventually arrested, 'Gafoor accepted in interview that the photofit could well have been him'.[9] Even allowing for the wisdom of hindsight, South Wales Police had made a serious error of judgement in shifting the focus of the investigation from finding the man in the photofit to pursuing the Cardiff Three.

(b) The Murder of Nikki Allan and the Trial of George Heron

In 1992, Nikki Allan, a seven-year-old girl, was murdered in a derelict Wearside warehouse after leaving her mother to walk home.[10] The police identified George Heron as a suspect

---

[3] See S Sekar, *Fitted In: The Cardiff Three and the Lynette White Inquiry* (London, The Fitted In Project, 1997); JL Williams, *Bloody Valentine: A Killing in Cardiff* (London, HarperCollins, 1995).

[4] *Paris*, above n 1, (1993) 97 Cr App R 99, 104.

[5] Pursuant to the Police and Criminal Evidence Act 1984 (PACE), s 76(2)(a).

[6] *Paris*, above n 1, (1993) 97 Cr App R 99, 103.

[7] South Wales Police, *Lynette Deborah White Phase III Inquiry: Final Report pursuant to Section 73(1) The Police Act 1996 South Wales Police Misconduct Reference—35/2003* (Cardiff, South Wales Police, 2013) 3.

[8] See S Sekar, *The Cardiff Five: Innocent Beyond Any Doubt* (Hook Hants, Waterside Press, 2012); Sekar, above n 3.

[9] South Wales Police, above n 7, 19.

[10] My discussion of this case draws on George Heron's audio-taped and transcribed interview records, Northumbria Police's *Report of an enquiry into the practices and procedures adopted by police officers during interviews with George Heron* (1994), and interviews with the principal investigating officer, Detective Superintendent John Renwick; Heron's counsel, Mr Roger Thorn QC and Mr Robin Patton; and Dr Michael Stockdale and Greer Hogan (Northumbria Law School). I am grateful to them for their assistance, but the interpretation is mine.

after they were given reason to believe that his statements (about his knowledge of the dead girl and his movements on the night of the murder) to officers carrying out house-to-house inquiries were untrue. Witness statements placed Heron in the area from which Nikki Allan disappeared. However, the crucial witness who saw the girl walking away with a man described someone unlike Heron and did not identify Heron when an identification parade was held. Just as in the Cardiff Three case, investigators had evidence which did not fit their case theory: instead of changing their theory, they tried to fit evidence into it. As we will see, allegiance to this theory led them to misrepresent the witness' evidence in an attempt to obtain a confession from Heron. The focus on Heron, rather than on the man described by the witness, may mean that no-one will ever be brought to justice for killing Nikki Allan.

After his arrest, Heron was questioned for a total of almost eight hours in five interviews over three days, during which time he denied the murder some 120 times. The final interviews, in which admissions were made, were conducted by senior officers in the presence of a legal advisor.

By the time that George Heron's case came on for trial at Leeds Crown Court, the Court of Appeal's decision in *Paris, Miller and Abdullahi* had been handed down, and it clearly influenced the course of the proceedings. Ruling on the voir dire, Mr Justice Mitchell declared Heron's 'confession' inadmissible on grounds of oppression. In the crucial final interviews, the interrogators had misrepresented the strength of the evidence against him, repeatedly asserted his guilt, asked offensive questions about his sex life, and suggested that it was in his own interests to confess.[11] Without any confession, the prosecution's case collapsed and Heron was acquitted. Northumbria Police established an enquiry into 'the practices and procedures adopted by police officers during interviews' with Heron.[12] However, echoing South Wales Police, the head of Northumbria CID announced that 'there was no question of … "looking for anyone else"',[13] with the clear implication that the police believed George Heron was their man.

Heron went into hiding (a religious order took him in). Nikki Allan's family subsequently brought a successful civil action for 'battery leading to the death of Nikki Allan' against Heron, who did not appear to contest the case.[14] When the double jeopardy prohibition was relaxed to enable acquittals to be quashed on the basis of 'new and compelling evidence',[15] Nikki Allan's mother called for re-investigation of the case, including exhumation of her daughter's body.[16] Northumbria Police did reopen the investigation, leading to the arrest of another suspect (not George Heron) in 2014, but nobody was ever charged.

---

[11] Four interview records which included the crucial admissions were excluded. Mitchell J found that misrepresentation of identification evidence was enough to require exclusion under PACE s 76, but insisted that the interview records should be evaluated as a whole: they constituted 'a continuing injustice' and 'a tale of an insidious form of oppression'. He added that even if s 76 had been found to be inapplicable, he would have excluded the recorded admissions under the s 78 fairness discretion (Mitchell J, ruling on the voir dire in *R v Heron*, Leeds Crown Court, 1 November 1993, 23, 26).

[12] Northumbria Police, above n 10.

[13] Detective Chief Superintendent Barry Stewart, quoted in M Pithers, 'Nikki Allan defendant says he will sue police: Detectives "not looking for anyone else"', *The Independent*, 23 November 1993.

[14] Northumbria Police, above n 10, 42.

[15] Criminal Justice Act 2003, Part 10.

[16] 'Pympurnell', 'Is Justice blind—then can Nikki Allan have some?', blogpost 11 January 2012, my.telegraph. co.uk/members/pympurnell/ (accessed 13 January 2016).

(c) Two Case Studies in Integrity

Although criminal procedure in England and Wales was extensively reformed by the Police and Criminal Evidence Act 1984 (PACE), changes in institutional culture and working practices took longer to disseminate and embed. The judicial interventions in *Paris* and *Heron* clearly signalled that changes in police practices and training would be needed to keep pace with statutory reforms (and that judges were prepared to play their part in influencing such change through their decisions). Tom Williamson, the English police's leading expert in interrogation training, reported that the Cardiff Three and *Heron* decisions forced 'a fundamental reappraisal of how the police have traditionally gone about the investigation of the most serious crimes'.[17] The Royal Commission on Criminal Justice endorsed reform of interview training, after noting that, '[t]he risks inherent in certain interview techniques were vividly illustrated by the copy of the tape sent to us by the Chief Justice after the Court of Appeal had allowed the appeal of the Cardiff Three'.[18]

Most police observers could dissociate themselves from judicial criticisms of interviewing practices characterised as horrifying. In *Heron*'s case, by contrast, the investigators interviewed in a way that most long-serving police officers would have considered unexceptionable and standard, although some Northumbria Police officers who were aware of developments in interview methods were critical of the senior officers who took over the final stages of Heron's interrogation. The head of Northumbria CID announced that 'there would be a full review of the techniques used by his officers', but added that 'he did not accept that these had been oppressive'.[19] As the Northumbria Police report on the case drily observed, Mitchell J's ruling 'undoubtedly came as a surprise to many of those involved in the case'.[20] The principal interviewers were very experienced senior detectives (rather than the detective constables involved in the Cardiff Three case); a legal advisor (albeit not a qualified solicitor) had been present during audio-taped interviews without any complaint; and the tapes were 'vetted' by the Crown Prosecution Service and by a psychologist acting as an 'independent assessor'. The investigating officers' superior maintained throughout that, '[t]hese interviews were conducted properly by police in accordance with the Police and Criminal Evidence Act and much of the lines and styles used in the questioning of the suspect have been used over a number of years'.[21] However, these standard methods were clearly no longer regarded as acceptable by the criminal courts.

Paris and *Heron* paved the way for comprehensive reform of police questioning practices through the adoption of investigative interviewing and the 'PEACE' programme.[22] Notably, this new investigative interviewing strategy extended to witnesses as well as suspects—a vital lesson learnt from the Cardiff Three investigation, as we will see. It also precipitated reform

---

[17] T Williamson, 'A commentary on the ruling on voir dire', in Northumbria Police, above n 10, 49.

[18] *Report of the Royal Commission on Criminal Justice*, Cm 2263 (London, HMSO, 1993) 12–13.

[19] Detective Chief Superintendent Barry Stewart, quoted in Pithers, above n 13.

[20] Northumbria Police, above n 10, 25.

[21] DCS Stewart, quoted in *The Times*, 2 November 1993. Also see reports and letters in *The Times*, 23 and 24 November 1993.

[22] PEACE is a mnemonic for the investigative interviewing framework which consists of: planning and preparation; engage and explain; account; clarify and challenge; closure; and evaluation. See B Ord, G Shaw and T Green, *Investigative Interviewing Explained* (Chatswood, NSW, LexisNexis, 2004); T Williamson (ed), *Investigative Interviewing* (Cullompton, Willan, 2006); T Shepherd and A Griffiths, *Investigative Interviewing* (Oxford, Oxford University Press, 2013).

of the organisation and management of criminal investigations, with a view to neutralising the pernicious effects of prematurely narrow case theories, 'heroic' detective culture, and tunnel vision in evidence-gathering which have contributed so much to miscarriages of justice over the years. Notwithstanding strong local feelings about Heron's acquittal, the internal inquiry was—to the credit of Northumbria Police—thorough and objective, canvassing invited submissions from professional (including academic) experts. The final report was submitted to national police agencies with a clear message that change was required.

The cases of the Cardiff Three and George Heron were landmarks in the modern reform of criminal investigations. We will now reconsider their broader significance when re-examined through the lens of integrity. As the Introduction to this volume shows, 'integrity' has a range of meanings and potential implications for criminal proceedings. The following discussion develops the themes of integrity as a coherent and integrated set of process values; integrity as professional responsibility; integrity as truth-finding; and integrity as fairness. In conclusion, we will also consider a darker side to the 'integrity' of criminal process.

1. Integrity as Normative Coherence and Integration

A central meaning of integrity, for our purposes, is that important values and principles are integrated—and implemented—throughout a process, organisation or set of practices. On a holistic view, integrity implies normative coherence rather than fragmentation or irreconcilable conflicts in fundamental commitments. The reality of criminal process may not be accurately depicted by the systemic flow charts produced by administrators, but its fundamental values and commitments should be shared by its principal agencies and honoured at every stage of the process. Normative coherence presupposes effective communication between the component parts of the system. If particular parts of the criminal justice apparatus become isolated, alienated or disenfranchised, the aspiration to shared values may become more rhetorical than enacted.

Regarding police interrogation, communication about what happened in the interview room used to depend on verbal or written accounts supplied by those present. Courts conventionally accepted the police version of events. Sometimes a political commitment to 'law and order' was revealed, as judges lambasted counsel who dared to challenge the veracity of police accounts.[23] More prosaically, judges and magistrates were obliged to proceed on the basis of the evidence which came before them. If a confession or other evidence had been procured in accordance with accepted standards, they were generally content to work with what they had.

Electronic recording of police interrogation, introduced in England and Wales in the late 1980s,[24] was an innovation which had a major impact on investigative practice. When used properly, to provide a reliable record of the *entire* interaction between suspect and

---

[23] Cf D Dixon, *Law in Policing: Legal Regulation and Police Practices* (Oxford, Clarendon Press, 1997) 194–95.

[24] Implementing PACE Code of Practice E. England and Wales have generally relied on audio-taping, in contrast to Australian jurisdictions which have used audio-visual recording since the early 1990s: see D Dixon, *Interrogating Images* (Sydney, Institute of Criminology, 2007).

interrogators, electronic recording enables judges to overcome the practical obstacles which had formerly excluded them from the interview room, and to impose curial values and standards on police interrogators.[25] Had the courts in *Paris* and *Heron* been presented only with each suspect's final written 'confession', the problematic nature of their production would not have come to light. Even after Heron's acquittal, the interviewers found it hard to accept that there was a problem in how they obtained his admissions. It seems certain that the construction through suggestion and adoption of key phrases in Heron's confession would not have appeared in evidence had they not been electronically recorded. This is not to suggest that the police would have deliberately behaved improperly. Rather, in retrospect, the precise content of these crucial exchanges—the significance of which becomes apparent only when the tape recordings were subjected to forensic scrutiny—might not have been remembered or regarded as important.

Electronic recording should be understood as a potentially vital tool in securing the integrity of criminal justice, by promoting normative coherence between the interview room and the court. However, the proviso that electronic recording must cover the entire interaction, and not just a set-piece confession (as it does, for example, in many US jurisdictions[26]), must be underlined. Incomplete recordings present a partial picture of the interview which could potentially be very misleading and damaging to the suspect (and, indeed, to the police, if selective recording leads to adverse inferences of police impropriety), and for this reason should be regarded as a threat to integrity.[27] Nonetheless, even complete tape recordings themselves guarantee nothing. One of the troubling features of the Cardiff Three's case was that the most oppressive sections of the interrogations were not presented to the jury which convicted them.[28] The ways in which tape recordings of interrogations are, or are not, utilised in criminal proceedings implicate the professional responsibilities of police officers conducting interviews, of courts reviewing confessions adduced in evidence, and—crucially, for our purposes—of lawyers providing custodial legal advice to suspects in the police station and advocates presenting the defence and prosecution cases in court.

2. Integrity as Professional Responsibility: The Role of Legal Advisors

The integrity of criminal process is partly a function of the personal integrity of its key personnel. Corrupt, malevolent or merely incompetent police officers pose obvious threats

---

[25] Ibid. See also D Dixon, 'Video Technology and Police Interrogation' in GJN Bruisma and DL Weisburd (eds), *Encyclopaedia of Criminology and Criminal Justice* (New York, Springer, 2014).

[26] RA Leo, SA Drizin, PJ Neufeld, BR Hall and A Vatner, 'Bringing Reliability Back In: False Confessions and Legal Safeguards in the Twenty-First Century' [2006] *Wisconsin Law Review* 479; TP Sullivan, 'The Time has Come for Law Enforcement Recordings of Custodial Interviews, Start to Finish' (2006) *Golden Gate Law Review* 175; BL Garrett, 'Interrogation Policies' (2015) 49 *University of Richmond Law Review* 895.

[27] D Dixon, '"A Window into the Interviewing Process"? The Audio-visual Recording of Police Interrogation in NSW Australia' (2006) 16 *Policing and Society* 328.

[28] The trial was run twice. The first trial had to be abandoned when the trial judge died as the defence was completing its final submissions. The full interview record had been played in this trial. However, in the second trial, Miller's barrister presented only a section of the crucial interview. His performance is strongly criticised by Sekar, above n 3, ch 8.

to the integrity of criminal investigation. Defence lawyers also have crucial roles to play, as their failures in the Cardiff Three and *Heron* cases implicitly demonstrate. In an adversary system, defence lawyers are often perceived as the prosecution's antagonists and may be regarded as obstructing justice. Too little attention is paid to their (real or potential) role and responsibility in giving practical substance to process values, as reflected in section 58(1) of PACE.[29]

Mention has already been made of the fact that the presence of a solicitor during their interviews had not much helped the Cardiff Three. Referring specifically to Stephen Miller's treatment, the Court of Appeal remarked that 'the solicitor appears to have been gravely at fault for sitting through this travesty of an interview'.[30] George Heron's legal advisor, who was an unqualified solicitor's 'representative',[31] proved no more effective. At the conclusion of the last interview with Heron, he declared himself 'very pleased with the way it has been dealt with'. Ruling on the voir dire, however, Mitchell J expressed 'the very greatest concern' about the fact that Heron had not seen a qualified solicitor until he appeared in court, adding that '[t]his is a state of affairs which must never be allowed to occur again'.[32] Mounting concern at the failure of legal advisors to protect their clients' interests in these and other contemporary cases prompted major reforms, including programmes of training and accreditation and disavowal of the previously widespread practice of solicitors' firms using unqualified, ex-police, 'runners' as legal advisors.[33]

The role of defence lawyers in providing support and professional legal advice to police stations detainees needs to be understood as contributing to the integrity of criminal process by vindicating the values of an adversarial procedural system; even if it might sometimes be hard for police and prosecutors to appreciate their contribution through the din and fury of contested litigation. Sometimes, the defence lawyer's role is to facilitate communication between suspects and investigators, explaining the legal situation and encouraging cooperation when appropriate. On other occasions, exemplified by *Heron* and the Cardiff Three, defence lawyers need to stand up for the law's fundamental principles in protecting their clients. This lesson remains to be learnt in Australia, where restriction of the right to silence in New South Wales appears to have been designed primarily to exclude lawyers from interrogation rooms.[34]

---

[29] Providing that: 'A person arrested and held in custody in a police station ... shall be entitled, if he so requests, to consult a solicitor privately at any time.'

[30] *Paris*, above n 1, (1993) 97 Cr App R 99, 104.

[31] One of the stranger details of the story is that the principal solicitor of the firm who supplied the 'advisor' to Heron was actually in the police station at the same time, advising another suspect—who subsequently testified for the prosecution against Heron.

[32] Mitchell J, above n 11.

[33] See Dixon, above n 23, ch 6; E Cape, 'Assisting and Advising Defendants before Trial' in M McConville and G Wilson (eds), *The Handbook of the Criminal Justice Process* (Oxford, Oxford University Press, 2002); L Bridges and J Hodgson, 'Improving Custodial Legal Advice' [1995] *Criminal Law Review* 101.

[34] D Dixon and N Cowdery, 'Silence Rights' (2013) 17 *Australian Indigenous Law Review* 23. On European developments, see J Blackstock, JS Hodgson, E Cape, T Spronken and A Ogodorova, *Inside Police Custody: An Empirical Account of Suspects' Rights in Four Jurisdictions* (London, Intersentia, 2014).

3. Integrity and Truth-finding: Themes and Accounts

The idea of integrity in police interrogation may easily be assimilated to a conception of criminal investigation as a 'search for the truth'. To be sure, this is an appealing cliché: investigators conventionally say that they seek the truth, and how could anyone object to that? However, truth and interrogation have a more complex relationship than appears at first sight. All too often, investigators have already committed themselves to a 'truth', that is an explanation of the crime and identification of its perpetrator, *before* questioning begins. An interrogation is then less about investigation and discovery of new evidence than a concerted effort to get the suspect to accept and adopt the investigators' truth, their version of events. Indeed, according to the 'Reid Technique', the highly influential interrogation method promoted by US company John E Reid & Associates, investigators should only interrogate suspects whom they believe to be guilty.[35]

The perils of the Reid Technique as an instrument of truth-finding are all too apparent in the transcript of George Heron's interrogation. Investigators repeatedly rejected out of hand Heron's attempts to establish any truth challenging their own version:

A   I didn't kill her.
Q   Well I believe you did kill her George.
A   I didn't.
Q   I believe you did.
A   I didn't …

Q   George you've got to help to tell the truth about this.
A   I am telling the truth …

Q   Come on, the truth George, come on we're not going to mess about, you've told lies, there's lies all the way along the line, you know what happened to Nikki Allan.
Q   You do George and you know exactly, her death …
A   I don't …

Q   Well let's start telling the truth George, I'm just asking you a simple question, right, I believe I know the answer to it and I'm asking you to tell the truth.
A   I am telling the truth …

A   I didn't kill her.
Q   You can keep saying that over and over again but that doesn't mean to me that you didn't do it and you know sat there the truth … all the evidence is pointing straight in your direction …
A   I am not admitting to somet't I didn't do.
Q   We are not asking you to admit that you didn't do, we are asking for the truth about the murder of Nikki Allan …

---

[35] FE Inbau, JE Reid, JP Buckley and BC Jayne, *Criminal Interrogation and Confessions*, 5th edn (Burlington MA, Jones and Bartlett, 2013). For criticism, see D Dixon, 'Questioning Suspects: A Comparative Perspective' (2010) 26 *Journal of Contemporary Criminal Justice* 426.

Q   … why have you been telling lies?

Q   Now George you have been asked that question a few times tonight and you have never answered it. Are you going to tell us why you have been telling lies? It's because you have got something to hide isn't it? …

Q   Well why have you been telling lies? Why won't you answer?

A   How would you like to be accused of a murder that you didn't commit? …

Q   You might have convinced yourself you haven't killed Nikki but George at the end of the day you are going to have to face up to reality you are going to have to tell the truth …

Q   I'm just asking for the truth George, that is all I am trying to establish.

A   I am telling the truth.

In these exchanges, the police repeatedly demand their truth (acceptance of their version of events and a confession) while Heron responds by asserting an alternative truth (that he did not kill Nikki Allan). How and why do suspects making such staunch initial denials sometimes come to speak the investigators' truth? As we will see, Heron eventually made an admission to knowing that Nikki Allan was dead before this became public knowledge. His initial admission opened the door to an intensive period of questioning about the circumstances of her death, and the gradual merging or imposition of the investigators' truth into his 'confession'.

Experience of miscarriages of justice in the US warns of the dangers of apparently convincing confessions bolstered by information fed to suspects (often unwittingly) by investigators themselves.[36] *Heron* confirms these dangers, but not in an entirely straightforward way. Some of George Heron's initial statements did not fit with information already known to police; and some of his inaccurate admissions would, if true, have made the crime even more heinous than it actually was. Interviewers responded by steering Heron away from inaccurate admissions and, at crucial moments, supplying 'cues' to help him confess 'accurately'. Thus, when Heron's version of the killing departed from the medical evidence, he had to be corrected and prompted:

Q   How many times do you think?

A   I lost count …

Q   So you have hit her with a brick a couple of times on the head?

A   Yes.

Q   That is not all you did George is it? …

Q   Did that kill her George with the brick? George it didn't did it, George?

Q   There is more isn't there George …

A   Went to throttle her …

Q   But you hit her with something else didn't you?

A   Probably I can't remember.

Q   George think I know it's not very nice but just think what else did you hit her with …

A   Fist.

---

[36] R Leo, *Police Interrogation and American Criminal Justice* (Cambridge MA, Harvard University Press, 2008); BL Garrett, 'Contaminated Confessions Revisited' (2015) 101 *Virginia Law Review* 398.

Q   What else, howay George you used something else didn't you, George, we knowhoway, George what else did you do, come on.

A   Piece of metal.

Nikki Allan had neither been throttled nor punched. Heron had to be corrected until he eventually volunteered 'a piece of metal'. But what kind of metal?

Q   What did you do with it?

A   Hit her.

Q   Hit her where?

A   (Unintelligible).

Q   No you didn't George, tell us what you did with it …

Q   But you did something else to her didn't you, you say with a piece of metal, what did you do?

Q   Well George we know she died as a result of what happened, don't we?

A   Yes …

Q   And you've told us that you've hit her with a piece of metal, now you did something with that piece of metal didn't you I just want you to tell us what you did …

A   Stuck it between her legs.

Q   Stuck what between her legs?

A   Metal pipe.

Q   And what did it do?

A   Blood …

Q   Where did the blood come from? From her head?

A   From between her legs.

Q   From between her legs? Howay George, look us in the eyes and tell me the truth …

Q   Well I'm saying to you, that you did something else to her as well didn't you eh, didn't you George, George didn't you? …

A   Assaulted her.

Q   What do you mean you assaulted her?

Q   What did you do?

A   Tried to have sex with her …

Q   What did you do, George, you didn't try to have sex with her did you George?

A   No …

A   I don't remember.

Q   Yes you do, right we'll come back to that in a minute …

Nikki Allan was not assaulted in either of the ways suggested by Heron. The investigators had to bring him back to 'metal'. Again, what kind of metal?

Q   Now you'd hit Nikki when she was lying on the floor, you hurt her again didn'tyou George you hurt her with something …

A   Yes.

Q   What did you use? Come on.

A   Metal.

Q   A metal what?

A   Bar.

Q   Bar?
A   Well, a piece of metal.
Q   And what did you do with that piece of metal, was it a knife, George?
A   It was sharp.

In this crucial exchange, the investigator shifts from correcting Heron to prompting: not a bar, a knife. Well, 'it was sharp'. Mention of a knife is first introduced by the police, not by Heron. But in a subsequent exchange, Heron responds directly to the cue by mentioning a knife.

Q   … what sort of metal are we talking about?
A   Sharp.
Q   Sharp metal.
A   Metal.
Q   What are we talking about though, was it an object?
A   Small, sharp, metal …

Q   What was this sharp metal object?
A   Knife.

Taken in isolation, this final, brief exchange appears to record Heron admitting to using a knife to kill Nikki Allan. Viewed in the context of what came before in his interviews, however, Heron may have merely been echoing the interrogator's prompt that a knife was used.

At any rate, the police were now evidently making progress in winning Heron over to their case theory, their truth. The murder weapon was a knife. But where did it come from?

Q   It was sharp, where did you get it from. George … did you have it with you?
A   No.
Q   You must have had it with you.
A   I don't remember having it with me …

The investigators believed that the knife came from Heron's apartment, so another prompt is necessary: 'you must have had it with you'. Notably, the investigators' working theory begs at least two significant questions. First, why would Heron be walking about with a knife from his apartment, unless the assault was premeditated? Yet premeditation was at odds with the police theory of a panicked impulsive killing. Secondly, if Heron had used the knife to kill Nikki Allan, would he really have taken it home, washed away any detectable traces of blood, and replaced it in his kitchen drawer? Yet Heron was not questioned about these matters, presumably either because the police failed to notice their significance (blinkered by their attachment to a presumption of guilt) or, possibly, because they expected Heron's answers to be inconvenient for their preferred account.

The next issue to be resolved was how the knife was used:

Q   Now you have hit her with the brick, and she had another injury or injuries on her body … How did you do them?
A   Wounds.
Q   Wounds, how did you cause the wounds?
A   Metal wounds …

Again, the investigators cue their suspect by indicating that the victim suffered multiple wounds:

Q   So we have got you, causing Nikki wounds to the torso with a knife. Do you know how many blows you would have rained on her with the knife, George?
A   No.
Q   Was there a lot of blows, George?
A   Probably yes …

Finally, where did the killer leave Nikki Allan's body?

Q   Was she left where you hit her?
A   No …
Q   You moved her—where to?
A   Near the entrance.
Q   Near the entrance. That is not true is it George. We know where she was found.
A   Basement …

On numerous occasions during these exchanges, Heron evidently gives the 'wrong' answer (Nikki Allan was not throttled or sexually assaulted, or assaulted with a pole, or left near the entrance) and has to be corrected by the police. The suggestion that a knife was used originates with the police, and is later adopted by Heron. The manner in which the knife was wielded during the assault is heavily cued: asking Heron how many blows he 'rained down' on a victim and then inquiring whether there were 'a lot of blows' channelled him in the 'right' direction, though at times he seemed unsure and was possibly speculating.[37]

A perplexing characteristic of the Reid Technique is its surprising indifference to 'the truth' of any suspect's confession. Having already decided that a particular suspect committed the crime under investigation, the interrogator's primary objective is to ease the suspect into confessing by suggesting an account of what might have happened which the suspect is able to accept and adopt. The recommended tactic is to minimise the suspect's culpability or in some other way 'normalise' their offending, almost irrespective of what was actually done. The Reid Technique specifies 'Nine Steps of Interrogation'. The second step is 'Theme Development', wherein the interrogator presents 'a "moral excuse" for the suspect's commission of the offense or minimizing the moral implications of the conduct'. Some themes, it advises, 'may offer a "crutch" for the suspect as he moves towards a confession'[38] by 'presenting reasons and excuses that will serve to psychologically (not legally) justify the suspect's behavior':

> Additionally, the interrogator minimizes the moral seriousness of the suspect's criminal behavior. Blame is shifted from the suspect to some other person or set of circumstances that prompted him to commit the crime … It is highly recommended that the interrogator be prepared to present at least five reasons and excuses to the suspect as to why he committed the crime and at least five additional ways to minimize the suspect's criminal behavior.[39]

---

[37] Cf C Egan, *Murderer No More* (Sydney, Allen & Unwin, 2010) (describing a similarly hypothetical 'confession' procured from Andrew Mallard by Western Australian police).

[38] Inbau et al, above n 35, 202.

[39] LC Senese, *Anatomy of Interrogation Themes* (Chicago, John E Reid & Associates, 2009) 28–29.

Regarding sexual offences, Reid & Associates provide a long list of 'rape themes' for interrogators to deploy, most of which explicitly shift blame to the victim. Investigators are advised, for example, to '[b]lame the victim's style of dress for leading the suspect on' or '[b]lame the victim's actions … such as … rejecting the suspect's advances'.[40] While such victim-blaming has been roundly condemned and rejected in modern criminal justice, Reid & Associates *train* interrogators to blame victims. The costs of doing so extend well beyond the immediate investigation, as Coughlin observes:

> By using victim-blaming stories to make rapists comfortable confessing, the police risk reinforcing the misogynist conventions and impulses that lead some men to rape in the first instance, that make victims refuse to report rapes, and that make it so difficult for the system to make charges stick for any but the most violent rapes.[41]

An interrogation process which diverges so far from values championed elsewhere in the criminal justice process (especially regarding sexual assault law reform) is surely one lacking integrity.

George Heron's interrogators did *not* invite him to say that Nikki Allan was to blame for 'leading him on'. However, they did resort to a 'common-sense' account of her death, which encouraged Heron to cooperate and confess by minimising his blameworthiness. According to the interrogators' proffered 'theme', the victim must have done something (perhaps she screamed?) which provoked an uncharacteristic, panicked response only to be expected of anyone in similar circumstances. The alternative to this everyday story of momentary human frailty, Heron was made to see, was that Nikki Allan's killer must be some kind of 'monster':

Q   … I think she probably screamed when you took her to that place and then I think you probably panicked … You never took her there to do her any harm, you are not that type of lad are you, are you George? …

Q   What was it all about? Was it something that just went horribly wrong?
A   I didn't murder her.
Q   Was it something that just went horribly wrong?
A   I didn't murder her
Q   Why will you not address the question?
A   Why address the question when that would be admitting that I killed her when I didn't?
    …

A   I am not that evil.
Q   Well … perhaps you are not that evil but perhaps because of the predicament you are in maybes through no fault of your own … you maybes might have done something when you didn't know what you were doing.
A   I didn't kill her.
Q   You see I think possibly that it's never intended to be a deliberate killing, maybes one course of action was set upon, … and things got out of hand … and there was no option …

---

[40] Ibid 219–20.
[41] AM Coughlin, 'Interrogation Stories' (2009) 95 *Virginia Law Review* 1599.

Q   George, something snapped in you that night.
A   I never snapped.
Q   We all snap at times …

Q   Did she scream?
A   I don't know I didn't kill her.
Q   George did she scream?
A   I don't know I didn't kill her …
Q   Did Nikki scream or did you snap?
A   I didn't kill Nikki.

In these exchanges, in which the investigators hold firm to their presupposed 'truth', the killing is normalised as what 'an ordinary lad' might have done, snapping under pressure when something went 'horribly wrong'.

Eventually, Heron did admit to killing Nikki Allan, adopting the 'I panicked' rationalisation supplied by investigators. In the decisive phase of the interrogation, Heron accedes to the officers' accusation that he knew Nikki Allan was dead when people were still searching for her. He then began to give an account which fitted with the scream/panic theme provided to him earlier in the interviews:

A   I don't know what happened.
Q   Right you don't know what happened. Right you tell me what you think happened and we will start that way …
A   The only thing I remember is talking to Nikki outside the pub …
Q   What's the next thing you remember?
A   Being in the house watching the two children while everybody went out to search.
Q   But you knew she was dead, didn't you George, didn't you, didn't you son? Eh didn't you George? George come on, come on it will be better when it is all out. Didn't you know she was dead, didn't you son?
A   Yes …
Q   Tell [us] what happened, you have already told us that you did it because you said you knew she was dead when you went searching for her. Now come on tell us what you did and tell us what it was all about. Come on.
A   I panicked.

This was the 'truth' constructed in George Heron's police interviews.

In a valuable discussion, Coughlin describes how stock narratives structure interrogations and produce confessions:

> [T]he police confessional room is a space where the truth is produced by the interrogator's strategic use of narratives that exploit popular ways of thinking about the gap between legal liability and moral culpability … [B]y using interrogations stories, interrogators actively and inescapably shape the meaning of the facts by helping suspects to embed them in a coherent narrative that coincides with our normative judgments about which acts are blameworthy and which are not.[42]

As Coughlin concedes, it would be foolish to insist that interrogators should never employ narratives. Although the Reid Technique may do so in an unacceptable way, narratives are

---

[42] Ibid 1603, 1609.

a basic mode of human communication and 'the legal system invariably gains access to the meaning of facts through explanations that come in a narrative form'.[43] Officials distinguish between relevant and irrelevant information by selecting from a world of facts those which make sense of what investigators see by fitting or building an emergent account: 'What they want is *the story* that makes *some of the facts* comprehensible'.[44]

If narrative accounts necessarily construct our realities, what are the lessons for the integrity of custodial interrogation? First, police should stop invoking 'the search for truth' as a peremptory way of closing down discussion about what happens in interrogation rooms. If investigators find truth there, it is at least partly their own construction. Secondly, narratives do not provide a neutral structure. As Griffin argues in relation to trials:

> Narrative's indifference to objective facts, its invitation to readers to construct parts of the tale, and expectations it raises for their sequence, significance and coherence of evidence all risk distortions in fact-finding … If fact-finders process information in terms of stories rather than logic, then they are predisposed to some misleading elements from familiar plots.[45]

Unlike many fictionalised or stereotypical narratives, real-life events are frequently messy, confusing and inconclusive. Real violence to truth can be inflicted by attempts to 'order' stories and understandings by prematurely imposing certainty or 'closure'.

Heron was just such a case. George Heron's acquaintance with the victim and a lie he told about his whereabouts on the night of her death apparently justified police suspicion against him. But Heron's reaction to questioning needs to be properly contextualised, rather than viewed through the distorting lens of an idealised rationality. As a socially marginal inhabitant of an economically deprived community, Heron might be expected to relate to the police in the estranged and mistrustful manner characteristic of such areas.[46] Moreover, to say that Heron *lied* about his whereabouts to the officers conducting door-to-door inquiries is a prosecutor's explanatory overlay, rather than the facts speaking for themselves. The trial judge's ruling on the voir dire in *Heron* provides the following account:

> In answer to the question, 'Do you know the victim, yes/no' which is printed on the form, the word 'yes' is deleted. If the defendant said he did not know the child, that was not true … Another question on the form deals with his whereabouts, the question is in this form, 'Obtain details of movements' … All that is recorded against that question is, '9.30, 7/10/92, at Wear Garth, babysitting'.[47]

On any view, the record is fragmentary. How does one go from an incomplete *pro forma* recording only that the respondent said he was babysitting at a particular time to an accusation that he lied about his whereabouts? Asserting that he was babysitting did not necessarily imply that Heron never went outside that night. The fact that he was supposed to have been babysitting might explain why he never mentioned going out. Admittedly, the police record appeared to be corroborated by further reports 'that a young man bearing a strong resemblance in appearance to the defendant' had been seen in local pubs around the time of Nikki Allan's disappearance.[48] However, this evidence creates uncertainties of its own.

---

[43] Ibid 1622.
[44] Ibid 1599.
[45] LK Griffin, 'Narrative, Truth and Trial' (2013) 101 *Georgetown Law Journal* 285, 302.
[46] Northumbria Police, above n 10; B Campbell, *Goliath* (London, Methuen, 1993).
[47] See Mitchell J, above n 11.
[48] Ibid.

Heron's arrest (after police collected these witness statements) and his acquittal (after police misrepresented the statement of a witness who had seen Nikki Allan with a man shortly before her death) both relied on apparently uncritical acceptance of identification evidence. Yet the fallibility of such evidence was already well known by the 1990s,[49] and there is now a substantial body of research indicating that casual identification of strangers, in particular, is prone to error and should be treated with caution.[50]

Unexplained absences pose further unanswered questions. The prosecution was so reliant on Heron's confession that its exclusion by the trial judge caused the case to collapse. But why was there no forensic science evidence pointing to the killer's identity? Within hours of the murder, the police had identified both a crime scene and the suspect's residence where he allegedly cleaned his clothes and the murder weapon. Yet relevant physical evidence was never mentioned during Heron's interviews, and its absence was not raised in the ruling on voir dire or in the subsequent police inquiry. Similarly, the lack of forensic connection between the defendants and the crime scene in the case of the Cardiff Three should have raised fundamental questions about their involvement.

The messiness and uncertainty of real-life cases conflict with the general desire for clarity, to know 'one way or the other' who is responsible for high-profile crimes.[51] However, the resulting pressure for prompt resolution has often caused investigators to make mistakes. In homicide investigations especially, there are strong, media-fuelled expectations of the police to solve the case, to restore social order and security, and to provide 'closure'. Miscarriages of justice are a likely result when, under intense pressure to close a case, police officers fall prey to tunnel vision in actively constructing a case against a known suspect while contrary evidence is overlooked or ignored.[52]

The narrative process has legal consequences. Coughlin argues that when investigators offer accounts to suspects, they are negotiating moral, rather than legal, responsibility.[53] This is what Reid & Associates also claim,[54] but matters are not so straightforward. Police may be interrogating to get a confession as the basis to charge: but charge with what offence? How the account is constructed by interrogators and which options are presented to the suspect may well determine the type and gravity of offence to which a confession is ultimately made. Non-fatal offences against the person have overlapping definitions and various gradations, as do sexual offences. The classification of homicide as manslaughter rather than murder turns largely on the killer's intention. Suggestions of provocation, mental incapacity or lack of specific intent may each have important legal consequences. Heron's interrogators were evidently adept in negotiating these issues. Having persuaded Heron to admit killing Nikki Allan by mitigating his culpability for what happened, they

[49] Lord Devlin, *Report to the Secretary of State for the Home Department of the Departmental Committee on Evidence of Identification in Criminal Cases*, HC 338 (London, HMSO, 1976).

[50] EA Loftus, *Eyewitness Testimony* (Cambridge MA, Harvard University Press, 1996); GL Wells, 'Eyewitness Identification: Systemic Reforms' [2006] *Wisconsin Law Review* 615; BL Cutler (ed), *Reform of Eyewitness Identification Procedures* (Washington DC, American Psychological Association, 2013).

[51] K Schulz, *Being Wrong* (New York, Harper Collins, 2010). On the messy reality of criminal proceedings, see D Sklansky, 'Confined, Crammed and Inextricable: What *The Wire* Gets Right' (2011) 8 *Ohio State Journal of Criminal Law* 473.

[52] H Rossmo, *Criminal Investigative Failures* (Boca Raton FL, CRC Press, 2009).

[53] Coughlin, above n 41, 1645.

[54] Inbau et al, above n 35, 202–55.

subsequently needed to change tack, by introducing a very different account emphasising a blameworthy deliberate killing:

Q … when I asked you why you killed Nikki you said you didn't mean to kill her is that right?

A Yes.

Q Well George you hit Nikki with a brick across the head … on a number of occasions and you stabbed Nikki in the body, a number of times, when you did those actions, did you mean to kill her?

A No.

Q Well I put it to you that you must have done George. At the point of the attack upon Nikki you did …

Q … That to me shows a clear intention on your part to kill her at that stage.

Whatever Heron might have been led to believe he was admitting to, his interrogators were constructing an admission to murder by intentional killing.

Coughlin suggests that 'once the suspect endorses one of the plots the cops offer, the interrogation story … itself has the potential to *become* the past'.[55] Official or public 'truths' are those recorded in verdicts, case reports, newspapers and 'true crime' stories. But there is also another past, even if we cannot recover it: there was, for example, what really happened in the final minutes of Nikki Allan's short life. Although it is not always possible to access such truths, a criminal justice system built on integrity would surely seek to minimise the gap between what actually happened and the recorded past. Whilst it might be naive and idealistic to expect justice systems reliant on negotiated confessions, charges and guilty pleas[56] to take truth-finding so seriously, a criminal process committed to integrity should embrace that as its goal.

4. Integrity as Fairness

Common law systems of criminal procedure recognise procedural 'fairness' or 'due process' as an independent value extending beyond accurate fact-finding.[57] Unfair criminal procedure lacks normative integrity. A critical issue for the fairness of confessions concerns the extent to which suspects may lawfully be deceived, bullied or bribed by inducements into making admissions.[58] The unfairness of the interrogation tactics to which Stephen Miller of the Cardiff Three was exposed has already been described. Deception, denigration, relentless repetition and 'pounding' were similarly deployed against George Heron. From the perspective of the trial judge, deception via misrepresentation of evidence was particularly problematic.

---

[55] Coughlin, above n 41, 1609.

[56] Also see McConville and Marsh, Chapter 4 in this volume.

[57] See P Roberts and A Zuckerman, *Criminal Evidence*, 2nd edn (Oxford, Oxford University Press, 2010) ch 5.

[58] English and Australian courts are more vigilant than their US counterparts (see Leo, above n 36) in restricting the use of evidence obtained by deception: see *R v Mason* (1988) 86 Cr App R 349 (CA); but cf *R v Christou and Wright* (1992) 95 Cr App R 264 (CA); *R v Palmer; R v Gyamfi; R v Cooke* [2014] EWCA Crim 1681.

In the following exchanges, Heron's interrogators suggest that a witness statement put him with Nikki Allan shortly before her death. This was not true: as noted above, the witness who reported seeing Nikki Allan in the company of a man gave a description not resembling George Heron.

Q   And you walked away and she walked away with you didn't she, now again be careful of what you're saying. We have evidence, I'm asking for the truth, come on George …
A   I've been telling the truth.
Q   You haven't though George, you've told lie after lie man, you know as we go on the witnesses are saying hey there we go, I saw that, I saw George, there, bang …

Q   George, we haven't even started to tell you yet about the evidence we have got against you, you know we are not trying to trip you up …

Later, ruling on the voir dire, Mitchell J found that this passage constituted deliberate misrepresentation of the evidence, which was fatal to the admissibility of Heron's subsequent admissions.[59] Investigators were presumably hoping that Heron would be picked out in an identification parade held after the interviews. As it turned out, neither the principal 'witness' nor two others who had been in the area at the time of Nicki Allan's disappearance recognized Heron. The broader significance of the timing of the parade is that, if the standard was an investigative interview seeking to test a suspect's account against previously collected evidence, it should have been conducted *before* rather than after the interviews with Heron. The trial judge insisted that the identification parade should have preceded the interviews; or at latest should have been held when it became clear in interviews that Heron was maintaining his claim that he did not go out on the night in question. Different elements of an investigation should be coordinated in an integrity-based system.

Another well-worn tactic in the interrogation play-book is to switch to the role of 'good cop', possibly by offering suspects inducements to confess. Investigators sought to build rapport with Heron by expressing empathy for his predicament:

Q   George, you have probably been a poor soul who has been crying out for some sort of love is that right?
A   I always do but nobody listens.
Q   Well George I am prepared to listen to you here tonight.
A   That is not the type what I was …

Heron may have needed a friend, but one across the table of a police interview room was not quite what he had in mind.

More significantly, the police suggested to Heron—despite his repeated denials—that it would serve his best interests to confess:

Q   And I think it's going to be in your interest to tell the truth and to get it off your chest.
A   I didn't kill her …

Q   George the time has come where I think it is going to be in your interests to tell the truth.
A   I am telling the truth.

---

[59]   See Mitchell J, above n 11.

Heron's 'interest', at this moment, was portrayed as being seen in a more favourable light when his case went to court:

Q If we knew why you did it and what made you do it, well perhaps we could understand, but the way things stand we cannot fathom out the reason behind it ... Well wouldn't you feel better if you told us what it was all about?

A I didn't kill her.

Q And what made you do it.

A I didn't kill her.

Q George, if we have to prove it all the way through the courts and you are going to constantly deny it what are people going to think if you're convicted? ...

Q ... if we have got to prove it without you showing any emotion people are going to look on you as an evil monster and you're not are you?

A I didn't kill Nikki.

Such suggestions that confession was in Heron's best interest drew particular criticism from the trial judge. These inducements were also fatal to the admissibility of Heron's subsequent admissions.

The audio-record of the interviews plainly reveals the insistent pressure placed on Heron to acquiesce in and adopt the officers' case theory, their truth. The line between acceptably rigorous questioning and unacceptable harassment may be a fine one, but the trial judge was in no doubt that investigators had crossed it, making Heron's interrogation 'oppressive' under PACE:

> What occurred during that Friday night at that police station was an exercise in breaking the defendant's resolve to make no admissions. The means adopted to achieve that end meant, in effect, that regardless of the fact that his eventual confession may very well have been true, the prosecution were prevented from discharging the burden imposed on them by the two limbs of Section 76(2) [to disprove vitiating factors].[60]

The judge found it 'probable that, at some stage, the defendant began to feel the relief of unburdening himself and began to speak freely', presumably implying that Heron's admissions, or some of them, may have been true. But section 76(2) mandates the exclusion of admissions obtained by oppression 'notwithstanding that [they] may be true', and in the hardest of cases, the judge did his duty by putting the integrity of the justice process above the pressure for conviction and punishment of an accused child-killer. In the case of the Cardiff Three, where the prosecution had relied on confessions bullied out of Stephen Miller, a vulnerable and highly suggestible suspect with an IQ of 75,[61] it was even more obvious that a line had been crossed and that the Court of Appeal needed to intervene to protect the integrity of the process.

---

[60] Mitchell J, above n 11.
[61] Sekar, above n 3, 39–43.

Conclusion: Integrity Reconsidered

Criminal justice is conventionally discussed and evaluated in terms of some kind of balance between due process and crime control, liberty and security, police powers and suspects' rights, law and order. However, the balance metaphor is often criticised for its limitations and shortcomings.[62] Integrity may be a superior concept, emphasising adherence to laws which are deliberately designed to protect society (encompassing both victims *and* suspects) directly, in terms of procedural rights and remedies, and through the longer-term benefits of enshrining fundamental values. Integrity may demand short-term losses for long-term gains. Thus, in *Heron* a confession that 'may very well have been true'[63] was excluded, and the prosecution's case collapsed, but in the longer run the police were obliged to reform their interrogation methods, thereby becoming more efficient both in controlling crime and in respecting suspects' rights. As well as considering integrity as procedural fairness, the two case studies explored in this chapter have elucidated further strands of criminal process 'integrity' in terms of systemic normative coherence, professional responsibility, and commitment to truth-finding in criminal adjudication.

The conceptual limits of integrity must also be acknowledged. Its elasticity has been demonstrated by the way this account of *Heron* and the Cardiff Three has fitted comfortably within it. However, the assumption that the primary value underlying integrity is due process has to be open to challenge. Integrity may also mean the prioritisation of the state's interests in protecting itself, its servants and the status quo. Perhaps criminal justice lacks due process integrity *inevitably* in that it is the site of *conflicting* values, principles and interests.[64] Take criminal justice in the US as an example. If due process was primary, it becomes hard to explain the glacial pace of responses to demonstrated miscarriages of justice. Even introducing comprehensive electronic recording of interrogations is far off, despite clear evidence of its benefits when used properly in comparable jurisdictions.[65] Criminal justice is structured by numerous influences—political, economic and commercial—and a commitment to due process is just one factor influencing institutions, processes and outcomes.

The complex, competing priorities of criminal justice and a less attractive face of integrity were illustrated by legal activity following the belated identification of Lynette White's murderer. The conviction of Jeffrey Gafoor begged questions about the original investigation and the Cardiff Three's convictions. Some of these were similar to the questions about Heron's case: How were statements collected from witnesses? How was forensic evidence used? How were the inquiries managed so that they came to focus on those charged? How did inaccurate confessions come to be made? Crucially in the Cardiff Three case, why did investigators turn from the single, blood-stained man described by a witness to the belief that Lynette White had been killed by a group? While this question is not directly answered

---

[62]   See eg Dixon, above n 23; A Ashworth and M Redmayne, *The Criminal Process*, 4th edn (Oxford, Oxford University Press, 2010).

[63]   Mitchell J, above n 11.

[64]   A Sanders, R Young and M Burton, *Criminal Justice*, 4th edn (Oxford, Oxford University Press, 2010).

[65]   Dixon, above n 23; Garrett, above n 26.

in the official report on the investigation, the consequences of the shift in the focus of the investigation are exposed.[66]

Once committed to their case theory, investigators collected evidence to fit it. In this process, an

> unusually high number of witnesses ... changed their evidence in favour of the prosecution after the defendants had been either arrested and/or charged. Significantly ... none of these changes [was] as a result of new information and no reasons were given as to why these witnesses had just simply changed their accounts.[67]

The product was a prosecution case based on an account of Lynette White's murder flawed by 'huge inconsistencies in the evidence', posing 'many questions about its reliability'[68] and which (not just with the benefit of hindsight) was quite implausible. At least nine people were supposedly in the small bedroom where Lynette White died. 'The circumstances of the murder were such that it was highly likely that there would be forensic evidence linking those involved in the murder to the scene. There was no forensic evidence linking the original defendants ... to the scene'.[69] The prosecutors' account was based on statements about the murder from witnesses which, Gafoor's conviction showed, were false.

Perjury undermines the integrity of the criminal process. The authorities began an ill-fated action in response. The South Wales Chief Constable wrote to the Cardiff Three expressing regret about their conviction and committing to investigate any offences committed during the original investigation.[70] Three major (non-police) witnesses in the Cardiff Three trial were prosecuted, convicted and jailed for perjury and perverting the course of justice. They might be better regarded as victims than as criminals: their evidence against the Cardiff Three was 'based on pressure, intimidation, and threats [by] police officers'.[71] The three witnesses 'alleged that the false accounts given to the court had arisen from their fear of and acquiescence to threats and intimidation by the police officers who had dealt with them'.[72] These threats included that they would be charged with the murder and in one case that the witness' child would be taken into care.[73] In sentencing them to 18 months' imprisonment, the trial judge acknowledged that

> all three of you, vulnerable in different ways as you were, were seriously hounded, bullied, threatened, abused and manipulated by the police during a period of several months ... as a result of which you felt compelled to agree to the false accounts that they were suggesting to you.[74]

While conviction was inevitable (duress not being available as a defence to such charges), the lengthy jail sentences were very harsh.

Attention then shifted to the investigators. When eight former officers went to trial in 2011, the judge ordered disclosure of various documents to the defence. The prosecution

---

[66] South Wales Police, above n 7.
[67] Ibid 21.
[68] Ibid.
[69] Ibid 27.
[70] Ibid 5.
[71] Ibid 11.
[72] Ibid 21.
[73] Ibid 26.
[74] Ibid 44.

reported to the judge that four of the requested documents had been destroyed, submitting that it could 'no longer sustain a position maintaining that the court and the defendants can have the required confidence in the disclosure process … with all its importance to our criminal justice system'. No further evidence was offered, the judge was invited to direct the jury to return not guilty verdicts, and the defendants were acquitted. The planned prosecution of five other officers was abandoned.[75] In a notable example of chutzpah, one of the Cardiff Three's investigators, former Chief Inspector Mouncher, had his solicitor tell the world that he had 'always maintained the integrity of the original investigation', that 'he leaves the court with his professional reputation intact and his character unblemished', and that he was considering suing for false arrest. Other legal action and inquiries rumble on, with the government refusing to set up an inquiry into the collapse of the 2011 trial, an application by the Cardiff Three for judicial review of that decision, and a report by Devon and Cornwall Police on Operation Dalecrest, an inquiry into complaints from former police officers about the South Wales Police investigation into the original investigation.[76]

Notwithstanding the limited relevance of the missing documents (ironically, they concerned complaints against the police, principally by John Actie, one of the two defendants acquitted in the Cardiff Three trial), the integrity of the process was taken to require abandonment of any action against the police. It may invite accusations of hypocrisy to raise concerns about strict adherence to disclosure requirements. However, the Cardiff Three, the jailed witnesses and others affected had good reason to be cynical, particularly when, six weeks later, the supposedly destroyed documents were found in the possession of South Wales Police. A rather different kind of 'integrity' was preserved as the authorities, with relief, closed the book on the Cardiff Three case.

A lay concept of criminal justice integrity would include an expectation that the state should be prepared to punish its officials when they do wrong and to provide remedies to those wronged by them. However, the authorities appear to see such action as threatening integrity of a different sort. A notably consistent and regrettable feature of miscarriage of justice cases has been failure to bring to account those whose misconduct and criminal actions caused wrongful convictions. If the authorities have not been keen to see what Lord Denning notoriously called the 'appalling vista' of recognising that police had coerced confessions and lied in court (as in the case of the Birmingham Six), they have been even less keen to punish those involved when misconduct was beyond dispute.[77] Extra-judicially, Denning went further, agreeing with an interviewer that the integrity of the criminal process and 'the general cause of upholding the system of justice' required judges to 'put aside' miscarriage of justice cases.[78] Denning was unusual only in his forthright manner: his authoritarianism was characteristic of a much more widely held and deeply entrenched

---

[75] Independent Police Complaints Commission, *South Wales Police: Destruction of specific documents leading to the collapse of the R v Mouncher & others trial at Swansea Crown Court on 1 December 2011* (IPCC, 2013) 6.

[76] Ibid.

[77] *McIlkenny v Chief Constable of the West Midlands* [1980] QB 283, 323 (CA Civ); see also Dixon, n 23 above.

[78] C Mullin, *Error of Judgement* (Dublin, Poolbeg, 1987) 311–12. See also E Heward, *Lord Denning* (Chichester, Barry Rose, 1997) 223–30; C Palley, 'Lord Denning and Human Rights' in JJ Jowell and JPWB McAuslan (eds), *Lord Denning* (London, Sweet & Maxwell, 1984) 304–307, 363–64; AN Wilson, 'England, His England' *The Spectator*, 18 August 1990, 10; M McConville and L Marsh, *Criminal Judges* (Cheltenham, Edward Elgar, 2014).

commitment to systemic integrity. It would be a bad mistake to think that integrity is a concept which is monopolised by supporters of due process.

Another consistent feature of miscarriage cases has been a focus on the police rather than on other players in the process. Some comments have been made about the passive role of the defence legal advisors in the Cardiff Three and *Heron* cases. But what of the prosecutors and trial judges in the Cardiff Three trial, given the 'huge inconsistencies in the evidence' posing 'many questions about its reliability'?[79] For prosecutors, integrity must mean exercising independent judgement and not being uncritically swept along by the police case theory. It should also be pointed out that the way to the Cardiff Three's successful appeal was not easy. Stephen Miller's initial application for leave to appeal was turned down. His lawyers 'advised him that he had no further prospect of winning an appeal'. It was only 'by a number of accidents' that he 'found allies and renewed his application for leave to appeal'.[80] Without these 'accidents', the Cardiff Three might never have been acquitted, and Lynette White's murderer may never have been convicted.

A striking feature of these cases is the gap between ideals of legal certainty and criminal justice integrity on one side and the messy reality of life on the other. If integrity involves restoration (of order, of foundational values, of just relations) then there is little sense of restoration in the lives of those affected by the cases considered here. Some of them have suffered from systemic integrity being valued above what they would see as justice. The murders of Lynette White and Nikki Allan and the trials of the Cardiff Three and George Heron have had profound and continuing effects, not just on the criminal justice process, but also on those involved and their communities. If integrity is to be a defining principle of criminal justice, it must not be merely a synonym for due process.

---

[79] South Wales Police, above n 7, 21.
[80] Gareth Peirce, Foreword to Sekar, above n 3, x.

4

Factory Farming and State-Induced Pleas

MIKE MCCONVILLE AND LUKE MARSH[*]

Introduction

This chapter explores the consequences of the annexation of criminal justice systems by state-induced guilty pleas. We address all practices commonly referred to as 'plea bargaining' including, for example, direct or indirect offers from state officials (police, prosecutors or judges) to reduce a sentence in return for a guilty plea, offers to reduce the number of charges or to alter the charge(s) from a more serious to a less serious offence, and offers to present the 'facts' (the basis of the guilty plea) in a more favourable light. This state practice, developed in England and Wales and elsewhere, has come to subvert traditional understandings, values, principles and justifications on which those systems, both common law and civilian, were avowedly based. Participants in the process today have become entrapped in an elaborate charade in which they act out prescribed roles, whilst lawyers who invoke traditional process protections and safeguards are exposed to judicial criticism and censure.[1] Romily's orthodox contention that 'the object of penal laws is the protection and security of the innocent' sounds almost anachronistic.[2] The volte-face in penal rationalisations adopted by judges and prosecutors and increasingly enforced upon defence lawyers is eroding the integrity, both of individual practitioners and of the criminal justice system itself.

Our argument proceeds by developing the striking parallels between plea bargaining and the industrialisation of the global meat industry. Like factory farming, state-induced guilty pleas are portrayed as an inevitable or required response to *uncontrolled demand* rather than as a preferred model chosen for its inherent qualities. As with plea bargaining in England and Wales, the second half of the twentieth century saw the rapid rise of factory farming systems in the US and Europe. The US model of large-scale animal production is rapidly being adopted by a number of developing countries, including Argentina, Brazil, China,

[*] Special thanks are owed to Gary Edmond, John Jackson, Paul Roberts and Simon Young for their comments on successive drafts.
[1] On which see M McConville and L Marsh, 'Adversarialism goes West: Case Management in Criminal Courts' (2015) 19 *International Journal of Evidence and Proof* 172.
[2] S Romily, *Observations on the Criminal Law of England* (London, Cadell and Davies, 1810) Note D.

India, Mexico, Pakistan, South Africa, Taiwan and Thailand. Their scale is extraordinary.[3] In a single year, some 10 billion animals are fed into the US consumer market alone,[4] demonstrating how far agribusiness has infiltrated daily lives.[5] As with any criminal guilty plea system, factory farms evoke huge resonance within the public domain and yet both systems proliferate with the aid of self-serving disinformation and media management.

The depressing reality of most farming structures is supplanted by nostalgic, comforting images of farms through 'countrified labelling and advertising of animal products'.[6] The ideological functions of imagery recalls Lord Hewart's familiar but solemn mantra that it is in the public interest not only for justice to be done, but to be seen to be done.[7] The UK Ministry of Justice, eager to demonstrate that the state-induced guilty pleas process is 'working' with cost-efficiency programmes designed to deliver a 'simpler, swifter and more transparent service',[8] in fact shrouds from public gaze the reality of its architecture and questionable purpose.[9]

This is not to target individual factory workers implicated in the running of these systems; 'factory worker' is used here in a dual sense: farmhands who process livestock into food in high-volume, hi-tech bio-factories;[10] and lawyers, whose daily practice consists of processing the criminally-accused through guilty pleas. Impelled by economic winds that force them to push cattle and clients to unending levels of productivity, factory workers face increasingly compromised professional obligations. In an echo of the 'present trend [which] culminates in a way of farming beyond their financial reach',[11] criminal lawyers increasingly find themselves unable to do justice to a single case for fear of losing out on the volume of business ultimately needed to keep their firms or chambers afloat.[12] This is symptomatic of what the present Lord Chief Justice described as 'an age of retrenchment' for the legal profession.[13] The factory workers are thus also victims of the *system*, although

---

[3] The number of birds and mammals killed for research purposes each year serves as a useful comparator. In the US alone, where 20 to 40 million test subjects die annually, this would represent a meagre two days of food production business: DA Miller (ed), *Current Controversies—Factory Farming* (Detroit, Greenhaven Press, 2010) 85.

[4] Ibid.

[5] For example, approximately 74% of the world's poultry and 68% of eggs are now produced by factory farms: T Weis, *The Global Food Economy: The Battle for the Future of Farming* (London, Zed Books, 2007) 20. The UK now has some 2,000 chicken factories: G Monbiot, 'Faeces, bacteria, toxins: welcome to the chicken farm', *The Guardian*, 25 May 2015.

[6] P Singer (ed), *In Defense of Animals—The Second Wave* (Oxford, Blackwell Publishing, 2012) 104.

[7] *R v Sussex Justices, ex parte McCarthy* [1924] 1 KB 256.

[8] See www.justice.gov.uk/about/justice/transforming-justice/criminal-justice-system-efficiency-programme2/criminal-justice-system-efficiency-programme (accessed 25 September 2015). In this regard, President of the Queen's Bench Division, Sir Brian Leveson, *Review of Efficiency in Criminal Proceedings*, published in January 2015, represents the most significant development (*Leveson Review*), www.judiciary.gov.uk/wp-content/uploads/2015/01/review-of-efficiency-in-criminal-proceedings-20151.pdf (accessed 25 September 2015).

[9] Self-servingly, Auld LJ (the principal architect of the modern English and Welsh criminal justice process) maintained that the public should be better informed but *only* as to their own ignorance where it affects 'public confidence': the Right Honourable Lord Justice Auld, *Review of the Criminal Courts of England and Wales: Report* (October 2001) ch 4, 32.

[10] Also known as concentrated feeding operations (CAFOs), mainly found throughout Europe and America.

[11] J Mason and P Singer, *Animal Factories* (New York, Crown Publishers, 1980) 8.

[12] Michael Mansfield QC's Tooks Chambers, renowned for its criminal legal aid work, was one high-profile casualty of reduced fees. Its dissolution in October 2013 was (according to its website) a 'direct result of government policies on Legal Aid'.

[13] Lord Thomas of Cwmgiedd, 'Reshaping Justice', speech delivered to JUSTICE, 3 March 2014, www.judiciary.gov.uk/announcements/lcj-speech-reshaping-justice/ (accessed 25 September 2015).

in a different way to their respective 'produce' (animals for food, and defendants for guilty-plea fodder).

Glimpsing behind this factory wall, the sight would surely disturb. Suspended bodies of pigs sway gently as they arrive, one after the other, at a device that efficiently guillotines head to trotter. While systematic comparison between the slaughterhouse and criminal justice teeters towards the Orwellian, their respective modes of production and output streams share an eerie resemblance. Although increasing dissent is heard from those who toil within an adjudicative machine marked by dispassion,[14] the growing procession of discount-induced 'guilty-plea' clients filtering through the courts has generated little public concern. Calling that indifference into question is one function of this chapter's critical, at times provocative, discussion.

More generally, this chapter is concerned with issues of integrity raised by the commodification process that characterises each system. It consciously merges concerns about conveyor-belt justice with current controversies surrounding the global but faceless agribusiness.[15] These exchanges and interfaces can illuminate and inform contemporary understandings of criminal justice machinery. The central argument of this chapter is that the 'process' cannot be understood merely as an essentially technical activity, aimed at meeting the needs of the public[16]—particularly when the public is misled as to the case for those needs. Rather, state-induced guilty plea practices reflect and embody a presupposition of guilt wrapped in cost-efficiency discourses and ideologies, and in doing so serve to sideline issues of principle and integrity that would be expected to be the routine concern of lawyers and judges. This chapter explores a range of influences upon both systems, specifically addressing cross-cutting issues of ethics, integrity, professional responsibility, and quality. We conclude that the stranglehold on probity, evident in both, has begun to unravel in the case of factory food production[17] but risks permanent entrenchment in criminal justice.

1. Two Parallel Shadow Systems

To draw close parallels between the killing floor and the courtroom is to characterise *faithfully* rather than caricature *implausibly* these disquietingly synchronistic systems. Indeed, parallels in function between agribusiness and criminal justice, in particular state-induced guilty pleas, emerge unforced. Both of these substitute or *shadow systems* arose, it

---

[14] A 'no confidence' motion in the leadership of the Law Society was tabled for an emergency meeting in December 2013, and the Criminal Bar Association staged a 'mass non-attendance' day in protest at reductions in legal aid: O Bowcott, 'Critics of legal aid cuts force Law Society vote', *The Guardian*, 19 November 2013.

[15] On which see YN Harari, 'Industrial farming is one of the worst crimes in history', *The Guardian*, 25 September 2015.

[16] Leveson explains, in the context of demonstrating alleged cost savings by streamlining criminal proceedings including removal of juries in prescribed circumstances, that the general public 'has a proper interest in the financial and human cost of the criminal justice system and how best to apply its limited resources', *Leveson Review*, above n 8, ch 10, 87.

[17] See P Singer's retrospective piece 40 years after the publication of his seminal work, *Animal Liberation*: 'The abuse of animals won't stop until we stop eating meat', *The Guardian* (Online), 11 February 2015, www. theguardian.com/commentisfree/2015/feb/11/abuse-animals-meat-eating-industry-liberation-speciesism (accessed 25 September 2015).

is alleged by their proponents, in response to the breakdown of the formal system that they subverted: in the one, the traditional farm; in the other, the classically conceived adversarial jury trial.[18]

It is easy to observe the parallel trends towards greater concentration, labour-saving machinery, growth acceleration, and other factory methods. Deeper structural parallels between the two systems reflect their shared hunger for *normalisation* attributed to *uncontrolled demand*. Whereas industrialised food producers artificially spur this demand, since their profit margins rely on high volumes at low production costs, defendants are said to clog the courts[19] and their interests are sacrificed to systemic 'culture change' which now pervades the criminal process.[20] Caseload demands, it is said, necessitate imposed plea decisions, standardisation of production lines and economies of scale.[21] State-induced guilty pleas, like factory farming, coerce all actors (police, judge, lawyer, client and consumer) along conveyor-belts designed with economic efficiency as their ostensible motor.

These reconstituted offerings still purport to offer *consumer choice*, but of a wan and malnourished variety.[22] Whilst both systems celebrate choice in their operational maxims ('the customer is always right'; '(voluntary) confession is the queen of proof'), this chapter's comparative lens presents a host of bleak analogues exposing their artificiality. This section further develops the structural analogy in terms of: (a) units of production; (b) efficiency trade-offs; (c) de-sensitisation and demoralisation; and (d) invisibility and immunity to oversight.

(a) Units of Production: Standardised Processing Meeting 'Insatiable' Demand

Industrial food production and plea-bargaining systems have both been engineered to produce predictable outputs: a single (or restricted) commodity crop in one; a guilty plea in the other. The principal aim is to increase control over output through consistency of production methods. The rationalisation of how these systems have evolved in this way is the claim of *uncontrolled demand meeting constrained supply*. Just as the factories rely on the public's 'insatiable' (in reality untested, inestimable and largely self-generated) desire for cheap meat,[23] the criminal justice system pivots on its own produce—the guilty plea—reanimated

---

[18] In Britain, the concept of a fair trial is said to find its ideal expression in trial by jury: *R v CCRC ex parte Pearson* [2000] 1 Cr App R 141, [145].

[19] An unsubstantiated claim, constantly recycled in modern times since the report of the James Committee on *The Distribution of Criminal Business between Courts* Cmnd 6323 (London, HMSO, 1975).

[20] See eg *R (on the application of the DPP) v Chorley Justices* [2006] EWHC 175, [24].

[21] See M McConville and C Mirsky, *Jury Trials and Plea Bargaining* (Oxford, Hart Publishing, 2005); P Shattuck, 'Law as Politics' (1974) 7 *Comparative Politics* 127.

[22] Following *R v Turner* (1970) 54 Cr App R 352, defendants were said to have 'complete freedom of choice' over plea and defence counsel were 'completely free' to do their duty. In reality, guilty pleas were expected and counsel were subordinated to trial judges: see M McConville and L Marsh, *Criminal Judges: Legitimacy, Courts and State-induced guilty pleas in Britain* (Cheltenham, Edward Elgar, 2014) ch 3. The former Justice Secretary was sceptical: 'I don't believe that most people who find themselves in our criminal justice system are great connoisseurs of legal skills': C Baksi, 'Chris Grayling', *Law Society Gazette*, 20 May 2013. Impaired defendants were 'too thick to pick': HC Deb 27 June 2013, col 523.

[23] In China, for example, burgeoning appetite for cheap protein has only risen in line with economic growth, fabricated availability and a corresponding fall in the price of meat: Miller, above n 3, 112.

as the life-blood of the system. Collapse of the entire system is the operating threat looming over all activity, despite the absence of any actuarial basis for dire predictions.[24]

In fact, the earliest documented plea-bargaining process was not precipitated by caseload demands. The introduction of plea bargaining in the US, for example, emerged concomitantly with prosecutors being judged by success in securing convictions, however obtained.[25] This policy was accompanied by an official reconstruction of offending, utilising categories of dangerousness to regulate the lower classes, giving rise both to the system for mass production in the courts and a criminology that sought its legitimation through attributions of criminogenic traits and behaviour. Plea bargaining, in short, resulted in factory-style production rather than being caused by an explosion in case demand. Once inaugurated, bargaining allowed for and invited unrestricted and unthinking prosecution and a concomitant increase in caseload. Both factory systems are therefore heavily premised upon a *false need* for *standardisation* principally achieved by *homogenised output*.[26] In each category, the subject is reared to be identical. On classic Fordist principles, each output must be perceived by factory workers as a fungible and docile *unit of production*. Food-animals, a breed clinically distinct from the family pet,[27] are pumped full of hormones and bred to reproduce the standardised consumable as rapidly as possible. Constant manipulations of anatomy, physiology, heredity,[28] and environment are incorporated to keep health problems and other costs down so commodity production can proceed at profitable levels.

Defendants are likewise treated as identical. They are processed through plea and charge offers, 'not in any automatic way, but by carefully orchestrated lines of interaction, which render those defendants indistinguishable to judges and other observers'.[29] Accordingly, there is a *standard* discount of one-third for the category deemed most compliant (expressing an intention to plead guilty at the earliest opportunity), with lesser standardised discounts for those who resist longer. Stripped of their individuality, defendants appear as disembodied entries on a docket or court-list which has to be cleared so that the disposition of others, waiting in line, can be accelerated.[30] To accelerate proceedings further, court hearings in England and Wales are increasingly video-broadcast.[31] The growth of camera links in police stations and prisons has led to affectless virtual courts which supplant the

---

[24] While the guilty plea rate in England and Wales has risen from 56% in 2001 to the current rate of about 70%, the guilty plea rate has exceeded 50% for at least the last half century: cf M Zander, 'Are Too Many Professional Criminals avoiding Conviction?—A study in Britain's Two Busiest Courts' (1974) 87 *Modern Law Review* 28.

[25] McConville and Mirsky, above n 21.

[26] Despite the common law ideology of individualised judging, the Court of Appeal (Criminal Division) always gives a collegiate single judgment. Moreover, employing High Court and Circuit Court judges to supplement full-time justices of appeal may result in appeals being dealt with by judges drawn from the same (or lower) 'common room' as the trial judge, calling into question the independence of appellate review: J Richardson, 'Is the Criminal Appeal System Fit for Purpose?' (2013) 19 *Criminal Law Week* (May 20).

[27] For a reflective account of the process of 'de-animalisation' to 'foodstuff', see N Vialles, *Animal to Edible* (Cambridge, Cambridge University Press, 1994).

[28] It is doubly ironic that schools of criminology in the nineteenth century associated crime with physiological traits of groups of individuals deemed to be criminogenic.

[29] DW Maynard, 'Social Order and Plea Bargaining in the Courtroom' (1983) 24 *Sociological Quarterly* 233.

[30] This process of de-individualisation is assisted by disparaging stereotyping of defendants, often reinforced by media demonisation ('scroungers', 'mobs', 'thugs', 'bullyboys', 'feral' etc).

[31] See Damian Green MP, 'Digital courtroom unveiled as justice enters the Wi-Fi era', Press Release 11 April 2014, www.gov.uk/government/news/digital-courtroom-unveiled-as-justice-enters-the-wi-fi-era (accessed 25 September 2015).

need for presence, thereby reinforcing alienation.[32] By mandating prompt discussion of disposition in mechanised form via the sentence-discount, court actors themselves more easily become detached from any meaningful inquiry into the individual accused and reliant instead upon boilerplate formulations cognisable to the process. How much easier it is to deal with a 'chain snatch', a 'mugging' or a 'handbag dipping' than to deal with the individuals actually charged with those offences. Just as corporations treat farms as production sources rather than places of animal husbandry, so courts are being judged on caseload management and timely dispositions rather than performance indicators encapsulating orthodox criminal justice values, such as the accuracy of verdicts or the effectiveness of specific sentences imposed to address recidivism.[33]

Essential to this *standardisation* paradigm is the capacity to nurture tranquil populations. These systems cannot function properly unless the subject is incorporated into the activity 'willingly'.[34] To achieve spontaneous compliance, both systems deploy *sweeteners* and *penalties* as pacifiers. Factory farming relies on the natural proclivity of animals to feed to the point of immobility, thereby legitimating the use of devices such as holding crates and electrified baths. Similarly, the criminal justice system relies on its own brand of force-feeding to facilitate the desired reductive output. In a short stressful period, an intensive diet of legal concepts and technical words is fed to the accused, who is forced, via a sliding trough of reward, to decide whether or not to plead guilty before the offer—the sweetener—is withdrawn at the courtroom door, with the threat of significantly higher penalties for dilatory pleaders or those convicted after trial.[35] Sentence 'discounts', communicated by the very person supposedly charged with supporting the accused, facilitate this force-feeding by being calibrated so that even obdurate defendants can be rationalised into pleading.[36] And yet, discounts are routinely offered whether the case is problematic or whether the prosecution evidence (as disclosed) is stronger. In this, as in other commodification systems, process asphyxiates principle.

(b) Efficiency Trade-offs: The Real Cost of Doing Business

Both systems market themselves on low financial cost. Factory farms aim at efficiency at the lowest cost to produce 'cheap' meat for the public. State-induced guilty pleas are portrayed

---

[32] In a conference speech, Leveson presented a vision of criminal proceedings which will only marginalise the accused further; one where 'much of the preliminary work will be done by everyone in their ... *living room* or remote video suite'. Hearings will be 'conducted on line (either by *rapid exchange of text* or ... using video conferencing tools *we can all access from home*),' 'Modernising Justice Through Technology', 24 June 2015, 4–5, www.judiciary.gov.uk/announcements/speech-by-president-of-the-queens-bench-division-modernising-justice-through-technology/ (accessed 25 September 2015).

[33] The CPS registers a guilty plea as a 'successful' outcome, even where it is not always due. In fact, on this indicator, the rise in guilty pleas since 2003/2004 has obscured deteriorating performance by the CPS when judged by convictions secured at trial: K Sosa, *In the Public Interest: Reforming the Crown Prosecution Service* (London, Policy Exchange, 2012) 28.

[34] For further on the co-optation of the defendant, see McConville and Marsh, above n 22, 114 *et seq.*

[35] In fact, sweeteners, threats and sanctions are also directed at lawyers, whose effectiveness may be heavily contingent upon maintaining collegial relationships with trial judges. The UK Criminal Procedural Rules up the ante by imposing sanctions for non-compliance: see eg *R v SVS Solicitors* [2012] EWCA Crim 319.

[36] See eg *R v Nightingale* [2013] 2 Cr App R 7, [2013] EWCA Crim 405 for a recent example of an uninvited judge-initiated discount which, initially at least, proved impossible to refuse.

as less costly for the court system and hence for the public purse. In fact, no actuarial calculation is made by courts who simply assume that plea bargaining is justified on a cost–benefit or 'utilitarian' basis.[37] In reality, the 'savings', even in purely financial terms, are largely illusory. Most cases take several hearings to achieve a bargained disposition and most of these would be straightforward guilty pleas in any event. Hidden financial costs— in terms of the introduction into the system of cases that ought not to be prosecuted at all; new procedures and practice directions; novel institutions such as sentencing councils; and avoidable appeals, to name but some—are substantial.[38]

Although lower processing costs might superficially appear beneficial, the net result has been an all-round diminution in the *quality* of process.[39] This is evidenced, for example, by a recent report of HM Crown Prosecution Service Inspectorate (HMCPSI), which found that 'effective implementation of the advocacy strategy is being hindered by ... local approaches to allocating work which appear to be based on the pursuit of the maximum amount of savings, rather than achieving and developing good quality advocacy'.[40] Further expediency-induced errors emerge at sentencing. In *Attorney-General's Reference (No 71 of 2012)*,[41] for example, the Court of Appeal noted that only one of the pertinent authorities had been drawn to the attention of the sentencing judge and questioned 'how thorough was the attention of [the] parties to the sentencing exercise'. In other decisions, the Court of Appeal has lamented that 'the court was not well served by the advocates' appearing on either side[42] and has drawn attention to the 'embarrassment' of defence counsel in overlooking elementary procedural errors.[43] Low pricing in these contexts masks the true cost.

By design, cut-price mono-cultural practices make skilled factory workers superfluous. Just as high-tech machinery and production lines minimise human input and decision-making, so do filtering mechanisms such as Plea and Trial Preparation Hearings,[44] fixed-fee cases and Early Guilty Plea courts.[45] Whilst countries with the fewest farmers may be

---

[37] For further analysis of the 'utilitarian' justification, see McConville and Marsh, above n 22, ch 3.

[38] The rationality of the 'resources argument' is questionable on further grounds. For example, the sentencing discount is not indexed to factors such as case complexity that have direct resource implications. Nor is the cost of failed prosecutions (£25.1m, or 4.3% of the CPS's net operating costs, in 2011/2012) factored into the calculus: Sosa, above n 33, 8.

[39] Note the government's insipid ambition to achieve 'adequate' standards of representation: Ministry of Justice Consultation Paper CP 14/2013, *Transforming Legal Aid: Delivering a More Credible and Efficient System* (London, MoJ, 2013).

[40] HMCPSI, *Follow-Up Report of the Thematic Review of the Quality of Prosecution Advocacy and Case Presentation* (London, 2012), Chief Inspector's Foreword. A staggering 71% of Crown Advocates fail the CPS's own internal advocacy training course: ibid 47.

[41] [2012] EWCA Crim 3071. Also see *Attorney-General's Reference (Nos 61 and 62 of 2012)* [2012] EWCA Crim 2847, where the sentencing judge was reminded of a once-leading but now outdated authority with only fleeting reference to the leading case.

[42] *Attorney-General's Reference (No 50 of 2010)* [2010] EWCA Crim 2872, [3].

[43] *R v Shields* [2011] EWCA 2343. Also see *R v Abdalla Mohammed* [2010] EWCA Crim 2400; *R v Mateta* [2013] EWCA Crim 1372.

[44] Formerly known as 'Plea and Case Management Hearings' (PCMH).

[45] The Early Guilty Plea Scheme, operating at all Crown Court centres, expedites the plea process by reducing 'unnecessary paper work' and increasing 'productivity'. In exchange, defendants will 'secure maximum credit'. See webarchive.nationalarchives.gov.uk/20130128112038/http://www.justice.gov.uk/downloads/legal-aid/early-guilty-plea-scheme.pdf (accessed 25 September 2015).

regarded as the most 'advanced',[46] a dearth of adequately paid legal representatives is hardly the hallmark of civilisation.[47]

Affording undue priority to haste has led to wholesale erosion of the system's proclaimed founding values. Adopting Dworkin's terminology,[48] the framework of rules in criminal cases rests on the normative foundation that individuals have a right that criminal procedures attach the correct importance to the risk of *moral harm* and the related, and practically more important, right to *equal treatment* with respect to that evaluation. Both are 'strong' rights, trumping any unmediated balancing of gains and losses through simple cost–benefit calculations. Cost-efficiency has a legitimate role in the delivery of justice, but, as Dworkin argued, there are other, more pressing, values which must constrain it.[49]

(c) Desensitisation and Demoralisation

An enabling feature of the cost-efficiency model is its demoralising treatment of factory workers, their consequent desensitisation, and its accompanying effect upon the charges under their 'care'.[50] Pachirat's grim ethnography of the slaughterhouse exposes how workers compartmentalise their role in the production process, thereby psychologically distancing themselves from its overt brutality. In the criminal justice context, demoralisation has been exacerbated by legal aid strictures and specific policy initiatives.[51] A corrosive official culture (governmental and judicial) towards defence legal services has produced a new disciplinary ethos, encapsulated in the following remarkable judicial explication of disclosure obligations:

> The lawyer's duty is *not to give the accused advice on what to do.* The lawyer's duty is to explain the statutory obligation that he has and to explain the consequences which follow from *disobedience* of it.[52]

Defence lawyers discover that the traditional 'obligation of the Prosecution to prove its case in its entirety before closing its case' has 'an anachronistic and obsolete ring'.[53] They learn that the traditional approach to criminal justice has changed, in ways at odds with

---

[46] In Britain and the US, about 1% of the workforce is full time on the land: Miller, above n 3, 160.

[47] Growing numbers of barristers' chambers have declined to act in fraud cases following a 30% reduction in legal aid rates for 'Very High Cost Cases': see C Baksi, 'Prepare for trial, judge tells defendants in QC boycott case', *Law Society Gazette*, 24 January 2014; *R v Crawley* [2014] EWCA Crim 1028.

[48] R Dworkin, 'Principle, Policy, Procedure' in R Dworkin, *A Matter of Principle* (Cambridge MA, Harvard University Press, 1985). See further, S Guest, 'How to Criticize Dworkin's Theory of Law' (2009) 69 *Analysis* 2.

[49] Cf Lord Bingham in *R (Gillan) v Commissioner of Police for the Metropolis* [2006] UKHL 12, [2006] 2 AC 307, [1].

[50] T Pachirat, *Every Twelve Seconds: Industrialised Slaughter and the Politics of Sight* (New Haven, Yale University Press, 2011). This, of course, connects with a more general theme in the sociology of inhuman behaviour: see Z Bauman, *Modernity and the Holocaust* (Ithaca, Cornell University Press, 1989).

[51] The former Attorney-General for England and Wales unapologetically explained away 'death by a thousand cuts' to the independent Bar as an 'extremely painful' but necessary process: J Hyde, 'Grieve: legal aid cuts hurt, but Bar is just too big' *Law Society Gazette*, 30 September 2013. Judicial sentiment aligns with the Executive. Lord Thomas CJ, above n 13, 2–3, warned that 'there has been a change to the role of the State and the expenditure it is prepared to make' and, 'far from being immune' to attack, the justice system will 'continue to be cut'.

[52] *R v Rochford* [2010] EWCA Crim 1928, [25] (emphasis added).

[53] *Malcolm v Director of Public Prosecutions* [2007] EWHC 363 (Admin), [31] (Burnton J).

their professional loyalty towards their clients. Most extraordinary has been defence lawyers' increased role in the prosecution enterprise. Since each process 'participant' is required
to prepare and conduct the case in accordance with the 'overriding objective',[54] the defence
now bears the *duty* of 'convicting the guilty'.[55] The deeply counter-intuitive implication is
that lawyers representing defendants who concede factual guilt but wish to put the prosecution to proof, a right they have traditionally enjoyed (in legal rhetoric at least), now have
a duty to help convict their clients notwithstanding, for example, the prosecution's inability to prove its case because of the absence of witnesses or its reliance upon inadmissible
evidence. This bastardisation of the adversarial system has required the recharacterisation
of defence lawyers as obstacles to the mass disposition of cases, by conflating them with
devious and manipulative defendants and depicting them as exploiting the system's weak
spots.[56] Notwithstanding the continued efforts of many individuals of integrity within the
profession, a swelling corpus of firms appears unable to fulfil a committed defence function.

Daniel Newman's recent empirical study of attitudes and practices of the legally-aided
defence profession in England and Wales reveals a deep malaise within the system.[57]
Newman categorised firms under observation into two groups: '*radicals*' who represent a
'dying breed' of lawyers devoted to their client-base, and '*sausage factories*' which represent
self-interested working practices that put profitability before clients.[58] Far from Newman's
original ambition of 'draw[ing] out the positive elements of legally aided criminal defence',
the evidence produced a 'dispiriting picture'.[59] Regardless of categorisation, '[c]lients were
pushed from pillar to post, rushed through the system as criminals who no-one should or
did care about'.[60] In a sombre reflection of factory workers who are required to go about
their jobs calmly operating the (dis)assembly-line, as chicks are de-beaked and pigs evis-
cerated, lawyers exhibited a 'pervading cynicism', routinely assuming factual guilt 'whether
or not they had talked to [clients] or read their file'.[61] When clients asserted innocence,
lawyers were 'unsympathetic' and 'refused to believe them' and were 'openly derogatory'.[62]
A client's choice was often sidelined by lawyers who 'sought to fool their clients into the
choice of action favoured by the lawyer'.[63] Where this form of 'client abuse' did not succeed,
'confidence tricks' were employed to 'take advantage of their client's vulnerability'.[64]

---

[54] This is not immediately apparent from the Overriding Objective's first requirement that 'cases be dealt with
justly': Rule 1.1 (1).
[55] Crim PR Rule 1.2 (1)(a).
[56] Cf the Auld Report's casual reference, above n 9, ch 10, [8], to 'the problem … of the uncooperative or feckless defendant *and/or his defence advocate* who considers that the burden of proof and his client's right to silence
justifies frustration of the orderly preparation of both sides' case for trial' (emphasis added).
[57] D Newman, *Legal Aid Lawyers and the Quest for Justice*, (Oxford, Hart Publishing, 2013).
[58] Ibid 30.
[59] Ibid 143.
[60] Ibid 85.
[61] Ibid 47.
[62] Ibid 47–48.
[63] See also J Blackstock, E Cape, J Hodgson, A Ogorodova and T Spronken, *Inside Police Custody: An Empirical
Account of Suspects' Rights in Four Jurisdictions*, (Cambridge, Intersentia, 2013) 320 (finding that suspects might
be encouraged to accept a particular disposal 'without any proper evaluation of the evidence having taken place').
[64] Newman, above n 57, 119. Cf S Malik, 'Halal slaughterhouse staff investigated over alleged animal cruelty',
The Guardian, 3 February 2015.

Newman concludes that 'the nature of the lawyer–client relationship was such as to place clients' access to justice in jeopardy'.[65] His data demonstrate that some solicitors firms, supposedly the frontline of criminal defence work, may develop cultures and organisational practices which succumb to the 'bottom-line' and de-rail the rights of suspects and defendants.[66] A heightened risk of being channelled into the guilty-plea processing machine, perpetuated by barristers adopting a similar de facto presumption of guilt,[67] is the predictable outcome of *desensitised practices* adverse to the accused.[68] Whilst factory workers may begin with high ideals, the surrounding structures soon weaken their hold on the cardinal professional virtues that traditionally anchored ethical practice.

(d) Invisibility: Zones of Secrecy and Immunity from Oversight

The justificatory model located in cost-effectiveness is shielded from informed criticism owing to the *secrecy* or *lack of transparency* percolating through each system. On factory farms, there are countless 'zones and areas people normally don't see' sheltering harmful industry-standard practices such as gestation crates which confine pregnant sows for their entire lives.[69] The industrialised killing business 'depends on consumers not being able to see (or hear about) what they do'.[70] And in many US states, secrecy has been secured by anti-whistle-blower legislation frustrating public exposure by workers or investigative journalists.[71]

State-induced guilty pleas have also operated in the shadows, contrary to the adversarial system's espoused principles.[72] Historically, judges made strenuous efforts to engineer guilty pleas in the privacy of chambers and were largely successful in keeping informal 'discussions' under wraps, until *Turner*[73] in 1970 generated some, albeit still muted, debate. Attempts to standardise approaches emerged only after judges were caught out conducting plea negotiations in the privacy of chambers. Superior courts initially issued hypocritical

---

[65] Newman, above n 57, 143. Amongst the 'systematic reasons' explaining why 'a healthy relationship was difficult to achieve in practice', the 'most obvious' was 'reduced legal aid remuneration': ibid 147.

[66] One senior partner told Newman, ibid 86: 'You should go through the unused material, chase witnesses up, go the extra mile for the client. But you don't. You realize that you can't do that. At the end of the day, every case has to be about trying to make a profit.' A junior solicitor from a different firm echoed: 'It's got to be run now like a business to survive.'

[67] See also, A Mulcahy, 'The Justifications of "Justice"' (1994) 34 *British Journal of Criminology* 411.

[68] Also see Blackstock et al, above n 63, 408; D Alge, 'The Effectiveness of Incentives to Reduce the Risk of Moral Hazard in the Defence Barrister's Role in Plea Bargaining' (2013) 16 *Legal Ethics* 1.

[69] The battery hen cage is another notorious abuse, affording each bird less space than an A4 sheet of paper. At the end of their lives, the often emaciated birds are suitable only for food processing. See generally, Mason and Singer, above n 11.

[70] See eg J Safran Foer, 'The Truth About Factory Farming' (2010), www.whistleblower.org/press/gap-in-the-news/361 (accessed 25 September 2015); M Pollan, *The Omnivore's Dilemma: A Natural History of Four Meals* (New York, Penguin, 2006).

[71] 'Ag Gag' laws have been introduced in Utah, Iowa, Missouri, and Idaho, and actively considered in other jurisdictions, including Australia: S O'Sullivan, 'Ag gag laws: The Battle for animal welfare is a battle over information', *The Guardian* (online), 5 May 2014; J Firth, 'American agriculture's great cover-up', *Index on Censorship*, 13 July 2012, www.indexoncensorship.org/2012/07/us-agriculture-cover-up-ag-gag/ (accessed 25 September 2015).

[72] See generally, McConville and Marsh, above n 22.

[73] (1970) 54 Cr App R 352 (CA).

denials (hardly an indication of integrity) while keeping the judge's door ajar on spurious grounds.[74] The *ex post* rationalisation of plea negotiations later presented in the Auld Report was rapidly imported into case law.[75] Early plea with sentence discount could now be characterised as a 'right', which had to be conveyed to the defendant by every counsel in every case (irrespective of other considerations), with judicial orchestration downplayed.

The new aversion to trials dispenses with innumerable intricacies of the criminal process by pre-empting the full exploration of a case in open court. As Bibas argues:

> Instead of allowing juries to air and wrestle with the hard, troubling cases, prosecutors may hide them from view. If, for example, prosecutors bargain away most cases involving dubious confessions, they avert public scrutiny of police interrogation tactics. If they buy off credible claims of innocence cheaply, they cover up faulty investigations that mistakenly target innocent suspects. By pressing the easiest cases, prosecutors turn jury trials into rubber stamps or mere formalities.[76]

The Auld Report asserted

> It may not be 'the function of law to trust those who exercise lawful powers'. But a criminal justice process cannot sensibly be designed on a general premise that those responsible for law are likely to break it. In those cases where, unfortunately, the police or other public officers are dishonest, the criminal trial process itself is the medium for protection and exposure.[77]

Such traditional assurances ring hollow. First, concerted efforts by successive 'law and order' initiatives to promote non-trial dispositions has marginalised trial protections. Secondly, it is extraordinary that any judge could promote the trial as it operates in reality as a reliable 'oversight' mechanism for official wrongdoing, when an expanse of miscarriages of justice (in no small part the responsibility of trial and appellate judges) was plainly in view. In England and Wales, however, courts have not merely abandoned their former eulogies to adversarial justice. Trials are now positively disparaged as a costly impediment to justice, whilst lower class defendants (and their lawyers) are castigated for exploiting system weaknesses—formerly known as relying on due process guarantees to secure fair trials.

Perpetuating *invisibility* is an ever-increasing *immunity* to legal oversight. Both production systems are characterised by a lack of comprehensive and coordinated regulation. Both feature dubious minimum standards and legal safeguards so narrow in scope and poorly enforced that they are effectively illusory.[78] And both production systems are—in effect—*self-regulated* machines.[79] Whilst there is no statutory framework governing plea bargaining

---

[74] The legal profession and the government attempted to suppress revelations of plea bargaining by J Baldwin and M McConville, *Negotiated Justice* (London, Martin Robertson, 1977).

[75] *R v Goodyear* [2005] 1 WLR 2532, [2005] EWCA Crim 888; *R v Caley* [2012] EWCA Crim 2821.

[76] S Bibas, 'Plea Bargaining Outside the Shadow of Trial' (2004) 114 *Harvard Law Review* 2473. See also A Alschuler, 'The Changing Plea Bargaining Debate' (1981) 69 *California Law Review* 652; R Lippke, *The Ethics of Plea Bargaining* (Oxford, Oxford University Press, 2011).

[77] Auld Report, above n 9, ch 10, [154] (footnote omitted).

[78] Laws against animal cruelty exempt institutional exploitation of animals in intensive farms. In effect, if the treatment of the animal is customary in the industry/farm, it is exempt. See E Goodman, 'Animal Ethics and the Law' (2007) 79 *Temple Law Review* 1291; D Rook, 'The Legality of Factory Farming under UK Law' [2007] *Journal of Animal Welfare Law* 1; JB Ruhl, 'Farms, Their Environmental Harms, And Environmental Law' (2000) 27 *Ecology Law Quarterly* 263, 328 (noting that 'farms cause substantial harms to the environment, and that, with a few minor exceptions, environmental law at federal and state levels has all but licensed those harms').

[79] As Sosa, above n 33, 80, observes, 'unlike District Attorneys in the United States, none of the CPS leadership is directly elected … with no local line of accountability to communities. CPS staff are held to account internally

(though plenty of judicially created rules of practice), factory farming legislation (such as it is) is rendered nugatory by government acquiescence or lack of enforcement.[80] Although every US state has an animal cruelty law, most exempt common factory farming practices. Corporate entities resist legal intervention in part because they sponsor regulatory efforts themselves and are quick to threaten critics with defamation suits.[81] Successful lobbying by agribusiness partly reflects governmental dependence on the huge tax revenues they generate.

In the absence of formal oversight mechanisms or robust legislative constraint, common law courts have been left to improvise plea-bargaining practices with minimal transparency or effective accountability. *Sub rosa* law-making has only intensified under the conceptually protean Criminal Procedure Rules (Crim PR), a judicially-inspired procedural guide-book providing a safety net of self-regulation to validate the creation of new rules as 'law'. The Crim PR do not define 'case management', but its broad meaning is apparent from Rule 3.5(1):

> In fulfilling its duty under rule 3.2 the court may give *any* direction and take *any* step actively to manage a case unless that direction or step would be inconsistent with legislation, including these Rules. (emphasis added)

Here, case management is seen to afford judges almost unlimited powers, the *only* express limitation being that the court may not give a direction or take a step which would be inconsistent with legislation (which is patchy).[82] The Criminal Procedure Rule Committee is engaged in a process of expansion and revision. Subsequent amendments to the rules make more substantive amendments, which then become law.[83] The trajectory of the Crim PR is therefore captive to future case-law development insulated from systematic external scrutiny.[84] A self-certification model thus exists, propped up by untestable honour.[85] With no truly reliable watchdog guarding the coop, practices anathema to the integrity of the system are allowed to blossom and flourish unchecked by public scrutiny.

---

by the bureaucratic oversight of their local Chief Crown Prosecutor and ultimately the DPP, and CPS leadership is subject to the indirect ministerial accountability provided by the "superintendence" of the Attorney General.'

[80] For example, the prohibition against routine tail-docking of piglets is widely ignored and piglets are commonly deprived of straw and hay, contrary to European law: P Stevenson, 'EC Legislation on the Welfare of Farmed Animals On-farm' [2007] *Journal of Animal Welfare Law* 4.

[81] For example, the Soil Association was threatened with libel proceedings after objections were made to a proposed 25,000 pig farm: F Lawrence, 'Soil Association given libel warning after objection to huge pig farm', *The Guardian*, 18 January 2011. Tracy Worcester's film, *Pig Business*, was pulled by Channel 4 in January 2009 after a threat of libel by Smithfield Foods of America. The film was eventually broadcast, in heavily redacted form and to a much reduced audience, on *More4* later in 2009.

[82] There may also be implied limits. In *R (Kelly) v Warley Magistrates' Court* [2008] 1 Cr App R 195 it was held that Rule 3.5 did not entitle the court to override legal professional privilege, which is a fundamental right of the defendant.

[83] The latest iteration of the Crim PR 2015 came into force on 5 October 2015: www.justice.gov.uk/courts/procedure-rules/criminal (accessed 25 September 2015).

[84] See eg *R v Musone* [2007] 1 WLR 2467; *R v Jarvis* [2008] EWCA Crim 488; *R v Ensor* [2009] EWCA Crim 2519, [2010] 1 Cr App R 18; *R (Firth) v Epping Justices* [2011] EWHC 388 (Admin), [2011] 1WLR 1818.

[85] Cf J Booth, 'Trust the judges, says Grayling, on totally secret terror trial', *The Times*, 5 June 2014.

2. Casualties of the Machine

The structural parallel between factory farming and state-induced guilty pleas can be developed further in terms of the types of 'ecological' harm that each imposes on its respective environments, participants and consumers. Prominent amongst the 'casualties of the machine' are: (a) environmental degradation; (b) linguistic perversion; and (c) individual victims.

(a) Environmental Degradation

Whilst keeping the unpalatable reality of their operations behind closed doors, both 'industries' insist on imposing their excesses on society—be it the build-up of toxic waste, polluting air and streams, or a dangerously overcrowded prison population,[86] unchecked police impropriety[87] or perverse charging practices.[88]

In factory farming, environmental degradation has been shown to lead to wastage, destruction of biodiversity and disease transmission. Wastage permeates industrial farms in two senses. First, no matter how 'efficient' factory farms become, in the narrow sense of producing more output, they are widely demonstrated as wasteful processes.[89] Additionally, there is oversaturation of waste in concentrated areas, creating unproductive diseased 'dead-zones'.[90]

With state-induced guilty pleas, in addition to the obvious costs of mistaken and wrongful convictions,[91] waste is incurred by the need to introduce or intensify new court procedures to elicit pleas (including Plea and Trial Preparation Hearings pursuant to Crim PR 2015 Rule 3.13(b)); new procedures[92] and different forums to ascertain the factual basis for the plea ('*Newton* hearings')[93] or to expedite guilty pleas (the Early Guilty Plea Scheme[94]); new official bodies to establish a plausible procedural framework (latterly, the Sentencing

---

[86] J Doward, 'Rising jail population jeopardising safety', *The Observer*, 29 June 2014. Cf K Perry, 'Chris Grayling plans to build Britain's biggest prison', *The Telegraph*, 5 January 2014.

[87] For a catalogue of police misconduct, see McConville and Marsh, above n 22, ch 8.

[88] Evidence of CPS undercharging to bolster conviction rates is hard to obtain, but see eg 'Judge slams CPS for "wrong" assault charge', *Worcester News*, 9 August 2012; The Politics Show, 'CPS "undercharging"?', news.bbc.co.uk/1/hi/programmes/politics_show/7944791.stm (15 March 2009) (accessed 25 September 2015).

[89] One telling example: the production of a single kilo of beef consumes 16,000 litres of water: Miller, above n 3, 112.

[90] Industrial livestock production concentrates large numbers of animals in one area, leading to uncontrollable soil pollution: ibid 133.

[91] There are also less obvious financial costs of official wrongdoing, eg failure to disclose the involvement of a police undercover agent in *R v Barkshire* [2011] EWCA Crim 1885 and related trials (involving 26 accused) resulted in at least five separate official inquiries.

[92] See eg procedures set out in the following cases: *R v Tolera* (1999) 1 Cr App R 29 (CA); *R v Myers* (1996) 1 Cr App R (S) 187 (CA); *R v Beswick* (1996) 1 Cr App R (S) 343 (CA); *Attorney-General's Reference (No 81 of 2000) (R v Jacobs)* (2001) 2 Cr App R (S) 16 (CA); *Attorney-General's Reference (No 58 of 2000) (R v Wynne)* (2001) 2 Cr App R (S) 19 (CA).

[93] Following *R v Newton* (1983) 77 Cr App R 13 (CA). This case has spawned its own detailed jurisprudence, eg *R v Smith (PA)* (1986) 8 Cr App R (S) 169; *R v Myers* (1996) 1 Cr App R (S) 187; *R v Kerrigan* (1993) 14 Cr App R (S) 179 (CA); *R v Underwood* (2005) 1 Cr App R (S) 13, CA; *R v Dudley (Stephen Paul)* [2011] EWCA Crim 2805.

[94] See above n 45.

Council); the proliferation of appeals by defendants on aspects of plea or sentence discounts;[95] and Attorney-General's 'references' to the Court of Appeal on grounds of (alleged) undue leniency.[96] To which must be added various statutory provisions, court procedures, Practice Directions and Attorney-General's Guidelines that have had to be created to impose some semblance of order on proceedings that, to put it generously, continue to cause confusion in the ranks of the judiciary and the Bar.[97] Moreover, the official cost-saving rationale rests on an entirely false representation of system waste and the cause of waste.

In England and Wales, the allegation made by Auld was that calculating, uncooperative, feckless and devious (guilty) defendants were cynically exploiting procedural loopholes.[98] In particular, defendants caused trials to 'crack' by entering a guilty plea at the courtroom door, resulting in substantial wasted resources (time and money) as well as inconvenience and stress to potential witnesses. In fact, the evidence (including empirical research of the Royal Commission on Criminal Justice (1993)) demonstrated that 'waste' was exaggerated to the point of being fictitious; that a substantial proportion of trials 'cracked' because of decision-making by the prosecution; and that in only 6 per cent of cases did the trial 'crack' because the defendant changed his mind.[99]

Reliance on state-induced guilty pleas has produced narrowing diversity, also witnessed with factory farming methods. The legal profession becomes less representative of society (more socially advantaged, less ethnically diverse),[100] as increasingly few lawyers are able to afford to work in this constrained and denatured environment.[101] No less disconcertingly, experience is diluted as fewer lawyers tackle greater numbers of cases whilst the remainder become occasional players or defect to civil work. Under *Goodyear*, there is limited scope for professional advice anyway.[102] Duty-bound to instruct a client on the 'benefits' of pleading guilty within constricted time frames, an intensified client–lawyer narrative pre-supposing guilt has developed to deal with discounts at the outset, rather than approaching the issue from a position of presumptive innocence. So the meaning and quality of independent legal advice, as well as the fundamental values of criminal justice, are further casualties of environmental degradation.

---

[95] See eg *R v Kulah* [2007] EWCA Crim 1701; *R v Seddon* [2007] EWCA Crim 3022; *Thornton v Crown Prosecution Service* [2010] EWCA 346; *R v Newman* [2010] EWCA Crim 1566.

[96] For a recent example, see *Attorney-General's Reference (No 6 of 2011)* [2012] EWCA Crim 86.

[97] For example, the question whether the discount should be reduced or withheld where the case against the defendant is overwhelming remains controversial, despite serial interventions by the Sentencing Guidelines Council: see eg *R v Wilson (Paul Anthony)* [2012] 2 Cr App R (S) 77; *R v Simpson (Dean)* [2009] EWCA 423.

[98] Auld Report, above n 9, ch 10, [8].

[99] See M Zander and P Henderson, *Crown Court Study*, RCCJ Research Study No 19 (London, HMSO, 1993) Table 5.1.

[100] As noted by Sir Bill Jeffrey, *Independent Criminal Advocacy in England and Wales* (London, Ministry of Justice, 2014) [6.18]–[6.20].

[101] The Bar Council published results of a research survey in 2015 on the 'well-being' of members of the Bar. The report found that over half of the self-employed bar were 'disengaged', suffering from a 'lack of autonomy' and 'reduced status', www.barcouncil.org.uk/media/348371/wellbeing_at_the_bar_report_april_2015__final_.pdf (accessed 25 September 2015).

[102] The neutering of criminal defence proceeds through additional obligations and restrictions, eg prohibiting 'tactical' manoeuvres (*JL v DPP* (2009) EWHC 238) and enforcing compliance with expanded disclosure obligations: *R v Rochford* [2010] EWCA Crim 1928.

(b) Perversions of Language

One particular form of 'ecological degradation' meriting emphasis is the perversion of language, concepts and values characteristic of both agribusiness and industrial-scale plea bargaining. Ecologically unsound mono-cultures employ various legitimating strategies, redefining terms and basic frames of reference whilst capitalising on the language of the marketplace associated with modern modes of production to smooth over popular anxieties. The language characteristic of both production systems is marked by deliberate ambivalence and obfuscation. The rural idyll of 'farming' is not easily associated with the clinical reality of industrial factory processes. The traditional terminology and values of criminal adjudication similarly belie the realities of bargained pleas.

A guilty plea is meant to be voluntary, but 'choice' is fixed and forced. Much as animals have no influence over conduct shaping their welfare, a defendant's choice is rather a response to powerful constraints and threats from judges (or in the US, from prosecutors). Sentence determinations from assertive judges become, in this sanitised world, 'sentence indications' disguising the fact that, as reported cases show, defendants 'buckle' under these judicial decrees and prosecuting and defence counsel 'acquiesce'.[103] Access to coercive knowledge is converted into a 'right' of defendants and its enforced conveyance to clients becomes a 'responsibility' of counsel in discharge of their professional 'duty'.

(c) Individual Victims

Despite such linguistic contortions, the direct casualties of both systems have always been readily identifiable, yet neither process is arrested by this knowledge. When poultry is cheaper than the wire encaging it, overcrowding becomes inevitable, producing routine animal injuries and deaths—which are regarded as necessary and inconsequential costs of increased output. Personalised 'losses' in a criminal justice context are similarly weighed, and justified, as tolerable wastage. A system of state-induced pleas adversely affects individual defendants and their representatives, victims of crime,[104] police, prosecutors and judges. We can only briefly mention here a few of the more pressing concerns.

Defendants, both the factually guilty and the factually innocent, are the first obvious casualties of plea bargaining. The imposition of a substantially greater punishment upon those who elect to go to trial as against a similarly situated defendant who pleads guilty would appear to encroach on the presumption of innocence. As Ashworth and Redmayne argue, the presumption of innocence implies a right to put the prosecution to the proof.[105]

---

[103] See *Attorney-General's Reference (No 40 of 1996) (R v Robinson)* [1997] 1 Cr App R (S) 357; *Attorney-General's Reference (Nos 80 and 81 of 1999) (R v Thompson and Rodger)* [2000] 2 Cr App R (S) 138 (where it was said to be 'almost abusive' for the Attorney General to challenge sentences as unduly lenient where the judge had given an indication of his view and the prosecution had taken no exception to it).

[104] Victims of crime suffer secondary victimisation where, to induce the guilty plea, the offence committed is downgraded (for example, rape to indecent assault, robbery to theft) and/or a sentence less severe than that merited is imposed.

[105] A Ashworth, *The Criminal Process: An Evaluative Study*, 2nd edn (Oxford, Oxford University Press, 1998). See also A Ashworth and M Redmayne, *The Criminal Process*, 4th edn (Oxford, Oxford University Press, 2010).

Accordingly, the presence of a substantial discount to induce a defendant to give up this right imposes an unfair disincentive to its exercise. This concern was (noddingly) acknowledged by the Auld Report, but summarily set aside. According to Auld:

> A sentencing system should not be tailored or modified to encourage the [guilty defendant] to try his luck; or at least it should not reward him with the same sentence he would have received if he had not done so. Of course, no system can guarantee that individual defendants, however innocent, will not regard the likelihood of a lesser sentence as an incentive to trade it for the risk of conviction and a more serious sentence, or that lawyers will not sometimes advise their clients badly. But those are not reasons for rejecting a sentencing practice if *in general* it serves a proper sentencing purpose, operates justly and assists the efficient administration of justice.[106]

In other words, the sacrifice of innocent individuals is an inevitable and acceptable price paid for an otherwise legitimate sentencing regime. This rationale subsequently became official judicial policy in *Goodyear*. The aggregate 'benefit' to the collective is acceptable even where it knowingly and inevitably involves punishment of some who are innocent. Such reasoning cuts across the law's long-standing principled rejection of consequentialist thinking, encapsulated in the slogan that is better for the guilty, regrettably, to go unpunished to preserve the innocent from wrongful conviction.

The notion of inevitable and acceptable casualties contributes to an ethos of demoralised and alienated 'factory workers', for whom financial incentives displace ethical concerns.[107] Defendants, like penned pigs, are left feeding from offal; or put differently, the worst, most depleted parts of the criminal justice process, staffed by lawyers with too little time, too little experience or—worse—too little motivation to defend properly.[108] Given that payments for legally-aided work are lower than rates for privately funded work, there is adverse selection for quality in legal representation. Remuneration is typically fixed and not based on performance; therefore some level of moral hazard is inevitable.[109] Contracting for block services rather than for work performed on a case-by-case basis will tend to minimise individualised efforts to assess the possibility of securing acquittals whilst rewarding routinised case processing. This problem can only worsen if, as some research has concluded, most defence lawyers develop an expectation that cases will end in guilty pleas, and over time become inclined to presume guilt.[110]

Judges have always been central to plea-bargaining practices in England and Wales.[111] Courts stubbornly clung on to the practices they had themselves improvised, but struggled to find an acceptable ethical foundation.[112] A guilty plea was said to be evidence of remorse, until the thought occurred that pressurised 'remorse' should convince no-one.

---

[106] Auld Report, above n 9, ch 10, [105] (emphasis added).

[107] See Monbiot, above n 5, who notes that 15% of UK poultry workers suffer from chronic bronchitis.

[108] Current legal aid policies anticipate less experienced representation by junior lawyers, 'because they are the ones who will tend to do the simple guilty pleas': Baksi, above n 22, quoting the last Justice Secretary.

[109] See Alge, above n 68, 171, 180 (suggesting that 'the current fee structure is more likely to cause [the lawyer's] interests to diverge by indirectly providing incentives to "crack" a case').

[110] See eg N Garoupa and F Stephen, 'Why Plea-Bargaining Fails to Achieve Results in So Many Criminal Justice Systems: A New Framework for Assessment' (2008) 15 *Maastricht Journal of European and Comparative Law* 345; Newman, above n 57.

[111] Elected District Attorneys appear to have been the pivotal figures in the US, and today exploit vast sentencing differentials to eliminate most trials in both federal and state courts.

[112] For contemporary criticism of *Turner*'s 'deliberately induced ignorance' regime, see J Adams, 'The Second Ethical Problem in *R v Turner*, the Limits of an Advocate's Discretion' [1971] *Criminal Law Review* 252.

Relieving victims' stress, as an alternative rationalisation, encounters the inconvenient truth that reduced charges and discounted sentences often short-change both victims and justice. Some crimes have no (direct) victim. Of those that do, some victims would prefer to testify and inform the court of the true nature of the criminal offence and its impact on their lives. As for direct appeals to cost–benefit trade-offs dignified as 'utilitarian', Lord Gill exposed the poverty of such rationalisations in the Scottish case of *Gemmell*:

> The euphemism 'utilitarian value' may be thought to give the principle of discounting some ethical content; but sentence discounting is not an exercise in Benthamite philosophy. It is not based on any high moral principle relating to the offence, the offender or the victim. On the contrary, it involves the court's passing a sentence that, in its considered judgment, is less than the offence truly warrants … In some cases, there is a saving of inconvenience to [victims] and witnesses. In a small minority of cases there is a saving in jury costs. There is also a benefit to the criminal justice system in the avoidance of undue delay between arrest and sentencing. But the primary benefit that is realised in every case is the saving of administrative costs and the reduction of the court's workload.[113]

Having (rightly) abandoned 'remorse' as a justification, the English courts were forced to confront the conundrum that direct dealings between defendants and the judge would render any guilty plea involuntary, yet this was 'necessary' to produce the desired case resolution. What could be done? Detailed analysis is unnecessary to demonstrate how the Court of Appeal in *Goodyear* abased itself on the altar of cost-effectiveness.[114] In essence, voluntariness would not be impaired if the judge was invited to be involved by the defendant who, in turn, would be advised by counsel of the 'right' to have a 'sentence indication' from the judge. If counsel forgot that this 'right' existed or failed for other reasons to raise the matter, the judge would remind counsel accordingly. With this contrived performance, the problem of voluntariness and judicial pressure was rationalised away. These tortured, and utterly unconvincing, post hoc justifications are poor advertisements for the quality of common law judicial reasoning and the integrity of the judicial office—two more casualties of industrialised plea bargaining.

Conclusion

This chapter has, in the spirit of this volume, re-examined a familiar topic through novel lenses. Its unconventional methodology is calculated to challenge readers' complacent assumptions and prod their consciences. Stark comparison with modern factory farming encapsulates all that is endemically wrong with institutionalised plea-bargaining systems. A prevailing ideology of cost-effectiveness, coupled with economic pressures on lawyers and depleted legal aid, are hastening the perversion of a justice system to a factory-farming process. By juxtaposing the heartless treatment of animals with routine processing of the criminally accused, it can be seen that both systems are engineered, contrary to popular belief, to produce uniform outputs, sacrificing ethical integrity to cost-effective bulk processing. After prolonged exposure to plea bargaining, an informed general assessment can

---

[113] *Gemmell v HM Advocate* 2012 JC 223, [2011] HCJAC 129, [34].
[114] *R v Goodyear* [2005] 1 WLR 2532. For comprehensive criticism, see McConville and Marsh, above n 22, ch 4.

now be made. What was (and is) presented as an efficient way to streamline court processes and reduce hearing times is doing more harm than good.

This chapter identified parallels in both the structural organisation and harmful side-effects of factory farming and state-induced guilty pleas. But perhaps this is where the analogy between the two production systems runs out. Whilst plea bargaining shows no sign of abatement and is rapidly colonising other jurisdictions,[115] the factory farming model is being challenged by a growing number of biologists, ethicists and other critics.[116] The fact remains, however, that only a comparatively small number of the billions of animals consumed annually live and die outside the modern meat-packing industry. Yet the truths and consequences of mass food-animal production—the inhumane methods, health risks, environmental damage and ethical quandaries—are far from transparent. Just as we are insulated from the grim realities of factory farming, the side-effects of state-induced guilty pleas remain shielded from view: out of sight, and out of mind. Ultimately, we can never know precisely how many innocent persons are forced to make what they see as a rational decision to plead guilty, how many offenders receive less punishment than they deserve, or how many victims (actual and future) are sacrificed in the name of cost-effectiveness.

Just as genetically-engineered hormones to accelerate a pig's growth, and vaccination to enable more animals to huddle together, are dubious applications of technology, plea-bargaining strategies pervert the traditional ideals and rationales of criminal adjudication. Irrational on its own terms,[117] industrial plea bargaining advances a spurious logic of necessity, whilst quietly eviscerating the presumption of innocence, the burden and standard of proof, the distinction between factual guilt and legal guilt, exclusionary rules of evidence, and other normative cornerstones of the criminal trial. Reflective and intelligent trial systems which, for all their admitted shortcomings, sought to call the state to account for its intrusions into the lives of its citizens and conscientiously tried to discriminate between the innocent and guilty are replaced by a criminal agribusiness, the objective of which is to keep the production line—accurately styled 'the machinery of justice'—moving, with or without adequate quality control. The principal casualties in all of this, apart from the direct victims of coerced guilty pleas, are the integrity of judges and lawyers and the legitimacy of courts.

---

[115] R Rauxloh, *Plea Bargaining in National and International Law* (Abingdon, Routledge, 2012); J Turner, *Plea Bargaining Across Borders* (New York, Aspen Publishers, 2009).

[116] In California, the Prevention of Farm Animal Cruelty Act of 2008, adopted by a wide margin, prohibits various farming practices. Veal crates were banned in the UK in 1990; sow stalls since 1999. EU welfare standards for laying hens banned 'barren' battery cages. See, *Factory Farm Nation: 2015 Edition* for a comprehensive list of sources, www.foodandwaterwatch.org/reports/factory-farm-nation/ (accessed 25 September 2015).

[117] For example, empirical data question the efficacy of offering larger discounts for earlier pleas, given the psychological realities of offenders' motivation: W Dawes, P Harvey, B Mackintosh, F Nunney and A Phillips, *Attitudes to Guilty Plea Reductions*, Sentencing Council Research Series 02/11 (London, Sentencing Council, 2011); R Henham, *Sentencing and the Legitimacy of Trial Justice* (London, Routledge, 2012).

5

Negotiating Justice with Integrity in New South Wales

NICHOLAS COWDERY AM QC

Introduction

Can criminal justice be negotiated with integrity? This has become a vital question for modern criminal justice systems, not only in the common law world where the 'principle of opportunity' (prosecution discretion) is embraced, but also in civil jurisdictions under the 'principle of legality', traditionally committed to mandatory prosecution in any case in which evidential sufficiency is met.[1] Court-based criminal adjudication processes are costly, time-consuming, often delayed and heavily resource-intensive. Pragmatic pressures have led, over a long period of time, to increasing reliance on negotiated guilty pleas in common law jurisdictions. There is a danger—perhaps it is already a reality—that criminal justice in these legal systems has become a negotiated commodity, converting the process into 'a system of pleas, not a system of trials'.[2]

One might wonder whether just outcomes can simply be agreed between adversarial litigants. Does integrity not require some intervention by an independent adjudicator with power to assess the evidence and determine an appropriate disposition? Even if guilty pleas negotiated between the parties are acceptable in principle, there are further practical issues to consider, such as who should participate in these negotiations and how they should be conducted and evidenced. What are the benefits and risks of such a process? What safeguards should be in place? How should the outcome of negotiation be given practical effect?

This essay explores these pressing issues, taking the current law and practice of New South Wales (NSW), Australia, as a foil for broader common law and comparative reflections. It will be argued that the practical necessities of negotiated justice are compatible with integrity in the administration of criminal justice, but only if prosecutors themselves are conscientious in discharging their professional duties. There are undeniable risks and limitations in a system of negotiated pleas and there is no room for complacency in its design and operation.

---

[1] There is a trend in countries such as Germany, France and Switzerland to introduce elements of the common law's charge negotiation system, at least in relation to less serious offences: see G Gilliéron, *Public Prosecutors in the United States and Europe: A Comparative Analysis with Special Focus on Switzerland, France and Germany* (Switzerland, Springer, 2014).

[2] *Lafler v Cooper,* 132 S Ct 1376, 1385 (2012). Cf McConville and Marsh, Chapter 4 in this volume.

1. Procedural Context, Terminology and Theoretical Justifications

A criminal trial in the state of NSW is an adversarial procedure conducted, as in other common law jurisdictions, primarily between the Crown (the prosecution) and an accused person. The (alleged) victim is not a formal party to the proceedings and is not entitled to legal representation. The common law criminal justice process is not primarily directed at establishing the factual truth of disputed events. It is an *accusatorial* process, wherein the prosecution mounts and seeks to prove a case and the defence, in contested proceedings, seeks to thwart that proof by challenge and cross-examination and/or by presenting an affirmative opposing case. The question at the end of the trial is not 'what happened?': it is 'has the prosecution proved its case—what it says happened, the forensic truth it seeks to establish—beyond reasonable doubt?' The end result is a product of the interaction of all the agencies in the criminal justice system carrying out their particular functions: investigation, prosecution, defence and adjudication.

Charge negotiation processes in NSW began to be regularised in the late 1980s, when the office of Director of Public Prosecutions (DPP) was created.[3] Publicly available guidelines were introduced in 1987 by the Office of the DPP and further developed thereafter. On 18 September 2001 the Attorney General of NSW commissioned a major inquiry to review procedures, following public criticism of 'charge bargaining' where prosecutors had not communicated effectively with victims and police. The inquiry was conducted by The Hon Gordon Samuels, a former appeal court justice and Governor of NSW. The Samuels Report,[4] published in 2002, established the foundations for charge negotiation to become a well-integrated part of the prosecution process in NSW.

The starting point for Samuels was that an indictment should allege 'such charges as the Crown on the existing state of facts believes can be proved beyond reasonable doubt'. Whilst a guilty plea was a desirable outcome to the proceedings, it must not compromise what he characterised as the 'criminality principle':

> The optimum outcome of a criminal prosecution is resolution by a plea of guilty to a charge which adequately represents the criminality revealed by facts which the prosecution can prove beyond reasonable doubt, and which gives the sentencer an adequate range of penalty. A charge bargain must not compromise the principle—which I will call 'the criminality principle'—made up of these three ingredients.[5]

Samuels' 'criminality principle' is built on adversarial assumptions, according to which prosecutors enjoy considerable discretion in formulating charges and entering into plea negotiations. Prosecutorial discretion is more constrained where responsibility for determining guilt remains firmly with the court, as it supposedly does in Continental civil jurisprudence.[6]

---

[3] Director of Public Prosecutions Act 1986 (NSW).

[4] *Review of the New South Wales Director of Public Prosecutions' Policy and Guidelines for Charge Bargaining and Tendering of Agreed Facts* (NSW, 2002), www.lawlink.nsw.gov.au/report/lpd_reports.nsf/pages/report_gsamuels (accessed 9 August 2015).

[5] Ibid [8.1].

[6] However, theory and practice may diverge. In a recent empirical study of negotiated procedures in Germany, a majority of judicial respondents admitted to non-compliance with statutory requirements and in 'a significant

As explained in the next section, the Statement of Agreed Facts is central to plea negotiations in NSW. Building on a recommendation in the Samuels Report, the current (2007) edition of the NSW DPP's *Prosecution Guidelines* contains a detailed consolidated statement of formal requirements relating to agreed facts.[7] These *Guidelines*, which have a statutory basis,[8] set out criteria for the exercise of prosecutorial discretion to assist prosecutors in their decision making and to inform the defence, victims, police and members of the public.

Negotiation directed towards the resolution of issues in a case is commonly undertaken when, for example, the accused disputes elements of the charge but is prepared to admit facts that would constitute a less serious offence. It also occurs where a large number of charges may be negotiated to a smaller number that proceed, with or without the unprosecuted charges being taken into account on sentence. Discussions may be initiated by either prosecution or defence, and are generally conducted on a 'without prejudice' basis (meaning that concessions by either party cannot later be held against them). If a compromise agreement cannot be reached, the prosecution proceeds on the existing charge or charges.

In some jurisdictions, negotiations focus more on sentence than charge and involve a greater role for the courts in conducting negotiations or approving their outcomes. In NSW, however, the court has no involvement of that kind. A range of, more or less jurisdiction-specific procedural and evidential considerations influences the conduct and outcomes of plea negotiations, including:

— the extent of pre-trial disclosure by prosecution and defence;
— challenges to the admissibility of evidence;
— the reliability and persuasiveness of witnesses;
— engagement of and representations by any victim of crime;
— the prosecutor's assessment of the competence and completeness of the investigation;
— the confidence of investigators, prosecutors and defence representatives in the justice process;
— judgements of the accused's personal culpability;
— the parties' respective skills in negotiation; and
— the readiness of all parties to offer and accept reasonable terms of compromise.

There may well be other contextual factors at play, including, on occasion, legal representatives' personal motives. Plea negotiation is not necessarily a neat and orderly, linear process, and this may further complicate its description and evaluation.

(a) Terminological Clarifications

Discussions of negotiated justice are plagued by lack of clarity and consistency in basic terminology. In this context (as elsewhere) choice of terminology is important for the shades

---

percentage of cases, judges accepted a formal agreement of the prosecutor's factual allegations by the defendant as the sole basis for finding the defendant guilty, contrary to the law's demand of independently establishing the truth': JI Turner, 'Limits on the Search for Truth in Criminal Procedure: A Comparative View' in J Ross and S Thaman (eds), *Research Handbook on Comparative Criminal Procedure* (Cheltenham, Edward Elgar, 2015).

[7] The *Guidelines* are available on the Officer of the Director of Public Prosecutions (ODPP) website www.odpp.nsw.gov.au (accessed 16 January 2016) and are reproduced in standard practitioner works. See in particular Guideline 20, 'Charge Negotiation & Agreement; Agreed Statements of Facts; Form 1'.

[8] Director of Public Prosecutions Act 1986 (NSW), s 13.

of meaning that it may convey and for its further conscious or unintended implications. In fact, several different processes are covered by the umbrella term 'plea negotiations'. The particular focus of this chapter will be *charge negotiation*.

The Samuels Report defined charge bargaining (as it was then known) as a 'process by which the prosecutor agrees to withdraw a charge or charges upon the promise of an accused to plead guilty to others'.[9] It was stressed that the practice does not really involve 'a bargaining, bidding, haggling, or horse-trading process [and] it is not a process in which the prosecutor merely reduces the gravity of the charges in return for a plea of guilty'.[10] Samuels' criticisms of lax terminology prompted the Office of the DPP in NSW to adopt the language of 'charge negotiation' leading to a 'charge agreement', in an effort to dispel any impression of bargained or compromised justice achieved, perhaps, by unprincipled means. Similar shifts in terminology, replacing terms such as 'plea *bargaining*' and 'charge *bargaining*' that may evoke bartered justice[11] with more neutral descriptions, have occurred in other Australian states and in North America.

In the US Federal jurisdiction, for example, there are now three types of 'plea agreement': (i) 'charge agreements'; (ii) 'sentence agreements'; and (iii) 'mixed agreements' combining the two.[12] In the Australian state of Victoria the term 'plea negotiation' is preferred. Perras defines plea negotiation as:

> A proceeding whereby competent and informed counsel openly discuss the evidence in a criminal prosecution with a view to achieving a disposition which will result in the reasonable advancement of the administration of justice.[13]

The 1993 Martin Committee Report (Ontario) extolled the virtues of an even broader concept of 'resolution discussions':

> Resolution discussions … include much more than simply plea discussions, which may themselves be quite broad. Resolution discussions include any discussions between counsel aimed at resolving any issues that a criminal prosecution raises. In the Committee's view, there is no reason to draw any distinction between the resolution of issues that will shorten the trial, and the resolution of issues that will make a trial unnecessary.[14]

Unfortunately, the language of 'plea bargaining' has popular currency and remains a media staple. 'Plea bargaining' is arguably even more misleading than 'charge bargaining', inasmuch as the only plea ever in contemplation is one of guilty. It is invariably the *charge* that is under negotiation. Others might say that the plea itself is still under negotiation, because unless an acceptable 'bargain' can be struck about charges and facts, no plea will be forthcoming. Particular terminological preferences sometimes reflect the nuances of process in particular jurisdictions.[15]

---

[9] Samuels Report above n 4, [6.1], citing D Andrew, 'Plea Bargaining' (1994) *Law Institute Journal* 236.

[10] Ibid, quoting from K Mack and S Roach Anleu, *Pleading Guilty: Issues and Practice* (Melbourne, Australian Institute of Judicial Administration, 1995) 6.

[11] SA Cohen and AN Doob, 'Public Attitudes to Plea Bargaining' (1989) 32 *Criminal Law Quarterly* 85, 87.

[12] United States Attorneys' Manual, ch 9-27.000: www.justice.gov/usao/eousa/foia_reading_room/usam/title9/27mcrm.htm (accessed 16 January 2016).

[13] DW Perras, 'Plea Negotiations' (1979) 22 *Criminal Law Quarterly* 58, 58–59.

[14] *Charge Screening, Disclosure, and Resolution Discussions* (Ontario Ministry of the Attorney General, 1993) 282.

[15] Cf the Martin Committee's preference for 'resolution discussions', ibid, especially 275–291.

(b) Normative and Pragmatic Rationales

The new terminology of negotiation and agreement is intended to distance negotiated justice from the pejorative marketplace connotations of 'bargaining' and the impression of unprincipled deals concluded only for reasons of expediency (or worse). It also usefully prompts a shift in the traditional adversarial mindset. Charge negotiation is not simply a bargained contractual settlement acceptable to two adversarial parties. It is a process that must serve the general public interest in the administration of criminal justice.

Domestic and international experience teaches that negotiated justice is probably unavoidable, if only for pragmatic reasons of cost, time and efficiency.[16] Without some wholesale means of avoiding full-blown contested trials in the majority of cases, the court lists would surely expand and backlogs worsen and the criminal justice process would eventually grind to a halt under the weight of defended matters. However, the justification for adopting processes of negotiated justice is not entirely pragmatic.

The prosecution (and thus the police, community, victims and witnesses) all benefit from the savings of time, inconvenience and cost in dealing with a plea of guilty on agreed facts. There are significant practical and psychological benefits to be derived from timely resolution without a formal trial, for the accused, crime victims and witnesses. For the Martin Committee, for example, 'resolution discussions are an essential part of the criminal justice system in Ontario, and, when properly conducted, benefit not only the accused, but also victims, witnesses, counsel, and the administration of justice generally'.[17]

Critics often say that negotiated justice defeats truth-seeking, but the value of truth in adjudication should be viewed in the aggregate across all proceedings rather than focusing exclusively on factual rectitude in individual cases. Reflecting on the rapid growth of negotiated processes globally, Turner observes that, while negotiated outcomes may deflect the search for truth in individual cases, negotiation nonetheless 'yields a net benefit for truth-seeking across the board' when opportunity costs are factored into the equation:

> By freeing up resources that prosecutors and courts can use to pursue more offenders, the argument goes, plea bargaining may help resolve more cases and thus achieve an overall gain in criminal law enforcement.[18]

Rather than comparing negotiated justice with merely aspirational ideals, the actuality of criminal proceedings, in which compromise is an embedded fact of life, should be taken as the critical standard. For example, there is rarely enough time for trials to run as counsel would ideally like, for every pertinent question to be asked and all relevant evidence to be adduced. Efficiency demands and the practicality of jury trials require that on many occasions procedures must be truncated. This is the practical context in which the integrity of negotiated pleas must be understood and evaluated.

In NSW, in common with many other legal jurisdictions, 'doing more with less' is the government's favourite bureaucratic mantra. 'Juniorisation' of professional public services often accompanies reduced budgets, potentially leaving inexperienced practitioners without adequate supervision. There is also significant pressure to dispose of as many cases

---

[16] Turner, above n 6; citing M Damaška, 'Truth in Adjudication' (1998) 49 *Hastings Law Journal* 289, 301, 307.
[17] Martin Committee Report, above n 14, 281.
[18] Ibid.

as possible in summary proceedings—in the Local Court, in NSW—rather than by jury trial on indictment. This saves significant time and costs.[19] Accompanying this is pressure for a reduction in the severity of penalties being imposed, with a preference for diversion and non-custodial options for lower-level offending. Greater leniency in sentencing is not necessarily undesirable in itself; but it does reinforce the motivation and provide further incentives for negotiating charges downwards.

2. Charge Negotiation in New South Wales— Legal Framework and Process

The process of charge negotiation in NSW proceeds within a framework of overlapping legal and other normative regulations. The Criminal Procedure Act 1986 (NSW) comprehensively regulates criminal proceedings at all stages of the process, up to defended trials and pleas of guilty. This Act contains pre-trial case management procedures designed to reduce delays, including, since late 2013,[20] prescriptive requirements for timely pre-trial disclosure by both prosecution and defence (which, however, are very rarely used). In addition to formal legislation, the rules of the professional associations—the Bar Association and Law Society—also regulate disclosure obligations. Whilst full and prompt disclosure may facilitate charge negotiation directly, strictly time-tabled mandatory duties have been controversial and, if they were to be routinely enforced, would be likely to impose considerable additional time and cost burdens on both prosecution and defence; providing another incentive for negotiated outcomes rather than contested trials.

The present regime, if operated in the spirit intended, is calculated to promote the integrity of charge negotiation; albeit that, as in most aspects of criminal practice, good intentions may sometimes be subverted. One assumption, which may not necessarily always hold, is that defendants have the benefit of proper professional legal representation and advice on any plea agreement. The immediate incentive for the accused to plead guilty (following charge negotiation or otherwise) is the sentencing discount common, in one form or another, to all common law sentencing systems. NSW has enacted the principle of reduced sentence for guilty pleas in section 22(1) of its Crimes (Sentencing Procedure) Act 1999, which provides as follows:

(1) In passing sentence for an offence on an offender who has pleaded guilty to the offence, a court must take into account:

(a)   the fact that the offender has pleaded guilty, and
(b)   when the offender pleaded guilty or indicated an intention to plead guilty, and
(c)   the circumstances in which the offender indicated an intention to plead guilty,

and may accordingly impose a lesser penalty than it would otherwise have imposed.

---

[19] The Criminal Procedure Act 1986 (NSW) enables some indictable offences to be heard summarily in the Local Court. This underlines to prosecutors the desirability of charge negotiations resulting in summary process and holds out the incentive of generally reducing sentence tariffs for the accused.
[20] Criminal Procedure Amendment (Mandatory Pre-trial Defence Disclosure) Act 2013 (NSW).

Other discounts are available for facilitating the administration of justice (section 22A) and providing assistance to law enforcement authorities (section 23). In a guideline sentencing judgment on section 22 the Court of Criminal Appeal held that a sentencing judge should explicitly state that a plea of guilty has been taken into account.[21] The judge should quantify the effect of the plea on the sentence insofar as he or she believes it appropriate to do so. The discount should generally be assessed in the range 10 to 25 per cent (having particular regard to the timing of the plea). In some cases a plea, considered together with other factors, may change the nature of the sentence imposed but in other circumstances may not attract any discount. Section 35A additionally requires certification of a consultation process with police and victims before a negotiated charge and guilty plea may proceed to sentence.

The sentencing discount has attracted controversy. Some academic critics believe that it pressurises innocent people with poor cases to plead guilty. Popular sentiment is more likely to cavil at the notion of guilty offenders 'getting off lightly' with a reduced charge and punishment. Most prosecutors, however, are persuaded of its merits and it has become a routine part of modern criminal procedure.

After section 22 of the 1999 Act, the most important provision governing charge negotiation in NSW is Guideline 20 of the DPP's *Prosecution Guidelines* on 'Charge Negotiation and Agreement; Agreed Statements of Facts; Form 1'. A charge agreement in NSW must be concluded in a principled manner, in conformity with the Samuels 'criminality principle'. A formal written agreement as to the factual basis for sentencing, adopted by both parties, should virtually always form the centrepiece of any charge agreement. This is a vital safeguard of integrity in the negotiation process. It would usually be impossible to assess whether an agreement adequately reflects the criminality involved and provides adequate scope for sentencing (in accordance with the 'criminality principle') unless the facts to be taken into account by the sentencing judge are clearly indicated. In the experience of the author, failure to agree a precise and detailed statement of facts can produce lengthy delays and many days of courtroom argument, especially in the context of multiple charges. This can all be avoided if the charge agreement process concludes with an accurate and comprehensive agreement as to facts.

Preparing an agreed statement of facts concentrates the minds of both parties on the question of what exactly the plea entails and the factors relevant to sentence. In addition to addressing the elements of the offence, it is useful (but not always possible) to secure agreement on any circumstances of aggravation or mitigation. Aggravating and mitigating factors, more often than essential elements, give rise to later disputes concerning Statements of Agreed Facts. A plea of guilty technically goes no further than accepting an admission of the elements of the charge. Circumstantial detail, including motivation, intention and other subjective dimensions of the incident, add meaning, significance and colour to the bare legal elements, enabling the sentencing judge to gauge the offender's culpability and the harmfulness of the conduct more precisely. Circumstantial details also matter to victims, who typically want the true and full picture of the offending placed before the court.

Identifying which matters surrounding the commission of the offence should be included in, and what should be excluded from, a Statement of Agreed Facts is an integral part of the charge negotiation process. For the Crown, adequacy is the watchword: adequate reflection of the criminality involved and adequate scope for sentencing. Prosecutorial judgement,

---

[21] *R v Thomson; R v Houlton* [2000] 49 NSWLR 383; NSWCCA 309.

infused by experience, is required. If there is strong evidence of aggravation, the Crown should not usually agree to a statement of facts excluding it. The Crown must also bear in mind the principle acknowledged in Australia that facts that would elevate an offence to a more serious category may not be taken into account when sentencing for the lesser offence.[22] Defence representatives, for their part, must ensure that the accused is fully and appropriately informed of the available procedural options and their implications. From the defence perspective, it is likely to be important to press for the inclusion of mitigating circumstances in agreed facts, if there is any evidential basis for doing so.

In terms of practicalities, it is generally preferable for the first draft of a Statement of Agreed Facts to be prepared by the prosecution, which has access to all relevant materials resulting from the investigation. However, it would not be inappropriate in some cases for the defence to be invited to submit a draft for consideration, or even to volunteer one. Written confirmation of any concluded charge agreement and agreement as to facts should generally be sent by the prosecution to the defence. If circumstances permit, adoption of the agreed facts should be evidenced by the parties' signatures and initialled by the police and any victim. These formalities promote transparency and accountability in the process, and thus its procedural integrity. Where full agreement is not possible, it might still be useful and appropriate to conclude an agreed statement as to *most* of the facts relevant to sentence, but on the further understanding that evidence will be led in connection with still disputed aspects of the offence or its surrounding circumstances. The more precisely points of continuing disagreement can be isolated in advance, the better for all concerned.

3. The Prosecutor's Role and Responsibilities

A defensible process of charge negotiation and agreement depends upon the balanced satisfaction of two potentially competing public interests. There is the public interest in ensuring that criminal conduct is punished according to its deserts (an imprecise criterion in itself); and the public interest in conserving resources, reducing delay and ameliorating pressures on victims, witnesses and others involuntarily drawn into criminal proceedings. Formal criminal trial, with all that entails, is not the only way—and is very often not the best way—to balance the public interest for the benefit of society and the offender. Charge negotiation and procedures associated with it may provide better—more *just*—outcomes with propriety and integrity. Much depends in practice, however, on the quality of the actors in the process and their understanding of their professional roles and responsibilities.

The prosecutor is the central figure in charge negotiation. Common law courts have repeatedly stressed that, although the prosecutor is an adversarial litigant, he or she must also conduct proceedings as a 'minister of justice' in the public interest. As long ago as 1935, the US Supreme Court emphasised the prosecutor's special duty to abide by the law and foreswear 'foul blows':

> The United States Attorney is the representative not of an ordinary party to a controversy, but of a sovereignty whose obligation to govern impartially is as compelling as its obligation to govern at all,

---

[22]   Known as the *De Simoni* principle: *R v De Simoni* (1981) 147 CLR 383; [1981] HCA 31.

and whose interest, therefore, in a criminal prosecution is not that it shall win a case, but that justice shall be done. As such, he is in a peculiar and very definite sense the servant of the law, the two-fold aim of which is that guilt shall not escape or innocence suffer. He may prosecute with earnestness and vigour—indeed, he should do so. But, while he may strike hard blows, he is not at liberty to strike foul ones. It is as much his duty to refrain from improper methods calculated to produce a wrongful conviction as it is to use every legitimate means to bring about a just one.[23]

Twenty years later, Rand J of the Supreme Court of Canada wrote in *Boucher*:

It cannot be over-emphasised that the purpose of a criminal prosecution is not to obtain a conviction; it is to lay before a jury what the Crown considers to be credible evidence relevant to what is alleged to be a crime. Counsel have a duty to see that all available legal proof of the facts is presented: it should be done firmly and pressed to its legitimate strength, but it must also be done fairly. The role of the prosecutor excludes any notion of winning or losing; his function is a matter of public duty than which in civil life there can be none charged with greater personal responsibility. It is to be efficiently performed with an ingrained sense of the dignity, the seriousness and the justness of judicial proceedings.[24]

In common law systems, prosecutorial discretion is exercised independently of any inappropriate influence by government, politics, the media, the police or any individual or sectional interest in the community, including crime victims. It has never been the case that every evidentially supported charge laid against an accused must be prosecuted automatically. Conversely, a prosecution is not necessarily hamstrung by evidential difficulties if there is evidence to support a lesser charge.

The prosecutor's onerous duties as a minister of justice are as firmly embedded in Australian jurisprudence as they are in other common law jurisdictions.[25] The professional and personal demands placed on individual prosecutors by these high expectations should not be underestimated. Difficult judgement-calls sometimes have to be made in circumstances where there are no easy answers and reasonable minds might reach different conclusions.[26] Professional judgements must be made at every stage of a prosecution: in charging decisions, evidence selection, framing legal and factual arguments, communicating and interacting with other participants in the process and so on. Prosecutorial decision-making is not a scientifically exact process, with easily measurable outcomes or standardised performance benchmarks. Prosecutors are entrusted to carry out their functions to the highest achievable professional standards, in accordance with the law, departmental guidelines

---

[23] *Berger v United States*, 295 US 78, 88 (1935).

[24] *Boucher v R* (1954) 110 CCC 263, 270.

[25] In relation to England and Wales, see eg *R v H* [2004] 2 AC 134, [2004] UKHL 3, [13]; *R v Puddick* (1865) 4 F & F 497, 499 (Crompton J). Paragraph 2.4 of Crown Prosecution Service, *The Code for Crown Prosecutors* (London, CPS, 2013) stipulates that: 'Prosecutors must always act in the interests of justice and not solely for the purpose of obtaining a conviction.' See www.cps.gov.uk/publications/code_for_crown_prosecutors/ (accessed 21 November 2015).

[26] Addressing the XXth Annual Conference of the Canadian Federal Prosecution Service in June 2000, the Deputy Attorney General of Canada (and Minister responsible for the FPS), Morris Rosenberg, reflected: 'Carrying out the duties of a prosecutor is difficult. It requires solid professional judgement and legal competence, a large dose of practical life experience and the capacity to work in an atmosphere of great stress. Not everyone can do this. Moreover, there is no recipe that guarantees the right answer in every case, and in many cases reasonable persons may differ. A prosecutor who expects certainty and absolute truth is in the wrong business. The exercise of prosecutorial discretion is not an exact science. The more numerous and complex the issues, the greater the margin for error.'

and rules of conduct, exercising judgement throughout the course of the case in the pursuit of a just outcome. They must never forget that they contribute to but one part of a process—the criminal justice process—within the criminal justice system as a whole. Like all complex systems, the machine works best when each component part performs its allocated function effectively, meshing with the other parts without trying to exclude or supersede them. The result—a conviction or an acquittal, or indeed a hung jury and potential retrial—is produced by the process carried out by the whole system, not just by the prosecutor. If the outcome is to be judged, it should be viewed as the product of the system as a whole: *the system of justice* either wins or loses, if those problematic terms must be used at all.

Given that prosecutors do not 'win' cases by securing convictions or 'lose' prosecutions resulting in acquittal (however individual prosecutors may feel at the end of a long, hard-fought case) and that their performance is not assessed by any 'hit list' of convictions or results scorecard, there should be no formal professional incentive of that kind for negotiating charges to secure guilty pleas. Beyond diffuse structural pressures towards negotiated justice operating across the system, decision-making in individual cases is driven by contextual factors relating to the nature of the charges and the quality of the evidence. Defence lawyers in receipt of timely pre-trial disclosure may be in a position to identify opportunities for productive discussion just as readily as prosecutors and should act on them in the interests of their clients if they do. A negotiated outcome usually carries significant benefits for an offender. Negotiations 'without prejudice' provide some safeguard for the accused. Defence legal representatives, of course, must be alert to the possibility of an accused person seeking to plead guilty to an offence that he or she did not commit, possibly owing to family, financial or other pressures. It remains the prosecutor's duty throughout proceedings to continually screen cases to assess the strength of the admissible evidence available and the continuing appropriateness of any charge that is proceeding.

Legitimate opportunities for negotiation are presented where the conduct in question might constitute overlapping offences of varying gravity. To take a very simple example, on an indictment containing a charge under section 33 of the Crimes Act 1900 (NSW) of causing grievous bodily harm (GBH) with intent, the defence might offer a plea to section 35 of recklessly causing GBH (without the intent). GBH with intent carries a maximum penalty of 25 years' imprisonment; the punishment for reckless GBH is capped at ten years imprisonment. For many assaults resulting in GBH, a maximum penalty of ten years might give completely adequate scope for the sentencing judge to reflect the criminality involved in the accused's conduct. Obviously, if proof of intent might be difficult on the facts, the prosecutor might sensibly settle for a plea to the reduced recklessness charge. However, even where the Crown was confident of proving the more serious section 33 offence, the prosecutor might reason that the cost of a lengthy trial which will consume resources, time and money and cause grief for all concerned, is not justified if the likely sentence that would be imposed on conviction after a contested trial would be considerably less than the ten-year maximum for the lesser offence. In these circumstances, charge negotiation leading to a plea to section 35 reckless GBH may be the best means of achieving justice in conformity with the Samuels criminality principle.

Another common scenario involves multiple charges related to a course of offending, which is often found in relation to, for example, domestic burglary or child sexual assault. In such circumstances, pleas to a subset of the charges might be preferable to proceeding on all counts at the risk of producing an acquittal after a contested trial. Careful consideration must be given to charge selection and acceptable pleas. If a pattern of offending occurred over a considerable period of time it would usually be preferable to select representative charges reflecting the course of criminality during the entire period. The Statement of Agreed Facts might appropriately refer to admissions by the accused in relation to some or all of the other incidents. Multiple offences are also routine features of corporate crime and fraud prosecutions. Trials in relation to such matters are often complex and lengthy and a charge agreement could therefore have considerable benefits for the public as well as for the accused, victims and witnesses.

In contemplating charge negotiations, prosecutors need to make a realistic appraisal of the nature and quality of evidence available to prove each charge. Sometimes a victim's evidence, appearing solid enough on paper, may come to seem less persuasive or reliable during conference[27] or following committal proceedings. The witness may be confused, vague or forgetful rather than deliberately untruthful or dissembling. It might also be that a victim's statement includes material which is hearsay or which for other reasons is inadmissible at the trial or would not carry much weight with the fact-finder. The witness' evidence might be difficult to fit in with the prosecution's case as a whole. In such circumstances, the criminality principle requires that any negotiated plea adequately reflect the underlying criminality that can be demonstrated by the Crown's *admissible* evidence.

Some witnesses, having made complaints and given statements to the police, may be reluctant to proceed. This is not uncommon in cases of domestic violence and sexual assault. Some witnesses refuse point blank to testify. There may be particular reluctance to testify against a family member or friend. In other cases, a witness who does not actually refuse to give evidence is nevertheless in such a state of emotional turmoil that any testimony she or he might give is likely to be unconvincing or even incoherent. Sometimes the personal circumstances of the victim may have changed so significantly that further harm could be done by forcing him or her to testify (by applying to the court for a subpoena to require attendance[28]). In such circumstances, the prosecutor must assess whether or not the justice of the case requires the witness to be called; or whether a plea to a lesser charge, or one taken on the basis of a statement of agreed facts omitting allegations or aggravating factors initially alleged, would better serve the interests of justice; provided always that the Samuels criminality principle is observed.

These are the principal strategic factors that might motivate a prosecutor to enter into charge negotiations in any particular case. It is essential that the proper formalities are observed and that the process is conducted with professional propriety. A prosecutor's failure to follow proper procedures during charge negotiation, including appropriate consultation with those involved, is unprofessional and if publicly exposed can result in adverse media and political attention, distressed victims and complaints from the police (of the kind that led to the Samuels report). It may also contribute towards miscarriage of justice. This may be a rare occurrence, but when it happens it reflects badly (and unfairly and disproportionately) upon the professionalism of the prosecution and tends to diminish public confidence in the criminal justice process.

---

[27] Prosecutors are permitted, and in some circumstances actively encouraged, to interview witnesses (including complainants) in NSW. Cf Roberts, Chapter 7 in this volume.

[28] Criminal Procedure Act 1986 (NSW), s 222.

4. Victims and Police

The prosecution and defence are not the only interested parties in charge negotiations. Regard must also be had, in particular, to the concerns of victims and the police. The charge negotiation process in NSW is subject to formal duties of notification and certification.

Many common law jurisdictions nowadays formally articulate rights for victims. In NSW, The Charter of Victims' Rights has statutory force pursuant to section 6 of the Victims Rights and Support Act 2013 (NSW). Victims should be treated with courtesy, compassion and respect for their rights and dignity. In particular, victims should be kept informed of the progress of a prosecution and their views taken into account when key decisions are made. Section 35A of the Crimes (Sentencing Procedure) Act 1999 (NSW), inserted in 2011, for the first time imposed a duty upon the courts to ensure that charge negotiation processes have been conducted in compliance with NSW *Prosecution Guidelines* 19 and 20, including proper consultation. The fundamental rule is that victims must be informed when any charge negotiation is initiated and the views of the victim must be obtained and recorded before there is any formal decision concerning a charge agreement. Victims should have been made aware of the charges against the accused at the time of arraignment and the factual basis on which the prosecution is proceeding. It is not difficult to imagine the victim's confusion, and possibly anger, if the next thing that she or he hears about the matter after giving a police statement or following arraignment is that the accused has pleaded guilty to some less serious charge, or to fewer charges, than originally specified, possibly on substantially 'watered down' facts.

Accordingly, as soon as charge negotiations commence or are contemplated the victim must be contacted. The victim should be informed of the rationale and basic principles governing charge negotiation and agreement. The reasons why charge agreement is being considered in his or her particular case should be explained, and the version of the facts to be put forward discussed. This is not for the purpose of obtaining 'instructions' from a victim, because the complainant is not the prosecutor's client. Rather, it is a matter of sensitive handling and adequate briefing. The defence needs to understand the nature of this process, and that proper consultation may take time, especially if vulnerable victims are involved. Since a Statement of Agreed Facts is an integral part of any charge agreement, it follows that the victim must be kept informed of all aspects of the negotiation regarding its content. Sometimes much of what a victim believes to be relevant to a particular case actually has no legal significance for sentencing and will be excluded from an agreed statement of facts. This may require careful explanation to the victim. Still greater challenges of sensitive explanation attend circumstances where, for the sake of reaching a fair compromise, plea negotiations result in the exclusion of facts which show the offence in a more serious light and which the prosecution might have been able to prove.

In practice, charge negotiation frequently entails much last-minute to-ing and fro-ing involving changes to the indictment and to the proposed agreement as to facts. It may be difficult to keep the victim or police informed of all such developments as they occur, but every effort must be made to ensure that it is done, at all events, before final agreements are reached. Consultations must be recorded in compliance with the statutory duty.[29] If the

---

[29] Crimes (Sentencing Procedure) Act 1999 (NSW), s 35A.

victim has no objection to the proposed Statement of Agreed Facts, he or she should ideally initial or sign a copy of it indicating the absence of any objection. Failing that, victims should be asked to sign a copy of the document in acknowledgement of its existence and a record should be made of the fact and nature of any disagreement or objection.

It is equally important to keep the investigating officers informed about the progress of charge negotiations. The role of the prosecution and the desirability of negotiated pleas should be easier to explain to police officers than to some crime victims. However, it is still essential for the prosecutor to inform the police of all phases of the charge negotiation and to seek the views of the police as to any proposed charge agreement or Statement of Agreed Facts; not least because the police may have further relevant information to contribute. The process of informing the police and seeking and receiving their views should likewise be recorded in writing. A police representative should be invited to sign the Statement of Agreed Facts, by way of acknowledgement if not full agreement. Observing these formalities contributes to the transparency and accountability of the charge negotiation process, thus promoting its procedural integrity and acceptability to the community.

5. Judicial Supervision

In keeping with common law orthodoxy, Australian courts do not actively interfere with the prosecutor's discretion to enter into charge negotiations and secure agreed pleas of guilty. Judicial supervision is largely confined to ensuring that a plea of guilty is voluntary and fully informed. Prosecutorial decisions are judicially reviewable only for abuse of the court's process or manifest unfairness. In *Maxwell*,[30] for example, the High Court of Australia was confronted with a trial judge's refusal to proceed on the prosecutor's acceptance of a plea of guilty to manslaughter on an indictment for murder. Dawson and McHugh JJ reaffirmed the trial judge's obligation to accept an unequivocal plea of guilty from an accused as an admission of all the essential elements of the offence. It was said that, absent an abuse of process, the fact that the trial judge himself 'thought that the material placed before him was insufficient to establish diminished responsibility was no more relevant than is the view of a trial judge who disagrees with the verdict of a jury but is nevertheless required to sentence upon the basis of that verdict'. In other words, the sentencing judge is bound by the factual assumptions underpinning the accused's plea:

> In sentencing the accused, [the trial judge] was required to proceed upon the basis that, in killing his wife, the accused's mental responsibility for his acts was substantially impaired by reason of an abnormality of mind, notwithstanding any reservations which he may have entertained had the matter been one for his decision.[31]

---

[30] *Maxwell v R* (1996) 184 CLR 501, [1996] HCA 46 (citations omitted) (Toohey, Gaudron and Gummow JJ agreeing). More recently, see *Likiardopoulos v R* (2012) 247 CLR 265, [2012] HCA 37; and *R v Elias; R v Issa* [2013] HCA 31, [28]. The *Maxwell* decision is closely scrutinised by Jeremy Gans in Chapter 6 in this volume.

[31] *Maxwell v R* (1996) 184 CLR 501, [1996] HCA 46, [27], observing that 'a sentencing judge may be required by reason of the charge selected by the prosecution to take an artificially restricted view of the facts' and applying the principles elucidated by Gibbs CJ in *R v De Simoni* (1981) 147 CLR 383; [1981] HCA 31: '[T]he judge cannot act on a view of the facts which conflicts with the jury's verdict … [W]here the Crown has charged the offender with, or has accepted a plea of guilty to, an offence less serious than the facts warrant, it cannot rely, or ask the judge to rely, on the facts that would have rendered the offender liable to a more serious penalty.'

The respective roles of the parties and the court in the charge negotiation process were addressed in 2004 in the important High Court case of *R v GAS; R v SJK*.[32] Referring specifically to 'plea agreements' (the preferred terminology in the state of Victoria, where the appeal originated), the High Court laid down the following five general principles, which merit full quotation:

1. First, it is the prosecutor, alone, who has the responsibility of deciding the charges to be preferred against an accused person. The judge has no role to play in that decision ...

2. Secondly, it is the accused person, alone, who must decide whether to plead guilty to the charge preferred. That decision must be made freely ... Once again, the judge is not ... involved in the decision. Such a decision is not made with any foreknowledge of the sentence that will be imposed. No doubt it will often be made in the light of professional advice as to what might reasonably be expected to happen, but that advice is the responsibility of the accused's legal representatives.

3. Thirdly, it is for the sentencing judge, alone, to decide the sentence to be imposed. For that purpose, the judge must find the relevant facts. In the case of a plea of guilty, any facts beyond what is necessarily involved as an element of the offence must be proved by evidence, or admitted formally (as in an agreed statement of facts), or informally ... There may be significant limitations as to a judge's capacity to find potentially relevant facts in a given case. The present appeal provides an example. The limitation arose from the absence of evidence as to who killed the victim, and the absence of any admission from either appellant that his involvement was more than that of an aider and abettor.

4. Fourthly, as a corollary to the third principle, there may be an understanding, between the prosecution and the defence, as to evidence that will be led, or admissions that will be made, but that does not bind the judge, except in the practical sense that the judge's capacity to find facts will be affected by the evidence and the admissions. In deciding the sentence, the judge must apply to the facts as found the relevant law and sentencing principles. It is for the judge, assisted by the submissions of counsel, to decide and apply the law. There may be an understanding between counsel as to the submissions of law that they will make, but that does not bind the judge in any sense. The judge's responsibility to find and apply the law is not circumscribed by the conduct of counsel.

5. Fifthly, an erroneous submission of law may lead a judge into error and, if that occurs, the usual means of correcting the error is through the appeal process. It is the responsibility of the appeal court to apply the law. If a sentencing judge has been led into error by an erroneous legal submission by counsel, that may be a matter to be taken into account in the application of the statutory provisions and principles which govern the exercise of the appeal court's jurisdiction.

These principles reflect the traditional division of responsibility between prosecutors and courts.[33] The prosecutor is entitled to run the Crown's case without judicial interference, whilst sentencing is a matter of law for the judge. It follows that a prosecutor cannot promise a particular sentence to an accused as leverage in the charge negotiation process. Negotiations must proceed according to some conventional understanding of the 'going rate' of judicial sentences for guilty pleas in relation to particular offence categories. Prosecutors may exert some incidental influence on trial judges' sentencing decisions through skilful submissions regarding penalty. In NSW (and Victoria), for example, prosecutors 'may submit that a custodial or non-custodial sentence is appropriate' and 'must correct any error made by the opponent ... and must assist the court to avoid appealable error on the issue

---

[32] (2004) 217 CLR 198, [2004] HCA 22 (citations omitted).
[33] *Maxwell v R* (1996) 184 CLR 501, [1996] HCA 46, [28].

of sentence'.[34] Thus, it is open for prosecutors to offer to make particular submissions as to sentence as part of the charge negotiation process, even though they cannot guarantee any particular type or severity of punishment.

It is uncontroversial that prosecutors are under a duty to assist trial judges to ensure that any sentence imposed on an offender complies with legal requirements (which are characteristically complex and prone to frequent revision in response to prevailing political fashions).[35] However, Australian prosecutors' previously established practice of addressing the court on 'an appropriate range of severity of penalty' must now be read in light of the High Court's 2014 decision in *Barbaro and Zirilli*[36] and the new Legal Profession Uniform Conduct (Barristers) Rules 2015. *Barbaro and Zirilli* was an appeal from Victoria by two accused who had 'settled' their plea through a charge negotiation ('plea negotiation' in Victoria) predicated 'on the basis of what the prosecution had said to be its views of the available sentencing range'.[37] In the event, the trial judge refused to hear the prosecution's views on sentencing and the appellants complained that they had thereby been denied a valuable opportunity to secure a reduced sentence. A four-Justice majority of the High Court replied that the appellants' argument was founded on two flawed premises. First, there is in fact no general right or duty of a prosecutor to address the court on appropriate sentencing ranges. Secondly, such submissions, if permitted, would not relate to questions of sentencing law:

> The prosecution's statement of what are the bounds of the available range of sentences is a statement of opinion. Its expression advances no proposition of law or fact which a sentencing judge may properly take into account in finding the relevant facts, deciding the applicable principles of law or applying those principles to the facts to yield the sentence to be imposed. That being so, the prosecution is not required, and should not be permitted, to make such a statement of bounds to a sentencing judge.[38]

It was observed that a bare statement of sentencing range provides the judge with no explanatory justification for imposing a particular sentence; nor would Crown counsel necessarily be in a position to provide any elucidation, unless they also happened to have been personally involved in the pre-trial charge negotiations. The Court concluded that permitting prosecutors to express their views regarding the appropriate penalty range was wrong in principle and should not be done:

> If a sentencing judge is properly informed about the parties' submissions about what facts should be found, the relevant sentencing principles and comparable sentences, the judge will have all the information which is necessary to decide what sentence should be passed without any need for the prosecution to proffer its view about available range. If the judge is not sufficiently informed about what facts may or should be found, about the relevant principles or about comparable sentences, the prosecution's proffering a range … will not do anything to help the judge avoid specific error; it will not necessarily help the judge avoid imposing a sentence which the offender will later allege to be manifestly excessive. Most importantly, it will not assist the judge in carrying out the sentencing task in accordance with proper principle.[39]

---

[34] Legal Profession Uniform Conduct (Barristers) Rules 2015, Rule 95. See www.legislation.nsw.gov.au/sessionalview/sessional/sr/2015-243.pdf (accessed 9 August 2015).
[35] See eg Rule 95, ibid.
[36] *Barbaro v R; Zirilli v R* (2014) 88 ALJR 372, [2014] HCA 2.
[37] Ibid [5] (French CJ, Hayne, Kieffel and Bell JJ).
[38] Ibid [7].
[39] Ibid [23], [37]–[38] (citations omitted).

The impact of *Barbaro and Zirilli* on charge negotiation is difficult to gauge. On its face, it seems to imply that the prosecutor's scope for offering credible indications of likely sentence to encourage pleas of guilty is very limited. Justices Basten and Johnson of the NSW Supreme Court, writing extra-judicially, have suggested a different interpretation.[40] They argue that, rather than limiting submissions from a prosecutor, *Barbaro and Zirilli* should be read as an invitation to provide sentencing courts with *more* information to explain and contextualise the rationale for any suggested penalty range, including the facts of the particular case, the maximum penalty and standard non-parole period (if any), pertinent mitigating or aggravating factors, any sentences on co-offenders (if parity is an issue), sentencing statistics (if useful) and details of comparable cases. This interpretation finds support in a subsequent decision of the Victorian Court of Appeal.[41] *Barbaro and Zirilli* can be viewed as merely reinforcing the existing principle of law embedded in common law jurisdictions (including NSW and Victoria) that the sentencing role of the court cannot be pre-empted (though it may be structured and strongly influenced) by any 'agreement' concluded between the parties.

Accepting the constitutional role of the judge in sentencing, the fact remains that plea negotiation can only function if the prosecutor is at liberty to make representations on which the accused can reasonably rely. The Supreme Court of Canada recently observed that 'the binding effect of plea agreements is a matter of utmost importance to the administration of justice'.[42] It followed that 'the Crown may simply have to live with the initial decision that has been made', even if subsequent counsel would not have struck that deal and now wanted to resile from it:

> To hold otherwise would mean that defence lawyers would no longer have confidence in the finality of negotiated agreements reached with front-line Crown counsel, with whom they work on a daily basis. Further, if agreements arrived at over the course of resolution discussions cannot be relied upon by the accused, the benefits that resolutions produce for both the accused and the administration of justice cannot be achieved … [T]he situations in which the Crown can properly repudiate a resolution agreement are, and must remain, very rare.[43]

Some measure of finality in charge negotiation is equally imperative in NSW and it is to be hoped that the High Court in *Barbaro and Zirilli* has not upset the delicate balance mediating between the roles, expectations and responsibilities of the various actors at each stage of the process. Experience to date suggests that it has not done so. Charge negotiation must begin with the defence and prosecution, but any agreement reached is no mere 'contractual undertaking'. The primary parties have continuing obligations to the accused, victims, the community and the court. It is those obligations, rather than any bipartisan contractual bond, that require the prosecution to adhere to agreements reached. Whilst courts maintain overall supervision of the process (an essential guarantee of process integrity), there are fairly well-defined limits on direct judicial involvement in the negotiation process itself.

---

[40] J Baston and P Johnson, 'The Prosecutor's Role in Sentencing' (2014) 26 *Judicial Officers' Bulletin (NSW)* 47.
[41] *Matthews v R; Vu v R; Hashmi v R* [2014] VSCA 291.
[42] *R v Nixon* [2011] SCC 34.
[43] Ibid [48].

Conclusion: Meeting Integrity's Challenge for Negotiated Justice

In 2012, the US Supreme Court acknowledged 'the reality that criminal justice today is for the most part a system of pleas, not a system of trials. Ninety-seven percent of federal convictions and ninety-four percent of state convictions are the result of guilty pleas'.[44] In the previous year, the Canadian Supreme Court commented that 'plea resolutions help to resolve the vast majority of criminal cases in Canada and, in doing so, contribute to a fair and efficient criminal justice system'.[45] This picture is replicated across the common law world. In NSW, for example, 83 per cent of indictable criminal cases concluded in the District Court (the main court for indictable offences) between 2011 and 2013 were disposed of by pleas of guilty.[46] Guilty pleas are not always the outcome of charge negotiation: they may be prompted by the overwhelming strength of incriminating evidence, or to secure the maximum sentencing discount available for an early plea, or even by genuine remorse. But there is no doubt that charge negotiation can and does increase the proportion of pleas of guilty very significantly.

Does charge negotiation, as practised in NSW, erode the legitimacy of a criminal justice system founded on an ideology of fair trials that protect the rights of all those involved? The pragmatic benefits of negotiated justice, in terms of economy, efficiency and reduced delays, have long been recognised. Viewing the matter in the round, resources conserved through negotiated pleas can be redeployed to achieve justice in other cases. The benefits to victims and witnesses and others involved in the trial process from early settlement are also very significant in human terms. And there are obvious advantages to the guilty accused, not least a reduced penalty. Still, what critics persist in calling 'plea bargaining' attracts many familiar objections, including:

— the lack of an explicit basis in statute or at common law;
— the absence of measurement and reporting of the use of the process and its outcomes;
— circumvention of public and open justice and the embedded rights and protections intrinsic to trial proceedings;
— diminished accountability arising from lack of transparency in the process;
— the power reposed in the prosecutor to influence discretionary decision-making that should instead reside with the bench;
— limited trust and confidence in the prosecutor to conduct negotiations in accordance with best practice requirements and proper motivation in the interests of justice;
— the sense of injustice that may be felt by crime victims or police officers who consider that their views were ignored or not taken seriously enough; and
— an accused's sense of injustice, when feeling confused, duped or coerced into an unfavourable guilty plea arrangement.

---

[44] *Lafler v Cooper*, 132 S Ct 1376, 1385 (2012).

[45] *R v Nixon* [2011] SCC 34, [47].

[46] C Ringland and L Snowball, *Predictors of Guilty Pleas in the NSW District Court*, Bureau Brief Issue Paper No 96 (Sydney, NSW Bureau of Crime Statistics and Research, 2014) 5, www.bocsar.nsw.gov.au/Documents/BB/bb96.pdf (accessed 9 August 2015).

Possibly the most serious allegation against negotiated justice is that innocent people may plead guilty to crimes they did not commit, especially if a large sentencing discount is perceived as forcing their hand and defence legal representatives have self-interested motives for preferring guilty pleas to trials.[47] It seems undeniable, and indeed inevitable, that innocent people sometimes do plead guilty,[48] but there are no reliable statistics and it is difficult to get any sense of the magnitude of the problem. Access to high-quality legal advice and high standards of professional ethics should provide some safeguards in those jurisdictions, like NSW, where such provision is made. On the other side of the political argument, it might be said that some offences are too serious for plea or charge negotiation, or that it is inherently obnoxious for guilty offenders to 'get away' with a reduced penalty, especially in the teeth of compelling evidence.

One cannot reject these criticisms out-of-hand, especially in the absence of systematic empirical research on plea and charge negotiation practices in Australia.[49] It would be fatuous to deny that plea negotiation lacks the publicity, transparency, evidential scrutiny and community participation characteristic of full-blown contested jury trials. However, when negotiated outcomes are compared to the reality—as opposed to some idealised abstraction—of criminal adjudication, their principled, as well as pragmatic, merits should be recognised. Even civil jurisdictions, traditionally committed to judicially supervised inquiries into truth, are progressively endorsing the virtues of compromise. Negotiation is not an invitation to complacency. The Canadian Martin Committee wrote:

> [I]t is plain that resolution agreements must not undermine the integrity of the court, or otherwise bring the administration of justice into disrepute. While the sanctity of agreements entered into is an important principle of the administration of justice, Crown counsel's primary duty is to the integrity of the system. Accordingly, in the rare cases where these two values clash, the latter must prevail.[50]

Charge negotiation in NSW, and analogous negotiated justice practices across Australia, are conducted within a framework of law and professional ethics. The prosecutor is a minister of justice who acts at all times in the public interest. Charges must always conform to the Samuels criminality principle, taking account of evidential sufficiency and the rules of admissibility. Agreements may only be concluded after proper consultation with victims and the police. There may be scope for strengthening existing procedural safeguards by, for example, creating a register of charge agreements, requiring written copies to be filed with the court and establishing a reasonably accessible inquiry mechanism. Common law jurisdictions have adopted somewhat different positions on the question of whether, or to what extent, sentencing judges should regard themselves as constrained by prosecutors' charge agreements.

---

[47] PW Tague, 'Guilty Pleas or Trials: Which Does the Barrister Prefer?' (2008) 32 *Melbourne University Law Review* 242.

[48] See eg A Flynn, 'Plea-Negotiations, Prosecutors and Discretion: An Argument for Legal Reform' (2015) *Australian and New Zealand Journal of Criminology* Advance Access (reporting US Innocence Project data indicating an initial guilty plea rate of 10% amongst those subsequently exonerated).

[49] Though in relation to Victoria, see A Flynn and K FitzGibbon, 'Bargaining with Justice' (2011) 35 *Melbourne University Law Review* 31; A Flynn, 'Bargaining with Justice: Victims, Plea Bargaining and the Victims' Charter Act 2006 (Vic)' (2011) 37 *Monash University Law Review* 73; A Flynn, '"Fortunately We in Victoria Are Not in That UK Situation": Australian and United Kingdom Legal Perspectives on Plea Bargaining Reform' (2011) 16 *Deakin Law Review* 361.

[50] Martin Committee Report, above n 14; quoted with approval in *R v Nixon* [2011] SCC 34, [49].

Acting in accordance with statutory and practice obligations, a NSW prosecutor may sometimes properly withdraw a charge which the available evidence supports (and which, therefore, the prosecution could prove at trial) in return for a plea to a less serious charge. Such decisions require professional judgement and experience and reasonable minds will not always agree about the proper course of action. This is the individual prosecutor's professional burden, which no reviewing court (or external critic) can fully second-guess. When the result of a negotiation process conducted in the public interest and with appropriate consultation is a timely plea by a guilty offender, on agreed facts enabling the sentencing court to reflect the full measure of criminality in the punishment imposed, it seems that justice has been served with integrity.

6

The Integrity of Charging Decisions

JEREMY GANS

Introduction: Maxwell's Dictum

> The judge does not agree and he tells them
> So-o-o-o.
> But as the words are leaving his lips,
> A noise comes from behind.
> Bang! Bang! Maxwell's silver hammer
> Came down upon his head.[1]

In *Maxwell*, a 1996 judgment of the High Court of Australia, Gaudron and Gummow JJ remarked:

> The integrity of the judicial process—particularly, its independence and impartiality and the public perception thereof—would be compromised if the courts were to decide or were to be in any way concerned with decisions as to who is to be prosecuted and for what.[2]

The idea that courts should be loath to second-guess prosecutorial charging choices, given the distinct functions and informational asymmetries of their two offices, is a commonplace of the common law world.[3] However, as this chapter explains, Gaudron and Gummow JJ's absolutist approach to the 'integrity of the judicial process' when it comes to curial involvement in charging choices is a poor guide to the doctrinally blurred boundary between judicial and prosecutorial powers, which is instead delineated by multiple doctrines governing the relationship between courts, prosecutors and legislators in contexts where offence provisions overlap.

The chapter has two main parts. Section 1 analyses the particular charging choice in *Maxwell* itself, a prosecutor's decision to accept a plea to a lesser included offence (manslaughter) after charging a more serious one (murder). In Canada, judges who consider that the more serious charge is warranted may reject the plea, a stance attributed to protecting the court's integrity against entering an unwarranted acquittal. In England, judicial objections to the acceptance of a lesser plea may trigger a review of the charging decision up the

---

[1] *Maxwell's Silver Hammer*, John Lennon and Paul McCartney (EMI Music Publishing, Sony/ATV Music Publishing LLC, 1969).

[2] *Maxwell v R* [1996] HCA 46; (1996) 184 CLR 501, 534.

[3] See the recent affirmation of this approach by the Supreme Court of Canada in *R v Anderson* [2014] SCC 41, [46]–[47].

chain of prosecutorial accountability. In Australia, by contrast, the overriding imperative is to ensure that courts play no role in what charges are brought before them.

Section 2 examines how the phenomenon of multiple overlapping statutory provisions defining offences (notably for sexual crimes) justifies a variety of court interventions in prosecutorial choices. Where a particular charging choice is thought to circumvent the legislature's intent, courts have variously responded by reading down offences, treating certain choices as an abuse of the court's processes, applying doctrines preventing unprincipled verdicts or sentences, or manipulating doctrinal boundaries to influence charging practices. The array of doctrines, while highly variable across jurisdictions and times, shares a common hallmark: prioritising the legislature's intentions over maintaining a strict separation of curial and prosecutorial roles.

On sustained analysis, there is little value in pronouncements like Gaudron and Gummow JJ's that courts must never intrude on prosecutors' turf, lest one or both institutions lose their 'integrity'. Rather, common law courts can, should and do make choices about competing threats to the integrity of judicial process, particularly in light of parliamentary intentions when devising schemes of overlapping offence provisions.

1. Integrity in Prosecutorial Control

(a) Maxwell's Crime

On 24 August 1992, Brian Maxwell drove to the William Lawson Childcare Centre in the Sydney suburb of Prospect, picked up a sawn-off rifle and waited for his estranged wife, Marilyn, to return from dropping off their son, Guy.[4] Moments later, Maxwell's yellow raincoat was covered in her blood. He told a passer-by: 'I had to do it, it was the only way', adding (falsely) that 'I haven't seen my son in twelve months'. Fourteen months later at his arraignment for murder, he entered a plea of guilty to Marilyn Maxwell's manslaughter.[5] The prosecutor, citing two expert reports, told the court he accepted the plea 'on the basis of diminished responsibility in full satisfaction of the indictment'.[6] It took nine more years to finalise Maxwell's prosecution.

When Maxwell's sentencing hearing commenced, his trial judge observed that the expert reports mentioned by the prosecutor were founded on an unverified history provided by the defendant and contained conclusions that went beyond medical expertise.[7] Justice McInerney expressed his 'considerable doubt about whether [he could] ... accept the plea of not guilty to murder but guilty to manslaughter on the basis of diminished

---

[4] The facts are set out in *R v Maxwell* [1999] NSWSC 1085, while the best description of the proceedings is in *R v Maxwell* [2001] NSWCCA 362.

[5] The plea was the result of earlier communications between Maxwell's 'legal advisers' and 'the Crown': *R v Maxwell* (1994) 34 NSWLR 606, 607.

[6] *Maxwell v R* [1996] HCA 46; (1996) 184 CLR 501, 516.

[7] Details of the doctors' reports are found at *Maxwell v R* [1996] HCA 46; (1996) 184 CLR 501, 505. An example: 'Regarding the question of psychiatric defences, clearly Mr Maxwell was not psychotic and [*M'Naghten's*] rule does not apply. Automatism is also unavailable. The memory gaps are explained by his heightened emotions. This leaves diminished responsibility and I believe Mr Maxwell does have such a defence available to him.'

responsibility'.[8] He sought submissions from counsel. After a six-week adjournment, the prosecution successfully argued that the trial judge was entitled to and should reject Maxwell's plea. Justice McInerney's acceptance of the prosecution stance was upheld by the New South Wales (NSW) Court of Criminal Appeal.[9] However, in 1996, a majority of the High Court of Australia ruled that Maxwell's judge had exceeded his lawful jurisdiction.

The majority reasons in *Maxwell* were divided between two pairs of judges, neither of whose judgments referred to the other. Justices Dawson and McHugh identified two situations when a trial judge can reject a plea of guilty against the wishes of the parties. First: 'If it appears to the trial judge, for whatever reason, that a plea of guilty is not genuine, he or she must (and it is not a matter of discretion) obtain an unequivocal plea of guilty or direct that a plea of not guilty be entered.'[10] Secondly, 'in an appropriate case a court may need to give effect to its own right to prevent an abuse of its process'.[11] Neither situation applied to Maxwell's plea:

> In this case, McInerney J did not purport to act to save the court from an abuse of its process. He rejected the appellant's plea of guilty in the exercise of a discretion which he believed he had but which, in our view, he did not have.[12]

The other majority pairing, Gaudron and Gummow JJ, having identified the same two situations, observed that:

> [T]he real question is whether, notwithstanding a prosecutor's acceptance of a plea ... a court may either require an accused person to stand trial on the more serious offence charged in the indictment or, if the prosecutor declines to offer evidence, refuse to act on the plea. Framed in that way, the question largely answers itself.[13]

A fifth judge, Toohey J, dissented. The appeal was allowed and McInerney J's order setting aside Maxwell's plea of manslaughter was itself set aside.

(b)   Protecting Prosecutors

A backdrop to *Maxwell*, unstated in the High Court, was public criticism of the prosecutor's initial decision to accept Maxwell's manslaughter plea. The day after the plea was entered, the Shadow Minister for Women's Affairs, speaking in the NSW Parliament, asked the Attorney-General whether he would launch an investigation into both how the prosecution came to accept Maxwell's plea, and whether he would, either directly or by request to the NSW Director of Public Prosecutions (DPP), immediately appeal against the 'manslaughter verdict'.[14] Two days later, Sydney's leading broadsheet newspaper, *The Sydney Morning Herald*, cited Maxwell's case when repeating its call for the abolition of the defence of diminished responsibility, arguing that the defendant's psychiatric state is an issue for the

---

[8] *Maxwell v R* [1996] HCA 46; (1996) 184 CLR 501, 506.
[9] *R v Maxwell* (1994) 34 NSWLR 606.
[10] *Maxwell v R* [1996] HCA 46; (1996) 184 CLR 501, 511.
[11] Ibid 514.
[12] Ibid.
[13] Ibid 533.
[14] NSW Legislative Assembly, *Questions and Answers No 38*, 27 October 1993, [1903]. The questions were answered on 10 March 1994, with the Attorney-General noting that there was no manslaughter verdict and that there would be no immediate investigation given the trial judge's rejection of the plea and the ongoing appeal.

sentencing judge, not the prosecutor or the jury.[15] After another newspaper article suggested that the prosecutor's experts had 'hijacked' the homicide case, a further twist occurred when one of those experts reversed his conclusion that Maxwell's responsibility was diminished by a psychiatric condition, claiming that he had not seen the full brief of evidence.[16]

The High Court's ruling that judges cannot override pleas accepted by the prosecutor would have provoked further public disquiet were it not for the Court's unanimous observation in dicta that the prosecutor may be able to withdraw his acceptance of the plea, even years later, as Maxwell was still awaiting sentencing for manslaughter:

> [I]t is inappropriate to regard the prosecution as bound by its election if the interests of justice require its withdrawal. An accused may with leave withdraw a plea of guilty at any time before sentence or other disposal of the case and there is no reason why the prosecution should be placed in a lesser position with regard to its acceptance of a plea. That means, however, that before the prosecution may withdraw its acceptance it must obtain the leave of the court.[17]

When Maxwell's sentencing hearing resumed before a new trial judge almost two years after it began, a new prosecutor immediately asked for leave to withdraw the earlier acceptance of Maxwell's manslaughter plea.

We return to the Maxwell saga shortly. First, some observations on the High Court's stance are in order. A common thread links the Court's twin holdings that a prosecutor generally can, and a court generally cannot, override an earlier acceptance of a plea: the limits on judicial review of prosecutorial discretion. Justices Dawson and McHugh observed:

> The decision whether to charge a lesser offence, or to accept a plea of guilty to a lesser offence than that charged, is for the prosecution and does not require the approval of the court. Indeed, the court would seldom have the knowledge of the strengths and weaknesses of the case on each side which is necessary for the proper exercise of such a function. The role of the prosecution in this respect, as in many others, 'is such that it cannot be shared with the trial judge without placing in jeopardy the essential independence of that office in the adversary system'.[18]

The distance between courts and prosecutors, both in their institutional function and the information they have access to, are familiar rationales for not interfering in charging choices. The rationales are very strong, but not absolute: courts 'seldom' know enough to interfere, and their interference would place prosecutorial independence 'in jeopardy'. Thus, in Canada, where the Supreme Court recently reaffirmed the rationales, a 'deferential' standard of review was propounded, triggered by egregious and seriously threatening choices by the prosecutor.[19] By contrast, Gaudron and Gummow JJ expressed the position in terms of an absolute ban:

> It ought now to be accepted, in our view, that certain decisions involved in the prosecution process are, of their nature, insusceptible of judicial review. They include decisions whether or not to prosecute, to enter a nolle prosequi, to proceed ex officio, whether or not to present evidence and, which is usually an aspect of one or other of those decisions, decisions as to the particular charge to be laid or prosecuted.[20]

---

[15] 'Murder, not Manslaughter', *The Sydney Morning Herald*, 29 October 1993, 4.

[16] The (unidentified) article is discussed in *R v BWM* (1997) 91 A Crim R 260, 262.

[17] *Maxwell v R* [1996] HCA 46; (1996) 184 CLR 501, 515 (Dawson and McHugh JJ), see also 536 (Gaudron and Gummow JJ).

[18] *Maxwell v R* [1996] HCA 46; (1996) 184 CLR 501, 513, quoting *R v Apostilides* (1984) 154 CLR 563, 575.

[19] *R v Anderson* [2014] SCC 41, [50].

[20] *Maxwell v R* [1996] HCA 46; (1996) 184 CLR 501, 534.

As Australia's current Chief Justice has observed, absolute prohibitions on judicial review sit poorly with contemporary Australian constitutional principles:

> [T]he existence of the jurisdiction conferred upon this Court by s 75(v) of the Constitution in rela- tion to jurisdictional error by Commonwealth officers and the constitutionally-protected super- visory role of the Supreme Courts of the States raise the question whether there is any statutory power or discretion of which it can be said that, as a matter of principle, it is insusceptible of judicial review.[21]

Moreover, an absolute prohibition on judicial review of prosecutorial decision-making is at odds with other common law nations. As French CJ observed in 2003 in his previous role as a judge in Fiji:

> The court was helpfully referred, by counsel for the DPP, to a large number of cases in a variety of jurisdictions including New Zealand, Australia, the United Kingdom, Canada, Northern Ire- land, the United States, Hong Kong, Samoa, Guyana, Barbados and the European Court of Human Rights. Apart from an obiter statement by Gaudron and Gummow JJ in *Maxwell v R* ..., there is now little or no support for the proposition that such decisions are completely beyond the reach of judicial review albeit the occasions on which it may successfully be invoked are likely to be rare because of the width of the power and the mix of factors that may legitimately be taken into account in its exercise.[22]

These observations were later endorsed by the Privy Council, disapproving a decision of the Supreme Court of Mauritius that relied on *Maxwell* to rule that a decision to enter a *nolle prosequi* could not be judicially reviewed.[23]

Despite Australian state governments' occasional claims that *Maxwell* confers 'prosecuto- rial immunity',[24] subsequent events in Maxwell's case itself make it clear that the judgment does not bar adverse court findings about prosecutors' charging choices. When Maxwell appealed against his new trial judge's decision to allow the prosecution to withdraw its plea agreement, Hunt CJ at Common Law (CL) bluntly observed:

> The Crown prosecutor did not give evidence before the judge, so I have no explanation from him, but I am bound to say that, upon the material which was placed before the judge, the Crown pros- ecutor made a complete botch of the whole thing.[25]

This was no gratuitous criticism, but rather a key step in the Court of Criminal Appeal's own rationale for dismissing Maxwell's appeal, applying the High Court's test for judicial leave for a prosecutor to withdraw an acceptance of a plea. Hunt CJ at CL continued:

> If, as I would find, the Crown prosecutor simply made a complete botch of the whole thing but subsequently realised his error (whether or not as a result of the criticisms expressed by McInerney J), it was still in the interests of justice that the disputed but unresolved issues of fact which bear directly upon the applicant's guilt or otherwise of the murder charged be resolved.

---

[21] *Likiardopoulos v R* [2012] HCA 37; (2012) 291 ALR 1, [4].

[22] *Matalulu v DPP* [2003] FJSC 2; [2003] 4 LRC 712.

[23] *Mohit v DPP (Mauritius)* [2006] UKPC 20; [2006] 1 WLR 3343, [21].

[24] Attorney-General (Victoria), Second Respondent's Supplementary Written Submissions, (*Momcilovic v R*, M134/2010, High Court of Australia), 3 March 2011, www.hcourt.gov.au/assets/cases/m134-2010/Momcilovic_ Res2-Supp.pdf (accessed 18 January 2016) [20]. See also https://globalliberalmediaplease.net/files/policesupreme- submissions20121.pdf, 9, [28](a), where Victoria police cite *Maxwell* as authority for a 'prosecutorial immunity that prevents [defendants] from having the Informant's decision to proceed with the more serious charges reviewed'.

[25] *BWM* (1997) 91 A Crim R 260, 268.

As I said earlier, it would not be acceptable to the community on behalf of which the Crown prosecutes that a person charged with murder should be sentenced only for the substantially less serious
offence of manslaughter where those issues remain unresolved. Only in that way can the interests
of justice be served.[26]

So, *Maxwell* does not insulate prosecutors from judicial scrutiny of their discretionary
decision-making. Rather, as we now discuss, the purpose behind *Maxwell* is not to protect
prosecutors, but rather to protect judges.

(c) Protecting Judges

Despite Gaudron and Gummow JJ's confidence that the question of judicial authority to
reject prosecutorial plea decisions 'largely answers itself', the nine judges who considered
this question at all levels of the *Maxwell* proceedings split five–four on this issue, with the
High Court majority in the minority of a simple judicial head-count. The three judges
comprising NSW's Court of Criminal Appeal, as well as Toohey J dissenting in the High
Court, endorsed McInerney J's intervention, citing a Canadian decision, *R v Naraindeen*,[27]
in which such interventions were regarded as an appropriate, perhaps even necessary, part
of the judicial function.

These were the facts of *Naraindeen*. In the early morning of 21 April 1989, Toronto police
attended an apartment from which an ambulance had taken Ambrose Vereen to hospital
with a cut on his face. The apartment's owner, Naraindeen, readily admitted that he had
slashed Vereen with a steak knife after an argument about the latter's dancing. At his trial
in Ontario's provincial court later that year, the unrepresented accused indicated that he
wanted 'to plead not guilty to the charge of assault involving a weapon, but guilty to the
charge of simple assault'. After presenting the facts, the prosecutor indicated that he 'consented to the plea'. The transcript records the following comments from the trial judge:

> Let me see the information, please? I don't see, on those facts, how I can possibly find him not guilty
> of assault, of the charge of committing an assault using a weapon while committing an assault.
> I mean it's plain. How can I possibly find him guilty of a lesser offence?

After speaking with the defendant, the prosecutor advised the court that there would be
no guilty plea to the more serious offence. The trial judge then tried and convicted him of
assault involving a weapon, and the accused appealed.

The Ontario Court of Appeal reviewed English and Canadian practice on entering alternative pleas, observing that statutory provisions permitting the defendant to enter a plea
to a lesser included offence were introduced to avoid moot trials. The Court concluded
that 'the acceptance of the plea was not simply a matter for the accused and counsel for the
prosecution', but rather necessarily required some judicial involvement:

> [T]he prosecutor has primary responsibility for the enforcement of the criminal law ... This
> responsibility carries with it the power to decide whether or not to charge an accused and what
> charge or charges to lay. It includes the power to withdraw charges before the commencement
> of the trial. However, once the prosecutor has seen fit to bring the proceeding before a court, the

---

[26] Ibid.
[27] *R v Naraindeen*, 1990 CanLII 6731; 75 OR (2d) 120; 80 CR (3d) 66; 40 OAC 291.

accused has pleaded, and what is sought involves something more than merely not proceeding with a charge but, rather, the acquittal of the accused on the charge that brought him or her before the court, the court has a legitimate role to play in the decision made. The court is not gratuitously interfering with a prosecutorial decision. The prosecutor has ample and unfettered scope, short of asking the court to acquit on the charge before the court, to enforce the criminal law as he or she sees fit and to decide what charges will be prosecuted.[28]

The Court rejected an argument that such a judicial role would be contrary to the defendant's right to a fair hearing before an independent and impartial court under Canada's *Charter of Rights and Freedoms*.

The High Court majority in *Maxwell* distinguished *Naraindeen* in two ways. First, they noted that the relevant statutory provisions governing pleas to lesser offences were materially different; Canada's provision empowered 'the court … with the consent of the prosecutor' to accept a lesser plea, whereas the relevant NSW provisions empowered 'the Crown … [to] elect to accept such plea of guilty'.[29] Secondly, Dawson and McHugh JJ observed that the English practice relied upon by the Canadian court had apparently narrowed in recent years. They relied entirely on a remark made in a ground-breaking 1986 report by a committee led by Farquharson LJ into the role and responsibilities of the prosecutor advocate:

> In accepting a plea of guilty to a lesser offence or offences Counsel for the Prosecution is in reality making a decision to offer no evidence on a particular charge. It follows in our opinion that if Counsel is entitled to decide whether he should offer no evidence on the Indictment as a whole, as we think he is, then correspondingly, it must be for him to decide whether or not to proceed on a particular count in an Indictment.[30]

However, while this supports the view that judicial involvement in prosecutorial decision-making is not *required* to preserve judicial integrity, it does not support Gaudron and Gummow JJ's stronger claim that judicial involvement would compromise that integrity. Indeed, Dawson and McHugh JJ grudgingly conceded that judicial commentary was permitted.[31]

As the NSW Court of Criminal Appeal observed in *Maxwell*, the Farquharson Committee's remark was expressly qualified in the following terms:

(a) It is sometimes the practice when Prosecution Counsel decides to accept a plea to a lesser count for him to invite the approval of the Judge. Counsel may feel it appropriate to do so in cases where it is desirable to reassure the public at large that the course proposed is being properly taken, or when he has been unable to reach agreement with his Instructing Solicitor. As we have already said, Counsel is not bound to invite the Judge's approval but if he does so, then he must of course abide by the Judge's decision …

---

[28] Ibid [22].

[29] *Maxwell v R* [1996] HCA 46; (1996) 184 CLR 501, 513 (Dawson and McHugh JJ). See also 533 (Gaudron and Gummow JJ), contrasting Crimes Act 1900 (NSW), s 394A ('the Crown may elect to accept such plea of guilty') with *Criminal Code* (Can), s 606(4) ('the court may, with the consent of the prosecutor, accept that plea of guilty').

[30] Cited in *Maxwell v R* [1996] HCA 46; (1996) 184 CLR 501, 512. The guidelines were published in J Archbold, *Pleading, Evidence and Practice in Criminal Cases*, 43rd edn (London, Sweet & Maxwell, 1988) 336–42. Now see www.cps.gov.uk/publications/prosecution/farqbooklet.html (accessed 5 August 2015).

[31] *Maxwell v R* [1996] HCA 46; (1996) 184 CLR 501, 514: 'No doubt a court may, if it thinks it desirable to do so, express its view upon the appropriateness of a charge or the acceptance of a plea and no doubt its view will be accorded great weight. But if a court does express such a view, it should recognise that in doing so it is doing no more than attempting to influence the exercise of a discretion which is not any part of its own function and that it may be speaking in ignorance of matters which have properly motivated the decision of the prosecuting authority.'

(b)   … The Judge may take the view that Counsel's decision proceeds from caprice or incompe-tence, or simply that he entirely disagrees with the decision however carefully Counsel has arrived at it. The Judge cannot in such circumstances be expected to lend himself to a process which in his judgment amounts to an abuse or to injustice. While for the reasons already given the Judge cannot insist on Prosecution Counsel proceeding on the major charge he may decline to proceed with the case without Counsel first consulting with the Director of Public Prosecutions, on whether he should proceed in the light of the comments the Judge will have made. In an extreme case he may think it right to invite Counsel to seek the advice of the Attorney General …

(c)   Sometimes a decision has to be made to offer no evidence during the course of the trial; and similarly pleas of guilty may be tendered to lesser counts. While the Prosecution case is being presented the decision as to what course to take in these circumstances remains with Counsel.[32]

The NSW Chief Justice Murray Gleeson observed that, despite the different statutory word-ing, 'the consideration which so influenced the court in *Naraindeen* is present. What is involved is not only a conviction of the lesser charge but also an acquittal of the more seri-ous charge.'[33] Gleeson CJ, subsequently to become Chief Justice of Australia's apex High Court, concluded:

> Questions of this kind … arise at the margin between executive and judicial power. They are ordi-narily resolved in a practical way. However, there are occasions, such as the present, when it is necessary to mark out the limits of the powers, duties and authorities of the participants in the trial process.[34]

In short, as a counterpoint to Gaudron and Gummow JJ's supposedly self-answering ques-tion, the view in NSW, Canada and England was that the question was a 'practical' one that the various institutions involved would need to answer together to meet the requirements of particular cases.

The High Court majority neglected to consider the qualifications to the Farquharson guidelines, and its reasons for deviating from a more pragmatic, context-sensitive approach must remain a matter of speculation. It is probable, though, that what troubled the majority of the High Court was a prospect acknowledged (theoretically, anyway) in England, Canada and NSW, namely that the judge's inability to require the prosecution to proceed on a more serious charge—much less adduce evidence in support of it—'may, at least in theory, give rise to the possibility of something in the nature of a stalemate.'[35] The majority would surely have been underwhelmed by the Farquharson Committee's recourse to institutional pros-ecutorial arrangements to break this stalemate:

> In the final analysis, when these steps have been taken, the Judge has no power to prevent Counsel proceeding. Indeed any attempt by him to do so would give the impression that he was stepping

---

[32]   Cited in *R v Maxwell* (1994) 34 NSWLR 606, 610–11. The present guidelines (www.cps.gov.uk/publications/prosecution/farqbooklet.html (accessed 18 January 2016)) provide that: 'If Prosecution Counsel does not invite the Judge's approval of his decision … the final decision remains with Counsel.' However, '[i]n an extreme case where the Judge is of the opinion that the course proposed by Counsel would lead to serious injustice, he may decline to proceed with the case until Counsel has consulted with either the Director or the Attorney General as may be appropriate' and '[i]f Prosecution Counsel invites the Judge to approve the course he is proposing to take, then he must abide by the Judge's decision'.

[33]   *R v Maxwell* (1994) 34 NSWLR 606, 614.

[34]   Ibid 608–609.

[35]   *R v Maxwell* (1994) 34 NSWLR 606, 612 (Gleeson CJ). See also *R v Brown* (1989) 17 NSWLR 472.

into the arena and pressing the Prosecution case. However, we are of the opinion that the occasions when Counsel felt it right to resist the Judge's views would be rare.[36]

Whereas Gleeson CJ's proposed 'political resolution' might have been positively alarming:

If, notwithstanding McInerney J's rejection of the plea of guilty, the Crown had declined to lead any evidence against the appellant on the murder charge, then there was nothing that McInerney J could do to force the Crown to lead such evidence. What would have arisen was what was described earlier in these reasons as a stalemate; a collision between the executive and the judicial branches of government that might, if necessary, have required a political resolution. In the last resort, it may only be the responsibility of the Attorney-General to Parliament and the electorate that could break such a deadlock.[37]

Be that as it may, the puzzle remains why the *Maxwell* majority was concerned about judicial integrity in that case, where ultimately the prosecutor was more than willing to proceed with a more serious charge.

(d) Protecting Judgment

When Maxwell was finally tried for murder, events in his case took their strangest turn. No doubt aware of the publicity his case had received, Maxwell opted to be tried without a jury by a third trial judge (who, unlike the first two, had not expressed any view on the prosecutor's initial decision to accept the manslaughter plea). That new judge, Justice Bruce, took an unprecedented ten months to hand down his verdict of guilty of murder. This sparked further public controversy. It emerged that, while deliberating on Maxwell's plea of diminished responsibility, Bruce J was himself under investigation for a pattern of excessively delayed judgments, which he attributed to a depressive illness. Although the judge avoided the unprecedented event of dismissal for incapacity by the NSW Parliament,[38] the Court of Criminal Appeal held that his condition was too closely linked to Maxwell's defence of diminished responsibility to be compatible with the requirements of impartial adjudication:

During the period of time in which Justice Bruce was composing his judgment in this matter the proposition that a medical condition of depression had a significant effect on a person's capacity to perform his employment functions in an efficient and orderly manner was of critical personal significance to him. That same proposition was also at the heart of one of the disputes between the medical experts in these proceedings.[39]

The Court allowed Maxwell's appeal against conviction, concluding that 'both the accused and an informed independent observer, acting reasonably, could form the opinion that his Honour might not bring an impartial and unprejudiced mind to the resolution of the issues in the case'.[40]

---

[36] Cited in *R v Maxwell* (1994) 34 NSWLR 606, 611.
[37] *R v Maxwell* (1994) 34 NSWLR 606, 615.
[38] www.parliament.nsw.gov.au/Prod/parlment/hansart.nsf/V3Key/LC19980527008 (accessed 16 January 2016).
[39] *R v Maxwell* (1998) 217 ALR 452, 472.
[40] Ibid.

This was a rare instance of a finding of apprehended judicial bias in criminal proceedings. According to Gaudron and Gummow JJ, interventions into prosecutorial discretion, such as McInerney J's in the first trial phase, also threaten a criminal court's impartiality:

> [I]t may be that the impartiality of the judicial process is brought more directly into question by a decision at the behest or with the consent of a prosecutor that a plea previously accepted by the prosecutor should be rejected.[41]

The risk of bias arising from judicial involvement in prosecutorial decision-making is illustrated by Naraindeen's case, where the trial judge proceeded to try the indictment that his own ruling had obliged the prosecutor not to abandon. On appeal, the accused complained that the trial judge told the prosecutor that there was no need to call evidence of the knife as Vereen 'didn't get a cut on the side of his face from wishful thinking', barred the defendant from detailing Vereen's alleged assault on him and presumed in his reasons for judgment and sentence that the knife caused Vereen's scar (despite evidence to the contrary). The Ontario Court of Appeal held that the judge's remarks reflected both impatience and error, but dismissed the appeal because none of these evidential matters affected Naraindeen's guilt of the offence of assault with a weapon.

The problem of possible bias may be ameliorated by having any trial of a case where a judge has overruled a prosecutor's charging choice heard before a new judge. That is what happened in Maxwell's case, both at the hearing into whether the prosecutor's acceptance of the plea could be withdrawn, and at Maxwell's eventual trial for murder.[42] However, this solution will not preclude the possibility that repeated judicial criticism of prosecutors may leave the entire court system with a diminished capacity to secure a fair hearing for the accused. This further problem is coincidentally illustrated by the next set of events in Maxwell's tortured prosecution.

At Maxwell's second and final trial in 1999, Grove J, his fourth trial judge, commenced the reasons for his verdict by questioning a further agreement struck between the prosecutor and Maxwell's legal advisors, presumably to manage the potential forensic fallout from the adverse publicity that his case had attracted:

> [T]he hearing proceeded before me without a jury pursuant to s 32 of the *Criminal Procedure Act 1986*. The parties waived the rules of evidence pursuant to s 190 of the *Evidence Act 1995*. In the result, a substantial part of the trial was conducted by tender of statements by witnesses accompanied by transcripts of testimony given before Bruce J ... It is a disturbing observation that an accused citizen is potentially liable to the maximum available penalty known to our law upon judicial decision without any contribution to the finding of guilt by a jury of his peers and after a trial significantly conducted 'on paper'. I strongly urge the legislature to consider exempting crimes of the magnitude of murder from s 32 of the *Criminal Procedure Act* or at least restoring to the courts a power to insist upon trial by jury irrespective of any concert between an accused and the Director of Public Prosecutions avoiding it.[43]

---

[41] *Maxwell v R* [1996] HCA 46; (1996) 184 CLR 501, 535.

[42] Bruce J (and later Grove J) heard the trial; Adams AJ gave the prosecutor leave to vacate the earlier plea agreement; and McInerney J was the originally appointed judge.

[43] *R v Maxwell* [1999] NSWSC 1085, [5], [7]. The references to s 32 of the Criminal Procedure Act 1986 appear to be erroneous references to s 132 of the same statute.

As with the decision to plead guilty to a lesser offence, NSW law permitted Grove J to reject the agreement for a trial without jury only on limited grounds, none of which applied in Maxwell's case.[44] Justice Grove proceeded to convict Maxwell of murder.[45]

(e) Maxwell's Punishment

After Maxwell's conviction, Grove J's—and the NSW judiciary's—conflict with the prosecution was over. The prosecutor did not request a particular sentence.[46] And yet, Grove J still felt compelled by the earlier events to give Maxwell a lower sentence than would otherwise have been imposed. Justice Bruce, the only one of Maxwell's trial judges who did not express his disagreement with prosecutorial decision-making in this case, had originally sentenced Maxwell to 16 years' imprisonment, citing McInerney J's delays and Maxwell's own depression. Despite scepticism on both grounds, Grove J accepted the defence's submission that Maxwell's sentence should not exceed the penalty he would have received if his earlier conviction had not been quashed due to the sentencing judge's own tardiness and depression.[47]

Justice Grove's predicament was, of course, the product of the whole convoluted course of Maxwell's prosecution and, anyway, as the Court of Criminal Appeal observed, Grove J 'was not obliged' to follow convention.[48] But the issue is one of general principle. The prospect of a trial judge being forced to issue a sentence he disagreed with was central to the earlier dispute between McInerney J and the original prosecutor. Justice Toohey's dissent in the High Court appeal focused on the sentencing problems that flow from a dispute between judge and prosecutor. In particular, Toohey J endorsed the following remark by Gleeson CJ in the lower court:

> As a matter of principle, I regard as unacceptable a conclusion that a judge can be forced to sentence an offender on a factual basis which the judge cannot conscientiously accept. The present case provides a good example of the problem … McInerney J has made clear his opinion that, consistently with his judicial duty, he cannot (on the present state of the evidence) deal with this as a case of diminished responsibility. It would be otherwise, of course, if the matter had gone to a jury and the plea of diminished responsibility had the support of a jury's verdict. Judges do not have to agree with the verdict of a jury before they can conscientiously sentence an offender.[49]

---

[44] Criminal Procedure Act 1986 (NSW), s 132(2) provides: 'The court must make a trial by judge order if both the accused person and the prosecutor agree to the accused person being tried by a Judge alone.' This is subject only to s 132(5), which requires that the court is 'satisfied that the accused person has sought and received advice in relation to the effect of such an order from an Australian legal practitioner'. By contrast, Grove J did have a discretion to reject the parties' agreement to dispense with the hearsay rule so as to allow the trial to occur on the papers—see Evidence Act 1995 (NSW), s 190(1)—but apparently declined to exercise that discretion.

[45] *R v Maxwell* [1999] NSWSC 1085, [86].

[46] Prosecutorial restraint in this regard was subsequently endorsed by the High Court in *Barbaro v R; Zirilli v R* [2014] HCA 2; (2014) 253 CLR 58. See Cowdery's discussion of this case in Chapter 5.

[47] *R v Maxwell* [2001] NSWCCA 362, [53]–[55]. As a result, Maxwell became eligible for parole in 2002 shortly after the High Court (including one of the authors of the *Maxwell* dictum) rejected his final attempt to overturn his murder conviction: *Maxwell v R* [2002] HCATrans 308.

[48] *R v Maxwell* [2001] NSWCCA 362, [53].

[49] *R v Maxwell* (1994) 34 NSWLR 606, 612, endorsed at *Maxwell v R* (1996) 184 CLR 501, 524.

However, the majority rejected Toohey J's argument that binding judges to prosecutorial charging choices was quite different to binding them to the jury's verdict. Justices Gaurdon and Gummow expressly declined to draw any such distinction:

> [I]t was not open to McInerney J to reject the appellant's plea of guilty to manslaughter on the grounds suggested by the Court of Criminal Appeal, namely that it required him to sentence the appellant on a basis which he could not conscientiously accept. That, too, involves a review of the prosecutor's decision.[50]

According to Justices Dawson and McHugh, the correct approach was dictated by a 1981 High Court precedent:

> In *R v De Simoni* Gibbs CJ pointed out that a sentencing judge may be required by reason of the charge selected by the prosecution to take an artificially restricted view of the facts. He said:
>
> > This will be so also in cases where the jury's verdict is inconsistent with the view of the facts that the judge himself has formed, for the judge cannot act on a view of the facts which conflicts with the jury's verdict. However, where the Crown has charged the offender with, or has accepted a plea of guilty to, an offence less serious than the facts warrant, it cannot rely, or ask the judge to rely, on the facts that would have rendered the offender liable to a more serious penalty.[51]

In *De Simoni*,[52] the Court ruled that, because the prosecutor had charged the defendant with simple robbery, rather than the aggravated offence of robbery causing grievous bodily harm, the sentencing judge was precluded from taking account of the victim's serious injuries. The Court drew on a pattern of holdings in Australia, England and New Zealand,[53] to rule that sentencing judges' obligation to constrain their sentencing fact-finding consistently with the verdict before them extends not only to consistency with jury verdicts, but also to consistency with prosecutorial charging decisions. In particular, Australian sentencing judges must not find facts that amount to more serious charges than the one brought by the prosecutor, a rule now repeatedly referenced as the principle (or rule) in *De Simoni*.

The *De Simoni* principle supplies the final justification for the *Maxwell* holding, but also exposes the power it affords to prosecutors and the costs it imposes on courts. Any charging decision by a prosecutor is more than just a choice in favour of one charge. It is also a choice against bringing all other charges, including aggravated offences, that could have been prosecuted on the evidence. Prosecutorial decision-making effectively constrains the judicial role to this extent. Section 2 of this chapter will explore the context of overlapping charges in more detail. It will explain how this broader context, exemplified by overlapping sexual offences, has challenged the policy of non-interference by judges in prosecutorial charging choices.

---

[50] *Maxwell v R* (1996) 184 CLR 501, 536.
[51] Ibid 514–15.
[52] *R v De Simoni* [1981] HCA 31; (1981) 147 CLR 383, 389, 395 (Gibbs CJ, Mason J and Murphy J agreeing).
[53] Including *R v Bright* [1916] 2 KB 441; *R v Martini* [1941] NZLR 361; and *Lovegrove v R* [1961] Tas SR 106.

2. Integrity in Judicial Control

(a) Limiting the Scope of Criminal Offences

At an English criminal trial in the Chester Summer Assizes in 1884, 11-year-old Ann Smith was asked whether she had consented to sex with the accused. She gave the reply that counsel wanted and the jury accepted: she did not. Surprisingly, the question was put by defence counsel, who argued that her answer meant that the prosecutor had erred in charging William Neale with the misdemeanour of carnal knowledge of a girl under 12, rather than the felony of rape. While Neale's argument was rejected by his trial judge, and by the Court for Crown Cases Reserved,[54] a similar argument succeeded in Australia's High Court nearly 150 years later. As we now discuss, the law of overlapping sexual offences has proved to be a fertile ground for Australian and other courts to find reasons to become closely 'concerned with decisions as to who is prosecuted and for what'.

In 1989, a jury found that Akhandananda Saraswati, the leader of the Satyanandra Ashram in Mangrove Mountain, NSW, had abused a teenage resident by touching her breasts, buttocks and vagina, and having sex with her.[55] Saraswati's alleged abuse had occurred in 1983 when the complainant was aged 15. While this alleged conduct is easily recognisable as the child sexual offences of indecent assault and carnal knowledge,[56] the prosecution had instead charged Saraswati with the newer and lesser offence of an 'act of indecency', pursuant to what was then section 61E(2) of the Crimes Act 1900 (NSW).[57] This time, the prosecutor's choice to bring a less serious charge was criticised, not by the trial judge or the media, but by the defendant. The reason is that the more serious charges were barred by statute where the alleged victim was aged 14 or over and the alleged incident occurred 12 months or more before charges were laid.[58] Saraswati's case raised the question whether a long-standing statutory bar on delayed prosecutions of carnal knowledge or indecent assault involving older children could be outflanked by the later introduction of a broader offence, not covered by the bar.

The NSW Court of Criminal Appeal regarded the prosecutor's decision as unexceptional:

> The prosecutorial discretion extends to the formulation of a less serious charge upon which a conviction is certain rather than running the risk of alleging a more serious offence which the facts ultimately may not sustain. Thus, the Crown may charge manslaughter although an arguable case of murder exists; might charge, in respect of a girl under age, carnal knowledge rather than risk litigating the issue of consent; may charge common assault rather than assault occasioning actual bodily harm, etc. … Similarly, the Crown, having charged a more serious offence, retains the discretion to accept a plea to a lesser offence. Such is the practice.[59]

---

[54] *R v Neale* (1844) 1 Car & K 591, 174 ER 591.

[55] *R v Saraswati* (1989) 18 NSWLR 143.

[56] Crimes Act 1900 (NSW), ss 61E(1), 71 ('sexual assault category 4—indecent assault', 'carnally knowing girl between 10 and 16'), repealed respectively in 1989 and 1985.

[57] 'Sexual assault category 4—act of indecency', repealed in 1989.

[58] Crimes Act 1900 (NSW), s 78, applying to ss 61E(1), 71 and 72 (attempted unlawful carnal knowledge), where the alleged victim is aged between 14 and 16, repealed in 1992.

[59] *R v Saraswati* (1989) 18 NSWLR 143, 157.

The appeal court accordingly rejected Saraswati's argument that the 'act of indecency' offence should be construed as not extending to incidents already covered by the statute-barred offences:

> [I]f the proper construction of the provisions is that conduct which amounts to indecent assault or carnal knowledge can in no case support a conviction for act of indecency, the construction for which the appellant contends, the same construction would necessarily apply in circumstances where the statutory time-limit had not been exceeded. The consequence would be to deprive the Crown of its ordinary discretion to charge a lesser rather than a greater offence or, having charged the greater offence, to accept a plea to the lesser.[60]

However, a majority of the High Court took a different view. They did so just five years before a differently constituted majority in *Maxwell* ruled that trial judges could not (but prosecutors could) reverse an acceptance of a plea to a lesser charge.[61] True, *Saraswati* was concerned with judicial interpretation of a statute defining a crime, whereas *Maxwell* directly addressed the scope of judicial scrutiny of a prosecutor's charging decisions. However, the interpretation adopted in Saraswati's case was also expressly designed to limit prosecutorial choices.[62]

Justice Gaudron, a member of the *Saraswati* majority and later a co-author of the *Maxwell* holding, stressed that an approach limiting prosecutorial options was forced on her by the rules of statutory interpretation:

> It is a basic rule of construction that, in the absence of express words, an earlier statutory provision is not repealed, altered or derogated from by a later provision unless an intention to that effect is necessarily to be implied.[63]

Yet as Deane and Dawson JJ observed in dissent, Parliament's intentions in this case were a puzzle:

> One can only speculate about the rationale of that legislative intent. Perhaps it was simply that the offence of an 'act of indecency' is a less serious one. Perhaps it was that an 'act of indecency' is a comprehensive offence which does not involve the same degree of detailed particularisation as do the more serious offences of indecent assault, attempted carnal knowledge and carnal knowledge and that, for that reason, the recollection and evidence of the alleged victim may be less reliable in the case of the more serious offences. However, if considerations relating to the reliability of evidence underlay the legislative policy to be discerned in s 78, it is difficult to understand why the time limit is imposed in the case of the more serious offences only in a case where the alleged victim has reached fourteen years of age.[64]

While the dissentients read the ambiguity in legislative intent as offering prosecutors a choice between overlapping offences, Gaudron J saw it as mandating a construction that limited

---

[60]   Ibid 169.

[61]   *Saraswati v R* (1991) 172 CLR 1 (Toohey, Gaudron and McHugh JJ; Deane and Dawson JJ dissenting).

[62]   For a Canadian decision deprecating such an interpretative approach for a different pair of offences, see *R v Verrette* [1978] 2 SCR 838, 850. There, the Canadian Supreme Court criticised a lower court's reading of an 'indecency' requirement into the national ban on public nudity in order to remove prosecutors' 'temptation' (*R v McCutcheon* [1977] CA 103; 1 CR (3d) 39, 50 (Owen JA)) to invoke the ban in performance cases in order to avoid a similar requirement in an offence covering immoral entertainment: 'With deference, I do not think that we should endeavour to construe the Criminal Code so as to make the task of the prosecution easier or more difficult. The selection of the charges is entirely a matter for the Crown.' Cf *R v Quon* [1948] SCR 508.

[63]   *Saraswati v R* (1991) 172 CLR 1, 17.

[64]   Ibid 7.

prosecutorial choice by removing the overlap. The other two members of the *Saraswati* majority[65] stressed that any such construction of the offence provisions must not frustrate Parliament's purposes in enacting the lesser offence. In particular, McHugh J argued that the expression 'act of indecency' (unlike the clear words of the statutory bar) was malleable; while touching someone's breasts and buttocks, not to mention sex, are unambiguously 'acts' of 'indecency' in ordinary language, the offence's legislative history indicated that the words were directed at sexual conduct with children that did not involve contact with the child's body.[66] Acknowledging that removing the area of overlap between these sexual offences could have some surprising consequences—for instance, people accused of acts of indecency might defend themselves by leading evidence that they actually assaulted or had sex with a child—McHugh J noted that these dilemmas were simply a product of the fluid boundaries of sexual contact, which had long raised dilemmas for framing charges and applying the rule against double jeopardy.[67] Unlike the alternatives of rape and carnal knowledge addressed 150 years earlier in *Neale*, the offence of act of indecency was not introduced to free prosecutors from the burdens of proving what happened between an adult and a child, but rather to extend the law to encompass newly recognised types of child abuse.[68]

(b) Limiting Prosecutors

During the following decade, senior judges in the UK seemingly expressed some envy of their Australian counterparts, noting that *Saraswati* 'concerned the construction of [what] appears to have been a codifying Act susceptible of harmonious construction as a whole, rather than a consolidating Act of the "rag bag" nature'[69] of the Sexual Offences Act 1956. Michael Jones was accused of repeated sex with the 13-year-old daughter of his landlord and family friend, but was charged and convicted only with indecent assault in order to evade a statutory time limit on the more serious charges. On appeal to the House of Lords, Baroness Hale observed that the English statute, 'was a mess when it was enacted and became an ever greater mess with later amendments'.[70]

> It is not possible to discern within it such a coherent parliamentary intention as to require it to be construed so as to forbid prosecution for a 'mere' act of sexual intercourse after 12 months where that act properly falls within the definition of an indecent assault. Although we do have to try to make sense of the words Parliament has used, we do not have to supply Parliament with the thinking that it never did and words that it never used.[71]

Nevertheless, prior to the comprehensive reforms introduced by the Sexual Offences Act 2003, England's judges were repeatedly asked to—and did—supply the thinking that Parliament neglected. For example, in two cases in 2000 and 2001, the Law Lords plugged one

---

[65] McHugh J, with Toohey J agreeing (although the pair would later disagree in *Maxwell*).
[66] *Saraswati v R* (1991) 172 CLR 1, 27.
[67] Ibid.
[68] Ibid 26.
[69] *R v Jones* [2002] EWCA Crim 2983; [2003] 1 WLR 1590, [20] (Potter LJ).
[70] *R v J* [2004] UKHL 42; [2005] 1 AC 562, [89].
[71] Ibid.

gap in the 1956 legislation by reading a *mens rea* requirement into the offences of indecent assault and indecency with children, relying on the general principle of statutory interpretation that moral culpability is a precondition of (*malum in se*) criminal liability.[72] However, this creative approach was less readily available in Jones' 2004 appeal.

In contrast to the statutory bar considered in *Saraswati*, the English statutory time limit was limited to underage 'sexual intercourse',[73] which courts (like some US presidents) struggle to clearly distinguish from other sexual contact. Because the Australian solution of removing the overlap between offence provisions was not viable, Lord Steyn framed the dilemma as one of resolving conflicting institutional roles:

> In our system of government Parliament has the primary responsibility for the bulk of the criminal law which is statute based. The role of the courts is to interpret and apply statutes. The courts must loyally give effect to the statutes as enacted by Parliament. The judiciary may not render a statutory provision, such as a time limit, nugatory on the ground that it disagrees with the reason underlying it. The CPS as an independent law enforcement agency carry out duties of a public character. It must act fairly and within the law. It must observe statute law as Parliament framed it. In our parliamentary democracy nobody is above the law. The powers of the CPS are extensive but not extensive enough to permit it to take decisions intended to evade the clear intent of Parliament.[74]

The remaining members of the majority held that the prosecutor's decision to bring a lesser charge 'cut across the intention of Parliament'.[75] This juxtaposition of prosecutorial discretion and parliamentary intention is in stark contrast to the *Maxwell* dictum of judicial non-involvement in prosecutorial decisions. However, the House of Lords relied on a doctrine that Gaudron and Gummow JJ expressly described as a qualification to their own dictum: 'of necessity, a court always retains power to prevent abuse of its process, including its criminal process'.[76]

The House of Lords held that, even though:

> The present case is not easily accommodated under any of the traditional categories of abuse of process … it is plain as a pike staff that the CPS policy under challenge in the present appeal was intended to circumvent the intent of Parliament in creating a time limit for prosecutions.[77]

The chief difficulty with the abuse of process doctrine, however, is that distinguishing between a legitimate exercise of prosecutorial discretion and its abuse is almost never 'plain as a pike staff'.[78] As Baroness Hale observed in *Jones*, Parliament's purposes in enacting the statutory bar—be they defunct concerns about complaints motivated by unplanned pregnancies, contemporary concerns about fair trials for stale matters or limiting prosecutions to meritorious cases—are all squarely considerations for prosecutors:

> At one extreme will be the teenage romance between a boy and a girl who have since gone their separate ways, where no possible personal or public interest would be served by prosecution. At the

---

[72]   *B v DPP* [2000] UKHL 13, [2000] 2 AC 428; *R v K* [2001] UKHL 41, [2002] 1 AC 462. These offences have all now been superseded by the Sexual Offences Act 2003.

[73]   Sexual Offences Act 1956, s 37(2) and schedule 2, para 10(a).

[74]   *R v J* [2004] UKHL 42; [2005] 1 AC 562, [38].

[75]   Ibid [49].

[76]   *Maxwell v R* (1996) 184 CLR 501, 535.

[77]   *R v J* [2004] UKHL 42; [2005] 1 AC 562, [38] (Lord Steyn; Lords Bingham and Rodger agreeing, ibid [27] and [66]. See also Lord Clyde ibid [49]).

[78]   Also see Whitfort, Chapter 10 in this volume.

other will be prolonged and serious abuse of a position of trust by a person who might well be left to do it again unless action is taken. It will all depend upon the circumstances, in which the interests of the accused, the victim and of society will all play their part. A just and humane prosecution policy should be capable of taking all these factors into account.[79]

Baroness Hale would have dismissed Jones's appeal because the 'balance of interests' in his case supported prosecution.[80]

Tellingly, Gaudron and Gummow JJ's 'abuse of process' qualification in *Maxwell* had its own qualification:

It follows from the nature of a criminal trial, in which the prosecution bears the onus of proving guilt beyond reasonable doubt, that it cannot be an abuse of process to proceed on a lesser charge, whether by acceptance of a plea ... *or otherwise*, merely because there is evidence which, if accepted, would sustain a conviction for a more serious offence.[81]

In the same case, Dawson and McHugh JJ declared that '[a] mere difference of opinion between the court and the prosecuting authority could never give rise to an abuse of process'.[82] The balance of these statements is obviously directed to protecting traditional negotiated plea arrangements from curial intervention.[83] However, Gaudron and Gummow JJ's expansive language covers charging decisions too, which is justifiable in light of the *Maxwell* court's reliance on the principle in *De Simoni*, which equates decisions not to charge with acquittals (including on the basis of lesser pleas), for some purposes.

A year after the *Jones* decision, in *McNeil*,[84] Scotland's High Court of Justiciary was confronted with a different method of circumventing a statutory bar on child sexual offence prosecutions.[85] The Court considered that the bringing of the more serious (and, incidentally, non-statute-barred) charge will sometimes be appropriate, and hence a matter that falls within the legitimate scope of prosecutorial discretion. Starting from first principles:

Where in Scotland the Crown prosecutes on a charge of rape (inevitably on indictment) it is right to assume, in the absence of compelling reasons to the contrary, that it does so on the basis, first, that it has before it information which, in the considered judgment of Crown counsel, supports such a charge and, second, that it is in the public interest to prosecute on that charge.[86]

Interpreting Scottish law on alternative verdicts,[87] the Court held that, after the more serious charge had been preferred and tried, a finding of guilt on the lesser included child sexual offence would be a permissible verdict, notwithstanding the statutory bar to its independent prosecution.[88] Although not addressed by the Court, it is implicit that the lesser conviction may also follow from a guilty plea by the defendant. However, these remarks are subject to the enigmatic qualification that there is an 'absence of compelling reasons' to contradict the Court's implicit trust in the prosecutor's judgement.

---

[79] *R v J* [2004] UKHL 42; [2005] 1 AC 562, [89]–[90].
[80] Ibid [91].
[81] *Maxwell v R* [1996] HCA 46; (1996) 184 CLR 501, 535 (emphasis added).
[82] Ibid 514.
[83] See further, Cowdery, Chapter 5 in this volume.
[84] *McNeil v HM Advocate* 2006 JC 71; [2005] HCJAC 113.
[85] Sexual Offences (Scotland) Act 1976, s 4(1), since repealed.
[86] *McNeil v HM Advocate* 2006 JC 71; [2005] HCJAC 113, [13].
[87] Sexual Offences (Consolidation) (Scotland) Act 1995, s 14, since repealed.
[88] *McNeil v HM Advocate* [2005] ScotHC HCJAC 113, [13].

(c) Limiting Judgments

In the 1998 Australian High Court case of *Pearce*, decided two years after *Maxwell*, Kirby J (who did not sit in the earlier case) observed:

> In the normal case, in accordance with conventions which are ordinarily observed, prosecutors for the Crown can be trusted not to abuse their powers. As a matter of practicality, in most cases, their decisions have a profound effect on the course which the criminal process follows. Prosecutors must therefore be conscious of the vast expansion of statutory offences that has occurred during this century. This development has inevitably presented a risk of overlap and duplication of charges arising out of the same facts and circumstances ...
>
> The multiplication of statutory crimes has necessitated the adoption of rules and practices to avoid outcomes offensive to a sense of justice ... There are very strong inhibitions upon the interference of courts in the exercise of prosecutorial decisions. On the other hand, especially in recent times, judges have been unwilling to surrender entirely to the conscience of a prosecutor the fairness of subjecting an accused to the peril of prosecution and punishment for multiple offences arising out of the same facts and circumstances.[89]

An exemplar of such 'rules and practices' is supplied by a 1974 Canadian case, *R v Kienapple*,[90] in which the accused, John Kienapple, was charged and convicted of both rape and unlawful carnal knowledge of a 13-year-old in relation to a single assault.[91] A majority of the Supreme Court of Canada quashed Kienapple's unlawful carnal knowledge conviction, as amounting to de facto double jeopardy:

> If there is a verdict of guilty on the first count and the same or substantially the same elements make up the offence charged in a second count, the situation invites application of a rule against multiple convictions ... In the circumstances of the present case, the superadded element of age ... does not operate to distinguish unlawful carnal knowledge from rape. Age under fourteen is certainly material where consent to the sexual intercourse is present; but once that is ruled out, as it is in the present case, it becomes meaningless as a distinguishing feature of the offences of rape and unlawful carnal knowledge.[92]

A later Court explained that the 'ban on multiple convictions for the same delict' is triggered when two charges share both a 'factual nexus' (that is, 'the charges are founded upon the same act') and a 'legal nexus', established either by one offence being an aggravated version of the other or (as in *Kienapple* itself) where 'there is no additional and distinguishing element that goes to guilt' separating the two offences.[93] The latter condition is to be assessed by 'ascertaining Parliament's intention in creating different offences', that is, was there 'a legislative intent to increase punishment in the event that two or more offences overlap'?[94]

---

[89] *Pearce v R* [1998] HCA 57; (1998) 194 CLR 610, [95]–[96].
[90] *R v Kienapple* [1975] 1 SCR 729.
[91] The two offences as specified by *Criminal Code* (Can), ss 143 and 146.
[92] *R v Kienapple* [1975] 1 SCR 729, 751, 755 (Laskin J, Judson, Spence, Pigeon and Dickson JJ agreeing). A later decision clarified that trial judges dealing with overlapping convictions should stay one of them until the appeal against the main conviction was finally resolved: *R v Provo* [1989] 2 SCR 3.
[93] *R v Prince* [1986] 2 SCR 480, [34].
[94] Ibid.

The 'Kienapple principle' replaces ad hoc approaches to regulating double jeopardy and double punishment arising from multiple overlapping charges.[95] In Australia, Hayne J, in a Victorian appeal, ruled that a man could not be convicted of both rape and causing serious injury for a horrific (but single) act of digital penetration of a baby's vagina. He added that he should not 'be taken as embracing tests that have evolved in this regard in the Supreme Court of Canada'.[96] Hayne J acknowledged the limits on interference in prosecutorial discretion set out in *Maxwell* the previous year, and reiterated shortly afterwards in *Pearce*.[97]

However, the High Court's main reason in *Pearce* for taking a hands-off approach to multiple prosecutions for the same act or omission (in that case, charges of assault and breaking-and-entering, each with intent to cause grievous bodily harm) was the *De Simoni* principle:

> The short answer to the contention that the charging of both counts was an abuse of process is that because the offences are different (and different in important respects) the laying of both charges could not be said to be vexatious or oppressive or for some improper or ulterior purpose. To hold otherwise would be to preclude the laying of charges that, together, reflect the whole criminality of the accused and, consonant with what was held in *R v De Simoni*, would require the accused to be sentenced only for the offence or offences charged, excluding consideration of any part of the accused's conduct that could have been charged separately.[98]

As Kirby J noted:

> Although addressed to the principles governing punishment, necessarily whilst it stands [*De Simoni*] has consequences for the exercise of prosecutorial discretions. In many cases, prosecutors will, understandably, frame the charges contained in the counts of an indictment in terms of several overlapping offences. They will do so to avoid the risk that an accused might escape punishment for circumstances of aggravation appearing in the elements of separate offences.[99]

Judicial restraint in this context has a strong practical dimension. The principle in *De Simoni* is complex to apply and therefore potentially open to divergent approaches reflecting particular courts' views about how prosecutors should handle overlapping offences. A recent Australian illustration concerned a similar pair of offences to those considered in *Kienapple*: rape and sexual penetration of a child.[100] In 2010, a teenager pleaded guilty to three charges of sexual penetration of a 14-year-old when he was 16 years of age, charges that the prosecutor had brought in lieu of rape 'after a lengthy process had been undertaken with the victim and her family'.[101] However, following a dispute about whether or not the sexual penetration had been accompanied by violence, the defence argued in Victoria's Children's Court that the principle in *De Simoni*[102] precluded the sentencing magistrate from taking violence into account, absent a rape conviction. When the magistrate called

---

[95] Ibid [14].

[96] *R v Sessions* [1998] 2 VR 204, 315.

[97] *Pearce v R* [1998] HCA 57; (1998) 194 CLR 610, [30], [96]. Strangely, the High Court makes no reference to *Kienapple*.

[98] *Pearce v R* [1998] HCA 57; (1998) 194 CLR 610, [31]. But cf [97]–[98].

[99] Ibid [98].

[100] The offences are prescribed by the Crimes Act 1958 (Vic), ss 38 (rape) and 45 (sexual penetration of a child under 16).

[101] *ADA v Bruce* [2011] VSC 338, [9].

[102] See Section 1(e), above.

for further submissions, the prosecution responded by preferring rape charges against the accused and the magistrate rejected the defence's arguments that these charges were an abuse of process. Although the defendant appealed these decisions to the Supreme Court, they were never ruled upon.

Rather, seeking to avoid a bruising contest about a rape charge in the child sexual offence proceeding before him, Osborn J accommodated the principles in *De Simoni* to child sexual offences, relying heavily on a close analysis of the inferences supported by evidence of violence or non-consent:

> (f)   If the Crown adduces evidence of violence or lack of consent upon the plea hearing relating to a charge of sexual penetration of a child under 16, the Crown cannot invite the Court to infer from that evidence that the accused had the specific intention which would render the acts in issue rape ...
>
> (h)   It cannot follow simply from the submission of evidence either as to the mode of penetration or the victim's state of mind that the Crown is inviting the sentencing Court to draw an inference beyond reasonable doubt that the prisoner had the specific intent which would demonstrate guilt of rape.
>
> (i)   The fact that such evidence might form a basis for such a conclusion ... if rape were charged, does not make it inadmissible as evidence of objective aggravating factors with respect to the offence charged.[103]

Despite its strained distinctions and doubtful citations, this summary had the desired result. After Osborn J had set out this understanding, the dispute about the rape charges was adjourned indefinitely, as the prosecution and defence 'now accepted before me that the original sexual penetration charges provide an adequate vehicle for the resolution of the Crown case against the accused if [these] principles ... are applied to it'.[104]

In framing his summary, Osborn J relied on a recent five-judge Victorian Court of Appeal ruling, *Clarkson*,[105] for the proposition that consent is not usually a mitigating factor in sentencing for child sexual penetration; a ruling that comes close to equating child sexual penetration with rape of a child, just as the Supreme Court of Canada did 36 years earlier in *Kienapple*. However, *Clarkson* was concerned only with sentencing for child sexual penetration and made no mention of the possibility of rape charges or *De Simoni*. Indeed, the Court's isolated comment about aggravating factors, on which Osborn J relied, was, literally, parenthetical:

> (On the other hand, proven absence of consent will significantly increase both the gravity of the offence and the culpability of the offender. Proof that the offender knew or suspected that the child was not consenting would found a charge of rape.)[106]

---

[103] *ADA v Bruce* [2011] VSC 338, [16]. The dubious authority for Osborn J's views on evidence of violence (not discussed in the Court of Appeal decision) is a comment—quite possibly taken out of context—in *Poulton v WA* [2008] WASCA 97, [4]. Cf *WD v R* [2012] VSCA 100, [25] (when sentencing for sexual penetration the judge was in error merely for mentioning evidence of violence in her sentencing remarks).

[104] *ADA v Bruce* [2011] VSC 338, [13]. Justice Osborn added: 'For the sake of completeness I record that counsel for the first defendant indicated to this Court that he would request the Director of Public Prosecutions to intervene in and further facilitate the expeditious resolution of this matter.'

[105] *Clarkson v R; EJA v R* [2011] VSCA 157; (2011) 32 VR 361, [30]–[32].

[106] Ibid [36], citing *R v Sulemanov* [2007] VSCA 288, [12]–[13] (which primarily related to the accused's awareness of consent and likewise made no reference to the *De Simoni* principle).

This passage demonstrates the artificiality of the principle in *De Simoni*, as well as the courts' willingness to distinguish[107] or perhaps simply forget[108] the rule altogether when they are minded to achieve a particular policy outcome, in this case avoiding bruising contests about consent in sentencing hearings for child sexual offences.

(d) Limiting Punishment

McHugh, Hayne and Callinan JJ were surely right to observe in *Pearce* that, '[t]o an offender, the only relevant question may be "how long"'.[109] The English courts readily adopted a rule to insulate offenders from excessive punishments arising from prosecutorial charging practices in the context of overlapping sexual offences. In *Quayle*,[110] the prosecution had deliberately brought charges of indecent assault because the maximum penalty for unlawful sexual intercourse with a girl under 13 was regarded as insufficient to reflect the underlying course of criminality. The Court of Appeal held that the sentence should nevertheless be capped by the lesser maximum, where the charged conduct fell within the area of overlap:

> In principle, it may sound odd that the technical maximum for the touching of a girl's breast between the ages of 13 and 16 is 10 years whereas the maximum for unlawful sexual intercourse with her is 2 years' imprisonment. It is submitted that the right approach for the court, in respect of something which is, in truth, no more than unlawful sexual intercourse, is not to award more than two years if she is between the ages of 13 and 16. The court has sympathy with that submission and so far as the two counts which relate to the offences committed between the ages of 13 and 16 are concerned, we think it right to substitute sentences of two years.[111]

In the period when indecent assault charges were being brought to avoid the statutory time limit for the charge of sexual intercourse with a child under 16 the English courts adopted the lesser sentence option, mindful of potential unfairness to the accused:

> The maximum sentence for … [unlawful sexual intercourse with a girl under the age of sixteen] … is 2 years' imprisonment. The only reason why the learned judge was able to pass a sentence of three years was because the offence charged originally was time-barred, and accordingly, there was substituted for it what might seem the lesser offence of indecent assault, rather than unlawful sexual intercourse. An offence of indecent assault, since 1985, carries a maximum sentence of 10 years. Accordingly, the learned judge's sentence was strictly lawful in terms of the maxima imposed by Parliament, but the unfairness of the situation is clear: had it not been for the time-bar, the appellant could not have been sentenced to more than two years' imprisonment. It would be unfair that he should be sentenced to more than that, simply because the case had been delayed in coming to court.[112]

---

[107] See eg *R v Saraswati* (1989) 18 NSWLR 143, 170.

[108] Cf *Singh v R* [2013] VSCA 300, [28]–[29].

[109] *Pearce v R* [1998] HCA 57; (1998) 194 CLR 610, [45].

[110] *R v Quayle* (1993) 14 Cr App R (S) 726, extracted in *R v Jones* [2002] EWCA Crim 2983; [2003] 1 WLR 1590, [18].

[111] Ibid.

[112] *R v Hinton* [1995] 16 Cr App R (S) 52, extracted in *R v Jones* [2002] EWCA Crim 2983; [2003] 1 WLR 1590, [16].

This remained the 'now settled practice of this court in treating 2 years' imprison-ment as the maximum sentence appropriate to a charge of indecent assault brought in' such circumstances,[113] until the House of Lords in 2004 scotched this charging practice altogether.[114]

In Australia, a similar practice developed in some courts, especially in relation to overlaps between general fraud offences (which typically carry higher penalties) and more specific charges. In the 1982 case of *Scott v Cameron*, the defendant, who claimed unemployment benefits despite being employed, was charged with a general fraud offence under the fed-eral Crimes Act (carrying a maximum penalty of two years' imprisonment) rather than a specific offence of making false statements to a social services officer (with a six-month maximum penalty).[115] Justice White of the Supreme Court of South Australia wrote:

> Counsel for the respondent correctly said that the prosecution had an absolute discretion whether to lay the complaints under one section or the other. But it is for the Court, not the prosecution, to impose the appropriate sentence. And the Court's discretion is not to be fettered by the prosecutor's choice, at least in those cases where the facts are such that the prosecution could have been equally appropriately brought under one section or the other. Indeed, it seems to me that the prosecution would more appropriately have been brought under s 138 of the *Social Services Act* because that section deals specifically with this type of offence and contains the maximum penalty chosen by the legislature therefor. On the other hand, s 29C of the *Crimes Act* is a general blanket section designed to cover all kinds of false statements which might be made in all kinds of circumstances to all kinds of departments for all kinds of purposes. Where, as here, the facts reveal a general 'run of the mill' series of offences, it seems to me that the specific section ought to be used, while the more gen-eral provisions of s 29C of the Crimes Act should be reserved for particularly serious cases where it is quite obvious that the offending is far beyond the maximum penalty contemplated by the section. If there is administrative dissatisfaction with the level of penalties imposed by the Courts for breaches of s 138, then the position should not be cured administratively but cured either legis-latively by seeking an increased maximum penalty or by launching an appropriately researched test appeal through the court system.[116]

Over a decade later, in *R v Liang and Li*, the full court of the Supreme Court of Victoria formulated a general rule for sentencing conduct covered by overlapping offences:

> [A]lthough it is for the prosecuting authority in its absolute discretion to determine which particu-lar charge it will lay against an accused person, it is none the less relevant and proper for the judge on sentence to take into account as a relevant sentencing principle the fact that there was another and less punitive offence which not only could have been charged but indeed was as appropriate or even more appropriate to the facts alleged against the accused.[117]

Justice White's concern that 'the Court's discretion is not to be fettered by the prosecutor's choice' seems to mirror the Canadian approach[118] to protecting judicial integrity where some of the decisions include quite blunt criticisms of prosecutors' charging selections. Likewise, Winneke P in *Liang* expressed his concern that the prosecutor's general fraud charge in that case (in preference to a specific offence relating to the use of telephones,

---

[113] *R v Jones* [2002] EWCA Crim 2983; [2003] 1 WLR 1590, [41].
[114] *R v J* [2004] UKHL 42; [2005] 1 AC 562.
[115] The two offences were Crimes Act 1914 (Cth), s 29C and Social Services Consolidation Act 1947 (Cth), s 138.
[116] *Scott v Cameron* (1980) 26 SASR 321, 325–26.
[117] *R v Liang and Li* [1995] VSC 178; (1995) 82 A Crim R 39, 44.
[118] *R v Naraindeen*, 1990 CanLII 6731; 75 OR (2d) 120; 80 CR (3d) 66; 40 OAC 291.

where the accused were alleged to have participated in a scam involving a public phone booth) was problematic on two grounds: it betrayed a misunderstanding of Australian telecommunications law, and exposed the defendants to disproportionate penalties.[119] These cases predated *Maxwell* (albeit in *Liang* only by a year) and were little applied in ensuing decades. Unsurprisingly, on the first occasion it considered the rule in 2013, the High Court rejected the 'principle in *Liang and Li*', citing *Maxwell*:

> There is an undeniable tension between the statement in *Liang* that it is 'relevant and proper' for the judge to take into account the existence of another offence which the judge considers to be 'as appropriate or even more appropriate' and the recognition that the selection of the charge is within the 'absolute discretion' of the prosecutor. That the 'principle' can be traced to decisions that date to more than 30 years ago and that it has been applied (albeit infrequently) in a number of Australian jurisdictions does not mean that it should be accepted as part of the common law of Australia if, as appears, it is inconsistent with recognition of the separation of prosecutorial and judicial functions, which in this country has a constitutional dimension ... The time for debate as to any claimed abuse arising out of the selection of the charge is before the entry of a plea. After an offender has been convicted of an offence it risks compromising the impartiality and independence of the court to require that it sentence by reference to an offence of which the offender has not been convicted but which it considers the prosecution should have charged.[120]

Indeed, the High Court went further, holding that '[c]onsideration of different offences for which an offender might have been convicted is merely a distraction'.[121] This dictum appears entirely to preclude a sentencing judge from referring to the maximum punishments fixed by parliament for overlapping or similar offences as yardsticks for imposing proportional punishment in analogous cases.

A majority of the High Court recently applied *Maxwell* to reject a constitutional challenge to a scheme that set a mandatory penalty for a broadly-defined aggravated people-smuggling offence.[122] Given that the aggravated offence covered all instances of the standard Australian people-smuggling venture (that is, by overcrowded boat), the scheme effectively afforded the prosecutor a choice between a five-year minimum sentence for the defendant (by charging the aggravated offence) or a sentence at the judge's discretion (by charging the simple offence).[123] Commencing with a citation of *Maxwell* and later cases,[124] the Court began with 'the general proposition that it is for the prosecuting authorities (not the courts) to decide who will be prosecuted and for what offences' and continued:

> The decisions which a prosecutor makes about what offences to charge may well affect what punishment will be imposed if the accused is convicted. But that observation does not entail, as the appellant's argument necessarily assumed, that the prosecutor exercises judicial power in choosing to charge an aggravated form of offence rather than the simple form of that offence.

> If, as in this case, one available charge is of an offence for which a mandatory minimum penalty is provided and there is another available charge of a different offence for which no minimum

---

[119] *R v Liang and Li* [1995] VSC 178; (1995) 82 A Crim R 39, 42–43.

[120] *Elias v R; Issa v R* [2013] HCA 31; (2013) 248 CLR 483, [33], [35].

[121] Ibid [36].

[122] *Magaming v R* [2013] HCA 40; (2013) 87 ALJR 1060 (French CJ, Hayne, Crennan, Kiefel and Bell JJ).

[123] Migration Act 1958 (Cth), s 236B(3)(c) fixes the mandatory minimum sentence. The two offences are ss 233A (offence of people smuggling) and 233C (aggravated people smuggling, involving at least five people).

[124] *Magaming v R* [2013] HCA 40; (2013) 87 ALJR 1060, [20].

penalty is prescribed, the prescription of a mandatory minimum penalty for one of the offences does not lead to any different conclusion.[125]

Gageler J, in a lone dissent, applied the principle expressed by Lord Diplock in *Hinds*:

> What Parliament cannot do, consistently with the separation of powers, is to transfer from the judiciary to any executive body … a discretion to determine the severity of the punishment to be inflicted upon an individual member of a class of offenders.[126]

Gageler J would have invalidated the mandatory minimum sentence. In response to the majority's reliance on *Maxwell*, and their objection that 'involving a court in an inquiry into a forensic choice made by a participant in a controversy actually or potentially before the court' would compromise judicial integrity, the dissentient was not prepared to acquiesce in any situation where the prosecution's choice pre-empts the court's own supervisory jurisdiction.[127]

Conclusion: Maxwell's Mantra

> Maxwell Edison, majoring in medicine,
> Calls her on the phone.
> 'Can I take you out to the pictures,
> Joa-oa-oa-oan?'[128]

Comprehensive reform of England's sexual offences law in 2003 failed to end courtroom disputes about the appropriateness of charging choices in that jurisdiction. One innovation was a special provision by which youthful defendants under 18 years of age are subject to reduced penalties for committing sexual offences against children.[129] However, there is nothing to stop a prosecutor charging a youthful defendant with a more serious general sexual offence that could be committed by or against anyone. In 2008, on an appeal by a 15-year-old defendant who pleaded guilty to the charged offence of 'rape of a child under 13' on the basis that the 12-year-old complainant 'willingly agreed to have sexual intercourse', Lord Hoffmann remarked:

> If the prosecution has been unduly heavy handed, that may be unfair and unjust, but not an infringement of human rights. It is a matter for the ordinary system of criminal justice. It would be remarkable if [ECHR] article 8 [the right to respect for private life] gave Strasbourg jurisdiction over sentencing for all offences which happen to have been committed at home. This case is another example of the regrettable tendency to try to convert the whole system of justice into questions of human rights.[130]

---

[125] Ibid [38]–[39].

[126] *R v Hinds* [1977] AC 195, 226.

[127] *Magaming v R* [2013] HCA 40; (2013) 87 ALJR 1060, [68], [70].

[128] *Maxwell's Silver Hammer*, John Lennon and Paul McCartney (EMI Music Publishing, Sony/ATV Music Publishing LLC, 1969).

[129] Sexual Offences Act 2003, s 13.

[130] *R v G* [2008] UKHL 37; [2009] 1 AC 92, [10].

While the appeal was dismissed, the majority holding was narrow and the deciding vote,[131] as well as the later judgment of the European Court of Human Rights,[132] relied heavily on the Court of Appeal's revision of the 15-year-old's sentence from a 12-month detention and training order to a conditional discharge. That ruling rested on the court's conclusion that 'this was an offence that fell properly within the ambit' of the provision for child offenders,[133] rather than the one charged. This was an unembarrassed application of what Australian courts would refer to as the former principle in *Liang and Li*.

Lord Hoffmann's view that prosecution and sentencing are not a matter for courts applying human rights law, while perhaps debateable in Europe, sits well with *Maxwell*'s dictum. However, as the foregoing discussion has shown, whatever the normative merits of Gaudron and Gummow JJ's remarks, they are only partially descriptive of practice. There are numerous situations and legal bases in Australia, England and Canada where courts may be and sometimes are 'in any way concerned with decisions as to who is to be prosecuted and for what'.[134] These include judicial interpretations of statutory offences that reduce the impact of prosecutorial discretion in circumstances where the underlying conduct is covered by overlapping charges;[135] courts' findings that certain prosecutorial charging choices are an abuse of process;[136] doctrines restricting certain sorts of trial outcomes and sentencing in light of prosecutors' charging choices (and the manipulation of those limitations to influence charging choices);[137] and sentencing doctrines that take into account the penalty regime for a 'more appropriate' charge the prosecution could have made.[138]

To be sure, each doctrine is limited, many are uncertain, some are controversial and one has recently been disapproved by the High Court itself.[139] Their common element is that each doctrine is an exercise in interpreting parliamentary intentions with respect to schemes of overlapping offences. This is obviously the case when the question before the court concerns the proper interpretation of one or more offence definitions. It is no less explicit where abuse of process arguments target prosecutorial charging choices as being contrary to parliamentary intention or, indeed, unlawful in light of a statutory rule, such as a limitation period. The role of parliamentary intention is implicit in courts' deployment of doctrines relating to convictions, fact-finding and charging choices, and in their susceptibility to further legislative intervention and revision. The statutory basis of each doctrine suggests the need for caution in generalising too readily from individual decisions. Rather, it is likely that the operation of all these overlapping doctrines will vary depending

---

[131] See B Malkani, 'Article 8 of the European Convention on Human Rights, and the Decision to Prosecute' [2011] *Criminal Law Review* 943, 946, noting that 'three of the five judges'—Lords Hope, Carswell and Mance, with Baroness Hale also willing to discuss the point—'held that prosecutorial policy and decision-making does come within the ambit of Article 8'.

[132] *G v UK* (2011) 53 EHRR SE25; [2012] Crim LR 46, [39].

[133] *R v G* [2006] EWCA Crim 821; [2006] 1 WLR 2052, [51].

[134] *Maxwell v R* [1996] HCA 46; (1996) 184 CLR 501, 534.

[135] For example, *Saraswati v R* (1991) 172 CLR 1.

[136] For example, *R v J* [2004] UKHL 42; [2005] 1 AC 562.

[137] For example, *R v Kienapple* [1975] 1 SCR 729; *R v De Simoni* [1981] HCA 31; (1981) 147 CLR 383.

[138] For example, *R v Kienapple* [1975] 1 SCR 729 and the former rule in *R v Liang and Li* [1995] VSC 178; (1995) 82 A Crim R 39.

[139] *Elias v R; Issa v R* [2013] HCA 32; (2013) 87 ALJR 853, rejecting *R v Liang and Li* [1995] VSC 178; (1995) 82 A Crim R 39.

on the particular overlapping offences under consideration. Moreover, in jurisdictions with a statutory or constitutional human rights law, they will squarely and uncontroversially be shaped by those laws.

What exactly does *Maxwell* add to this picture? In my view: nothing. Or, more precisely, it should add nothing, if Australian lawyers and courts do their jobs properly. Not only are there plenty of ways Australian courts can review prosecutorial choices, but the scope of those doctrines depends on other, well-developed rules regulating the relationship between the courts and prosecutors and, more specifically, Parliament's intentions for each pair of offences. Neither the relationship between courts and prosecutors nor Parliament's intentions for particular overlapping offences is susceptible to general pronouncements (at least, not by a court). Hence, *Maxwell's* holding in the name of 'integrity' is reduced to: a lazy argument for prosecutors bristling at being questioned; a convenient shorthand for judges who are not inclined to second-guess prosecutors; and lip service for judges who are so inclined. *Maxwell* is any number of legal clichés: a hard case,[140] a lamp post,[141] and a 'vibe'.[142] What it is not, is 'seriously considered dicta',[143] let alone a 'common law principle'[144] and still less a 'constitutional' requirement.[145] Its date with Mr Edison is long overdue.

---

[140] 'Hard cases, it has frequently been observed, are apt to introduce bad law': *Winterbottom v Wright* (1842) 10 M & W 109, 116; 152 ER 402, 406 (Rolfe B).

[141] That is, 'as a drunkard uses a lamp post, for support rather than for illumination': see D Ogilvy, *Confessions of an Advertising Man* (London, Longmans, 1964) 100.

[142] 'It's the vibe of the thing, your Honour', says Dennis Denuto in the Australian comedy classic film *The Castle* (Working Dog Productions, 1997).

[143] *Farah Constructions Pty Ltd v Say-Dee Pty Ltd* [2007] HCA 22; (2007) 230 CLR 89, [34]; cf *Beveridge v Whitton* [2001] NSWCA 6, [30].

[144] *Pantazis v R* [2012] VSCA 160; (2012) 217 A Crim R 31, [62].

[145] *Elias v R; Issa v R* [2013] HCA 31; (2013) 248 CLR 483, [33].

7

Prosecutors Interviewing Witnesses: A Question of Integrity

PAUL ROBERTS[*]

Introduction

Pre-trial witness preparation by prosecutors is commonplace in many legal systems, but has traditionally been frowned upon in England and Wales. It therefore marked a signal departure from established prosecutorial practice when, in 2007, Crown Prosecutors were given a new power to conduct pre-trial interviews with potential prosecution witnesses (PTWI), including complainants.[1] The advent of PTWI was variously characterised in official publications and media reports as 'fairly radical',[2] 'a fundamental change to our legal system',[3] and even 'revolutionary';[4] and it continues to resonate with subsequent developments in English criminal justice policy, including the recent, and widely publicised,[5] initiative to expand Crown Prosecutors' role in witness familiarisation at court.[6] Such familiarisation involves, 'meeting the prosecutor in advance; and having their questions answered ... help[ing] a witness to feel prepared for their court experience and able to give their best evidence'.[7] It does not extend to discussing the *content* of the witness's

[*] I am grateful to participants in the Hong Kong University and University of New South Wales workshops for their critical feedback and suggestions, and especially to Mike McConville and Jeremy Gans, the discussants for my paper. Candida Saunders and my three co-editors made many helpful suggestions for improving previous drafts. The early stages of researching and writing were supported by AHRC Research Leave grant AH/F005970/1. A short visit to the Oñati International Institute for the Sociology of Law provided the ideal environment to work on the manuscript, with thanks to Adam Czarnota, Susana Arrese Murguzur and the MA class of 2014/15 for their warm hospitality during a cold March in the Basque Country.
[1] P Roberts and C Saunders, 'Introducing Pre-Trial Witness Interviews—A Flexible New Fixture in the Crown Prosecutor's Toolkit' [2008] *Criminal Law Review* 831.
[2] Crown Prosecution Service, *Pre-Trial Witness Interviews by Prosecutors: A Consultation Paper* (London, CPS, 2003) 5.
[3] 'CPS announces the roll out of two key justice initiatives', CPS Press Release, 1 April 2008, www.cps.gov.uk/news/latest_news/122_08/ (accessed 1 March 2015).
[4] C Dyer, 'Criminal justice revolution to secure more convictions: plan for prosecutors to interview witnesses before trial will end ancient rule' *The Guardian*, 11 November 2005.
[5] DPP Alison Saunders appeared on BBC Radio 4's flagship *Today* programme at 07:50 on 19 January 2015 to announce the consultation: see www.bbc.co.uk/programmes/b04y9y6r (accessed 1 March 2015). And see A Hill, 'DPP Proposes New Guidelines to Help Victims and Witnesses in Court', *The Guardian*, 19 January 2015.
[6] CPS, *Speaking to Witnesses at Court—Draft CPS Guidance for Consultation* (London, CPS, January 2015).
[7] Ibid 1.

testimony.[8] PTWI was introduced by the Crown Prosecution Service (CPS) 'for the purpose of assisting a prosecutor to assess the reliability of a witness's evidence or to understand complex evidence'.[9] Since its national implementation in 2008, Crown Prosecutors[10] in England and Wales may interview a complainant or other witness whenever it would enable them 'to reach a better informed decision about any aspect of the case'. National roll-out of PTWI was preceded by a pilot study evaluation, in which I participated as an academic consultant and researcher.[11]

Drawing on empirical data collected as part of the PTWI Evaluation Pilot, this chapter explores the extent to which prosecutors' interviews with witnesses can usefully be conceptualised as posing 'questions of integrity', in terms of three interweaving strands of analysis. First, there are epistemic issues pertaining to the 'integrity of the evidence'. How does pre-trial interviewing affect the type and quality of information that is later available to factfinders at trial? What bearing, if any, do the prosecutor's interventions have on the probative value of witness testimony? Are there any further implications for the way in which testimonial evidence should be regulated or evaluated? A second strand of integrity analysis concerns prosecutors' professional ethical responsibilities. How should pre-trial witness interviewing be conducted in the light of the prosecutor's dual roles as an adversarial party and a 'minister of justice'?[12] Thirdly, pre-trial witness interviewing leads naturally into more expansive discussions of the theoretical and normative questions raised in this volume's Introduction, concerning the legitimacy and normative foundations of criminal proceedings as a whole. Integrity in this holistic sense is engaged most acutely by the risks of evidence 'contamination' and 'witness coaching', which in turn implicate the cogency of institutional (including judicial) responses to these risks and the potential for procedural unfairness and constraining defence rights.

Pre-trial witness preparation, together with its evil twin 'witness coaching', rarely figure in scholarly analyses of English criminal proceedings or in British textbooks on Evidence or Criminal Process.[13] Whilst this chapter's central methodological ambition (reflecting the

---

[8] '[W]hat is being proposed is limited and within the boundaries of our current system … All that the provision of the information on the likely nature of the defence case does is reduces the risk that the witness will feel "ambushed" in the witness box … This will help them give their best evidence and at the same time improve the experience of those witnesses who have felt that they were not given sufficient support to deal with the stresses of cross-examination': *Consultation on Speaking to Witnesses at Court—Summary of Responses* (11 September 2015), www.cps.gov.uk/consultations/speaking_to_witnesses_at_court_responses.html (accessed 21 November 2015).

[9] *Pre-trial Witness Interviews: Code of Practice (for the Purpose of the CPS Pilots)* (London, CPS, 2005) [2.1].

[10] That is to say, lawyers employed by the CPS. During the PTWI Pilot, barristers—members of the independent Bar instructed as Crown advocates by the CPS—could *attend* PTWI interviews, but not conduct them. CPS Guidance now states that interviews may also be conducted 'by an independent advocate on the authority of a designated Crown Prosecutor': *Pre-Trial Witness Interviews—Guidance for Prosecutors*, www.cps.gov.uk/legal/p_to_r/pre_-trial_witness_interviews/#a04 (accessed 21 November 2015).

[11] P Roberts and C Saunders, *Interviewing Prosecution Witnesses: A Socio-Legal Evaluation of the Pre-Trial Witness Interview Pilot* (London, CPS, 2008); REF2014 Impact Case Study, *Piloting Pre-Trial Witness Interviews (PTWI) by Crown Prosecutors—Facilitating the Practical Implementation of Criminal Justice Policy* (University of Nottingham, 2013), impact.ref.ac.uk/casestudies2/refservice.svc/GetCaseStudyPDF/32981 (accessed 19 January 2016).

[12] A theme developed in the previous two chapters by Cowdery (Chapter 5) and Gans (Chapter 6) and by Edmond in Chapter 9.

[13] It would be invidious to name names, because the issue is *structural*—it relates to the way in which the disciplinary domains of Evidence and Procedure are constructed in English legal, or more broadly common law, scholarship—rather than to the idiosyncrasies of particular texts or authors. The question is this: why do these topics fall between the cracks in orthodox disciplinary taxonomies, so that they are lucky to attract passing mention, let alone extended critical analysis, in the received pedagogical canon?

volume as a whole) is to promote critical discussion of procedural integrity beyond its two existing doctrinal beachheads,[14] a subsidiary programmatic objective is to shine a spotlight into a neglected, and it might be thought unavailingly prosaic, corner of criminal process; one with under-appreciated theoretical significance and growing importance for criminal practitioners in England and Wales.

1. Tight-lipped: The English Law and Practice of Witness Preparation/Coaching

Witness preparation is widely regarded as legitimate, sensible and even necessary, or at all events a benign and unremarkable feature of litigation, 'in many common law jurisdictions'. Prevailing practice goes unquestioned, and the suggestion that there is anything problematic or untoward in pre-trial contact between prosecutors and witnesses would very likely be met with puzzlement. Prosecutors in Australia,[15] Canada[16] and New Zealand, for example, interview key witnesses as part of their routine trial preparations.[17] Elsewhere, the risks of inappropriate influence amounting to 'witness coaching' have generated critical discussion. Notably, witness preparation has been considered by the US Supreme Court[18] and is quite extensively debated amongst American legal scholars

---

[14] That is, abuse of process and the exclusion of improperly obtained evidence, as discussed by Whitfort (Chapter 10) and Chau (Chapter 11) in this volume. Generally, see P Roberts and A Zuckerman, *Criminal Evidence*, 2nd edn (Oxford, Oxford University Press, 2010) 22, 188–91; P Mirfield, *Silence, Confessions and Improperly Obtained Evidence* (Oxford, Clarendon Press, 1997) 28ff; IH Dennis, 'Reconstructing the Law of Criminal Evidence' [1989] *Current Legal Problems* 21; AAS Zuckerman 'Illegally-Obtained Evidence—Discretion as a Guardian of Legitimacy' [1987] *Current Legal Problems* 55. But cf A Ashworth, 'Exploring the Integrity Principle in Evidence and Procedure' in P Mirfield and RJ Smith (eds), *Essays for Colin Tapper* (Oxford, Oxford University Press, 2003).

[15] Legal Services Council (NSW & Vic), www.legalservicescouncil.org.au/ (accessed 19 January 2016), Legal Profession Uniform Conduct (Barristers) Rules 2015 (27 May 2015 No 243), Rule 70 (expressly permitting 'questioning and testing in conference the version of evidence to be given by a prospective witness, including drawing the witness's attention to inconsistencies or other difficulties with the evidence'; but barristers 'must not encourage the witness to give evidence different from the evidence which the witness believes to be true'). The parallel provision for solicitors is Legal Profession Uniform Law Australian Solicitors' Conduct Rules 2015, Rule 24 ('Integrity of Evidence—Influencing Evidence'). Also see B Hancock and J Jackson, *Standards for Prosecutors* (The Hague, International Association of Prosecutors, 2009) 101–102. According to a document prepared by the New South Wales Bar Association on 'Witness Preparation' (May 2012): 'Barristers who attempt to present a case in Court without taking the time to prepare are either geniuses, or just lazy, lousy advocates. 99.9% are in the second category ... One vital aspect of preparing the case is the preparation of witnesses for the giving of evidence ... It is increasingly the task of Counsel to take proofs of evidence from litigants and witnesses'.

[16] See Public Prosecution Service of Canada, *Deskbook* (2014) [2.23], [3.17], [3.3.8], [4.1], [4.2], www.ppsc-sppc.gc.ca/eng/pub/index.html (accessed 19 January 2016); *R v Regan* [2002] 1 SCR 297, 2002 SCC 12 (surveying practices in different provinces, and concluding that 'in some Canadian jurisdictions, *pre-charge* interviews by the Crown are a regular, even common practice. In these jurisdictions at least, it appears that public policy is served by the practice': ibid [91], emphasis added).

[17] SV Vasiliev, 'From Liberal Extremity to Safe Mainstream? The Comparative Controversies of Witness Preparation in the United States' (2011) 9 *International Commentary on Evidence*, Article 5; Office of the Attorney General, *Pre-Trial Witness Interviews by Prosecutors—Report* (London, 2004) Part 3 ('The Foreign Experience').

[18] *Geders v United States*, 425 US 80, 89–90; 96 S Ct 1330, 1336–37 (1976) (holding that risks of improper coaching had to be accepted as incidental to securing the accused's Sixth Amendment right to effective assistance of counsel: *Powell v Alabama*, 287 US 45 (1932)).

and practitioners.[19] Pre-trial 'witness proofing' has also lately become a contentious issue in international criminal proceedings.[20] Considerable variability in routine practices and cultural attitudes towards pre-trial interviewing underlines a general methodological caveat in comparative legal studies: it is vital to pay fastidious attention to the precise details and broader institutional contexts of legal practices across jurisdictions,[21] in this instance, to the range of activities that may be lumped together under the portmanteau term 'witness preparation'. Prosecutors might conceivably interview witnesses at various stages of criminal proceedings, for different purposes and with a range of practical effects. The roles and responsibilities of 'prosecutors' are not uniform across jurisdictions and legal traditions and cultures.[22] Criminal proceedings organised along inquisitorial lines should be expected to manage the production of witness evidence differently to those rooted in adversarial assumptions. Alternative models of adversarial procedure might well conceptualise and evaluate witness preparation differently, depending on each legal system's detailed specification of the relationship between the parties and the court and the division of responsibilities between them.

The English position is both muted and, in terms of the common law average, relatively conservative.[23] British academic literature on pre-trial witness preparation remains parlous, and would have been virtually non-existent but for the introduction of PTWI and

---

[19] See eg BL Gershman, 'Witness Coaching by Prosecutors' (2002) 23 *Cardozo Law Review* 829; B Allison, 'Witness Preparation from the Criminal Defense Perspective' (1999) 30 *Texas Tech Law Review* 1333; FC Zacharias and S Martin, 'Coaching Witnesses' (1999) 87 *Kentucky Law Journal* 1001; L-Col Henley, 'Horse-Shedding the Evidence—Twenty Do's and Don'ts of Witness Preparation' [1998] *Army Lawyer* (February) 38; JS Solovy and R Byman, 'Witness Coaching is a Good Thing', *The National Law Journal*, 13 September 1999; JD Piorkowski Jr, 'Professional Conduct and the Preparation of Witnesses for Trial: Defining the Acceptable Limitations of "Coaching"' (1987) 1 *Georgetown Journal of Legal Ethics* 389; JS Applegate, 'Witness Preparation' (1989) 68 *Texas Law Review* 277.

[20] R Karemaker, BD Taylor III, and TW Pittman, 'Witness Proofing in International Criminal Tribunals: A Critical Analysis of Widening Procedural Divergence' (2008) 21 *Leiden Journal of International Law* 683; K Ambos, '"Witness Proofing" before the International Criminal Court: A Reply to Karemaker, Taylor, and Pittman' (2008) 21 *Leiden Journal of International Law* 911; S Vasiliev, 'Proofing the Ban on "Witness Proofing": Did the ICC Get it Right?' (2009) 20 *Criminal Law Forum* 193; JD Jackson and YM Brunger, 'Witness Preparation in the ICC: An Opportunity for Principled Pragmatism' (2015) 13 *Journal of International Criminal Justice* 601.

[21] Cowdery, in Chapter 5 of this volume, makes a similar point in relation to variable practices of 'plea bargaining'. For another telling illustration of significant comparative variation in the minutiae of criminal procedure, see P Marcus, 'Judges Talking to Jurors in Criminal Cases: Why US Judges Do It So Differently from Just About Everyone Else' (2013) 30 *Arizona Journal of International and Comparative Law* 1.

[22] See eg D Nelken, 'Can Prosecutors be Too Independent? An Italian Case Study' in T Daems, D van Zyl Smit and S Snacken (eds), *European Penology?* (Oxford, Hart Publishing, 2013); J-M Jehle and M Wade (eds), *Coping with Overloaded Criminal Justice Systems: The Rise of Prosecutorial Power Across Europe* (Berlin, Springer, 2006); RM White, 'Investigators and Prosecutors or, Desperately Seeking Scotland: Re-formulation of the "Philips Principle"' (2006) 69 *Modern Law Review* 143; J Hodgson, *French Criminal Justice* (Oxford, Hart Publishing, 2005); JD Jackson, 'The Effect of Legal Culture and Proof in Decisions to Prosecute' (2004) 3 *Law, Probability and Risk* 109; DT Johnson, 'Prosecutor Culture in Japan and the USA' in D Nelken (ed), *Contrasting Criminal Justice: Getting From Here to There* (Aldershot, Ashgate, 2000); G Di Federico, 'Prosecutorial Independence and the Democratic Requirement of Accountability in Italy' (1998) 38 *British Journal of Criminology* 371; J Fionda, *Public Prosecutors and Discretion: A Comparative Study* (Oxford, Oxford University Press, 1995); WT Pizzi, 'Understanding Prosecutorial Discretion in the United States: The Limits of Comparative Criminal Procedure as an Instrument of Reform' (1993) 54 *Ohio State Law Journal* 1325.

[23] Prosecutions in Scotland are structured differently; pre-trial interviewing ('precognition') by prosecutors (procurators fiscal) is one significant point of contrast in criminal proceedings north and south of the Scottish border. See eg *Heggiev v HM Advocate* 2010 SCL 350, [2009] HCJAC 96. Cf *Mowbray v Crowe* 1994 SLT 445.

the roughly contemporaneous litigation described later in this section.[24] Appellate courts in England and Wales seemingly did not mention witness coaching, even casually, until recent decades. By the 1990s one can find isolated dicta in the case law, such as Farquarhson LJ's observation in *R v Skinner* that 'any rehearsal of the evidence of witnesses or the coaching of witnesses are practices to be strongly discouraged'.[25] A few years later in an unreported case Lord Bingham CJ remarked that it was 'a matter of the utmost importance that nothing should be done which amounts to rehearsing the evidence of a witness, or coaching the witness so as to encourage the witness to alter the evidence originally given'.[26] The Court of Appeal elaborated on these isolated warnings when, in 2005, it was presented with the opportunity to address the perils of witness coaching directly.

The case of *Momodou and Limani*[27] arose out of a major disturbance at the newly-opened Immigration Detention Centre at Yarl's Wood, Bedfordshire, in February 2002. The Centre was operated by Group 4, a well-known private security firm.[28] On the night in question, a seemingly minor incident involving the restraint of a female detainee, Eunice, quickly escalated into a full-scale riot precipitating widespread destruction of property, intimidation of staff, and many escapes. Half of the Centre was burnt to the ground, and the ensuing criminal investigation involved the largest forensic examination ever undertaken in Europe. Fatalities were grimly anticipated, yet through some miracle of good fortune, no detainees or staff actually perished in the conflagration. Henry Momodou—'Big Henry'—was said to have been an instigator of the riot, wielding broken chair legs and breaking windows. He was convicted of violent disorder (though acquitted of arson) and sentenced to four years' imprisonment. Limani, another apparent ringleader, was captured on CCTV urging others to join the disturbance. He was also convicted of violent disorder and sentenced to four years' imprisonment.[29] On appeal, both defendants complained inter alia that Group 4 had coached its staff to testify as prosecution witnesses at their trial.

As it later emerged in court, Group 4 employees had undergone three different phases of 'counselling' or preparation for trial, organised by Group 4. First, relevant Group 4 staff were offered 'trauma de-briefing' immediately after the incident. Secondly, they attended witness preparation training organised by Bond Solon, a specialist commercial supplier of such programmes.[30] Thirdly, a series of 'group counselling' sessions was provided by

---

[24] A Watson, 'Witness Preparation in the United States and England & Wales' (2000) 164 *Justice of the Peace* 816. Now see also P Cooper, 'Witness Familiarisation and Special Measures Come of Age' (2012) 156 *Solicitors Journal* 10; L Ellison and J Wheatcroft, '"Could You Ask Me That in a Different Way Please?" Exploring the Impact of Courtroom Questioning and Witness Familiarisation on Adult Witness Accuracy' [2010] *Criminal Law Review* 823; L Ellison, 'Witness Preparation and the Prosecution of Rape' (2007) 27 *Legal Studies* 171; L Dobbs and D Etherington, 'Witness Coaching in Criminal Cases' *The Barrister*, 13 January 2004.

[25] (1994) 99 Cr App R 212, 216 (CA).

[26] *R v Roberts (Michael Harry) and Roberts (Jason Lee)*, CA Transcript 97/3023/Z5, 6 April 1998; (1998) 162 JP 691 (summary).

[27] [2005] 1 WLR 3442, [2005] 2 Cr App R 6, [2005] EWCA Crim 177.

[28] Rebranded G4S, the company subsequently attained notoriety in relation to its provision of security staff at the London 2012 Olympics: see eg SP Chan, 'Timeline: How G4S's Bungled Olympics Security Contract Unfolded', *The Telegraph*, 21 May 2013.

[29] A third inmate pleaded guilty and received a sentence of 1-and-a-half years. Numerous others were acquitted, either at the direction of the judge or by the jury following contested trials.

[30] See www.bondsolon.com/ (accessed 21 November 2015). According to its website, 'Bond Solon is the leading provider of Witness Familiarisation training in the UK … provid[ing] witness training on behalf of the majority of the top 100 leading law firms across the UK and directly to companies for a variety of legal forums including arbitrations, civil, criminal and family courts, tribunals, select committees and inquiries'. These courses promise

consulting psychiatrists. It subsequently proved impossible to say for sure which staff had attended which, if any, of these three phases of counselling/preparation, since accurate records of participation were not kept. However, it was clear that several key witnesses who testified at trial had been through one or more of these processes. The situation was further complicated by Group 4's own status as a potential defendant in corporate manslaughter proceedings (before it was established that nobody had died) and as a civil litigant against the police authority claiming damages under the Riot Damages Act 1886. Group 4 were apparently reluctant to cooperate fully with the police investigation. At various stages of the proceedings the police, and subsequently the CPS (on counsel's advice), wrote to Group 4 expressing very serious reservations about its attitude towards the police investigation and its exposure of potential witnesses in anticipated criminal proceedings to counsellors and consultants hired by Group 4.

As it turned out, Group 4's attempts at witness preparation seriously backfired on the prosecution at trial, as Crown counsel had all along feared. In the absence of full documentation, it had to be assumed that all Group 4 employee-witnesses had been exposed to procedures which risked contaminating their evidence. The prosecution candidly volunteered this concession in opening its case at trial, and the judge directed one acquittal explicitly on that basis. The trial then proceeded on the remaining charges. Although witness coaching of any description was roundly condemned in the trial judge's summing-up, and the jury was directed to take procedural irregularities into account in evaluating the testimony of Group 4 employees, Momodou and Limani were still convicted. On appeal, the defence argued that the proceedings in their entirety should have been stayed as an abuse of process.[31] Despite entertaining serious reservations about Group 4's irregular witness preparation measures, the Court of Appeal concluded that the accused had suffered no material prejudice:

> [T]he way in which the 'training' issue was left to the jury meant that it was damaging to the credit-worthiness of every witnesses who received it. In the result, looking at the evidence overall, the arrangements for training ... do not undermine the safety of the conviction.[32]

In dismissing the defendants' appeals, however, the Court of Appeal took the opportunity to issue the following general guidance on the limits of appropriate witness preparation:

> There is a dramatic distinction between witness training or coaching, and witness familiarisation. Training or coaching for witnesses in criminal proceedings (whether for prosecution or defence)

---

to 'mitigate against risk of poor witness performance in court' and 'thoroughly prepare witnesses for their appearance in a hearing', including 'eliminating' (no less!) 'the effects of nervousness or over-confidence'. For comparative discussion, see N LeGrande and KE Mierau, 'Witness Preparation and the Trial Consulting Industry' (2004) 17 *Georgetown Journal of Legal Ethics* 947 (noting the proliferation of litigation consultants offering witness preparation services in the US and the absence of any regulatory framework or enforceable professional standards for consultants).

[31] Generally, see AL-T Choo, *Abuse of Process and Judicial Stays of Criminal Proceedings*, 2nd edn (Oxford, Oxford University Press, 2008); Whitfort, Chapter 10 in this volume.

[32] [2005] EWCA Crim 177, [67]. 'Unsafety' is now the single criterion for allowing criminal appeals in England and Wales, pursuant to the Criminal Appeal Act 1968, s 2 (as amended). However, this does *not* necessarily imply factual innocence, 'because of the fundamental constitutional requirement that even a guilty defendant is entitled, before being found guilty, to have a trial which conforms with at least the minimum standards of what is regarded in this jurisdiction as being an acceptable criminal trial': *R v Hanratty (Deceased)* [2002] 2 Cr App R 419; [2002] EWCA Crim 1141, [95].

is not permitted. … The witness should give his or her own evidence, so far as practicable uninfluenced by what anyone else has said, whether in formal discussions or informal conversations. The rule reduces, indeed hopefully avoids any possibility, that one witness may tailor his evidence in the light of what anyone else said, and equally, avoids any unfounded perception that he may have done so. … These dangers are present in one-to-one witness training. Where however the witness is jointly trained with other witnesses to the same events, the dangers dramatically increase. Recollections change. Memories are contaminated. Witnesses may bring their respective accounts into what they believe to be better alignment with others. They may be encouraged to do so, consciously or unconsciously. They may collude deliberately. They may be inadvertently contaminated. Whether deliberately or inadvertently, the evidence may no longer be their own. Although none of this is inevitable, the risk that training or coaching may adversely affect the accuracy of the evidence of the individual witness is constant. So we repeat, witness training for criminal trials is prohibited.[33]

Several aspects of this considered judicial policy pronouncement are noteworthy. First, deliberate witness coaching is unambiguously forbidden; euphemisms like 'counselling' or 'training'will not wash. When the Court of Appeal directs that 'witness training for criminal trials is prohibited' it is referring to a particular sort or set of inappropriate practices, not to the description these practices happen to bear in a personnel training company's advertising literature,[34] in criminal practitioners' common parlance, or elsewhere.

Secondly, the Court offers guidance for demarcating the permissible from the impermissible in witness preparation: '[t]here is a dramatic distinction between witness training or coaching, and witness familiarisation.' What are the tangible contours of this 'dramatic' distinction? The Court expressly stated that genuine trauma counselling for distraught employees in the aftermath of a terrifying experience is legally unproblematic: 'It was not unreasonable for employers to do everything they could to alleviate the pressures and stresses endured by those members of their staff who were involved in or witnessed this incident.'[35] Witnesses' pre-trial familiarisation with courtroom layout, etiquette and procedure was likewise endorsed, being characterised by the Court as '[s]ensible preparation for the experience of giving evidence, which assists the witness to give of his or her best at the forthcoming trial'.[36] In a criminal process orientated to systematic 'rebalancing' in favour of victims' rights,[37] witness familiarisation is coming to be viewed as a primary official responsibility and legitimate 'consumer' expectation. The CPS has recently committed itself to

---

[33] [2005] EWCA Crim 177, [61].

[34] Cf M Solon, 'Why is it worth it?' (2015) 165 *New Law Journal* 10 (20 November); M Solon, 'Witness Familiarisation: Are You an Abramovich or a Nigella?' *Legal Hub*, 14 March 2014, www.legalhub.co.uk/ (accessed 19 January 2016) (contending, with no sense of irony, that '[n]o one is claiming that witness familiarisation can influence the outcome of a case, which will be decided on the evidence, but it can make a huge difference to the confidence of the witness and the impression which he or she creates').

[35] [2005] EWCA Crim 177, [58]. The Court continued: 'In its immediate aftermath, we can well understand why little, if any, thought was given to the position of potential witnesses who might become involved in any subsequent prosecutions of any detainees. At that time there was no process to be abused. Litigation, civil or criminal, would have been far from the mind of any of these potential witnesses'.

[36] Ibid [62].

[37] Home Office, *Criminal Justice System Review: Rebalancing the Criminal Justice System in Favour of the Law-abiding Majority* (2006), webarchive.nationalarchives.gov.uk/20060904182404/homeoffice.gov.uk/ documents/cjs-review.pdf/ (accessed 19 January 2016); Home Office, *Justice for All*, Cm 5563 (London, The Stationery Office, 2002); JD Jackson, 'Justice for All: Putting Victims at the Heart of Criminal Justice' (2003) 30 *Journal of Law and Society* 309.

piloting new arrangements for speaking to witnesses at court and training all relevant staff.[38] The traditionally axiomatic ban on pre-trial contact between witnesses and barristers has been relaxed to accommodate familiarisation.[39] The decisive consideration for the Court of Appeal in *Momodou* was that legitimate witness familiarisation need not, and preferably should not, involve any discussion about the substance of the witness's evidence. Witness familiarisation is unproblematic to the extent that it is confined to providing generic advice about the process of testifying in court and offering 'tea and sympathy'-style reassurance and moral support to the witness. The line is crossed when *the content* of testimony becomes the subject of conversation.[40]

This is evidently what occurred in the Bond Solon and consultant psychiatrist-led sessions in *Momodou*. The Bond Solon training, in particular, was—the Court of Appeal found—'wholly inappropriate and improper'.[41] Herein lies a third noteworthy aspect of the *Momodou* guidance. The Court was naturally concerned about deliberate collusion or 'tailor[ing] ... evidence in the light of what anyone else said', but added that even 'any unfounded perception of impropriety would be troubling. On elementary first principles, procedural rectitude is partly a matter of public perception: justice must not only be done, but must manifestly be seen to be done.[42] This common law axiom is now reinforced by European human rights law principles and jurisprudence.[43] Several well-established rules of English criminal procedure reflect the concern that a witness might 'trim' his evidence as a consequence of being exposed to other witnesses' pre-trial statements or courtroom testimony. Witnesses are not allowed to sit in court and observe trial proceedings until after they have testified themselves.[44] Nor should any witness have access to another witness' statement or proof of evidence prior to going into the witness-box.[45] Witnesses

---

[38] *CPS Action Plan in Response to Victim and Witness Survey* (2015), www.cps.gov.uk/publications/research/index.html (accessed 19 January 2016).

[39] The Bar Council's *Written Standards for the Conduct of Professional Work* (2006) [6.1.2] unambiguously states: 'There is no longer any rule which prevents a barrister from having contact with any witness.' Pre-trial contact with witnesses whom counsel expects to call in-chief is positively encouraged in relation to (i) experts; and (ii) lay witnesses of fact 'especially when the witness is nervous, vulnerable or apparently the victim of criminal or similar conduct, to ensure that those facing unfamiliar court procedures are put as much at ease as possible': ibid [6.1.4].

[40] CPS insists that its proposed familiarisation arrangements are 'limited and within the boundaries of our current system', and that 'prosecution advocates, both those employed by the CPS and those from the independent Bar, know where the line should be drawn': *Consultation—Summary of Responses*, above n 8. Nonetheless, the practical challenges for legal professionals of holding this line *whenever* they meet with lay witnesses of fact should not be underestimated. The legally acceptable parameters of witness familiarisation might well be very clear in the lawyer's mind, but the witness may have other expectations and perceptions.

[41] [2005] EWCA Crim 177, [45].

[42] 'It has long been a fundamental principle of English law that justice must not only be done, but must be seen to be done': *Re S-W (Children)* [2015] EWCA Civ 27, [43] (King LJ). The *locus classicus* is Lord Hewart CJ's celebrated dictum in *R v Sussex Justices, Ex parte McCarthy* [1924] 1 KB 256, 259 (KBD) that 'it is not merely of some importance but is of fundamental importance that justice should not only be done, but should manifestly and undoubtedly be seen to be done'.

[43] *Hanif and Khan v United Kingdom* (2012) 55 EHRR 16; *Axel Springer AG v Germany* (2012) 55 EHRR 6, [80]; *Borgers v Belgium* (1993) 15 EHRR 92; *Hauschildt v Denmark* (1990) 12 EHRR 266; *Piersack v Belgium* (1983) 5 EHRR 169.

[44] Described as 'good practice ... in the normal course of things', with the proviso that departures may trigger exclusion under PACE 1984, s 78: *R v Carty* [2011] EWCA Crim 2087, [10]; *R v Smith (Joan)* [1968] 1 WLR 636, (1968) 52 Cr App R 224 (CA). An exception is made for expert witnesses, enabling them to advise the instructing party on responding to expert testimony adduced by an opponent.

[45] *R v Richardson* (1971) 2 QB 484, 490 (CA); *R v Skinner* (1994) 99 Cr App R 212 (CA).

who have already testified may sit in the public gallery, if they wish, but must not seek to communicate with those who have yet to be called or otherwise influence their evidence.[46] Section 79 of the Police and Criminal Evidence Act 1984 (PACE) (legislating the pre-existing common law rule)[47] imposes similar discipline on the accused, by ensuring that if the accused elects to testify in his own defence he must do so before calling any other defence witness. Lady Justice Hale (as she then was) summarised the general position in judicial review proceedings brought by an applicant who claimed that a police officer had deliberately run him over in an attempted vehicular homicide, and who sought—unsuccessfully, as it transpired—to secure access to witness statements collected as part of an investigation by the Police Complaints Authority:[48]

> Contamination is not generally a problem in the civil and family jurisdictions which start from the proposition that witnesses are doing their best however misguided or mistaken their best may be. It is however a problem in the criminal jurisdiction which does not start from that proposition. Witnesses (apart from police officers) must be kept apart and not allowed to see one another's witness statements for two reasons: there is a risk either (a) that they will deliberately trim their evidence to fit in with the evidence of others (ie act dishonestly) or, perhaps more seriously (b) that their honest evidence will be disbelieved because the accusation of trimming can be made to discredit it.[49]

Deliberate trimming or collusion, or colourable suspicion of either, are not the only forensic risks presented by pre-trial contact between witnesses or irregular exposure to another witness's testimony. Contamination of evidence may occur subconsciously, without a witness's deliberate connivance or conscious awareness. English trial process has long sought to insulate itself from testimony infected by 'innocent contamination'.[50] The plasticity and malleability of human memory, extensively researched by cognitive and behavioural scientists, exacerbates these risks.[51] In Judge LJ's pithy encapsulation in

---

[46] *R v B* [2008] EWCA Crim 238; *R v Mendy* (1976) 64 Cr App R 4 (CA).

[47] *R v Morrison* (1911) 6 Cr App R 158 (CCA); approved as 'an authoritative statement which this court reiterates and endorses as correctly stating the law' by *R v Smith (Joan)* [1968] 1 WLR 636, 637 (CA).

[48] The PCA was superseded by the Independent Police Complaints Commission (IPCC), from April 2004, pursuant to the Police Reform Act 2002. See www.ipcc.gov.uk/ (accessed 19 January 2016).

[49] *R (Green) v Police Complaints Authority* [2002] EWCA Civ 389, [81]. Simon Brown LJ agreed that 'evidence may be contaminated, and … therefore, disclosure would risk hindering or frustrating the very purpose of the investigation, the bringing to book of police officers who properly ought to be prosecuted or disciplined': ibid [55]. Chadwick LJ concurred in the result on narrower grounds. Baroness Hale's exemption for police officers contrasts with Farquharson LJ's observation in *R v Skinner* (1994) 99 Cr App R 212, 216 (CA), that avoiding any appearance of collusion in the production of witness statements 'is particularly important in the case of police officers because, as is well known, they are the only ones who give evidence fortified by the use of notes made at the time. In such a case, as indeed is the case here, witnesses can be attacked for giving evidence on grounds that they are giving not a true account of what happened, but something which has been affected by the discussions they have had with somebody else.'

[50] See eg *R v N* [2011] EWCA Crim 730; *DPP v Boardman* [1975] AC 421, 444 (Lord Wilberforce), 459 (Lord Cross) (HL).

[51] EF Loftus, D Wolchover and D Page, 'General Review of the Psychology of Witness Testimony' in A Heaton-Armstrong, E Shepherd, G Gudjonsson and D Wolchover (eds), *Witness Testimony: Psychological, Investigative and Evidential Perspectives* (Oxford, Oxford University Press, 2006); G Cohen, 'Human Memory in the Real World'; and G Davies, 'Contamination of Witness Memory', both in A Heaton-Armstrong, E Shepherd and D Wolchover (eds), *Analysing Witness Testimony* (London, Blackstone Press, 1999); GH Gudjonsson, *The Psychology of Interrogations, Confessions and Testimony* (London, Wiley, 1992) ch 5. For judicial recognition, see eg *R (Saunders) v IPCC* [2008] EWHC 2372 (Admin), [13].

Momodou, whenever there has been pre-trial discussion between witnesses about the facts of the case, '[w]hether deliberately or inadvertently, the evidence may no longer be their own'.[52]

A fourth consideration highlighted by the *Momodou* judgment opens up the epistemological foundations of judicial evidence to closer scrutiny. Contamination of evidence may occur in private conversations between two witnesses, or between one witness and a lawyer or therapist. The danger is especially acute, however, in group 'counselling' or preparation sessions, in which witnesses share their perceptions and recollections with each other. Witnesses exposed to new information, imparted directly or through more subtle hints and behavioural cues, will naturally seek to integrate it into their own perceptions and recollections, as postulated by theoretically cogent[53] and empirically grounded narrative or 'story' models of testimony and common-sense inferential reasoning.[54] Epistemic modesty demands that we all must sometimes concede the fallibility of our memories and perceptions. If, for example, a witness discovers that particular details of his account are contradicted by three other independent witnesses, who all appear confident in their recollections, the witness might well be inclined to think himself mistaken, and to revise his story accordingly. Moreover, once such adjustments are made it may be tempting to persuade oneself that the original telling contained remediable errors and to adopt the 'cleaned-up' version as authentic; especially when invited to re-tell the story many months later in a criminal trial.[55] It is plausible that such interactions will tend to produce a kind of cognitive 'reversion to the mean' whereby a (more or less) coherent narrative is formulated, with its rough edges knocked off and inconsistencies edited out, essentially through a process of group confabulation.

These psychological processes may operate even in the absence of institutional or partisan pressures to produce an agreed 'authentic' account. But in *Momodou*, the forensic risks inherent to group witness preparation were exacerbated by conflicts of interest, at several levels.[56]

---

[52] [2005] EWCA Crim 177, [61].

[53] RJ Allen, 'Factual Ambiguity and a Theory of Evidence' (1994) 88 *Northwestern University Law Review* 606; MS Pardo, 'Juridical Proof, Evidence, and Pragmatic Meaning: Toward Evidentiary Holism' (2000) 95 *Northwestern University Law Review* 399; MS Pardo and RJ Allen, 'Juridical Proof and the Best Explanation' (2008) 27 *Law and Philosophy* 223. But cf DM Risinger, 'John Henry Wigmore, Johnny Lynn Old Chief, and "Legitimate Moral Force": Keeping the Courtroom Safe for Heartstrings and Gore' (1998) 49 *Hastings Law Journal* 403; D Menashe and ME Shamash, 'The Narrative Fallacy' (2005) 3(1) *International Commentary on Evidence*, Article 3 and replies by Allen (Article 5) and Burns (Article 4).

[54] N Pennington and R Hastie, 'A Cognitive Theory of Juror Decision Making: The Story Model' (1991) 13 *Cardozo Law Review* 519; R Hastie and N Pennington, 'The OJ Simpson Stories: Behavioral Scientists' Reflections on the *People of the State of California v Orenthal James Simpson*' (1996) 67 *University of Colorado Law Review* 957; L Ellison and VE Munro, '"Telling Tales": Exploring Narratives of Life and Law within the (Mock) Jury Room' (2015) 35 *Legal Studies* 201. Generally, see W Twining, 'Lawyer's Stories' in W Twining, *Rethinking Evidence: Exploratory Essay,* 2nd edn (Cambridge, Cambridge University Press, 2006); BJ Foley and RA Robbins, 'Fiction 101: A Primer for Lawyers on How to Use Fiction Writing Techniques to Write Persuasive Fact Sections' (2001) 32 *Rutgers Law Journal* 459.

[55] 'Both adults' and children's memories are highly sensitive to the passage of time. Although some knowledge and experiences are stored for decades, a great deal of information is lost or becomes inaccessible due to decay or interference': JR Spencer and R Flin, *The Evidence of Children: The Law and the Psychology*, 2nd edn (London, Blackstone Press, 1993) 299.

[56] A similar situation arose in the aftermath of the Hillsborough disaster inquiry, where police officers' initial eyewitness accounts underwent 'an extensive process of review and alteration of the recollections and their transition to multi-purpose statements', largely with a view to excising comments unfavourable to South Yorkshire Police: Hillsborough: *The Report of the Hillsborough Independent Panel*, HC 581 (London, The Stationery Office, 2012) Part 11, hillsborough.independent.gov.uk/ (accessed 21 November 2015).

Individual Group 4 employees may have been concerned that their own conduct, for example in the initial restraint of the detainee Eunice, would be regarded as excessive and a precipitating cause of the riot, for which they could be held personally responsible. Group 4 was also itself a potential criminal defendant, directly or vicariously liable for the conduct of its employees. Those employees who underwent witness training must have been aware that their employer had a direct interest in the substance of their testimony: indeed, this surely explains why Group 4 went to such lengths to prepare its employees' testimony in the first place, with the possible bonus of developing evidence in anticipation of its civil action against the police.[57] Small wonder that the trial court in *Momodou* held its nose when invited to draw from this poisoned testimonial well. Even Crown counsel was embarrassed by the situation, and made factual stipulations diminishing the credibility of prosecution witnesses that were, if anything, excessively favourable to the defence.

The Court of Appeal's pronouncements in *Momodou* usefully clarify the parameters of legitimate witness preparation in English law, yet the judgment remains question-begging in several vital respects. Consider, to begin with, the Court's enigmatic assertion that, '[t]he witness should give his or her own evidence, so far as practicable uninfluenced by what anyone else has said, whether in formal discussions or informal conversations.' Now, of course the witness should give 'his or her own evidence'. The principle of orality,[58] buttressed by a phalanx of familiar procedural requirements and evidentiary doctrines (not least, the common law hearsay prohibition[59]), demands that witnesses should provide percipient evidence of what was seen, heard, smelt, felt or tasted by the witness him- or herself with his or her own unaided senses.[60] However, this elementary statement of legal principle is liable to convey a very misleading picture of how in practice witness testimony is actually generated.[61] For one thing, criminal proceedings often involve substantial delays, in which memories may corrode or, alternatively, acquire new layers of imaginative reinterpretation. For another, by the time that witnesses testify in court, they will often already have repeated or re-read their evidence on several occasions, each repetition offering a further opportunity for omission or embellishment. Thirdly, and most significantly for

---

[57] The Court of Appeal remarked: 'We have not heard evidence or representations on behalf of Bond Solon or Group 4, but the inference that Group 4 was concerned to protect its intended civil proceedings is inescapable': [2005] EWCA Crim 177, [39].

[58] Roberts and Zuckerman, above n 14, 291–97 and 465–68. The 'principle of orality' has been discussed explicitly by the European Court of Justice (eg *Baustahlgewebe GmbH v EC Commission* (Case C-185/95 P) [1999] 4 CMLR 1203 [77]–[96]) but not, in so many words (that I can find), by any English or Scots court. However, the *principle* of orality—however articulated—is indisputably integral to traditional common law conceptions of criminal trial procedure: see eg *Arthur JS Hall & Co v Simons* [2002] 1 AC 615, 692 (HL) (Lord Hoffmann describing 'The substantial orality of the English system of trial and appellate procedure'); *R v Derodra* [2000] 1 Cr App R, 41, 47 (CA) (Buxton LJ referring to 'the pervasive orality, and the principle of testament by identified witnesses, of the English criminal trial'); *A v HM Advocate* [2012] HCJAC 29, 2012 JC 343, [22] ('the starting point in all criminal trials in Scotland remains parole evidence').

[59] The relationship between the epistemology of testimony and the common law hearsay prohibition is insightfully explored by MS Pardo, 'Testimony' (2007) 82 *Tulane Law Review* 119. The admissibility of hearsay evidence in English criminal trials is now principally governed by the Criminal Justice Act 2003, ss 114–18, which relaxes the common law prohibition whilst retaining nearly all of the pre-existing inclusionary exceptions.

[60] Spectacles and hearing aids are permitted, but may open the witness up to cross-examination to credit. See eg *R v Herman* [2009] EWCA Crim 1211, [9], [25]; *R v Manahan* [2004] EWCA Crim 117, [7].

[61] See generally, A Heaton-Armstrong, D Wolchover and A Maxwell-Scott, 'Obtaining, Recording and Admissibility of Out-of-Court Witness Statements' in Heaton-Armstrong et al (eds) (2006), above n 51; D Wolchover and A Heaton-Armstrong, 'Recording Witness Statements' [1992] *Criminal Law Review* 160.

our purposes, *witnesses never produce their own evidence unaided.* A witness statement provided to the police is, generally speaking, written by the police officer taking the statement, to be sure from information obtained from the witness, but frequently—sometimes tragi-comically—employing the unmistakable idiom of police professional jargon. Real people never say things like, 'On May, 23 around midday I was proceeding in a westerly direction along High Street, when I saw the man I now know to be the defendant advancing towards me in a menacing fashion'.[62] The statement which the police officer writes becomes the witness' statement when the witness reads it over (or has it read back to them by the police officer)[63] and signs it, authenticating the statement and adopting it as their own. This performance is aptly characterised, from a sociological perspective, as an institutionally structured co-production. What emerges from the statement-taking process is not identical to what would have emerged if the witness had been given pen and paper and left to write unsupervised in a corner of the interview room.

The same theoretical analysis applies to tape-recorded and video-recorded statements. Granted that, by comparison with written transcriptions, statements produced by electronic media are more obviously and literally 'in the witness's own words', they are still elicited through a series of answers to questions formulated with particular investigative objectives in mind.[64] A tape-recorded or video-recorded statement might well begin with a 'free narrative' phase where the witness is invited to 'say what happened in your own words', but sooner or later the style of the interview will switch to a more directive approach. In this later phase of the interview the questioner employs relatively closed questions in an effort to focus attention on particular points of interest on which the witness's response is desired. The evidential fruits of this process resemble the contents of the more traditional police-transcribed witness statement precisely to the extent that investigative interviewing is always a joint enterprise, a co-production of witness and police (or other investigative) interviewer. After the witness has spoken to tape or camera,[65] moreover, lawyers often edit out irrelevant or otherwise inadmissible material to make the statement fit for presentation in court.[66]

Socio-legal scholars' talk of the 'construction' of legal cases[67] is liable to make practitioners exceedingly nervous; especially if 'construction' is taken to imply strongly relativistic or

---

[62]   This particular illustration may be rather music hall, but the methodological point is sound and generalises.

[63]   A somewhat controversial, if entirely pragmatic, extension of the general practice: *R v McGillivray* (1993) 97 Cr App R 232 (CA); *R v Kelsey* (1982) 74 Cr App R 213 (CA); *R v Ascough* [2014] EWCA Crim 1148.

[64]   The police interview transcripts, reproduced by Dixon in Chapter 3 of this volume, graphically illustrate the goal-orientated nature of investigative interviewing, there pursued to excess.

[65]   Of course, the performance could conceivably have been pre-scripted *before* the camera rolls: cf M McConville, 'Videotaping Interrogations: Police Behaviour On and Off Camera' [1992] *Criminal Law Review* 532.

[66]   See eg Consolidated Criminal Practice Directions [2015] EWCA Crim 1567, CPD V Evidence 16A.1 (directing that: 'Where the prosecution proposes to tender written statements in evidence ... it will frequently be necessary for certain statements to be edited. This will occur either because a witness has made more than one statement whose contents should conveniently be reduced into a single, comprehensive statement, or where a statement contains inadmissible, prejudicial or irrelevant material'); *R v Greenwood* [2005] 1 Cr App R 7, [2004] EWCA Crim 1388 (formal admissions); *R v Wood* [1987] 1 WLR 779 (CA).

[67]   M McConville, A Sanders and R Leng, *The Case for the Prosecution: Police Suspects and the Construction of Criminality* (London, Routledge, 1991); A Sanders, 'Constructing the Case for the Prosecution' (1987) 14 *Journal of Law and Society* 229; D Sudnow, 'Normal Crimes: Sociological Features of the Penal Code in a Public Defender Office' (1965) 12 *Social Problems* 255. For vivid illustrations of the processes of 'constructing' scientific evidence, see E Cunliffe, *Murder, Medicine and Motherhood* (Oxford, Hart Publishing, 2011); G Edmond, 'Azaria's Accessories: The Social (Legal-Scientific) Construction of the Chamberlains' Guilt and Innocence' (1998) 22 *Melbourne University Law Review* 396; P Roberts, 'Science in the Criminal Process' (1994) 14 *Oxford Journal of Legal Studies* 469.

sceptical connotations.[68] Professionals and policy-makers involved in the practical administration of criminal justice understandably worry that 'construction' could be construed as 'fabrication', and nobody wants to be responsible for producing fabricated evidence. Still, every experienced practitioner knows perfectly well that the preceding two paragraphs state an elementary, if seldom so bluntly articulated, truth. In police and lawyers' jargon, witnesses are 'statemented', which—if it were really a proper word—would certainly be a verb. Being statemented is something that is *done to* witnesses by police and legal professionals, or at least a process through which the former, innocents abroad in the strange land of criminal law, are conducted by the latter, their expert local guides.

Let me be absolutely clear about the practical implications of this analysis. My epistemology of judicial evidence does *not* imply that there is anything necessarily untoward in the sociological co-production of witness statements by lay witnesses and police or legal professionals. Criminal litigation as currently designed and performed simply could not function on a daily basis unless evidence was carefully selected, organised, packaged and presented by professionals making sound judgements of relevance and determining which facts have to be proved by what evidence in order to substantiate criminal charges or successfully defend them. In reality, a lay witness of fact is probably going to need considerable professional assistance to (in Judge LJ's words) 'give of his or her best at the forthcoming trial'.[69]

This realisation need not flatly contradict the Court of Appeal's injunction that 'the witness should give his or her own evidence, so far as practicable uninfluenced by what anyone else has said, whether in formal discussions or informal conversations'.[70] But it does lay considerable stress on the qualification *so far as practicable*. It would certainly be *possible* to keep witnesses isolated from police investigators and legal professionals (though not from family members, work colleagues or other acquaintances with whom witnesses might potentially discuss their evidence) and thereafter closeted in evidential purdah prior to testifying in court. But this is hardly realistic in our current system of litigation, in which evidence has to be carefully scrutinised, evaluated and prepared for trial by many hands and through successive procedural stages. So Judge LJ's 'practicable' must mean 'appropriate' or 'desirable', which only restates the essential conundrum: in what ways, and to what extent, is it appropriate or desirable for a witness's evidence to be influenced by their interactions with any third party, be they police investigator, interviewing lawyer, therapist or counsellor, or work colleagues unfortunate enough to find themselves in the midst of a prison riot? At what point in such interactions, or by reference to which of their characteristics or

---

[68] Cf D Nicolson, 'Taking Epistemology Seriously: "Truth, Reason and Justice" Revisited' (2013) 17 *International Journal of Evidence and Proof* 1; RK Greenstein, 'Determining Facts: The Myth of Direct Evidence' (2009) 45 *Houston Law Review* 1801; A Green, 'How the Criminal Justice System Knows' (1997) 6 *Social and Legal Studies* 5.

[69] [2005] EWCA Crim 177, [62]. My point is conceptual and epistemological. It opens up many further practical and normative questions concerning the manner in which police and lawyers perform their evidentiary tasks—eg concerning the extent to which victims' accounts are authentically documented and reproduced in legal proceedings and their voices heard in court—which I do not pursue here. For further discussion, see eg H Baillot, S Cowan and VE Munro, '"Hearing the Right Gaps": Enabling and Responding to Disclosures of Sexual Violence within the UK Asylum Process' (2012) 21 *Social & Legal Studies* 269; A Cretney and G Davis, 'Prosecuting Domestic Assault: Victims Failing Courts, or Courts Failing Victims?' (1997) 36 *Howard Journal of Criminal Justice* 146; KL Scheppele, 'Just the Facts, Ma'am: Sexualized Violence, Evidentiary Habits, and the Revision of Truth' (1992) 37 *New York Law School Law Review* 123.

[70] [2005] EWCA Crim 177, [61].

qualities, might one be obliged to conclude that the witness is no longer giving 'his or her own evidence' but rather channelling a collective (re)construction? Or again, under what circumstances would the integrity of criminal proceedings be imperilled by the perception, or a fortiori by the reality, that intolerable coaching has taken place?

The witness training in *Momodou*, conceded by trial counsel to be 'wholly inappropriate and improper',[71] was undertaken by an ostensibly reputable service provider. Group 4 did not try to conceal what it had done: to the contrary, it sought to justify putting its employees through the Bond Solon witness training programme, and refused to desist when called upon to do so by the police and the CPS. This was not an instance of clandestine witness coaching, either flagrant or indirect. Training of this kind does not attract legal professional privilege and can always be challenged and criticised in litigation (assuming that opposing parties know about it).[72] *Momodou* occupies the perplexing and ill-defined borderlands between permissible witness preparation and impermissible witness coaching. The Court of Appeal claimed to discern a 'dramatic distinction' between familiarisation and training, yet the Bar Council's contemporaneous *Guidance* stated that 'the line between (a) the legitimate preparation of a witness and his/her evidence for a current or forthcoming trial or hearing and (b) impermissible rehearsing or coaching of a witness, may not always be understood'.[73] Barristers, as a professional group with copious experience, are perfectly at ease both with conceptual distinctions and with drama, so any lingering misunderstandings are presumably indicative of deeper, more intractable complexities.

That conjecture is reinforced by the opinion of experienced police investigators, who advise that 'there is a very fine line to be drawn between the legitimate process of questioning a witness's account of events in order to investigate the allegations effectively, and contaminating that witness's evidence'.[74] It also chimes with the experience of foreign jurists.[75] According to one US commentator, the boundaries of legitimate witness preparation in his jurisdiction are so loosely formulated that 'evidence at trial … has the palm prints and fingerprints of the lawyers all over it as the evidence is shaped, reshaped, and sometimes distorted a bit for adversarial advantage'.[76] Similar concerns have been expressed in

---

[71]   Ibid [45].

[72]   There is 'no property in a witness' in English law, before, during or after trial: see eg *R v Deeney* [2011] EWCA Crim 893, [34] (characterising this aphorism as 'lawyers' vernacular'). Either side is perfectly entitled to request an interview with the other party's witnesses, and under reformed disclosure rules, the defence must notify the prosecution of any witnesses it proposes to call at trial as well as receiving a witness list from the prosecution: see Criminal Procedure Rules (Crim PR) 2015, Part 15; and *Code of Practice for Arranging and Conducting Interviews of Witnesses Notified by the Accused*, issued pursuant to s 21A of the Criminal Procedure and Investigations Act 1996. A witness in court could always be asked by an opposing litigant whether she has previously undergone any kind of witness training programme. Conceivably, even a witness who is not called to testify in the first instance could be compelled to answer such questions by an opponent, by invoking the compulsory process of the court and, if necessary, having her declared hostile, pursuant to Criminal Procedure Act 1865, s 3. Of course, legal permissibility does not necessarily indicate sensible forensic strategy.

[73]   Bar Council, *Guidance on Witness Preparation* (2005).

[74]   Letter dated 26 February 2002 from South Yorkshire Police to the Court of Appeal, quoted in *R (Green) v Police Complaints Authority* [2002] EWCA Civ 389, [28].

[75]   In *State v Earp*, 571 A 2d 1227, 1235 (Md 1990), for example, the Maryland Court of Appeal cautioned that 'the line that exists between perfectly acceptable witness preparation … and impermissible influencing of the witness … may sometimes be fine and difficult to discern'.

[76]   WT Pizzi, *Trials Without Truth* (New York, New York University Press, 1999) 126.

Hong Kong.[77] In truth, *pace Momodou*, the distinction between witness coaching and witness preparation/familiarisation remains (dramatically) under-determined and (perilously) imprecise. Only in terms of the legal consequences of falling on one side of the line or the other is the distinction, after *Momodou*, dramatically clear.

2. From Doctrine to Process: The Advent of Pre-trial Witness Interviewing

Until quite recently, prosecutors in England and Wales were de facto insulated from the ethical dilemmas[78] and evidentiary responsibilities shouldered by defence solicitors in criminal proceedings. Witness statements were taken exclusively by the police and neither Crown Prosecutors nor members of the independent Bar instructed as Crown advocates had any pre-trial contact with lay witnesses of fact.[79] Anticipating accusations of 'witness-coaching' (well-founded or otherwise) from their adversarial opponents in court, barristers[80] appearing in criminal cases in England and Wales have traditionally internalised a strict cultural taboo against any pre-trial contact with witnesses other than the accused. However, various factors have lately combined to prompt critical reconsideration of prosecutors' institutional isolation from witnesses, which might be perceived as aloof, disengaged or alienating. Prominent policy drivers include safeguarding the rights and interests of complainants and (especially, vulnerable) witnesses,[81] improving the quality

---

[77] See *HKSAR v Cho Wing-nan* (unreported), DCCC 360/2011, Reasons for Sentence (30 April 2012), [32], discussed by M Jackson (Chapter 8) in this volume. PTWI was rejected in Hong Kong partly on the basis of 'genuinely held concerns that a PTWI scheme could lead to problems of coaching of witnesses and contamination of evidence': Legislative Council Panel on Administration of Justice and Legal Services, *Pre-Trial Interviewing of Witnesses by Prosecutors*, LC Paper No CB(2)1599/09-10(01), May 2010, www.legco.gov.hk/yr09-10/english/panels/ajls/papers/aj0524cb2-1599-1-e.pdf (accessed 19 January 2016) [12].

[78] The classic discussion is MH Freedman, 'Professional Responsibility of the Criminal Defense Lawyer: The Three Hardest Questions' (1966) 64 *Michigan Law Review* 1469.

[79] Expert witnesses are not included in the PTWI scheme, since contact between prosecutors and experts has always been permitted: see P Roberts and C Willmore, *The Role of Forensic Science Evidence in Criminal Proceedings*, RCCJ Research Study No 11 (London, HMSO, 1993) 18–21. Discussions with expert witnesses raise distinctive practical, epistemological and ethical issues. In addition to Edmond (Chapter 9) in this volume, see Crim PR 2015, Part 19; T Ward, 'Expert Witnesses: Role, Ethics and Accountability' in G Bruinsma and D Weisburd (eds), *Encyclopedia of Criminology and Criminal Justice* (New York, Springer, 2013) 1494; J Sanders, 'Expert Witness Ethics' (2007) 76 *Fordham Law Review* 1539; GC Harris, 'Testimony for Sale: The Law and Ethics of Snitches and Experts' (2000) 28 *Pepperdine Law Review* 1.

[80] Note that England and Wales still operates a 'split profession' in which barristers (specialist advocates at the independent Bar) and solicitors are separate branches with their own professional training, qualifications, regulatory authorities and rules of conduct. In criminal trials on indictment, barristers are briefed by 'the professional client', ie CPS employee or defence solicitor. This functional and cultural divide has doubtless served to reinforce and preserve barristers' distance from witnesses, in comparison with most other common law jurisdictions with a single professional qualification (eg 'attorney-at-law') or the possibility of joint qualification as a solicitor *and* barrister.

[81] The *Code of Practice for Victims of Crime* (London, Ministry of Justice, 2015) guarantees various service rights to information and support, including 'key entitlements' to be 'informed if the suspect is to be prosecuted or not … [s]eek a review of the police or CPS's decision not to prosecute … [and m]eet the CPS advocate and ask him or her questions about the court process'. On the broader reform context, see Roberts and Zuckerman, above n 14, ch 10; J Doak, 'Victims' Rights in Criminal Trials: Prospects for Participation' (2005) 32 *Journal of Law and Society* 294; L Ellison, *The Adversarial Process and the Vulnerable Witness* (Oxford, Oxford University Press, 2001).

of evidence, boosting conviction rates and promoting efficiency in the administration of justice.[82]

In comparative law terms, England and Wales was a very late adopter of a national prosecution agency. The CPS was established only in 1986.[83] At that time, the traditional ban on counsel's pre-trial contact with witnesses was widely assumed—possibly without much reflection—to apply *mutatis mutandis* to Crown Prosecutors. It cohered with the philosophy of maintaining a strict separation between the investigative and prosecutorial phases of criminal proceedings, which had been influential in the CPS's original design and creation.[84] By the early years of the twenty-first century, however, both the Attorney General and the Director of Public Prosecutions (DPP) were publicly expressing their dissatisfaction with what was now being characterised as an unreasonable fetter on effective case-preparation by prosecutors.

The proximate impetus for reform in England and Wales appears to have been the collapse of the first Damilola Taylor murder trial.[85] Although criminal policy-making is often reactive,[86] and sometimes for that reason ill-considered and poorly executed, agitation for witness interviewing by prosecutors may have been building for some time.[87] Perhaps also because it chimed with a clutch of contemporary policy priorities, the proposal struck

---

[82] On the drive for efficiency in English criminal procedure, see A Edwards, 'The Other Leveson Report—The Review of Efficiency in Criminal Proceedings' [2015] *Criminal Law Review* 399; J McEwan, 'From Adversarialism to Managerialism: Criminal Justice in Transition' (2011) 31 *Legal Studies* 519; M McConville and L Marsh, 'Adversarialism Goes West: Case Management in Criminal Courts' (2015) 19 *International Journal of Evidence and Proof* 172.

[83] Prosecution of Offences Act 1985. See J Rozenberg, *The Case for the Crown* (Wellingborough, Equation, 1987) (suggesting at 79 that 'one can only marvel at the fact that until 1986 nobody had succeeded in taking the power to prosecute out of the hands of the police'); A Sanders, 'The New Prosecution Arrangements: (2) An Independent Crown Prosecution Service?' [1986] *Criminal Law Review* 16.

[84] As set out in the Philips Royal Commission on Criminal Procedure, *Report*, Cm 8092 (London, HMSO, 1981) [7.6]–[7.7]: 'It is a central feature of our proposals that there should be a division of functions between the police and prosecutor ... [W]e would leave with the police complete responsibility for investigating offences ...'

[85] In particular, prosecutors' embarrassment surrounding 'Witness Bromley', whose evidence was discredited at trial after a video-tape came to light showing her singing 'I'm in the money' (taken to be a reference to the reward-money she expected to receive in return for her testimony) whilst waiting to give her statement in a police interview-room: see S Laville, 'Damilola judge rejects witness as a liar', *The Telegraph*, 28 February 2002; N Hopkins, 'Secrets and lies of a far from expert witness', *The Guardian*, 28 February 2002. Two other teenagers were subsequently convicted of Damilola's manslaughter: S Tendler, 'Justice for Damilola as brothers convicted six years on', *The Times*, 10 August 2006.

[86] Relaxation of the double jeopardy prohibition was likewise precipitated by the collapse of the first Stephen Lawrence murder trial: see P Roberts, 'Double Jeopardy Law Reform: A Criminal Justice Commentary' (2002) 65 *Modern Law Review* 393. Generally, see M McConville and L Bridges (eds), *Criminal Justice in Crisis* (Cheltenham, Edward Elgar, 1994).

[87] In his JUSTICE Tom Sargant Memorial Lecture on 'Prosecuting by Consent—A Public Prosecution Service in the 21st Century' (19 October 2004), justice.org.uk/wp-content/uploads/2004/10/Prosecuting-by-Consent. pdf (accessed 19 January 2016), DPP Ken Macdonald presented pre-trial witness interviewing as 'a natural part of giving prosecutors a greater role in advising the police and the responsibility for determining the charge'. Rather than a departure from orthodox principles, it was more in the nature of purging embedded irrationalities: '[F]ar from interviewing [victims] pre-trial, we did not even talk to them. It was almost as if they were unclean. The sight of a prosecutor talking to a victim would provoke a furious complaint to a judge or a lacerating, or supposedly lacerating, cross-examination. In my view, this world of criminal lawyers was becoming more and more unreal; and more and more divorced from what the community wanted and expected from us. Because what this approach absolutely guaranteed was the disengagement of victims and witnesses from the prosecution and trial process. Disengagement implies that they were once engaged; perhaps it would be more accurate to describe it as non-engagement.'

an instant chord and was taken up with enthusiasm. Two policy papers were issued, the first by the CPS in 2003[88] and the second by the Office of the Attorney General in 2004,[89] both of which (notwithstanding some initial reservations) came down decisively in favour of relaxing the prohibition on pre-trial contact between prosecutors and witnesses. The upbeat tone and leading rationales for reform are conveyed by the following extract from Attorney General Lord Goldsmith QC's paper:

> [I]t is striking that it is only in England and Wales that prosecutors do not have direct access to witnesses even in order to assess their credibility and reliability—even though there is no reason why an impartial public prosecution service should not undertake this role. If my vision of the CPS as a world class prosecuting service, admired and respected, and seen by all as a champion of victims and justice is to be realised, this must change. … [T]he interests of justice in ensuring that a prosecutor is able to explore all necessary aspects of a witness's evidence before reaching a prosecution decision outweigh the potential risks.[90]

Whilst the Attorney General's reference to assessing 'credibility and reliability' might imply a static conception of testimony, as something pre-constituted and available for detached appraisal, the idea of 'explor[ing] all necessary aspects of a witness's evidence' at least strongly hints at a more dynamic relationship between interviewer and witness. It is suggestive of an important distinction, further explored below, between 'evidence' *qua* information known to the witness which could usefully be conveyed to the factfinder and 'evidence' *qua* the witness' ultimate testimony in the courtroom (which could be less or more, or more *and* less, than she actually knows).

(a) PTWI Pilot and Evaluation

Under the superintendence of the DPP, a Code of Practice for prosecutors conducting pre-trial witness interviews was drawn up,[91] and employed in a Pilot project covering four (out of 42) CPS Areas.[92] The Pilot ran for 15 months between January 2006 and April 2007. During this time almost 100 CPS cases were assessed for suitability for witness interviewing by a small, handpicked group of prosecutors who had undergone a dedicated training

---

[88] Crown Prosecution Service, *Pre-Trial Witness Interviews by Prosecutors: A Consultation Paper* (London, CPS, 2003).

[89] Office of the Attorney General, above n 17.

[90] Ibid 3, 20. As a matter of fact, although pre-trial witness interviewing and preparation are routine across much of the common law world, England and Wales was not the 'only' jurisdiction maintaining the traditional ban, which continues to apply, for example, in Malaysia and Hong Kong. See Legislative Council Panel on Administration of Justice and Legal Services, above n 77; LegCo Panel on Administration of Justice and Legal Services, *Information Paper on Pre-trial Interviewing of Witnesses by Prosecutors*, LC Paper No CB(2)2327/07-08(05), 23 June 2008, www.legco.gov.hk/yr07-08/english/panels/ajls/papers/aj0623cb2-2327-5-e.pdf (accessed 21 November 2015); *Submission of the Hong Kong Bar Association—Pre-Trial Witness Interview By Prosecutors*, 16 October 2009, www.hkba.org/whatsnew/submission-position-papers/2009/20091016a.pdf (accessed 21 November 2015).

[91] *PTWI Code of Practice*, above n 9. Now see *Pre-trial Witness Interviews: Code of Practice* (February 2008) (as amended), www.cps.gov.uk/victims_witnesses/resources/interviews.html (accessed 21 November 2015) (PTWI Code of Practice).

[92] CPS was consolidated (back) into 13 Areas in 2010, in order 'to realise economies of scale … take full advantage of developments in technology and … ensur[e] that we were in the best possible position to face the challenge of the budget reductions required between 2011–2015': CPS, *Annual Report and Accounts 2010–2011*, HC 1000 (London, The Stationery Office, 2011) 1 (Director's Letter to the Attorney General).

programme. Some 53 interviews were actually conducted in 47 Pilot cases.[93] Drawing directly on this useful (if modest) practical experience, PTWI was rolled out to Crown Prosecutors nationally from April 2008.[94]

The PTWI Pilot Evaluation incorporated a significant socio-legal element, augmenting the CPS's own comprehensive internal monitoring. This chiefly comprised 12 in-depth semi-structured research interviews with PTWI-trained prosecutors, and two group debriefing meetings extending over three days with a larger pool of about 20 prosecutors. Although the Pilot Evaluation itself sampled only four CPS Areas, our research covered what was then the entire population of PTWI-trained lawyers and relevant cases. The socio-legal component aimed to investigate patterns of action, strategies, motivations, attitudes and opinions, and to identify good practice and potential problems and pitfalls, rather than to quantify case outcomes or establish causation.[95] With the benefit of exceptional 'outsider-insider' access, the study generated rich qualitative data documenting prosecutors' first, occasionally faltering, steps in getting to grips with the operational and legal challenges of pre-trial witness interviewing.

Initial prosecutor training consisted of attendance at (up to) three, two-day CPS in-house training events, incorporating discussions of hypothetical cases and more hands-on practical simulations and interview role-plays. Though hardly comprehensive, this was probably about as much 'theory' as prosecutors could usefully take on-board before immersing themselves in 'live' casework. Prosecutors reported general satisfaction with their training. Several could draw on previous experience of interviewing clients and witnesses in their 'past lives' as defence solicitors, but for the rest—including younger, career-prosecutors— witness interviewing was a novel undertaking.

The challenges of becoming an effective forensic interviewer, and the pitfalls of poor technique, have been extensively documented, for example, in relation to child victims and witnesses[96] and also in the context of police interviews with suspects.[97] As part of the Pilot Evaluation, we wanted to explore how prosecutors were adapting themselves to unfamiliar practical demands in dealing with witness testimony. The remainder of this section, incorporating previously unpublished empirical data, explores prosecutors'

---

[93] Pilot case 'vital statistics' and key findings are summarised in Roberts and Saunders, above n 1.

[94] Joint Statement to Parliament of Baroness Scotland AG and Vera Baird MP, Solicitor General, HL Deb 27 November 2007, vol 696 cols 142–43WS; HC Deb 27 November 2007, vol 468 col 24WS. See Attorney General's Office Press Release, 'National rollout of Pre-trial witness interview scheme—Prosecutors, victims and criminal justice system set to benefit' (27 November 2007); L McGowan, 'Prosecution Interviews of Witnesses: What More will be Sacrificed to "Narrow the Justice Gap"?' (2006) 70 *Journal of Criminal Law* 351.

[95] Numbers and percentages are reported, here and in other published work, only for the purposes of indicating broad trends. For fuller methodological discussion, see P Roberts and C Saunders, 'Piloting PTWI: A Socio-Legal Window on Prosecutors' Assessments of Evidence and Witness Credibility' (2010) 30 *Oxford Journal of Legal Studies* 101.

[96] See eg K London, 'Investigative Interviews of Children: A Review of Psychological Research and Implications for Police Practices' (2001) 4 *Police Quarterly* 123; JM Wood and S Garven, 'How Sexual Abuse Interviews Go Astray: Implications for Prosecutors, Police, and Child Protection Services' (2000) 5 *Child Maltreatment* 109; JA Quas, GS Goodman, S Ghetti and AD Redlich, 'Questioning the Child Witness: What Can We Conclude From the Research Thus Far?' (2000) 1 *Trauma, Violence & Abuse* 223.

[97] In addition to Dixon (Chapter 3) in this volume, see eg SM Kassin, SA Drizin, T Grisso, GH Gudjonsson, RA Leo and AD Redlich, 'Police-Induced Confessions: Risk Factors and Recommendations' (2010) 34 *Law and Human Behavior* 3; T Williamson (ed), *Investigative Interviewing* (Collumpton, Willan, 2006); J Baldwin, 'Police Interviewing Techniques: Establishing Truth or Proof?' (1993) 33 *British Journal of Criminology* 325.

strategic approaches to pre-trial witness interviewing and considers the impact of interviews on the progression and termination of Pilot cases. Section 2(b) describes questioning styles and strategies focused on reviewing and checking witnesses' statements, and highlights opportunities—which were not always grasped in Pilot cases—for eliciting additional information. Section 2(c) discusses more 'probing', and potentially problematic, questioning styles and strategies, and begins to tease out their further evidentiary and practical implications for the conduct of criminal prosecutions.

(b) More Information

PTWI was designed to afford witnesses an additional opportunity to tell their story in their own words and to allow prosecutors to explore any unresolved issues 'for the purpose of assisting a prosecutor to assess the reliability of a witness's evidence or to understand complex evidence'.[98] Following national roll-out, the model of interviewing trialled in the Pilot was extrapolated to all CPS Areas, with some minor modifications to the PTWI Code of Practice and supported by internal *Guidance for Prosecutors*.[99] In every case, the witness will already have made one or more statements to the police.[100] Notwithstanding the prosecutor's expanded role, the police unequivocally remain the primary takers of witness statements in English criminal proceedings. The PTWI Code of Practice now prescribes that accredited prosecutors[101] 'may conduct a pre-trial interview with a witness when they consider that it will enable them to reach a better informed decision about any aspect of the case'.[102] This generic objective is obviously very broad. It encompasses deciding not to charge or to discontinue[103] evidentially weak cases, as well as building up prosecutions destined for trial. In terms of conducting the interview itself:

> [T]he witness may be asked about the content of their statement or other issues that relate to reliability. This may include taking the witness through their statement, asking questions to clarify and expand evidence, asking questions relating to character, exploring new evidence or probing the witness's account.[104]

The clear implication is that interviews may generate new information, not only in the sense of better informing the prosecutor about matters already known to the witness, but more substantially in terms of testing the witness's reactions to newly discovered evidence

---

[98] PTWI Code of Practice, above n 91, [2.1].

[99] www.cps.gov.uk/legal/p_to_r/pre_-trial_witness_interviews/index.html (accessed 21 November 2015).

[100] As a precondition of PTWI, 'no interview should be conducted until the witness has provided to the police a signed witness statement or has taken part in a visually recorded evidential interview': PTWI Code of Practice, above n 91, [2.4].

[101] 'A PTWI may be conducted by a Crown Prosecutor designated by the Chief Crown Prosecutor (CCP) for their Area, Deputy Chief Crown Prosecutor (DCCP) or Head of Division (HoD) to conduct such interviews, or by an independent advocate on the authority of a designated Crown Prosecutor': *PTWI Guidance for Prosecutors*, above n 10. Designated prosecutors must also complete the relevant CPS training course, though this requirement can be waived in 'exceptional cases'.

[102] PTWI Code of Practice, above n 91, [2.2].

[103] Pursuant to the Prosecution of Offences Act 1985, ss 23 and 23A. See Crim PR 2015, Part 12; *R (Gujra) v Crown Prosecution Service* [2013] 1 AC 484, [2012] UKSC 52.

[104] PTWI Code of Practice, above n 91, [2.3] (substituting 'their' for 'his/her', as per the version on the CPS website www.cps.gov.uk/victims_witnesses/resources/interviews.html, accessed 19 January 2016).

and exploring issues, such as character and credibility, the legal salience of which is unlikely to be appreciated by lay witnesses. The PTWI Code of Practice anticipates the need for an investigating officer to take follow-up statements from witnesses to capture, in legally competent form, new information arising from interviews with prosecutors.[105] On the other hand, '[p]re-trial interviews must not be held for the purpose of improving a witness's evidence or performance' and '[p]rosecutors must not under any circumstances train, practise or coach the witness or ask questions that may taint the witness's evidence. Leading questions should be avoided.'[106] Here one may detect a transposition of the central equivocation previously identified in the *Momodou* judgment: if the pre-trial interview has the effect—possibly intended—of making the witness's testimony at trial more complete, more coherent, better phrased, purged of irrelevancies or problematic diction or editorialising, or otherwise polished up and rounded out, in what sense has their 'evidence or performance' *not* been 'improved'?

As part of their induction programme, PTWI Pilot prosecutors had been exposed to a fairly standardised sequential model of interviewing.[107] This begins with formal introductions followed by a 'rapport-building' phase, before proceeding to the interview proper. According to the prevailing philosophy,[108] forensic interviews should begin with relatively open-ended questions, gradually focusing down on more targeted, progressively 'closed' questioning as the flow of the interview appears to demand. This sequential model was reflected in prosecutors' descriptions and recollections of the interviews they had conducted in Pilot cases. Open questioning was frequently translated into 'walking the witness through their statement', although this was not deemed appropriate in every case. Members of the public, we were informed, have a tendency to 'gallop through their testimony' and consequently need to be guided methodically through examination-in-chief to ensure that their testimony is comprehensive and effective. Confronted with the novelty of pre-trial interviewing, analogies to courtroom testimony came easily to prosecutors:

> It did seem very much to develop into an examination-in-chief. I was anxious to ask open questions so that they could give their response. If you're an advocate and you start asking open questions you almost slip into examination-in-chief mode. (CPS Prosecutor # 1)[109]

---

[105] 'Where, in the course of an interview, the witness provides further evidence which is material to the case, a further witness statement should be taken (or visual interview conducted) by a police officer': ibid [8.2].

[106] Ibid [7.1].

[107] Now also see *Pre-Trial Witness Interviews—Guidance for Prosecutors*, Annex B: 'Detailed Guidance for Prosecutors on Conducting Interviews', www.cps.gov.uk/legal/p_to_r/pre_-trial_witness_interviews/#a06 (accessed 21 November 2015).

[108] The step-wise approach to interviewing was first endorsed by the *Memorandum of Good Practice on Video Recorded Interviews with Child Witnesses for Criminal Proceedings* (Home Office, 1992): see R Bull, 'Obtaining Evidence Expertly: The Reliability of Interviews with Child Witnesses' (1992) 1 *Expert Evidence* 5; J McEwan, 'Where the Prosecution Witness is a Child: The Memorandum of Good Practice' (1993) 5 *Journal of Child Law* 16. It is also integral to the 'PEACE' model of investigative interviewing adopted by the British police: see College of Policing, *Investigative Interviewing*, www.app.college.police.uk/app-content/investigations/investigative-interviewing/#peace-framework (accessed 21 November 2015). Now see generally, Ministry of Justice, *Achieving Best Evidence in Criminal Proceedings: Guidance on Interviewing Victims and Witnesses, and Guidance on Using Special Measures* (March 2011 revision), www.cps.gov.uk/publications/docs/best_evidence_in_criminal_proceedings.pdf (accessed 19 January 2016).

[109] Interviewees are designated 'CPS Prosecutor # 1' through to 'CPS Prosecutor # 17'. To further protect respondents' anonymity all PTWI-trained prosecutors are described as female (in reality, five prosecutor interviewees were male). Verbatim quotations were tape-recorded. Respondents reported their own personal experiences, judgements and opinions which do not purport to represent CPS policy.

Several prosecutors remarked that the character of the interview, and the witness' perceptions of it, could be influenced as much by the *style* of questioning as by its content. As CPS Prosecutor # 2 observed: 'You can ask the, "Could you tell me? Could you explain to me?"… There is a way of asking a question that isn't a challenge'. PTWI should not be an alienating experience for complainants and other potential prosecution witnesses, which, quite apart from humanitarian concerns,[110] would be counter-productive for securing the witness's cooperation and achieving best evidence. As CPS Prosecutor # 4 remarked:

> The last thing you want is the witness picking up the nearest thing to hand and hurling it across the room at you. Alternatively, getting up, stamping their feet and saying, 'Well, I'm glad that I'm not bothering with this case', and stomping out the room.

Referring to Pilot [CASE 47], CPS Prosecutor # 8 suggested that PTWI allowed a more iterative approach to questioning that, if utilised skilfully, might encourage and enable witnesses to communicate their evidence more effectively than would be possible in the more formal and procedurally constrained environment of the courtroom. For example, the prosecutor could periodically invite the witness to back-track and clarify key points in their story. Such circumlocution would generally be frowned upon in examination-in-chief at trial, yet—as CPS Prosecutor # 8 reflected—it more closely approximates natural conversation:

> Because people aren't thinking in the way that you're thinking. … [Y]ou know where you're trying to go with it and you think everybody's going to be entirely linear about their description of the event, because that's how time moves. And it's not how it works.

In numerous Pilot cases, prosecutors felt that they had been able to elicit additional information from a complainant or to resolve apparent contradictions in police statements without being confrontational, even where the new information or clarification tended to undermine the complainant's story. In [CASE 14], for example, CPS Prosecutor # 2 was able to ascertain that the complainant had *not* mentioned being raped during an earlier complaint to the police. In relation to the currently alleged assault, moreover, the complainant admitted that she had gone to bed with the accused voluntarily whilst her strapping teenage son was asleep in the same room:

> So we just went on to the next question. But there you've got a scenario: You've got a six-foot-four bloke in the room. You say that this ex-husband, who you're frightened of, is in effect raping you, and you don't do anything. You don't cry out at all. You're looking at it from a jury point of view: how is a jury going to take that on board? What is a jury going to say when you say 'Did he say anything to you beforehand?', and the witness says 'He had been making advances towards me' before she'd gone out that night. Well, if someone had been making advances towards you before you went out that night, so that you knew maybe there was going to be trouble, you wouldn't come back and get into that bed with him. (CPS Prosecutor # 2)

In these situations, the prosecutor is undoubtedly putting the complainant's account to the test, not 'to trip her up' deliberately, as CPS Prosecutor # 7 emphasised in relation to another Pilot case, but possibly 'if she wasn't quick enough … to catch her out' in a half-truth or

---

[110] On humane treatment as a foundational principle of criminal procedure, see P Roberts, 'Theorising Procedural Tradition: Subjects, Objects and Values in Criminal Adjudication' in A Duff, L Farmer, S Marshall and V Tadros (eds), *The Trial on Trial Volume Two: Judgment and Calling to Account* (Oxford, Hart Publishing, 2006), reprinted in P Roberts (ed), *Theoretical Foundations of Criminal Trial Procedure* (Farnham, Ashgate, 2014); Roberts and Zuckerman, above n 14, 21–22.

an evasion. CPS Prosecutor # 2 acknowledged that it was hard for a lawyer *not* to slip into cross-examination mode in these circumstances.

The methodical interviewing strategy of 'walking the witness through their police statement' is not always deemed suitable. Pilot cases varied enormously in their levels of seriousness and complexity.[111] Where a witness has made several police statements, possibly in relation to multiple incidents, it may be impractical (as well as unnecessary) to attempt to cover all this ground during PTWI. In [CASE 76], for example, the complainant was involved in two separate prosecutions against the same defendant. CPS Prosecutor # 10 explained that her predominant concern in planning an interview was to narrow down the issues in order to avoid confusing either herself or the complainant:

> I can see the file now, the Crown Court one's like that [*gestures to indicate deep file*] and there's also a really big history of it. I wouldn't necessarily go through every incident with her ... [W]hat I would probably do in the preparation for that is sit down and pick out the bits that I needed to talk to her about and be very specific and maybe only show her those statements relating to what I'm going to ask her about. I don't want to get her confused and me to have a false impression of her—because I've been the one to confuse her. So I'd have to be really careful with that.

In several other Pilot cases the interviewing lawyer took a conscious tactical decision to focus the interview on just one or a small cluster of specific issues requiring clarification. In [CASE 38], for example, it was one particular aspect of the complainant's video-recorded statement that CPS Prosecutor # 5 wished to pin down:

> So with her I went straight to it, and just said to her: 'You've told us in your statement that you've been raped up until the age of twelve, but there's something I need to clarify with you, and this is the question. We have this information. Do you remember making a complaint about being raped at 15?' And of course, she then went into it. But that's probably the only one where I've been that specific and that's because I needed to be.

Evidently, this more focused approach to eliciting new information is informed by prosecutors' anticipation of potential vulnerabilities in the witness's testimony (including credibility factors)[112] which are likely to be targeted by defence cross-examination if the case goes to trial.

Pilot [CASE 14] represents a further interesting variation on the theme of *not* taking the witness through their statement. CPS Prosecutor # 2 concentrated on the circumstantial details surrounding the incident with an eye to corroborating material aspects of the complainant's allegation.[113] When no supporting details were forthcoming during PTWI, the prosecution was abandoned:

> I didn't go through the rapes at all with her ... I wanted to know what happened before the rape, and what happened afterwards ... What I was trying to do was just ask her factually about certain

---

[111] Pilot cases are profiled in Roberts and Saunders, above n 1. In brief, rapes and other sexual assaults constituted about a third of all PTWI Pilot cases, and there were also serious physical assaults, kidnapping, robbery, aggravated burglary, actual bodily harm, burglary, theft, common assault and harassment. Roughly 20% of Pilot cases were pre-charge.

[112] See Roberts and Saunders, above n 95, 123–33.

[113] In the sense of logically supporting the truth of the complainant's testimony, rather than 'corroboration' in the technical legal sense of providing independent proof of a particular offender's criminality: cf *R v Baskerville* [1916] 2 KB 658 (CCA); *R v Makanjuola* [1995] 1 WLR 1348 (CA). CPS *Guidance*, above n 10, advises prosecutors preparing for PTWI to 'go through all the key witness statements and cross-refer them. You should note who corroborates who and any inconsistencies or gaps in the evidence.'

aspects that had come to light after she had made the initial complaint. So we didn't actually go into the details of the actual incident itself. We went into everything else to see how much she would make a compelling witness before the court. We didn't have any other evidence—just her. And that was why we came to that conclusion.

This was one of 16 Pilot cases in which proceedings were abandoned ($n = 6$), or never even formally charged ($n = 10$), following the prosecutor's interview with the complainant. Taken together, this accounts for 40 per cent of the 40 *finalised* cases in which interviews were actually conducted during the Pilot Evaluation.[114] In some of these cases, PTWI was effectively the 'last chance saloon' for achieving the standard of evidential sufficiency needed to charge or avoid discontinuance, thereby enabling the prosecution to proceed. On the other side of the balance sheet, ten Pilot cases were discontinued *without* conducting a witness interview; and there were several clear instances of non-charging or discontinuance precipitated by new information obtained during PTWI.[115]

This range of case outcomes confirms the dual role anticipated for pre-trial interviews. Timely interviews with key witnesses can accelerate efficient disposal of cases already suspected on the basis of paper file review to be evidentially shaky, or which are revealed to be so in the course of the interview. Alternatively, prosecutors may be better informed and equipped to prepare more thoroughly for trials in cases meeting the standard of evidential sufficiency prescribed by the Code for Crown Prosecutors for continuing a prosecution.[116] As part of this assessment, '[p]rosecutors should consider whether there are any reasons to question the reliability of the evidence, including its accuracy or integrity'.[117] The Evaluation Pilot demonstrated PTWI's potential to fulfil the policy objectives of enhancing the quality of prosecutions and promoting administrative efficiency; but it also highlights why interviews or their outcomes might prove contentious, especially in relation to prosecutions of rape and sexual assault in which high levels of case 'attrition' have been regarded as problematic for many decades.[118] PTWI in principle covers all offences,[119] but—for a

---

[114] Roberts and Saunders, above n 1, Figure 3.

[115] In [CASE 56], for example, it became apparent that the complainant had been the initial aggressor: 'She said that they were both drunk when it happened; she'd pushed him first. She basically puts the blame on herself and says that any injuries she got were caused in the struggle ... In effect, once she's gone through it all in detail, you look at her credibility and the situation's changed' (CPS Prosecutor # 12).

[116] Prosecutions may proceed to trial only if there is a 'realistic prospect of conviction', interpreted as a '51%' or 'more likely than not' test, and prosecution is in the public interest: *The Code for Crown Prosecutors* (London, CPS, 2013), Part 4, www.cps.gov.uk/publications/code_for_crown_prosecutors/ (accessed 21 November 2015). For critical discussion, see A Ashworth and M Redmayne, *The Criminal Process*, 4th edn (Oxford, Oxford University Press, 2010) 199–209; M Burton, 'Reviewing Crown Prosecution Service Decisions Not to Prosecute' [2001] *Criminal Law Review* 374; A Ashworth, 'The "Public Interest" Element in Prosecutions' [1987] *Criminal Law Review* 595; G Williams, 'Letting Off the Guilty and Prosecuting the Innocent' [1985] *Criminal Law Review* 115; P Worboys, 'Convicting the Right Person on the Right Evidence' [1985] *Criminal Law Review* 764.

[117] *Code for Crown Prosecutors*, above n 116, [4.6].

[118] See eg J Temkin and B Krahé, *Sexual Assault and the Justice Gap: A Question of Attitude* (Oxford, Hart Publishing, 2008); CJS, *Narrowing the Justice Gap* (London, The Stationery Office, 2002), www.cps.gov.uk/Publications/docs/justicegap.pdf (accessed 19 January 2016); L Kelly, J Lovett and L Regan, *A Gap or a Chasm? Attrition in Reported Rape Cases*, Home Office Research Study 293 (London, Home Office RDS, 2005), webarchive.nationalarchives.gov.uk/20110218135832/rds (accessed 19 January 2016); J Gregory and S Lees, 'Attrition in Rape and Sexual Assault Cases' (1996) 36 *British Journal of Criminology* 1.

[119] 'Interviews will normally be of most value in serious indictable-only cases. However, nothing precludes the holding of an interview in either-way or summary only cases.' *PTWI Guidance for Prosecutors*, above n 10.

variety of reasons[120]—it may have particular salience for prosecutions of rape and sexual assault, which constituted about a third of all Pilot cases. Although prosecutors 'should swiftly stop cases which do not meet the evidential [Code test] … and which cannot be strengthened by further investigation',[121] the question may be asked whether prosecutors did everything they reasonably could to build up salvageable cases.[122] The CPS has dedicated policies in relation to both sexual assault[123] and domestic violence[124] which partly overlap with PTWI.

(c) Probing Questions

Sooner or later in the course of an interview the PTWI prosecutor must decide how far to go in subjecting the witness' police statement(s) and oral replies to critical scrutiny and testing. Some measure of guidance on this vital issue is provided by the PTWI Code of Practice, as we have seen, and these messages were reinforced through the Pilot prosecutors' training programme. Amplifying the Code of Practice's injunction (citing *Momodou*) that prosecutors 'must not under any circumstances train, practise or coach the witness or ask questions that may taint the witness's evidence', CPS Guidance now advises prosecutors to 'be very careful during the interview and in all dealings with witnesses that you do not taint a witness's evidence':

> Do not ask leading questions. You should not tell the witness what other witnesses have said. This may cause them to change their evidence. Similarly, your questions should not be suggestive that another witness has given different evidence. … Under no circumstance should you ever suggest to a witness that he/she might be wrong (they may be right and other witnesses may be wrong) or indicate approval or disapproval in any way to any answer given by the witness. Never suggest the answer to a question. To do so goes beyond coaching into the territory of fabricating evidence.[125]

But at the same time, 'probing' questioning is not only permitted but positively endorsed. Prosecutors are told that they will 'need to go through the evidence of the witness … and

---

[120] Offence seriousness and the central importance of complainants' testimony in sustaining allegations of sexual assault, which typically takes place in private with no other witnesses, are two material factors. A third is the sheer increase in prosecuted cases: see N Padfield, 'Editorial: The Growing Number of Convicted Sex Offenders' [2015] *Criminal Law Review* 927; P Radcliffe, GH Gudjonsson, A Heaton-Armstrong and D Wolchover (eds), *Witness Testimony in Sexual Cases: Evidential, Investigative and Scientific Perspectives* (Oxford, Oxford University Press, 2016).

[121] *Code for Crown Prosecutors*, above n 116, [3.3].

[122] See further, L Ellison, 'Promoting Effective Case-Building in Rape Cases: A Comparative Perspective' [2007] *Criminal Law Review* 691; L Ellison 'Prosecuting Domestic Violence Without Victim Participation' (2002) 65 *Modern Law Review* 834; Y Moreno and P Hughes, *Effective Prosecution: Working in Partnership with the CPS* (Oxford, Oxford University Press, 2008).

[123] *CPS Policy for Prosecuting Cases of Rape* (London, CPS, 2012); *Legal Guidance—Rape and Sexual Offences* (stating that, '[t]he use of pre-trial witness interviews (PTWI) is considered an effective tool in rape cases. This will particularly apply in cases where the decision to prosecute is "borderline"'), www.cps.gov.uk/legal/p_to_r/rape_and_sexual_ offences/ (accessed 21 November 2015).

[124] *Domestic Abuse Guidelines for Prosecutors*, www.cps.gov.uk/legal/d_to_g/domestic_abuse_guidelines_for_ prosecutors/#a60 (accessed 21 November 2015).

[125] 'Detailed Guidance for Prosecutors on Conducting Interviews', above n 107, 3.

check everything they have to say for accuracy' and '[l]ook for signs of exaggeration or over confidence'. Furthermore:

> Probing questions may cause a witness to modify his/her evidence. *This course is absolutely necessary*. It is much better to know as soon as possible that evidence has been over-emphasised or misstated … Closely questioning your witness can have considerable benefits. … Where there is significant conflict between witnesses that cannot be resolved by careful questioning, alternative accounts may be put to the witness for comment so long as the source of the alternative account is not attributed. If this is done, it should never be suggested to the witness that they adopt the alternative account.[126]

This is all sound practical advice (not available in so many words to prosecutors participating in the Pilot), and the PTWI Code's general statements of principle are entirely unobjectionable. There remain, nonetheless, indistinct borderlines and considerable scope for interpretational latitude in translating generic guidance into interview practice. What, exactly, is a 'probing' question? How *probing* are such questions allowed to be? How is one to determine *ex ante* whether a particular probing question might influence the witness to alter her evidence in some way? Won't drawing a witness's attention to particular parts of her statement necessarily, at some level, affect the witness's own perception of her evidence—if only by indicating the prosecutor's special interest in that portion of her testimony? This is the somewhat uncertain terrain that PTWI prosecutors in the Pilot, and subsequently all CPS lawyers electing to conduct pre-trial interviews with potential prosecution witnesses, were and are obliged to negotiate.

One response we observed during the Pilot was pronounced caution. Thus, CPS Prosecutor # 10 had made every effort to keep her interview questions in Pilot [CASE 20] 'very neutral, very open … so that it would come from them and there'd be no accusations that you put words in their mouths … I wouldn't say it was terribly probing because I really don't want to be accused of coaching'. Along similar lines, CPS Prosecutor # 7, reflecting on a disappointing outcome in [CASE 10], felt that the value of PTWI had been limited, owing to the impossibility of full-blown cross-examination:

> [I]f you really want to get to the truth you almost want to cross-examine them, but feel that you can't. You do feel you're a little bit sort of hidebound. Not that you want to upset them, but if you really want to test them, you almost want to go hammer and tongs and you can't and I think that is a little difficult. … I think I wish I could have probed more. … But then you don't want to prejudice the case by doing it, by doing this [interview] that hopefully might help the case. If you go too far and ruin it, then that's not helping anybody.

Constraints on more probing cross-examination were felt to be inherent to the structural relationship between the prosecution and Crown witnesses, and not merely formal requirements of criminal procedure law or prosecutorial ethics:

> If I was defending, that's what you'd be doing. You'd say, 'Come on, you're scared, you've had a knife pressed in but you stay in the garden? Come on. Didn't happen, did it? You weren't *that* scared'. And obviously, we can't do that under any circumstances, even forgetting the [PTWI Code of Practice]. The witness would be so aghast; and I think this is probably where the problem is, that whilst we are independent and it's prosecution, they are our witness … So you're never going to get a true trial

---

126 Ibid 3–4.

vision of how this woman will react to cross-examination. You're never going to get that, because you can't, and probably quite rightly shouldn't, go that far. (CPS Prosecutor # 7)

Whilst it is only natural—and humane—for prosecutors to be solicitous of complainants' feelings, we have seen that charges may be abandoned or prosecutions discontinued if the interview fails to resolve material omissions, inconsistencies or puzzling features of the complainant's account (or accounts, where there are serial disclosures or multiple witness statements) to the prosecutor's satisfaction. In Pilot [CASE 4], for example, CPS Prosecutor # 1 judged that it would not have been in the spirit of the occasion to press the two complainants further about apparent discrepancies in their respective police statements: 'I did explore things by asking questions, by saying, "Let's break this down" … Where they did depart from their statements, I didn't challenge them about that, because I felt that then that would put them on the spot and they would feel threatened.' The case was promptly discontinued following the interview.

Contrasting with these relatively cautious approaches, other prosecutors insisted that more searching questioning might be required, at least in the later stages of the interview, if the potential benefits of PTWI were to be fully realised. They described their general interviewing styles as adaptations of examination-in-chief blended with elements of cross-examination on crucial points of detail requiring further clarification. In CPS Prosecutor # 8's pithy summation: 'It's examination-in-chief segueing into cross-examination, but not in a hostile way. It's examination-in-chief in so far as you draw out of them initially their version of events and then you have to press them; have to press them for particulars.' Along similar lines, CPS Prosecutor # 5 explained, 'there'll probably be an appropriate stage to ask them a question which is more of a cross-examination-type question'.

The difference between probing questioning during PTWI and outright cross-examination is well-illustrated by [CASE 22], in which a toxicology report indicated that the complainant had ingested cocaine on the night of the alleged offence. She had not mentioned this in her police witness statement. In the earlier part of her pre-trial interview, the complainant more or less confirmed what she had already told the police about her alcohol consumption. CPS Prosecutor # 4 takes up the narrative in the following post-interview reflections:

> I then simply said, 'Anything else?' Which is an open question; it's not being led at her. … And that's when the information about cocaine came out, which she explained away, which was a really big bonus of the interview. If she had come out and said, nothing else, I wouldn't have then hit her with, 'Well, we've a forensic science statement here saying you've got a cocktail of things in your blood-stream including cocaine, which heightens sexual arousal, what have you got to say about that then?' That's not the way it would have gone at all. It would have been, 'What if it were to be suggested that you may have ingested other substances?'—or some word other than ingested, which is perhaps less lawyerly—and see where that led. If that was, 'Well, no, I never touch drugs', then it would have had to be pressed further: 'If it were to be suggested that you took heroin?' … So you'd have to approach that subject, hopefully, in a tactful way.

In [CASE 36], where a domestic assault had apparently taken place in the presence of a child (a significant public interest factor in maintaining the prosecution, even if the complainant retracts), a materially different picture of the incident emerged in response to Prosecutor # 6's questioning:

> [A]ccording to her initial statement, a child was present *in the room* during this incident. But during the witness interview, she revealed that the child hadn't actually been present in the room,

the child had been present in the *house*. … And she was saying to me, in the PTWI, 'Well, the child wasn't present and she didn't hear a thing' … She didn't volunteer that information because I asked her in a roundabout way. I said, 'Who was in the house? Where was Alice?[127]' And she told me where Alice was, and I … went through the statement to her and said, 'Well, that's not consistent'. [To which she replied] 'Oh, well, you see what I meant was …' And you know, she appeared completely credible with what she was saying. It was just a case of when the police officer had taken the statement, he'd written it down one way and what she meant was something slightly different.

CPS Prosecutor # 6's willingness to probe the complainant's account in [CASE 36] might be contrasted with CPS Prosecutor # 7's more tentative approach to discrepancies in the complainant's various witness statements in [CASE 52] (which had a crucial bearing on charge selection).[128] CPS Prosecutor # 7 laid out her options in preparing for the interview:

Do I just say to her, 'What age do you think you were? Why do you think you were that age?' and leave it there? Or, if it's still very [vague]—whether I go on that extra mile and say, 'Look I've got two different things in two statements, which is it?' And I suspect I perhaps shouldn't do that … Because then, is there an element that you've coached her? She's not given you the answer that you want and you're saying, 'Look, it's got to be one of these two, which is it?'

It is apparent from prosecutors' remarks and reported experiences in Pilot cases that the limits and appropriate style of PTWI interviews remained somewhat imprecise and negotiable. This was only to be expected, in view of the variability of individual cases and the limited guidance prosecutors had received on the more refined aspects of interviewing style and substance. On one view, prosecutors sometimes need to be 'cruel to be kind', by challenging witnesses through robust questioning in order to give them an opportunity to forestall discontinuance or pre-charge 'No Further Action'. Yet coaching witnesses and evidence contamination are expressly forbidden. CPS Prosecutor # 7 encapsulated the essential dilemma:

You don't want to ask questions that will invalidate the whole case by going too far. But equally, you don't want to not go far enough and then think, well … I haven't really covered that aspect and I'm still none the wiser. You'd feel you've wasted everybody's time, really.

The line between legitimate questioning and unlawful witness coaching was acknowledged by several prosecutors to be 'very thin' (CPS Prosecutor # 9), creating the potential for legal challenges. Another prosecutor specifically drew attention to the inherent ambiguity in the notion of 'rehearsing' a witness's evidence, and its potential implications for PTWI:

You're always going to be wary about going too far, because you don't want the defence to accuse you of coaching them. … I'm still concerned because, to me, every time you pick up a statement and you go through it again, it's a rehearsal. I mean, I know that's not maybe the word you should use, but the more they go over and over it, the more prepared they are … [T]here's this big … shift towards looking after your victims and witnesses and actually they really are quite important: it's nice to be nice to them instead. But I still *can't* in some ways get my head around the fact … You *are* investigating, you *are* rehearsing them. Because every time you take them through a statement you must be rehearsing them a little bit. (CPS Prosecutor # 10)

Several prosecutors shared the rueful sentiment that, '[u]ntil it *is* tested in court, we're not going to know, are we?' (CPS Prosecutor # 5).

---

[127] Names have been changed to preserve anonymity, in accordance with standard research protocols.
[128] If the complainant had been 15 years old at the material time, the accused's conduct would have constituted unlawful sexual intercourse with a minor ('statutory rape') irrespective of the complainant's consent in fact.

Seven years later (and counting), the Court of Appeal has still not commented on the legality or acceptable parameters of pre-trial witness interviewing. This is partly a simple numbers game. Cases involving interviews comprise a tiny fraction of the CPS's overall caseload, and only a small subset of interviews—those leading to charges, successful prosecutions and convictions at first instance—is even capable of giving rise to arguments on appeal. It is also, however, all of a piece with the paucity of English legal doctrine addressing witness preparation in general. The Chief Crown Prosecutor responsible for running the PTWI Pilot observed, in 2009, that whilst '[o]ver 200 pre-trial witness interviews have now taken place … [i]n no case has there been a serious challenge, let alone a successful challenge, to the process or to a prosecutor's conduct of an interview'.[129] In its latest public pronouncements, CPS presents the absence of defence challenge or judicial rebuke as proof positive of successful implementation:

> Prosecution advocates have been conducting pre-trial witness interviews with victims of alleged sexual offences for some years. These have not resulted in a rise in abuse arguments, rehearsed evidence or unfair trials. Instead we have seen better quality evidence which is in the interests of all concerned.[130]

According to the CPS's 2015 consultation on witness familiarisation, '[p]rosecutors can have confidence that providing their discussion with a witness is aimed at assisting the witness to give their best evidence and avoids rehearsing them as to the evidence they should give then there should be no risk that coaching has occurred'.[131] But a close reading of *Momodou* lends no direct support to PTWI, and might even arguably militate against it.

Recall Judge LJ's admonition that '[t]he witness should give his or her own evidence, so far as practicable uninfluenced by what anyone else has said, whether in formal discussions or informal conversations'.[132] Surely, the epistemological realities of testimony, as a collaborative institutional construction, unavoidably pose the risk that almost *any* interaction between prosecutor and witness will affect the witness's testimony, in substance or form. Prosecutors realistically told us that 'even innocently, [it is] possible to influence what the witness says' (CPS Prosecutor # 3). After all, 'even where the interviewing party does not coach overtly, a look or gesture can convey to the witness that this was the "wrong" answer'.[133] In CPS Prosecutor # 17's balanced appraisal: 'Witness coaching will always be a risk—if a lawyer doesn't fear this possibility the potential dangers are likely to be greater. However, the benefits of PTWI should outweigh this risk, generally.'

The possibility that a witness's evidence might be innocently or inadvertently contaminated during PTWI is reminiscent of broader judicial concerns about witness testimony, which we have learnt to live with and accommodate as an acceptable cost of our traditional

---

[129] R Marshall, 'A Response' [2009] 8 *Archbold News* 6.

[130] *Consultation—Summary of Responses*, above n 8.

[131] CPS, *Speaking to Witnesses at Court*, above n 6, 6.

[132] *R v Momodou and Limani* [2005] 1 WLR 3442, [61]. Although not specifically directed at PTWI, Judge LJ's concerns might conceivably be extrapolated to certain aspects of pre-trial interviewing. Of course, the CPS 'was acutely aware of the relevant case law', and *Momodou* in particular, in formulating the PTWI Code of Practice: Marshall, above n 129. But the point is that there is not very much relevant case law, and what does exist is not as clear or definitive as prosecutors might ideally wish.

[133] J Lewis, 'Witness Testing: The Crown's New Weapon' [2009] 8 *Archbold News* 4, 5.

model of adversarial criminal adjudication.[134] English courts have tended to be pragmatic about epistemic threats to truth-finding that they feel powerless to control.[135] As prosecutors who participated in the Pilot evidently grasped, to the extent that such risks of contamination cannot be eliminated entirely they need to be managed and, if possible, ameliorated. Tape-recording of interviews and full pre-trial disclosure to the defence are important and feasible safeguards when prosecutors are permitted to discuss evidential matters with witnesses. After some initial equivocation, both audio-recording[136] and disclosure[137] were integral to the PTWI package implemented in England and Wales and in operation today.

3. Appraising the Integrity of PTWI

Three elementary axioms of criminal procedure frame the preceding discussion. First, witnesses of fact should testify truthfully to their own unaided and uncorrupted perceptions. In the common law witness oath's time-honoured idiom, those called to testify in criminal trials are enjoined to tell 'the truth, the whole truth, and nothing but the truth'.[138] Secondly, police and prosecutors must never 'coach' witnesses. Besides being in flagrant breach of professional legal ethics, witness coaching may constitute serious criminality[139] attracting custodial punishments.[140] Thirdly, witnesses should be assisted by criminal justice professionals and by the courts to give their 'best evidence'. Testifying in criminal proceedings is meant to be a dignified, solemn inquiry into contested allegations of criminal wrongdoing, not an obstacle course, coconut shy or memory test.[141] Empirical data from the PTWI Pilot Evaluation speak to a sociologically well-documented truism, widely intuited by criminal practitioners, but seldom expressly articulated: the third elementary axiom is in tension with the other two. Moreover, that tension is fundamental and, fundamentally, inescapable. PTWI was launched into this somewhat uncertain procedural environment, translating abstract theoretical conundrums into practical challenges for prosecutors.

---

[134] See eg *R v Lamb* [2007] EWCA Crim 1766; *R v Momodou and Limani* [2005] 1 WLR 3442, [61]; *R v H* [1995] 2 AC 596 (HL); *R v W(C)* (1994) 99 Cr App R 185 (CA).

[135] *R v Richardson* [1971] 2 QB 484 (CA); *R v Westwell* [1976] 2 All ER 812 (CA).

[136] Paragraph 8.1 of the PTWI Code of Practice, above n 91, mandates that '[a] comprehensive audio recording of the interview must be made'. The Criminal Bar Association advocated video-recording: *Criminal Bar Association Response to Pre-Trial Witness Interviews by Prosecutors—A Consultation Paper* (CBA, July 2003) [23].

[137] 'The record of a pre-trial interview will generally be unused material ... [S]ubject to the application of public interest immunity, the recording of the interview will be supplied automatically to the defence': PTWI Code of Practice, above n 91, [8.1].

[138] Cf *R v Southwood* (1860) 1 F & F 356, ER 762 (Watson B holding that an oath 'to "true answer make" ... will do'). Likewise, 'a witness statement must contain the truth, the whole truth and nothing but the truth on the issues it covers': *Cummings v Ministry of Justice* [2013] EWHC 48 (QB), [6] (quoting the White Book).

[139] Including suborning perjury *contra* Perjury Act 1911, s 7; *R v Kellett* [1976] QB 372, 391–92 (CA); and perverting the course of justice: *R v Toney* [1993] 1 WLR 364 (CA).

[140] *Attorney General's Reference (No 17 of 2008)* [2008] RTR 29, [2008] EWCA Crim 1341; *R v Archer* [2003] 1 Cr App R (S) 86, [2002] EWCA Crim 1996. A Hong Kong illustration is given by M Jackson (Chapter 8) in this volume.

[141] 'Giving evidence is not a memory test': *R v Davies* [2011] EWCA Crim 1177, [29]. This is, of course, the underlying rationalisation for the fiction of 'refreshing memory' from previous witness statements: see eg *Attorney General's Reference (No 3 of 1979)* (1979) 69 Cr App R 411 (CA); *R v Langton* (1876) 2 QBD 296 (CCR).

It might be claimed that PTWI is orientated towards preparing *the prosecutor* rather than the complainant or other potential witness, and as such raises no serious objections under *Momodou*. PTWI, as we have seen, performs a range of functions at different stages in (contemplated) criminal proceedings, so one must be wary of over-generalising about its objectives and case-specific effects. Nonetheless, in numerous Pilot cases prosecutors' pre-trial interviews with witnesses affected the nature of testimony at trial, either directly in terms of what the witness said[142] or did not say in their statements or testimony, or because the prosecution was equipped with new information which informed the way in which the witness' testimony was elicited through examination-in-chief in the courtroom.[143] In this way, prosecutors were able to pre-empt unhelpful distractions later in the proceedings or focus the witness's mind on the essential facts at issue (whilst filtering out irrelevance), without any perceptibly adverse impact on the authenticity or reliability of the witness's evidence.

A sociologically realistic conception of the integrity of judicial evidence should be capable of accommodating justice professionals' sincere and competent efforts to help witnesses negotiate the unfamiliar demands of criminal litigation and to present their best evidence to the court in the interests of justice. Given the highly acculturated and 'artificial'[144] nature of witness testimony, however, its epistemological integrity is dependent on other contextual considerations and dimensions of integrity. A second pillar of integrity in criminal process is constituted by professional legal ethics. It is vital that prosecutors understand their role as ministers of justice[145] and put this ethical theory into practice in all their professional conduct, including pre-trial witness interviewing.[146] The prosecutor's role in England and Wales imposes its own normative demands and practical expectations arising from the structural dynamics of adversarial criminal procedure. Thirdly, PTWI implicates broader considerations of procedural fairness, due process, the legitimacy of verdicts, legal rights and intrinsic values; the institutional manifestations of ethical commitments which, in aggregate, underwrite the coherence and normative integrity of comprehensive conceptions of criminal adjudication, criminal procedure, and criminal justice, properly conceived, as applied political morality.[147]

---

[142]   This is most obviously true in Pilot cases such as [CASE 2], [CASE 38] and [CASE 47] where PTWI revealed new information and follow-up police statements were taken.

[143]   In Pilot [CASE 1], [CASE 38] and [CASE 54], for example, problems in the complainants' police statements were cleared up, leaving the interviewing prosecutors with a much more positive assessment of complainants' credibility. In several other cases, PTWI revealed the need for special arrangements to enable the witness to testify effectively.

[144]   Modern life hardly takes place in the fabled 'state of nature'. But testimony can be characterised as 'unnatural' to the extent that it is generated, scripted, presented and tested in circumstances far removed from most people's everyday experiences.

[145]   'The prosecutor is a minister of justice ... and he must not seek to get a conviction at all costs. He must recognise his duty to act fairly, and ... not to mislead the jury, nor to erect a case on the basis of material which simply is incapable of supporting it': *R (Thayalanayagam) v Home Secretary* [2006] EWHC 3330 (Admin), [52]. And see *Lobban v R* [1995] 1 WLR 877, PC; and Cowdery (Chapter 5) and Gans (Chapter 6) in this volume.

[146]   Thus, CPS *Guidance*, above n 10, Annex B, reminds Crown Prosecutors to explain to witnesses, at the outset of a pre-trial interview, that prosecutors 'act for the public at large, not any individual'. Moreover: 'This is particularly important in the case of witnesses who are complainants, because they may labour under the misapprehension that you are their lawyer. It is essential that they understand that the prosecution has to consider other interests apart from those that concern the complainant.'

[147]   See further, P Roberts, 'Introduction' in Roberts (ed), above n 110; P Roberts, 'Groundwork for A Jurisprudence of Criminal Procedure' in RA Duff and S Green (eds), *Philosophical Foundations of Criminal Law* (Oxford, Oxford University Press, 2011).

Whatever else it is or can be, PTWI is an occasion of human interaction, with elements of spontaneity and unpredictability. In the final analysis, prosecutors must always use their *professional judgement* in deciding how to take the witness through his or her statement, what aspects of the witness's evidence to focus on, whether to ask that 'probing' follow-up question, how it should be phrased, and so on; as indeed they must exercise professional judgement in deciding whether or not to invite any particular witness for interview in the first place.[148] Prepared scripts or strategies may have to be revised midstream or abandoned entirely if the interview takes an unexpected turn or the witness becomes hostile, confused or distressed. These micro-features of criminal litigation are characterised by discretionary decision-making, sensitive to myriad circumstantial details which vary enormously from one case to the next. Compliance with ethical norms is best secured, not through the mechanical application of prescriptive rules of conduct, but by cultivating an ethos of ethical professionalism which should infuse practitioners' choices and conduct, so that ethical practice and decision-making become inculcated almost as reflex second-nature.[149]

Prosecutors should not require heroic mental exertions to think themselves into behaving like ministers of justice; they should already feel it, if not exactly in their bones, then at least as part of their professional persona or regulation workplace attire;[150] without which they should feel half-naked and embarrassed to stand before the court as the community's representative calling for justice. Lawyers with significant experience of private practice (including defence work) prior to joining the CPS should readily grasp these professional ethical imperatives. It will be an ongoing challenge for CPS staff training and professional development, in relation to pre-trial witness interviewing and more generally, to ensure that the same foundational commitments to ethical practice are absorbed by baby prosecutors many of whom, these days, grow up in the CPS without having known any other professional legal life.

Critics might well think that prosecutors' ethical integrity is a rather precarious hook on which to hang the legitimacy of a novel procedure like PTWI which is capable of influencing charging practice and materially affecting the course and outcomes of criminal trials. However, prosecutors' ethical professionalism does not stand alone as a safeguard of integrity in criminal process. Institutional procedures and practices are designed to cohere with and, ideally, to reinforce prosecutors' ethical decision-making in individual cases. It is evident that forensic risks associated with witness interviewing by litigants arise only in adversarial procedural systems in which 'the parties' are responsible for gathering, marshalling and presenting their own evidential cases to the fact-finder, and for testing their opponents' evidence in court.[151] Adversarial theory has developed its own legitimising doctrines and

---

[148] PTWI case selection and 'triggering criteria' are elucidated by Roberts and Saunders, above n 95, 108–23.

[149] Extrapolating from the more general argument for regarding professional ethics as fundamentally a question of practical attitude rather than formalistic rule-compliance: see eg FC Zacharias, 'Integrity Ethics' (2009) 22 *Georgetown Journal of Legal Ethics* 541. This argument, in turn, extends the classical tradition of viewing ethical behaviour as the product of virtuous character and practical wisdom—perceptively applied to the legal profession by AT Kronman, 'Living in the Law' (1987) 54 *University of Chicago Law Review* 835.

[150] With a respectful nod to GJ Postema, 'Integrity: Justice in Workclothes' (1997) 82 *Iowa Law Review* 821.

[151] Vasiliev, above n 17, 26–27 (noting that 'witness preparation is not regarded as part of the regular function of lawyers and has no place in the criminal process on the Continent').

procedural checks and balances to try to ensure that criminal adjudication achieves, in Ho's resonant phrase, 'justice in the search for truth'.[152]

Nobody could think that the highly artificial format for eliciting courtroom testimony, through stylised examination-in-chief and cross-examination, is calculated to capture spontaneous utterances or to obtain the witness' account of events in an unmediated narrative form. Modern criminal trials no longer resemble the unscripted altercation that might have occurred in eighteenth-century courtrooms.[153] Today, notoriously, lawyers control the flow of witness testimony through their tactical choices and questioning styles and strategies. Whilst the traditional model of witness testimony has undergone signifi-cant reform in recent decades, in response to cogent criticisms,[154] its saving grace is surely that questioning takes place in open court where everybody can see not only what the wit-ness said, and how she said it, but also what she was asked, and in what manner, to elicit particular responses. Open justice communicates public ownership of criminal charges[155] and formalises the witness' testimonial commitment to their evidence, traditionally by swearing an oath to be truthful. Trial testimony is both presented and tested in the physi-cal presence of the fact-finder, and in a way that ensures to each party a fair opportunity of challenge and reply. This is the pith of the still cherished principle of orality.[156] Pro-cedural reforms introduced in England and Wales to enable vulnerable or intimidated witnesses to present their evidence with the assistance of 'special measures' have, for the most part, striven to preserve these features of transparency and fair opportunity for chal-lenge.[157] The European Court of Human Rights likewise stresses openness and adversarial testing as integral to 'equality of arms' and the right to a fair trial guaranteed by ECHR Article 6.[158]

As a general proposition, the transparency of criminal proceedings tends to diminish as we retrace the progression of cases backwards from the public trial into the pre-trial phases and beyond into criminal investigations. Whereas criminal trials are generally open to the press and to the public, the flow of information during criminal investigations is tightly controlled, and some information protected by public interest immunity (PII) is never

---

[152] HL Ho, *A Philosophy of Evidence Law—Justice in the Search for Truth* (Oxford, Oxford University Press, 2008). Generally, see eg Roberts and Zuckerman, above n 14, 52–65; JD Jackson and SJ Summers, *The Interna-tionalisation of Criminal Evidence* (Cambridge, Cambridge University Press, 2012); MR Damaška, *The Faces of Justice and State Authority* (New Haven, Yale University Press, 1986); S Haack, 'Epistemology Legalized: Or, Truth, Justice, and the American Way' (2004) 49 *American Journal of Jurisprudence* 43; LL Fuller, 'The Forms and Limits of Adjudication' (1978) 92 *Harvard Law Review* 353; P Roberts, 'Paradigms of Forensic Science and Legal Process: A Critical Diagnosis' (2015) 370 *Philosophical Transactions B* Art 20140256.

[153] JH Langbein, *The Origins of Adversary Criminal Trial* (Oxford, Oxford University Press, 2003).

[154] See eg Ellison and Wheatcroft, above n 24; E Henderson, 'All the Proper Protections—The Court of Appeal Rewrites the Rules for the Cross-Examination of Vulnerable Witnesses' [2014] *Criminal Law Review* 93; LCH Hoyano and C Keenan, *Child Abuse: Law and Policy Across Boundaries* (Oxford, Oxford University Press, 2007) Part IV; L Ellison, 'The Mosaic Art? Cross-Examination and the Vulnerable Witness' (2001) 21 *Legal Studies* 353.

[155] The powerful idea of trials being a public 'calling to account' for criminal wrongdoing has been developed by RA Duff, *Answering for Crime* (Oxford, Hart Publishing, 2007); A Duff, L Farmer, S Marshall and V Tadros, *The Trial on Trial Volume Three: Towards a Normative Theory of the Criminal Trial* (Oxford, Hart Publishing, 2007).

[156] Above n 58.

[157] Roberts and Zuckerman, above n 14, ch 10; LCH Hoyano, 'Striking a Balance Between the Rights of Defend-ants and Vulnerable Witnesses: Will Special Measures Directions Contravene Guarantees of a Fair Trial?' [2001] *Criminal Law Review* 948.

[158] See eg *Valchev v Bulgaria* (2014) 58 EHRR SE16, [74]; *Dowsett v United Kingdom* (2004) 38 EHRR 41.

revealed, even if the case goes ahead and results in criminal convictions.[159] Much preparatory casework is conducted in police stations and CPS offices which are inaccessible to the public (and often to researchers) as well as to the accused and their legal representatives. Many aspects of case-building are de facto insulated from independent scrutiny, even when the information concerned is not confidential or privileged. Why should it be otherwise in an adversarial procedural system, in which each 'party' is responsible for developing its own case for trial? Part of the answer is that the system is *not* 'adversarial' in many of its evidence-gathering features. This is obvious, as socio-legal researchers have long insisted,[160] in relation to criminal investigations conducted by the police,[161] and almost inevitably so at the earlier stages of an investigation before there is a named suspect for the defence to represent. This structural adversarial deficit grows in practical significance and complexity, however, to the extent that out-of-court statements of one kind or another are now routinely admitted in criminal trials to a far greater extent than has traditionally been the case in common law systems. In combination with the impact of the Criminal Procedure Rules, facilitating and encouraging proactive judicial case management,[162] pre-trial events and decision-making are becoming more significant in modern English criminal litigation at the expense of the once pre-eminent and largely free-standing public trial.[163]

PTWI extends the general trend towards pre-trial evidence management, with its implicit risks of loss of transparency and fair opportunity for adversarial challenge. However it might be packaged or spun in official pronouncements, prosecutors' pre-trial interviews with witnesses are information-gathering events with the potential to generate new evidence or to affect the witness's testimony at trial. It would seem essential to the legitimacy of this procedure that it be conducted with an appropriate degree of transparency, so that pre-trial interactions between prosecutors and witnesses are always in principle open to retrospective scrutiny by the defence and, in the event of any defence objection or challenge, by the court. It would be possible in many (post-charge) cases to invite a defence legal representative to attend the interview. This might well upset some complainants and other witnesses, and besides would not necessarily be viable or appropriate, since the prosecutor might then be obliged to divulge or indirectly reveal aspects of prosecutorial strategy. Alternatively, independent counsel could attend, as they did in several Pilot cases. But again, this is unlikely to be practicable in many or most cases, especially if PTWI occurs pre-charge.

---

[159] Crim PR 2015, Part 15.3; *R v Davis, Rowe and Johnson* [1993] 1 WLR 613 (CA). Non-disclosure of 'unused material' is ECHR Article 6-compliant provided that it is 'strictly necessary' in the public interest and 'any difficulties caused to the defence by a limitation on its rights must be sufficiently counterbalanced by the procedures followed by the judicial authorities': *Fitt v UK* (2000) 30 EHRR 480, [44]–[45]; *McKeown v United Kingdom* (2012) 54 EHRR 7; *R v Austin* [2014] 1 WLR 1045, [2013] EWCA Crim 1028.

[160] See eg McConville, Sanders and Leng, above n 67, 81, 181 (arguing that 'the police are engaged in an inquisitorial task—an attempt to secure "facts" and identify offenders').

[161] The inquisitorial character of police investigation is confirmed by Paragraph [3.5] of the Code of Practice, issued pursuant to the Criminal Procedure and Investigations Act 1996, s 23, which mandates that '[i]n conducting an investigation, the investigator should pursue all reasonable lines of enquiry, whether these point towards or away from the suspect'.

[162] Crim PR 2015, Part 3. See Lord Thomas of Cwmgiedd, 'The Criminal Procedure Rules: 10 Years On' [2015] *Criminal Law Review* 395; R Denyer, *Case Management in Criminal Trials*, 2nd edn (Oxford, Hart Publishing, 2012).

[163] JD Jackson, 'Silence and Proof: Extending the Boundaries of Criminal Proceedings in the United Kingdom' (2001) 5 *International Journal of Evidence and Proof* 145.

The obvious solution, adopted in the Pilot and subsequently implemented nationally under the PTWI Code of Practice,[164] is tape-recording and full and timely disclosure to the defence; essentially the same solution, in other words, that was implemented by PACE 1984 to overcome the yawning transparency-deficit traditionally associated with police interrogation of suspects.[165] CPS Guidance to prosecutors reinforces the principle that, 'subject to the application of public interest immunity, the recording of the interview will be supplied automatically to the defence as unused material'.[166] Electronic recording and routine disclosure are not, however, a panacea for PTWI. Prosecutors may be concerned that some witnesses will not speak freely if they know that a recording of their interview will be disclosed to the defence and probably heard (or viewed) by the accused. But it would hardly be ethical to conceal disclosure requirements from the witness.[167] PII issues could conceivably arise in relation to certain information;[168] and there may be prosecutorial reluctance to disclose sensitive personal information which is not directly relevant to the issues and could only be used to launch more or less speculative attacks on the witness's general character and testimonial credibility.[169] Moreover, relevancy is a dynamic and relative standard[170] and there may be pragmatic difficulties of longer-term storage and retrieval in later proceedings. The adequacy of prosecution disclosure of 'unused material' is a perennial bone of contention in English criminal litigation.[171] Nonetheless, even if prosecutors may face

---

[164] PTWI Code of Practice, above n 91, Part 8.

[165] Now see PACE Code of Practice E on Audio Recording Interviews with Suspects (2013); and Code of Practice F on Visual Recording with Sound of Interviews with Suspects (2013), www.gov.uk/guidance/police-and-criminal-evidence-act-1984-pace-codes-of-practice#pace-codes-of-practice (accessed 19 January 2016). For comparative discussion, see Weisselberg (Chapter 15) in this volume. Without tape-recording, the interview extracts reproduced by Dixon (Chapter 3) would not have been available for critical dissection.

[166] *PTWI Guidance for Prosecutors*, above n 10.

[167] The CPS's witness advice leaflet (which is, in general, notably understated and at pains to avoid raising false hopes) explains that a 'recording of the interview will generally be made available to the defence solicitor unless it contains sensitive material. In most cases the defence will already have received a copy of your witness statement … They will not have been given your address unless it is relevant to the case.'

[168] 'You've got risks to [witnesses] also in disclosing the tape. There might be things on the tape that might well be sensitive. If it's sensitive or in some way might cause a risk to them, we've always got the situation where we might have to remove parts of the tape' (CPS Prosecutor # 6).

[169] Notably, CPS Prosecutor # 3 was adamant that the revelation of fresh impeachment material during PTWI in [CASE 25] did not constitute new information that should be disclosed, even though 'it made her look odd … There are counsel who would certainly have done anything to undermine her credibility and so they may well have brought that up'. The possibility of generating contradictions in a witness's accounts or additional impeachment material were mentioned by several Pilot prosecutors as risk factors in conducting an interview. CPS Prosecution # 10 was particularly forthright on this issue: '[CPS colleagues] have been saying, "Oh here's a domestic violence case. The victim's saying she doesn't want to come to court. I think you should interview her". Well, why should I interview her? She's only saying she doesn't want to come to court. It's not a case where her evidence needs clarifying … I don't want to give that victim an opportunity of coming in and saying to me, "Well not only do I not want to come to court, but it didn't happen like this". Or, "I told lies". Because her credibility's screwed in the future, isn't it it?' Information that could be used to cross-examine prosecution witnesses and '[a]ny material that might go to the credibility of a prosecution witness' must normally be disclosed: CPS *Disclosure Manual* (2005), [12.7]–[12.12], www.cps.gov.uk/legal/d_to_g/disclosure_manual/ (accessed 21 November 2015).

[170] As CPS Prosecutor # 14 noted: 'Material on the tape may not be undermining or assisting at the start of the trial but may well become so as the witness gives evidence. Unless the trial counsel has listened to the tape, important material may be overlooked.'

[171] Judiciary of England and Wales, *Magistrates' Court Disclosure Review* (May 2014); Lord Justice Gross, *Review of Disclosure in Criminal Proceedings* (Judiciary of England and Wales, September 2011); H Quirk, 'The Significance of Culture in Criminal Procedure Reform: Why the Revised Disclosure Scheme Cannot Work' (2006) 10 *International Journal of Evidence and Proof* 42; D Ormerod, 'Improving the Disclosure Regime' (2003) 7 *International Journal of Evidence and Proof* 102; R Leng, 'The Exchange of Information and Disclosure' in M McConville and G Wilson (eds), *The Handbook of the Criminal Justice Process* (Oxford, Oxford University Press, 2002).

difficult or uncomfortable choices in isolated cases and there are resourcing implications for the CPS, procedural fairness, evidential reliability and public confidence in the administration of justice combine to demand maximum transparency through full and timely disclosure of witness interviews with prosecutors.

Conclusion

This chapter presents a detailed case study of 'integrity' as a conceptual and normative heuristic for analysing criminal process. Critical evaluation of the introduction of pre-trial witness interviewing by Crown Prosecutors in England and Wales prompts broader reflection on the epistemological integrity of evidence, the ethical integrity of prosecutors (and prosecutions), and the normative institutional integrity of criminal proceedings. A fourth, slightly submerged theme is the conceptual coherence and structural integrity of adversarial criminal adjudication. As well as contributing to the book's overarching methodological ambitions, the chapter draws attention to a topic that too rarely features in legal scholarship, partly because pre-trial procedure is systematically downplayed in trial-centred conceptions of the Law of Evidence; partly because witness interviewing is easily written off as prosaic and uninteresting, when in fact—as I hope to have shown—it offers an illuminating window into the micro-dynamics of evidence construction and case-building in criminal proceedings. The integrity triptych comprising (1) the epistemology of juridical evidence, (2) professional ethics and (3) institutional political morality, which forms the chapter's analytical scaffolding, is offered up as a highly flexible and adaptable theoretical framework for depicting the features and contours of criminal process and evaluating proposals for procedural reform.

Although, according to *Momodou*, the distinction between acceptable witness preparation and illegitimate 'coaching' is 'dramatically clear',[172] the PTWI Evaluation Pilot confirms the forensic truism that almost *any* pre-trial interaction between criminal justice professionals and lay witnesses to crime is liable to impact on the way in which a witness ultimately testifies in court, in the literal sense that the witness's testimony is different—in substance or form—to what it would otherwise have been in the absence of that interaction. Witness testimony, in short, is *constructed* through goal-orientated institutionalised practices of information management, case building, formal presentation and adversarial testing. Deliberately falsifying evidence or suborning perjury are different matters entirely, and are already unambiguously forbidden by professional ethical responsibilities and the criminal law.

From the perspective of a sociologically realistic epistemology of testimony, these plain institutional facts pose no existential challenge to the integrity of judicial evidence.[173] They

---

[172] [2005] EWCA Crim 177, [61].

[173] See further, M Damaška, 'Truth in Adjudication' (1998) 49 *Hastings Law Journal* 289; AI Goldman, *Knowledge in A Social World* (Oxford, Oxford University Press, 1999); D Walton, *Witness Testimony Evidence: Argumentation, Artificial Intelligence and Law* (Cambridge, Cambridge University Press, 2007); DA Schum and JR Morris, 'Assessing the Competence and Credibility of Human Sources of Intelligence Evidence: Contributions from Law and Probability' (2007) 6 *Law, Probability and Risk* 247.

should only trouble those harbouring naive conceptions of witness testimony as a kind of 'automatic writing', as though witnesses were inert lightning rods passively channelling forensic truth. In reality, as every practitioner knows, witness evidence, in the form of legally admissible statements or trial testimony, is created, not found. We saw in Section 1 of this chapter, however, that English legal doctrine has not really grasped these episte-mological complexities or fully addressed their practical ramifications. Whilst it is not difficult to identify straightforward instances of compliance or deviation, there are many conceivable scenarios in which the 'distinction between witness training or coaching' and witness familiarisation, characterised by the Court of Appeal as '[s]ensible preparation for the experience of giving evidence, which assists the witness to give of his or her best at the forthcoming trial',[174] could not be described as 'dramatic', or even readily discernible.

The PTWI Pilot Evaluation helped to firm up CPS Guidance on witness interviewing and inform its ongoing staff training programme.[175] Some aspects of good practice, such as the ban on group preparation or any direct rehearsal of witness testimony, are explicit and well rationalised.[176] Crown Prosecutors in England and Wales arguably benefit from more detailed instruction and advice than their counterparts in other common law juris-dictions.[177] It is debateable how much further it would be desirable, or possible, to go in providing concrete legal guidance, given the infinite variability of cases and circumstances. Prosecutors' interviewing strategies and techniques are always, in practice, going to be influenced by contextual professional judgements and personal styles and temperament. In frontline operational decision-making, professional ethical standards play an irreduc-ible role in maintaining the integrity of processes and outcomes. Ethical instruction is plausibly most effective when directed towards cultivating integrity in the performance of professional duty, rather than issuing peremptory directives for rote-learning and robotic application. Personal professionalism, moreover, must be buttressed by structural institu-tional design which both coheres with adversarial precepts and promotes the foundational values of criminal adjudication embedded in our legal traditions.

As experience with pre-trial witness interviewing accumulates, the CPS must build on its successes in improving the quality of prosecutorial decision-making and performance, whilst seeking to address shortcomings and areas of ongoing contention (including the extent of pre-trial disclosure) identified in the Pilot Evaluation. Future developments in interviewing practice or other pre-trial interactions with witnesses, whether styled 'familiarisation' or something else, must continue to be structured by a robust normative framework and effective accountability, in which the 'hard working soft law' of detailed pro-fessional guidance will almost certainly exert more practical influence than loose legislative frameworks or question-begging legal precedents.

---

[174] [2005] EWCA Crim 177, [62].

[175] CPS, *Annual Report 2007–2008*, HC 538 (London, The Stationery Office, 2008) 21 (reporting that 180 Crown Prosecutors had completed the training programme).

[176] *R v Arif*, The Times, 17 July 1993; *R v Shaw* [2002] EWCA Crim 3004. But cf G Davies, 'Witness Familiari-sation: Welcome Relief for Witnesses', *The Barrister*, www.barristermagazine.com/barrister/archivedsite/issue27_index.html (claiming that, '[p]rovided the sessions and, particularly the mock cross-examination, follow the [Bar Council] Guidance, there does not appear to be any reason why witnesses cannot be trained in groups'). Also see R Mahoney, 'Witness Conferences' (2000) 24 *Criminal Law Journal* 297.

[177] Vasiliev, above n 17, 36, 43, characterises CPS Guidance as 'comprehensive and highly detailed' and regards the regulation of witness preparation under PTWI as 'immeasurably more rigid' than comparable common law jurisdictions.

8

Integrity, Immunity and Accomplice Witness Testimony

MICHAEL I JACKSON

Introduction

The use of immunised accomplice witnesses by the prosecution has long been a feature of criminal trials in England and those jurisdictions such as Hong Kong which adopted the English criminal justice system.[1] This practice has been disparaged as 'unsavoury' and 'distasteful',[2] even 'unethical',[3] but 'turning Queen's evidence' in return for immunity from prosecution has been regarded as a 'necessary evil' and legally sanctioned as an essential tool in the fight against serious crime. This is particularly true of those forms of criminal activity which normally take place in secrecy, such as trafficking in dangerous drugs, terrorism, fraud and—the subject of this chapter—corruption-related offences.

Not surprisingly, granting immunity to such witnesses is usually said to be 'exceptional'. It is justified by the public interest in prosecuting the co-accused of the immunised witness. Yet in recent years, as technology has enabled participants in corruption-related crimes to operate at a distance from each other, frequently crossing jurisdictional boundaries, the practice of inducing accomplices to give evidence for the prosecution under immunity has increasingly become a necessary, even critical, feature of successful prosecutions of such offences. Indeed, identifying and 'turning' accomplices has become a key strategy of many law enforcement agencies responsible for the investigation and prosecution of corruption-related offences, including the Independent Commission Against Corruption (ICAC) in Hong Kong.

This development poses a problem for the integrity of the administration of criminal justice, since immunised accomplice witnesses present obvious risks. First, there is the 'unsavoury' spectacle of individuals who have committed offences not being prosecuted for their offending, contrary to the general public interest in their prosecution and conviction.

---

[1] There are two further categories of immunity witnesses, namely undercover law enforcement agents, who are granted immunity in advance of going undercover, and informers, who are not accomplices in the offences being investigated, but may seek immunity for other offences in return for giving information. These categories of immunity witness also potentially present dangers to the integrity of the criminal justice system, but will not be discussed in this chapter.

[2] *R v Turner (Bryan)* (1975) 61 Cr App R 67, 79 (Lawton LJ).

[3] L Radzinowicz, *A History of English Criminal Law*, Vol 2 (London, Stevens & Sons, 1956) 53.

Secondly, there is a risk, potentially substantial, that the agents of the investigating authority may engage in improper conduct in handling such witnesses, either at the initial stage of inducing accomplices to give evidence against their co-accused, or in their subsequent preparation of such witnesses for trial. If misconduct occurs, and it comes to light, this may then lead to an application by the accomplice's erstwhile co-accused to permanently stay criminal proceedings against themselves for abuse of process, one of the principal manifestations of the integrity principle in the administration of criminal justice.[4] Thirdly, accomplice witnesses testify under a heavy suspicion of fabrication and falsity, and trial judges will often be confronted with further challenges either to the admissibility of their evidence, or by the need for warnings as to their reliability and credibility. Here, the integrity of the administration of the criminal justice system is again challenged.

An important feature of the practice of using immunised accomplice witnesses is that the discretion falls to the relevant prosecuting authority tasked with the responsibility for making decisions concerning prosecution and ancillary matters, not to the investigating agency. But at the same time, it is also a feature of English common law systems that the exercise of the discretion to prosecute or not prosecute, and of ancillary discretions such as granting immunity, is not generally open to challenge or review by the courts.[5] As a result, it more often than not falls to the courts to 'police' the legitimacy of the use of immunised accomplice witnesses in any particular case. But the judiciary has generally been reluctant to exercise its undoubted jurisdiction to protect the administration of criminal justice by staying proceedings or excluding evidence merely in order to 'discipline' or 'punish' investigating agencies for the misconduct of their officers. This chapter contends that the use of immunised accomplice witnesses can, as a result, have a 'corrupting' or 'corrosive' effect on the administration of criminal justice, potentially leading to a culture of impunity on the part of investigating agencies.

The following discussion explores this 'corrupting' effect, and the risks it poses to procedural integrity, by examining the use of immunised accomplice witnesses in corruption-related prosecutions in Hong Kong against a backdrop of historical and contemporary common law practice. Responsibility for investigating corruption in Hong Kong falls to the ICAC, which has enjoyed remarkable success in eliminating public sector corruption in Hong Kong. But its sheen, burnished over the 40 years since the ICAC was established, has been dulled in recent years for a variety of reasons, including the discovery and reporting of questionable conduct by its investigating officers inter alia in relation to immunised accomplice witnesses.[6]

This chapter first outlines the nature of immunity and the parties and processes involved in granting it. It will then identify the potential risks to the administration of criminal justice posed by immunised accomplice witnesses, and the control mechanisms that are potentially available to reduce these risks. In the final section, the 'corrupting' effect is exemplified by a case study of linked proceedings, beginning in 2010 and culminating in 2015, involving egregious misconduct by three ICAC officers in their handling and preparation for trial of a particular immunised accomplice witness—misconduct which, it is argued, may have

---

[4]   See Whitfort, Chapter 10 in this volume.
[5]   See Gans, Chapter 6 in this volume.
[6]   See eg S Young, 'Prosecuting Bribery in Hong Kong's Human Rights Environment' in J Horder and P Alldridge (eds), *Modern Bribery Law: Comparative Perspectives* (Cambridge, Cambridge University Press, 2013) 267.

been indicative of a 'culture of disregard' or impunity among ICAC investigating officers. Lessons learnt, and the possibilities and limits of further institutional reform, are briefly canvassed in the conclusion.

1. Immunity from Prosecution in Common Law Theory and Practice

Immunity from prosecution first appeared in England as a form of confession known as 'approvement', whereby those charged with treason or felony confessed their guilt and then give evidence against others whom they had exposed, thereby entitling themselves to a pardon.[7] During the eighteenth century, the courts recognised a further practice, whereby accomplices who made a 'full and fair confession of the whole truth, are in consequence thereof admitted evidence for the Crown and that evidence is afterwards made use of to convict the other offenders.[8] Unlike approvement, such accomplices had no right to a pardon, 'yet the usage, lenity and the practice of the Courts is to stop the prosecution against them and they have an equitable title to a recommendation for the [Queen's] mercy.[9]

During the eighteenth and nineteenth centuries, the courts accepted that such accomplices, upon 'turning Queen's evidence', are competent witnesses for the prosecution, despite the prospect of immunity from prosecution. But trial judges also took to warning juries of the dangers of convicting on accomplice evidence—including accomplices testifying for the prosecution—without corroboration. Over time, this 'corroboration warning rule' became mandatory, but in the latter years of the twentieth century it has commonly been abolished, including in England and Wales and in Hong Kong, re-vesting judges with a discretion about giving such a warning.[10]

Of course, the prosecuting authorities may simply decide *not* to prosecute an accomplice, if it is not in the public interest to do so.[11] But if an accomplice is to be called as a prosecution witness, immunity is necessary to overcome the privilege against self-incrimination: without immunity, accomplice witnesses would have the 'right' when called to testify not to answer any question in court or produce any document which might incriminate them.[12] Immunity provides the legal means of circumventing that privilege.[13]

---

[7] W Blackstone, *Commentaries to the Laws of England*, 1st edn, vol 4 (Oxford, Clarendon Press 1765-69), 324. See further discussion in *R v Turner (Bryan)* (1975) 61 Cr App R 67, 77–78.

[8] *R v Rudd* (1775) 1 Cowp 331, 344 (Lord Mansfield).

[9] Ibid.

[10] It was abolished in England by the Criminal Justice and Public Order Act 1994, s 32; and in Hong Kong in 1994 by the Criminal Procedure Ordinance (Cap 221), s 60.

[11] See AHY Chen, 'Focus on the Discretion Whether to Prosecute: Prosecutorial Discretion, Independence and Accountability' (1998) 28 *Hong Kong Law Journal* 406.

[12] See Li CJ in *Fu Kin Chi v Secretary for Justice* (1998) 1 HKCFAR 85, 96: 'At common law, a person has the privilege from being compelled to answer questions, the answers to which might tend to expose him to any punishment or penalty.' Its application to immunity witnesses is explicitly stated, eg in New Zealand's *Prosecutions Guidelines*, [12.2]: 'Unless the potential witness has already been charged and sentenced he or she may be justified in declining to give evidence on the grounds of self-incrimination.'

[13] *HKSAR v Leung Kai Chung* [2002] 1 HKLRD 771, [52], per Stock JA: 'the privilege against self-incrimination goes once an immunity is granted, because there is then no risk of exposure to criminality in the sense intended by the privilege'.

However, most accomplices testifying for the prosecution are not granted immunity. Instead, they are prosecuted and convicted prior to testifying, either receiving a discounted sentence, or having their sentencing deferred until after they have testified. This practice accords with the public interest in bringing those who commit crime to justice whenever possible, and prosecution codes commonly make this expectation explicit. For example, paragraph 11.1 of the Hong Kong *Prosecution Code*[14] commences the section on 'Immunity from prosecution' with the following declaration:

> In principle it is desirable that the criminal justice process should operate without the need to immunise witnesses to testify to the involvement of others in criminal offending, but it is recognized that in some cases that is an appropriate course. As a general rule, an accomplice should be prosecuted, irrespective of whether or not he or she is to be called as a witness. The preferable course is for a cooperating accomplice to be dealt with after the trial, and ordinarily he or she will receive a discount on sentence to reflect the nature and extent of his or her cooperation.

In *R v P and Blackburn*,[15] the English Court of Appeal, commenting on the practice of giving sentencing discounts (rather than complete immunity) to accomplice witnesses, as provided for by sections 73 and 74 of the then recently enacted Serious Organised Crime and Police Act (SOCPA) 2005, articulated several rationales for doing so:

> There never has been, and never will be, much enthusiasm about a process by which criminals receive lower sentences than they otherwise deserve because they have informed on or given evidence against those who participated in the same or linked crimes, or in relation to crimes in which they had no personal involvement, but about which they have provided useful information to the investigating authorities. However ... this is a longstanding and entirely pragmatic convention. The stark reality is that without it major criminals who should be convicted and sentenced for offences of the utmost seriousness might, and in many cases, certainly would escape justice. Moreover the very existence of this process, and the risk that an individual for his own selfish motives may provide incriminating evidence, provides something of a check against the belief, deliberately fostered to increase their power, that gangs of criminals, and in particular the leaders of such gangs, are untouchable and beyond the reach of justice. The greatest disincentive to the provision of assistance to the authorities is an understandable fear of consequent reprisals. ... The solitary incentive to encourage co-operation is provided by a reduced sentence, and the common law, and now statute, have accepted that this is a price worth paying to achieve the overwhelming and recurring public interest that major criminals, in particular, should be caught and prosecuted to conviction.[16]

Granting outright immunity from prosecution is more exceptional. This policy is often stated explicitly. Hong Kong's *Prosecution Code*, issued by the Department of Justice, provides that '[i]n certain *exceptional* circumstances a witness may be granted immunity from prosecution'.[17] Similar statements can be found in parallel guidelines issued by the Crown

---

[14] HKSAR Department of Justice, *Prosecution Code* (2013), available on the Department of Justice website, www.doj.gov.hk/eng/public/pubsoppaptoc.html (accessed 17 August 2015). The *Prosecution Code* resulted from a substantial revision of the previous *Statement of Prosecution Policy and Practice* (2009), with the assistance of Nicholas Cowdery QC, former DPP of NSW.

[15] [2008] 2 Cr App R (S) 5, [2007] EWCA Crim 2290.

[16] Ibid [22].

[17] *Prosecution Code*, above n 14, [11.3] (emphasis added). Ultimate responsibility for prosecution lies with the Department of Justice, headed by the Secretary for Justice, pursuant to Article 63 of the Basic Law of the HKSAR: 'The Department of Justice of the Hong Kong Special Administrative Region shall control criminal prosecutions, free from any interference.' Prior to the Basic Law coming into effect on 1 July 1997, the Department of Justice was known as the Attorney General's Chambers.

Prosecution Service (CPS) in England and Wales,[18] and by the Australian Commonwealth Director of Public Prosecutions (DPP).[19]

(a) Immunity and Public Interest

The essential rationale for granting immunity lies in the public interest in securing the conviction of those accused of serious crime. Thus New Zealand's *Prosecution Guidelines* declare that: 'Immunities are to be used sparingly and only in cases where it is demonstrably clear that without the evidence given under immunity the prosecution case is unlikely to succeed, or there is a risk it will be significantly weakened.'[20] New South Wales' *Prosecution Policy* likewise states that: 'It must be able to be demonstrated in all cases that the interests of justice require that the immunity be given.'[21]

These statements broadly reflect the common law position. Addressing the competence and admissibility of immunised accomplice evidence, the English Court of Appeal in *Turner* surveyed the common law relating to giving 'Queen's evidence', and observed:

> It is in the interest of the public that criminals should be brought to justice; and the more serious the crimes the greater is the need for justice to be done. Employing Queen's evidence to accomplish this end is distasteful and has been distasteful for at least 300 years to judges, lawyers and members of the public.[22]

The Hong Kong Court of Appeal elaborated on these sentiments in *HKSAR v Leung Kai Chung*.[23] Both the long-standing nature of encouraging testimonial turncoats, and judicial ambivalence towards the practice, were illustrated by a passage from Chitty's nineteenth-century treatise on criminal law:

> The law confesses its weakness by calling in the assistance of those by whom it has been broken. It offers a premium to treachery, and destroys the last virtue which clings to the degraded

---

[18] CPS, *Queen's Evidence—Immunities, Undertakings and Agreements under SOCPA 2005* (*Queen's Evidence*), [6]: 'Only in the most exceptional cases will it be appropriate to offer full immunity.' See also CPS, *SOCPA Agreements: Practical Notes for Defence Advocates* (2014).

[19] Commonwealth DPP, *Prosecution Policy of the Commonwealth: Guidelines for the Making of Decisions in the Prosecution Process; Guidelines and Directions Manual: Undertakings, offers of assistance and induced statements* (2012), [1]: Immunity from prosecution for specified Commonwealth offences, acts or omissions, under the Director of Public Prosecutions Act 1983, s 9(6D), 'will only be provided … in exceptional circumstances'.

[20] Crown Law, New Zealand, *Prosecution Guidelines* (2013) [12.7].

[21] Office of the DPP, *Prosecution Policy and Guidelines: Guideline 17* (2007).

[22] *R v Turner (Bryan)* (1975) 61 Cr App R 67, 79.

[23] *HKSAR v Leung Kai Chung* [2002] 1 HKLRD 771. In this case the Court of Appeal was confronted with oral offers of immunity, shortly before trial, compounded by the trial judge's direction that the immunised witnesses were not obliged to give answers which might incriminate them. Referring to (then subsisting) *Prosecution Policy*, Stock JA, for the Court, observed, ibid [42]: 'None of this is new to the Department of Justice. It accords with its long-standing stated, as well as actual, policy and practice. What happened in this case was that that practice was not followed.' See also *R v Chan Wai-Keung* [1995] 1 HKCLR 123 (PC), where Lord Mustill commented: 'It has been recognized for centuries that the practice of allowing one co-accused to "turn Queen's evidence" and obtain an immunity from further process by giving evidence against another was a powerful weapon for bringing criminals to justice, and although this practice "has been distasteful for at least 300 years to judges, lawyers and members of the public", and although it brings with it an obvious risk that the accused will give false evidence under this "most powerful inducement", the same very experienced Court which so stigmatized this practice was willing to accept that it was in accordance with the law.'

transgressor. Still on the other hand, it tends to prevent any extensive agreement among atrocious criminals, makes them perpetually suspicious of each other, and prevents the hopelessness of mercy from rendering them desperate.[24]

Moreover, noted the *Leung* court, 'another and signal advantage' is that, 'since it is in the public interest that criminals be brought to justice, the use of accomplice evidence, if necessary or helpful to that end, is admissible'. By the same token: 'That principled approach is accompanied by a practical concern, namely, the risk of false evidence induced by the hope or the real prospect of advantage which is nurtured by the accomplice who is turned prosecution witness.'[25]

Thus, despite deeply felt principled objections, the public interest sometimes justifies the grant of complete immunity from prosecution. Given the need to exercise discretion on the basis of the public interest, it falls to senior officials with responsibility for prosecutions to determine whether or not to grant immunity, and not to the investigating agencies themselves. In England, six 'specified prosecutors' are empowered to grant immunity, and, in some circumstances, must first consult with the Attorney General. In New Zealand, the Solicitor-General is made responsible. In Australia, the discretion falls to the relevant Attorney General, at both Commonwealth and state levels. In Hong Kong, the power vests in the DPP, as Head of the Prosecutions Division of the Department of Justice,[26] in accordance with the *Prosecution Code*'s requirement that grants of immunity be made only 'at directorate level'.[27]

The criteria to be considered at common law in determining whether or not to grant immunity from prosecution in England and Wales were summarised by the Attorney General in a written answer to the House of Commons on 9 November 1981. Three sets of considerations must be addressed:

(a)   whether, in the interests of justice, it is of more value to have a suspected person as a witness for the Crown rather than as a possible defendant;
(b)   whether, in the interests of public safety and security, the obtaining of information about the extent and nature of criminal activities is of greater importance than the possible conviction of an individual; and
(c)   whether it is very unlikely that any information could be obtained without an offer of immunity and whether it is also very unlikely that any prosecution could be launched against the person to whom the immunity is offered.

In addition, immunised accomplice witnesses may be admitted into witness protection schemes, now commonly provided for by statute,[28] or give their evidence anonymously,[29]

---

[24] J Chitty, *A Practical Treatise on the Criminal Law*, Vol I (London, Samuel Brooke, 1826) 769, quoted in *HKSAR v Leung Kai Chung* [2002] 1 HKLRD 771, [40].

[25] Ibid [40]–[41].

[26] Subject to the overriding authority of the Secretary for Justice, who is the head of the Department of Justice. Generally, see S Young, 'Prosecutions Division of the Department of Justice' in M Gaylord, D Gittings and H Travers (eds), *Introduction to Crime, Law and Justice in Hong Kong* (Hong Kong, Hong Kong University Press, 2009) 111.

[27] *Prosecution Code*, above n 14, [11.4].

[28] See eg Witness Protection Ordinance (Cap 564) (HKSAR); SOCPA 2005, ss 82–94 (England and Wales).

[29] For example, Coroners and Justice Act 2009, Part 3 (England and Wales).

again, usually pursuant to statutory witness anonymity schemes. Each of these types of immunity may generate their own issues regarding the integrity of the criminal trial, or even lead to the criminal prosecution of those who breach disclosure prohibitions.[30] These topics are beyond the scope of the present discussion.

(b) Forms and Grounds of Immunity

A grant of immunity may take one of two forms, or encompass both together: an immunity or indemnity against prosecution, and an undertaking not to use the evidence of the immunised witness in any subsequent prosecution against the witness.[31] Both procedural mechanisms, it is contended, present similar challenges to the integrity of the criminal justice system.

The existence of these two distinct forms in which immunity may be granted is sometimes explicit in the law or guidelines relating to immunity witnesses, but not always so. In England, for example, the law relating to immunity witnesses is now regulated by sections 71 to 75B of SOCPA 2005.[32] A clear distinction is drawn between offering 'immunity from prosecution' for any offence by way of an 'immunity notice', pursuant to section 71, and the offer of an undertaking under section 72 (called a 'restricted use undertaking') not to use information provided by a person against that person in any criminal proceedings.[33] The responsibility for offering each form of immunity falls to named 'specified prosecutors', including the DPP and the Director of the Serious Fraud Office (or their designates).[34] If a specified prosecutor 'thinks that for the purposes of the investigation or prosecution of an indictable offence ... it is appropriate', then he may offer immunity from prosecution or a restricted use undertaking.[35] If full immunity is being considered, then ordinarily the Attorney General should be consulted.[36] Detailed advice on the exercise of these powers is set out in guidelines issued, for example, by the CPS[37] and the Serious Fraud Office, including draft immunity notices and restricted use undertakings. However, the common law power to grant immunity still exists.[38]

---

[30] See eg *So Wing Keung v Sing Tao Ltd* (10 Aug 2004) HCMP 1833/2004 (CFI); appeal dismissed by CA on jurisdiction grounds, [2005] 2 HKLRD 11.

[31] An immunity may sometimes extend to civil proceedings; see eg Director of Public Prosecutions Act 1983 (Aus Cth), s 9.

[32] SOCPA 2005, s 71(7) excludes cartel offences under the Enterprise Act 2003, s 188, from the immunity notice procedure; immunity in relation to such offences is addressed in s 190(4) of the 2003 Act.

[33] This also includes proceedings under Part 5 of the Proceeds of Crime Act 2002 relating to civil recovery of the proceeds etc of unlawful conduct. This part of SOCPA also provides for agreements relating to reduction in sentence (s 73) and post assistance review of sentence (s 74) for offenders who assist or offer to assist investigators or prosecutors in relation to offences.

[34] SOCPA 2005, s 71(4)(a)–(d). Specified prosecutors may in turn designate other prosecutors for the purposes of offering immunity or restricted use notices: ss 71(4)(e) and 72(7).

[35] The restriction to indictable offences was inserted by the Coroners and Justice Act 2009, s 113.

[36] CPS, *Queen's Evidence*, above n 18, [15].

[37] Ibid.

[38] Ibid [38].

In Australia, the Commonwealth DPP is expressly empowered, pursuant to subsections 9(6) to (6C) of the Director of Public Prosecutions Act 1983, to 'give to a person an undertaking' that answers and statements made by him or her in giving evidence in criminal and related proceedings, and any information, document or other thing obtained as a direct or indirect result of such answers 'will not be used in evidence against the person' and, further, where such an undertaking is given, that any such answers, statements, etc are 'not admissible in evidence against the person in any civil or criminal proceedings' in a federal, state or territorial court.[39] The DPP is additionally empowered 'where the Director considers it appropriate to do so', to give 'an undertaking that the person will not be prosecuted' for Commonwealth offences. Similar powers exist at state level. In New South Wales (NSW), for example, sections 32 and 33 of the Criminal Procedure Act 1986 expressly confer power on the NSW Attorney General, '(a) to grant indemnity from prosecution' and '(b) to give an undertaking that an answer, statement or disclosure will not be used in evidence'. Pursuant to section 19 of the Director of Public Prosecutions Act 1986 (NSW), entitled 'Indemnities and undertakings', the NSW DPP may request the state Attorney General to exercise his immunity powers, although the NSW DPP himself is expressly prohibited from granting such an indemnity or giving such an undertaking.[40] In both Commonwealth and NSW jurisdictions, detailed guidance on the exercise of these powers and procedures to be followed is contained in relevant prosecution policies and guidelines, which similarly include draft forms of immunity and undertaking.[41]

In New Zealand, as mentioned above, immunity is addressed in the *Prosecution Guidelines* issued by the Crown Law Office.[42] Guideline 12, entitled 'Immunities from Prosecution', specifies that: 'Immunity takes the form of a written undertaking from the Solicitor-General[43] to exercise the power to stay if the witness is prosecuted for nominated offences.'[44]

In each case, the relevant factors to be taken into account in deciding whether or not the public interest justifies granting immunity, and the form it should take, are elaborated in the relevant prosecution codes or guidelines.[45] As mentioned, in England and Wales, the offence in respect of which accomplice evidence is to be given must be serious.[46] This is

---

[39] There is a necessary exception for criminal proceedings based on the falsity of evidence given by the immunised accomplice witness: Director of Public Prosecutions Act 1983, s 9(6).

[40] Director of Public Prosecutions Act 1986 (NSW), s 19(2).

[41] See Prosecution Policy of the Commonwealth (Cth, August 2014); Prosecution Policy (NSW, 2007). In NSW, a draft immunity by the Attorney General is attached to an *Interagency Protocol for Indemnities and Undertakings* dated 1 June 2007.

[42] Crown Law, above n 20.

[43] Under New Zealand constitutional law, the overriding responsibility for prosecutions falls on the Attorney General. However, in practice, the prosecution process is superintended by the Solicitor-General, and administered by Crown Solicitors, who are private practitioners appointed to prosecute under warrant issued by the NZ Governor-General.

[44] Crown Law, above n 20, [12.3]. The power to stay is provided in the Crimes Act 1961, s 378, which entitles the Attorney General (and thus the Solicitor-General, pursuant to the Constitution Act 1986, s 9A) to stay proceedings. Paragraph [12.3] stipulates that immunity protects the witness from both Crown and private prosecutions.

[45] CPS, *Queen's Evidence*, above n 18, [8]–[10] (England and Wales); Crown Law, above n 20, [12.7] (New Zealand); Office of the DPP, above n 41 (NSW).

[46] SOCPA 2005, ss 71 and 72. In addition, CPS guidelines expressly state that, 'as a rule, non-prosecution agreements should only be considered in serious cases': *Queen's Evidence*, above n 18, [13(a)].

also a general requirement in New Zealand, according to the *Prosecution Guidelines*;[47] but it is not expressly required under the NSW Guidelines. In addition, in accordance with the Attorney General's written statement, immunity should normally only be considered where there is limited likelihood of securing the evidence from other sources. Other common factors include the likely credibility of the proposed accomplice witness and the reliability of his or her evidence,[48] the relative degree of culpability of the proposed accomplice witness,[49] and whether any other inducement for giving evidence may have been offered or sought.[50]

(c) Accomplice Immunity in Hong Kong

In Hong Kong, accomplice immunity remains a common law procedure, but is addressed in the *Prosecution Code*.[51] Paragraph 11, headed 'Immunity from Prosecution', succinctly covers both informers and accomplice witnesses, and refers to the 'granting of an immunity', without further elaboration.[52] The usual terms of any such immunity, which can be granted only on the authority of the DPP,[53] are apparently along the following lines:[54]

> I hereby inform you that on condition that you give full and true evidence at the trial of [DEFENDANT] in connection with the alleged offence [ABC] ... no prosecution will be instituted against you in respect of the offence of [ABC] or any other offences connected with the said offence which have been disclosed by you or which may be disclosed by you in the course of your testimony during the said proceedings. Should you fail to give full and true evidence at the aforesaid trial, the Secretary of Justice shall not be bound by any undertaking given in this document and you may be prosecuted for the said offence or any other offence connected with the said offence.[55]

The immunity offered in Hong Kong seemingly entails, as in New Zealand, an undertaking not to prosecute ('no prosecution will be instituted'), but not an express undertaking not to use statements, information etc, disclosed by an immunised accomplice witness in subsequent proceedings.[56] According to the *Prosecution Code*, immunity should be given to the witness in writing and copies of it made available to the defence before the trial and thereafter to the trial court.[57]

---

[47] Crown Law, above n 20, [12.7]: 'Before agreeing to give immunity, the Solicitor General will almost invariably need to be satisfied of at least the following matters: That the offence in respect of which the evidence is to be given is serious.'

[48] *Queen's Evidence*, above n 18, [11]–[14] (England and Wales); Crown Law, above n 20, [12.7.3] (New Zealand); Office of the DPP, above n 41, Guideline 17(h) (NSW).

[49] *Queen's Evidence*, above n 18, [13](b) (England and Wales); Crown Law, above n 20, [12.7.4] (New Zealand); Office of the DPP, above n 41, Guideline 17(c) (NSW).

[50] Crown Law, above n 20, [12.7.6] (New Zealand); Office of the DPP, above n 41, Guideline 17(l) (NSW).

[51] *Prosecution Code*, above n 14, [11].

[52] Regarding informers, ibid paragraph [11.2] states: 'An informer should be used as a prosecution witness only if the interests of justice demand it.'

[53] Ibid [11.4].

[54] As set out in *HKSAR v Leung Kai Chung* [2002] 1 HKLRD 771, [43].

[55] The form goes on to record that the immunity does not apply to any offence of perjury etc committed by the witness in giving testimony during any such proceedings.

[56] It is not clear whether the form of immunity may have changed as a result of the 2013 revisions to the *Prosecution Code*.

[57] Ibid [11.4].

The factors to be taken into account by the DPP (or his Deputy Directors) in determining whether to grant immunity are adumbrated by paragraph 11.3 of the *Prosecution Code*, echoing many of the considerations found in similar codes in other jurisdictions:[58]

The decision to grant an immunity and the balancing process involved will be strongly influenced by:

(a) the nature of the evidence the witness may be able to give and its significance to the prosecution of the case;

(b) the antecedents of the witness;

(c) his or her perceived credibility (including the fullness of his or her disclosure of facts and matters within his or her knowledge) and any discernible motive for not telling the whole truth (including the receipt, promise or expectation of a benefit);

(d) his or her level of involvement in the offence being prosecuted (which should generally be lower than that of the offender being prosecuted);

(e) the presence of any supporting evidence.

Notably, there is no express restriction of immunity to serious cases or serious offences, unlike in England and New Zealand. Nonetheless, in *Leung*, the Hong Kong Court of Appeal emphasised the 'serious' nature of this discretion and identified key procedural safeguards to be followed in granting immunity:

[T]he grant of an immunity is a serious matter, not to be treated lightly or, as we find happened in this case, loosely. A decision to grant an immunity is a decision which should be made only by those duly authorised to make it, and the terms of the immunity to be granted must receive careful attention. The person to whom it is offered is entitled to know precisely what is properly expected of him if the immunity is to hold good, and in respect of precisely what conduct the immunity extends, subject to the overriding consideration that what is expected is the full truth.[59]

In Hong Kong, as elsewhere, it is necessary for the investigating officers as a first step in this process, after arresting or otherwise identifying a potential accomplice witness, to take a statement of his or her evidence, called a 'non-prejudicial statement' (NPS) in Hong Kong. Consent to the taking of an NPS as a first step in offering immunity must be sought from the Prosecutions Division.

2. Integrity Management

The essential challenges posed by the use of immunised accomplice witnesses to the 'integrity' of the administration of criminal justice are, first, that it is contrary to the public interest not to prosecute persons who have committed crimes; secondly, that such accomplice witnesses may have sought or been offered questionable inducements, in addition to prosecutorial immunity, in return for agreeing to give evidence; and thirdly, that their

---

[58] In the previous *Statement of Prosecution Policy and Practice*, the list of factors was preceded by the following statement: 'The central issue in deciding whether to give an accomplice an immunity is whether in the overall interests of justice the prosecution of the accomplice should be foregone in order to secure that person's testimony in the prosecution of another.'

[59] *HKSAR v Leung Kai Chung* [2002] 1 HKLRD 771, [41].

evidence may be unreliable and lack credibility or even be untruthful and involve fabrication or false allegations.

Managing these challenges and their consequential risks to the integrity of the administration of criminal justice falls to three key institutional entities: (1) the investigating agency, whose officers interact with an accomplice witness from the point of initial contact during an investigation through to the end of any trial that may take place; (2) the relevant prosecuting authority, vested with the discretion to offer immunity; and (3) the judiciary, tasked with the overall responsibility of ensuring a fair trial and protecting the integrity of the trial process and the administration of criminal justice. But there is always a risk of 'something going wrong', either through a failure of management or absence of effective oversight. Although this risk is greatest in relation to the investigating agency and its officers, the prosecuting authority may also be at fault: either as a result of misconduct in the formal procedures for granting immunity, or in relation to the exercise of the discretion to offer immunity itself, such as its exercise for political objectives. Inadequate judicial supervision of accomplice witness immunisation procedures further imperils integrity.

In light of the well-known risks inherent in reliance on immunised accomplice evidence, it is essential that each of the three main institutional agencies takes appropriate steps, and is subject to effective control mechanisms, to prevent these risks from crystallising, where possible, and to institute remedial measures when prevention fails.

(a) Investigating Agency

Not surprisingly, controls are most intensive in relation to the investigating agency and its officers. They encompass both *internal* and *external* mechanisms. Broadly speaking, two *internal* mechanisms are available. The first comprises an investigating agency's Code of Ethics[60] and its specific internal rules and practices for dealing with potential accomplice witnesses. These are usually set out in written form, and investigating officers are required to comply with them. Internal agency rules will likely mandate, for example, the recording of all meetings. This form of control involves a 'rules-based' mechanism, with breach of the rules leading to disciplinary proceedings or, in more egregious cases, to prosecution of the officers involved for offences such as misconduct in public office or perverting the course of justice (which is what happened in the case study presented in Section 3, below).

The second internal control mechanism operates by way of an internalised culture of integrity, according to which investigating officers automatically monitor their conduct not only to ensure compliance with explicit rules, but also to recognise when they may be entering a zone of ethical uncertainty or danger, so that officers can proceed with heightened caution to ensure that their conduct remains beyond reproach. This 'values-based' approach, as it is known, has become a key component of anti-corruption strategies and

---

[60] According to the ICAC's *Code of Ethics*, as displayed on its webpage at http://www.icac.org.hk/en/about-icac/mp/index.html, the first obligation of ICAC Officers is to 'adhere to the principles of integrity and fair play'. Likewise, in the Introduction to Hong Kong's *Prosecution Code*, above n 14, it is asserted that: 'A prosecutor is expected to discharge his or her duties with professionalism, skill and integrity, and to operate within the framework of defined and clear prosecution policy guidelines.'

'integrity management' in recent years.[61] It is intended to help those 'entrusted with positions of responsibility' to minimise conflicts of interest, and thereby reduce the risk of corruption. As Mulgan and Wanna elucidate:

> Integrity cultures ... may be broadly understood as the set of endorsed social understandings, behaviours and practices that affect how people think and act. Cultures are commonly distinguished from the formal organizational structures, such as institutions and legal rules. ... Accordingly, while the quality of legal regulation is certainly an important factor in affecting the extent of malfeasance or corruption, research has repeatedly shown that underlying cultural values and informal expectations among the actors involved are equally, if not more, influential. For this reason, much of the emphasis in building ethical environments and in combating corruption has moved from legal enforcement of ethical rules towards trying to change cultural attitudes in the direction of greater support for integrity and greater intolerance of corrupt behaviour.[62]

Although directed at 'those entrusted with positions of responsibility', the notion of an 'integrity culture' is equally applicable to those entrusted with the investigation of corruption by those in positions of responsibility. It presupposes both compliance with the internal rules, and also respect for the rule of law in the conduct of investigations including, specifically, in the handling and preparation of potential accomplice witnesses.

Turning to *external* controls, three such mechanisms can be identified. The first, specifically related to immunised accomplice witnesses, derives from the fact that the decision to offer immunity generally falls to the relevant prosecuting authority, not the investigating agency itself. In Hong Kong, this means that to initiate the immunity process ICAC investigators must first obtain the consent of the Prosecutions Division of the Department of Justice to their taking of an NPS from the proposed immunised accomplice. In due course, ICAC officers will have to present a case file in support of their recommendation for immunity to the Prosecution Division for independent scrutiny and assessment. Misconduct by the investigating officers in their handling of a potential accomplice witness may come to light at this stage. Of course, this control mechanism may be impotent if improper conduct has not been recorded, or if the evidence purportedly to be given by the witness is less than truthful. This was alleged to be a feature of ICAC misconduct in the *Raymond Ng* case study examined in Section 3(b), below. Quashing Ng's conviction due to alleged misconduct by three ICAC officers in their handling of Ng's erstwhile associate, Cheung (CCH), Stock VP recounted:

> On 29 May 2008, consent was given by counsel in the Department of Justice for the ICAC to take from CCH a non-prejudicial statement; meaning a statement that is not [to] be used against its maker in the event of the maker's prosecution for the offence or offences which it discloses but the purpose of which is for the witness to disclose what he knows of the offence or offences for which others have been arrested and, depending on the utility of the evidence thus disclosed, in respect of which the witness may become a prosecution witness, in exchange for an immunity from prosecution.[63]

---

[61] In relation to law enforcement in Australia, see L Porter and T Prenzler, *Police Integrity Management in Australia: Global Lessons for Combating Police Misconduct* (Boca Raton FL, CRC Press, 2012).

[62] R Mulgan and J Wanna, 'Developing Cultures of Integrity in the Public and Private Sectors' in A Graycar and RG Smith (eds), *Handbook of Global Research and Practice in Corruption* (Cheltenham, Edward Elgar, 2011) 416–28. For a discussion of these two approaches in relation to anti-corruption activities in Hong Kong, see I Scott, 'The Hong Kong ICAC's Approach to Corruption Control', ibid 401–15.

[63] *HKSAR v Ng Chun To Raymond* [2013] 5 HKC 390, [69]–[71] (CA).

In the absence of any written representations to the Department of Justice, however, the only evidence before the Hong Kong Court of Appeal regarding the giving of consent was a note signed by an investigating ICAC officer purportedly recording a conversation about consent with counsel in the Department of Justice. The note recorded Cheung's allegedly 'passive and minor role in the scam', his 'minimal' personal gain, and his lack of any 'direct dealing with the corrupt agents'. Stock VP observed:

> We were not provided with the records of interview with CCH which, prior to that Note, had taken place but the suggestion that CCH played a passive and minor role in [the] scam is, on its face and in the light of what we now know, false; as is the suggestion that CCH had no direct dealing with the corrupt agents. This is suggested to be another example of those in the ICAC playing fast and loose with the truth and to be evidence of a design to target [Ng] by sleight of hand.[64]

Furthermore, given the generally close working relationship between investigating agencies and prosecuting authorities, and their joint interest in prosecuting the corrupt and fraudulent, there is an ever-present risk that the case file may be less zealously scrutinised than it should be, making an offer of immunity all too routine and undemanding. As Young suggests:

> The use of immunity is open to abuse … if defendants are prepared to lie in order to ensure their own release. There now exists a general sentiment among defense lawyers that the Prosecutions Division may be granting immunity without proper scrutiny of the proffered evidence. Such sentiments, whether valid or not, make it imperative for prosecutors to properly weigh the decision to grant immunity so as not to run the risk of eroding confidence in the integrity of the trial process or of convicting innocent defendants.[65]

The second external control over investigating agencies and their officers is the judicial jurisdiction to stay proceedings[66] or exclude evidence[67] on grounds of investigative impropriety. Until the early 1980s, the perils of immunised accomplice evidence were simply accepted as a 'necessary evil', and there was relatively little a co-accused could do at trial to challenge its admissibility or uses, save by inviting the trial judge to give a corroboration warning. The possibility of misconduct associated with such witnesses prior to trial was simply not the concern of the courts, reflecting a more general philosophy confining judicial responsibility for ensuring the fairness of trials to proceedings in the courtroom itself. But today, as summarised by Roberts and Zuckerman[68] and mentioned in this book's Introduction, the position is very different, both as a result of statutory provisions empowering the courts to refuse to admit evidence if its admission may have an adverse effect on the fairness of the proceedings,[69] and also as a result of the judiciary claiming for itself the jurisdiction to stay criminal proceedings permanently in order to protect the integrity of judicial process in a more holistic sense.

---

[64] Ibid [71].

[65] Young, above n 26, 124.

[66] Also see Whitfort, Chapter 10 in this volume.

[67] Also see Chau, Chapter 11 in this volume.

[68] P Roberts and A Zuckerman, *Criminal Evidence*, 2nd edn (Oxford, Oxford University Press, 2010) 176–78.

[69] Notably, PACE 1984, s 78 furnished trial judges in England and Wales with a new statutory discretion to 'refuse to allow evidence on which the prosecution proposes to rely to be given if it appears to the court that, having regard to all the circumstances, including the circumstances in which the evidence was obtained, the admission of the evidence would have such an adverse effect on the fairness of the proceedings that the court ought not to admit it'.

In Hong Kong, this judicial oversight has gained additional purchase with the entrenchment of constitutionally guaranteed due process rights (including the generic right to fair trial), first via the Hong Kong Bill of Rights Ordinance,[70] and then, since 1 July 1997, by way of the Basic Law of the Hong Kong Special Administrative Region (HKSAR).[71] Since then, the Hong Kong courts, especially at the level of the Court of Final Appeal (CFA), Hong Kong's supreme court, have fully taken on board the need to protect fundamental rights and freedoms in the laws of Hong Kong, including those concerning the criminal process. Simon Young, speaking of the development in Hong Kong of 'visible demands and expectations of the public' for greater integrity and accountability on the part of the Hong Kong government, including its law enforcement agencies, has observed that the 'CFA's public law jurisprudence has served to build and reinforce strong societal values that recognize the importance of the rule of law and respect for human rights, which it is said to "lie at the heart of Hong Kong's separate system".'[72]

However, the judiciary has signalled that it will not exercise its discretion to grant a permanent stay merely as a means of 'disciplining' or 'punishing' investigating agencies such as the ICAC for the misconduct of its officers. Agencies' internal disciplinary mechanisms are the proper forum, save in exceptional cases, when bad faith, rather than mere indiscipline or indiscretion, is proved. By the time that such witnesses appear at court, immunity in hand and ready to testify, a court will all too often find itself confronted with demands to continue proceedings and admit the evidence of such witnesses despite whatever concerns it may still entertain about alleged official impropriety or lingering doubts about the credibility of immunised witnesses. It is all too easy for a court to distance itself from the misconduct and let the trial proceed, pronouncing that the serious nature of the alleged offences and the well-known difficulties in prosecuting corruption and fraud tip the public interest balance in favour of proceeding.

The third, more diffuse mechanism of external control comes via the media and public opinion. The significance of the media in exposing misconduct and shaping public opinion, and of public opinion itself, to the exercise of judicial oversight of the integrity of the administration of criminal justice, has been highlighted elsewhere in this volume.[73] Potential misconduct in relation to accomplice witnesses who have been granted immunity 'in the public interest' is both grist to the media gossip mill, and also a prime candidate for public condemnation and enquiry about the legitimacy of the administration of criminal justice (as we will see in relation to the *Raymond Ng* saga, discussed in Section 3).

(b) Prosecuting Authority

Turning to the second official participant in the immunisation process, the relevant prosecuting authority vested with responsibility for offering immunity, control mechanisms are fewer. At the procedural level, errors or difficulties with the offer or terms of an immunity

---

[70] Cap 383.
[71] See S Young, 'Human Rights in Hong Kong Criminal Trials' in P Roberts and J Hunter (eds), *Criminal Evidence and Human Rights: Reimagining Common Law Procedural Traditions* (Oxford, Hart Publishing, 2012).
[72] Young, above n 6, 282, quoting the CFA in *Ng Ka Ling v Director of Immigration* (1999) 2 HKCFAR 4, [29].
[73] See Young, Chapter 1.

may possibly be taken up before the trial court, by way of an application either to stay proceedings, or to exclude the accomplice witness' testimony.[74] But beyond this, judicial control over the actual exercise by prosecuting authorities of their discretion to prosecute, and over ancillary decisions such as offering immunity, all grounded in 'the public interest', is very limited and generally considered 'exceptional'. In the UK, for example, the amenability of the DPP to judicial review was explored by the House of Lords in *R v DPP, ex parte Kebeline*,[75] where Lord Steyn emphatically stated that, 'absent dishonesty or mala fides or an exceptional circumstance, the decision of the Director to consent to the prosecution of the applicants is not amenable to judicial review'.[76] The general principle at English common law is that, although 'a decision by the Director not to prosecute is susceptible to judicial review ... the power of review is one to be sparingly exercised'.[77]

A similar view was adopted in colonial Hong Kong,[78] and this position was broadly preserved on 1 July 1997, when the Basic Law of the HKSAR came into effect on the Mainland's resumption of sovereignty over Hong Kong. Article 63 of the Basic Law expressly provides that '[t]he Department of Justice of the [HKSAR] shall control criminal prosecutions, free from any interference'. As such, the prior common law position is preserved, but the Hong Kong courts have also endorsed the view that the Secretary for Justice must exercise his powers within the limits of constitutional propriety.[79] This qualification potentially makes the exercise of prosecutorial discretion amenable not only to appeal but also to judicial review, although this is only likely to occur in 'the rarest of cases'.[80] In relation specifically to the discretion to grant immunity, Silke VP in *R v Tsui Lai-ying*[81] reviewed well-known English authorities including *Gouriet*,[82] *Padfield*[83] and *CSSU*,[84] as well as the Hong Kong decision in *Cheung Sou-yat v R*,[85] and concluded that 'there may, in exceptional circumstances, be a right to review the exercise' of the powers of the Attorney General.[86]

In the absence of robust judicial supervision, control over the exercise of prosecutorial discretion is primarily left to the political arena, specifically via accountability in the legislature, reinforced by media scrutiny and public opinion. Transparency and a measure of accountability have been prompted by the preparation and publication of prosecution codes, albeit that Hong Kong was a relatively late-adopter.[87] Ultimately, however, heavy reliance is placed on the personal integrity of the individuals entrusted with the responsibility of exercising these prosecutorial discretions.

---

[74] The Court of Appeal in *HKSAR v Leung Kai Chung* [2002] 1 HKLRD 771, for example, considered shortcomings of the procedures for offering and granting immunity employed in that case.

[75] [2000] 2 AC 326.

[76] Ibid 371.

[77] *R v DPP ex parte Manning* [2001] QB 330, [23] (Lord Bingham of Cornhill CJ).

[78] See *Keung Siu Wah v Attorney General* [1990] 2 HKLR 238 (CA).

[79] See eg *RV v Director of Immigration* [2008] 4 HKLRD 529 (CFI).

[80] R Gordon and J Mok, *Judicial Review in Hong Kong* (Singapore, LexisNexis, 2009) [10-50]–[10-53]. For a recent discussion, see *D v Director of Public Prosecutions* [2015] 4 HKLRD 62 (CFI).

[81] [1987] HKLR 857 (CA).

[82] *Gouriet v Union of Post Office Workers* [1978] AC 435 (HL).

[83] *Padfield v Minister of Agriculture* [1968] AC 997 (HL).

[84] *Council of Civil Service Unions v Minister for the Civil Service* [1985] AC 374 (HL).

[85] [1979] HKLR 630 (CA).

[86] *R v Tsui Lai-ying* [1987] HKLR 857, 873 (CA).

[87] Hong Kong's first *Statement of Prosecution Policy and Practice* was published in 1993. This was superseded in 2013 by the current *Prosecution Code*, above n 14.

(c) Judiciary

The third official participant in the immunisation triad is the judiciary, particularly trial judges, who are most immediately responsible for determining applications for stays and evidentiary exclusion, and issuing accomplice evidence corroboration warnings. Supervision and control over lower courts' trial management decisions is maintained by the appellate process and infrequent judicial review.

In summary, although both external and internal controls exist, a significant accountability gap is apparent in the effective scope of judicial control over prosecuting authorities in the exercise of their discretion to offer, or withhold, immunity to or from accomplice witnesses. This gap is an inevitable feature of the administration of criminal justice, for exercise of the discretion involves consideration of a host of factors relevant to and affecting the public interest, including political and other factors, which naturally fall outside the scope of judicial process and which it would be unacceptable to have to explain or justify to a court.

This accountability gap, or rather knowledge of it by investigating officers, poses the greatest risk to the integrity of the criminal justice system from the use of immunised accomplice witnesses. For this knowledge, combined with the evident reluctance of the judiciary to stay proceedings or exclude evidence from immunised accomplice witnesses, potentially encourages a feeling of 'disregard' or even impunity amongst investigating officers in relation to their handling of potential immunity witnesses. And perceived impunity breeds contempt. Where reliance is increasingly placed on the testimony of immunised accomplice witnesses, as it has been in corruption cases in Hong Kong, perceived impunity may become 'received wisdom' within the minds of investigating officers. In the absence of vigilant scrutiny by the prosecuting authority, a misplaced sense of invulnerability has the potential to corrupt the integrity of the investigating officers, thereby weakening a major pillar of the overall integrity of the criminal justice system.

The next section substantiates this contention by reference to a case study in Hong Kong involving serious misconduct by three ICAC officers in their handling and preparation of an immunised accomplice witness. The officers' misconduct led not only to their prosecution, but also to a succession of applications to stay proceedings or exclude evidence, and multiple appeals against conviction. The backdrop to this litigation was a very real concern, expressed by counsel and commented on by the courts, that the misconduct of the ICAC officers may not have been an isolated instance of unbecoming conduct, but was rather a product of a 'culture' of disregard or collective misconduct.

3. Case Study: The ICAC's Unbecoming Use of Immunised Accomplice Witnesses

For over 40 years, Hong Kong's dedicated anti-corruption agency, the ICAC, has effectively and mostly successfully carried out its task of eliminating corruption in Hong Kong.[88] Fully

---

[88] The ICAC was established in 1974. See generally, I McWalters, *Bribery and Corruption Law in Hong Kong*, 2nd edn (Hong Kong, LexisNexis, 2010) ch 1. For fuller historical accounts, see HJ Lethbridge, *Hard Graft in*

resourced, armed with an array of statutory[89] and common law offences at its disposal,[90] and endowed with most of the investigative and enforcement powers required by a modern anti-corruption investigating agency,[91] the ICAC is often held up to other jurisdictions as a model agency of its kind.[92]

(a) Public and Private Corruption

For much of its history, the ICAC focused on public sector corruption, and it has achieved considerable success in eradicating the endemic public sector corruption that previously held sway in Hong Kong. Part of this success is attributable to its extensive—even 'draconian'—investigative powers, encompassing statutory powers to issue notices[93] compelling defendants and other persons believed to be acquainted with facts relevant to an investigation to answer questions and furnish material documentation. Such powers have, in general, withstood intermittent constitutional challenge and remain central to the ICAC's investigative weaponry.

Annual ICAC surveys disclose, however, that the prosecution of public sector corruption now constitutes only a relatively minor percentage of annual investigations and prosecutions. The ICAC's principal focus in relation to the public sector is now on prevention and education, along with the development of 'integrity management' systems. Over the past decade, the ICAC has increasingly redirected its investigative focus onto what it terms 'private sector' corruption, based on several offences in section 9 of the Prevention of Bribery Ordinance dealing with the bribery of 'agents'.[94] ICAC officers are equipped with a similar array of investigative and enforcement powers in relation to non-state or 'private sector' corruption, save only for those facilitating access to information pertaining specifically to public sector corruption.

Hong Kong (Hong Kong, Oxford University Press, 1985); RPL Lee (ed), *Corruption and its Control in Hong Kong* (Hong Kong, Chinese University Press, 1981).

[89] Principally found in the Prevention of Bribery Ordinance (Cap 201) (PBO). See generally, McWalters, above n 88. Election corruption is covered by the Elections (Corrupt and Illegal Conduct) Ordinance (Cap 554). At the international level, the United Nations Convention Against Corruption (UNCAC) had been ratified by the Central People's Government and entered into force for PRC including Hong Kong SAR.

[90] In particular, misconduct in public office. See McWalters, above n 88, ch 14; M Jackson, 'A Functional Approach to Misconduct in Public Office' [2012] *Journal of Commonwealth Criminal Law* 342.

[91] Pursuant to both the Independent Commission Against Corruption Ordinance (Cap 204) and the Prevention of Bribery Ordinance (Cap 201).

[92] B Cook, 'ICAC useful model for British crime fighters', *South China Morning Post*, 1 May 1993; K Kwok, 'Hong Kong's graft-busters a model for Asia Pacific, says US official', *South China Morning Post*, 14 September 2014; cf S Lo, 'Hong Kong's anti-corruption model won't work on mainland China', *South China Morning Post*, 4 September 2013. Scott, above n 62, 401, observes that the ICAC is 'often regarded as a model of the way in which efforts to prevent and control corruption should be implemented'. However, '[a]lthough features of the ICAC model have been adopted elsewhere, it is difficult to replicate the entire syndrome of characteristics because they are underpinned in Hong Kong by unique political and cultural factors'.

[93] For example, pursuant to s 14 of the Prevention of Bribery Ordinance (Cap 201).

[94] Section 9 criminalises corrupt transactions by and with 'agents', which s 2(1) defines broadly to include 'public servants'. However, it is not general 'practice' to prosecute public servants under subss 9(1) and (2): see McWalters, above n 88, 354. In addition, an ICAC investigation into public or private sector corruption may subsequently evolve into a broader investigation of fraudulent and other activities, pursuant to the ICAC Ordinance (Cap 204), s 10.

In all cases, once an ICAC investigation has produced sufficient evidence to warrant prosecution, it then falls to the Prosecutions Division of the Department of Justice in Hong Kong (headed up by the DPP) to carry forward the prosecution of the case. As we have seen, this includes determining whether or not to offer immunity to accomplices in return for their testimony. Whilst the introduction of values-based measures and integrity management systems has been strategically important in recent years in relation to the public sector, their introduction in the private sector has been less effective. The ICAC has worked with private sector organisations in an attempt to provide guidance on integrity management and to create voluntary cooperative mechanisms,[95] but with only modest impact thus far.

Investigation of private sector corruption mostly depends on traditional investigative techniques and measures. Despite the ICAC's extensive powers, private sector corruption has proved impervious, necessitating resort to less transparent sources of evidence, including covert surveillance, informers and undercover operatives, on the one hand, and the evidence of corrupt and fraudulent accomplices on the other.[96] Some form of immunity from prosecution often then becomes the price of securing 'full and truthful' testimony. My own basic survey of reported cases prosecuted by the ICAC in Hong Kong over the past decade in the District Court[97] suggests that immunised accomplice witnesses now feature in roughly a quarter of ICAC cases prosecuted at this level.[98] Furthermore, problematic issues concerning the immunisation process or the credibility or reliability of the immunised witnesses or their evidence often featured prominently either at trial or on appeal.

Much can go wrong in securing or presenting immunised accomplice evidence, ranging from a politicised exercise of the discretion to offer immunity, to improper 'coaching' of witnesses or inappropriate contact during the course of giving evidence, resulting in increasingly frequent (though mostly unsuccessful) applications to stay proceedings on the ground of abuse of process, or to exclude 'improperly obtained' evidence, and a proliferation of appeals against 'unsafe and unsatisfactory' convictions.[99] We now turn to a detailed study of one such case, and its broader ramifications.

(b) A Case of Conduct Unbecoming

Raymond Ng was known locally in Hong Kong as the 'King of Warrants', due to the 'huge profits' seemingly generated by his extensive trading in derivative warrants, a form of stock

---

[95] See eg its 'Corporate Ethics Programme', www.icac.org.hk/en/services/cep/index.html (accessed 17 August 2015).

[96] Commenting on the crisis of public confidence besetting the ICAC in recent years, Young, above n 6, 283, noted the historical emergence of this 'two-pronged' strategy by the ICAC in corruption and fraud related investigations, based on covert operations and immunity witnesses.

[97] The majority of the more serious charges are brought in the District Court before a District Court judge. Fewer cases are prosecuted in the Court of First Instance before a judge and jury.

[98] Search of District Court decisions (both reasons for verdict and reasons for sentence) since 2005 involving charges either under the PBO or resulting from an ICAC investigation. Ten out of 42 such cases, all involving private sector corruption or fraud, involved immunised accomplice witnesses. Figures for the past three years are: one of two cases in 2015; none of three cases in 2014; and one of four cases in 2013.

[99] The general grounds for allowing an appeal against conviction in Hong Kong, as specified by s 83(1) of the Criminal Procedure Ordinance (Cap 221), replicate those originally enacted in s 2(1) of the Criminal Appeal Act 1968 (England and Wales), namely: '(a) that the conviction should be set aside on the ground that under all the circumstances of the case it is unsafe or unsatisfactory; or (b) that the judgment of the court of trial should be set aside on the ground of a wrong decision on any question of law; or (c) that there was a material irregularity in the course of the trial.'

market speculation much favoured in Hong Kong.[100] On 28 May 2008, Ng was arrested, along with several others including Cheung Ching Ho, during the early stages of an ICAC investigation into alleged fraudulent warrant trading.[101] Following his video-interview, ICAC officers identified Cheung as a potential accomplice witness, and the very next day sought 'urgent legal advice' from the Department of Justice as to whether a non-prejudicial statement could be taken from him, as an initial step towards possibly offering him immunity. Given the alleged urgency of the matter, a somewhat informal procedure was used at this initial stage, possibly including misleading representations as to Cheung's role and significance in the alleged fraud, and concerning his level of contact with various allegedly corrupt agents. Consent having been given, three ICAC officers, including Kevin Cho, a chief ICAC investigator with extensive experience, then began a lengthy process of taking an NPS from Cheung, with the intention that he be immunised and called as the first prosecution witness (PW1) at Ng's trial. Ultimately, several accomplices testified under immunity against Ng and his co-defendants.[102]

Not long before, in 2007, the practices of the ICAC in handling and preparing immunised witnesses for trial had attracted adverse judicial comment in *Lee Wing Kan v HKSAR*.[103] Lee had been convicted of conspiracy to defraud, following a District Court trial involving two immunised prosecution witnesses, both of whom had been prepared for trial by the ICAC. Amongst other grounds of appeal, it was alleged that ICAC officers had undertaken what were described as 'memory refreshing exercises' with these two witnesses, during which, amongst other things, the witnesses were given a summary of each paragraph in their previously taken statements. The Hong Kong Court of Appeal rejected Lee's appeal against conviction,[104] concluding that the memory refreshing exercise was acceptable, save for the use of the summaries. Rejecting further leave to appeal, the Court of Final Appeal agreed. Chief Justice Li remarked:

> The Court of Appeal rightly condemned this practice, stating that it must stop. As it pointed out, this practice gave rise to the possible danger that: 'witnesses may feel compelled to agree with the summary given to them and to adopt it in their testimony later whether or not the phraseology used in the summary had been strictly accurate'.[105]

So Cho and his fellow ICAC officers ought to have been well aware of judicial concern about the ICAC's practices in handling immunised accomplice witnesses, and—thus being on notice—should have exercised extra caution in preparing Cheung for trial to ensure their conduct was above reproach.[106] Instead, seemingly undeterred, the ICAC officers brazenly

---

[100] P Moy, '"King of Warrants" on market fraud charges', *The Standard*, 1 December 2009.

[101] Ultimately, Ng (D1) was charged with five counts of conspiracy to defraud, four with Leo Lam (D2) and one with Polly Sun (D3), plus one count of doing an act with intent to pervert the course of public justice. The ICAC's jurisdiction extends to such categories of non-corruption offences should they come to light during a corruption-focused investigation. Ng's wife, Cheng Yuen Yi (D4), was also charged, with 17 counts of money laundering sums exceeding HK$100 million, being the alleged proceeds of Ng's fraudulent warrant trading activities.

[102] This included Lee Wai Ming (PW2), whom Ng had allegedly approached and asked not to cooperate with the ICAC, giving rise to the charge of doing an act with intent to pervert public justice.

[103] Unreported CFA Determination, FAMC 28/2007 (18 September 2007).

[104] Unreported CA Judgment, CACC 199/2006 (9 March 2007).

[105] *Lee Wing Kan v HKSAR* (unreported), FAMC 28/2007 (18 September 2007), [8]. See also *HKSAR v Tse Sui Luen* (unreported), DCCC 350/2006 (24–25 April 2008); *HKSAR v Tse Tat Fung* [2010] 5 HKC 455.

[106] In *HKSAR v Ng Chun To Raymond* [2013] 5 HKC 390, [60], the CA noted that the internal ICAC circular drawn up to give effect to these warnings was not issued until over a year later.

engaged in a series of improper practices in preparing Cheung for trial, including frequent meetings with him dubiously conducted away from ICAC premises, in coffee shops and tea houses, allegedly to ensure Cheung would give 'true and full evidence' at Ng's trial. Unfortunately for the ICAC officers, Cheung secretly recorded some of these meetings.

A few days before the trial of Ng and his co-defendants commenced, Cheung received his immunity from prosecution from the Department of Justice. When called to give evidence as PW1, Cheung initially complied, but then, on the second day, refused to testify.[107] The case against Ng and others continued, with other immunised accomplices testifying. Some four months later, Ng was convicted on four counts of conspiracy to defraud and the single count of perverting the course of public justice,[108] and sentenced to four years imprisonment.[109] His wife, Cheng (D4), was convicted on all 17 counts of money-laundering and sentenced to three years imprisonment.[110] Having lost his immunity when he refused to testify, Cheung was then prosecuted in 2011 on charges relating to the same fraudulent warrant trading. Not surprisingly, he applied to the District Court judge to stay the proceedings based on his having been improperly handled by the three ICAC officers prior to Ng's trial. He produced his secret audio recordings in support and gave evidence of all the alleged improper practices. In response, the prosecution called six of his alleged co-conspirators, all of whom had likewise been immunised for Ng's trial, to deny that their testimony had been coached by ICAC officers. When this stay application was eventually rejected by the District Court judge, in large part owing to the gravity of the offences with which Cheung was charged,[111] Cheung pleaded guilty and was sentenced to 25 months' imprisonment.

The three ICAC officers were subsequently prosecuted, on charges of doing acts tending to pervert the course of public justice and misconduct in public office, both contrary to the common law.[112] Cheung gave evidence at their trial, at which the prosecution, bolstered by Cheung's audio recordings, alleged that the three officers had variously: (i) taught Cheung what to say in the trial; (ii) shown him the witness statements of other immunity witnesses; (iii) told Cheung to memorise his witness statements; (iv) taught Cheung how to lie about his evidence; and (v) hinted to Cheung that he could read his own witness statement even after he had commenced giving evidence. Having listened to Cheung's evidence, the District Court judge commented, with a whiff of understatement, that Cheung was 'not entirely a witness of truth'. But the judge nonetheless found the charges proved and convicted all three ICAC officers, sentencing them to terms of imprisonment ranging from 18 to 30 months.

---

[107] *HKSAR v Ng Chun To Raymond* (unreported), DCCC 405 & 895/2009, Reasons for Sentence (28 April 2010).

[108] Following Cheung's refusal to testify, the prosecution decided to offer no evidence against Ng in relation to the count of conspiracy to defraud against him and Polly Sun (D3), leading to Ng's acquittal on that charge. However, Ng remained a named co-conspirator for the purposes of prosecuting Sun (D3).

[109] *HKSAR v Ng Chun To Raymond* (unreported), DCCC 405 & 895/2009, Reasons for Sentence (28 April 2010).

[110] Lee (D2) pleaded guilty to three counts of conspiracy to defraud after PW2 had testified and was sentenced to 28 months' imprisonment. Sun (D3) was convicted on the single count of conspiracy to defraud and sentenced to two years: *HKSAR v Ng Chun To Raymond* (unreported), DCCC 405 & 895/2009, Reasons for Sentence (28 April 2010).

[111] *HKSAR v Cheung Ching-ho* (unreported), DCCC 1443/2009, Reasons for Sentence (31 May 2011).

[112] *HKSAR v Cho Wing Nin* (unreported), DCCC 360/2011, Reasons for Verdict (13 April 2012); *HKSAR v Cho Wing Nin* (unreported), DCCC 360/2011, Reasons for Sentence (30 April 2012).

Cho reportedly became the most senior ICAC officer ever convicted, and all three achieved the dubious distinction of becoming the first ICAC officers to be convicted of perverting the course of justice.

The sentencing judge expounded on the broader ramifications of the three ICAC officers' 'inexcusable' conduct:

> The ICAC is perhaps the most potent weapon Hong Kong possesses against corruption. That is why great and sometimes even draconian powers are conferred upon this institution and its officers. The exercise of those powers must be done with the utmost of integrity and any abuse of that power must be punished. It is of paramount importance that public confidence in this cornerstone institution be maintained in order for Hong Kong to continue to remain a relatively corruption free society.[113]

Moreover, Cho and his colleagues had been the foolish architects of their own downfall:

> If they had adhered to the internal guidelines of the ICAC, whatever trap that Cheung … might have set for them would not have worked. If they had maintained their integrity, they would not have succumbed to the temptation of crossing the line from merely refreshing the witness' memory to coaching him.[114]

But cross the line they did.

Media headlines announced that 'Conviction Ends ICAC Officers' Stellar Run',[115] but the ICAC's public embarrassment arising from this case was far from over. There were to be three further public airings of the officers' misconduct. Chronologically, the first and third occasions were the successful appeals against conviction by Ng and his wife in 2013,[116] and Ng's subsequent retrial in 2015.[117] Sandwiched between these two sets of proceedings, in February 2014, was the three ICAC officers' own—unsuccessful—appeals against their convictions for perverting the course of justice.[118]

Inevitably, the appeals against conviction by Ng and Cheng rested primarily on the egregious misconduct of the ICAC officers. Had this been revealed prior to trial, it was submitted, it would have mandated a permanent stay of the criminal proceedings as an abuse of process. Not so, ruled the Court of Appeal, concluding that on balance neither the prospective 'fair trial' limb nor the 'affront to justice' limb of the abuse of process test had been made out 'in the particular circumstances'. However, the non-disclosure of the ICAC officers' conduct had still prevented Ng from receiving a fair trial and rendered Cheng's money-laundering convictions unsafe, obliging the Court to quash their convictions.[119] Ng was eventually re-tried on four charges of conspiracy to defraud in early 2015; and despite witness Cheung's absence from the re-trial, Ng was convicted once again and sentenced to four-and-a-half years' imprisonment.[120] His wife had already served her sentence, precluding any retrial in her case.

---

[113] *HKSAR v Cho Wing-nan* (unreported), DCCC 360/2011, Reasons for Sentence (30 April 2012) [31].

[114] Ibid [32].

[115] D Lee and S Cheung, 'Conviction Ends ICAC Officers' Stellar Run', *South China Morning Post*, 1 May 2012.

[116] In the same proceedings, the Secretary for Justice sought review of the sentences imposed on Ng and Cheng; this application fell away once the convictions were quashed.

[117] *HKSAR v Ng Chun To Raymond* (unreported), DCCC 405/2009, Reasons for Verdict (9 January 2015).

[118] *HKSAR v Cho Wing Nin* (unreported), CACC 178/2012 (28 February 2014).

[119] The question whether Ng and Cheng should be re-tried was considered at a later hearing, described below in text to n 129.

[120] *HKSAR v Ng Chun To Raymond* (unreported), DCCC 405/2009, Reasons for Sentence (30 January 2015).

The most illuminating discussion for present purposes is found in the judgment of the Hong Kong Court of Appeal in the 2013 appeals of Ng and his wife. The court, in addressing the question whether a permanent stay was warranted on the 'affront to justice' limb,[121] was invited to take into account the possibility of a 'wider malaise'. There were 'indicia of a systemic disregard by the ICAC for the rule of law', which, it was submitted, should be taken into account in assessing whether on balance it would be appropriate for the Court to exercise its discretion to issue a permanent stay. Elaborating, Stock VP observed:

> It is contended, in other words, that this is more than a case of three errant officers who were a law unto themselves. If it were 'just' such a case, the fact that the particular officers have been prosecuted and imprisoned would carry greater weight in the balancing exercise which has to be conducted, than if this law enforcement authority at large embraced or permitted a culture of disregard for the rule of law. ... The argument on behalf of the applicants is that what happened in the present case evidenced a deliberate disregard for earlier warnings and, that aside, reveals systemic eagerness improperly to bolster the credibility of prosecution evidence.[122]

The Hong Kong Court of Appeal reviewed the law relating to permanent stays of criminal proceedings, emphasising that the 'affront to justice' test is not whether the court is 'offended or even outraged by the prosecutorial misconduct disclosed', nor whether 'the public, possessed of the facts, would be offended or outraged', but rather 'whether "the court's sense of justice and propriety", or ... public confidence in the proper administration of justice, is or would be offended "if [the court] is asked to try the accused *in the particular circumstances of the case*"'.[123] This, observed Stock VP, is 'what distinguishes the punitive or disciplinary function, which is not the court's remit, from that which is the court's remit, namely to administer justice in individual cases by a process the integrity of which remains intact'.[124] The court registered both its natural sense of outrage at the ICAC officers' misconduct, and the concern that this might not be an isolated transgression:

> Given the nature and gravity of the misconduct in this case, the outrage-driven temptation to stay the proceedings is considerable, not least when the facts of this case as well as the facts revealed by a number of previous cases lead to a concern whether the attitude of these officers, that the end justifies the means is, in this particular agency, limited to this handful of officers or is more widespread.[125]

In this instance, however, the 'outrage-driven temptation to stay' was counterbalanced by at least four circumstantial factors, namely: (i) the seriousness of the charges and the substantial sums involved; (ii) the fact that Cheung's evidence was not actually relied on and would not be used at the retrial; (iii) there was no evidence of similar misconduct in handling other immunised witnesses; and (iv) it could not be legitimately said in this case that 'but for the misconduct, there would have been no trial or that had the misconduct been revealed to the prosecuting authority before trial no charges would have been brought'.[126]

---

[121] There was no argument that it was impossible for Ng to receive a procedurally fair re-trial: *HKSAR v Ng Chun To Raymond* [2013] 5 HKC 390, [115].

[122] Ibid, [64], [67], quoting from *Warren v Attorney General for Jersey* [2012] 1 AC 22, [35] (Lord Dyson JSC).

[123] *HKSAR v Ng Chun To Raymond* [2013] 5 HKC 390, [87]. Also see Whitfort, Chapter 10 in this volume.

[124] *HKSAR v Ng Chun To Raymond* [2013] 5 HKC 390, [88].

[125] Ibid [107].

[126] Ibid [108].

Such was the weight of these countervailing considerations, suggested Stock VP, that 'the interests of justice require a trial notwithstanding the misconduct which has been revealed; or, put the other way round, the prospect of a trial of these applicants, notwithstanding that misconduct, does not offend the conscience of the Court'.[127]

Lest it be thought the Court of Appeal was thereby condoning flagrant misconduct and perhaps even encouraging more widespread, systemic rule-breaking, Stock VP, in an Addendum, revisited the officers' misconduct and its profound implications for the rule of law:

> The function of the court is to render judgment in particular cases. It is generally not part of our remit to ask and determine whether the type of conduct revealed by this and a few other cases to which we have referred is part of a wider unhealthy attitude to the rule of law within the particular agency with which this case has been concerned. Yet anyone reading the facts of this case and the facts of one or two of the earlier cases to which we have referred is bound to ask that question to which there may well, justifiably, be a comforting answer. The organisation is a powerful one, armed, for good policy reason, with Draconian powers. It is therefore most particularly important for those powers to be exercised with an understanding of and true respect for the rule of law. The rule of law is not a sound bite. Understanding what the rule of law *actually* means in its many manifestations and *why* respect for it is the cornerstone protection for all members of our society— protection for those who wield power as much as for those who are affected by the exercise of power—is vital. Individual officers in this or any other organisation to whom this message is not effectively imparted may insufficiently appreciate that disdain for the rule of law in a particular case in order to achieve what they perceive to be the 'right' result is to contribute slowly but surely to the destruction of the checks and balances which have been designed over time to provide the public and individuals with a respected system of justice. It may well be that this is a message which is already sufficiently imparted but if it requires further specific attention, the expression of our concern may encourage that attention to be provided.[128]

Fine words of admonition, which the Court of Appeal had the chance to reiterate in a subsequent hearing, when it was submitted on behalf of Ng that 'an order for retrial may appear to be an indirect endorsement by [the Court of Appeal] of deliberate misconduct by the ICAC officers, an appearance, in other words, that the ends justifies the means'.[129] This was the same issue that had recently confronted the UK Supreme Court in *Maxwell*;[130] and the outcome in *Raymond Ng* was also the same. Ordering a retrial, Stock VP rejected the applicant's submission, maintaining that 'our judgment [on the merits] makes sufficiently clear our gross distaste for the conduct of the convicted ICAC officers whilst at the same time making equally clear the basis, in law and on the facts, upon which we nonetheless declined to order a permanent stay of proceedings'.[131]

Admonition there may be, yet one is left with a palpable sense that the 'serious' nature of corruption and fraud offences will inevitably predispose a court, 'on balance' and having regard to 'the particular circumstances', towards declining to exercise its integrity jurisdiction. This arguably leaves a deficit in the effective management of those charged with

---

[127] Ibid [109].
[128] Ibid [176].
[129] (Unreported), CACC 178/2010 (19 Nov 2013), [11].
[130] *R v Maxwell* [2011] 1 WLR 1837, [2010] UKSC 48.
[131] (Unreported), CACC 178/2010 (19 Nov 2013), [17].

handling immunised accomplice witnesses. All too aware of the court's tacit endorsement of their conduct, law enforcement agents and prosecutors may be emboldened in their exploitation of immunity to further the prosecution of corruption cases.

Conclusion

This chapter has explored the threats to criminal process integrity posed by the use of immunised witness evidence. The tactic of turning erstwhile accomplices into prosecution witnesses has a long history in the common law, and remains a routine feature of certain types of prosecutions, including those involving the corruption and related fraud offences that were the focus of the preceding discussion, in many legal jurisdictions today. Persuading known offenders to 'turn Queen's evidence' has always been a morally problematic prosecutorial gambit, which can only be justified by the countervailing public interest in bringing (even) more serious offenders to justice.

Moreover, the procedures through which witness testimony is immunised are themselves open to abuse. Section 2 of this chapter summarised attempts to achieve effective 'integrity management' through internal and external procedural controls, but prosecutors' operational discretion is difficult to constrain as Section 3's case study of the *Raymond Ng* prosecution in Hong Kong demonstrates. Despite the Hong Kong Court of Appeal's refusal to stay the proceedings against Ng and his co-defendants, it seems clear that the misconduct of the ICAC officers in that case was not merely the result of personal failings, but was instead the product of a systemic culture of reliance on immunised accomplice witnesses in ICAC prosecutions of private sector corruption. This telling illustration demonstrates why and how immunised accomplice witnesses present special risks to the integrity of the criminal justice process, all the more so when prosecutorial success comes to depend on the availability and testimony of such witnesses. When anti-corruption agencies such as Hong Kong's ICAC succeed, this inevitably breeds the expectation of further success. But if that further success depends in substantial part on the use of 'Queens evidence', as has commonly come to be the case in Hong Kong in relation to private sector corruption, then, it has been argued, reliance on such witnesses brings with it a potentially corrupting or corrosive effect on the conduct of investigating officers. In due course, this has the potential to spill over into the trial process and undermine the integrity of the administration of Hong Kong's criminal justice system.

How should policymakers and institutions respond to such systematic corrupting influences? Revised statutory frameworks setting out responsibilities more clearly, and prescribing the procedures to be followed, would be one positive initiative. In Hong Kong, for example, the Witness Protection Ordinance[132] sets out in some detail selection criteria for inclusion in a protection programme,[133] and the nature and contents of a 'Memorandum of Understanding' to be signed by any such witness,[134] with express statutory provision

---

[132] Witness Protection Ordinance (Cap 564).
[133] Ibid s 4.
[134] Ibid s 6.

for review of a decision of the approving authority.[135] A comparable statutory framework could perhaps be drafted in relation to immunity witnesses, with a clear statement of relevant criteria and, possibly, mechanisms for making decisions of the 'approving authority' reviewable and thus more accountable. But ultimately, just as the Witness Protection Ordinance provides that the relevant approving authority 'has the sole responsibility of deciding whether or not to include a witness in the witness protection programme', so also must it be accepted that the prosecuting authority's assessment whether or not 'the public interest' justifies offering immunity to an accomplice in return for his or her testimony must remain an operational judgement largely immune from formal institutional review, except at the political level.

Section 2 of this chapter described control and review mechanisms to reduce the risks of misconduct in relation to immunised accomplice witnesses. Yet, as with all such discretionary decision-making, the proper grant of witness immunity must eventually depend upon the personal and professional integrity of those entrusted with the responsibility of selecting and handling accomplice witnesses. As one Hong Kong commentator, contemplating the ultimate responsibility for prosecutorial discretion, has rightly said, 'in the final analysis, there seems to be no way to achieve a perfect institutionalization of the principle of accountability of the independent prosecution authority', so that guardianship of the public interest depends ultimately upon 'the unimpeachable integrity of the holder of the office whatever the precise constitutional arrangements in the State concerned'.[136]

---

[135] Ibid ss 13–14.
[136] Chen, above n 11, 411 (quoting a communique issued after the Commonwealth Law Ministers' Conference in Winnipeg in 1977).

9

Expert Evidence and the Responsibilities of Prosecutors

GARY EDMOND[*]

Introduction

A system that allows prosecutors, police, and prosecution experts to present scientific evidence without effective challenge, a system that is adversarial in name and theory but non-adversarial in reality, is likely to create habits and attitudes conducive to the abuse of scientific evidence.[1]

The work of prosecutors is central to the integrity of the criminal trial process. This chapter reconsiders the professional obligations of prosecutors with respect to forensic science and medicine evidence. Drawing upon long-standing prosecutorial responsibilities, accepted in most common law jurisdictions, it endeavours to explain why conventional interpretations of obligations, rules and norms are no longer suited to decisions to prosecute, plea negotiations and many trial and pre-trial practices involving expert evidence. Continuing adherence to traditional practices and commitments, in the face of alarming evidence about the quality of much forensic science and medicine, means that fundamental criminal justice system objectives and trial protections are being denuded of substantial value and the integrity of many criminal proceedings undermined.

Rather than merely criticise and insist on the need for more rules and more aggressive disciplinary responses, this chapter is an exercise in consciousness-raising and reconceptualisation. It suggests that fresh (and uncontradicted) insights into serious and widespread problems with the forensic sciences and medicine, in conjunction with evidence of trial and appellate frailties, require prosecutors to reconsider their approaches to adducing and presenting incriminating expert evidence. The chapter identifies the primary obligations of the prosecutor given the accusatorial trial's preoccupation with truth and justice (that is, rectitude and fairness).[2] It infuses these obligations—particularly the prosecutor's role as

[*] This research was supported by the ARC (FT0992041 and LP120100063). The author would like to thank University of New South Wales (UNSW) workshop participants, especially Paul Roberts, Jill Hunter, Michael Jackson, John Jackson, Peter Chau and Nick Cowdery, as well as several anonymous commentators. The argument is developed at greater length in G Edmond, '(Ad)Ministering Justice: Expert Evidence and the Professional Responsibilities of Prosecutors' (2013) 36 *UNSW Law Journal* 921.

[1] KC McMunigal, 'Prosecutors and Corrupt Science' (2007) 36 *Hofstra Law Review* 437, 443.

[2] See eg *Polk County v Dodson*, 454 US 312, 318 (1981) (Powell J); *Mackey v Montrym*, 443 US 1, 13 (1979) (Burger CJ); *R v Handy* [2002] 2 SCR 908; *Dietrich v R* (1992) 177 CLR 292; *M v R* (1994) 181 CLR 487; *Grey v R* (2001) 184 ALR 593; *R v Soma* (2003) 212 CLR 299; *Mallard v R* (2005) 224 CLR 125; *Libke v R* (2007) 230 CLR 559.

a 'minister of justice'—with substance, by suggesting ways of rehabilitating prosecutorial performance so that contemporary practice might be reconciled with long-standing commitments and aspirations.

Without restricting the discussion to a particular jurisdiction or set of professional rules, the chapter invokes broad principles (and some specific rules that appear to be widely accepted) governing the conduct of criminal trials. The discussion focuses predominantly on prosecutors, even though other participants—including investigators, judges, defence lawyers, expert witnesses and jurors—have vital roles to play in criminal proceedings. Without wanting to trivialise the important responsibilities held by these other participants (and the need for parallel responses), the prosecutor's position is special, indeed pivotal. Prosecutors are in the best position to regulate the appearance—in both senses—and reliance placed upon forensic science and medicine evidence. For, 'the prosecutor dominates the system, has exclusive control of the evidence, and decides … how that evidence will be used'.[3]

1. Background and Institutional Context

The broader institutional context includes two decades of critique, sometimes trenchant, of many forensic science and medicine techniques routinely used in investigations and routinely admitted in criminal proceedings.[4] The context also includes revelations about the inconsistent, though typically poor, performance of adversarial legal systems in response to forensic science and medicine.[5]

These two factors, the value of forensic science evidence and the performance of the trial, are intimately related. Prosecutors and judges have played important roles in the (premature) recognition and social legitimation of many types of expert evidence.[6] Significantly, trial procedures facilitated admission and reliance, while oft-valorised safeguards did not necessarily expose widespread and serious deficiencies with forensic science and

---

[3] B Gershman, 'Misuse of Scientific Evidence by Prosecutors' (2003) 28 *Oklahoma City University Law Review* 17, 18. See also B Green and F Zacharias, 'Prosecutorial Neutrality' [2004] *Wisconsin Law Review* 837; E Luna and M Wade, 'Prosecutors as Judges' (2010) 67 *Washington & Lee Law Review* 1413.

[4] Influential scholarly criticisms include DM Risinger, M Denbeaux and MJ Saks, 'Exorcism of Ignorance as a Proxy for Rational Knowledge: The Lesson of Handwriting "Expertise"' (1989) 137 *University of Pennsylvania Law Review* 731; DL Faigman, *Legal Alchemy: The Use and Misuse of Science in the Law* (New York, WH Freeman, 1999); DM Risinger et al, 'The *Daubert/Kumho* Implications of Observer Effects in Forensic Science: Hidden Problems of Expectation and Suggestion' (2002) 90 *California Law Review* 1; MJ Saks and J Koehler, 'The Coming Paradigm Shift in Forensic Identification Science' (2005) 309 *Science* 892; MA Berger, 'What Has a Decade of *Daubert* Wrought?' (2005) 95 *American Journal of Public Health* 59; PJ Neufeld, 'The (Near) Irrelevance of *Daubert* to Criminal Justice' (2005) 95 *American Journal of Public Health* 107.

[5] The context includes observational studies of trial practices, including some of my own. For analyses of specific techniques, their methodological problems and legal responses in Australia, see G Edmond et al, 'Law's Looking Glass: Expert Identification Evidence Derived from Photographic and Video Images' (2009) 20 *Current Issues in Criminal Justice* 337; G Edmond, K Martire and M San Roque, 'Unsound Law: Issues with ("Expert") Voice Comparison Evidence' (2011) 35 *Melbourne University Law Review* 52; E Cunliffe and G Edmond, 'Gaitkeeping in Canada: Mis-steps in Assessing the Reliability of Expert Testimony' (2014) 92 *Canadian Bar Review* 327.

[6] See eg J Campbell Moriarty, '"Misconvictions", Science and the Ministers of Justice' (2007) 86 *Nebraska Law Review* 1, 2–3.

medicine evidence. This dismal track record casts a pall over criminal justice practice and exposes the complacency of assumptions maintained (and defended) by prosecutors, defence lawyers, judges and those recognised by courts as *experts*.[7] Unavoidably, this backdrop must inform the way we approach professional obligations and rules (and adjectival law), and the way we evaluate the performances of lawyers, judges and experts.[8]

(a) The Forensic Sciences (Including Forensic Medicine)

Recent and authoritative reviews of the forensic sciences have exposed serious and widespread problems. A surprisingly large number of forensic science techniques have never been formally evaluated and are of unknown value.[9] Some of those that are reliable are not practised in ways conducive to the production of reliable results. The long and symbiotic relationship between courts, police, investigators, technicians and forensic analysts has produced a range of practices and conventions that are not sufficiently attentive to the actual value of techniques and the capabilities of analysts. Effectiveness in disposing of cases, witness experience, and judicial acceptance have often played more conspicuous roles in the admission of expert opinion than formal scientific evaluation, transparency and attention to jury comprehension.[10] In order to convey some sense of these problems and their magnitude, the obvious place to begin is a report by the US National Academy of Sciences (NAS).[11]

In 2006, following congressional appropriation, the NAS established a committee under the auspices of the National Research Council (NRC), comprised of eminent scientists and biomedical researchers, engineers, mathematicians, physicians and lawyers, to inquire into the condition of the forensic sciences. The resulting report, *Strengthening the Forensic Sciences in the United States: A Path Forward* (the NRC Report) published in 2009, was remarkably critical in tone. To its surprise, the Committee identified serious problems across the forensic sciences, and expressed genuine doubts about the evidentiary value of many techniques used routinely in criminal investigations and prosecutions.[12] The Committee found endemic problems, particularly the lack of scientific rigour, in relation to research, standards (and their application), and threats from contextual bias.

---

[7] 'Expert' is italicised to reinforce the point that in many cases we do not know whether those proffering opinions actually possess expertise (or 'specialised knowledge'). Generally, I have preferred 'forensic analyst' because many of those recognised by courts as 'experts' or 'forensic scientists' do not possess formal scientific qualifications.

[8] On the implications for admissibility practice, see eg G Edmond, 'Specialised Knowledge, the Exclusionary Discretions and Reliability: Reassessing Incriminating Expert Opinion Evidence' (2008) 31 *University of New South Wales Law Journal* 1. G Edmond, 'The Admissibility of Forensic Science and Medicine Evidence under the Uniform Evidence Law' (2014) 38 *Criminal Law Journal* 136.

[9] It is important, by way of caveat, to acknowledge that there are some very reliable techniques and interpretive practices in use.

[10] See eg Special Issue, 'Impressions and Expressions' (2013) 45 *Australian Journal of Forensic Sciences* 248.

[11] National Research Council of the National Academies, *Strengthening the Forensic Sciences in the United States: A Path Forward* (Washington DC, The National Academies Press, 2009) (NRC Report). For a more detailed review of the NRC Report, see G Edmond, 'What Lawyers Should Know about the Forensic "Sciences"' (2015) 36 *Adelaide Law Review* 33.

[12] NRC Report, see also H Edwards, 'Solving the Problems that Plague the Forensic Science Community' (2009) 50 *Jurimetrics* 5. Judge Edwards was co-chair of the NRC Committee.

Introducing its Report, the Committee explained:

> The law's greatest dilemma in its heavy reliance on forensic evidence ... concerns the question of whether—and to what extent—there is *science* in any given forensic science discipline.[13]

The Committee emphasised both the importance and feasibility of undertaking research, particularly validation studies:

> One particular task of science is the validation of new methods to determine their reliability under different conditions and their limitations. ... To confirm the validity of a method or process for a particular purpose (eg, for a forensic investigation), validation studies must be performed.[14]

And yet:

> Little rigorous systematic research has been done to validate the basic premises and techniques in a number of forensic science disciplines. The committee sees no evident reason why conducting such research is not feasible ...[15]

The Committee placed considerable emphasis on gauging and reporting uncertainty and error:

> All results for every forensic science method should indicate the uncertainty in the measurements that are made, and studies must be conducted that enable the estimation of those values. ... [T]he accuracy of forensic methods resulting in classification or individualization conclusions needs to be evaluated in well-designed and rigorously conducted studies. The level of accuracy of an analysis is likely to be a key determinant of its ultimate probative value.[16]

Validation studies determine the conditions in which techniques work, as well as indicating margins of error. They provide an empirical foundation for the development of standards and protocols and help to inform the way results should be reported.[17]

On standards, the Committee found:

> Often there are no standard protocols governing forensic practice in a given discipline. And, even when protocols are in place ... they often are vague and not enforced in any meaningful way. In short, the quality of forensic practice in most disciplines varies greatly because of the absence of adequate training and continuing education, rigorous mandatory certification and accreditation programs, adherence to robust performance standards, and effective oversight. These shortcomings obviously pose a continuing and serious threat to the quality and credibility of forensic science practice.[18]

Significantly, the absence of basic research means that even where standards are in place they are not necessarily empirically warranted or effective.

Lack of research also manifested itself in wide discrepancies in the terms used by forensic scientists to express conclusions in their reports and courtroom testimony:

> [T]he forensic science disciplines have not reached agreement or consensus on the precise meaning of ... terms. ... This imprecision in vocabulary stems in part from the paucity of research in forensic science and the corresponding limitations in interpreting the results of forensic analyses.[19]

---

[13] NRC Report, above n 11, 9, 87.
[14] Ibid 113.
[15] Ibid 189.
[16] Ibid 184, 122.
[17] G Jackson, C Aitken and P Roberts, *Case Assessment and Interpretation of Expert Evidence*, RSS Practitioner Guide No 4 (London, Royal Statistical Society, 2014).
[18] NRC Report, above n 11, 6.
[19] Ibid 185–86.

The Committee also voiced concern about widespread indifference to threats from contextual bias. There was, it explained, a conspicuous need for 'research programs on human observer bias and sources of human error in forensic examinations':

> Such programs might include studies to determine the effects of contextual bias in forensic practice (eg, studies to determine whether and to what extent the results of forensic analyses are influenced by knowledge regarding the background of the suspect and the investigator's theory of the case).[20]

While these findings and their implications might be unsettling, the Committee's conclusions with respect to 'identification' (or comparison) techniques used routinely in criminal investigations and prosecutions (for example, voice, image, foot, shoe and tyre mark, ballistics, latent fingerprints and tool marks comparisons and so on) are disturbing. The Committee concluded that:

> With the exception of nuclear DNA analysis ... no forensic method has been rigorously shown to have the capacity to consistently, and with a high degree of certainty, demonstrate a connection between evidence and a specific individual or source. ... The simple reality is that the interpretation of forensic evidence is not always based on scientific studies to determine its validity. This is a serious problem.[21]

In light of the lack of research and widespread failure to use (or even recognise the need for) orthodox methodological practices to support techniques routinely relied upon by investigators and used in criminal proceedings, the NRC Report captures the Committee's scepticism regarding the ability of legal institutions to identify and address endemic shortcomings.[22] Rather than rely on legal responses, the Committee recommended 'upstream' solutions directed towards establishing a national institute of forensic science capable of providing research leadership, undertaking or supervising the 'missing' research, developing research-based standards and managing quality control.[23]

Significantly, the NRC is not alone in its critical appraisal. More recent reports focused specifically on latent fingerprint evidence—one of the oldest techniques in the forensic science arsenal—issued by the National Institute of Standards and Technology and the National Institute of Justice (NIST/NIJ) in the US and Lord Campbell's Inquiry in Scotland, also identified serious limitations with underlying assumptions, comparison practices, the expressions used by fingerprint examiners, and a dearth of underpinning research.[24] It is striking that the lack of research, weak methods and superficial standards, misleading expressions and inattention to threats from bias were identified through external reviews, rather than by lawyers and judges, years or even decades after many forensic science techniques first appeared in criminal trials. In the case of latent fingerprint evidence, the clear implication is that latent fingerprint examiners have historically exaggerated the value of

---

[20] Ibid 24, 191.

[21] Ibid 7–8, 87.

[22] Ibid 85, 12, 53, 96, 109, 110.

[23] See also JL Mnookin et al, 'The Need for a Research Culture in the Forensic Sciences' (2011) 58 *UCLA Law Review* 725.

[24] Expert Working Group on Human Factors in Latent Print Analysis, *Latent Print Examination and Human Factors: Improving the Practice through a Systems Approach* (Washington DC, US Department of Commerce, National Institute of Standards and Technology, National Institute of Justice, 2012) 1 (NIST/NIJ Report); Lord Campbell, *The Fingerprint Inquiry Report* (Edinburgh, APS Group Scotland, 2011) (Campbell Report). See also Edmond, above n 11.

their opinions—characterising them as positive evidence of identification—in thousands of investigations and prosecutions, and continue to do so.[25] The reports also expose the surprising lack of sophistication and insight acquired by lawyers and judges across decades of contested adversarial proceedings. Moreover, as the NRC Report insisted, the dearth of underlying research, the lack of validation studies and information about error, indifference to bias, and inattention to the effects of different forms of expression on decision-makers all extend beyond latent fingerprint comparison to other forensic techniques. Serious problems persist with ballistics and tool marks, shoe, foot and tyre prints, bite marks, the use of images and voice recordings, gait, hair, fibre and document comparison, soil analysis and so on.[26] These techniques, most lacking formal validation and research-based standards, are routinely adduced by prosecutors and admitted and relied upon in courts, in Australia, England, Canada, New Zealand, Hong Kong and the US.[27]

It might be tempting to think that problems with the forensic sciences in the US and Scotland are jurisdictionally constrained. For a variety of reasons such a response seems misguided. Investigators in most advanced liberal democracies routinely rely on the techniques and practices criticised in the NRC, NIST/NIJ and Campbell reports. While there are some important differences in the organisation, training and funding of the forensic sciences, as well as in legal practice and cultures across jurisdictions, most of the fundamental concerns explained in the reports have direct application to Australia, England, Canada, New Zealand, Hong Kong and the US. Most conspicuous, and most detrimental to jurisdictional claims of exceptionalism, is the shared dearth of research, particularly validation studies. Notably, the NRC, NIST/NIJ and Campbell reports did not appeal to research available in other jurisdictions or alternative jurisdictional examples—within or beyond the common law adversarial tradition—as a potential solution to the serious problems they each identified and confront. The reports confirm the breadth of the research crisis. In almost all cases, because of the universal nature of the modern sciences, if there is no research available to attentive publics in the US then there is no relevant research elsewhere (and vice versa). This, in effect, means that many of the criticisms in the NRC Report, especially those critical of the paltry research base, apply more or less across the board. The lack of research is not a jurisdictional problem but a global one.

(b) Implications for Trials

These troubling revelations should prompt urgent reconsideration of conventional legal practice as an effective regulatory mechanism for expert testimony in criminal proceedings. The failure of lawyers and judges to have recognised these problems unilaterally suggests that trials and appeals have very real limitations when it comes to regulating and evaluating forensic science and medicine evidence. To the extent that prosecutors and judges trivialise or disregard these issues, criminal justice systems are seriously compromised and likely

---

[25] G Edmond, MB Thompson and JM Tangen, 'A Guide to Interpreting Forensic Testimony: Scientific Approaches to Fingerprint Evidence' (2014) 13 *Law, Probability and Risk* 1.
[26] NRC Report, above n 11, ch 5.
[27] See eg *Western Australia v Rayney (No 3)* [2012] WASC 404; and the discussion of the forensic pathology evidence against Kathleen Folbigg in E Cunliffe, *Murder, Medicine and Motherhood* (Oxford, Hart Publishing, 2011).

to produce inconsistent, and inappropriate, responses to incriminating expert evidence. Simultaneously, they threaten the goal of doing justice in the pursuit of truth,[28] and thus the procedural and substantive integrity of criminal proceedings. Insufficient attention to the reliability of expert evidence and the effectiveness of trial processes means that legal institutions are likely to mismanage incriminating expert evidence into the foreseeable future.

While prosecutors in earlier decades might reasonably have claimed ignorance of the deep structural and epistemic problems with many forms of forensic science and medical testimony, the same cannot be said for prosecutors practising today. In the wake of authoritative reports and continuing scholarly engagement bearing directly on these issues, today's prosecutors are on notice. In assessing, adducing and relying upon forensic science and medicine evidence, they are obliged to be conversant with and attend to the concerns of mainstream scientific organisations and the attentive community of scholars.

2. Prosecutorial Obligations: What is Required of a 'Minister of Justice'?

The primary obligations of prosecutors have been elucidated in influential common law judgments from England, Canada, Australia and the US as well as by supranational organisations.[29] These formulations, many long-standing, encapsulate the obligations owed by the prosecutor that flow from the presumption of innocence, accusation by the state and the adversarial nature of proceedings. In many jurisdictions (including New South Wales), they are supplemented by detailed codes or rules and, conspicuously in recent decades, influenced by human rights discourses.[30] It is my contention that the primary professional obligations of the prosecutor are a consequence of his or her privileged position as a representative of the state, in conjunction with the objectives of the accusatorial trial—concerned as it is with truth and justice.[31] How we understand prosecutorial obligations and performance must depend, in part, on what we know about the evidence adduced and the abilities of various legal actors to understand and evaluate it. Decisions about incriminating expert evidence unavoidably depend upon the effectiveness of actual (rather than putative) trial and appellate processes. In consequence, prosecutors must consider the actual abilities of the decision-maker—whether judge or jury—as well as the effectiveness of legal safeguards.

Convergent judicial statements from around the common law world tend to reinforce prosecutors' primary obligation 'not to press for a conviction' but rather to regard

---

[28] HL Ho, *A Philosophy of Evidence Law: Justice in the Search for Truth* (Oxford, Oxford University Press, 2008).

[29] Prosecutors' duties were discussed in general terms in Chapters 5 (Cowdery) and 6 (Gans) in this volume. Also see FC Zacharias, 'Structuring the Ethics of Prosecutorial Trial Practice: Can Prosecutors Do Justice?' (1991) 44 *Vanderbilt Law Review* 45; FC Zacharias, 'The Professional Discipline of Prosecutors' (2001) 79 *North Carolina Law Review* 721; D Luban, 'The Conscience of a Prosecutor' (2010) 45 *Valparaiso University Law Review* 1.

[30] See eg G Boas, *The Milosevic Trial: Lessons for the Conduct of Complex International Criminal Proceedings* (Cambridge, Cambridge University Press, 2007). See generally, J Gans et al, *Criminal Process and Human Rights* (Sydney, Federation Press, 2011).

[31] See the discussion in JD Jackson and SJ Summers, *The Internationalisation of Criminal Evidence: Beyond the Common Law and Civil Law Traditions* (Cambridge, Cambridge University Press, 2012) ch 1.

themselves more 'as "ministers of justice" assisting in its administration'.[32] Prosecutors must 'act with fairness and detachment and always with the objectives of establishing the whole truth in accordance with the procedures and standards which the law requires to be observed and of helping to ensure that the accused's trial is a fair one'.[33] In a much-cited passage, Justice Rand of the Supreme Court of Canada stressed that 'the purpose of a criminal prosecution is not to obtain a conviction … The role of prosecutor excludes any notion of winning or losing'.[34] Most jurisdictions have, in addition to such common law formulations, a code or set of guidelines to assist prosecutors to understand and manage their multiple obligations and discretions.[35] In New South Wales, for example, these guidelines draw upon and reiterate common law authority emphasising prosecutors' primary responsibilities as 'ministers of justice'.[36] Most prosecutors are also subject to bar rules. The New South Wales Barristers' Rules restate prosecutors' duties to 'fairly assist the court to arrive at the truth' by adducing only reliable and admissible evidence, sticking to reasonable arguments, avoiding bias and inflammatory language, and presenting the prosecution's case fully, firmly and fairly.[37] Reinforcing international convergence around these core principles, the International Association of Prosecutors' (IAP) *Standards of Professional Responsibility and Statement of the Essential Duties and Rights of Prosecutors* are to similar effect.[38]

These formulations place a premium on truth, justice and fairness, as well as the need for reasonable evidentiary foundations. Many of the statements require prosecutors to act objectively, impartially and 'with fairness and detachment'.[39] In theory and practice, if there is doubt about what a prosecutor should do, 'seeking justice' should always predominate over adducing or pressing evidence and securing a conviction. In the capacity of a 'minister of justice', the prosecutor is obliged to seek truth fairly. This must imply prosecuting only

---

[32] *Berger v United States*, 295 US 78, 88 (1935). See also *R v Banks* [1916] 2 KB 621, 623 and *R v Puddick* (1865) 4 F & F 497, 499 (though this approach to 'advocacy' may not be compatible with modern authority).

[33] *Whitehorn v R* (1983) 152 CLR 657, 663–64.

[34] *Boucher v R* (1954) 110 CCC 263, 270. Also see Cowdery, Chapter 5 in this volume.

[35] ES Podgor, 'The Ethics and Professionalism of Prosecutors in Discretionary Decisions' (2000) 68 *Fordham Law Review* 1511.

[36] Office of the Director of Public Prosecutions (NSW), 'Prosecution Guidelines of the Office of the Director of Public Prosecutions for New South Wales' (1 June 2007). Guideline 2 affirms: 'A prosecutor is a "minister of justice". The prosecutor's principal role is to assist the court to arrive at the truth and to do justice between the community and the accused according to law and the dictates of fairness.' See also *Gilham v R* [2012] NSWCCA 131; *Wood v R* [2012] NSWCCA 21.

[37] Legal Profession Uniform Conduct (Barristers) Rules (May, 2015), rr 83–89. See also Law Society of New South Wales, 'Professional Conduct and Practice Rules' (7 October 2013) r A62–72.

[38] Specifically, pursuant to IAP, *Standards of Professional Responsibility and Statement of the Essential Duties and Rights of Prosecutors* (7 October 2013) Statements 3 and 4: 'Prosecutors shall perform their duties without fear, favour or prejudice. In particular they shall: (a) carry out their functions impartially; … (c) act with objectivity; (d) have regard to all relevant circumstances, irrespective of whether they are to the advantage or disadvantage of the suspect; (e) in accordance with local law or the requirements of a fair trial, seek to ensure that all necessary and reasonable enquiries are made and the result disclosed, whether that points towards the guilt or the innocence of the suspect; (f) always search for the truth and assist the court to arrive at the truth and to do justice between the community, the victim and the accused according to law and the dictates of fairness. … Prosecutors shall perform an active role … in the institution of criminal proceedings, they will proceed only when a case is well-founded upon evidence reasonably believed to be reliable and admissible, and will not continue with a prosecution in the absence of such evidence.'

[39] S Levine, 'Taking Prosecutorial Ethics Seriously: A Consideration of the Prosecutor's Ethical Obligation to "Seek Justice" in a Comparative Analytical Framework' (2004) 41 *Houston Law Review* 1337.

as vigorously as *the evidence* and *procedural due process* allow. The prosecutor cannot ignore the frailties of the evidence, the actual constraints and limitations of the system, or the circumstances attending the individual trial or appeal.

In relation to evidence and proof, there are explicit expectations 'that all available legal proof of facts is presented',[40] 'to assist the court to arrive at the truth'[41] and 'to ensure that the accused's trial is a fair one'.[42] The prosecutor's response to incriminating expert evidence should be driven by the need for both an accurate outcome and a fair process. The more detailed guidelines tend to require, and this would seem particularly apposite to dealing with incriminating expert evidence, that the prosecution should proceed using 'evidence reasonably believed to be reliable and admissible'.[43] In *Boucher* this was characterised as using 'credible evidence … pressed to its legitimate strength'.[44] Rule 83 of the New South Wales Barristers' Rules requires 'a full and firm presentation of [the] case'. The International Association recommends that 'all necessary and reasonable enquiries are made and the results disclosed'—whether they point 'towards the guilt or the innocence of the suspect'.[45] Prosecutors, in short, are responsible for the integrity of proof. While concerns other than conviction should motivate their performance, prosecutors carry the burden of removing all reasonable doubts about the guilt of the accused.

Crucial to the operation of the accusatorial trial, particularly in a system purporting to be rational, the tribunal of fact (and trial and appellate judges) 'must be capable of understanding *and* evaluating all evidence and any disagreement—however complex or technical—with which it is presented'.[46] In consequence, the prosecutor has a non-revocable obligation to set out both the incriminating expert evidence and its limitations in a manner that is simultaneously accurate and comprehensible to lay persons.[47] Obliged to act with fairness and detachment, to make enquiries and disclose results, and present the case fully, prosecutors must not transfer to the judge or to the accused, via his lawyer, the obligation to explain incriminating expert evidence and its limitations. Failure to identify, disclose and explain limitations with expert evidence is inconsistent with the goals of truth and justice, inconsistent with the responsibilities of a minister of justice, and seems to have a subversive tendency to dilute the burden and standard of proof.

It is fruitful to reflect on the responsibilities of prosecutors, both the injunctions of appellate courts and the more particularised guidelines and professional rules, in the light of recent revelations about the forensic sciences summarised in Section 1 of this chapter. Widespread failure to appreciate, or proactively to disclose, evidentiary weaknesses, suggests that prosecutorial obligations need rethinking. It is not safe to assume that the defence

---

[40] *Boucher v The Queen* (1954) 110 CCC 263, 270 (Rand J) ('Boucher').

[41] Office of the Director of Public Prosecutions (NSW), 'Prosecution Guidelines of the Office of the Director of Public Prosecutions for New South Wales.' (1 June 2007) Guideline 2.

[42] *Whitehorn v The Queen* (1983) 152 CLR 657, 663.–4 (Deane J).

[43] American Bar Association, 'Model Rules of Professional Conduct' (7 October 2013) r 3.8. See www.americanbar.org/groups/professional_responsibility/publications/model_rules_of_professional_conduct/model_rules_of_professional_conduct_table_of_contents.html.

[44] *R v Boucher* (1954) 110 CCC 263, 270.

[45] IAP, above n 38, Statement 3. See also: Gershman, above n 3, 28.

[46] G Edmond and A Roberts, 'Procedural Fairness, the Criminal Trial and Forensic Science and Medicine' (2011) 33 *Sydney Law Review* 359, 372.

[47] RJ Allen and JS Miller, 'The Common Law Theory of Experts: Deference or Education' (1993) 87 *Northwestern University Law Review* 1131.

and the trial judge will compensate for the omissions and oversights of the prosecutor (and expert witnesses).[48] Before turning, in the next section, to reconsider prosecutorial obligations in light of the overarching commitment to truth and justice, it is worth spelling out the broader institutional significance of expert evidence that is unreliable or speculative (that is, of unknown reliability) in the accusatorial trial.

There is no place in a rational system of criminal prosecution for forensic science and medicine that is not demonstrably reliable. This would seem incontrovertible in jurisdictions that explicitly require expert evidence to be relevant and reliable (for example, in Canada and US federal courts), but it would also seem to provide the most serviceable guide to prosecutors in jurisdictions where admissibility standards—and the interpretation of prosecutorial responsibilities—are lax.[49]

In the absence of appropriate studies and research, neither the NRC nor any other scientific organisation or attentive commentator has suggested that we should admit evidence and leave ordinary citizens to work out the value of the techniques and derivative opinions based on what transpires at trial. While explaining limitations and notorious risks, such as the biases that can flow from exposing forensic analysts to gratuitous information, might place the value of the incriminating opinion evidence in a clearer light, this illumination cannot overcome the fundamental obligation on the state to evaluate the techniques it relies upon and avoid risky procedures, especially where techniques are in routine use. Where techniques have not been evaluated, despite now widely recognised dangers, it is inappropriate for lawyers and judges to speculate about the value of the derivative opinions at trial or abandon responsibility for assessment to jurors. Where there are doubts, the commitment to truth and the fair (that is, 'full and frank' or 'warts and all') presentation of expert evidence, including the identification and explanation of methodological deficiencies, should override strategic (and selective) representations that might advance the prosecution's case and the chance of victory while disadvantaging the accused both procedurally and substantially. Where there is little experimental evidence substantiating a technique, prosecutors should not lead incriminating opinions, let alone present them as expert.

Whatever the prosecutor does, she should not connive at subverting fact-finding in a manner detrimental to the accused, or adopt strategies likely to produce substantial unfairness or error. There is, in my submission, a non-derogable obligation to present expert evidence fairly. That obligation falls squarely on the state, and therefore on the prosecutor, and indirectly on the judge, as the state's representatives in the administration of justice. A fair proceeding, centrally concerned with rectitude through the elimination of reasonable doubts, is obliged to have expert evidence presented in a manner that is balanced and enables the tribunal of fact to evaluate it rationally.[50]

---

[48] D Medwed, *Prosecution Complex: America's Race to Convict and Its Impact on the Innocent* (New York, New York University Press, 2012) 98.

[49] On lax admissibility standards, see Law Commission, *Expert Evidence in Criminal Proceedings in England and Wales*, Report No 325 (2009) [3.3] and [6.10].

[50] G Edmond, 'Forensic Science Evidence and the Conditions for Rational (Jury) Evaluation' (2015) 39 *Melbourne University Law Review* 77.

3. Obligations in Context: Rethinking Prosecutorial Responsibilities

It would be premature to offer a confident answer to the question of whether existing frameworks and normative guidance (rules and codes) will be adequate to meet the challenges posed to orthodox criminal practice by scientific evidence.[51] What we can say is that insufficient attention has been directed to this issue, given what we now know about the questionable value of many forms of forensic science and medicine evidence. Presenting forensic science and medicine evidence in ways that endeavour to convey the actual value of the evidence could hardly be thought to be an unreasonable imposition on a 'minister of justice'.[52] This section endeavours to encourage prosecutors to reconsider their professional obligations in relation to forensic science and medical testimony. Prosecutorial responsibilities and practices should be indexed to both the methodological shortcomings of scientific evidence and the limitations of traditional legal practice in dealing with them.

Unreliable, weak and speculative forensic science and medicine evidence would be far less of a problem if conventional trial mechanisms consistently identified and conveyed limitations with expert evidence.[53] Unfortunately, the rules regulating the admission and examination of expert evidence appear to operate inconsistently and are often surprisingly weak. Notwithstanding the need to identify and convey infirmities to facilitate the rational assessment of evidence (and guilt), the kinds of problems with expert evidence identified in the various reports are neither systematically identified nor explained in courtrooms. Indeed, the identification and explanation of evidentiary infirmities occurs so haphazardly that the phrases 'admissibility standards' and 'trial safeguards' might be thought misnomers.[54] Admissibility rules, trial safeguards, jury participation and scope for appellate review, currently afford less security than safeguards genuinely indexed to truth and justice ought to provide.

---

[51] US commentators have been inclined to advocate greater regulation through additional rules: see eg M Raeder, 'See No Evil: Wrongful Convictions and the Prosecutorial Ethics of Offering Testimony by Jailhouse Informants and Dishonest Experts' (2007) 76 *Fordham Law Review* 1413, 1450; MJ Saks, 'Scientific Evidence and the Ethical Obligations of Attorneys' (2001) 49 *Cleveland State Law Review* 421, 426; PC Giannelli and KC McMunigal, 'Prosecutors, Ethics and Expert Witnesses' (2007) 76 *Fordham Law Review* 1493, 1535; Medwed, above n 48, 165. See also FC Zacharias, 'Specificity in Professional Responsibility Codes: Theory, Practice, and the Paradigm of Prosecutorial Ethics' (1993) 69 *Notre Dame Law Review* 223; E Yaroshefsky, 'Wrongful Convictions: It Is Time to Take Prosecution Discipline Seriously' (2004) 8 *University of the District of Columbia Law Review* 275.

[52] It may have resource and competency implications, but these are separate issues. See generally, PA Joy, 'The Relationship between Prosecutorial Misconduct and Wrongful Convictions: Shaping Remedies for a Broken System' [2006] *Wisconsin Law Review* 399, 407.

[53] There is also the problem of lay decision-making in legal contexts. This is not simply a question of jury (and judicial) competence, but the more complex issue of evaluating evidence in circumstances that are not always conducive to decision-making.

[54] Claims that trials are effective can be refuted by the routine failure to identify or concede the kinds of concerns identified by the NRC Committee. Where are the judicial references to the failure to undertake validation studies and proficiency tests, the significance of not having access to error rates, the way that analysts have exaggerated their abilities, the potentially corrosive potential of contextual factors and biases, the need for caution with experience and confidence, and so on?

One of the clearest expressions of doubt about traditional trial safeguards (outside the NRC Report) can be found in the English Law Commission's report on *Expert Evidence in Criminal Proceedings in England and Wales*:

> Cross-examination, the adduction of contrary expert evidence and judicial guidance at the end of the trial are currently assumed to provide sufficient safeguards in relation to expert evidence … However, … it is doubtful whether these are valid assumptions.[55]

This assessment is consistent with the work of innocence projects, criminal cases review commissions and my own observations of criminal trials and appeals in Australia.[56] It is also consistent with the NRC Report, insofar as common law systems have allowed unreliable and speculative evidence into trials for decades on the erroneous assumption that techniques are inherently reliable and/or that significant limitations will be exposed (or disclosed), explained and understood.[57]

The historical record clearly shows that conventional trial safeguards, particularly in the way they have traditionally been understood and resourced, are not sufficient to deal with unreliable, and most forms of speculative and 'shaky', expert evidence.[58] Trials do not provide a credible assessment of new, emerging or impugned techniques. Techniques should be formally assessed prior to their appearance in criminal proceedings. When experts and lawyers appeal to earlier accommodating admissibility decisions and previous convictions as evidence for the reliability of techniques and opinions, they are making a category error[59] as admissibility decisions and convictions, including those withstanding appeals, cannot provide scientific legitimation or substitute for formal evaluation. Validation studies and rigorous proficiency tests provide evidence of ability and accuracy.

Techniques in routine use should be evaluated to determine whether they do what analysts claim, as well as to gauge their levels of accuracy. Analysts should be proficient and preferably experienced with techniques that have been evaluated. Evaluation should be independent—separate from litigation and the courtroom. While the criminal trial might on occasion hold experts to account, it is not a genuine, well-calibrated test or credible substitute for independent empirical evaluation.[60] Admissibility decisions and success withstanding cross-examination typically tell us more about admissibility standards and the resourcing and relative competence of lawyers and judges, than they reveal about the actual value of techniques or the expert opinions derived from them.[61]

---

[55] Law Commission, above n 49, [1.20].

[56] See Weisselberg, Chapter 15 in this volume. See also KA Findley, 'Innocents at Risk: Adversary Imbalance, Forensic Science, and the Search for Truth' (2008) 38 *Seton Hall Law Review* 893; BL Garrett, *Convicting the Innocent: Where Criminal Prosecutions Go Wrong* (Cambridge MA, Harvard University Press, 2011).

[57] NRC Report, above n 11, 85.

[58] See G Edmond and M San Roque, 'The Cool Crucible: Forensic Science and the Frailty of the Criminal Trial' (2012) 24 *Current Issues in Criminal Justice* 51. The term 'shaky' is taken from *Daubert v Merrell Dow Pharmaceuticals, Inc*, 113 S Ct 2786, 2798 (1993), where the US Supreme Court explained that: 'Vigorous cross-examination, presentation of contrary evidence, and careful instruction on the burden of proof are the traditional and appropriate means of attacking shaky but admissible evidence.'

[59] A notorious example is *United States v Harvard*, 117 F Supp 2d 848 (SD Ind, 2000).

[60] See S Jasanoff, *Science at the Bar: Law, Science and Technology in America* (Cambridge MA, Harvard University Press, 1995). Cf G Edmond, 'The Building Blocks of Forensic Science and Law: Recent Work on DNA Profiling (and Photo Comparison)' (2011) 41 *Social Studies of Science* 127.

[61] See G Edmond et al, 'How to Cross-examine Forensic Scientists: A Guide for Lawyers' (2014) 39 *Australian Bar Review* 174.

(a) Admissibility Standards and Prosecutorial Integrity

The responsibilities of prosecutors are not necessarily fulfilled by adherence to conventional practice or compliance with existing adjectival rules. Admissibility standards governing expert evidence are a case in point. 'Weak forensic evidence', as Medwed notes, 'continues to pour, not drip, into criminal trials'.[62] Medwed is concerned with practice in the US in the aftermath of *Daubert v Merrell Dow Pharmaceuticals, Inc.*[63] Similar problems persist in Canada in the aftermath of the reliability shift associated with *R v DD*, *R v L-JL* and *R v Trochym*,[64] and will no doubt continue to haunt English practice, following the rather half-hearted implementation of the Law Commission's proposals through delegated legislation and court rules.[65] Australian admissibility jurisprudence is largely inattentive to the reliability of techniques. Our judges have preferred to focus their attention on less informative heuristics such as the existence of a 'field', formal qualifications, the experience of the analyst and tortured inquiries into the (admissibility of) facts underlying the opinion.[66]

Satisfying the often misguided, and frequently undemanding, standards regulating the admission of incriminating expert evidence neither fulfils nor ends prosecutorial responsibilities. Regardless of whether there is a formal admissibility standard stipulating 'reliability', the prosecutor should be attentive to the reliability (or probative value) of incriminating expert evidence, as well as its potential to mislead.[67] The prosecutor should not, as a minister of justice, adduce insufficiently reliable evidence or permit forensic science and medicine evidence to be presented in terms stronger than empirical evidence will, or could, allow. Where there are serious doubts about opinions, or limited empirical support for techniques, prosecutors should not—regardless of historical practices—adduce the evidence, given that accusatorial systems and adversarial mechanisms have repeatedly shown themselves incapable of responsibly handling unreliable, 'shaky' and speculative forms of incriminating expert opinion.[68]

---

[62] Medwed, above n 48, 102.

[63] *Daubert v Merrell Dow Pharmaceuticals, Inc*, 113 S Ct 2786 (1993).

[64] *R v DD* [2000] 2 SCR 275; *R v L-JL* [2000] 2 SCR 600; *R v Trochym* [2007] 1 SCR 239. See, also G Edmond et al, 'Admissibility Compared: The Reception of Incriminating Expert Opinion (ie Forensic Science) Evidence in Four Adversarial Jurisdictions' (2013) 3 *University of Denver Criminal Law Review* 31.

[65] See I Dennis, 'Editorial: Tightening the Law on Expert Evidence' [2015] Crim LR 1; *Consolidated Criminal Practice direction* [2015] EWCA Crim 1567, CPD V 19A. The Ministry of Justice apparently declined to proceed with the Law Commission's draft Criminal Evidence (Experts) Bill on costs grounds: *The Government's response to the Law Commission report: Expert evidence in criminal proceedings in England and Wales* (Law Com No 325) (21 November 2013). See also, G Edmond, 'Is Reliability Sufficient? The Law Commission and Expert Evidence in International and Interdisciplinary Perspective' (2012) 16 *International Journal of Evidence and Proof* 30.

[66] See generally, *Clark v Ryan* (1960) 103 CLR 486; *R v Bonython* (1984) 38 SASR 45; *HG v R* (1999) 197 CLR 414; *Makita (Australia) Pty Ltd v Sprowles* (2001) 52 NSWLR 705; *Velevski v R* (2002) 187 ALR 233; *Dasreef Pty Ltd v Hawchar* (2011) 85 ALJR 694. Cf *Tuite v R* [2014] VSCA 148.

[67] Irrespective of the jury's ultimate decision-making responsibility, prosecutors and judges should attend to the probative value of incriminating expert opinion evidence.

[68] Desirable as *reliability* seems to be—as a prophylactic capable of eliminating the worst of the problems with incriminating expert evidence—it has not been widely embraced by prosecutors (or judges), even in jurisdictions with explicit reliability-based admissibility standards to inform their practice.

When adducing and presenting incriminating expert evidence the prosecutor must assess the ability of the jury to understand and evaluate the evidence.[69] The analytical and reasoning process, as well as the basis for the opinion, should be transparent or capable of being made transparent.[70] Greater transparency may well reveal or expose limitations and errors.[71] Greater attention to the lay assessment of evidence, particularly empirically-derived probabilistic forms of expression, should improve fact-finding. Prosecutors should carefully consider the way that experts express their opinions. They should aim to avoid misleading impressions and to maximise comprehension by decision-makers.

To be sure, the reliability of techniques and derivative opinions is sometimes open to reasonable disagreement.[72] In such cases, prosecutors acting in good faith would seem obliged to identify substantial limitations (and credible criticism) unilaterally if they decide to adduce the evidence.[73] In all cases prosecutors should not wait for the defence to object before drawing the court's attention to issues that bear on the admissibility or weight of incriminating expert evidence. In practice, the prosecutor should not simply promote the positive case and leave the defence to contest admissibility and expose limitations. Where the prosecutor has a well-founded belief that the techniques are reliable and there is evidence to support that contention they might lead the evidence, but only on condition that any presentation is 'warts and all' *and* the defence is capable of making reasonable submissions and calling appropriate witnesses in response.

Where state laboratories and forensic analysts have not undertaken evaluation of their techniques, and thereby developed appropriate standards and empirically predicated terminology for interpreting their findings and communicating their opinions, the prosecutor cannot ignore, and should be reluctant to excuse, such oversights.[74] The prosecutor is obliged to take these omissions into account when considering whether to lead expert evidence. Where evidence has not been assessed, and where notorious methodological vulnerabilities (such as contextual biases) persist, it may be that the evidence has little or even no probative value, and is therefore logically irrelevant—regardless of how it might be represented, or historically has been understood and presented, in criminal trials.

In most areas of forensic science and medicine, and especially in relation to techniques that are in routine use, experience should not be used to ground admissibility. Even though most admissibility rules exempt 'experience'-based expertise from the general common law prohibition on witnesses expressing 'opinions', unambiguous scientific research confirms that experience is generally incapable of grounding techniques and can be misleading.[75]

---

[69]   See eg *R v Gilham* [2012] NSWCCA 131, [405]: 'It is in the discharge of the different but allied obligations of the expert and the Crown Prosecutor that the jury is educated and informed about matters in issue between the Crown and the accused which are beyond the jury's experience.'

[70]   See *Dasreef Pty Ltd v Hawchar* (2011) 85 ALJR 694; and *Davie v Magistrates of Edinburgh* [1953] SC 34, 40.

[71]   Attention should, therefore, be paid to the manner in which opinion evidence and its foundations are presented in reports and testimony. See eg *HG v R* (1999) 197 CLR 414; *Makita (Australia) Pty Ltd v Sprowles* (2001) 52 NSWLR 705; *R v Morgan* [2011] NSWCCA 257.

[72]   DS Caudill, 'Lawyers Judging Experts: Oversimplifying Science and Undervaluing Advocacy to Construct an Ethical Duty?' (2011) 38 *Pepperdine Law Review* 675.

[73]   See eg *General Medical Council v Meadow* [2006] EWCA Civ 1390, [206].

[74]   See Special Issue, above n 10.

[75]   See eg D White et al, 'Passport Officers' Errors in Face Matching' (2014) 9 *PloS ONE* e103510. More generally, see D Kahneman, P Slovic and A Tversky (eds), *Judgment under Uncertainty: Heuristics and Biases* (New York, Cambridge University Press, 1982); D Kahneman and G Klein, 'Conditions for Intuitive Expertise: A Failure to Disagree' (2009) 64 *American Psychologist* 515.

Where techniques can be evaluated experimentally, they should be. Moreover, contesting the value of experience at trial can be problematic. It is difficult to explain the limits of experience effectively, particularly where the confident analyst is a very experienced investigator who has used the impugned technique, and been allowed to express untested opinions, for years and perhaps decades. In such cases, defence challenges tend to appear (and are often portrayed by prosecutors as) implausible, self-serving and desperate. The important issue is expertise, not experience. Experience, even long experience, is a poor substitute for independent evidence of actual ability. Experience is useful once a technique has been properly tested and evaluated, so that we have an idea of the value of the experience and how practices might be refined to improve performance. Experience alone is generally incapable of validating a technique.

(b) Exclusionary Discretions

Prosecutors should pay attention to the risk of unfair prejudice to the accused, in addition to complying with formal admissibility standards.[76] If the probative value of expert evidence is low, the risk of unfair prejudice will often be considerable. Where the probative value of the evidence is unknown there are serious risks that limits will not be clearly conveyed, the jury might defer to the expert (particularly authoritative, experienced and/or confident witnesses), and that the evidence will be misunderstood or over-valued.

While the jury is free to approach expert evidence and combine it with other evidence in a common-sense fashion, a rational trial process cannot ignore the need to provide the decision-maker with pertinent information about validity, competence and accuracy. Moreover, a jury should not be entitled to attribute any weight it deems appropriate to an expert's opinion—especially if validation studies and indicative error rates exist.[77] The probative value of an opinion must be constrained by objective data circumscribing the value and accuracy of techniques. Conversely, the absence of such information should raise cautionary flags. It signals the need to seriously consider whether expert evidence should be adduced at all, and how it can legitimately be presented, if properly admitted. If the jury is unlikely to appreciate, or is incapable of appreciating, limitations with techniques and opinions, reasonable doubts pointing towards acquittal may be overlooked.

The prosecutor's obligation not to lead (and trial judges' derivative obligation to exclude) insufficiently reliable expert evidence is especially important because, on settled evidentiary principles, the persuasive burden is on the party adducing the evidence. Relying on exclusionary discretions imposes the onus on the party challenging admission. Given the need to present evidence fairly, in conjunction with a fair process, prosecutors should not exploit low admissibility standards to deflect responsibility for unpacking (un)reliability onto the accused. The accused should not bear the risk of systematic failures to evaluate techniques or proficiency, or be exposed to heightened risk of a jury's misunderstanding or

---

[76] In many jurisdictions there may be additional obligations to attend to waste of time, resources and the risk of confusion.

[77] Because the probative value of many techniques can be gauged—even if in some range—prosecutors and judges should not allow a jury to assign to the evidence (almost) any value. Generally, interpretations should be guided by validation studies and indicative error rates. See, eg Edmond, Thompson and Tangen, above n 25.

over-valuing the evidence when it is presented at trial. The accused should not be obliged to prove that 'shaky' techniques are in fact 'shaky'.

(c)   Prosecutors and Experts must Disclose and Explain Serious Limitations with Expert Evidence

Notwithstanding the ability (at least in theory) of the defence to call rebuttal experts, in many cases the need to call such witnesses should be pre-empted by the prosecutor's 'full and frank' presentation of any incriminating expert evidence it intends to rely upon. It is simply not good enough for a 'minister of justice' to adduce opinions that are not demonstrably reliable, or do not include or respond to notorious limitations and criticisms, without disclosing that information. The defence should be obliged to respond only to an even-handed presentation of incriminating expert evidence that openly acknowledges non-trivial problems and limitations. The need for disclosure, along with the ability to explain limitations and oversights, should influence the decision to adduce incriminating expert evidence and will substantially reduce the need for the defence—whether or not they can afford it and regardless of whether such assistance is available to them—to adduce rebuttal expert evidence.[78]

The obligation to explain limitations should expose prosecutors to the facts that many forensic science and medicine techniques have not been evaluated and that a good deal of analysis is undertaken by individuals with few formal qualifications and without systematic experience. While such analysts *may* have formidable practical abilities, they may not be qualified to identify and explain cognitive, methodological and statistical problems with their practices and operating assumptions. Latent fingerprint examiners are a good example. While recent research confirms examiners' ability to discriminate between prints with relatively few errors,[79] their historical claims about a match being the equivalent of positive identification and the technique being infallible are, as the NRC and two subsequent inquiries concluded, 'unrealistic'.[80] If assistance is required to explain to fact-finders the limitations of latent fingerprint evidence, it may be that fingerprint examiners themselves are unable (or unwilling) to respond. In such circumstances, it will be incumbent on the prosecutor to call the evidence of cognitive scientists or statisticians to facilitate jury understanding of evidentiary limitations.[81]

Timely disclosure of limitations should be required for admissibility. It should not, however, guarantee admissibility. Expert evidence should be sufficiently reliable for admission and susceptible to presentation in a manner such that limitations can be explained at trial and rationally evaluated within trial and appeal constraints, before the prosecutor

---

[78]   In many areas, such as latent fingerprint and ballistics comparisons, for example, there is no ready supply of non-aligned 'experts' available to the defence.

[79]   B Ulery et al, 'Accuracy and Reliability of Forensic Latent Fingerprint Decisions' (2011) 108 *Proceedings of the National Academy of Sciences of the United States of America* 7733; J Tangen, M Thompson and D McCarthy, 'Identifying Fingerprint Expertise' (2011) 22 *Psychological Science* 995.

[80]   NRC Report, above n 11, 143. See also Mnookin et al, above n 23.

[81]   Though we should not assume that formal 'tuition' will provide a solution. See K Martire et al, 'The Psychology of Interpreting Expert Evaluative Opinions' (2013) 45 *Australian Journal of Forensic Sciences* 305.

adduces it. Merely conceding oversights, such as the failure to validate, does not provide rational means of evaluating expert evidence and should not provide a 'backdoor' to the courtroom.[82]

Prosecutors should require experts to produce reports and testimony that comply with jurisdictional reporting obligations—often outlined in codes of conduct.[83] Expert reports should clearly identify limitations with the analysis and conclusions, and draw the reader's attention to both supportive and critical literatures. They should be a resource for the parties and the court. The expert is, after all, supposed to operate impartially and has a fundamental duty to the court. Prosecutors cannot simply accept expert witnesses' self-serving claims that they have complied with their professional and legal duties, particularly if the method is not explained or there are no references to relevant studies, standards and protocols, limitations or error rates.[84]

(d) Admissibility Compromises and Faulty Combinations

Prosecutors should generally be reluctant to obtain admission for unreliable and speculative techniques and opinions on the basis of admissibility compromises, that is, dubious attempts to 'spilt the difference' by allowing experts to testify on a restricted basis or subject to overt caveats or concessions.[85] The problem with admissibility compromises, such as where an analyst comparing CCTV images of an offender with reference photographs of the accused is restricted to describing similarities and prevented from making a positive identification (even though they believe they can), is that the compromises are not based on any independent evidence of ability.[86] This is why underlying research, such as validation studies, is fundamental. Studies provide information on performance and limitations, and assist with the formulation of standards, expression and evaluation of opinion evidence.[87] In the absence of such studies, expressions of opinion (including many forms of qualified expression) are speculative and may be impenetrable *ipse dixit*.[88]

Prosecutorial screening and judicial admissibility determinations are vitally important because, once incriminating expert evidence is admitted, it no longer stands by itself. It is frequently presented as independent *even when it is not*, and as corroborative of other inculpatory evidence *even though it might not be*. Because forensic scientists are routinely

---

[82] Contrast the English approach in *R v Atkins* [2010] 1 Cr App R 8, [2009] EWCA Crim 1876; *R v Otway* [2011] EWCA Crim 3; *R v Dlugosz* [2013] 1 Cr App R 32, [2013] EWCA Crim 2.

[83] See eg Chief Justice Allsop, Federal Court of Australia, 'Expert Witnesses in Proceedings in the Federal Court of Australia', Practice Note CM 7, 4 June 2013. See also B Found and G Edmond, 'Reporting on the Comparison and Interpretation of Pattern Evidence: Recommendations for Forensic Specialists' (2012) 44 *Australian Journal of Forensic Sciences* 193.

[84] In *R v Wood* [2012] NSWCCA 21, [728]–[730], the expert's flagrant failure to adhere to the code of conduct was said to be an issue for weight rather than admissibility.

[85] S Cole, 'Splitting Hairs? Evaluating "Split Testimony" as an Approach to the Problem of Forensic Expert Evidence' (2011) 33 *Sydney Law Review* 459.

[86] See eg *R v Tang* (2006) 65 NSWLR 681.

[87] D McQuiston-Surrett and MJ Saks, 'The Testimony of Forensic Identification Science: What Expert Witnesses Say and What Factfinders Hear' (2009) 33 *Law and Human Behavior* 436; Martire et al, above n 81.

[88] See eg *Morgan v R* (2011) 215 A Crim R 33, [76]; *Honeysett v R* [2013] NSWCCA 135; *R v Gilham* [2012] NSWCCA 131.

exposed to potentially prejudicial domain irrelevant information (that is, contextual information about the case or its investigation which is not required for the analysis), if treated as independent support for the case against the accused, incriminating expert evidence may be over-valued by the fact-finder.

Prosecutorial screening and admissibility gatekeeping ought to focus attention on the value of techniques and opinions isolated from any other evidence relevant to the accused's guilt.[89] When considering the admissibility of incriminating expert evidence, in most cases prosecutors and judges should not consider the existence of other incriminating evidence or the overall strength of the case against the accused. For *admissibility*, techniques and derivative opinions should stand or fall on their own merits. It does not matter if the case is strong or weak, the admissibility of expert evidence should generally be considered independently. Once admitted at trial, however, forensic science and medicine evidence no longer stands, or needs to be assessed, on its own. The tribunal of fact may combine any admissible evidence, bolstering the weak with the strong as part of its interpretation of the facts. Decision-makers should not, however, ignore dependence and contamination if these were present in the production of incriminating expert opinions.

Despite the fact that forensic analysts are regularly exposed to domain irrelevant information, issues of contextual bias and cross-contamination tend to arise only rarely, and perfunctorily, in trials. Contextual bias and cross-contamination introduce serious threats to incriminating expert opinions, diluting their independence from other evidence and eroding the standard of proof. If, for example, a forensic analyst is exposed to prejudicial information that is not relevant to the analysis, then there is a real risk that this information will influence, and even contaminate, the interpretation. Studies have demonstrated that exposure to domain irrelevant information has the ability to lead fingerprint examiners to shift between classifying the same pair of prints as a match and a non-match, and to cause biologists to include or exclude a profile from a mixed sample when interpreting mixed DNA profiles.[90] The effects of contextual bias may persist notwithstanding the analyst's experience or training and regardless of whether they are aware of the risks. Cognitive biases are not moral or ethical failings. Rather, they are a product of cognitive architecture, experience and socialisation.[91] They typically operate unconsciously, hidden from the analyst. In consequence, as part of their concern with the reliability of incriminating expert evidence and the fair and impartial presentation of that evidence, prosecutors ought to consider the circumstances in which any expert evidence was developed. And, in presenting the case, they should refrain from suggesting that forensic science evidence provides independent support for, or corroborates, other evidence unless they are confident that the analyst was not affected by domain irrelevant information and other known threats to accuracy.

---

[89] See A Burke, 'Improving Prosecutorial Decision Making: Some Lessons from Cognitive Science' (2006) 47 *William & Mary Law Review* 1587; A Burke, 'Talking about Prosecutors' (2010) 31 *Cardozo Law Review* 2119.

[90] I Dror, D Charlton and A Péron, 'Contextual Information Renders Experts Vulnerable to Making Erroneous Identifications' (2006) 156 *Forensic Science International* 74; I Dror and G Hampikian, 'Subjectivity and Bias in Forensic DNA Mixture Interpretation' (2011) 51 *Science & Justice* 204.

[91] I Dror, 'The Paradox of Human Expertise: Why Experts Get It Wrong' in N Kapur (ed), *The Paradoxical Brain* (Cambridge, Cambridge University Press, 2011).

(e) What About Defence Lawyers?

It might be argued that the exacting interpretation of prosecutorial obligations developed in this chapter gives defence lawyers an easy time. To some extent that may be true. However, the presence of a defence lawyer does not provide prosecutors with grounds for adducing insufficiently reliable scientific or medical evidence, or a justification for abandoning responsibility for identifying and explaining limitations, including potentially debilitating limitations, for the benefit of decision-makers. Similarly, the fact that limitations *might* be successfully explained to the tribunal of fact during an adversarial proceeding—through cross-examination, rebuttal expertise or in a closing address—is no excuse for making defence lawyers the primary bulwark against unreliable and speculative incriminating opinions. Limitations and uncertainties raised, and conceded, by the prosecutor are likely to make a greater impression on the fact-finder. While the defence obviously has a role to play in relation to incriminating expert evidence, that role emerges once the prosecutor has clearly explained the incriminating expert evidence, 'warts and all'.

Where techniques and opinions adduced by the state and admitted are unreliable, speculative or 'shaky', the obligations upon defence lawyers become onerous. In such circumstances, the defence should ordinarily challenge admissibility. Where the contested evidence is admitted they are often obliged to attempt to expose limitations with the evidence in a manner that the jury can readily comprehend. Generally, prosecutors should be reluctant to prevent the defence from calling rebuttal experts from *relevant* fields. Where an expert called by the defence is explaining a methodological or technical problem, prosecutors should not seek to trivialise the issue unfairly. The fact that these may be research scientists, often from fields or disciplines different to the forensic analysts presenting the state's incriminating opinion evidence, should make little material difference.[92] We should not forget that the vast majority of the (many) problems with forensic science and medicine identified in recent decades—including the need to refine DNA processing, interpretation and reporting—were identified by those who were not practising forensic analysts.[93] Most of the criticisms, subsequently endorsed by the NRC Committee and other independent bodies, were first identified and explained by attentive scholars.[94] The significance of these problems was often downplayed by forensic practitioners, and their professional associations, and discounted by courts.

Presenting incriminating expert evidence fairly will often require that the defence be allowed to adduce critical evidence from cognate areas of expertise. While scope for rebuttal tends to be conceived as important, in many adversarial contests, we should not assume that allowing (or expecting) the defence to rebut the opinions of experienced investigators represents an appropriate counter to insufficiently reliable expert evidence or an effective way to facilitate the evaluation of expert evidence. Forensic science and medicine evidence, adduced by the prosecutor and admitted by the trial judge, is very likely—regardless of its

---

[92] Cf *R v Weller* [2010] EWCA Crim 1085; and *R v Otway* [2011] EWCA Crim 3. See also SA Cole, 'A Cautionary Tale about Cautionary Tales about Intervention' (2009) 16 *Organization* 121.

[93] See J Aronson, *Genetic Witness: Science, Law, and Controversy in the Making of DNA Profiling* (Piscataway NJ, Rutgers University Press, 2007); DH Kaye, *The Double Helix and the Law of Evidence* (Cambridge MA, Harvard University Press, 2010).

[94] See above n 4.

actual value—to exert a much stronger influence on decision-makers than methodological criticisms, often technical in nature, adduced by the defence.[95]

No matter how prosecutors (re)interpret their professional responsibilities in response to growing awareness of the mutual frailties of the forensic sciences and the accusatorial trial, defence lawyers will continue to have substantial obligations in relation to the conduct of the trial and scope for appeal. Defence lawyers have important roles to play even in relation to basically reliable techniques and competent analysis. For, there are always real dangers of error—from the collection of samples to the presentation of results—even where the underlying techniques are demonstrably reliable.[96] Defence lawyers need to maintain vigilance to ensure that prosecutors and experts meet their professional obligations to present incriminating evidence fairly. They must be ready to intervene to correct any unfairness, misrepresentation or ambiguity and to develop legitimate differences or alternative interpretations.

Conclusion: If Prosecutors will not Step Up, Where does that Leave Procedural Integrity?

> Prosecutors are the most powerful players in the criminal justice system, capable of determining who should be charged and with what crimes. The duty to serve as a minister of justice is designed to limit abuse of this power and to compensate for the imbalance of resources that so often places the defense at a disadvantage. Demanding more of prosecutors than of other lawyers also fosters greater confidence in the legitimacy and accuracy of the criminal justice system.[97]

This chapter has been critical of the restrictive manner in which prosecutors have interpreted and applied their professional obligations with respect to expert evidence. Insensitivity to the limits of forensic science and medicine evidence means that prosecutors may, to varying degrees, be oblivious to their complicity in the creation of many of the problems that now require attention. Prosecutors continue to adduce, and judges to admit, expert opinions derived from techniques that have never been evaluated without explaining, or apparently recognising, the significance of such oversights. Rather than require evidence of ability and accuracy, courts have accepted, and sometimes preferred, apparent utility and the non-systematic experience of those they deemed experts. Premature legal recognition and continuing reliance on insufficiently reliable techniques and opinions cannot continue. Existing practice is not consistent with criminal adjudication's overarching aspirations or the well-established obligations of prosecutors and judges. Indeed, it threatens the primary goal of the accusatorial trial—doing justice in the pursuit of truth.[98]

Historically, responsibility for identifying and explaining limitations with incriminating expert evidence has 'fallen between stools'. Prosecutors have been guided by liberal

---

[95] Edmond and San Roque, above n 58.

[96] Human involvement introduces the risk of error: see eg FHR Vincent, *Inquiry Into the Circumstances that Led to the Conviction of Mr Farah Abdulkadir Jama*, PP No 301, Session 2006-10 (Melbourne, Victorian Government Printer, May 2010).

[97] Medwed, above n 48, 2.

[98] Ho, above n 28.

admissibility standards and a commitment to allowing the jury free rein in determining the weight of evidence. In all common law jurisdictions, judges have accommodated expert evidence on the ground that trial safeguards are effective and the jury is responsible for fact-finding. Judges, as a professional group, are yet to fully appreciate the extent of problems with forensic science and medicine, summarised in Section 1 of this chapter, or to face up to their own complicity in this unfortunate state of affairs. Forensic analysts have, in general, been willing to testify whenever called upon. Too often, they have proffered confident opinions that were not empirically grounded, and only occasionally (and often reluctantly) made appropriate concessions. Experts sometimes rationalise their dissembling on the grounds that nobody asked them the pertinent questions, or they invoke previous involvement in investigations and appearances in court as evidence of their ability and accuracy. Defence lawyers have generally performed poorly at identifying and effectively explaining the shortcomings of incriminating expert evidence. Given these unsatisfactory performances it seems incumbent upon prosecutors to take the lead.

Apprised of the deep-seated problems rehearsed in this chapter, prosecutors should begin to re-evaluate their practices in ways that improve the quality of incriminating expert evidence relied upon in and out of court. They should do this regardless of judicial gatekeeping and admissibility standards, regardless of the quality of the defence and resources available to the defence, and regardless of how forensic analysts and their institutional representatives respond to authoritative calls for reform. Prosecutors have formal obligations to systematically address notorious problems with forensic science and medicine in the exercise of their discretions and in their trial and appellate practice. They are 'repeat players ... with access to vast sources of information'.[99] Though not necessarily well resourced, on average prosecutors are better resourced and better organised than defence lawyers and those accused of criminal offences. They are also in a much better position than judges to undertake inquiries and review specialist literatures.[100] Prosecutors need to securely anchor the administration of criminal justice to what is *known* beyond the courts. If prosecutors do not interpret their obligations in ways that require them to confront and address problems with forensic science and medicine evidence, and take pains to engage with exogenous knowledge, effective responses to systematic problems are unlikely to materialise.

There can be little doubt that the vast majority of prosecutors are decent, conscientious lawyers. For a variety of reasons, however, they have not adapted their professional responsibilities and obligations to the changed circumstances and understandings of forensic science and the accusatorial trial. This chapter has endeavoured to provide some assistance in helping prosecutors to begin to reconceptualise the contemporary meaning and significance of their professional responsibilities in the light of emerging revelations and burgeoning critical literatures. The alternative, legal indifference to consensual scientific opinion beyond the courts, is likely to produce embarrassing errors, undermine limited public confidence, and perpetuate increasingly fraught relations between mainstream science and law. Prosecutors' professional integrity demands a more proactive, critical assessment of ostensibly incriminating expert evidence, and the integrity of criminal process depends upon it.

---

[99] Medwed, above n 48, 20.
[100] See G Edmond, D Hamer and E Cunliffe, 'A little ignorance is a dangerous thing: Engaging with exogenous knowledge not adduced by the parties' (2016) 28 *Griffith Law Review* (forthcoming).

10

Stays of Prosecution and
Remedial Integrity

AMANDA WHITFORT

Introduction

It is well established in the United Kingdom, Australia and Hong Kong that where a court finds there has been an abuse of process by the prosecution it has an inherent power to order the criminal proceedings to be stayed permanently. A stay of proceedings may be permitted on two bases. An application may be made on the basis that a fair trial is not possible (for reasons such as pre-trial publicity or delay), or on the much rarer basis that whilst a fair trial is possible the application for a stay should be granted anyway as the criminal justice system would otherwise be affronted. This chapter focuses on the latter kind of stay.

It was the House of Lords' decision in *R v Horseferry Road Magistrates Court, ex parte Bennett*[1] that placed police misconduct squarely in the frame as a basis for ordering a stay of prosecution. In that case the court proceeded on the basis that the defendant had been unlawfully brought into the UK as a result of collusion between the South African and British police. Regardless of the merits of the case against him, the actions of those tasked with bringing the case to court had effectively undermined the state's right to prosecute it. As Lord Lowry observed:

[T]he court, in order to protect its own processes from being degraded and misused, must have the power to stay proceedings which have come before it and have only been made possible by acts which offend the court's conscience as being contrary to the rule of law. These acts, by providing a morally unacceptable foundation for the exercise of jurisdiction over the suspect taint the proposed trial and, if tolerated, will mean the court's process has been abused … It may be said that a guilty accused finding himself in the circumstances predicated is not deserving of much sympathy, but the principle involved goes beyond the scope of such a pragmatic observation and even beyond the rights of those victims who are or may be innocent. It affects the proper administration of the rule of law.[2]

---

[1] [1994] 1 AC 42.
[2] Ibid 76.

The decision has since been frequently cited in Australia[3] and Hong Kong,[4] although it is strictly binding in neither. In all three jurisdictions, however, there is a consensus that stay applications should be rarely sought and even more rarely allowed.

Recent cases in these jurisdictions have demonstrated that the appellate courts experience real difficulties in determining when prosecutorial conduct which could justify a stay has occurred, and what should be done about it. In his dissenting judgment in the recent High Court of Australia case, *Moti*,[5] Heydon J lamented the inarticulate nature of the test for a stay and called for increased clarity in judicial explanations. He warned that without clearer guidance from the superior courts as to the principles which would justify a stay, this area of law will continue to be riddled with inconsistencies.[6] The situation in the UK is equally opaque. In *Warren v Attorney General of Jersey* the Privy Council held that rigid classifications as to the circumstances in which a stay might be ordered are 'undesirable'.[7] In Hong Kong, the Court of Appeal has recently softened its earlier hardline view that when investigating authorities engage in a deliberate breach of legal professional privilege, a stay is generally warranted.[8]

Section 1 of this chapter considers the jurisprudence of stay proceedings in Hong Kong. In allowing a stay in *HKSAR v Wong Hung Ki*, the Court of Appeal observed that any comparison of cases where stays have succeeded or failed in Hong Kong has limited value.[9] Quoting the House of Lords in *R v Latif*,[10] Stock VP ruled that an 'infinite variety of cases' can arise in which, even though a fair trial is possible, it would be 'contrary to the public interest in the integrity of the criminal justice system that a trial should take place' and 'general guidance as to how the discretion should be exercised in particular circumstances will not be useful'.[11] He observed that a judge must 'weigh in the balance the public interest in ensuring that those that are charged with grave crimes should be tried and the competing public interest in not conveying the impression that the court will adopt the approach that the end justifies any means'.[12] In *HKSAR v Wong Hung Ki*,[13] a deliberate violation by investigating officers of a suspect's right to legal professional privilege was judged sufficient to justify a stay. In the subsequent case of *HKSAR v Ng Chun To Raymond*, however, Stock VP, giving judgment for the court, appeared to soften his earlier view that official misconduct in the bringing of a prosecution should attract a stay, insisting that 'the discretion to stay is not a disciplinary jurisdiction'.[14]

Section 2 considers three recent decisions in Australia and the UK where the response of the appellate courts to serious misconduct differed widely. All three judgments demonstrate how inarticulate the courts have been in identifying what the test for a stay should be

---

[3] See eg *Mokbel v DPP (Victoria)* (2008) 202 A Crim R 319, 334.
[4] See eg *HKSAR v Lee Ming Tee* (2001) 4 HKCFAR 133, 183.
[5] *Moti v R* (2011) 245 CLR 456.
[6] Ibid [89].
[7] *Warren v Attorney General of Jersey* [2012] 1 AC 22, [26].
[8] *HKSAR v Ng Chun To Raymond* [2013] 5 HKC 390, [95].
[9] [2011] 1 HKLRD 183, 212, [86].
[10] [1996] 1 WLR 104, 113.
[11] [2011] 1 HKLRD 183, 212, [86].
[12] Ibid.
[13] Ibid [89].
[14] *HKSAR v Ng Chun To Raymond* [2013] 5 HKC 390, [86].

and when an application for a stay should succeed. They highlight the real need for authoritative guidance in this critically important application of judicial discretion.

In Section 3 consideration is given to the boundaries that have been drawn by the appellate courts on their powers to order a stay for an affront to justice. These limitations have now severely curtailed the exercise of the discretion in the UK and Hong Kong. There are problems, however, in all three jurisdictions which arise from the reluctance of the appellate courts to define with any clarity what the test for ordering a stay is, and what it requires of the courts.

In conclusion, the chapter calls for the appeal courts to articulate a clear test which would bring to an end the uncertainty that currently attaches to applications for stays in all three jurisdictions.

1. Hong Kong

The prosecution of Hong Kong's longest running and most expensive case to date, *HKSAR v Lee Ming Tee*,[15] commenced three times, and twice a permanent stay was ordered. On both occasions the Court of Final Appeal (HKCFA) unanimously reversed the stay. The case began in 1992 when, on the basis of complaints about share placements and other intelligence, the Chairman of the Hong Kong Securities and Futures Commission (SFC) wrote to the Financial Secretary and recommended an investigation into the Allied Group of companies, a group with over 100 subsidiaries.[16] A billionaire by the name of Lee Ming Tee was its chairman and Ronald Tse a director and financial controller. A steering group was set up to monitor an investigation of the companies. Representatives of the Financial Secretary, the SFC and the Attorney General's Chambers sat on the committee. It was recognised at the outset that criminal investigation of the company's officers may be necessary and the police were kept informed. An inspector was formally appointed under Hong Kong's Companies Ordinance (hereafter 'the Ordinance').[17] Part of his role was to obtain evidence in a form admissible in criminal or civil proceedings in respect of any matter which may constitute fraud or other offence against Hong Kong law that is identified in the course of the investigation'.[18] He had the power to compulsorily obtain documents and information, and examine officers of the companies, who were legally bound to answer his questions. The Ordinance provided, however, that if persons under examination invoked their privilege against self-incrimination then the answers they gave could not be used as evidence against them in subsequent criminal proceedings. After becoming a subject of inquiry, Ronald Tse brought judicial review proceedings challenging the compulsion powers of the inspector for violation of his rights and freedoms under the Hong Kong Bill of Rights. He lost.[19]

---

[15] *HKSAR v Lee Ming Tee & Securities and Futures Commission (Third Party)* (2003) 6 HKCFAR 336.

[16] For a full history see Simon NM Young, 'Defending White Collar Crime in Hong Kong: A Case Study of the *Lee Ming Tee* case' (2006) 36 *Hong Kong Law Journal* 35.

[17] Pursuant to s 143 of the Companies Ordinance (Cap 32).

[18] *HKSAR v Lee Ming Tee* (2001) 4 HKCFAR 133, 145.

[19] *R v Allen, ex parte Ronald Tse Chu-fai* (1992) 2 HKPLR 266.

Throughout 1992 and early 1993, Allied Group company documents were obtained and scrutinised. Company officers were interviewed. The inspector advised the steering group that there might be evidence of fraud. The police were alerted and given access to documents and interview transcripts, including written answers to questions put by the inspector in correspondence. They were also permitted to attend meetings of the steering group. Substantial sums having been spent by government to carry out the inspection (eventually reaching HK\$46 million), there was pressure within the steering committee to publish the fruit of their labour. The Attorney General's Chambers warned that publication of the inspector's report might compromise a future trial. Legal advice was considered. The report was eventually finalised in August 1993 and over the following month a series of police raids was conducted on the offices of Allied Group companies. On the last day of the raids, a press conference was held by the Financial Secretary where an abridged version of the report was released to the public. The police raids, the press conference and the report received widespread media coverage. An extensive task force was set up by the police to prepare a case against Lee and Tse and both were subsequently committed for trial, in 1999, on charges of conspiracy to defraud and publishing a false statement of account.

Prior to the first trial in 2000, the defendants sought a permanent stay of the proceedings against them.[20] Pang J ordered a stay on the basis that the Financial Secretary and the inspector had abused their statutory powers and violated the defendants' rights by handing over the materials they had revealed to the police. They had further (Pang J held) engaged in official misconduct by putting forward a misleading affidavit and correspondence in connection with judicial review proceedings commenced by the defendants in 1993 for perceived bias and lack of independence in the inspection process.[21] Pang J considered that the conduct of the inspector and members of the steering committee constituted an affront to the criminal justice system. The pre-trial publicity of the case against the defendants at the press conference, the release of the report and the attendant publicity which had attached to the series of raids on the Allied Group offices in 1993 had also rendered a fair trial impossible. However, the HKCFA took a different view.[22]

In determining the appeal, Ribeiro PJ of the HKCFA ruled that, under Article 63 of the Hong Kong Basic Law, the decision whether or not to bring a prosecution fell entirely with the Secretary for Justice. Generally, where a prosecution is brought, the court has a duty to try the case. However, in exceptional cases, the court also has the unquestionable power to stay proceedings brought by the Secretary for Justice, where such a course is justified. That jurisdiction rests on the court's inherent power to prevent abuse of its own processes.[23] Referring to *Connelly v DPP*,[24] Ribeiro PJ observed that the executive cannot be left as sole arbiter of what is fair. However, in the case before them, the HKCFA found that the official misconduct complained of in the judicial review fell 'very far short of an abuse of process which amounts to an affront to the public conscience and requires the criminal proceedings to be stayed'.[25] In regard to the action of the Inspector and Financial Secretary in handing

---

[20] *HKSAR v Lee Ming Tee* [2000] HKEC 854.
[21] See *R v Attorney General, ex parte Allied Group Ltd* (1993) 3 HKPLR 386.
[22] *HKSAR v Lee Ming Tee* (2001) 4 HKCFAR 133.
[23] Ibid 148.
[24] *Connelly v DPP* [1964] AC 1254.
[25] *HKSAR v Lee Ming Tee* (2001) 4 HKCFAR 133, 185.

over compulsorily obtained materials to the police, the Court found that the sharing of information was arguably permissible under the Companies Ordinance. Further, while the pre-trial publicity had made it difficult for Lee and Tse to receive a fair trial, it had not been made impossible and the lapse of six years between the publication of the report and the trial reduced some of the potential prejudice. The case was remitted to the High Court for trial.

After the second trial in the Court of First Instance was abandoned for incurable prejudice, an application for a stay was again made,[26] this time for prosecutorial breach of the common law duties of disclosure. In the course of presenting the prosecution's case at the second trial a forensic accountant named Li was called as an expert witness. He gave evidence of examining the share transactions of the Allied Group in preparation for the trial. Li's evidence went largely unchallenged, but on the last day of trial the defence learned that the witness had himself held a non-executive position on the board of directors of a company suspected of engaging in the same kind of misconduct alleged against the defendants (illicit share-trading). His entire board had been forced to resign in response to the allegations against them. The defence contended that non-disclosure of these matters undermined the credit of the witness to such an extent that recalling him would not assist the jury. They argued that inadequate disclosure had resulted in a fatally flawed trial and applied for the jury to be discharged. The application was granted. The defence then discovered that other relevant matters relating to Li had also been withheld. He was found to have been investigated over a two-year period by the SFC for illicit placement of shares in another company. This matter had not even been disclosed to the prosecution authorities. Shortly before Li gave evidence for the prosecution, the SFC closed the case against him for insufficient evidence. A second stay of proceedings against Lee and Tse was granted. Ruling on the application, Seagrott J considered that the investigation was relevant to the defence case and should have been disclosed by the witness Li and the SFC. He ruled that in closing the case against Li the SFC had consciously, and strategically, removed an impediment to his giving evidence as a prosecution expert.[27]

This second stay, too, was subsequently reversed by the HKCFA. The Court found that while the SFC investigation should have been disclosed to the prosecution (and in turn, to the defence), absent a finding of misconduct by the SFC a permanent stay of proceedings was not warranted.[28] The prosecution could not be blamed for breaching its duty of disclosure as prosecutors were equally in the dark about the investigation into Li. The case was, yet again, remitted for trial, and the defendants eventually pleaded guilty to a much reduced charge sheet.

Another high-profile Hong Kong case in which a complaint of prosecutorial misconduct formed the basis of a stay application was *HKSAR v Kissel (Stay: Media)*.[29] In *Kissel*, the Hong Kong Court of First Instance was asked to consider an application for a permanent stay of the charge of murder brought against Mrs Kissel, dubbed by the media 'the milkshake murderer'. Kissel, an expatriate banker's wife, had been convicted of drugging

---

[26] *HKSAR v Lee Ming Tee* [2002] HKEC 1554.

[27] Ibid [147]. Although Li was not an accomplice, there were clearly suggestions of similar conflicts of interest to those addressed by M Jackson in Chapter 8 of this volume.

[28] *HKSAR v Lee Ming Tee & Securities and Futures Commission (Third Party)* (2003) 6 HKCFAR 336, 396.

[29] [2011] 3 HKLRD 1.

her husband and then bludgeoning him to death in their luxury Hong Kong home. She had rolled his body in a carpet, put it behind the sofa and two days later asked the building's caretakers to stow it in a downstairs store room. The Hong Kong press and public were riveted. Kissel was eventually convicted but successfully appealed on the basis of mistakes made by the prosecutor and judge at trial. Her conviction having been quashed, Kissel sought a stay of proceedings when her case was listed for re-trial. The application was made on several grounds, including that a fair trial could not be achieved due to adverse pre-trial publicity relating to inadmissible material and prejudicial evidence, which was wrongly admitted at the first trial. In ruling on the application, the court considered it extremely rare for pre-trial publicity to result in a permanent stay of proceedings. The court found that in most cases where special care is taken to counteract the effects of possibly prejudicial publicity, a properly directed jury can be trusted to deliver its verdict on a fair basis.[30] In exceptional cases, however, the quality and extent of the prejudice may render a fair trial impossible, no matter how careful and prudent the trial judge in his conduct of proceedings and directions to the jury.[31] The court ruled that the facts of the *Kissel* case were not exceptional enough to warrant a stay.

It was also argued in support of the stay application that, even if a fair trial were possible, it would be an affront to the public conscience to permit a prosecution to proceed as the question of a re-trial had only arisen because of the prosecutorial misconduct at the first trial. The conduct complained of involved improper cross-examination of the defendant and improper comments to the jury. At the first trial, Kissel claimed she had experienced ongoing memory loss since the date of the offence and could not remember killing her husband. She was cross-examined as to why she had not mentioned she was suffering from memory loss at her bail applications. Specifically, she was challenged as to why others who had seen her at the time of the offence, both professionally and personally, had not raised the alarm as to the possibility she was suffering from amnesia. Over counsel's objections, the judge required Kissel to speculate on the views taken by others, who were not called as witnesses. Unsurprisingly, her explanations evidently failed to impress the jury.

Another argument advanced in support of a stay was that the prosecution had wrongly relied at trial on the hearsay assertions of two witnesses: the victim's close friend Byrna O'Shea and one Frank Shea, a private detective whom the victim had hired to spy on his wife. O'Shea gave evidence that in the weeks before his death the victim had told her he thought his wife may be trying to kill him. Shea gave evidence that the victim suspected that his wife was poisoning his whisky. In the prosecution's closing speech these statements were referred to as 'prophetic'. Further, the prosecutor invited the jury to treat the hearsay statements as evidence that Kissel had been poisoning her husband. He submitted that there was a causal link between the earlier poisoning attempts and the victim's death; Mr Kissel's guilt over suspecting his wife of treachery stopping him from acting quickly enough to save himself. In the judgment overturning the first conviction the Court of Final Appeal ruled the submissions of the prosecutor 'grossly prejudicial and quite improper'.[32]

In determining the application for a stay, Macrae J found that—even absent bad faith—a prosecutor's breach of professional duty might be such as to make it wrong for proceedings

---

[30] A similar decision was reached by the High Court of Australia in *Dupas v R* (2010) 241 CLR 237.
[31] *HKSAR v Kissel (Stay: Media)* [2011] 3 HKLRD 1, 10.
[32] *Kissel v HKSAR* (2010) 13 HKCFAR 27, [130].

against a defendant to continue.[33] However, in this case, none of the prosecutorial misconduct at the original trial resulting in the dissemination of inadmissible evidence and improper comment in the press came anywhere near engaging the power to halt the prosecution. Weighing the public interest in bringing serious crimes to trial and consideration of policy and justice, there was no abuse of process which would justify a stay. Kissel was convicted of murder on her re-trial. A challenge to that conviction recently failed.[34]

Where an application for a stay is founded on an allegation of entrapment or abduction, recent UK authority has suggested that the application is likely to succeed.[35] While Hong Kong has no abduction cases to examine, some guidance is given in the Court of Appeal's decision in *HKSAR v Wong Kwok Hung*[36] as to what would be required before a stay for entrapment should be ordered. In that case the defendant had been convicted of soliciting and accepting bribes. As chairman of the incorporated owners of a housing estate he asked for a substantial payment in return for his support for a private bus company's application to renew its licence to provide a bus service to residents of the building. The Independent Commission Against Corruption (ICAC) used the bus operator to investigate the defendant further. He was asked to contact the defendant on numerous occasions to try to get him to solicit a bribe. Relying on the decision in *Looseley*,[37] McMahon J, giving judgment for the Court of Appeal, ruled that in determining whether the circumstances were exceptional enough to warrant a stay, a judge should consider whether the police officer 'did no more than provide the defendant with an unexceptional opportunity to commit the offence. If that is so, then it may well be that no entrapment had taken place.'[38] Further, in situations where the type of criminal activity concerned was normally carried out in secrecy and was consequently difficult to detect, more pro-active policing strategies were both necessary and excusable.[39] A question of proportionality may also arise. The judge should consider the nature and seriousness of the suspected crime and whether the investigating officers' actions went too far given the nature of the offence. Where the actions of the officers were found to have gone beyond what was reasonable or necessary, then the question of whether they amounted to an affront to the public conscience would still need to be considered before a stay could be granted.[40] In this case, the actions of the ICAC had not crossed the threshold into disproportionality.

Such sentiments were echoed in a subsequent Court of Appeal decision, *HKSAR v Fung Hin Wah*.[41] In that case the defendant was a high-ranking police officer suspected of providing protection to criminals involved in vice clubs. He was exposed by undercover officers of the ICAC posing as night club operators. They met with the defendant, ostensibly

[33] *HKSAR v Kissel (Stay: Media)* [2011] 3 HKLRD 1, 25.
[34] *HKSAR v Kissel* [2014] HKEC 779.
[35] *Warren v Attorney General of Jersey* [2012] 1 AC 22 [26]. And see *R v Looseley* [2001] 1 WLR 2060, [2001] UKHL 53, [42], where Lord Hoffmann stated: 'the entrapped defendant is not ordinarily complaining that the admission of certain evidence would prejudice the fairness of his trial. He is saying that, whatever the evidence, he should not be tried at all. The appropriate remedy, if any, is therefore not the exclusion of evidence but a stay of the proceedings.'
[36] [2007] 2 HKLRD 621.
[37] [2001] 1 WLR 2060, [2001] UKHL 53.
[38] [2007] 2 HKLRD 621, 628.
[39] Ibid 631.
[40] Ibid 638.
[41] [2012] 1 HKLRD 374.

seeking advice on how to avoid attracting police attention to unlawful activities in their club. The defendant was covertly recorded offering advice about police raids, how to facilitate a liquor licensing application and how to handle the supply of dangerous drugs. He was charged with misconduct in public office. At his trial, a stay application was made on the basis that the undercover officers had entrapped him into committing the crime. The court ruled that the accused took the initiative to commit the offence, whilst the ICAC officers had done no more than provide the opportunity for him to do so. The court reiterated that the use of undercover operations is an essential weapon in the armoury of the law in uncovering serious crime, justifying resort to proactive policing.[42]

In a case which did cross Hong Kong law's threshold requiring a stay, *HKSAR v Wong Hung Ki*,[43] the appellants were charged with conspiracy to offer an advantage to public servants and falsifying accounts. The District Court refused their applications for a permanent stay of proceedings after it was discovered that the ICAC had audio-recorded a lunch meeting at a public restaurant where one of the defendants obtained legal advice from his lawyers. The appellants successfully appealed against their convictions and the Court of Appeal ordered a permanent stay of proceedings on the basis that the ICAC had deliberately infringed legal professional privilege by recording and listening to a privileged conversation (without believing that the meeting constituted an attempt to pervert the course of justice).[44] The Court declared this an abuse of process of such gravity that it threatened the rule of law in Hong Kong.[45] In giving the Court of Appeal's judgment granting the stay, Stock VP stated:

> We are concerned in this case with serious offences, albeit not as serious as the murder cases represented by *R v Grant* … We are concerned also with a principle which lies at the heart of the rule of law. The cases are replete with expressions about the fundamental character of legal professional privilege; that the honouring of it in practice is vital to the operation of the adversarial system; that suspects, whether in fact guilty or not, must have recourse to confidential legal advice; that deliberate eavesdropping upon such privileged communications is without question unlawful and viewed by the courts with such disapprobation that they will in general divorce themselves from proceedings tainted by this category of illegality … When one considers the public conscience in this context, there is necessarily implicit the notion of a public that is sufficiently informed to appreciate the manner in which a deliberate infringement of legal professional privilege undermines the rule of law and why *principle is more important than the individual case.*[46]

It should be noted that in the case of *Warren v Attorney General for Jersey*[47] (discussed below) the Judicial Committee of the Privy Council has since disavowed the Court of Appeal's decision in *R v Grant*.[48] Whilst the deliberate invasion of a person's legal professional privilege is a serious affront to the integrity of the justice system and may often lead

---

[42] Ibid 390.

[43] [2011] 1 HKLRD 183.

[44] Which would have thus fallen within the so-called crime/fraud exception to legal professional privilege established in *R v Cox and Railton* (1884) 14 QBD 153.

[45] [2011] 1 HKLRD 183, 215.

[46] Ibid 212 (emphasis added).

[47] *Warren v Attorney General of Jersey* [2012] 1 AC 22.

[48] [2005] 3 WLR 437.

to a stay, the Privy Council found it will not always do so. The Board emphasised that the particular circumstances of each case must always be taken into account.[49]

In light of *Warren*,[50] the Hong Kong Court of Appeal has softened its view on whether gross misconduct by those charged with investigating an offence, in and of itself, warrants a stay. In *HKSAR v Ng Chun To Raymond*,[51] the appellants sought to overturn their convictions for conspiracy to defraud, and other crimes, involving the trading of derivatives. The offending conduct had involved a highly sophisticated fraud on the investing public which had generated the defendants over HK\$140 million. The appellants claimed their trial had been an abuse of process as officers from the ICAC, involved with investigation of the case, had 'coached' the main prosecution witness, Cheung. Cheung had received immunity from prosecution in exchange for his agreement to give evidence against the appellants, but on the day he was due to testify, he refused to do so. The trial proceeded without his evidence and the appellants were convicted anyway. His immunity having been revoked, Cheung was prosecuted for his part in the frauds. Seeking a stay of his prosecution, Cheung revealed that he had received extensive coaching on his evidence from ICAC officers before the appellants' trial. The officers involved met with Cheung on 54 occasions for coaching purposes. They told him that if asked about the meetings in the witness box, he should say they did not talk about his evidence but discussed general matters only. In fact, the officers spent hours rehearsing Cheung's evidence and advising him how to answer questions put to him at court most convincingly. ICAC officers told Cheung what his accomplices had said in their statements and asked him to add corroborating facts when he testified. They advised him how to avoid revealing to the court an unrecorded deal he had made with them as to non-confiscation of his assets. They told him to lie to the court about having approached his accomplices to assist the ICAC. They explained that he would be ordered by the court not to discuss his evidence with them, once he started testifying, and purchased phone cards to allow him to keep in touch with them without detection.

The stay application failed, but the officers involved in the coaching were convicted of conspiracy to pervert the course of justice and misconduct in public office.[52] The appellants in *Ng Chun To Raymond*[53] claimed they were denied a fair trial as, had they known about the coaching of Cheung, they would have cross-examined other immunised witnesses who did testify as to whether they, too, had been similarly coached. They further claimed that, but for the impropriety of the ICAC officers, the case against them might never have been brought and, had the trial judge known of the officers' misconduct at their trial, he would have granted them a stay.

The Court of Appeal quashed the convictions on the basis that non-disclosure of the coaching meetings had precluded a fair trial, but was not persuaded that the trial judge would have stayed the trial had he been aware of the ICAC officers' misconduct. Stock VP found that while the officers involved in the abuse had behaved unlawfully, and outrageously so,[54] a court should not utilise its discretion to stay a case for disciplinary purposes.[55]

[49] *Warren v Attorney General of Jersey* [2012] 1 AC 22, [36].
[50] Ibid.
[51] [2013] 5 HKC 390.
[52] *HKSAR v Cho Wing Nin* [2014] HKEC 330.
[53] *HKSAR v Ng Chun To Raymond* [2013] 5 HKC 390.
[54] Ibid [59].
[55] Ibid [86].

Quoting Lord Dyson in *Warren*, the court acknowledged that 'it may not always be easy to distinguish between (impermissibly) granting a stay "in order to express the court's disapproval of official conduct pour encourager les autres" and (permissibly) granting a stay because it offends the court's sense of justice and propriety'.[56] The court found that before a stay can be legitimately granted, consideration needs to be given not only to the misconduct concerned but also the other relevant factors in the case. These included 'the gravity of the offence with which the accused is charged, the availability of a sanction against the miscreant, and whether the misconduct was perpetrated in bad faith or in circumstances of urgency'.[57]

The stance taken by the Court of Appeal in *Wong Hung Ki*,[58] that official misconduct in the bringing of a prosecution should attract a stay, appears to have softened. The Court in *Ng* criticised passages from the earlier judgment suggesting that the ICAC's cavalier approach to privileged communications had provided the basis for the stay.[59] Stock VP explained that those passages were 'likely to be read as suggesting that a deliberate snub to the rule of law may give rise to such a sense of outrage as *of itself* to warrant a stay of proceedings'; whereas '[t]he suggestion that in general a deliberate violation of a suspected person's right to legal professional privilege of itself renders the associated prosecution an abuse is a suggestion which goes too far'.[60] Having regard to all the circumstances of the case, the Court in *Ng Chun To Raymond* refused to order a stay of proceedings. The interests of justice required a trial, in spite of the ICAC officers' misconduct.[61]

The Hong Kong jurisprudence reviewed in this section indicates Hong Kong courts' extreme reluctance to allow stay applications for official impropriety in criminal proceedings. These decisions also demonstrate the difficulty in predicting what the courts will do when faced with an application for a stay.

2. Comparative Jurisprudence: Recent Australian and UK Cases

In the extraordinary case of *Moti*,[62] the High Court of Australia stayed the prosecution of the former Attorney General of the Solomon Islands, an Australian lawyer, for child sex offences. The stay was granted on the basis that Moti had been wrongfully extradited by the Solomon Islander authorities with the connivance of the Australian government, which had provided the necessary travel documentation for Moti and his guards to land in Australia, knowing that those documents would be used to facilitate an unlawful deportation. At the time of his removal from the Islands' capital city, Honiara, Moti had seven days left

---

[56] *Warren v Attorney General of Jersey* [2012] 1 AC 22, [37] (quoting Lord Lowry in *R v Horseferry Road Magistrates Court, Ex parte Bennett* [1994] 1 AC 42, 75).
[57] *HKSAR v Ng Chun To Raymond* [2013] 5 HKC 390, [89].
[58] [2011] 1 HKLRD 183.
[59] Ibid [94].
[60] *HKSAR v Ng Chun To Raymond* [2013] 5 HKC 390, [95].
[61] Ibid [116].
[62] *Moti v R* (2011) 245 CLR 456.

to appeal against his deportation to Australia. The court found that the Australian Acting High Commissioner in Honiara had correctly objected that to deport Moti before the expiration of the appeal period would be unlawful. Unfortunately, her advice was ignored.

Six of the seven High Court Justices sitting on the case ruled in favour of a permanent stay of the charges. They relied on the actions of Australian officials to justify the stay. Their conclusion that the deportation of Moti from the Solomon Islands was unlawful was a necessary but not, of itself, sufficient basis to constitute an abuse of process. In determining an abuse of process application the Court held that three propositions must be addressed.[63]

First, the trial of an indictable offence must generally be conducted in the presence of the accused.[64] The accused was present in Australia to answer the indictment because the Solomon Island officials had removed him in contravention of their own legislation. Secondly, if Australia seeks the extradition of a person from another country for the purpose of standing trial in Australia, for crimes against Australian law, the principles of double criminality and speciality would apply.[65] In this case, however, these protections were circumvented, as Moti was not formally extradited. Thirdly, as was identified in *Williams v Spautz*,[66] 'the public interest in the administration of justice requires that the court protect its ability to function as a court of law by ensuring its processes are used fairly by State and citizens alike'.[67] Further, 'unless the court protects its ability so to function in that way, its failure will lead to an erosion of public confidence, by reason of concern that the court's processes may lend themselves to oppression and injustice'.[68] Public confidence, in this context, was held to refer to the trust reposed constitutionally in the courts to protect the integrity and fairness of their processes.[69] The majority ruled that the actions of the Australian officials in the *Moti* case required the court to order a stay.

In a strong dissenting judgment, Heydon J criticised the abuse of process authorities in the UK and Australia for their inability to articulate clear rules as to when, or even why, a stay should be granted. He questioned the widespread assumption of the Australian and UK authorities that where an accused person is removed from one country and brought into another for trial, even though the removal does not create the risk of an unfair trial and the court has jurisdiction to try the case, there is a discretionary power, or perhaps even a duty, for the court to stay the prosecution in certain circumstances. As the correctness of the cases supporting what he called 'the assumed rule' was not challenged by the Commonwealth Director of Public Prosecutions in the *Moti* appeal, Heydon J did not pursue this matter in his judgment. However, he proceeded to launch a scathing attack on the inability of the authorities to articulate just what the 'assumed rule' was and what it required of the

---

[63] Ibid [53].

[64] *Lipohar v R* (1999) 200 CLR 485, [69].

[65] See eg *Truong v R* (2004) 223 CLR 122. The principle of double criminality requires that no person may be extradited whose deed is not a crime according to the criminal law of the State which is asked to extradite, as well as the State which demands extradition. The principle of speciality arises under s 42 of Australia's Extradition Act 1988 (Cth) and requires that unless he has first had the opportunity to leave Australia, a person may be tried only for the specific conduct in respect of which he was surrendered.

[66] (1992) 174 CLR 509.

[67] Ibid 520.

[68] Ibid.

[69] *Moti v R* (2011) 245 CLR 456, [57].

courts. Despite the decision of the majority, his final, dissenting, conclusion was that the assumed rule does not exist.[70]

In reaching this decision, Heydon J considered first those authorities which had tried to articulate the assumed rule. In *Levigne v Director of Custodial Services*, a decision of the New South Wales Court of Appeal, Kirby P lent support to the view that the law mandated 'the entitlement of the courts to protect the integrity of their own process and to uphold that integrity and the perception of it in the eyes of the parties, of the community and of the judges themselves'.[71] However, as Heydon J noted, Kirby P did not pinpoint what the test actually was. In the same case, McHugh J underscored the importance of balancing the public interest in preventing unlawful conduct against the public interest in having the charge determined. He said that 'conduct which might be regarded as constituting an abuse of process in respect of a comparatively minor charge may not have the same character in respect of a serious matter'.[72]

In the House of Lords, the majority speeches in *R v Horseferry Road Magistrates Court, ex parte Bennett*[73] concurred in endorsing the existence of a judicial power for the courts to refuse to try an accused person brought within their jurisdiction in deliberate abuse of extradition procedures. However, as Heydon J observed, prior to the decision in *Moti*, the assumed rule had only been considered by the High Court of Australia once before, in *Truong*.[74] In giving their judgments in that case, Gummow and Callinan JJ used the assumed rule as authority for the requirement that an appellant must show deliberate disregard of the extradition laws by the Australian authorities or knowing misconduct before the court can order a stay for abuse of process. Kirby J formulated a somewhat wider proposition, to bring within the scope of the power to stay 'serious cases where, whatever the initial motivation or purpose of the offending party, and whether deliberate, reckless or seriously negligent, the result is one which the courts, exercising the judicial power, cannot tolerate or be part of'.[75]

Heydon J also noted the Full Court of the Federal Court of Australia's comment in *Bou-Simon v Commonwealth Attorney General*[76] that the formulations of the test 'all differ somewhat'.[77] Judicial articulations of the guiding principle ranged from a requirement of 'deliberate abuse'[78] to the need for 'something so gravely wrong as to make it unconscionable that a trial should go forward, such as some fundamental disregard for basic human rights or some gross neglect of the elementary principles of fairness'.[79] According to *Truong*, even well motivated but 'seriously negligent' conduct might suffice.[80] In light of his review

---

[70] Ibid [86].
[71] (1987) 9 NSWLR 546, 557.
[72] Ibid 565.
[73] [1994] 1 AC 42.
[74] *Truong v R* (2004) 223 CLR 122.
[75] Ibid [135].
[76] (2000) 96 FCR 325.
[77] Ibid [34].
[78] *R v Martin* [1998] AC 917, 927 (Lord Lloyd of Berwick).
[79] Ibid 946–47 (Lord Clyde).
[80] (2004) 223 CLR122, [135].

of the authorities, Heydon J questioned the notably indeterminate language used in the leading cases on abuse of process:

> There are references to 'acts which offend the court's conscience', to an act which is 'an affront to public conscience', to what 'offends the court's sense of justice and propriety' and to acts which 'by providing a morally unacceptable foundation for the exercise of jurisdiction over the suspect taint the proposed trial'. There are references to 'basic human rights'. There are references to 'unworthy conduct'. It has been said that the 'issues … are basic to the whole concept of freedom in society'. There are references to 'the dignity and integrity of the judicial system' and to the need for the prosecution 'to come to court with clean hands'. There are references to 'the public interest in the integrity of the criminal justice system'. These exercises in rhetoric do not assist in defining the relevant test.[81]

Ultimately it was this inability in the judgments to define the 'assumed test' that led Heydon J to doubt its very existence.[82]

Even assuming that the test for granting a stay could be identified, Heydon J was perplexed by the character of the jurisdiction. If absolute and non-discretionary, he questioned whether any illegality would suffice to attract it, however trivial. If so, it was undesirable because of its extremity. If, however, its scope was narrower, as the cases suggested, the indeterminacy of the rule would create uncertainty and difficulties in predicting its application.[83] As Heydon J observed:

> The proposition that in some ill defined circumstances an indeterminate duty may apply, or a discretion may be exercised or a balancing exercise performed, in an unpredictable way, to stay a prosecution which will [otherwise] operate fairly is one which requires weighty justifications … A contravention of the laws of a foreign state which results in the bringing of an accused person before the courts of another state is an evil thing. To stay the trial, however, does not right that evil. It creates a second evil … The criminal is to go free because the official has blundered.[84]

Heydon J went on to question the reliance of the courts on public confidence as a reason to entertain the assumed rule. Allegations that particular rules promote or damage public confidence are common,[85] however, the expression has tended to become an automatic reflex, to be used in almost every context in which an attempt is made to enlist community sentiment as rhetorical reinforcement for the argument.[86] Heydon J observed:

> The expression is beginning to lack meaning. It usually postpones or evades problems. It does not face them or solve them. At least that is so in this particular field … Might it not be better for the courts not to keep looking over their shoulders by worrying about their reputation or any perceived level of confidence in them? Should they not simply concentrate on doing their jobs diligently, carefully, honestly and independently, whatever the public or the community think?[87]

Heydon J took the view that the misconduct of the Australian authorities in Moti's case would be better dealt with through collateral disciplinary sanctions. He found this was

---

[81] *Moti v R* (2011) 245 CLR 456, [86] (citations omitted).
[82] Ibid.
[83] Ibid [89].
[84] Ibid [90]–[91].
[85] Ibid [100].
[86] Ibid [101].
[87] Ibid.

much more likely to deter similar conduct in the future than a stay, which has no direct impact on the officials responsible. He argued that, while allowing the trial to proceed may risk bringing the administration of justice into disrepute, immunising the accused by staying the proceedings against him defeated justice entirely. The other six Justices comprising the majority of the High Court of Australia, however, thought otherwise.

In stark contrast to the decision in *Moti*, two subsequent UK cases demonstrate that even where the police have engaged in really serious misconduct, their actions may be insufficient to stay a prosecution. This is so, even where the police misconduct produced the only evidence to support the charge. In the first case, *Warren v The Attorney General of Jersey*,[88] the police were investigating a large-scale conspiracy to import cannabis into Jersey, in part by hire car, driven through Holland, Belgium and France. They requested permission from the state authorities in each country to put tracking and audio devices on the vehicle carrying the drugs. Despite the Dutch and French refusing to grant permission to install an audio device, the police went ahead and installed it anyway. The evidence provided by the audio device was instrumental in allowing the case against Warren to be brought and prosecuted successfully. The trial judge refused to order a stay of proceedings based on serious prosecutorial misconduct and both the Jersey Court of Appeal and the Judicial Committee of the Privy Council rejected appeals against that refusal.

The Privy Council ruled that, while it was well established that the court would grant a stay where it concluded that in all the circumstances it would offend the court's sense of justice and propriety to try the accused, the court was required to strike a balance between the public interest in ensuring those accused of serious crime were tried and the principle that executive misconduct must not bring the criminal justice system into disrepute. There was considerable weight in favour of a stay. The police had misled the authorities of Jersey and two foreign states, and the prosecution was only made possible because the police had procured the vital evidence unlawfully. However, the Board took the view that it was not the general function of criminal courts to discipline the police. Important factors identified by the Board as weighing against a stay included the fact that the offence charged was very serious, Warren was a professional drug dealer and had only recently been released from prison for a similar offence, the police had relied on legal advice from the Senior Crown Advocate on the conduct of the operation, no attempt had been made to mislead the court and there was a real urgency to act before the crime was concluded.[89]

The refusal to order the stay in this case is perhaps surprising, given the very deliberate action taken by the police to act outside the law. Of particular concern, however, is the Board's characterisation of the judge's ruling as not 'perverse or one which no reasonable judge could have reached'.[90] In other words, there must be irrationality in a decision to refuse a stay or mistake as to the relevant facts or law, before an appeal court should intervene. As has been noted by Patrick O'Connor, this restrictive approach to abuse of process cases adopted in *Warren*[91] (and repeated in the second case, *R v Maxwell*,[92] discussed below)

---

[88] *Warren v Attorney General of Jersey* [2012] 1 AC 22.
[89] Ibid 38.
[90] Ibid [51].
[91] Ibid.
[92] [2011] 1 WLR 1837, [2010] UKSC 48.

is a new development. In both *Latif*[93] and *Looseley*,[94] the House of Lords did not confine its review to mistake or irrationality but considered the merits of the earlier decisions. The limitation sits uncomfortably with the court's duty to protect the integrity of the criminal justice system.[95]

In *Warren*,[96] the Board provided some guidance as to when the exercise of the discretion to order a stay is warranted in the UK. Their Lordships drew on the useful summary of pertinent factors enumerated in Andrew Choo's book, *Abuse of Process and Judicial Stays of Criminal Proceedings*.[97] Such factors include the seriousness of any violation of rights, bad faith or malicious police misconduct, improper motives, whether the actions were carried out in exigent circumstances, the availability of a direct sanction against the person(s) responsible and the seriousness of the offence with which the defendant is charged.[98] The Board considered that entrapment and abduction cases should generally attract a stay.[99] Where, but for the abuse of power, the defendant would not be before the court, the court should consider this a relevant, but not necessarily determinative, factor.[100] The Board added that while all these factors might be relevant in undertaking the balancing exercise, there was no attempt to enumerate a comprehensive list. So the test remains open-ended in its application, and therefore somewhat uncertain in practice.

The non-interventionist approach to stays adopted in *Warren* also features in the subsequent UK Supreme Court decision, *R v Maxwell*.[101] In that case the Court of Appeal had ordered a retrial in a murder case where the original conviction had been quashed for serious police misconduct relating to an informant's evidence. Lord Brown found it 'hard to imagine a worse case of sustained prosecutorial dishonesty designed to secure and hold a conviction at all costs'.[102] The main prosecution witness was a professional criminal turned supergrass. Whilst awaiting sentence on his own robbery offences, he provided information to police about a robbery and murder, which led to the appellant and his brother being charged and prosecuted. After allegations were made that the police were planning to pay the witness money after his release from prison, the Criminal Cases Review Commission investigated the case. The Criminal Cases Review Commission found that the police had deliberately misled the court, the Crown Prosecution Service, and counsel by lying about a host of benefits provided to the informant and his family to secure his continuing cooperation. These included money, visits to brothels, access to heroin and protection from prosecution for further offences. On one occasion the police forged a custody record when its enforced disclosure to the defence would have revealed their actions. To stop Maxwell's application for leave to appeal succeeding, two senior officers had perjured themselves in the Court of Appeal.

---

[93] [1996] 1 WLR 104, HL.
[94] [2001] 1 WLR 2060, [2001] UKHL 53.
[95] For a fuller discussion, see P O'Connor, '"Abuse of Process" after *Warren* and *Maxwell*' [2012] *Criminal Law Review* 672.
[96] [2012] 1 AC 22.
[97] 2nd edn (Oxford, Oxford University Press, 2008) 132.
[98] *Warren v Attorney General of Jersey* [2012] 1 AC 22, [24].
[99] Ibid [26].
[100] Ibid [30].
[101] [2011] 1 WLR 1837.
[102] Ibid [83].

On the basis of these findings, the Court of Appeal had no choice but to quash Maxwell's convictions. Meanwhile, Maxwell himself had made a series of admissions of guilt after his conviction which was necessary to establish his case with the Criminal Cases Review Commission. The Crown applied for a re-trial on the basis of this strong, fresh and untainted evidence provided by Maxwell himself. The Court of Appeal ordered a re-trial and the Supreme Court dismissed an appeal against that order by a majority of three to two. The Supreme Court found that Parliament had given the Court of Appeal a broad discretion to determine when the interests of justice required a re-trial and a decision as to the exercise of that discretion should only be disturbed if it was 'plainly wrong, in the sense that it is one which no reasonable court could have made or if the court took into account immaterial factors or failed to take into account material factors'.[103]

In contrast to *Warren*,[104] this decision related to an appeal against an order for re-trial rather than a refusal to grant a stay, but again the higher court allowed the decision of the lower court to stand, on the basis that it was not irrational or mistaken in law or fact. Over a period of 11 years, the police in *Maxwell*[105] continually and deliberately undermined the integrity of the justice system they were duty bound to uphold. Without their systematic abuse of the criminal justice system, Maxwell would not have been convicted and probably would not have confessed. Despite meeting this 'but for' test, irrationality or mistake were considered the main criteria for appellate review of a decision not to order a retrial. Upholding the integrity of the process did not demand a more intensive degree of scrutiny.

3. Extrapolating Principled Guidance

It is characteristic of stay jurisprudence that the UK Supreme Court in *Maxwell* acquiesced in the Court of Appeal's decision to prioritise the public interest in prosecuting the accused, over the need to maintain the integrity of the criminal justice system, on narrow, rationality grounds. The trial judge's original refusal of a stay therefore remained undisturbed. There was scant consideration of whether the lower court's decision was right in substance.

Lord Dyson dismissed the issue, stating that while the decision to refuse a retrial for prosecutorial misconduct was analogous to cases where a retrial was refused for an affront to public justice 'the analogy should not be pressed too far. The question whether the interests of justice require a retrial is broader than the question whether it is an abuse of process to allow a prosecution to proceed (whether or not by retrial)'.[106] Later he stated:

> The Court of Appeal considered that the fact that the admissions would not have been made but for the conviction which had been obtained by prosecutorial misconduct was a factor militating against a retrial; but it was no more than one of a number of relevant factors to be taken into account in the overall decision of whether the interests of justice required a retrial.[107]

---

[103] Ibid [19].
[104] [2012] 1 AC 22.
[105] [2011] 1 WLR 1837.
[106] Ibid [21].
[107] Ibid [26].

Lord Rodger, concurring, elaborated: 'Of course, if the Court of Appeal reached a decision on retrial which no reasonable Court of Appeal could have reached, then doubtless this Court could intervene to put matters right. But that is not the position in this case.'[108]

Dissenting, Lord Brown argued that, regardless of the stage in the criminal process at which the balancing exercise arises, be that at trial, on appeal or when consideration is being given to a re-trial, the question is always the same: What do the interests of justice require?[109] Mere avoidance of irrationality would not seem to be enough. As the other dissentient, Lord Collins, recognised, 'the interests of justice demand the application of the integrity principle. In this case it means that there should be no retrial on evidence which would not have been available but for a conviction obtained (and upheld) as a result of conduct so fundamentally wrong that for the criminal process to act on that evidence would compromise its integrity'.[110]

In the recent decision of *HKSAR v Ng Chun To Raymond*,[111] the Hong Kong Court of Appeal appears to have imported from *Warren*[112] the requirement to demonstrate irrationality before a decision on a stay will be overturned. Referring to the decision of the Board, Stock VP observed that their Lordships found it impossible 'to characterise the decision to refuse a stay in this case as perverse, or one which no reasonable judge could have reached'.[113] In Australia, the High Court has placed no such limitation on its right to review the discretion to order a stay in the name of preserving procedural integrity. However, none of the appellate courts in these three jurisdictions has yet provided clear guidance to their lower courts as to what the test for a stay for an affront to public justice is, and when the discretion of the court to order a stay should be exercised. Without a clear, settled and reasonably determinate test the lower courts face uncertainty in exercising their powers and any evaluation of an order in the appeal courts is compromised.

So what should the test be, and when should it be exercised? Whether a decision to stay is just must play a central role in first instance decision making and appellate review. If appeal courts limit their intervention in a stay decision to criticise only the irrational or the clear mistake of law or fact then something vitally important is lost. The merits of the decision warrant consideration. Of course, it is never enough to justify a review for the appeal court simply to say it would have exercised the discretion differently, but there should be a better articulation of the principles guiding the exercise of the discretion in the trial courts, if the decisions made are to be properly validated.

For these reasons it is vitally important that the courts go further than simply stating that the determination of which cases should be stayed is fact sensitive and that attempting to give further guidance as to when the discretion to order a stay should be exercised is pointless. As Heydon J noted in *Moti*, the current authorities 'do not assist in defining the relevant test. Indeed they cast doubt on whether there is any relevant test'.[114] Such a situation is

---

[108]   Ibid [44].
[109]   Ibid [98].
[110]   Ibid [115].
[111]   [2013] 5 HKC 390.
[112]   [2012] 1 AC 22.
[113]   *HKSAR v Ng Chun To Raymond* [2013] 5 HKC 390, [105].
[114]   (2011) 245 CLR 456, [86].

extremely unsatisfactory. In high profile cases such as *Ng Chun To Raymond*,[115] *Maxwell*[116] and *Moti*,[117] where executive misconduct is placed under an especially intense spotlight, the public interest in the justice system working fairly is at its highest.

If we attempt to extrapolate from the leading common law cases on the courts' jurisdiction to stay proceedings for abuse of process on the grounds of an 'affront to justice', what principles or other normative criteria for decision-making can be gleaned? From the Hong Kong cases reviewed in this chapter the following six points emerge:

(1)   If the actions of the prosecution are arguably permissible under the law, then a stay should not be ordered (*Lee Ming Tee*).

(2)   An express finding of misconduct is generally required before a stay is warranted (*Lee Ming Tee and SFC*).

(3)   Absent bad faith, a prosecutor's breach of professional duty might be enough to grant a stay (*Kissel*).

(4)   Providing an opportunity for a defendant to commit a crime is not enough to warrant a stay, actual encouragement is required before a stay may be considered necessary (*Wong Kwok Hung*).

(5)   Where a serious crime is normally carried out in secrecy the police may be more proactive in their undercover operations without inviting criticism (*Fung Hin Wah*).

(6)   A sense of outrage at misuse of executive power is not in itself enough to warrant a stay. All the circumstances specific to the particular case must be balanced together. Such circumstances may include the gravity of the offence with which the accused is charged, the availability of a sanction against the miscreant, and whether the misconduct was perpetrated in bad faith or in exigent circumstances (*Ng Chun To Raymond*).

The Australian cases contribute two further points:

(7)   An unlawful deportation for prosecution does not, of itself, necessitate a stay; other relevant factors also need to be considered (*Moti*).

(8)   Where the actions of the state use the court's processes unfairly, the court should protect its integrity by ordering a stay (*Moti*).

Finally, UK and English law generate the following additional principles:

(9)   Factors relevant to the balancing exercise required to determine a stay include the seriousness of the offence, the seriousness of the misconduct of the state's agents, the urgency, emergency or necessity in which the action was taken and the availability of other sanctions for misconduct (*Warren*).

(10)   A stay will normally be ordered in cases of abduction or entrapment (*Warren*).

(11)   While a deliberate breach of legal professional privilege will often be a serious enough affront to the justice system to warrant a stay, it must be balanced against

---

[115] [2013] 5 HKC 390.
[116] [2011] 1 WLR 1837.
[117] (2011) 245 CLR 456.

other factors such as the seriousness of the offence and whether the actions caused prejudice to the accused (*Warren*, disapproving *Grant*).

(12)   Where the state's officers have previously been warned by the court, but have persisted in their misconduct, the warning will be a relevant factor in determining a stay (*Warren*).

(13)   The fact that the prosecution would not have taken place but for the state's misconduct is relevant but not decisive (*Maxwell*).

While a review of the leading cases thus enables one to identify and elucidate a list of the considerations a court might consider relevant in determining whether to order a stay, it does no more than that. It does not produce a comprehensive or integrated set of criteria for judicial decision-making. Clear guidance to the trial court as to how to balance the relevant factors is conspicuously absent from the judgments of all three jurisdictions.

Is it too much to expect the courts to provide clearer guidance? Does the infinite variety of cases in which an abuse of process might be said to have occurred necessitate that the best that can be hoped for is a list of factors which might tip the scales, depending on how they are balanced? Surely it is not too much to expect enough guidance to assist the trial courts to determine how heavily they should weigh a breach of legal professional privilege against the seriousness of the crime exposed or how serious police misconduct must be before it overrides the public interest in bringing criminal offenders to justice. The decisions of the courts, in all three jurisdictions, demonstrate that a clear articulation of the test for granting a stay is still very much in a primitive state of evolution.

Conclusion

Through detailed examination of an expanding jurisprudence, this chapter has highlighted the reluctance of appellate courts in Hong Kong, Australia and the UK to provide a clear test for when an affront to public justice has occurred which would warrant the stay of an otherwise fair trial. The absence of clear guidance is regrettable. The trial courts have a responsibility to try cases unless there are proper and cogent reasons not to do so. What those reasons are should ideally be clearly articulated by the appeal courts for the benefit of certainty in criminal adjudication.

In *Latif*, Lord Steyn made the following pertinent observations:

> If the court always refuses to stay such proceedings, the perception will be that the court condones criminal conduct and malpractice by law enforcement agencies. That would undermine public confidence in the criminal justice system and bring it into disrepute. On the other hand, if the court were always to stay proceedings in such cases, it would incur the reproach that it is failing to protect the public from serious crime.[118]

The courts must indeed have a free hand to determine when it is in the best interests of the criminal justice system to grant a permanent stay of proceedings. But the interests of the criminal justice system are wide and if integrity is to be preserved the need for clear principles guiding this most critical exercise of judicial discretion should not be overlooked.

---

[118] [1996] 1 WLR 104, 112.

11

Excluding Integrity? Revisiting Non-Consequentialist Justifications for Excluding Improperly Obtained Evidence in Criminal Trials

PETER CHAU*

Introduction

This chapter revisits non-consequentialist justifications for excluding a piece of *reliable* evidence which is improperly obtained (say, through torture or an illegal search) in criminal proceedings. By non-consequentialist justifications, I refer to principles which claim that the improperly obtained evidence should be excluded even if by doing so we do not produce any further good contingent consequences such as deterrence of misconduct by investigatory agents. The two most prominent non-consequentialist justifications offered in the literature are the protective principle and the integrity principle.

The plan for this chapter is as follows. Section 1 introduces the deterrence principle, the protective principle, and the integrity principle. Section 2 surveys some objections raised against the protective principle in the literature. I will argue that they are not decisive; at most they show that the protective principle is not the only justification for excluding improperly obtained evidence rather than that the protective principle is mistaken. Section 3 notes that the integrity principle encounters serious problems. Section 4 introduces a third non-consequentialist principle, distinct from both the protective principle and the integrity principle, which can be called the no-profit principle. I claim that the no-profit principle avoids some of the objections against the protective principle and can cover some cases where we think that improperly obtained evidence ought to be excluded but which are not covered by the protective principle. Should we then abandon the integrity principle and justify the exclusion of improperly obtained evidence in criminal trials only by the no-profit and protective principles? The concluding section suggests otherwise. Without the integrity principle, it is hard to explain an intuition, held by many, that we should be more ready to exclude improperly obtained evidence in criminal trials than in non-punitive civil proceedings.

* I am grateful to participants in the Hong Kong and Sydney conferences, in particular my respondents Paul Roberts and Amanda Whitfort, for their feedback; and to Frank Choi for written comments.

Two further points about the aim and scope of this chapter should be noted. First, I will not investigate in detail the question of what amounts to 'improper' conduct in obtaining evidence. Some official conduct, such as torture and illegal searches, are clearly improper, and these are assumed as paradigmatic cases. The question that interests me is why the impropriety of an act should bear on the admissibility, in criminal trials, of any evidence resulting from the improper conduct. Secondly, the following discussion is normative, not doctrinal. My aim is to examine what the justification for excluding improperly obtained evidence should be from the perspective of political morality, not to articulate a principle (or principles) which can account for all judicial decisions (some of which may not be legally, let alone morally, sound). References to decided cases, therefore, are merely illustrative.

1. Deterrence, Protection and Integrity

Deterrence, or the disciplinary approach, used to be the dominant justification for excluding reliable but improperly obtained evidence in criminal trials.[1] According to this principle, we should exclude improperly obtained evidence because that would deter people (usually law enforcement officers) from using improper methods to obtain evidence in future.

Two telling objections have been levelled against the deterrence principle. The first is that exclusion of evidence is not an effective means of deterrence. For a policeman, he may not have much to fear from using improper investigatory methods if all that could possibly happen is that the evidence obtained would be ruled inadmissible.[2] Second, some people would feel that it is unfair to admit such evidence against the accused, no matter what the consequences are, but the deterrence principle cannot capture this sense of unfairness.[3]

Deterrence is one of the most prominent consequentialist justifications for excluding reliable but improperly obtained evidence in criminal trials. Its perceived failure has led theorists to explore non-consequentialist justifications. Two of them are particularly prominent in the theoretical literature.

The first is the protective principle, the proponents of which include Andrew Ashworth, Jerry Norton, and William Schroeder.[4] This principle starts with the idea that an individual should not suffer loss because of a breach of his rights. It then claims that since the defendant's rights were breached in the improper evidence-gathering process, he should not suffer loss as a result of the breach. The only way to ensure that he does not suffer loss is to exclude the improperly obtained evidence.

---

[1] A Ashworth, 'Exploring the Integrity Principle in Evidence and Procedure' in P Mirfield and RJ Smith (eds), *Essays for Colin Tapper* (Oxford, Oxford University Press, 2005) 112.

[2] P Roberts and A Zuckerman, *Criminal Evidence*, 2nd edn (Oxford, Oxford University Press, 2010) 187. See also A Duff, L Farmer, S Marshall and V Tadros, *The Trial on Trial Volume 3: Towards a Normative Theory of Criminal Trial* (Oxford, Hart Publishing, 2007) 228; P Mirfield, *Silence, Confessions, and Improperly Obtained Evidence* (Oxford, Oxford University Press, 1998) 21–23.

[3] Ashworth, above n 1, 112.

[4] A Ashworth, 'Excluding Evidence as Protecting Rights' [1977] *Criminal Law Review* 723; J Norton, 'The Exclusionary Rule Reconsidered: Restoring the Status Quo Ante' (1998) 22 *Wake Forest Law Review* 261; W Schroeder, 'Restoring the Status Quo Ante: the Fourth Amendment Exclusionary Rule as a Compensatory Device' (1983) 51 *Washington Law Review* 633.

The second prominent non-consequentialist justification for excluding improperly obtained evidence in criminal trials is the integrity principle, defended by Antony Duff et al, Ian Dennis, Paul Roberts and Adrian Zuckerman, amongst others.[5] The integrity principle builds on the increasingly influential idea that in order to blame an offender through a legitimate and proper process, it is insufficient that the offender is blameworthy. In addition, the blamer must exhibit integrity, in the sense of moral coherence, in blaming the offender.[6] To use an oft-cited example, suppose a brutal murderer, without accounting for his own murder, blames another person for perpetrating a minor assault. This act of blaming is defective, even if the attacker who commits minor assault is genuinely blameworthy, because the murderer adopts a morally incoherent stance in blaming. The murderer's pair of actions suggests, on the one hand, that harming another is something that should be condemned by blaming the attacker, while on the other hand, harming another is not something that should be condemned by refusing to account for his own murder. The integrity principle suggests that if the court admits improperly obtained evidence in convicting the defendant, the court would similarly adopt a morally incoherent stance: on the one hand, the court condemns violation of rights by convicting the defendant; but on the other hand, the court does not take the violation of the defendant's rights seriously in admitting the evidence.[7]

2. Objections to the Protective Principle

Seven prominent objections have been raised against the protective principle in the literature. I will argue that none of them is decisive. They at most show that the protective

---

[5] Duff et al, above n 2, 226; I Dennis, *The Law of Evidence*, 4th edn (London, Sweet & Maxwell, 2010) 49–56; Roberts and Zuckerman, above n 2, 188; discussed (without being endorsed) in Ashworth, above n 1, 108. See also HL Ho, 'State Entrapment' (2011) 31 *Legal Studies* 71; F Stark, 'Moral Legitimacy and Disclosure Appeals' (2010) 14 *Edinburgh Law Review* 205; L Hoyano, 'What is Balanced on the Scales of Justice? In Search of the Essence of the Right to a Fair Trial' [2014] *Criminal Law Review* 4.

[6] Can there be a *broader* integrity theory for excluding improperly obtained evidence that focuses *not* on the moral incoherence between admitting the evidence and the *blaming message sent out to the defendant in a criminal trial*, but rather on the moral incoherence between admitting the evidence and the *aim of doing justice which is the aim of every judicial proceeding*? The broader integrity theory would apply to any judicial proceedings, whether criminal or civil, and seems to be adopted by Lord Bingham in *A v Home Secretary* [2006] 2 AC 221, [92]–[95] (HL). The difficulty with the broader integrity theory is that while it is hard to explain why admitting the improperly obtained evidence is incoherent with the condemnatory message sent out to the defendant in a criminal trial (see Section 3, below), it is even harder to explain why admitting the improperly obtained evidence is inconsistent with, say, the aim of doing justice in a tort or administrative proceeding. Moreover, whatever the status of the broader integrity theory as an independent basis for excluding improperly obtained evidence in criminal trials, I will suggest later that the narrower integrity theory, which focuses on blame, must be part of the justification for excluding improperly obtained evidence in criminal trials and hence merits attention in its own right.

[7] I set aside the question of whether there are constraints on just blaming *besides* moral coherence of the blamer. For exploration of issues concerning the blamer's standing to blame, see eg GA Cohen, 'Casting the First Stone: Who Can, and Who Can't, Condemn the Terrorists' (2006) 58 *Royal Institute of Philosophy Supplement* 113; T Scanlon, *Moral Dimensions: Permissibility, Meaning, Blame* (Cambridge MA, Harvard University Press, 2008) 177; A Smith, 'On Being Responsible and Holding Responsible' (2007) 11 *Journal of Ethics* 465; A Duff, 'I Might be Guilty but You Can't Try Me: Estoppel and Other Bars to Trial' (2003) 1 *Ohio State Journal of Criminal Law* 245; A Duff, 'Blame, Moral Standing, and the Legitimacy of Criminal Trial' (2010) 23 *Ratio* 123.

principle is not the only justification for excluding improperly obtained evidence, rather than that it is mistaken.

(a) The Disproportion Objection

The first objection can be called the *disproportion objection*. The protective principle, as defined here, is a general principle that does not distinguish between the nature of the breach and the kind of crime charged against the defendant. Accordingly, under the protective principle, there is a duty to exclude improperly obtained evidence even if the breach of the defendant's right is minor and the defendant's crime is a serious one. However, according to Roberts and Zuckerman, in cases where the breach of the defendant's right is minor and the defendant's crime is serious, the improperly obtained evidence should not generally be excluded.[8]

In reply to this objection, as Antony Duff et al explain, a proponent of the protective principle need not take the principle to be an absolute one. Accordingly, it is perfectly consistent for an advocate of the protective principle to accept that in cases where the breach is minor and the defendant's crime is serious, the protective principle is trumped by another moral principle (for example, the importance of doing retributive justice) such that the evidence should not be excluded in those cases.[9]

(b) The Other Remedies Objection

The second objection, which can be called the *other remedies objection*, is that even if the defendant should be protected from suffering loss caused by a breach of his right and hence deserves a remedy, the remedy should not take the form of exclusion of evidence.[10] The breach of the defendant's right in the evidence-gathering process should be addressed in a separate civil action against the evidence-gathering agent.[11]

Two replies can be made in response to this objection. The first reply is that the alternative protective remedy, for example, an action in tort, is often time-consuming and costly for the defendant to pursue.[12] The second reply is that, independent of efficiency concerns, the best remedy to a person whose right was breached seems to be restoring him as closely as possible to the status quo. Using an analogy in contract law, it seems that the ideal remedy for breach of contract, ignoring efficiency issues, should be specific performance rather than damages because specific performance would put the claimant in the same position as

---

[8]   Roberts and Zuckerman, above n 2, 184. See also P Duff, 'Admissibility of Improperly Obtained Evidence in the Scottish Criminal Trial: the Search for Principle' (2004) 8 *Edinburgh Law Review* 152, 165.

[9]   Duff et al, above n 2, 231–32.

[10]   Roberts and Zuckerman, above n 2, 184. See also Ashworth, above n 1, 113, 116 (discussing related points in a different context).

[11]   For discussions of possible remedies, see D Ormerod, 'ECHR and the Exclusion of Evidence: Trial Remedies for Article 8 Breaches?' [2003] *Criminal Law Review* 61; R Myers, 'Fourth Amendment Small Claims Court' (2013) 10 *Ohio State Journal of Criminal Law* 567.

[12]   Ashworth, above n 1, 118; A Taslitz, 'Hypocrisy, Corruption, and Illegitimacy: Why Judicial Integrity Justifies the Exclusionary Rule' (2013) 10 *Ohio State Journal of Criminal Law* 419, 425.

if the breach had not taken place.[13] Analogously, since excluding the evidence would produce a situation closer to the status quo than admitting the evidence and compensating the defendant separately, the protective principle encapsulates a principled reason for choosing exclusion of evidence as the preferred remedy.[14]

(c) The Special Remedy Objection

The third objection, which can be called the *special remedy for the guilty objection*, claims that if we provide exclusion of evidence as a form of protective remedy then we are 'committed to the perverse contention that only the [actually] guilty (along with a few innocents who appear guilty) should enjoy a special remedy for the violation of their rights'.[15] This is because if no incriminating evidence was obtained in the right-violation (say, an illegal search), then this remedy is not helpful to the victim whose right was breached.[16]

In reply one might ask, why is this supposed to be a problem? It is entirely plausible that if a right-violation caused loss to a victim, then some additional remedy should be available to him as compared to the situation where the right-violation did not cause any loss. It is true that the right to have the improperly obtained evidence excluded is helpful only to a person against whom incriminating evidence is found. But the general right which this specific right is based on, namely the right not to suffer because of a breach of one's rights, protects everyone, and hence no one is offered any special treatment. By analogy, a person whose car was damaged wrongfully enjoys a compensatory remedy which is unavailable to people who do not own cars or people whose cars were not damaged wrongfully. But that does not mean that the owner of a damaged vehicle enjoys any special protection in tort law because that specific remedy is derived from the general right not to suffer tortious damage, a right which protects everyone.[17]

A further four objections to the protective principle share a similar structure, in that they all assert that the principle produces counter-intuitive results in certain cases. The four objections can be differentiated, and will now be scrutinised, in terms of the following three dimensions: whether *the victim of right-violation* is the defendant himself, whether the *right-violator* is a state agent, and whether the right violation occurred in an *investigatory process*.

(d) The Identity of the Victim of Right-violation Objection

According to the fourth objection, which can be called the *identity of the victim of right-violation objection*, the protective principle cannot explain why there is a reason to exclude

---

[13] Duff et al, above n 2, 232.

[14] Also see A Slavny, 'Negating and Counterbalancing: A Fundamental Distinction in the Concept of a Corrective Duty' (2014) 33 *Law and Philosophy* 143; Schroeder, above n 4, 654.

[15] Roberts and Zuckerman, above n 2, 185 (noting that this objection is 'regularly levelled' against the protective principle, without endorsing it).

[16] See also Duff, above n 8, 170–71.

[17] That there should be an *extra* remedy available to those against whom incriminating evidence is found does not mean that there should be *no* remedy available to those whose right was breached but against whom no incriminating evidence is found. Exclusion of evidence is just one form of remedy amongst many.

evidence where the person whose right was breached by the investigatory agent is not the defendant himself. As an example, suppose that the police improperly searched the home of a friend of the defendant and discovered some evidence against the defendant there. In such a case, the remedy under the protective principle, if any, should be provided to the defendant's friend, not to the defendant.[18]

In reply, I agree that there is a reason to exclude the evidence in such a case and that the protective principle cannot explain it. But how damaging is this objection against the protective principle? Perhaps we should not expect to find a principle that can do all the justificatory work on its own. It is entirely possible that some cases of exclusion are justified by one principle, while other cases of exclusion are justified by another principle. The fact that the protective principle does not cover all cases of justified exclusion does not mean that it is not a correct principle. By way of analogy, the fact that we are justified in punishing some persons who are not morally guilty (for instance, in strict liability cases) does not, per se, show that retributivism is not a good justification of punishment; it only shows that retributivism is not the complete story, and must be supplemented by other justifications of punishment practices.[19] Similarly, as long as we give up the understandable but unjustifiable presupposition that there exists only one justification for excluding improperly obtained evidence, the fact that the protective principle cannot cover all cases of justified exclusion should not be seen as a decisive objection to it.

(e) The Non-investigatory Private Right-violator Objection

The fifth objection, which can be called the *non-investigatory private right-violator objection*, focuses on a case in which the defendant's right was breached by a private agent in a non-investigatory process. To borrow an example from Duff and colleagues, suppose the defendant stole some goods, but his own home was later burgled. The police, in apprehending the burglar, discovered some evidence that can be used to prove the defendant's guilt of the original theft.[20] According to Mike Redmayne, there is no reason to exclude the evidence in such a case. Yet the protective principle would wrongly suggest that there is a duty to exclude, since if the evidence were admitted the defendant would suffer as a result of a violation of his rights.[21]

In reply, I agree that there is no duty to exclude in such a case. But it is unclear that the protective principle would call for exclusion in such a case, at least after some reasonable clarifications and refinements of the protective principle. It seems that the most plausible normative basis of the protective principle is *corrective justice*: a person has a duty to make sure that no one suffers loss because of *his* breach of others' rights.[22] Corrective justice is

---

[18] Duff et al, above n 2, 232.

[19] See eg J Gardner, 'Crime: in Proportion and in Perspective' in A Ashworth and M Wasik (eds), *Fundamentals of Sentencing Theory* (Oxford, Oxford University Press, 1998) 32–33. Cf Duff et al, above n 2, 233.

[20] Duff et al, above n 2, 238.

[21] M Redmayne, 'Theorizing the Criminal Trial' (2009) 12 *New Criminal Law Review* 287, 307.

[22] But cf P Roberts, 'Excluding Evidence as Protecting Constitutional or Human Rights?' in L Zedner and J Roberts (eds), *Principles and Values in Criminal Law and Criminal Justice: Essays in Honour of Andrew Ashworth* (Oxford, Oxford University Press, 2012) 182, 185–86 (advocating a more pluralistic and contextual analysis).

a bilateral principle: the duty to protect arises *only in relation to the right-violator, not for other persons.* For example, if I broke into your house and damaged it, it is *me* who has a duty to ensure you do not suffer loss by compensating you. A stranger has no duty to restore you to the status quo. Accordingly, the best interpretation of the protective principle is *not* one which claims that the state should ensure that no person suffers as a result of a breach of that person's rights, no matter who the right-violator is, but rather the more limited principle that the state should ensure that no one suffers as a result of the *state's* breach of his rights.[23] Once we understand the protective principle in this more refined manner, it becomes clear that it does not mandate evidentiary exclusion in the thief and burglar case above.[24]

(f) The Investigatory Private Right-violator Objection

According to the sixth objection, which can be called the *investigatory private right-violator objection*, if we understand the protective principle in the more refined manner just suggested (as applying only to instances where the defendant's right was violated by *the state*), then we will run into trouble with the following cases. Some people believe that there is a duty to exclude evidence obtained by a private agent in an illegal investigatory process, for example, an illegal search by a private detective hired by the victim or telephone-tapping by journalists. However, if we understand the protective principle to be based on corrective justice, then the protective principle cannot justify exclusion in such cases. Since it was not the state who breached the defendant's rights, the state is not under any duty to provide a remedy.[25]

Two replies can be made to this objection. First, I wonder whether there is really a duty to exclude evidence in cases where it was someone other than a state official who obtained the evidence improperly. In other words, I am not sure whether the sixth objection highlights a weakness rather than a strength of the refined protective principle. Commentators are by no means unanimous on this point. Notably, Duff et al, in their fairly comprehensive treatment, remain undecided whether the duty to exclude improperly obtained evidence applies primarily to *official* misconduct.[26] Secondly, even if we accept that there is a duty to exclude in such cases and that the refined protective principle cannot account for it, that only shows (as before in relation to the *identity of the victim of right-violation objection*) that the refined protective principle is not the complete story rather than that its story is false.

---

[23] Duff et al, above n 2, 230.

[24] Another possible reply on behalf of the protective theorist is that the protective principle is concerned with preventing a person from suffering loss as a result of a breach, not of any of his rights, but of some of his *constitutional rights* only. Since the relevant constitutional rights are primarily rights *against the government*, the defendant is not entitled to a protective remedy if the improper evidence-gathering act was performed by a private agent. See Norton, above n 4, 302 (n 324); Schroeder, above n 4, 672–73.

[25] Duff et al, above n 2, 233.

[26] Ibid 239–40. In the objection's favour, however, *A v Home Secretary* [2006] 2 AC 221 (HL) held that evidence obtained by torture could not be admitted even though the evidence was obtained by a foreign agent over whom the UK authorities exercised no control.

(g) The Non-investigatory Official Right-violator Objection

According to the seventh objection, which can be called *the non-investigatory official right-violator objection*, there is no duty to exclude evidence in criminal trials, even if it is improperly obtained by a state official, if the official is not acting in the course of a criminal investigation.[27] Suppose, for example, that state officials destroyed the defendant's house illegally for some reason unrelated to crime investigation, for example, in the course of general intelligence-gathering or as an expression of police power. Entirely unexpected to the state officials, evidence suggesting guilt of the defendant, which was stored inside the house, was revealed after the house was destroyed. Some believe that there should be no duty to exclude this piece of evidence since it was not obtained for an investigatory purpose, yet the protective principle will suggest that there is a duty to exclude in such a case. Hence, the protective principle is too broad.

Two replies can be made to this objection. First, one may wonder if there is really no duty to exclude at all if the evidence was obtained by a state official's improper non-investigatory act. Suppose that a state official tortures a person *for fun* (and therefore not acting in an investigative capacity) and the person, in a semi-unconscious state, reveals his guilt of a wrongdoing which was previously unknown. Is it too far-fetched to believe that the court should reject the evidence in such a case? Secondly, assuming for the sake of argument that there is no duty to exclude in such cases, I am not certain that the refined protective principle *must* imply otherwise. Official agents who are acting in an investigatory capacity may properly be seen as belonging to the same overarching entity as the criminal courts and the prosecution, as they all contribute towards the practical implementation of criminal justice, such that under corrective justice criminal courts and the prosecution have a duty to make sure that the defendant does not suffer because of breach of his rights by official agents acting in an investigatory capacity. However, there is certainly an argument for claiming that official agents who are not acting in an investigatory capacity should *not* be seen as belonging to the same overarching entity as the criminal courts and the prosecution, and hence the criminal courts and the prosecution are under no remedial duty of corrective justice in relation to losses inflicted by state agents with whom they have no relevant association.

3. The Integrity Principle's Problem

The integrity principle suffers from a well-known problem. Recall the murderer we mentioned in Section 1 who, without accounting for his own wrongdoing, condemns the perpetrator of a minor assault. This murderer, we said, clearly exhibits moral incoherence. But why must a criminal court suffer from the same type of moral incoherence if it admits improperly obtained evidence and convicts the defendant partly on that basis? Unlike the murderer who did not condemn his own wrongdoing, the criminal court can

---

[27] This argument is not explicitly put forward by Duff et al, but is suggested by their remarks on the importance of the distinction between improper investigation and other improper conduct and their contention that the principle of integrity applies mainly to the former: see Duff et al, above n 2, 233–34, 238–39, 251.

denounce the evidence-gathering act in its judgment. The criminal court may even convict the evidence-gathering agent in another proceeding, if the evidence-gathering method involved criminality.[28] One may argue that the public will inevitably perceive the court as not condemning the wrongful evidence-gathering method if the court makes use of the resulting evidence. However, many people would be sceptical about the idea that we should judge the merits of a policy by the public's perception of it.[29]

Duff et al try to support the integrity principle by claiming that, in order to be serious in our condemnation of a wrongdoing, we must adopt the attitude that no good comes from the wrongdoing; or at least the attitude that even if the wrongdoing can produce some incidental goods, there is no value in the directly intended outcome of it. Since the evidence obtained from, say, an illegal search is the directly intended object of the wrongful evidence-gathering method, if the court admits the evidence it would treat some of the directly intended outcomes of the wrongful evidence-gathering method as good, and hence it would fail to condemn the wrongful evidence-gathering method in full sincerity.[30]

There is some intuitive appeal to Duff et al's position, but their argument needs considerable development as it stands. Taken at face value, it seems *irrational* to adopt the attitude that a wrongdoing cannot produce any directly intended good outcome since, after all, counter-examples readily spring to mind. For example, suppose we kill three innocent persons to save one person. That is assuredly a wrongdoing; but just as clearly, the wrongdoing produced a good (saving one innocent person) as a directly intended outcome of it. If it is puzzling why Duff et al deny this conclusion, their argument cannot take us any further. Why exactly would the court lack coherence in blaming the defendant without adopting this seemingly irrational attitude? Duff et al's argument seems radically question-begging in its present form.

4. The No-Profit Principle

While the protective principle and the integrity principle are the most prominent non-consequentialist justifications for excluding improperly obtained evidence canvassed in the literature, they do not exhaust all possibilities. This section outlines another candidate, which can be called the no-profit principle. Though sometimes mentioned in legal judgments,[31] the no-profit principle is not, to my knowledge, developed in detail in the academic literature discussing evidentiary exclusion.[32]

According to the no-profit principle, the reason why improperly obtained evidence should be excluded is because the state, or the polity, should not *benefit* from a wrongdoing. The idea that one should not be allowed to profit from a wrongdoing can be illustrated

---

[28] Duff et al, above n 2, 251. See also Ashworth, above n 1, 116; Redmayne, above n 21, 305–306; A Ashworth and M Redmayne, *The Criminal Process*, 4th edn (Oxford, Oxford University Press, 2010) 361–62.

[29] Ashworth, above n 1, 111. For related distinctions, see Mirfield, above n 2, 24–25.

[30] Duff et al, above n 2, 251.

[31] See eg *Murray v United States*, 487 US 533, 542 (1988) (Scalia J noting that 'government should not profit from its illegal activity').

[32] It receives only cursory treatment in Duff et al, above n 2, 105, 107–108.

by the famous case of *Riggs v Palmer*.[33] In that case, a grandson who was the main current beneficiary of his grandfather's will murdered his grandfather in order to secure his anticipated legacy and pre-empt the risk of being disinherited. The New York Court of Appeals invoked the no-profit principle to deny the grandson his inheritance. Extrapolating to the present context, the principle can be refined by asking two further questions. First, is the polity only precluded from benefiting from *its own* wrongdoing? Can it still be allowed to benefit from *others'* wrongdoings consistently with the principle? Secondly, is the polity only precluded from benefiting from the *intentional* outcomes of the wrongdoing? Alternatively, is it also precluded from benefiting from the *incidental* effects of the wrongdoing as well? Answering these questions would yield some possible variations of the no-profit principle, but I will not attempt that task here. My immediate objective is to show how the no-profit principle is distinct from both the protective principle and the integrity principle.

The no-profit principle may at a first glance appear similar to the integrity principle. For example, they both seem to be based on the idea that there is something problematic about making use of the fruits of wrongful evidence-gathering methods. However, there are also substantial differences. According to the integrity principle, the reason why we cannot make use of the fruits of the wrongful evidence-gathering method is because in doing so we adopt an attitude that is *incoherent with the condemnatory message sent out in convicting the defendant*. The main burden of the integrity principle is to explain why the court must still be viewed as adopting an attitude that is incoherent with the condemnation of the defendant even if the court, in addition to making use of the fruits of the wrongful evidence-gathering method, also condemns the wrongful evidence-gathering method and, in appropriate cases, takes steps to punish the miscreant agent. In contrast, the no-profit principle does not face this problem. The basis for excluding the evidence, under the no-profit principle, lies simply in the idea of fairness, not in any alleged incoherence between admitting the evidence at trial and the condemnatory message sent out in convicting the defendant. According to the no-profit principle, even if making use of the fruits of the wrongful evidence-gathering method is entirely coherent with the condemnatory message sent out in convicting the defendant, the state simply should not be allowed to make use of the evidence as a matter of fairness. Since the no-profit principle is based on fairness, a general principle that applies even in non-blaming contexts, it is broader than the integrity principle and can be applied to non-criminal proceedings, unlike the integrity principle which applies specifically to proceedings involving blame. For example, suppose I obtained evidence from you illegally and tried to adduce that evidence in a civil dispute between us. This would not be forbidden by the integrity principle but it might well be forbidden by the no-profit principle.

The no-profit principle is also fundamentally different from the protective principle in its shape and normative implications. The no-profit principle is a gain-based principle, while the protective principle is a loss-based principle. Significantly, the no-profit principle appears to have conceptual resources, after suitable refinements, to address three of the objections to the protective principle surveyed above, namely, the identity of the victim of right-violation objection, the investigatory private right-violator objection, and the non-investigatory official right-violator objection. First, the no-profit principle can explain why

---

[33] 115 NY 506 (1889).

there is a duty to exclude when the evidence is obtained from an illegal search of a person other than the defendant, since the no-profit principle is concerned with preventing gain by the state rather than preventing loss to the defendant. Secondly, the no-profit principle may justify (assuming that we do endorse) exclusion where the evidence was obtained improperly by a private agent in an investigatory process, since one may claim that the state should not benefit from the intentional fruits of a wrongdoing perpetrated by another person or entity. Thirdly, the no-profit principle may explain (again, assuming that we want to do so) why there is no reason to exclude evidence obtained by an official agent in a non-investigatory process. The no-profit principle, as mentioned above, can naturally be formulated to disregard incidental fruits obtained unintentionally.

Conclusion: Is the Integrity Principle Redundant?

This chapter has argued that familiar objections to the protective principle are not decisive. Those objections at most suggest that the protective principle is not the complete justification for excluding improperly obtained evidence in criminal proceedings, rather than establishing that the protective principle is mistaken. I have also argued that there is another non-consequentialist principle, which can be called the no-profit principle, which avoids some of the standard objections against the protective principle. In particular, the no-profit principle seems to be able to cover some cases where we think there is reason to exclude improperly obtained evidence but which are not covered by the protective principle, like the case in which the illegal search was targeted against a person other than the defendant. The integrity principle, meanwhile, faces a serious problem in explaining why admitting improperly obtained evidence is incoherent with the condemnatory message conveyed by a criminal court in convicting and punishing the defendant.

In light of these considerations, it may be alluring to think we should just give up the integrity principle altogether, and justify the exclusion of improperly obtained evidence in criminal trials either by the no-profit principle alone or taken in conjunction with the protective principle. Yet there is a powerful intuition which is hard to account for without the integrity principle. If we accept that intuition, then it seems to follow that the integrity principle must be at least part of the justification for excluding improperly obtained evidence in criminal trials.

Compare two hypothetical scenarios. In the first case, the police obtain evidence against the accused through telephone-tapping and the prosecution tries to adduce it in a criminal trial. In the second case, some governmental officers obtain evidence against a person also through telephone-tapping and the evidence is adduced by the government against that person in an action for tort or an administrative proceeding which is not punitive in nature. Many people believe that the argument for exclusion is stronger in criminal cases.[34] This intuition can easily be explained by the integrity principle. The integrity principle

---

[34] Courts in England are certainly more willing to exclude improperly obtained evidence in criminal than in civil cases: see eg *Olden v Serious Organised Crime Agency* [2010] EWCA Civ 143. The US Fourth Amendment exclusionary rule is not always applicable to deportation proceedings: *INS v Lopez-Mendoza*, 468 US 1032 (1984).

focuses on the right to blame wrongdoers, and blaming is intrinsic to criminal proceedings but not civil or other administrative proceedings.[35] The protective principle and the no-profit principle, by virtue of their general nature, will have a hard time accounting for that distinction. If a right-violator has a general duty to prevent his victim from suffering loss caused by his breach of the victim's rights, then the government has a duty not to use the evidence improperly obtained by its officials against the other party; especially bearing in mind that non-punitive proceedings may have very serious consequences for the parties, such as losing custody of their children or being deported.[36] Similarly, if there is a duty not to profit from a wrongdoing, then the government should be denied the evidence in both cases.[37]

This argument does not aim to show that the protective principle or the no-profit principle are incorrect, in the sense that they are not sound justifications for excluding improperly obtained evidence. The argument simply demonstrates that these principles are not exhaustive, and that the integrity principle must be part of the complete picture.

A critic wanting to reject the integrity principle might attempt three responses. First, it might be argued that the protective principle and/or the no-profit principle adequately explain why we should be more willing to exclude improperly obtained evidence in criminal trials than in civil or administrative proceedings. But, at least at present, I cannot see how this argument can succeed. The protective theorist may argue that the loss caused by a criminal conviction is greater than, say, losing a deportation proceeding and hence the duty to protect is stronger in criminal proceedings. But that does not seem to me to be a general truth about the comparative gravity of different kinds of legal proceeding: losing a deportation case would very often be a more disastrous outcome to a party than being convicted of a minor crime.[38]

---

[35] Some writers argue that US deportation proceedings are punitive in nature: see eg E Rossi, 'Revisiting *INS v Lopez-Mendoza*: Why the Fourth Amendment Exclusionary Rule Should Apply in Deportation Proceedings' (2013) 44 *Columbia Human Rights Law Review* 477. This is debateable, but nothing turns on the choice of example. My point here is simply that there is a stronger duty to exclude improperly obtained evidence in punitive proceedings than in non-punitive proceedings, whichever is which.

[36] Norton, above n 4, 303.

[37] For the idea that criminal law has a distinctive aim and hence the evidence rules proper for a criminal trial need not be proper for a civil trial, see Dennis, above n 5, 49–57; Duff et al, above n 2, 101–102; Roberts and Zuckerman, above n 2, 12, 188.

[38] Are there other resources internal to the protective principle to justify the distinction between the exclusion of improperly obtained evidence by government officers in civil cases and the exclusion of such evidence in criminal cases? According to one familiar argument, while *criminal* courts and government officials belong to the same overarching entity, the *civil* courts do *not* belong to the same overarching entity as government officials; *ergo* a civil court, unlike a criminal court, is not under a corrective justice duty to prevent or remedy losses arising from official illegality. This argument rests on three assumptions, the plausibility of which cannot be investigated in this chapter. First, civil courts are fundamentally different from criminal courts in their relationship with government officials. The second assumption turns on a distinction between the corrective justice duty *of the government* (as a party to the proceeding) and the corrective justice duty *of the courts*. No matter whether the proceeding is civil or criminal, the government, as a party to the proceeding, has the same corrective justice duty to prevent the other party from suffering loss caused by the wrongdoings of its agents and accordingly the same corrective justice duty *not to make use of the evidence*. Therefore, if the protective theorist believes that the reason for exclusion is weaker in the civil case than in the criminal case, he must assume that the reason for exclusion is not solely based on the corrective justice *duty of the government not to make use of the evidence*. Thirdly, there is the disputable (see above n 22) assumption that the protective principle is grounded in corrective justice.

Secondly, one might ascribe the intuition to rationales other than the integrity principle, the protective principle, or the no-profit principle. But *what* would that missing rationalisation be? A protective theorist might argue that while the reason to protect, and hence the reason *for* excluding the improperly obtained evidence, is equally strong in both cases, the reason *against* exclusion in the deportation trial, namely the need to deport the persons who really should be deported, is stronger than the reason against exclusion in the criminal trial, namely the need to convict the truly guilty. Hence we should be more willing to exclude evidence in criminal trials than in deportation cases, all things considered.[39] Yet is it really true that proper conviction and punishment of the guilty is less important than regulating immigration? In any case, it is hard to accept that the conviction of the truly guilty is, in general, less important than reaching the right substantive outcome in a civil case.

Finally, thirdly, one may simply reject the claim that we should be more ready to exclude improperly obtained evidence in a criminal trial than in a non-punitive civil proceeding like a deportation case. Some people may not share the intuition that criminal trials import different considerations. Not much more need be (or can be) said to them. For those who feel the intuitive force of the thought experiment, there is a theoretical cost to be paid for abandoning integrity as part of the moral rationale for evidentiary exclusion. Nonetheless, if the theoretical objections against the integrity principle are otherwise decisive, we should bite the bullet and revise our initial intuition as a matter of reflective equilibrium.[40] Whether that would be a justified course to take depends on a deeper investigation of the normative content and institutional implications of the integrity principle.

---

[39] Cf Justice O'Connor's judgment in *INS v Lopez-Mendoza*, 468 US 1032 (1984) (characterising evidentiary exclusion in criminal trials as a function of cost–benefit analysis).

[40] On 'reflective equilibrium', see J Rawls, *A Theory of Justice*, rev edn (Oxford, Oxford University Press, 1999) 40.

12

Unbecoming Jurors and Unreasoned Verdicts: Realising Integrity in the Jury Room

JOHN JACKSON*

Introduction

In an article written over ten years ago I observed that the jury system in the common law world has survived throughout the years by being able to adapt to different legal and political cultures.[1] It might have been more accurate to say that this is one of the reasons why it has survived in criminal cases. In many but not all parts of the common law world[2] the demise of the civil jury has been remarkable. In his Hamlyn lectures 30 years ago Lord Hailsham illustrated this quite graphically when he said that at the time of the Great War—over a century ago now—almost every issue of fact that had to be determined before the superior courts in England and Wales outside the Chancery Division was tried by a jury.[3] Yet by 1983 the civil jury was arguably a thing of the past. One of the reasons for this decline would seem to be that jurors were increasingly considered less suited than professional judges to the role that was expected of them in modern civil litigation.

There is much greater support for the role of the jury continuing in criminal cases, at least in England and Wales, where it has been argued that the jury fulfils broader functions. It plays an important educative role in informing citizens about the workings of the criminal process and about the content of the criminal law, and makes the criminal law more transparent and accessible.[4] In these ways it can be claimed that the jury plays

* Thanks are due to participants at the UNSW conference and at a seminar at the City University, London in May 2013 for their comments on earlier drafts of this chapter. Special thanks are due to Mark Coen, Jonathan Doak, Nancy Marder, Paul Roberts and Simon Young for their detailed comments on earlier drafts and to Thom Brooks, Niamh Howlin, Jill Hunter and Luke Marsh for providing me with ideas and assistance.

[1] JD Jackson, 'Making Juries Accountable' (2001) 50 *American Journal of Comparative Law* 477.

[2] The US civil jury is still a potent force: see R Litan (ed), *Verdict: Assessing the Civil Jury System* (Washington, Brookings Institution, 1993).

[3] Lord Hailsham, *Hamlyn Revisited: The British Legal System Today* (London, Stevens, 1983).

[4] See M Redmayne, 'Theorising Jury Reform' in A Duff, L Farmer, S Marshall and V Tadros (eds), *The Trial on Trial (2): Judgment and Calling to Account* (Oxford, Hart Publishing, 2006) 99 (suggesting that arguments for the jury can be classified as belonging to three broad perspectives: court-centred (good fact-finders), citizen-centred (good governance) and defendant-centred (offering protection to defendants)). See also T Brooks, 'The Right to Trial by Jury' (2004) 21 *Journal of Applied Philosophy* 197, 204.

an important instrumental role in promoting the integrity of the criminal law and the criminal justice system as a whole. There has been less satisfaction, however, about the way jurors have conducted themselves in certain cases—regarding what might be described as the personal integrity of jurors.[5] In recent years, periodic crises of confidence have sparked debate and suggestions for reform to prevent jurors acting prejudicially or otherwise flouting their obligations, the latest example being the Law Commission's proposals to deal with jurors who try to search for details of the case they are trying on the internet.[6] These crises of juror misconduct have gone hand in hand with a more general expectation that jurors should be made more accountable for their behaviour, which would seem to be linked to growing demands for all manner of public bodies to be made more accountable.[7] So long as juries were traditionally *of* the community they did not need to be accountable *to* the community any more than to a hierarchical bureaucratic authority.[8] But the increasingly diverse nature of communities from which juries are chosen has engendered less confidence in their ability to apply undifferentiated community standards in their decision-making.

Against this backdrop, it is imperative to consider how best to ensure that jurors do not fall short of their obligations. Section 1 of this essay argues that an undue focus on individual juror impropriety has diverted attention away from how we want the jury as a collective decision-making body to act, and that there should be clearer standards in this regard. There is a need to shift the debate away from the personal integrity of jurors towards the 'institutional' integrity of the jury as a decision-making body in the criminal process. The focus here is on a third kind of integrity—the integrity of the criminal process—which can be differentiated both from the integrity of the criminal justice system as a whole (including substantive criminal law) and from the personal integrity of individual jurors.[9] Comparative and empirical scholarship has illuminated the important role that the jury plays in promoting the adversarial features of an oral and public trial.[10] But the openness

---

[5]   But cf J Hunter, *Jurors' Notions of Justice* (Sydney, University of New South Wales, 2013) 35, for empirical evidence that jurors *do* attach importance to personal integrity in terms of abiding by the instructions given to them by the judge.

[6]   See Law Commission, *Contempt of Court (1): Juror Misconduct and Internet Publications* (London, Stationery Office, 2013).

[7]   Jackson, above n 1.

[8]   MR Damaška, 'Structures of Authority and Comparative Criminal Procedure' (1975) 84 *Yale Law Journal* 480.

[9]   Some commentators have distinguished between the integrity or 'legitimacy' of the criminal justice process as a whole, and narrower aspects of integrity such as the principle of judicial integrity, the integrity of the trial and the integrity of the verdict. See A Ashworth, 'Exploring the Integrity Principle in Evidence and Procedure' in P Mirfield and RJ Smith (eds), *Essays for Colin Tapper* (London, Butterworths, 2003); L Hoyano, 'What is Balanced in the Scales of Justice? In Search of the Essence of the Right to a Fair Trial' [2014] *Criminal Law Review* 3. Cf IH Dennis, 'Reconstructing the Law of Criminal Evidence' (1989) 42 *Current Legal Problems* 21; TRS Allan, 'The Concept of a Fair Trial' in E Attwooll and D Goldberg (eds), *Criminal Justice* (Stuttgart, Franz Steiner Verlag, 1995).

[10]   The link between the principles of the public oral criminal trial and the jury was made long ago by the nineteenth-century German criminal law scholar, CJA Mittermaier, who used this thesis to argue against the introduction of the 'Schöffengericht' mixed court in Germany: see A Koch, 'CJA Mittermaier and the 19th Century Debate About Juries and Mixed Courts' (2000) 72 *Revue International de Droit Pénal* 347. For more recent explorations, see E Knittel and D Seiler, 'The Merits of Trial by Jury' (1972) 30 *Cambridge Law Journal* 316, 318; J Jackson and S Doran, *Judge without Jury: Diplock Trials in the Adversary System* (Oxford, Clarendon Press, 1995); J Jackson, 'The Value of Jury Trial' in Attwooll and Goldberg, above n 9, 79.

that juries help promote during the course of the trial stands in sharp contrast to the secrecy of their deliberations in the jury room. Section 2 contends that, as jurors become more active in their role as fact-finders, and more easily exposed to extraneous material, greater scrutiny may be required of these closed proceedings with more directive judicial guidance specifying how deliberations should be conducted. Section 3 then confronts the question whether the greater 'judicial' responsibilities that such guidance entails should extend to mandating reasoned decisions for jury verdicts. Section 4 explores possible answers with the benefit of lessons drawn from comparative experience, and the essay concludes with a brief recapitulation of the main arguments and their implications for the integrity of trial by jury.

1. Falling Short: Periodic Crises of Confidence in the UK's Jury Systems

Periodic crises of confidence over the course of the past 30 years have prompted the question whether juries, as presently constituted, can be trusted to conform with their oath to 'faithfully try the defendant and give a true verdict according to the evidence'.[11] It would be an exaggeration to claim that these crises have threatened the very survival of the criminal jury; there remains enduring support for the system, not least by prominent members of the legal profession and judiciary.[12] But three particular concerns have come to light during this period, each of which has evoked a considerable degree of soul-searching.

The first concern which manifested itself most prominently in the 1980s and 1990s, until the passage of the Criminal Justice Act 2003, was that many juries were insufficiently representative of the population as a whole, and that this could skew decisions in favour of 'criminals'. Secondly, doubts have arisen from time to time, especially since the passage of the Human Rights Act 1998, as to whether the system sufficiently guarantees an independent and impartial tribunal, which is an essential component of a fair trial under Article 6 of the European Convention on Human Rights (ECHR). A third concern which has manifested itself more recently has been whether jurors' increasing access to extraneous information about the case they are deciding exacerbates the risk that verdicts are based unduly on such information rather than on the evidence in the case. These three concerns may be summarised as relating to: (a) representativeness; (b) impartiality; and (c) reliance on extraneous material.

---

[11] *Criminal Practice Directions 2015* [2015] EWCA Crim 1567, CPD VI 26E.1.

[12] See eg the remarks of Lord Judge CJ, 'Jury Trials', Judicial Studies Board Lecture, November 2010, reported at http://www.lawgazette.co.uk/analysis/lord-chief-justice-fears-new-threats-to-jury-trial/58173.fullarticle (accessed 23 February 2016). Although this support remains strong, there have been calls from time to time for experiments to be made with other modes of trial, such as the Schöffengericht system of a judge sitting with lay assessors or more simply with trials by judge alone. See eg G Williams, *The Proof of Guilt*, 3rd edn (London, Stevens, 1963) 299–300; L Blom-Cooper, 'Judge and Jury, or Judge Alone' (2004) 44 *Medicine, Science and the Law* 6. Lord Hailsham himself argued in favour of greater experimentation with mixed courts in his Hamlyn lectures; and in his *Review of the Criminal Courts of England and Wales* (London, Stationery Office, 2002) Lord Justice Auld favoured greater use of this mode of trial (see Ch 7, [21-35]). See J Jackson, 'Modes of Trial: Shifting the Balance towards the Professional Judge' [2002] *Criminal Law Review* 249.

(a) Representativeness

Throughout the 1980s and 1990s there were persistent allegations that many of those summoned for jury service were able to opt out of serving and those who actually sat on juries were often unfit for such service. A newspaper survey in *The Times* in 1988, backed up by evidence assembled by the Criminal Bar Association, claimed that the discretion to excuse individuals from jury service was so wide that people with property, education and wide experience were under-represented and that the selection of jury panels, and of individual jurors from the panels, was haphazard and primitive.[13] Home Office research in 1999 indicated that 38 per cent of those summonsed for jury service were excused.[14] In addition, large sections of the population were ineligible because of their occupation. The result, it was claimed, was that juries had gone from being, in Lord Devlin's resonant phrase, 'middle-aged, middle-minded and middle-class' to becoming predominantly young, unemployed or manual workers.[15] This concern about juries being unrepresentative in a very different manner from the past led occasionally to periodic media panic that jurors were often criminals themselves, or were 'eye-balled' or intimidated by the accused or his family members or associates seated in the public gallery into arriving at perverse verdicts.[16] One particular example arose out of the acquittal of a defendant in a high-profile murder case in 1993 which prompted a spate of media reports about how juries were representative of an 'increasingly undereducated and lawless population' which was pre-disposed against conviction.[17]

Although steps were taken in 1988 to make the jury in England and Wales more representative of the community at large by abolishing peremptory challenges, concerns about representativeness resurfaced in Auld LJ's *Review of the Criminal Courts of England and Wales* in 2001.[18] Lord Justice Auld was particularly concerned that excusals from jury service were 'depriving juries of the experience and skills of a wider range of professional and otherwise successful and busy people', creating the impression 'voiced by many … that jury service is only for those not important enough or clever enough to get out of it'.[19] In the light of this finding, Auld recommended that everyone should be eligible for jury service, save for the mentally ill, and no one should be excused as of right but only upon good cause. These proposals were enacted in section 321 and Schedule 33 to the Criminal Justice Act 2003, and as a result there has been a considerable narrowing of the exemptions from jury service and a potential broadening of the pool of persons who actually make up juries.[20]

While these new rules enable juries to draw upon a wider body of experience, Auld considered that there remained certain types of cases that were unsuited for jury trial. Prominent among these were particular kinds of serious or complex fraud cases which

---

[13] F Gibb, 'The Jury on Trial', *The Times*, 24–26 October 1988.

[14] Home Office RDS, *Jury Excusal and Deferral*, Research Findings No 102 (London, HMSO, 1999).

[15] Lord Devlin, *Trial By Jury* (London, Stevens, 1956) 20.

[16] Gibb, above n 13.

[17] See *R v Wood* (1996) 1 Cr App R 207, where the Court of Appeal commented that fairness demands that pressure should not be put on juries by the press or anyone else.

[18] Auld Report, above n 12.

[19] Ibid ch 5, [13].

[20] R Taylor, M Wasik and R Leng, *Blackstone's Guide to the Criminal Justice Act 2003* (Oxford, Oxford University Press, 2003) 66.

have long been the subject of debate.[21] Drawing upon a 'culmination of calls' over the years for these cases to be tried without a jury,[22] Auld recommended that, as an alternative to trial by judge and jury, provision should be made for a judge to try such cases either with the assistance of selected lay members or, where the defendant consented, by the trial judge alone. Auld also considered that all young defendants charged with offences that merited a sentence of greater severity than the Youth Court could impose should no longer be tried by a judge and jury but instead by a Youth Court consisting of a judge of appropriate seniority sitting with at least two experienced magistrates. The only exception would be cases in which the defendant was charged jointly with an adult. Finally, drawing attention to the non-jury mode of trial by judge alone instituted for terrorist cases in Northern Ireland, Auld considered that defendants should be able to opt for trial by judge alone with the consent of the court in relation to a wide range of offences. This could provide 'a simpler, more efficient, fairer and more open form of procedure than is now available in many jury trials, with the added advantage of a fully reasoned judgment'.[23]

The variety of cases identified in the Auld Report as being unsuitable for jury trial seemed to erode the principle that jury trial is the most suitable mode of trial for *all* serious cases. Parliament was stirred to embark on its own scrutiny of cases unsuited to jury trial. In the event, however, all of Auld's recommendations for non-jury trial proved too controversial and none was enacted, with the exception of the serious fraud proposals which were then never brought into force.[24] Auld LJ's own recommendations for widening the pool of jury experience seemed to pre-empt his argument that certain cases were too complex for juries to deal with.[25] Concerns about jury tampering, however, could not be alleviated by widening the jury pool. Parliament *was* persuaded to enact section 44 of the Criminal Justice Act 2003, which made provision for a judge to order non-jury trial where there is evidence of a 'real and present' danger that jury tampering would take place during a particular trial.[26]

(b) Impartiality

The Auld reforms broadening the jury pool seemed to defuse criticism that juries were insufficiently experienced to try complex cases and to allay the pervasive concern that was prevalent pre-Auld that juries could too easily succumb to rendering perverse verdicts. Prejudice, of course, whether conscious or unconscious, can always afflict individual jurors, but when personal bias manifests itself amongst a widely diverse group, it may be cancelled out by the views of other jury members.[27] This expectation emphasises the importance

---

[21] See eg Lord Roskill, *The Fraud Trials Committee Report* (London, HMSO, 1986).

[22] D Corker, 'Trying Fraud Cases Without Juries' [2002] *Criminal Law Review* 283, 285.

[23] Auld Report, above n 12, ch 5, [117].

[24] Taylor et al, above n 20, 55–56. Criminal Justice Act 2003, s 43 has since lapsed; and further attempts at resurrection failed: S Doran, 'Trial by Judge Alone' in C Montgomery and D Ormerod, *Fraud: Criminal Law Procedure* (Oxford, Oxford University Press, 2008) C5.

[25] Jackson, above n 12.

[26] Ibid 56–61. This provision has been invoked only rarely: M Kennedy, 'Legal History Made As Four Stand Trial Without Jury', *The Guardian*, 10 January 2010. And see *Twomey and Cameron and Guthrie v UK*, Application Nos 67318/09 and 22226/12, 28 May 2013.

[27] See *R v Abdroikov* [2007] UKHL 37, [2007] 1 WLR 2679, [37]–[38].

of jurors acting collectively in the enterprise of reaching a verdict, working positively as a body and not just individually, to prevent prejudice infecting the deliberations in the case, a responsibility to which we shall return.

While the Auld reforms may have gone some way to reduce the risk of actual bias on the part of juries, the courts have stressed the importance of assessing a tribunal's impartiality from an 'objective' as well as a 'subjective' point of view.[28] The question is not just whether the tribunal has in fact been biased, but also whether an objective and fair-minded observer would have legitimate doubts as to the impartiality of the tribunal. Two particular concerns have arisen in recent years. The first is that it is still possible—given the UK's demographics—for a randomly selected jury to contain only white jurors in cases where race becomes an issue, with the result that prejudice may ensue.[29] Auld recommended the introduction of a scheme for selecting juries consisting of up to three people from any particular ethnic group in cases where the court considered that race might be an important issue in the case.[30] This proposal did not find favour with the legislature. It would seem that in any circumstances where 'generic' bias manifests itself, the only recourse is to hope that any prejudiced or discriminatory behaviour is brought to light.[31] It will then be for the judge to provide sufficient guarantees to exclude any objectively justified or legitimate doubts as to the impartiality of the tribunal.[32] Given the secrecy of juror deliberations, bias can only come to light if jurors take the responsibility to speak up and expose unacceptable attitudes. This suggests again that it is not enough for jurors to act impartially in their decision-making as individuals. We may legitimately require of the 'good' juror, acting with integrity, that he or she raise any concerns about other jurors being biased, in the first instance with their fellow jurors and then, if this fails to make any headway, to expose any instances of prejudice to the judge.[33]

The second concern relates to the practice of permitting those with experience of the administration of justice to sit on a jury. Justice professionals might not approach the case with the same openness of mind as others unconnected with the legal system. Until the 2003 Act there was a long-standing rule that members of the legal profession and others associated with the administration of justice should be ineligible for jury service.[34] Auld did not see why the undoubted risk of bias should be any greater than in the case of many others who are not excluded from juries and are trusted to put their prejudice aside.[35] Another risk, however, is that system insiders may exert a disproportionate influence on other jurors

---

[28] *Piersack v Belgium* (1983) 5 EHRR 169, [30]. See also *Porter v Magill* [2002] 2 AC 357.

[29] The issue of racial bias and racism within the criminal justice system has received much exposure since *The Stephen Lawrence Inquiry: Report of an Inquiry by Sir William Macpherson of Cluny*, Cm 4262-I (London, Home Office, 1999). However, empirical data do not support systematic racial bias in jury verdicts: see C Thomas, *Are Juries Fair?* MoJ Research Series 1/10 (London, Ministry of Justice, 2010) 25–26.

[30] Auld Report, above n 12, ch 5, [52]–[62].

[31] See N Vidmar, 'Pretrial Publicity in Canada: A Comparative Perspective on the Criminal Jury' (1996) 79 *Judicature* 49 (distinguishing 'generic prejudice' from case-specific 'interest prejudice'). See also N Vidmar (ed), *World Jury Systems* (Oxford, Oxford University Press, 2000).

[32] *Sander v United Kingdom* (2001) 31 EHRR 44.

[33] *R v Thompson* [2010] EWCA Crim 1623, [2011] 1 WLR 200, [6] (holding that juror misconduct must immediately be drawn to the attention of the trial judge, or to the other jurors).

[34] See Morris Committee, *Report of the Departmental Committee on Jury Service*, Cmnd 2627 (London, HMSO, 1965).

[35] Auld Report, above n 12, ch 5, [30].

precisely because of their experience with the justice system.[36] Generally speaking, a line has been drawn by both the English courts and the European Court of Human Rights (ECtHR), whereby the mere fact that jurors have held positions as police officers or even prosecutors does not by itself give rise to any justified fears of bias. However, where such jurors have a direct connection with the instant case—if, for example, they are an employee of the prosecuting authority, or they have had some connection with the witnesses or the defendant—stricter scrutiny is required.[37] In *Hanif and Khan v UK*,[38] a juror, who was a serving police officer, knew one of the officers who testified at trial that one of the accused was alone in a car where a quantity of heroin was found. The accused claimed that he had a passenger in the car. The Court of Appeal upheld the convictions on the basis that it was not possible on the evidence to conclude that there had been a passenger. According to the Court, no fair-minded observer would believe that the jury's conclusion might have been brought about as a result of partiality on the part of the police officer juror. The ECtHR, however, considered that although there was nothing to suggest that the police officer juror had actually been biased:

> [W]here there is an important conflict regarding police evidence in the case and a police officer who is personally acquainted with the police officer witness giving the relevant evidence is a member of the jury, jury directions and judicial warnings are insufficient to guard against the risk that the juror may, albeit subconsciously, favour the evidence of the police.[39]

The Court dismissed the argument that the evidence as a whole may have favoured the police officer's account on the ground that it was not for the ECtHR to make its own assessment of the evidence presented at trial.

The ECtHR's refusal to consider the weight of the evidence as a whole in determining the question of bias emphasises the importance that is attached to the manner in which a decision is reached, as opposed to whether the decision itself is factually correct. In determining this question, the Court has focused less on whether the tribunal was subjectively biased than on whether there were objective doubts about its impartiality. Of course, the fact that, as the Court found, the individual police officer juror may have subconsciously favoured the evidence of the police does not necessarily in itself raise a doubt as to whether the jury as a whole was biased. There would appear to be a gap in the reasoning here, for in order to conclude that there was bias on the part of the jury deciding on the crucial conflict of evidence between the police evidence and the defence evidence, any bias on the part of the police officer juror must have disproportionately affected the jury as a whole (or raised an objectively justified suspicion that it had done so). While other jurors could be expected to resist any 'generic' bias on the part of the police officer juror, the fact that the juror knew the police witness (for over ten years and had worked with him on three occasions in the investigation of the same incident) meant that he had 'special' knowledge which could have unduly swayed an otherwise impartial jury.

---

[36] P Hungerford-Welch, 'Police Officers as Jurors' [2012] *Criminal Law Review* 320.
[37] *R v Abdroikov* [2007] UKHL 37, [2007] 1 WLR 2679. See also *R v Khan* [2008] EWCA Crim 531; *Re Purcell's Application* [2008] NICA 11; *Armstrong v UK*, Application No 65282/09, 9 December 2014.
[38] (2012) 55 EHRR 16.
[39] Ibid [148].

(c) Extraneous Material

A related concern that arises from a juror's access to 'special knowledge' about a witness is that this knowledge may be shared with jurors and used against one of the parties in the case without the details being presented and scrutinised in open court. The exclusion of the parties from 'special knowledge' goes to the heart of a concern that has recently attracted considerable attention. Through the internet, in particular, jurors are now able to access extraneous material about the case much more easily than in the past. This additional information may then influence the outcome of the case, in defiance of jurors' oaths to give a true verdict according to the evidence in court. This kind of misconduct strikes at the heart of a fair trial. Such material may have improperly influenced the jury without a warning by the judge as to how it should be assessed. More fundamentally, as Lord Judge CJ observed:

> If material is obtained or used by the jury privately, whether before or after retirement, two linked principles, bedrocks of the administration of criminal justice, and indeed the rule of law, are contravened. The first is open justice, that the defendant in particular, but the public too, is entitled to know of the evidential material considered by the decision-making body; so indeed should everyone with a responsibility for the outcome of the trial, including counsel and the judge, and in an appropriate case, the Court of Appeal Criminal Division. This leads on to the second principle, the entitlement of both the prosecution and defence to a fair opportunity to address the material considered by the jury when reaching its verdict.[40]

Convictions may be found unsafe where there is any prospect that the defendant has been adversely affected in any of these ways by the jury's exposure to extraneous material.[41]

That the problem of extraneous material is quite widespread has been illustrated by a number of appeals.[42] The Criminal Cases Review Commission disclosed to the Law Commission that since 2006 it had been invited to investigate at least 27 cases concerning allegations about juror misconduct. Complaints ranged from jurors using mobile phones in court and having inappropriate access to information about the proceedings to having impermissible contact with someone connected to the case they were trying.[43] Cheryl Thomas' research on juries in England and Wales found that 12 per cent of jurors surveyed in high-profile cases attracting media attention admitted looking for information on the internet, although in other, more routine cases this figure reduced to 5 per cent.[44] Further follow-up research at Crown Court centres revealed that 23 per cent of jurors questioned were 'confused about the rule on internet use', 7 per cent of jurors admitted to looking up information about the legal teams in their trials and 1 per cent admitted to searching for information about parties in the case (other than the defendant).[45] The previous Lord Chief Justice regarded the problem of internet misuse as posing a tangible threat to the very survival of the jury system.[46]

---

[40] *R v Karakaya* [2005] EWCA Crim 346, [2005] 2 Cr App R 5, [24].

[41] Cf *R v Karakaya* [2005] EWCA Crim 346, [2005] 2 Cr App R 5; *R v Marshall and Crump* [2007] EWCA Crim 35.

[42] A list of cases is cited in the Law Commission's Consultation Paper No 209, *Contempt of Court* (London, Stationery Office, 2012) [4.1].

[43] Ibid [4.27].

[44] Thomas, above n 29.

[45] C Thomas, 'Avoiding the Perfect Storm of Juror Contempt' [2013] *Criminal Law Review* 483, 490–91.

[46] Auld Report, above n 12.

2. Integrity in the Jury Room

When reflecting on documented examples of juror misbehaviour, it is important to emphasise the distinction between individual misconduct and its effect on the jury as a whole. One juror's misconduct will not jeopardise the decision-making of an entire jury unless it impacts on the other jurors; and this in turn depends on how other jurors respond. The collective nature of jury deliberations has been somewhat neglected in the anxieties generated by individual misconduct. Remedial action can, of course, be taken against individual jurors for various kinds of misconduct. The Law Commission's consultation paper cited numerous instances of juror behaviour which have been deemed to be misconduct and may amount to contempt of court.[47] Judges have been instructed to warn jurors, as soon as they are sworn in, that behaviour such as discussing the case with anyone outside the jury, carrying out any inquiries or research into any aspect of the case themselves or taking account of media reports, may well amount to contempt which is an offence punishable with imprisonment.[48] Following consultation, the Law Commission recommended that there should be a special criminal offence of intentionally seeking information related to the case that the juror is trying and Parliament has now created several offences which are designed to combat juror misconduct in this respect.[49] While the creation of such offences may be the best means of conveying a consistent message to jurors in all cases of what exactly is being prohibited, and may have some deterrent value,[50] the effectiveness of such an offence will be dependent on jurors disclosing their own misconduct or that of other jury members to the judge. This would seem to necessitate a direction that not only informs juries of the offence and of their need to act with personal integrity within the law, but also appeals to their collective responsibility to bring in a verdict in a manner that forecloses any reliance on extraneous information and respects the integrity of the trial process.

Following a series of criminal appeals involving juror irregularity, Lord Judge CJ in *R v Thompson*[51] emphasised the importance of the jury's collective responsibility. The verdict of the jury, he said, was the verdict of them all (or the requisite statutory majority), and their collective responsibility was not confined to the verdict:

> It begins as soon as the members of the jury have been sworn. From that moment onwards, there is a collective responsibility for ensuring that the conduct of each member is consistent with the jury oath and that the directions of the trial judge about the discharge of their responsibilities are followed. Where it appears that a member of the jury may be misconducting himself or herself, this must *immediately* be drawn to the attention of the trial judge by another, or the other members of

---

[47] Law Commission, above n 42, 62–63.

[48] See Judicial Studies Board, *Crown Court Bench Book: Directing the Jury* (2010). For high-profile examples of jurors sentenced to imprisonment for contempt, see *AG v Dallas* [2012] EWHC 156 (Admin), [2012] 1 WLR 991; *AG v Fraill* [2011] EWCA Crim 1570, [2011] 2 Cr App R 21.

[49] Criminal Justice and Courts Act 2015, ss 71(1), 72 and 73. The Irish Law Reform Commission has recommended a specific offence prohibiting jurors from making independent investigations and internet searches: LRC 207-2013, *Jury Service* (Dublin, Law Reform Commission, 2013).

[50] But this is doubted by JR Spencer, 'The Law Commission's Consultation Paper on Contempt of Court' [2013] *Criminal Law Review* 1, 2. The Law Commission, above n 6, [3.49], [3.61]–[3.65], noted that jurors may be loath to get their fellow jurors into trouble, and that comparative experience provides no clear evidence of the mooted deterrent effect of criminalisation. See also Hunter, above n 5.

[51] [2010] EWCA Crim 1623, [2011] 1 WLR 200.

the jury. So, if for example, an individual juror were to be heard saying that he proposed to decide the case in a particular way regardless of his oath to try it on the evidence, or he were demonstrating a bias based on racism or some other improper prejudice, whether against a witness or the defendant, these things must be reported to the trial judge. So must outside interference, such as imparting information of views apparently gathered from family or friends, or using a mobile phone during deliberations, or conducting research on the internet. The collective responsibility of the jury for its own conduct must be regarded as an integral part of the trial itself.[52]

This is an important statement in emphasising that juror behaviour in the jury room is part of the trial. It does not, of course, form part of the open proceedings of the trial but it can be said to be part of its closed proceedings. Private deliberations cannot be regulated directly by the judge (except perhaps after the fact); they are perforce secret and so they must instead be regulated by the jurors themselves. But in giving directions on how jurors should behave, there is a risk that too much emphasis may be put on jurors' responsibility to respond to irregularity. Rather than emphasise what jurors should *not* do and the procedures for remedying misconduct, the integrity of the closed proceedings as a whole might be better served if clearer instructions were given as to how jurors *should* conduct themselves in the jury room.

At the end of the trial, judges sum up on the evidence and expend much time on directing jurors in terms of what Roberts and Zuckerman call 'forensic reasoning rules'.[53] But in her research, Thomas found that jurors would like more instruction on how they should go about the task of deliberation.[54] In *R v Thompson* the Court of Appeal acknowledged this research finding but considered that, like any other body of individuals called upon to examine evidence before reaching a conclusion, each deliberating jury would have its own dynamics and ways of working. Trial judges could therefore give only general guidance, in terms of reminding the jury that each member has an equal responsibility for the verdict, that it is inevitable that different views will be expressed about different features of the case, and that there must be reasonable give and take between the members of the jury, with an opportunity for each to be heard and his or her opinions considered.[55] Yet this would appear to fall short of the type of guidance juries want. In a follow-up study, Thomas found a desire for more concrete guidance about numerous aspects of jury deliberation, including what to do when confused about a legal issue, how to ensure that jurors are not unduly pressurised into reaching a verdict, how to start deliberations and what to do 'if something goes wrong during deliberations'.[56] Judges have always been reluctant to give jurors any blueprint for their deliberations. But jurors could be given more direction on how to act

---

[52] Ibid [6]. Generally, see *Crown Court Bench Book*, above n 48, 9.

[53] P Roberts and A Zuckerman, *Criminal Evidence*, 2nd edn (Oxford, Oxford University Press, 2010) 662–63.

[54] Thomas, above n 29, 39–40. See also J Goodman-Delahunty, N Brewer, J Clough, J Horan, J Ogloff and D Tait, *Practices, Policies and Procedures that Influence Juror Satisfaction in Australia: Report to the Criminology Research Council July 2007* (Canberra, Australian Institute of Criminology, 2008) 139.

[55] [2010] EWCA Crim 1623, [2011] 1 WLR 200. Cf the wording of the '*Watson*' direction', articulated in *R v Watson* [1988] QB 690, 700, which may be given by judges as part of the summing-up or as a last resort after a jury is still unable to reach a majority verdict: 'Each of you has taken an oath to return a true verdict according to the evidence. No one must be false to that oath but you have a duty not only as individuals but collectively. That is the strength of the jury system. Each of you takes into the jury box with you your individual experience and wisdom. You do that by giving your views, listening to the views of others. There must necessarily be discussion, argument and give and take within the scope of your oath. This is the way in which agreement is reached. If unhappily, one of you cannot reach agreement, you must say so.'

[56] Thomas, above n 45, 496–97.

with the integrity that is required of any *judicial* body adjudicating in a criminal trial. In particular, they could be told more about what responsibilities they have as a body, and not just individually, to adhere to their pledge to give a 'true verdict according to the evidence'.[57]

Guidance to jurors might begin by emphasising that, although they come from the community as citizens, their role in the proceedings is to act as a quasi-judicial body, with special responsibilities. The nature of the lay judicial role is, assuredly, somewhat different from that of the professional judge.[58] There has been much debate about the propriety of jurors exercising a power of 'nullification'.[59] The oath that judges swear—to do right after the law[60]—is absent from the jurors' oath which (as we have seen) is to 'faithfully try the defendant and give a true verdict according to the evidence'. I have argued elsewhere that although jurors do not need to bring in a verdict according to the law, they are bound to determine the case on the merits in accordance with the evidence.[61] This responsibility allows them to maintain some 'role distance'[62] from the classic judicial responsibility to uphold the law. However, this distance only extends towards jurors' refusal to apply the full rigour of the law to the defendant; it does not entitle them to convict upon some extra-legal standard.

Three sets of responsibilities would seem to come into play when directing juries on how to perform their 'judicial' role in accordance with their oath: (a) responsibilities that jurors owe to each other; (b) responsibilities in fact-finding; and (c) responsibilities to ensure fairness to the parties.

(a) Responsibilities Jurors Owe to Each Other

The first set of responsibilities comprises those which individual jurors owe to each other in the exercise of their collective function. Although jurors do not expressly swear to engage in group deliberations, by implication the oath 'to give a true verdict according to the evidence' bids them to do more than come to a personal view of the evidence. They must engage in the act of reaching a collective verdict, which is rendered possible only through joint deliberation.[63] So long as they act within the role assigned to them, that is, to decide the

---

[57] Cf US guidance on jury deliberations: American Judicature Society, *Behind Closed Doors: A Guide for Jury Deliberations* (Des Moines IA, American Judicature Society, 1999). I am grateful to Nancy Marder for this reference.

[58] Jackson and Doran, above n 10, 223, 293–94.

[59] See RF Schopp, 'Verdicts of Conscience: Nullification and Necessity as Jury Responses to Crimes of Conscience' (1996) 69 *Southern California Law Review* 2039; T Brooks, 'A Defence of Jury Nullification' (2004) 10 *Res Publica* 401; M Mattravers, '"More than Just Illogical": Truth and Jury Nullification' in A Duff, L Farmer, S Marshall and V Tadros (eds), *The Trial on Trial (1): Truth and Due Process* (Oxford, Hart Publishing, 2006); Redmayne, above n 4; K Crosby, 'Controlling Devlin's Jury: What the Jury Thinks, and What the Jury Sees Online' [2012] *Criminal Law Review* 15.

[60] Judges in England and Wales swear 'to do right to all manner of people after the laws and usages of this Realm, without fear or favour, affection or ill will': see www.judiciary.gov.uk/about-the-judiciary/introduction-to-justice-system/oaths (accessed 26 January 2016). For further discussion, see J Gardner, *Law as a Leap of Faith* (Oxford, Oxford University Press, 2012) chs 7 and 10.

[61] Jackson, above n 1, 523. See also AAS Zuckerman, 'Law, Fact or Justice?' (1986) 66 *Boston University Law Review* 487.

[62] E Goffman, 'Role Distance' in *Encounters: Two Studies in the Sociology of Interaction* (Indianapolis, Bobbs-Merrill, 1961).

[63] See the terms of the *Watson* direction, above n 55, which states that there must necessarily be discussion, argument and give and take within the scope of the oath.

case in accordance with the evidence, jurors must respect each others' views. This extends to respecting personal conscience and not being bullied into violating it.[64] There should also be respect for the confidentiality of their discussions. Judges, of course, already emphasise the importance of confidentiality in their charge to the jury.[65] This may seem to sit oddly with the new emphasis being placed on the need for judges to alert jurors to bring 'any concerns' about fellow jurors to the attention of the judge. However, delays in reporting irregularities may infect the entire jury and its process of deliberation in such a way that it may be necessary to abort the whole trial when disclosures are finally made.[66] If jurors wait until after the trial to allege misconduct, it may be too late to investigate, absent an allegation that extraneous material was used to reach the verdict.[67] But judges need to be careful about what they ask jurors to report. In *Thompson*, the Lord Chief Justice acknowledged that when judges after the trial receive letters complaining about aspects of the deliberation process, it is hard to avoid the conclusion that the complaint is no more than a protest at the verdict. This suggests that judges should encourage jurors to report only serious irregularities tantamount to a breach of the juror's oath.

(b) Fact-finding Responsibilities

A second set of responsibilities relates to jurors' specific duties as triers of fact. The requirement to give a true verdict according to the evidence is aimed at ensuring that jurors do their best to act in accordance with the tenets of what Twining characterises as the 'rationalist tradition': making judgements under uncertainty by reasoning inductively from admissible, relevant evidence, using the 'available stock of knowledge about the common course of events … supplemented by specialized scientific or expert knowledge'.[68] If they do this, we might say that they are acting with the epistemic integrity that is demanded of them, although this does not mean, of course, that they will always make correct judgements. As already mentioned, jurors will be guided by the judge on how to approach the evidence. However, there has been considerable discussion about jurors' capacity to follow judicial directions.[69] It has been argued that giving these directions to juries at the close of evidence does not assist their understanding.[70] Constructivist learning theory, proposing that learners construct knowledge for themselves, is now widely accepted by behavioural scientists.[71] One implication is that greater efforts should be made to encourage jurors

---

[64] As Judge LCJ said in *R v Thompson* [2010] EWCA Crim 1623, [2011] 1 WLR 200, [9], continuing confidence in the jury system presupposes that jurors do not violate their consciences and can resist pressures to conform. See TA Green, *Verdict According to Conscience* (Chicago, University of Chicago Press, 1985).

[65] *Crown Court Bench Book*, above n 48, 9.

[66] See eg *R v Thakrar* [2008] EWCA Crim 2359, [2009] Crim LR 357 (jurors' failure to report misconduct was itself misconduct).

[67] *R v Mirza, Connor and Rollick* [2004] AC 1118 (HL).

[68] W Twining, *Rethinking Evidence: Exploratory Essays*, 2nd edn (Cambridge, Cambridge University Press, 2006) 76, Table 1, Model II, [6].

[69] See generally, J Horan, *Juries in the 21st Century* (Annandale NSW, Federation Press, 2012) ch 3; C Ellsworth and A Reifman, 'Juror Comprehension and Public Policy: Perceived Problems and Proposed Solutions' (2001) 6 *Psychology, Public Policy and the Law* 788; NS Marder, 'Bringing Jury Instructions into the Twenty-First Century' (2006) 81 *Notre Dame Law Review* 449.

[70] Horan, above n 69, 77–78.

[71] B Schäfer and W Wiegand, 'It is Good to Talk—Speaking Rights and the Jury' in Duff et al, above n 4.

to raise issues with the judge while the trial is still proceeding. Horan has observed that trial by judge alone has been modified to take into account the benefits of construction-ist learning theory; judges are active participants in trials.[72] By contrast, jurors are still discouraged from taking any active role in the trial proceedings. They are often required to absorb oral evidence without resort to written or visual aids, and are discouraged from asking questions.[73] Research in other jurisdictions indicates that juries may be helped in evaluating the evidence when they are encouraged to be more active, for example, by asking questions through the judge.[74]

The argument for encouraging greater juror participation, however, is not just about improving the quality of deliberations and fact-finding; it is also calculated to make jurors aware of their responsibilities and instil confidence in their decision-making role. When they cannot make sense of the evidence or they have a particular concern about its mean-ing or salience, jurors need to raise this first with each other, and then if necessary with the judge. For how can jurors act with integrity to their oath if they passively allow evidence to go over their heads or fail to engage with the evidence as best as they can?

It is one thing to encourage questions about evidence that has been admitted; quite another to encourage questions about perceived gaps in the evidence. Judges often tell jurors not to speculate about missing evidence. Yet it would appear that jurors are often alive to gaps in the evidence in a case.[75] It might be preferable to encourage jurors to raise these concerns with the judge and the parties than to leave them to draw inferences against parties from missing evidence—or worse, as discussed below, to go off and make their own inquiries. The problem of gaps in the evidence may be less pronounced than in the past. There has been a trend across the common law world in favour of admitting more relevant evidence, particularly in the form of hearsay and bad character evidence.[76] Some years ago, the point was made that with better educated and more literate jurors, the value of the old restrictive rules of evidence was being re-evaluated and many were being discarded or modified.[77] But the admission of more information can create its own difficulties for jurors. In relation to the changes that have been made to the admissibility of bad character evidence in the Criminal Justice Act 2003, Roberts and Zuckerman have noted the shift in focus from evidentiary exclusion to judicial directions as the principal institutional mechanism for

---

[72] Horan, above n 69, 77–78.

[73] See M Coen and L Heffernan, 'Juror Comprehension of Expert Testimony: A Reform Agenda' [2010] *Criminal Law Review* 195, 205208.

[74] See L Heuer and S Penrod, 'Juror Notetaking and Question Asking During Trials' (1994) 18 *Law and Human Behavior* 121; S Diamond, M Rose and B Murphy, 'Jurors' Unanswered Questions' (2004) 41 *Court Review* 20, available at http://www.law.northwestern.edu/faculty/fulltime/diamond/papers/unansweredQuestions.pdf (accessed 23 February 2016); BM Dann, V Hans and D Kaye, *Testing the Effects of Selected Jury Trial Innovations on Juror Comprehension of Contested mtDNA Evidence: Final Technical Report* (2004), available at www.ncjrs.gov/pdffiles1/nij/grants/211000.pdf (accessed 23 February 2016).

[75] W Young, N Cameron and Y Tinsley, *Juries in Criminal Trials Part Two—A Summary of the Research Find-ings*, Preliminary Paper 37, vol 2 (Wellington, NZ Law Commission, 1999) [4.8]–[4.11]. Jurors may, in particular, speculate about the accused's concealed criminal past: see L Laudan and RJ Allen, 'The Devastating Impact of Prior Crimes Evidence and Other Myths of the Criminal Justice Process' (2011) 101 *Journal of Criminal Law and Criminology* 493; M Coen, 'Hearsay, Bad Character and Trust in the Jury: Irish and English Contrasts' (2013) 17 *International Journal of Evidence and Proof* 250.

[76] Whilst this is so in England and Wales, following the enactment of the Criminal Justice Act 2003, not all jurisdictions have followed this liberalising trend: see Coen, ibid.

[77] *R v H* [1995] 2 AC 596, 613 per Lord Griffiths, cited in Roberts and Zuckerman, above n 53, 592.

neutralising potential prejudice.[78] The admissibility of bad character evidence can raise difficulties even when juries try to follow cautionary directions. Where, for example, bad character evidence is admitted to establish the accused's propensity to engage in conduct indicative of the crime charged, this inevitably invites some speculation about other aspects of the accused's past and may implicitly encourage independent background research on the accused. This brings us to a third set of responsibilities shouldered by juries, concerning the fairness of trial proceedings.

(c) Fairness to the Parties

Judicial summings-up naturally try to forestall unfairness towards witnesses and defendants during jury deliberations. But the question is whether enough is really done to explain to juries why it is particularly unfair for them to engage in independent research, given jurors' increasing access to extraneous information. In England and Wales, the present guidance in the Crown Court Bench Book requires judges to explain that in an open system of justice, in which the parties themselves decide what evidence to adduce at trial, it is upon that evidence alone that the jury must reach a verdict.[79] Jurors are warned against seeking further information because the prosecution and defence would be unaware of it and unable to respond to it. But it must be questioned whether this is a sufficient explanation, given the fact-finding responsibilities already adverted to which require juries to take an open and inquiring attitude towards the evidence.

The difficulty here is that juries are being asked to do something that seems counter-intuitive to ordinary experience.[80] In a high-profile English trial of a celebrity defendant for perverting the course of justice, much publicity was given to '10 questions' that the jury asked of the judge.[81] One question was whether a juror can come to a conclusion based on a reason that was not presented in court and has no facts or evidence to support it, either from the prosecution or defence. The jury was criticised by the trial judge for misunderstanding its essential function. It is impossible to know for certain exactly what the jury meant by such a question, and it would be a mistake to generalise about jury behaviour from a single case.[82] Empirical data suggest, however, that jurors do not seem to appreciate the importance or do not understand the logic of restricting themselves to the information presented by the parties and the judge. In an illuminating empirical study in New South Wales, Hunter et al found that a prevalent misconception amongst certain jurors was that a juror's task is to determine the true facts in a case rather than whether the prosecution has proven a defendant's guilt beyond reasonable doubt.[83] In their words, they prioritised 'objective truth' over 'procedural truth', or 'truth' over 'proof'.[84]

---

[78]   Roberts and Zuckerman, ibid 660.

[79]   *Crown Court Bench Book*, above n 48, 9.

[80]   According to Hunter, above n 5, 39, 'everyone's every day experiences endorse thorough research for important decision-making—for choosing a child's school, buying a car or choosing a job, a career, a new appliance or where to live. Most activities reward diligence in gaining an improved understanding of the world in which decisions are made. Not so jury duty.' See also Horan, above n 69, 168.

[81]   C Davies, 'Vicky Pryce Trial: 10 Questions Jury Asked Judge', *The Guardian*, 20 February 2013.

[82]   C Thomas, 'Exposing the Myth' (April 2013) *Counsel Magazine* 25.

[83]   J Hunter, D Boniface and D Thomson, *What Jurors Search For & What They Don't Get: Pilot Study—Juror Comprehension & Obedience to Judicial Directions Against Juror Investigation* (Sydney, UNSW, 2010). See also Hunter, above n 5.

[84]   Hunter et al, above n 83, 16; Hunter, above n 5, 18.

Existing judicial directions to counteract the problem of juror investigation and research were categorised by Hunter et al as related either to the integrity of the trial process or to matters of personal significance for the investigating juror. In their sample cases, they found that no trial judge provided a jury with a completely comprehensive explanation of the personal and procedural consequences that might follow should a juror disregard a direction not to engage in investigation or research. Hunter et al suggest that more should be done to link the features of 'adversarial justice' together to illustrate why it is both 'completely unnecessary and deeply inappropriate' for jurors to engage in extra-curial investigation or research. The Judicial Commission of New South Wales' suggested directions in the Criminal Trial Courts Bench Book provide illustrations explaining the nature of the criminal trial and the jury's function within it. They now spell out why making inquiries offends against the juror's oath to give a true verdict founded squarely on the evidence presented in open court.

Although these guidelines would appear to be improvements on existing directions, it may be asked whether they do enough to integrate the fact-finding responsibilities of the jury with standards of procedural fairness. The guidelines make reference to the frustration that jurors may feel about a lack of evidence but then go on to say, in effect, that jurors must put up with this, since making inquiries about anything to do with the case is 'not your function', which is instead, 'to decide on the evidence that has been placed before you whether the case for the Crown has been proved beyond reasonable doubt'.[85] Jurors may well understand from this why they must not go away and conduct independent research and make inquiries unconnected with the evidence in the case. But their job *is* to test the evidence that is placed before them to determine whether, taken in the round, it reaches the standard of proof beyond reasonable doubt. They do this in the light of examination by trial counsel, but at the end of the day jurors have to satisfy themselves, one way or another—and this is where the motivation to seek out further information gains a foothold.

Rosemary Pattenden has suggested that the distinction between extraneous and non-extraneous material is built on sand, because jurors must necessarily bring to the deliberations their own experience of life and general knowledge.[86] She is critical of one case where the Court of Appeal in England and Wales quashed a conviction for possession of an offensive weapon after a judge failed to warn the jury not to act on any experiment carried out after receiving a report that a jury member had attempted to bring a pair of clippers into the court building to demonstrate some point in connection with the case.[87] Pattenden contrasts this with the example of a juror who shares information which he knows about knives with the rest of the jury. The former juror is errant but the latter juror does the 'right thing'. She goes on to suggest that the distinction between general knowledge and illicit non-evidential material becomes even more tenuous when the internet is brought into the equation. A juror who is a lawyer would be allowed to pass on his knowledge about the meaning of a legal term but a lay member who looks the term up on the internet to refresh his memory from something the judge has said has

[85] New South Wales Judicial Commission, *Criminal Trial Courts Bench* Book, [1-480] available at www.judcom.nsw.gov.au/publications/benchbks/criminal (accessed 26 January 2016).

[86] R Pattenden, 'Investigating Irregularities—United Kingdom (England and Wales)' (2010) 14 *International Journal of Evidence and Proof* 362.

[87] *R v Thompson* [2010] EWCA Crim 1623, [2011] 1 WLR 200, [84].

misbehaved.[88] The Court of Appeal has suggested that experts sitting on a jury may not 'introduce entirely new evidence into the case, let alone doing so at a time when neither party had been put on notice of it and given the opportunity to test it, and where the appellant in particular had not been given any opportunity to provide an explanation of it'.[89] But there is a fine line between using one's specialised knowledge in analysing the evidence given in a case and actually giving new evidence oneself.[90]

A more realistic approach may be to concede that, while jurors are theoretically prohibited from checking up details on the internet, it is impossible in this day and age to prevent them from doing so, short of a form of sequestration that would bar access to the internet altogether. Better in these circumstances to concentrate on bringing home to jurors the important 'judicial' responsibilities they have. By swearing that they will try the case according to the evidence, jurors are by implication undertaking not to consider evidence which has not been admitted into court and has not been disclosed to the parties. The rationale for this restriction, it might be stressed, is not simply to satisfy some formal notion of 'procedural' fairness, but to ensure that evidence is properly tested before being acted upon. Upholding the integrity of the trial process is not to prioritise due process independent of truth-finding, but rather mandates finding the truth through a process of 'adversarial' argument. Failure to subject evidence to this process can result in flawed outcomes.[91]

It would seem to follow that if, by *whatever* means, jurors are aware of any information which has not been presented to the parties, their 'judicial' role requires that before sharing it with their fellow jury members, they must first disclose it to the judge so that the judge can decide how to proceed in consultation with the parties. Having considered counsel's submissions, the judge may decide to discharge the juror, along with the entire jury if there is a risk of contamination. Alternatively, the judge may decide that the disclosure would not risk an unfair trial.

3. From Reasonable Verdicts to Reasoned Verdicts

We have established that jurors assume important 'judicial' responsibilities to ensure that their deliberations are based on the evidence that has been adduced before them. But the juror's oath pledges jurors not only to try the defendant according to the evidence but also to 'give a true verdict according to the evidence'. Should jurors' responsibilities thus extend to giving a reasoned decision for their verdict?

---

[88] Professional guidance to barristers and solicitors states that, if selected for jury service, they serve as private citizens and should not proffer legal advice or opinions: Bar Council, *Guidance for the Bar Called for Jury Service* (June 2004); Law Society, *Solicitors Called for Jury Service—Guidance*, 29 September 2005.

[89] *R v Fricker*, The Times, 13 July 1999.

[90] See N Haralambous, 'Juries and Extraneous Material: A Question of Integrity' (2007) 71 *Journal of Criminal Law* 520. The distinction between expert opinion and factual testimony is not always easy to apply: see eg *R v Abadom* [1983] 1 All ER 364.

[91] In Hunter et al's study, above n 83, 36, the dangers of flawed information, potential irrelevance and misleading jurors unskilled in its assessment rated as the most persuasive reasons for not engaging in private inquiries. On the relationship between 'adversarial' challenge and truth finding, see JD Jackson and SJ Summers, *The Internationalisation of Criminal Evidence* (Cambridge, Cambridge University Press, 2012) 362–63.

Much has been written in recent years about whether the defendant's right to a fair trial requires a reasoned judgement. The Grand Chamber of the ECtHR in *Taxquet v Belgium* took the view that a fair trial entailed that the accused, and indeed the public, must be able to understand the verdict. This was 'a vital safeguard against arbitrariness'.[92] In proceedings conducted before professional judges the accused's understanding of his or her conviction stems primarily from the reasons given in the judicial decision. No such reasons are furnished by general jury verdicts. Yet the Grand Chamber drew back from the Chamber's ruling, which appeared to require that all decisions in criminal cases, including those given by lay juries, must be accompanied by reasons. The Grand Chamber in *Taxquet* accepted that, in the case of assize courts sitting with a lay jury, Article 6 does not require the lay jury to give reasons, although it does require an assessment of whether sufficient safeguards were in place to avoid any risk of arbitrariness and to enable the accused to understand the reasons for his conviction.

One of the safeguards specifically mentioned by the ECtHR is that directions or guidance are provided by the presiding judge to the jurors on the legal issues arising or the evidence adduced. Given this framework, it may often be relatively straightforward to infer why and more or less how a criminal jury has arrived at its verdict.[93] The Lord Chief Justice has considered that 'a properly structured summing up followed by a verdict of the jury ... provides a complete understanding to the defendant and to the public of the reasons why the jury decided that the case against the defendant has been proved'.[94] In its admissibility decision in *Judge v UK*[95] where the applicant complained that a Scottish jury had convicted him of serious sexual offences without giving reasons, the ECtHR seemed to agree. According to the Court:

> [I]n Scotland the jury's verdict is not returned in isolation but is given in a framework which includes addresses by the prosecution and the defence as well as the presiding judge's charge to the jury. Scots law also ensures there is a clear demarcation between the respective roles of the judge and jury: it is the duty of the judge to ensure the proceedings are conducted fairly and to explain the law as it applies in the case to the jury; it is the duty of the jury to accept those directions and to determine all questions of fact. In addition, although the jury are 'masters of the facts' ... it is the duty of the presiding judge to accede to a submission of no case to answer if he or she is satisfied that the evidence led by the prosecution is insufficient in law to justify the accused's conviction ... These are precisely the procedural safeguards which were contemplated by the Grand Chamber ... in *Taxquet*. In the present case, the applicant has not sought to argue that these safeguards were not properly followed at his trial. Nor has he suggested that the various counts in the indictment were insufficiently clear. Indeed, the essential feature of an indictment is that each count contained in it must specify the factual basis for the criminal conduct alleged by the prosecution: there is no indication that the indictment upon which the applicant was charged failed to do so. It must, therefore, have been clear to the applicant that, when he was convicted by the jury, it was because the jury had accepted the evidence of the complainers in respect of each of the counts in the indictment and, by implication, rejected his version of events.[96]

---

[92] *Taxquet v Belgium* [2012] 54 EHRR 26.
[93] P Roberts, 'Does Article 6 of the European Convention on Human Rights Require Reasoned Verdicts?' (2011) 11 *Human Rights Law Review* 213.
[94] Lord Judge CJ, above n 12.
[95] Application No 35863/10, 8 February 2011.
[96] Ibid [36]–[37].

It is important here to unravel the different strands of reasoning that a defendant and the public can draw from a verdict that has followed a contested trial. There is a difference between an accused understanding *what* evidence has been accepted in order to lead to his or her conviction, *why* that evidence has been accepted and *how* the decision was actually reached. The fact that the judge may have ruled that there is a case to answer implies rational evidential support for the conviction and the ECtHR also stressed the availability of procedural mechanisms in Scots law for quashing any conviction found on appeal to be a miscarriage of justice. But a reasonable verdict is not necessarily *reasoned*. Where, as on the facts in *Judge*, the evidential issue is whether to believe the complainer's evidence or whether to believe the defendant's evidence and a verdict of guilty follows, it is easy to understand that the reasons for the conviction were that the jury believed the complainer and not the defendant. But in a more complex case such as *Taxquet* where there were eight defendants allegedly involved in a conspiracy to murder and Taxquet was convicted of the pre-meditated murder of a government minister and the attempted pre-meditated murder of the minister's partner, a general verdict in itself (or, as was the case in *Taxquet*, simple 'yes' or 'no' answers to questions about the defendant's level of involvement and planning) may not be enough to explain his role in the conspiracy, especially since several co-conspirators were cleared of premeditation.

It is not enough to assert that the allegations against the defendant have been proved. There needs to be some evidence which the defendant can understand linking him or her to the elements of the charge. This is why closed material proceedings which have increasingly become a feature of the landscape in deportation and immigration cases in the UK are so problematic.[97] The ECtHR has held that where detainees are facing lengthy periods of detention they must be provided with sufficient information about the allegations against them to enable them to give effective instructions to the special advocate who will represent their interests in the closed proceedings.[98] But even if this minimal standard of disclosure is satisfied, when the closed proceedings end with a decision against the detainee which does not explain how the evidence links him to the allegations, he may not understand why the allegations have been upheld.[99]

In criminal cases the defendant has the benefit of knowing all the evidence against him, an opportunity to contest it and a careful summing up which should explain on what evidential basis a jury is at liberty to convict the defendant of the offences charged. As counsel for the UK government argued in *Taxquet*, in the course of a summing up a judge can give directions about the proper approach, or particular caution, to adopt in respect of certain evidence as well as providing the jury with information about the applicable legal rules. On that account the judge clarifies the constituent elements of the offence and sets out the chain of reasoning that should be followed in order to reach a verdict based on the jury's findings of fact. Where there is a verdict of guilty reached upon the basis of a summing up which articulates the route or, as may happen, the various routes argued by the prosecution

---

[97] The Justice and Security Act 2013 extends this mechanism in civil proceedings. See J Jackson, 'Justice, Security and Right to a Fair Trial: Is the Use of Secret Evidence Ever Fair?' [2013] *Public Law* 720.

[98] *A v United Kingdom* (2009) 49 EHRR 29; followed in *Secretary of State for the Home Department v AF* [2009] UKHL 28, [2010] 2 AC 269.

[99] Cf *Bank Mellat v HM Treasury (No 1)* [2013] UKSC 38, [2014] AC 700, [69] (any party who has been excluded from a closed hearing should be told as much as possible about the court's reasoning and the evidence and arguments it received).

towards liability, then the defendant will arguably be given a sufficient understanding of the reasons for the verdict.

But even if a defendant is indirectly given a sufficient understanding of the reasons for the verdict, should the jury *itself* not explain its own reasoning? Since the verdict is a 'performance' act that not merely declares the defendant's guilt but makes a normative judgement upon the accused from which grave consequences can follow, is the accused not owed a direct explanation *from* the jury as to what the reasons are for its verdict?[100] Duff et al have argued that those calling an accused to account forfeit moral standing if they fail to communicate the normative grounds for their verdict.[101] In certain recent decisions the UK Supreme Court has emphasised the importance of avoiding a sense of injustice on the part of those subject to legal decision-making.[102] As Lord Reid put it, 'justice is intuitively understood to require a procedure which pays due respect to persons whose rights are significantly affected by decisions taken in the exercise of administrative and judicial functions'.[103] Giving reasons is generally considered an important aspect of the judicial role, but juries have not traditionally been conceived as exercising a significant 'judicial' function in pronouncing their verdict.

Unlike appointed 'officials', juries pass a very personal judgement on their peers.[104] Although unified into a panel, each juror retains an individual voice. There is no single 'official' condemnation that comes with the verdict, but rather a series of what may be very individual and different reasons each justifying the verdict as a matter of conscience. In such circumstances, so long as defendants have confidence in their peers as a group of randomly selected community members who can be expected to share similar values as themselves, they can accept an unreasoned verdict, without feeling any sense of injustice. Conversely, the more that values within the community diverge and a normative rift opens up between different sections of the community, the more likely a sense of injustice may be created by a verdict that is unexplained. A feeling of injustice might be particularly engendered on the part of those who are extradited from foreign countries and found guilty by an unaccountable jury completely unconnected to their community back in their home country. If they are extradited from countries which have no tradition of jury trial and where reasons are given as a matter of course by any tribunal adjudicating on the guilt of an accused, a sense of injustice might be further compounded by the lack of reasons given for their guilt.[105]

Rather than asking what is owed to defendants, we might instead consider what is required to do justice to the integrity of the criminal process. This raises a set of questions having less to do with the accused's sense of injustice than with the institutional integrity of what is owed by jurors as a judicial body intent on giving 'a true verdict according to the evidence'. We have seen that this task involves a commitment towards three distinct

---

[100] On 'performative' utterances, see JL Austin, *How To Do Things With Words* (Oxford, Oxford University Press, 1962) 1–11.

[101] A Duff, L Farmer, S Marshall and V Tadros, *The Trial on Trial (3): Towards a Normative Theory of the Criminal Trial* (Oxford, Hart Publishing, 2007) 218–20. See also J Gardner, 'The Mark of Responsibility' (2003) 23 *Oxford Journal of Legal Studies* 157.

[102] See eg *Osborn v Parole Board; Booth v Parole Board; In re Reilly* [2013] UKSC 61, [2014] AC 1115.

[103] Ibid [68].

[104] But cf R Lippke, 'The Case for Reasoned Criminal Trial Verdicts' (2009) 22 *Canadian Journal of Law and Jurisprudence* 313, 321 (arguing that jurors act as temporary state officials and should therefore fully and publicly justify their acts to satisfy the condition of political legitimacy).

[105] I owe this point to Paul Roberts.

responsibilities: collective deliberation, rational fact-finding and fairness towards the parties within the context of the adversarial trial. The question then is whether a requirement to give reasons might contribute positively towards these ends and, if so, whether reasons for jury verdicts should become mandatory.

At one level, requiring reasoned verdicts would seem to aid the deliberation process as it would encourage jury members to engage in deliberation together rather than reach conclusions by means of arithmetical vote-counting. There has been some debate in the jury research literature as to whether jury deliberations are evidence-driven or verdict-driven.[106] The former reasoning model starts with a review of the evidence without reference to the verdict and works towards agreeing upon the single most credible story of the events at the time of the alleged crime. The latter mode begins with a public ballot and embarks on deliberation by citing evidence in support of a specific verdict position. Both styles of deliberation may in fact be adopted by jurors, sometimes during the course of a single deliberation.[107] The evidence-driven approach might seem closer to the deliberative ideal of being open to persuasion without feeling under pressure from other jurors.[108] However, it is by no means clear whether a requirement to give reasons would encourage this mode of deliberation. Such a requirement might encourage jurors to develop a single story in the evidence-driven mode, but it might also, on the other hand, merely encourage early vote-taking with subsequent deliberations amounting to little more than *ex post facto* rationalisation of a fait accompli.

Would requiring reasons enhance the quality of the jury's deliberations and improve the rationality of jury decision-making? The supposed rationality of jury deliberations has been widely debated.[109] While many share an aspirational vision of juror rationality,[110] others argue that heuristics and biases infect individual juror decision-making, and when jurors share a particular bias, group processes can magnify its effect.[111] Whatever view is taken about the rationality of jury decision-making, however, it is hard to see how a requirement to give reasons would eradicate the biases that may infect decision-making. In recent years common law jurisdictions have encouraged trial judges to provide more structured summings-up to aid juror comprehension of the issues. Written directions to juries—variously styled 'question trails', 'decision trees', structured question paths', 'flow charts' or 'routes to verdict'—are carefully tailored to the law and the evidence in the case, with the aim of assisting juries to adopt a logical, sequential approach to their deliberations.[112]

---

[106] See R Hastie, S Penrod and N Pennington, *Inside the Jury* (Cambridge MA, Harvard University Press, 1983) 163–65; PC Ellsworth, 'Are Twelve Heads Better than One?' (1989) 52 *Law and Contemporary Problems* 247.

[107] J Fordham, 'Illustrating or Blurring the Truth: Jurors, Juries, and Expert Evidence' in B Brooks-Gordon and M Freeman (eds), *Law and Psychology: Current Legal Issues Volume 9* (Oxford, Oxford University Press, 2006) 338.

[108] Hastie et al, above n 106, 165.

[109] See eg C Callen (ed), *Visions of Rationality in Evidence Law Symposium* (2003) 4 *Michigan State Law Review* 847–1364.

[110] See E Swift, 'Aspirational Optimism about Evidence Law' (2003) 4 *Michigan State Law Review* 1337, 1344 (characterising aspirational rationality as the consensus view of participants in Callen (ed), above n 109).

[111] E Beecher-Monas, 'Heuristics, Biases, and the Importance of Gate-Keeping' (2003) 4 *Michigan State Law Review* 987; C Sunstein, *Going to Extremes* (New York, Oxford University Press, 2011). Contemporary research on biases and heuristics originates from A Tversky and D Kahneman, 'Judgment under Uncertainty: Heuristics and Biases' (1974) 185 *Science* 1124.

[112] See eg J Ogloff, J Clough, J Goodman-Delahunty and W Young, *The Jury Project 1—A Survey of Australian and New Zealand Judges* (Canberra, Australian Institute of Judicial Administration, 2006). See also *R v Green* [2005] EWCA Crim 2513; *R v Thompson* (2010) EWCA Crim 1623, [2011] 1 WLR 200, [13]. The New South Wales Law Reform Commission has given support to integrated directions and written question trails, particularly in

While such efforts may encourage juries to structure their reasoning process in a more orderly manner around the key questions to be determined, however, they do nothing in themselves to address any biases that might taint the deliberative process. Requiring reasons would make juries justify their answers to the questions asked. But the degree to which this would actually improve the quality of jury decision-making is debatable. Accountability of this kind may help to concentrate jurors' minds on how to justify the decision reached, but to the extent that reasons are merely *ex post facto* rationalisations of mental processes, they do not act as a constraint on the process of reaching the decision in the first place.

At this point, it may be argued that requiring reasons at least provides a basis for evaluating whether the jury is able to provide a rational justification for the verdict. In permitting the case to be heard by a jury, a judge is signifying that a verdict of guilty may be justifiable on the evidence, but when the jury enters the deliberation room we have no means of knowing how rational its members will be in coming to their decision. Accountability for the decision, on this argument, is not about improving decision-making, but rather about enabling an effective challenge to be made to a decision-making process that is necessarily opaque and lacking in transparency. At present, we are reliant on individual jurors to complain about any impropriety in the jury room to trigger further investigation by the judge. If reasons were required for the verdict there would at least be a basis for scrutinising in every case whether the jury has provided a rational justification for its verdict.

So long as the evidential basis for the jury's decision-making remains confined to information presented by the parties in open court, and litigants can influence judicial directions informing jurors how trial evidence should be considered and tested, it can be argued that the parties have sufficient 'input' control into the process to ensure that unreasoned verdicts are not tainted by adversarial deficit. As Damaška has explained, it is mainly through the parties' influence on what evidentiary material 'the procedural Sphinx hears and sees that the parties feel they can affect the outcome of the case'.[113] Evidence law thus becomes a means not only of correcting factual error—it becomes the means of shoring up 'ex ante the legitimacy of inscrutable jury verdicts'.[114] The more relaxed the evidentiary standards become, however, with ever less probative and more potentially prejudicial evidence entrusted into the jury's care (albeit under evidentiary instruction), the more an adversarial deficit is likely to emerge in terms of the parties' ability to challenge how exactly such evidence was handled in the closed confines of the deliberation room. Add to this the increasing ease with which jurors are able to obtain access to extraneous information (albeit in the teeth of stern judicial warnings against undertaking such inquiries) and the argument for greater scrutiny of their decision-making becomes all the stronger.

If it were simply the case that juries were being asked to assess information and reach decisions in a manner which corresponded with their behaviour in everyday life, they might be trusted not to deviate from 'natural' processes of decision-making. But this is very far from the case. The kind of forensic reasoning rules on which judges instruct juries do not always reflect common-sense decision-making. Admittedly, some of the more egregious examples of 'unnatural' reasoning, such as requiring juries to distinguish between evidence

---

complex cases: see New South Wales Law Reform Commission Report 136, *Jury Directions* (Sydney, New South Wales Government, 2012) [6.168].

[113] MR Damaška, *Evidence Law Adrift* (New Haven, Yale University Press, 1997) 44.
[114] Ibid 46.

going to issues in the case and evidence going to credibility,[115] are in decline. But we have seen that directions that attempt to limit the jury's reasoning to the evidence adduced in the trial grinds against a natural curiosity towards thorough investigation. The idea that juries should restrict themselves to a prescribed evidential database does not conform to the way in which decisions are made in everyday life. Although steps are being developed to equip juries with normative guidance, the more these norms depart from the natural inclinations of rational decision-makers and take on a specifically 'judicial' character designed to assure the adversarial integrity of the trial, the more, it can be argued, that juries should be required, like any other judicial body, to give some assurance that they arrived at their decision in a legally competent manner.

Of course, requiring a reasoned judgment would not *guarantee* that juries have in fact delivered on their oath to act only upon the evidence. What the discipline of reason-giving can do, however, is offer some means of scrutinising not only whether a verdict can be supported on the evidence but also whether the tribunal itself can justify the verdict on the basis that proper considerations were taken into account and that improper considerations were disregarded.[116] It may be that the judge's summing-up once played this justificatory role. However, as juries are being required to play a more demanding 'judicial' role themselves within the closed parts of criminal proceedings, affording full integrity to this process would seem to require some explanation of how jurors applied the summing up in their deliberations and verdict.

4. Towards More Reasoned Judgments: A Comparative Overview

If this argument is accepted in principle, there remain, of course, considerable practical difficulties in requiring reasons from a body of 12 persons who, although required to deliberate together, can reach individual conclusions on the facts by different routes. It is sometimes said to be impossible to require jurors to give full reasons for their decisions, at least in more complex cases.[117] There are certainly limits to the degree to which detailed reasons can be formulated. In order to consider how juries might be required to produce more reasoned verdicts, it is useful to advert to the practice in European countries which have retained—or in some cases resurrected—the 'traditional' jury within their criminal justice system but have been inclined to scrutinise jury verdicts more searchingly than common law countries generally do.[118]

---

[115] See eg S Lloyd-Bostock, 'The Effect on Juries of Hearing about the Defendant's Previous Criminal Record: A Simulation Study' [2000] *Criminal Law Review* 734.

[116] See *Flannery v Halifax Estate Agencies Ltd* (2000) 1 WLR 377, 383 (Henry LJ).

[117] See eg Blom-Cooper, above n 12, 14. But cf Lippke, above n 104, 324–25.

[118] The Grand Chamber in *Taxquet v Belgium* [2012] 54 EHRR 26, [43], uses the term 'traditional' to characterise the 'trial-by-jury' model, the 'defining feature of which is that professional judges are unable to take part in the jurors' deliberations'. On difficulties of nomenclature and the variety of models of lay adjudication in Europe, see JD Jackson and N Kovalev, 'Lay Adjudication and Human Rights in Europe' (2006) 13 *Columbia Journal of European Law* 83. A surprisingly large number of continental systems operate a 'traditional' jury system. The Grand Chamber in *Taxquet* counted ten Council of Europe states; Switzerland has since defected, but Georgia has joined the list: see S Thaman, 'Should Criminal Juries Give Reasons for their Verdicts?' (2011) 86 *Chicago-Kent Law Review* 613, 619.

During the course of the nineteenth century most European countries followed the approach taken in France and introduced a system of trial by jury in criminal cases that allowed jurors to base their decisions on their *intime conviction*.[119] Unlike the unvarnished general verdict of 'guilty' or 'not guilty', however, continental juries were required to return an itemised special verdict or 'question list' which asked jurors to address the basic elements of the charged crimes and any possible excuses or justifications. In many jurisdictions the French characterisation of a judicial decision as an *intime conviction* has gradually been developed to require a more overtly reasoned verdict.[120] Thus, for example, Article 120(3) of the Spanish Constitution specifically requires that 'reasons shall always be given for judgments'. When Spain re-introduced jury trial after the Franco era, the Spanish Supreme Court had to interpret how this requirement was to be applied to jury decisions. Thaman describes how the Court has vacillated between a 'flexible' approach, requiring little more than the jury restating the evidence presented at trial, and a more 'demanding' approach, requiring the jury to articulate why and how it arrived at its determination of the facts, very much resembling the explanation demanded of professional judges in 'motivating' a judgment.[121]

In the light of the first *Taxquet* decision, which put so much emphasis on the need for reasons in criminal cases as a safeguard against arbitrariness, it appeared for a while that there were only two choices facing countries with the traditional jury system: either move to require juries to give reasons or abolish trial by jury altogether. Belgium followed Spain in requiring reasons whilst the traditional juries in Switzerland and Denmark have been phased out altogether. Various approaches have been adopted to assist the jury in giving reasoned decisions. One is to invite the judge into the deliberation room after the jury has reached its verdict to help it to draft reasons. The risk here, however, is that the reasons end up being those of the professional judge and not those of the jury. Alternatively, the jury might be permitted to summon the clerk of the court or some suitably qualified lawyer to draft the reasons.[122] Again, however, the danger of domination by the professional lawyer is one that might be too much to tolerate for a common law culture dedicated to the preservation of lay decision-making. Another approach is to ensure proper input by the professional judge *before* the jury deliberates, requiring the judge, in consultation with counsel, to put suitably detailed questions to the jury. When the questions are in 'closed' format (inviting yes/no answers) the jury's determination resembles a special verdict, but such verdicts are not fully reasoned.[123] Where the questions are of a more 'open' nature, however, the jury is able to construct a fuller, more nuanced narrative. A third approach is to give the jury free rein to explain its verdict within the parameters of the judge's directions but to enable the judge to refuse to accept the reasons if they are not adequately articulated. This exercise of judicial control is analogous to common law judges' power to direct an acquittal

---

[119] All European countries introduced jury trials in the 19th century with the exception of the Netherlands and Luxembourg: N Vidmar, 'The Jury Elsewhere in the World' in Vidmar (ed), above n 31, 429–32.

[120] Damaška, above n 113, 21.

[121] Thaman, above n 118, 634. See also S Thaman, 'Spain Returns to Trial by Jury' (1998) 21 *Hastings International & Comparative Law Review* 241; M Jimeno-Bulnes, 'A Different Story Line for Twelve Angry Men: Verdicts Reached by Majority Rule—The Spanish Perspective' (2011) 82 *Chicago-Kent Law Review* 759, 766.

[122] This was the procedure adopted in the Canton of Geneva and is the procedure used in Spain: Thaman, above n 118, 627, 629. For discussion of the role played by the secretary in drafting reasons, see Thaman, above n 121, 374–76.

[123] This was the pre-*Taxquet* Belgian model: see P Traest, 'The Jury in Belgium, Lay Participation in the Criminal Trial in the XX1st Century' (2001) 72 *Revue Internationale de Droit Pénal* 27.

(for example, for insufficiency of evidence) at any time before the jury retires, except that it would be exercised *after* the jury has returned its reasoned verdict. The precise parameters of this judicial jurisdiction have been disputed in Spain. Judges assuredly have the power to refuse to accept reasons that are clearly contradictory on their face. In these circumstances, the jury will be instructed to 'repair' its material omissions. More controversy surrounds the question whether a judge can refuse to accept reasons considered to be insufficient or inadequate.[124]

These different approaches are not mutually exclusive and others could no doubt be devised. The continental experience with reasoned verdicts has attracted mixed reviews over time. Esmein judged the system a 'fertile' one.[125] For Mannheim, however, it rested on 'the fundamental mistake' of believing that the more numerous and detailed the questions were, the more jurors could be limited to the pure facts of the case.[126] This arrangement proved so confusing and impracticable in Germany that, according to another commentator, it was one of the reasons why the jury system was abolished in favour of the mixed court system in 1924.[127]

Two general lessons might be drawn from the continental experience. First, where enough judicial guidance is given in advance of the jury retiring and where, in particular, written instructions are provided, it is not impossible to require juries to give reasoned verdicts. One does not have to look to continental jurisdictions to vindicate this claim. Despite the demise of the civil jury, several common law countries have retained an inquest system where juries sit to deliver verdicts in certain cases. These are often special verdicts answering closed questions. However, a more narrative style has become increasingly common where inquests are the instrument by which the UK meets its procedural obligation under Article 2 of the ECHR (right to life) to investigate any death implicating agents of the state.[128] In such cases, coroners are required to elicit a jury's conclusion on the central issues—by what means and in what circumstances did the deceased meet his death?—extending beyond proximate causation. Although short verdicts in the traditional form will sometimes enable the jury to express its conclusion on these issues, the UK Supreme Court has said that a change of approach incorporating narrative elements may be required in certain circumstances.[129] Examples of such verdicts can be found in recent high-profile cases where juries were asked to draw detailed conclusions in relation to fatal shootings by security forces in Northern Ireland.[130] Findings in such cases are inevitably controversial,

---

[124]   Thaman, above n 118, 649–50.

[125]   A Esmein, *A History of Continental Criminal Procedure with Special Reference to France* (Boston, Little, Brown & Co, 1882; trans J Simpson 1913) 416.

[126]   H Mannheim, 'Trial by Jury in Modern Continental Law' (1937) 53 *Law Quarterly Review* 99, 107. For some of the difficulties with the Spanish system, see Thaman, above n 118, 670–72.

[127]   F Gorphe, 'Reforms of the Jury-System in Europe: France and Other Continental Countries' (1937) 27 *American Institute of Criminal Law & Criminology* 155, 158.

[128]   See eg *Taylor v UK* (1994) 79 DR 124, 137; *McCann v UK* (1995) 21 EHRR 97, [161]; *Powell v UK* Application No 45305/99, 4 May 2000; *Salman v Turkey* (2002) 34 EHRR 425, [104]; *Jordan v UK* (2001) 37 EHRR 52, [105]. Such an obligation was recognised in respect of state killings preceding the entry into force of the Human Rights Act 1998: *Re McCaughey* [2011] UKSC 20, [2012] 1 AC 725. Cf *Re McKerr* [2004] UKHL 12, [2004] 1 WLR 807.

[129]   *R (Middleton) v HM Coroner for the Western District of Somerset* [2004] UKHL 10, [2004] 2 AC 182.

[130]   See eg the narrative verdict returned by an inquest jury in the case concerning the shooting of two IRA men, McCaughey and Grew, by SAS soldiers: B McCaffrey, 'Jury Says SAS Justified in Shooting IRA Man on Ground', *The Detail*, 31 March 2012; www.thedetail.tv/issues/87/shoot-to-kill/jury--says-sas-justifed-in-shooting-ira-man-on-ground (accessed 26 January 2016).

prompting the question whether coroners' inquests are an appropriate forum for meeting Article 2 obligations. But narrative verdicts do at least expose the jury's reasoning in a manner that would otherwise be far more opaque if a peremptory verdict were recorded instead.[131] It has since been confirmed that such verdicts may be returned in non-Article 2 inquests as well.[132]

Whether it is desirable to require juries to provide detailed narratives in criminal cases is another question. Here, juries are required to consider whether a number of elements in a criminal offence charged have been proved rather than more simply what led to a particular death. Although the jury must reach a conclusion that each element of the offence has been proved beyond reasonable doubt,[133] it does not have to agree collectively on the weight to be given to all the items of proof that make up the evidence for each element.[134] To insist that 12 jurors, or even a weighted majority of jurors, should agree on the weight to be attached to each item of proof might lead to an increase in hung juries in circumstances where juries in fact agree on the guilt of a defendant, albeit for different reasons. Even on the Continent where there has never been such a demand for unanimous or weighted majority verdicts,[135] we have seen that there has been controversy over how fully reasoned a jury verdict should be. We concluded in the previous section that, while reasoned decisions may not necessarily enhance the epistemic integrity of rational decision-making, they can enhance the adversarial integrity of the trial process by opening up a closed decision-making process to more effective scrutiny. The question then arises whether greater adversarial scrutiny of this process might still be achieved without incurring the practical difficulties of requiring a fully reasoned decision from the jury.

Which brings us to a second general lesson arising from continental experience, concerning judicial activism in helping juries to justify their verdicts. Although these various intrusions into the jury's decision-making process would be more controversial if transposed to a common law environment, many common law jurisdictions have permitted judges to influence and sometimes even dictate the ultimate verdict. Under what is sometimes called the 'thirteenth juror' rule, defendants in the US may file a motion of acquittal on the ground that the evidence presented was legally insufficient for a conviction.[136] Other jurisdictions permit trial judges to exercise considerable influence over the jury's reasoning in the course of their summings-up. We have seen that common law jurisdictions, including England and Wales, are intensifying this influence by encouraging judges to provide written step-by-step directions to juries that take the form of questions to be answered. In his *Review of the Criminal Courts of England and Wales* Auld LJ went a step further by recommending that juries be required to answer these questions publicly on the basis of the evidence presented

---

[131] For example, the narrative verdict returned by the jury in respect of the killing of Mark Duggan which led to the London riots in August 2011: V Dodd, 'Mark Duggan family reacts with fury to inquest verdict of lawful killing', *The Guardian*, 8 January 2014.

[132] *R (Longfield Care Homes Ltd) v HM Coroner for Blackburn* [2004] EWHC 2467 (Admin). See C Dorries, *Coroners' Courts: A Guide to Law & Practice* (Oxford, Oxford University Press, 2014) [9.116]–[9.123].

[133] *R v Brown (Kevin)* (1984) 79 Cr App R 115.

[134] See JC Smith, 'Satisfying the Jury' [1988] *Criminal Law Review* 335; Roberts, above n 93.

[135] See Jackson and Kovalev, above n 118, 113–14; EJ Leib, 'A Comparison of Criminal Jury Decision Rules in Democratic Countries' (2008) 5 *Ohio State Journal of Criminal Law* 629.

[136] See R Allen, W Stuntz, JL Hoffmann and D Livingston, *Comprehensive Criminal Procedure* (New York, Aspen, 2001) 1283. For commentary see S Doran, 'The Necessarily Expanding Role of the Criminal Trial Judge' in S Doran and J Jackson (eds), *The Judicial Role in Criminal Proceedings* (Oxford, Hart Publishing, 2000).

in court.[137] Auld LJ rightly predicted that his proposals for a public particularisation of a jury's verdict would meet with great opposition. Special verdicts have fallen into disuse in criminal cases.[138] But they are not foreign to Anglo-American jury tradition and continued in use in England and Wales until the end of the eighteenth century.[139] Judges sometimes today require explanations for voluntary manslaughter verdicts when the factual basis of the conviction is unclear on its face.[140]

Special verdicts deal with the practical objection that jurors are not trained judges skilled in written self-justification. Of course, there is no guarantee that in answering judicially prescribed questions juries will always confine themselves to the relevant evidence and applicable law. But special verdicts do ameliorate the adversarial deficit that has been exposed when juries retire to the deliberation room and return simply to proclaim a general verdict. In discussing the manner in which states should comply with their Article 2 procedural obligation to investigate suspicious deaths, the UK Supreme Court stressed the legitimate interest that the deceased's family or next of kin be afforded an appropriate level of participation in the conduct of the investigation and that an uninformative jury verdict will be unlikely to meet that expectation.[141] The Court went on to stress the importance of involving parties in making submissions on the means of eliciting the jury's factual questions and on any questions to be put, although the coroner would naturally have the final say. Adversarial process is at least as important in a criminal trial; yet although parties may have some input into judicial directions on the law, the failure to require juries to answer specific questions means the parties have less influence over how juries should go about reaching their verdict during their closed deliberation. Once the jury retires, the parties' role comes to an end except when the jury notifies the judge of any matters on which they require further assistance. It has been argued that framing directions to juries in the form of specific questions, after input from both the prosecution and defence, would enable the jury to identify more clearly the issues they have to decide and enter into an exchange in open court on the questions they were having difficulty resolving.[142] The greater interaction between jury and judge that this innovation would facilitate would not only benefit juries. It would also provide a mechanism for the parties to gain an insight into what the jury is thinking, thereby promoting the integrity of adversarial proceedings throughout the deliberation stage.

There remains the objection that requiring juries to answer questions would unduly inhibit juries exercising their constitutional role of bringing in a verdict on the merits, against the law and the evidence, sometimes referred to as a perverse verdict. Juries could still be empowered to issue a general verdict after answering each question put and have the final say on whether to convict or acquit the accused, although questions would then

---

[137]   Auld Report, above n 12, ch 5, [52]–[55].

[138]   See *R v Hendrick* (1921) 15 Cr App R 149, *R v Bourne* (1952) 36 Cr App R 125.

[139]   See JH Baker, 'Criminal Courts and Procedure 1550–1800' in Baker, *The Legal Profession and the Common Law* (London, Hambledon Press, 1986), Thaman, above n 118, 661. For contemporary US practice, see K Nepveu, 'Beyond "Guilty" or "Not Guilty": Giving Special Verdicts in Criminal Jury Trials' (2003) 21 *Yale Law & Policy Review* 263.

[140]   See eg *R v Cawthorne* [1996] 2 Cr App R (S) 445.

[141]   *R (Middleton) v HM Coroner for the Western District of Somerset* [2004] UKHL 10, [2004] 2 AC 182, [18]. See also *R (Amin) v Secretary of State for the Home Department* [2003] 4 All ER 1264, [31].

[142]   Moses LJ, 'Summing Down the Summing Up', Annual Law Reform Lecture 2010, www.barcouncil.org.uk/media/100359/lj_moses_summing_down_the_summing-up.pdf (accessed 26 January 2016).

remain about the scope of any appellate review. Ultimately, the scope to be given to the jury's constitutional or governance role has to be balanced against the need to recognise, as we have argued, that modern juries are now effectively assigned an important quasi-judicial responsibility in exercising their fact finding role. This responsibility is best regulated by injecting greater openness into the relationship between the judge, the parties and the jury.

Conclusion

It is an open question how long the 'traditional' jury will be able to hold out against ever more pressing arguments that juries should provide greater justification for their verdicts. In its Grand Chamber judgment in *Taxquet* the ECtHR exempted the jury from this requirement, on the ground that other procedural safeguards enable defendants to understand the reasons for their conviction. However, this rationale addresses only one dimension of a more complex issue. The important 'judicial' responsibilities which, it has been argued, are bestowed on contemporary jurors have constituted them into a body of more than merely private citizens when they take the oath to try the case and give a verdict in accordance with the evidence. When jurors were less sophisticated and had little access to the outside world once they had retired to deliberate, they could concentrate upon judging their fellow peers as citizens in the manner in which they were directed by the judge. Nowadays, however, jurors are more active in their analysis of evidence, reflecting the learning needs of a modern age. Their obligations and responsibilities in the administration of criminal justice must be rethought accordingly. Just as courtroom procedure must conform with modern fair trial standards, jurors' obligation to be fair to the parties extends, I have argued, to the closed proceedings in the jury room as well. It follows that procedural mechanisms must be crafted to enable juries to discharge this judicial role in a more fully integrative manner, by indicating the basis for their decisions, just as professional judges and tribunals must do.

Reflecting on the importance of procedural reform 30 years ago, Lord Hailsham speculated that the time had come to experiment with the idea of judges sitting with juries in a mixed court. After all, tribunal hearings already operated in this fashion and it is what many jury systems transmogrified into in continental Europe. Reform in this direction is not inevitable. There is still strong support in the UK for retaining the traditional jury. Appellate courts are, however, increasingly requiring that jurors be made aware of their 'judicial' responsibilities in the deliberation room and exhorting them to act more like lay judges than purely private citizens. Unless we give further thought to what these 'judicial' responsibilities entail for the integrity of the trial process, we risk undermining confidence in an institution that, for many centuries past, has done much to instil integrity into the administration of criminal justice.

13

Remorse and Demeanour in the Courtroom: Cognitive Science and the Evaluation of Contrition

SUSAN A BANDES[*]

Introduction

Though it occurred over a decade ago, the story of the first encounter between former US President George W Bush and Russian President Vladimir Putin still elicits bemused scepticism. On meeting Putin in 2001, the former president famously declared: 'I looked the man in the eye. I found him to be very straightforward and trustworthy and we had a very good dialogue. I was able to get a sense of his soul.'[1] The notion of looking into Putin's eyes and seeing his soul met with scorn not only because of a widespread consensus that President Bush had misread President Putin's soul,[2] but also because the entire soul-reading enterprise sounds mystical and irrational, and inappropriate for questions of governance. Given the legal system's emphasis on rationality, one might expect that premising decisions on the ability to read the soul would be frowned upon in the courtroom as well. Thus it is perhaps surprising how much stock the criminal justice system places in the ability to resolve questions of deep character by looking into the eyes of litigants and witnesses, reading their body language, and evaluating other aspects of what the legal system calls 'demeanour' and 'credibility'. The evaluation of remorse in criminal proceedings provides a striking example of the legal system's faith in its ability to evaluate 'deep character'[3] or the condition of a defendant's soul.

[*] For their extraordinarily helpful comments on earlier drafts, I am grateful to John Deigh, Neil Feigenson, Jeffrie Murphy, Song Richardson, Carol Sanger, Susannah Scheffer, Jordan Steiker, and to Gary Edmond, Simon Halliday, Jill Hunter, Mehera San Roque, Paul Roberts and the other participants in the UNSW workshop. For excellent research assistance I thank Devin DiDominicus, Michael Grothouse, Jennifer James, Rachel Milos and Robin Wagner. Many of this essay's arguments are prefigured in SA Bandes, 'Remorse, Demeanor, and the Consequences of Misinterpretation: The Limits of Law as a Window into the Soul' (2014) 3 *Journal of Law, Religion and State* 170.
[1] CA Robbins, 'Mr Bush Gets another Look into Putin's Eyes', *New York Times*, 30 June 2007. http://www.nytimes.com/2007/06/30/opinion/30sat3.html?_r=0 (accessed February 16, 2016).
[2] Ibid.
[3] JG Murphy, 'Remorse, Apology, and Mercy' (2007) 4 *Ohio State Journal of Criminal Law* 423, 437.

The principle that remorse should play a role in sentencing decisions 'is well settled in the common law world'.[4] The principle is reflected in case law, statute and the rules governing sentencing advisory bodies. In the criminal justice context, crucially important decisions about life and liberty hinge on whether offenders are perceived as appropriately remorseful.[5] In capital cases in the US juries determine both guilt and sentence.[6] Several studies based on interviews with former capital jurors have concluded that the perceived remorsefulness of the defendant is a crucial factor in determining whether the defendant is sentenced to death.[7] In a significant majority of cases, it was found to be *the* crucial factor.

More surprisingly, although one might assume that remorse becomes relevant only *after* guilt or innocence is determined, studies demonstrate that in fact the evaluation of remorse takes place throughout the trial as well as during sentencing, and that perceptions of remorse can also affect the determination of guilt or innocence. The trier of fact observes the defendant's reactions while the crime is being recounted in testimony and determines whether these reactions are appropriately remorseful. In a murder case, for example, a defendant's 'cold, unemotional demeanour' has in some cases been 'taken as evidence that she was the kind of person who could have committed such a crime and could potentially repeat it'.[8] Scott Peterson's high profile murder conviction in the US exemplifies the potential implications of failing to appear remorseful: 'The prosecution had portrayed his unflinching behavior [at trial] as the cool calculation of a killer.'[9] In cases where the defendant has admittedly caused the death, as in many vehicular homicides, whether the defendant appears visibly distressed at the account of the crime at trial may affect the severity of the verdict.[10] This sort of evaluation may easily run afoul of rules against judging an accused person by his character rather than by his actions. Moreover, the demand for remorse has had an especially

---

[4]   See M Proeve and S Tudor, *Remorse: Psychological and Jurisprudential Perspectives* (Farnham, Ashgate, 2010) 136–38 (summarising the legal authorities governing remorse in Australia, Canada, England, Wales, New Zealand, Singapore and the United States).

[5]   In some instances the role of remorse or acceptance of responsibility is explicitly encoded in a statute: ibid. But remorse has been shown to influence judges in the absence of such statutory guidance as well.

[6]   In capital cases in the US, juries determine guilt and then, in a separate proceeding known as the penalty phase, determine whether a death sentence will be imposed. *Lockhart v McCree*, 476 US 162 (1986). In a small and dwindling number of US states, juries also determine sentence in non-capital cases: see MB Hoffman, 'The Case for Jury Sentencing' (2003) 52 *Duke Law Journal* 951, 953.

[7]   See Scott Sundby, 'The Capital Jury and Absolution: The Intersection of Trial Strategy, Remorse, and the Death Penalty', 83 *Cornell L Rev* (1998), 1551, 1563; C Haney, L Sontag and S Constanzo, 'Deciding to Take a Life: Capital Juries, Sentencing Instructions, and the Jurisprudence of Death' (2010) 50 *Journal of Social Issues* 149; T Eisenberg, SP Garvey and MT Wells, 'But Was He Sorry? The Role of Remorse in Capital Sentencing' (1998) 83 *Cornell Law Review* 1599, 1604–607; WS Geimer and J Amsterdam, 'Why Jurors Vote Life or Death: Operative Factors in Ten Florida Death Penalty Cases' (1987–88) 15 *American Journal of Criminal Law* 1, 16–17. See also M Kimberly Maclin, Corynn Downs, Otto H Maclin, and Heather M Caspers, 'The Effect of Defendant Facial Expression on Mock Juror Decision-Making: The Power of Remorse', (2009) *North American Journal of Psychology*, 323 (finding that mock jurors are significantly more likely to reach a lenient verdict when a defendant's facial expression indicates remorse).

[8]   DT Robinson, L Smith-Lovin and O Tsoudis, 'Heinous Crime or Unfortunate Accident? The Effects of Remorse on Responses to Mock Criminal Confessions' (1994) 73 *Social Forces* 175, 176 (using the US case of Pamela Smart as an example of this phenomenon). One might argue that lack of remorse is not the appropriate descriptive term for the cold demeanour or lack of distress jurors observe in such a situation. In the mock juror studies recounted here, jurors were specifically asked about the role of remorse. But when no such direct evidence exists, either from mock juror studies, interviews with former jurors, or judicial statements, the precise motivation of the jurors becomes a matter of speculation by the press or other observers.

[9]   DE Murphy, 'At Peterson Sentencing, a Family's Anger', *New York Times*, 17 March 2005, A20.

[10]   For example, a vehicular homicide might be classified as voluntary or involuntary depending on the defendant's demeanour as the crime is described in court. See Robinson, Smith-Lovin and O Tsoudis, above n 8.

pernicious effect on the wrongly convicted, whose perceived lack of remorse at trial and sentencing, and subsequent refusal to admit to a crime, can increase their punishment.[11]

Remorse affects assessments of guilt and punishment in several other criminal justice contexts as well.[12] Lack of remorse is viewed as a primary indicator of a psychopathic personality or antisocial personality disorder.[13] The lack of remorse can lead to more punitive sentences, more restrictive prison conditions, and denial of parole or a pardon or clemency.[14] In the juvenile context, it can lead to transfer of an adolescent accused of a felony from juvenile to adult court.[15]

Decision-makers attempting to evaluate a defendant's remorse may have access to various sources of information, depending on the type of proceeding. In a criminal trial, for example, the defendant may testify. He may talk to forensic psychologists or probation officers or others who can attempt to evaluate his state of mind. The defendant's conduct during or after the crime may give rise to inferences about his level of remorse.[16] In capital cases, however, the defendant rarely takes the stand at the guilt phase or the penalty phase. In such cases, the defendant's facial expression and body language as he sits silently in court are among the most influential factors in the jury's evaluation of his level of remorse. And even where other sources of information are available, the defendant's demeanour remains a powerful influence on the fact-finder. In short, the question of whether remorse can be accurately evaluated in the courtroom is of enormous practical import.

In light of these practical consequences, investigation of whether the legal system can evaluate remorse with any accuracy is both essential and overdue. As this chapter will discuss, there is currently no evidence that remorse can be accurately evaluated based on facial expression and body language in the courtroom. Even more troubling, there is ample evidence that evaluation of remorse is influenced by factors that ought to play no role in determining culpability or sentence. Specifically, remorse is particularly difficult to evaluate when the fact-finder and the defendant are of different racial or ethnic groups, or when the defendant is a juvenile, or mentally ill, or intellectually disabled, or under the influence of psychotropic medication. Thus decisions affecting life and liberty are influenced by

---

See also MacLin, Downs, MacLin and Caspers, above n 7 (reporting on a mock jury experiment in which remorse judged by facial expression influenced decisions on guilt and innocence).

[11] R Weisman, 'Showing Remorse: Reflections on the Gap between Attribution and Expression in Cases of Wrongful Conviction' (2004) 46 *Canadian Journal of Criminology and Criminal Justice* 121. Failure to confess or otherwise 'accept responsibility' for the crime even prior to trial may also contribute to the perception of lack of remorse.

[12] See PH Robinson, SE Jackowitz and DM Bartels, 'Extralegal Punishment Factors: A Study of Forgiveness, Hardship, Good Deeds, Apology, Remorse, and Other Such Discretionary Factors in Assessing Criminal Punishment' (2012) 65 *Vanderbilt Law Review* 737, 745–47. Expressions of remorse may also affect the conduct and resolution of civil suits: MV Day and M Ross, 'The Value of Remorse: How Drivers' Responses to Police Predict Fines for Speeding' (2011) 35 *Law and Human Behavior* 22; BH Bornstein, L Rung and MK Miller, 'The Effects of Defendant Remorse on Mock Juror Decisions in a Malpractice Case' (2002) 20 *Behavioral Sciences and the Law* 393. See also JK Robbenolt, 'Apologies and Legal Settlement: An Empirical Examination' (2003) 102 *Michigan Law Review* 460.

[13] R Weisman, 'Remorse and Psychopathy at the Penalty Phase of the Capital Trial: How Psychiatry's View of "Moral Insanity" Helps Build the Case for Death' (2007) 41 *Studies in Law, Politics, and Society* 187.

[14] Robinson et al, above n 8, 176.

[15] MG Duncan, '"So Young and So Untender": Remorseless Children and the Expectations of the Law' (2002) 102 *Columbia Law Review* 1469.

[16] For example, his acceptance of responsibility at the guilt phase, or an early confession, or actions taken after the commission of the crime that suggest a desire to help the victim: see S Sundby, above n 7.

assessments of remorse, despite the absence of evidence that remorse *can* be accurately evaluated, and despite evidence that evaluation of remorse is influenced by race, ethnicity and other irrelevant and often pernicious factors.

To determine whether remorse can be appropriately evaluated in a courtroom, it is necessary to ask what role remorse is meant to play in the criminal law. Is a demand for remorse—or a penalty for the lack of remorse—consistent with the standard deterrent, rehabilitative or retributive aims of punishment? Is it consistent with the more recent focus on the expressive aims of punishment, or on restorative justice? This is a theoretical question, but it is closely entwined with certain practical considerations.

Remorse connotes an internal state—a condition of the soul. As Jeffrie Murphy argues, the determination that one is appropriately remorseful is more a judgement of deep character than an evaluation of state of mind. As I will suggest, the weight accorded to remorse may be a function of certain assumptions about what a remorseful person will do in the future. That is, the attempt to evaluate remorse may be a proxy for other questions that could be addressed more directly, such as the possibility of recidivism or future dangerousness. If remorse is valued for its action tendencies—its association with a desire to atone and become a better person, for example—it becomes crucial to distinguish remorse from other emotions or states that have different action tendencies. Notably, there is little evidence that remorse can be distinguished from stigmatic shame in a courtroom; yet shame is not associated with a desire to behave better in the future, and in fact has been correlated with higher rates of recidivism. Indeed, the entire question of what emotions discourage recidivism is an empirical issue, and one that needs far more study.

A criminal justice system administered with integrity will design institutions and procedures that address not only the explicit reliance on remorse but also its off the record evaluation in jury rooms and other decision-making venues. This is not to suggest that addressing the problem is a simple matter. Explicit reliance on remorse may be minimised, but evaluating a defendant's remorse is part of human nature. It is not clear that the legal system is capable of evaluating blameworthiness without reference to remorse. This chapter argues for minimising the role of remorse where possible, for clarifying why remorse is important and addressing those goals more directly, and for using jury instructions, expert witnesses and other tools to channel and educate decision-makers on the limitations and pitfalls of evaluating remorse.

1. Questioning Recourse to Remorse as 'A Window into the Soul'

There is substantial evidence that perceptions of a defendant's remorse have a causal effect on judgment: that jurors,[17] judges,[18] parole boards,[19] probation officers[20] and other

---

[17] See above, n 7.

[18] R Zhong, M Baranoski, N Feigenson, L Davidson, A Buchanan and HV Zonana, 'So You're Sorry? The Role of Remorse in Criminal Law' (2014) 42 *Journal of the American Academy of Psychiatry and the Law* 39; RS Everett and BC Nienstedt, 'Race, Remorse, and Sentence Reduction: Is Saying You're Sorry Enough?' (1999) 16 *Justice Quarterly* 99.

[19] R Weisman, *Showing Remorse: Law and the Social Control of Emotion* (Farnham, Ashgate, 2014) 84–91.

[20] Everett and Nienstedt, above n 18.

decision-makers treat remorse as one of the determinative factors in their decisions.[21] In some of these venues, the decision-maker has access to the subject's own description of his emotions and attitudes, for example through in-court testimony, forensic interviews, or pre-sentence reports. In some situations, evidence of the defendant's behaviour during or after the incident in question may bear on remorse. But in many cases—especially capital cases in the US—the defendant's in-court demeanour is the major determinant of whether he is adjudged appropriately remorseful. In most capital cases, the defendant does not testify, which makes the question of how jurors assess remorse all the more complex. Indeed, the US Supreme Court explicitly recognised the importance of remorse and of facial expressions as a means of demonstrating remorse, observing in a capital case that 'serious prejudice could result if medication inhibits the defendant's capacity … to demonstrate remorse or compassion … [A]ssessments of character and remorse may carry great weight and, perhaps, be determinative of whether the defendant lives or dies'.[22]

There is a growing body of evidence about what can go wrong with the process of evaluating remorse. Conversely, there is little or no evidence that remorse can be accurately evaluated based on demeanour or body language. This state of affairs—in which life or death decisions are based on popular belief, or what I will call folk knowledge, that is at best unsubstantiated and at worst demonstrably wrong—poses several pressing questions. First, what more can be learned about the dynamics of evaluating remorse? Secondly, even if we determine that a remorseful countenance can be accurately identified, what significance should this have for the criminal justice system? And finally, if evaluation of remorse is ineradicable, what can be done to improve upon an evaluative process that is demonstrably riddled with error and bias?

Turning to the most basic question, when decision-makers evaluate remorse, what is it precisely that is being evaluated? What indicia do they seek out? Unfortunately, even when the term 'remorse' appears in judicial or legislative contexts, it is not defined.[23] It is necessary to turn to sources such as interviews with judges and jurors to understand what decision-makers mean by the term. Or more precisely, to understand 'what expectations … these decision-makers have for the *display and communication* of remorse'.[24]

A comparison between apology and remorse places the difficulty of evaluating remorse in sharp relief. An apology is an outward manifestation, generally verbal in nature. Its existence is externally ascertainable. An apology might be sincere or insincere, and these underlying motivations are far less observable. However, whether an apology is sincere may not matter. For example, Brent White has argued that in some contexts, such as a court-mandated apology by a public entity or official for a violation of civil rights, it is primarily the content and public nature of the apology that matter to the litigant. Whether the apology rests

---

[21] Although lack of remorse is linked to detrimental outcomes in almost every context, there is some evidence that when a defendant shows remorse before culpability has been established, his remorse may be taken as an indicator of guilt: BH Bornstein, L Rung and MK Miller, 'The Effects of Defendant Remorse on Mock Juror Decisions in a Malpractice Case' (2002) 20 *Behavioral Sciences and the Law* 393.

[22] *Riggins v Nevada*, 504 US 127, 143–44 (1992) (Kennedy J concurring).

[23] See eg US Sentencing Guidelines, discussed below n 51; *Riggins v Nevada*, 504 US 127 (1992).

[24] R Weisman, 'Being and Doing: The Judicial Use of Remorse to Construct Character and Community' (2009) 18 *Social and Legal Studies* 47.

on sincere emotion may be entirely irrelevant to the goals of the litigation.[25] Remorse, by contrast, is an internal state and therefore is far less susceptible to measurement. Professor Weisman provides an articulate description:

> While an apology may *refer* to the anguish and pain that the offender feels at having broken the norms of community, an expression of remorse *shows* or *demonstrates* this pain by making the suffering visible. Conventional usage in law and psychiatry describes expressions of remorse as 'signs', 'symptoms', 'manifestations', or 'demonstrations'. What this suggests is that remorse is communicated through gestures, displays of affect, and other paralinguistic devices. Both the apology and the expression of remorse can be communicated through simple linguistic formulae such as 'I am sorry'. With the former, we are likely to attend to the words. With the latter, we focus on how the words are expressed, the feelings that accompany the words; expressions of remorse are shown rather than stated.[26]

This description accords with Murphy's contention that to evaluate remorsefulness is to claim to be able to evaluate 'deep character'[27] or the soul. As Justice Kennedy observed in his concurring opinion in *Riggins v Nevada* (in which the Court ordered a retrial where the defendant was so heavily medicated he was unable to show remorse), sentencers must attempt to 'know the heart and mind of the offender'.[28] The evaluation of deep character requires some fine distinctions.

Most prominently, the remorse the offender displays must be remorse for the harm caused by the crime; not remorse for getting caught or having to suffer the consequences.[29] This demand for sincere, non-instrumental remorse presents an obvious challenge in legal settings, in which a defendant has every incentive to appear remorseful—and in which a convincing show of remorse may be a matter of life or death. Indeed, it might be argued that the very act of advocating for a more lenient sentence calls the sincerity of the offender's remorse into question. This has been called one of the 'central paradoxes'[30] of factoring remorse into the punishment calculus. If indeed the remorseful offender suffers for the harm he caused and sincerely wishes to atone for it, some argue that he ought to welcome punishment, not use his remorseful state as a means of reducing it.

At bottom, the function of remorse is to separate the act from the offender; to identify those situations in which the act is a deviation from the offender's character rather than an expression of it.[31] Somewhat counter-intuitively, facial expression and body language, unlike testimony, are regarded as spontaneous, 'natural', and non-manipulable, and thus as transparent windows into true feelings of remorse.[32]

---

[25] B White, 'Say You're Sorry: Court-Ordered Apologies as a Civil Rights Remedy' (2006) 91 *Cornell Law Review* 1261. See also J Ainsworth, 'The Social Meaning of Apology' and L Kern Griffin, 'Insincere and Involuntary Public Apologies', both in PH Robinson, SP Garvey and K Kessler Ferzan (eds), *Criminal Law Conversations* (New York, Oxford University Press, 2009) 199–203.

[26] Weisman, above n 11, 125.

[27] Murphy, above n 3, 437.

[28] *Riggins v Nevada*, 504 US 127, 143–44 (1992) (Kennedy J concurring).

[29] Weisman, above n 24, 58 ('He must be suffering for the suffering he caused; not the suffering he endured').

[30] Ibid 53.

[31] Ibid 50.

[32] Weisman, above n 19, 11.

2. Demeanour in the Theatre of Contrition

> Make eye contact with the jury, but not homicidal maniac eye contact.[33]

Let us now put to one side the question whether sincere remorse is germane to legal decision-making, to consider an empirical question: Can remorse actually be ascertained from viewing demeanour? The question urgently requires an answer because decision-makers (as well as the media, which shape public perception about crime and punishment) believe demeanour can be ascertained in this manner, and serious legal consequences flow from this belief. The available evidence indicates that there are no consistent criteria by which remorse is currently measured, that instead remorse is often in the eye of the beholder, and that when criteria are articulated, they are often based on inaccurate assumptions. These problems afflict juries, judges, parole officers, and other legal actors. There is also ample evidence that evaluation of remorse is heavily influenced by factors such as race, ethnicity, mental disability and age.

Sociologist Craig Haney and colleagues, in their study of California capital jurors, reported that one of the major factors in their decision was 'whether or not the defendant expressed remorse (based only on in-court observations of the defendant)'.[34] In the opinion of most jurors, capital defendants simply did not express appropriate emotion during the penalty-phase proceedings.[35] Defendants cannot opt out of this evaluative process. The prevailing assumption is that 'what is not shown is also not felt'.[36] In interviews, capital jurors made statements along the lines of 'I was waiting for the defendant to express remorse for what he had done. I did not hear any of that remorse'.[37] As Scott Sundby reports of his own interviews with former capital jurors:

> Jurors scrutinize defendants through the trial and are quick to recall details about demeanour, ranging from attire to facial expressions ... Mostly jurors deduced remorselessness from the defendant's general demeanour—mainly his lack of emotion during the trial as the prosecution introduced horrific evidence. The defendant's perceived boredom or indifference made jurors angry. Some saw them as cocky and arrogant, indicating they lacked human compassion.[38]

Thus, much rides on an appropriate showing of remorse, yet exhibiting appropriate remorse through facial expression poses a challenge. Beverly Lowry gives this description of Karla Faye Tucker's attempt to follow her lawyer's instructions during her capital murder trial. The lawyer

> had told her to try to look dignified and calm and so she was trying to look unmoved by the proceedings and when she did they said she was cold and when she looked out into the courtroom and

---

[33] Cartoon caption by Gahan Wilson, 'Defense Attorney Instructing his Client', *The New Yorker*, 13 August 2007.

[34] Haney et al, above n 7, 163.

[35] Ibid. See also ME Antonio, 'Arbitrariness and the Death Penalty: How the Defendant's Appearance During Trial Influences Capital Jurors' Punishment Decision' (2006) 24 *Behavioral Sciences and the Law* 215, 223 (finding that when jurors viewed the defendant in the courtroom as emotionally involved, sorry and sincere they were much more likely to favour a life sentence than when they viewed the defendant in the courtroom as emotionally uninvolved and bored).

[36] Weisman, above n 13, 203.

[37] Ibid.

[38] Sundby, above n 16, 1563.

smiled at [her father] Larry Tucker, the press reported that she had smiled at someone else, and so she never looked out in the courtroom again.[39]

Alex Kotlowitz conducted interviews with the men and women who served as jurors in the capital trial of a young man named Jeremy Gross. His account captures how growing understanding and empathy toward a defendant can transform a jury's interpretation of demeanour. A jury of men and women who strongly favoured the death penalty convicted Gross of a brutal murder, yet spared his life at the penalty phase of the trial.[40] Kotlowitz reports that the jurors, having learnt about Gross's own brutal childhood, gradually came to understand him and even to empathise with various aspects of his life. At first, jurors could not look him in the eye, and they judged him to be cold and indifferent. As they got to know more about him, they began to view what they initially thought was indifference as shame. This re-reading of his demeanour was, in their accounts, crucial to their eventual decision to spare him.[41]

People are far less adept at evaluating demeanour than they believe, and than the legal system assumes them to be.[42] This problem is greatly exacerbated by empathic divides in situations where demeanour must be evaluated across cultural,[43] ethnic[44] or racial lines,[45] or where juvenile[46] or mentally impaired[47] defendants are being judged. Bowers and colleagues, for example, found that:

> [O]bserving the same defendant and interpreting the same mitigating evidence, black jurors saw a disadvantaged upbringing, remorse, and sincerity, while white jurors saw incorrigibility, a lack of emotion, and deceptive behavior ... where a white juror sees black witnesses as faking or putting on, a black juror sees them as sincere. Where a white female juror interprets the black defendant's demeanor as hard and cold, a black male juror sees him as sorry. Even when a white female juror sympathizes with the anguish of the black defendant's mother, she blames the defendant for it and rationalizes that his execution will be in his mother's best interest.[48]

The empathic divide between the white juror and the black defendant is deep and tenacious. Moreover, the problems of lack of articulable or consistent criteria, reliance on inaccurate folk knowledge, and the influence of irrelevant or pernicious variables are not

---

[39] B Lowry, *Crossed Over: A Murder, A Memoir* (New York, Alfred A Knopf, 2002) 171.

[40] Note that in this case jurors and defendant were all white, eliminating one potential barrier to empathy (email from Alex Kotlowitz to Susan Bandes, 12 September 2003).

[41] A Kotlowitz, 'In the Face of Death', *The New York Times Magazine*, 6 July 2003, 32.

[42] See eg JA Blumenthal, 'A Wipe of the Hands, A Lick of the Lips: The Validity of Demeanor Evidence in Assessing Witness Credibility' (1993) 72 *Nebraska Law Review* 1157; OG Wellborn III, 'Demeanor' (1991) 76 *Cornell Law Review* 1075.

[43] Duncan, above n 15, 1499 (discussing problems of judging demeanour of juveniles in homicide cases).

[44] Everett and Nienstedt, above n 18 (finding that both race and ethnicity affected evaluations of expressions of remorse).

[45] See generally, SL Johnson 'The Color of Truth: Race and the Assessment of Credibility' (1996) 1 *Michigan Journal of Race & Law* 261; JW Rand 'The Demeanour Gap: Race, Lie Detection, and the Jury' (2000) 33 *Connecticut Law Review* 1. In relation to defendants with mental disabilities, see eg G Stobbs and MR Kebbell, 'Jurors' Perception of Witnesses with Intellectual Disabilities and the Influence of Expert Evidence' (2003) 16 *Journal of Applied Research in Intellectual Disabilities* 107.

[46] Duncan, above n 15.

[47] *Riggins v Nevada*, 504 US 127, 142 (1992) (Kennedy J concurring).

[48] WJ Bowers, BD Steiner and M Sandys, 'Death Sentencing in Black and White: An Empirical Analysis of the Role of Jurors' Race and Jury Racial Composition' (2001) 3 *University of Pennsylvania Journal of Constitutional Law* 171, 244–52.

confined to the jury. A recent ethnographic study by Zhong and colleagues, consisting of interviews with 23 sitting judges, found the judges in substantial disagreement about the indicators of remorse. The authors observed that '[b]ehaviors that suggested remorseful- ness to some judges suggested remorselessness to others'.[49] Furthermore, some judges were confident in their ability to perceive remorse, while others believed that true remorse is difficult to ascertain. Some judges placed great weight on demeanour or body language, but interpreted specific indicators quite differently. For example, '[s]ome judges believed that putting one's head down or hanging one's head was a sign of respect. Others said that it indicated an absence of remorse. Similarly, eye contact or lack thereof could be construed as either respectful or disrespectful.'[50]

Another study focused on the operation of the Federal Sentencing Guidelines, and spe- cifically on the question of whether the incidence of downward departures from standard sentencing ranges based on the defendant's 'acceptance of responsibility'[51] differs by race or ethnicity of the offender. The researchers found a pronounced difference in sentencing out- come based on both race and ethnicity. Although the information available to the decision- makers in these cases went well beyond demeanour evidence, it was clear that court actors responsible for sentencing, including prosecutors, judges and probation officers, placed sig- nificant emphasis on demeanour. The authors posited that cultural differences might affect the court officials' ability to perceive genuine remorse when it is expressed differently than in their own culture. They also observed that some 'culturally defined inhibitions [may] preclude the open demonstration of certain emotional expressions'.[52]

> For example, a judge in a region with a large Hispanic population commented on Hispanic males'
> difficulty in openly and publicly admitting guilt, 'to look you in the eye and say they're sorry'. Cul-
> tural values inculcated in certain racial/ethnic minorities may prohibit such required displays of
> remorse, just as a judge's cultural values may preclude him or her from perceiving a valid expres-
> sion of remorse from a member of a different racial/ethnic group.[53]

Cultural and social norms and display rules exacerbate the difficulty of evaluating the remorse of adolescents accused of serious crimes. As Duncan explains, remorse becomes a factor at a very early and significant stage in juvenile proceedings—the decision whether to try the accused as a juvenile or as an adult, known as the juvenile transfer hearing. Since remorse is viewed as a sign that rehabilitation may be possible, it is also viewed as consistent with the Juvenile Court's 'historical mission of rehabilitation'.[54] And remorse plays a simi- larly significant role at sentencing. Unfortunately, the folk knowledge view of what remorse looks like fails to account for several aspects of adolescent development.

---

[49] Zhong et al, above n 18 at 43.

[50] Ibid.

[51] Everett and Nienstedt, above n 18, 101 n 2. The US Federal Sentencing Guidelines provide recommended sentence ranges, and then specify ameliorating factors that may lead to a downward departure from the lowest recommended sentence: US Sentencing Commission, *Guidelines Manual* [3E1.1] (US Sentencing Commission, 2014), www.ussc.gov/sites/default/files/pdf/guidelines-manual/2014/GLMFull.pdf (accessed 26 January 2016). Acceptance of responsibility is one such factor. Although 'acceptance of responsibility' is not defined, the second application note mentions remorse as a relevant consideration in applying the guideline.

[52] Ibid 117.

[53] Ibid 117–18.

[54] Duncan, above n 15, 1476.

For one thing, comprehension of the nature and gravity of the crime may be long delayed for adolescents, appearing well after the commission of the offence[55] and even after trial and sentencing. For another, facial expression is likely to be an especially poor measure of remorse. Duncan describes a case in which the judge at the juvenile transfer hearing relied heavily on his own perception of the demeanour of a 14-year-old boy accused of murder to conclude that the boy had no remorse (noting 'the lack of any expression of emotion or remorse', characterising his face as 'impassive' and concluding that he was 'amoral').[56] Yet as one child psychiatrist put it: 'Fourteen-year-olds do not appear remorseful, almost categorically. They feel relatively powerless within the system and react by rebelliousness, which feels authentic to them'.[57] An indifferent or 'tough' front may be a protective shell. In many adolescent circles, youth may be 'required to be tough, alien, and mean', postures 'diametrically opposed to the qualities needed for remorse'.[58]

Mental disability poses an additional set of problems for the evaluation of remorse. As the Supreme Court has noted, psychotropic drugs may affect demeanour and interfere with a defendant's ability to exhibit appropriate remorse.[59] Mental illness or disability may itself render the defendant's facial expression or body language an unreliable indicator of his level of remorse. More to the point, the trier of fact, whether judge or jury, may not be cognisant of the effects of mental illness or medication on demeanour and body language generally, or on their impact on the ability to display what is considered appropriate remorse.[60]

3. Does (Demonstrable) Remorse Exist?

It is possible, as discussed below, that concerns about reading remorse from facial expression and body language can be partially ameliorated through jury instructions, expert testimony, judicial training, and other institutional interventions. But there is a more basic antecedent and ontological question: are there any external observable indicia that can be said to reflect 'actual remorse'?

There is a flourishing branch of cognitive psychology and neuroscience focusing on the interpretation of facial expressions, including 'micro' expressions, defined as expressions that are so fleeting they are difficult for the untrained eye to see. It is controversial whether internal emotions are ever precisely identifiable by physical indicia like expression, body language, or physiological signals such as flushing or blushing, and whether these indicia remain constant across cultures and contexts for any group of emotions.[61] Researchers

---

[55] R Aviv, 'No Remorse', *The New Yorker*, 2 January 2012, 55, 63. This is problematic when investigative, mental health or legal personnel interpret the absence of 'same day contrition' as evidence of remorselessness: Duncan, above n 15, 1491.

[56] Ibid 1499.

[57] Ibid.

[58] Ibid.

[59] *Riggins v Nevada*, 504 US 127, 142 (1992).

[60] Zhong et al, above n 18.

[61] The field encompasses two prominent approaches to measuring facial expression: the component approach, which involves objective description and measurement of changes in facial behaviour (see eg P Ekman, WV Friesen and S Ancoli, 'Facial Signs of Emotional Experience' (1980) 39 *Journal of Personality and Social Psychology* 1125); and the judgement approach, which builds on Darwin's *The Expression of Emotions in Man and Animals* (1872)

have argued that some emotions, such as anger, fear, pride or shame, do have physiological correlates.[62] Others argue, to the contrary, that all emotions are cultural and social constructs, rather than 'natural kinds'.[63] Yet even among those who believe in the existence of basic, cross-cultural, physiologically identifiable emotions, there is disagreement about how many such basic emotions exist. It may be possible to identify positive or negative expressions generally, or even basic expressions such as happiness, anger, fear, surprise, disgust and sadness, but for other emotions, their expression may be too variable or too culturally influenced to be universally identifiable.[64] In particular, there is as yet no evidence that facial expressions, body language, or other physiological markers exist that can identify feelings of remorse.[65] Michael Proeve and Steven Tudor, in their comprehensive study of remorse, refer to shame, guilt and regret, as well as contrition and repentance, as 'retractive' emotions. They define these as emotions that involve a retreat from a particular action that would otherwise be 'seen as belonging to or associated with the self'.[66] In other words, these are the emotions associated with wishing one had behaved differently. Proeve and Tudor conclude that remorse has been the least investigated of this group of emotions, and that thus far, there is 'little evidence of a distinct profile for remorse'.[67]

One study investigated the ability to distinguish between embarrassment, shame and guilt. Embarrassment was defined as a reaction to transgression of social norms; shame as a reaction to the failure to live up to central personal expectations; and guilt as a reaction to violation of obligatory moral standards. Using these definitions, guilt is the closest of these emotions to remorse. The study found that while embarrassment and shame may have distinct facial displays, there was no evidence that there is an identifiable facial display of guilt as a discrete emotion.[68] A more recent article surveyed the scholarship on the distinction between shame and embarrassment, and found no consensus about how to distinguish or even define the two concepts, and no consensus on the facial displays associated with either one.[69] Yet if remorse is valued for its likelihood to lead to atonement or to improved

and other work, and which explores the assumption that facial expressions for certain emotions are innate and universal: see eg P Ekman, 'An Argument for Basic Emotions' (1992) 6 *Cognition and Emotion* 169.

[62] See eg JL Tracy, AF Shariff, W Zhao and J Henrich, 'Cross-cultural Evidence that the Pride Expression is a Universal Automatic Status Signal' (2013) 142 *Journal of Experimental Psychology: General* 163; JL Tracy and D Matsumoto, 'The Spontaneous Expression of Pride and Shame: Evidence for Biologically Innate Nonverbal Displays' (2008) 105 *Proceedings of the National Academy of Sciences* 11655.

[63] The argument is made in a seminal, and much debated, article by LF Barrett, 'Emotions as Natural Kinds?' (2007) 1 *Perspectives on Psychological Science* 28.

[64] D Roberson, L Damjanovic and M Kikutani, 'Show and Tell: The Role of Language in Categorizing Facial Expression of Emotion' (2010) 2 *Emotion Review* 254 (citing findings that people respond most strongly to the facial expressions of individuals of their own race).

[65] But see JM Grohot, 'Can you Fake Feeling Remorse?' *PsychCentral*, 10 February 2011, psychcentral.com/blog/archives/2011/02/10/ (accessed 20 January 2016) (reporting on a Canadian study identifying indicators of fake remorse, including a greater range of emotional expressions, swinging from one emotion to another quickly, and speaking with hesitation).

[66] Proeve and Tudor, above n 4, 31.

[67] Ibid 70.

[68] D Keltner and BN Buswell, 'Evidence for the Distinctness of Embarrassment, Shame, and Guilt: A Study of Recalled Antecedents and Facial Expressions of Emotion' (1996) 10 *Cognition and Emotion* 155.

[69] WR Crozier, 'Differentiating Shame from Embarrassment' (2014) 6 *Emotion Review* 267. Definitions of shame employed included 'the involvement of core aspects of the self, and the impact upon the self': ibid 270. This injury to one's core conception of oneself is also a feature of many definitions of remorse.

behaviour, it becomes crucial to distinguish it from an emotion like shame, which may instead lead to a withdrawal from society and continued antisocial behaviour.[70]

One important lesson of such studies is that there is no consistent, widely accepted terminology for emotional states. The definitions used in these studies, variable as they are, all fall within the realm of common usage as well as accepted scholarly usage. And that should be a problem for the criminal justice system, in which emotion states like 'remorse' have no consistent meaning and no articulated criteria, and yet wield tremendous power. To complicate matters further, recall that even if guilt or remorse could be identified as discrete emotions correlated with identifiable facial expressions, the legal system demands still more from the display. The defendant must display remorse that is attributable to his distress at the crime and the harm caused by the crime, and not to his selfish distress at being caught up in the criminal justice system. It is difficult to imagine a scenario in which facial expression could be reliably correlated with such a fine-grained moral assessment of internal attitudes. Even more problematic, remorse generally describes a more complex and dynamic process, consisting not only of a backward-looking reaction to the wrongdoing, but a forward-looking desire to atone for it.

This complication contains the seeds of a larger objection to the legal uses of remorse. Remorse appears to be more than simply an emotion. If it is an emotion, it is not a transient one. We might describe a defendant as appearing angry or cold or sad as he sits in the courtroom. Our description might or might not be accurate, but it is plausible that we can discern these emotional states from observation. Perhaps even regret or shame can plausibly be discerned by observing demeanour. The term remorse, on the other hand, implies a less transient state; and even if fleeting remorse is possible, it hardly seems to be an attitude that should merit leniency. Remorse is a state of mind, or a process. It implies a painful path leading to acceptance of personal responsibility for the harm one has caused; a desire to atone or to make restitution; or even a desire to transform oneself. It does not seem plausible that this complex and unfolding state can be discerned from outward manifestations such as demeanour.

This is not a concern about fakery or sincerity. Fakery is always possible in the courtroom; the problem of insincere performance (often abetted by coaching) is hardly confined to remorse. The point, rather, is that even assuming genuine, sincere remorse, it is simply not something that can be conveyed solely by facial expression and body language.[71] This objection to reading remorse from demeanour shares common ground with some of the powerful arguments Jeffrie Murphy has made against the legal uses of remorse. With dry wit, Murphy observes:

> Issues of deep character are matters about which the state is probably incompetent to judge—it cannot even deliver the mail very efficiently, after all—and which, for that reason and others, might well be regarded as simply none of the state's business.[72]

Murphy's objections, both normative and practical, are premised on the notion that remorse is an aspect of deep character. One of these objections concerns the invasion of

---

[70] Proeve and Tudor, above n 4, 70. Empirical studies show that stigmatic shame is associated with an increased likelihood of recidivism, as compared to guilt: ibid 90–91.
[71] Weisman, above n 19, 11.
[72] Murphy, above n 3, 437.

an autonomous personal sphere. The law may ask us to conform our behaviour to certain norms, but it should have no dominion over our internal thoughts, desires and souls. The related practical objection is more germane to this chapter: even if it were permissible for the state to pass judgement on deep character, it has no viable means of discerning that character.

Murphy concludes, albeit with some ambivalence, that remorse should be accorded little weight at the sentencing stage.[73] Granting his point about the difficulties of evaluation, there is the vexing question of whether remorse *can* be kept off-limits. I doubt it is possible for the criminal justice system simply to put questions of remorse aside when assessing punishment.[74] Remorse is too deeply ingrained in the fabric of judgements of culpability and sentencing. Remorse is regarded as a measure of whether the defendant's bad act is consistent with his general character or a deviation from it. As Weisman puts it, successfully expressed remorse communicates the message that 'the self that *condemned* the act is more real than the self that committed the act'. A failure to communicate remorse indicates, conversely, that 'the self that committed the offending act is the true self'.[75]

Remorse suggests that a defendant will strive to avoid such aberrant and concededly wrong behaviour in the future rather than pose a continuing danger to society. Remorse has expressive value: it signals to the victim and to society that although there has been an injury to the social fabric, there has also been an acceptance of responsibility and even repentance. Feelings of remorse are often difficult to separate from other emotions an offender is expected to feel if he is to be readmitted to the community, such as empathy or compassion toward the victim or her family, shame at the act, or a desire to learn and change. Ultimately, the appropriate role of remorse in assessing punishment cannot be disentangled from the question of why we punish—a question that is unlikely to be definitively resolved.[76]

The preceding argument can be framed more critically. Evaluating remorse may be a flawed proxy for more relevant inquiries. We may believe that the remorseful defendant is less likely to re-offend.[77] Indeed, Weisman refers to a widespread belief that there is a correlation between remorse and reduced recidivism.[78] Judge Posner, for example, expressed this common notion in *United States v Beserra*:

> A person who is conscious of having done wrong, and who feels genuine remorse for his wrong … is on the way to developing those internal checks that would keep many people from committing crimes even if the expected costs of criminal punishment were lower than they are.[79]

---

[73] JG Murphy, *Punishment and the Moral Emotions* (Oxford, Oxford University Press, 2012) 161 (arguing, however, that remorse is an appropriate factor when the executive is determining whether clemency or a pardon is appropriate).

[74] It is also not clear to me that remorse, or at least distress and compassion and other emotions associated with remorse, can reliably be kept out of assessments of guilt in some cases—at least without corrective measures.

[75] Weisman, above n 19, 9.

[76] See D Allen, 'Democratic Dis-ease: Of Nature and the Troubling Nature of Punishment' in SA Bandes (ed), *The Passions of Law* (New York, New York University Press, 2000) 191, 206.

[77] At least one set of studies supports the conclusion that the importance accorded to remorse is based in large part on the assumption that the remorseful defendant is less likely to reoffend: GJ Gold and B Weiner, 'Remorse, Confession, Group Identity, and Expectancies About Repeating a Transgression' (2000) 22 *Basic and Applied Social Psychology* 291.

[78] Weisman, above n 19, 7.

[79] *United States v Beserra* 967 F 2d 254, 256 (7th Cir 1992), quoted in S Bibas and RA Bierschbach, 'Integrating Remorse and Apology into Criminal Procedure' (2004) 114 *Yale Law Journal* 85, 95.

But whether remorse in fact correlates with changed behaviour is an empirical question. This is a promising area for research, but one that has not thus far yielded any firm evidence of a correlation between remorse and reduced recidivism.[80] As Murphy points out, even for the *genuinely* remorseful, there is a very real danger of backsliding.[81] Whether the remorseful defendant poses less danger to society is likewise an empirical question. Although I know of no studies on the correlation between remorse and future dangerousness, there is ample evidence of the difficulty of predicting dangerousness,[82] and of the pernicious impact of racial stereotypes (including 'stereotypical racial appearance') on predictions of dangerousness.[83]

4. Regulating Remorse with Integrity

A full discussion of the theoretical justifications for involving the criminal justice system in the evaluation, elicitation and communication of remorse is beyond the scope of this chapter.[84] The relevant point for present purposes is a narrower, methodological one: all normative theories and justifications advanced in the literature are premised on the power of genuine remorse. They all assume that the evaluation of genuine remorse is a task that should, and by necessary implication *can*, be accomplished in a courtroom. Stephanos Bibas and Richard Bierschbach, for example, argue for the value to offenders and victims alike of an offender's face-to-face verbal expressions of remorse in the courtroom. They explain that to comply with their proposal, 'the offender should both feel sorry and express this sorrow'.[85] As the US Supreme Court put it in *Riggins*, the trier of fact attempts not just to evaluate or predict behaviour, but 'to know the heart and mind of the offender'.[86] Yet, as we have seen, there is no evidence that deep character of this sort can be assessed or illuminated by observing the facial expressions and body language of a defendant sitting silently

---

[80]   Weisman, above n 19, 7; Proeve and Tudor, above n 4, 90.

[81]   Murphy, above n 3, 439.

[82]   See eg T Grisso and PS Appelbaum, 'Is it Unethical to Offer Predictions of Future Violence?' (1992) 16 *Law and Human Behavior* 621.

[83]   See eg JL Eberhardt, PG Davies, VJ Purdie-Vaughs and SL Johnson, 'Looking Deathworthy: Perceived Stereotypicality of Black Defendants Predicts Capital-Sentencing Outcomes' (2006) 17 *Psychological Science* 383 (reporting that stereotypes, such as the belief that black people are more criminally inclined, can affect jurors' evaluation of credibility and blameworthiness); Bowers et al, above n 48; ME Antonio, 'If Looks Could Kill: Identifying Trial Outcomes of Murder Cases Based on the Appearance of Capital Offenders Shown in Black-and-White Photographs' in GR Burthold (ed), *Psychology of Decision Making in Legal, Health Care and Science Settings* (New York, Nova Science Publishers, 2007).

[84]   The restorative justice movement generally, and victim–offender mediation in particular, raise a host of theoretical, practical and empirical questions to which I cannot begin to do justice here. Essentially, they raise two important sets of questions. First, do these face-to-face encounters bring about the desired results? Secondly, what impact do they have on the fairness of the trial as a whole and on the defendants' constitutional protections? For an excellent and comprehensive discussion of remorse and restorative justice, see Proeve and Tudor, above n 4, ch 9.

[85]   Bibas and Bierschbach, above n 79, 90. Advocates for integrating remorse and apology into the criminal justice system have argued for the importance of face-to-face apologies to crime victims, in part because such apologies permit the communication of facial expression and body language.

[86]   *Riggins v Nevada*, 504 US 127, 142 (1992).

in a courtroom.[87] There is ample evidence that such assessments can be distorted by a host of factors, such as race, age, class and ethnicity. Even where additional clues such as verbal testimony are available, there is reason to be extremely sceptical of the legal system's ability to gauge genuine remorse.

As I have previously argued, however, evaluation of remorse, in some form or other, is probably impossible to prevent, given the existing dynamics of criminal proceedings, trials and sentencing.[88] We should therefore concentrate on helping decision-makers improve their evaluative abilities and understand the limitations of those abilities. Although it may be impossible to take remorse off the table entirely, criminal justice systems have many choices about how much weight to accord to remorse. For example, statutes such as the US Federal Sentencing Guidelines,[89] the Canadian Criminal Code,[90] and the Crimes Act 1914 in Australia[91] offer a sentence reduction for a convincing showing of remorse, and many US state courts have explicitly found the absence of remorse to be an appropriate aggravating factor when calculating criminal punishment.[92] The failure to display remorse and therefore accept responsibility for one's crime and its consequences is often an explicit reason for more severe probation recommendations, denial of parole,[93] or other decisions penalising defendants and prisoners.[94] In situations like these in which the role of remorse is made explicit, this role might either be minimised in recognition of the difficulties of assessing remorse perceptively, or defined and regulated more precisely.[95]

Regimes that emphasise restorative justice place a premium on acceptance of responsibility, remorse and apology. As Weisman demonstrates, in a restorative as opposed to a retributive regime, expressions of remorse play a significant role in determining whether to impose conditional sentences.[96] But even in a more traditional retributive setting, prosecutors are generally permitted to comment on the defendant's lack of remorse.[97] Such comments are

---

[87] Bibas and Bierschbach's argument, above n 79, 114–15, contemplates verbal apologies, in which the defendant's facial expression and body language would be among the indicia of sincere communication.

[88] S Bandes, 'Evaluation of Remorse is Here to Stay: We Should Focus on Improving its Dynamics', in Robinson et al (eds), above n 25, 198.

[89] See MM O'Hear, 'Remorse, Cooperation, and "Acceptance of Responsibility": The Structure, Implementation, and Reform of Section 3E1/1 of the Federal Sentencing Guidelines' (1997) 91 *Northwestern University Law Review* 1507.

[90] R Weisman, 'Detecting Remorse and its Absence in the Criminal Justice System' (1999) 19 *Studies in Law, Politics, and Society* 121, 123 (citing s 721(3)(a) of the Criminal Code as 'tantamount to requiring an evaluation of whether or not the offender shows remorse').

[91] Crimes Act 1914 (Cth), s 16A, cited in Proeve and Tudor, above n 4, 136.

[92] BH Ward, 'Sentencing without Remorse' (2006) 38 *Loyola University Chicago Law Journal* 131.

[93] Robinson et al, above n 8, 176.

[94] Indeed, as Weisman, above n 11, 128, has documented, one of many hurdles for the wrongfully convicted is their inability to satisfy the persistent demand that they accept responsibility for their crimes: 'A long list can be compiled from among the annals of the wrongfully convicted in Canada, in which parole was denied or temporary absences refused because of a continued assertion of innocence. Even when denial of parole is not expressly justified by lack of remorse, it may be based on the failure to participate in therapeutic or rehabilitative programs that will accept only those inmates who accept responsibility for their crimes, thereby barring those who continue to assert their innocence because they will not express remorse.'

[95] As Murphy, above n 73, 156 n 34, points out, the Federal Sentencing Guidelines do specify the conditions for a downward departure, and these include pleading guilty and other forms of cooperation with the government. In this context, the guidelines' use of the term 'remorse' is rather odd and perhaps misleading.

[96] Weisman, above n 11, 123. See also Proeve and Tudor, above n 4, 179–205 and ch 9.

[97] For an excellent and thorough discussion of these issues, see LL Levenson, 'Courtroom Demeanor: The Theater of the Courtroom' (2008) 92 *Minnesota Law Review* 573, 614–31.

especially problematic where the defendant chooses not to testify, because they may imply that the fact-finder may draw an unfavourable inference from the defendant's exercise of his right—in the US, a constitutional right and throughout Europe, a human right—not to testify. But as Laurie Levenson discusses, courts' difficulty in part flows from the ambiguous legal status and questionable relevance of non-testimonial demeanour. In the US, for example, there is a split between courts that regard demeanour as having no bearing on guilt or innocence, and therefore as an impermissible topic for prosecutorial comment, and courts that treat demeanour as a factor that may be considered and addressed in argument. The tension Levenson highlights spills over into the discussion of remorse. Prosecutors could be forbidden from commenting on a defendant's failure to exhibit remorse in the courtroom,[98] but this would not fully address the problem. Judges and jurors share the widely held belief that remorse can be and ought to be displayed in the courtroom, and this belief will hold sway whether or not the prosecutor comments. Thus educating fact-finders is crucial.

Jury instructions can play an important role. The US Supreme Court has upheld the 'anti-sympathy instruction', which commanded capital juries in California to put their sympathy aside when determining the defendant's sentence.[99] One critique of the anti-sympathy instruction is that it fails to define sympathy;[100] an instruction on remorse could attempt to address this definitional deficit. Given the strong empirical evidence that fact-finders habitually take remorse into account and accord it great weight, it is unlikely that drawing jurors' attention to remorse will introduce a notion which jurors would not otherwise consider. Judicial silence on remorse will not negate its powerful influence; it will simply leave jurors to their own devices. There is always the possibility that jury instructions will not have the desired effect, but as Levenson points out, the instructions have value in any case. Judicial instructions 'educate the jurors on how to use the information they perceive in the courtroom', communicating rules of law as well as rules of jury conduct.[101] Such instructions can remind the jury of the defendant's right not to testify at trial, and they can guide jurors in assessing the weight and relevance of remorse to the issue at hand. For example, they can inform jurors who are determining guilt or innocence that their verdict must be based on the defendant's acts and not his character.[102]

---

[98] See J Epstein, 'Silence: Insolubly Ambiguous and Deadly: The Constitutional, Evidentiary and Moral Reasons for Excluding "Lack of Remorse" Testimony and Argument in Capital Sentencing Proceedings' (2004) 14 *Temple Political & Civil Rights Law Review* 45. It is generally agreed that a capital defendant is entitled to have the jury instructed that it should draw no adverse inference from his failure to testify at the guilt phase: see *Griffin v California*, 380 US 609 (1965); *Carter v Kentucky*, 450 US 288 (1981) (general rule on instruction cautioning against adverse inference from failure to testify); and *Caldwell v State*, 818 S W 2d 790, 800 (Texas Crim App 1991) (comments on failure to express remorse as a result of failure to testify violate the 5th Amendment, but prosecutor may comment on testimony given during the guilt phase that denies responsibility for the crime). But cf *Burns v Secretary*, 720 F 3d 1296 (11th Cir 2013) (prosecutor may seek to demonstrate lack of remorse when defendant's remorse was raised by his witnesses in mitigation at the penalty phase; this is not necessarily a comment on his failure to testify).

[99] *California v Brown*, 479 US 538 (1986).

[100] SA Bandes, 'Repellent Crimes and Rational Deliberation: Emotion and the Death Penalty' (2009) 33 *Vermont Law Review* 489, 495–98. Another objection is that it singled out one emotion as off-limits, implying that all other emotions elicited by the testimony may appropriately guide the penalty-phase jury's decision.

[101] Levenson, above n 97, 629.

[102] Ibid 619–20.

Expert testimony would be helpful on several key issues. It could address the inherent limitations of demeanour evidence. More specifically, expert witnesses might explain and caution against the general difficulties of inferring remorse from facial expression, or the particular challenges posed by juveniles,[103] those with mental disabilities,[104] or demeanour assessments across racial lines. Empanelling more diverse juries would be another step in the right direction. And finally, it is important to remember that it is not just juries, but also judges, parole officers, probation boards and other decision-makers who often take an intuitive, 'I know it when I see it', approach to remorse. Exercises of official discretion might be better guided through the provision of more specific statutory or administrative criteria. In addition, training decision-makers about the psychological and sociological research on these issues, and the ways in which it contradicts widely accepted folk knowledge, is essential.

Conclusion

Evaluation of remorse in the courtroom poses both theoretical and practical challenges to the integrity of criminal justice systems. As a theoretical matter, the justifications for considering remorse as part of the punishment calculus have not been adequately articulated. Moreover, evaluation of remorse influences decisions of punishment based on unacceptable factors, such as race, ethnicity and mental disability. The criminal justice system at times explicitly promotes evaluation of remorse—as when prosecutors call attention to a defendant's lack of remorse, or when judges rely on remorse as a mitigating or aggravating factor in sentencing. More troubling, there is evidence that remorse exerts a silent yet quite pervasive effect on determinations of sentence and even guilt.

This chapter has advanced three conclusions, which in certain respects are in tension. The first conclusion is that, in the legal realm, serious consequences, including loss of life or liberty, hinge on whether a defendant displays what is regarded as appropriate remorse through facial expression and body language. The second conclusion, however, is that there is no good evidence that remorse can be evaluated through facial expression and body language, and significant evidence that evaluation of remorse is influenced by racial, ethnic and cultural factors, among other extra-legal or flat-out illegal considerations. The third conclusion is that, as long as we adhere to the long-standing traditions of open courtrooms in which demeanour is evaluated, it is likely to be difficult to entirely remove evaluation of a defendant's remorse from the process of assessing guilt and assigning punishment.

Legislators and policymakers must consider afresh what role remorse is meant to serve in the criminal justice system. This will depend on the particular legal context in question. For example, remorse may be relevant at a sentencing hearing, or in determining whether a prisoner should be released or pardoned, but not necessarily at trial. The appropriate role of remorse will also depend on our notions of what ends punishment is meant to serve.

---

[103] See Duncan, above n 15, 1517–18 (cautioning that though experts can be helpful, they are no panacea, in part because they may well disagree).

[104] Everett and Nienstedt, above n 18 (discussing contribution of mental health experts to judicial evaluation of remorse displayed by mentally ill offenders); Stobbs and Kebbell, above n 45.

Cognitive scientists, particularly those working in the burgeoning field of facial expression, ought to make the study of remorse and related emotions a priority. Is remorse something that can be identified or evaluated in a courtroom? What are the barriers to accurate evaluation? When decision-makers say they are evaluating remorse, what are they actually doing? Is there any correlation between remorse and future behaviour? The answers to these empirical questions should inform debates about the role of remorse in criminal process. They might also assist in the design of procedures—in the courtroom, the jury room and the judge's chambers—founded on a more realistic appraisal of human behaviour.

The legal system has many choices about when to demand showings of remorse or penalise a lack of remorse. The available evidence establishes that evaluating remorse from facial expression and body language is imprecise at best, and that it permits or even encourages selective empathy based on race, mental disability and other pernicious factors. Two methodological conclusions flow from the available evidence. First, criminal process policymakers and officials need to be better informed about cognitive science research on the evaluation of remorse. Secondly, until there is evidence that remorse can be identified or evaluated, a legal system concerned about the integrity of its procedures and outcomes ought to take every opportunity to minimise the occasions on which material consequences hinge on such shaky evaluations. To the extent this cannot be done, for example, where defendants are in an open courtroom and human nature leads decision-makers to evaluate their (apparent) remorsefulness, ameliorative steps—including cautionary jury instructions, judicial training and appropriate uses of expert testimony—should be taken. A more radical solution would be to screen the defendant from the decision-maker. This solution is unlikely to be adopted, but it does place in sharp relief the more basic antecedent questions: what do we expect to learn from demeanour evidence generally? Why do we place so much faith in it? And how well do existing procedures meet our aspirations?

14

Rape Law, Past Wrongs and Legal Fictions: Telling Law's Story with Integrity

JILL HUNTER*

Introduction—The Legal Landscape

That rape is wrong, and seriously wrong at that, can scarcely be doubted. Arguably, rape is among those wrongs which are never excusable [and probably] … among those wrongs which are never justifiable … [It appears on a] shortlist of wrongs which are crimes 'everywhere in the civilized world' and the decriminalisation of which 'no reasonable person could advocate'.[1]

Rape *is* a serious crime.

This chapter takes as its starting position that there is something about the law's approach to rape that sets it apart from other crimes. First, the prosecution of rape is pre-eminently a staging ground for hard-fought battles over fact and law. Proof of guilt is particularly fraught where sexual violence occurs between adults and behind closed doors. This is the classic intimate partner rape crime scene. It is here that, in the criminal trial, the private domain restricts a prosecution's evidentiary base and gives oxygen to conscious and sub-conscious real-rape stereotypes.[2] These trigger complex economic, social and psychological reactions in criminal law's actors that flow into all aspects of the criminal justice system. Arguably rape-in-marriage is now, and has been for centuries, at the extremity of rape law's comfort zone. For centuries, even its criminality was dismissed by the law and by sectors of society. However, statistics show that adult women who are victims of sexual assault are many times more likely to have been sexually assaulted by a person known to them than

* My thanks to Susan Bandes and Julie Stubbs for their inspiration.
[1] J Gardner and S Shute, 'The Wrongness of Rape' in J Horder (ed), *Oxford Essays in Jurisprudence*, 4th Series (Oxford, Oxford University Press, 2000) 193, quoting J Feinberg, *Harm to Others* (New York, Oxford University Press, 1984) 10.
[2] See M Randall, 'Sexual Assault Law, Credibility, and "Ideal Victims": Consent, Resistance, and Victim Blaming' (2010) 22 *Canadian Journal of Women and the Law* 397; B Krahe and J Temkin, *Sexual Assault and the Justice Gap: A Question of Attitude* (Oxford, Hart Publishing, 2008) 121 (reporting English studies indicating that 'the crucial determinant of judgments about rape cases is the extent to which people subscribe to rape myths'. Studies indicate that men subscribe to rape myths more than women). And see *R v Seaboyer* (1991) 83 DLR (4th) 193, 209: 'Like most stereotypes, they operate as a way, however flawed, of understanding the world and like most such constructs, operate at a level of consciousness that makes it difficult to root them out and confront them directly' (L'Heureux-Dubé J, dissenting).

by a stranger.[3] In all, one cannot help but be struck by the huge gulf between Gardner and Shute's positioning of rape and the law's disappointing track record on rape.

This chapter takes the 2012 Australian High Court case of *PGA v R*[4] as its focal point. *PGA* is a case study for analysing integrity in judicial decision-making. Further, the judgments in *PGA* may well offer food for thought to other jurisdictions facing historic rape-in-marriage prosecutions. Its majority judgment is also important if for no other reason than it rewrites legal history *internationally* by declaring that South Australia[5] was—*by many decades*—the very first common law jurisdiction to have stepped away from Hale's marital rape immunity.[6] The Soviet Union and Poland, previously seen as precocious outliers with respect to removing the immunity, are now joined by South Australia in the vanguard of extending the crime of rape into marriage.[7] This back-dated status of global leader arose because the Australian court was required to determine the status of a marital rape prosecution arising from events alleged to have taken place in 1963. Closer to home, the *PGA* decision also rewrites much of Australian criminal law history because South Australia was notably tardy in legislating away the vestigial remains of the immunity,[8] delaying even until 1992 and after the High Court decision in *R v L*[9] to do so. Elsewhere in Australia the immunity was statutorily removed in the 1980s.[10] In other words, prior to *PGA* creating this new official story, South Australia was in fact the straggler Australian jurisdiction.

Rape-in-marriage has been for centuries at the nadir of law's attitude to protecting rape victims and prosecuting rapists. In Anglo-based common law systems the marital rape immunity is attributed to Hale's 1736 proposition that:

> [T]he husband cannot be guilty of a rape committed by himself upon his lawful wife, for by their mutual matrimonial consent and contract the wife hath given up herself in this kind unto her husband, which she cannot retract.[11]

The immunity lingered until recent times. In many countries it still reflects the law.[12] Its durability is notable, and if we compare the immunity to Hale's other belief that reflected

---

[3] See n 106 and accompanying text, below.

[4] (2012) 245 CLR 355, [2012] HCA 21.

[5] And by implication also the non-Criminal Code states, New South Wales and Victoria.

[6] On the immunity's global stretch, see DJ Frank, BJ Camp and SA Boutcher, 'Trends in the Criminal Regulation of Sex, 1945 to 2005' (2010) 75 *American Sociological Review* 867. Sweden abolished it in 1965: see RA Elman, *Sexual Subordination and State Intervention: Comparing Sweden and the United States* (New York, Berghahn Books, 1996) 90.

[7] Statutory change only began in the 1980s in Canada, New Zealand, the US and Australia.

[8] Criminal Law Consolidation Act 1935 (SA), s 73(5), required the prosecution to prove aggravated conduct (including violence and threats of violence) for charges of rape, indecent assault, assault with intent to commit rape (or attempts to commit these crimes) upon a spouse.

[9] *R v L* (1991) 174 CLR 379, [1991] HCA 48.

[10] New South Wales removed the immunity in 1981: Crimes (Sexual Assault) Amendment Act 1981 (NSW); the Northern Territory in 1983: Criminal Code Act 1983 (NT); the Australian Capital Territory and Victoria in 1985: Crimes (Amendment) Ordinance (No 5) 1985 (ACT); Crimes (Amendment) Act 1985 (Vic). Western Australia, Tasmania and Queensland in 1985, 1987 and 1989, respectively, completely removed the immunity from their Codes: Acts Amendment (Sexual Assaults) Act 1985 (WA); Criminal Code Amendment (Sexual Offences) Act 1987 (Tas), Criminal Code, Evidence Act and other Acts Amendment Act 1989 (Qld).

[11] M Hale, *The History of the Pleas of the Crown* (1736), quoted by the majority in *PGA v R* (2012) 245 CLR 355, [2012] HCA 21, [39]. For Scotland, see *S v HM Advocate* 1989 SLT 469; D Hume, *Commentaries on the Law of Scotland, Respecting Crimes*, vol 1 (1797) 306.

[12] See eg United Nations (UN Women), *Progress of the World's Women, In Pursuit of Justice* (UN Women, 2011). Aside from the 52 countries that by 2011 had *explicitly* made marital rape a criminal offence, other countries are

women's position in his society,[13] namely, his belief in witchcraft,[14] we see a partial explanation for the immunity's resilience. However, while witchcraft itself (as opposed to fake sorcery) was written out of English criminal law by the Witchcraft Act 1735,[15] the marital rape immunity solidified under the rubric of the law of marriage and women's perceived duty to honour their vows and obey their husbands.[16] Law's preoccupation with conjugal rights conveniently distanced marital rape from the protection of the criminal law and any association with violence, injury and degradation. The immunity was firmly integrated into marriage law and was therefore by the second half of the twentieth century well placed for legal reinvention as a family law issue rather than a matter for criminal prosecution. This in turn facilitated its continuation for further decades. The blindness of the criminal law to rape-in-marriage matched the same affliction in criminal law enforcement of domestic violence. Until relatively recently, it too was prone to dismissal by police and prosecutors as merely a private or family matter.[17] As we shall see, it is no coincidence that these forms of criminality are, in legal history terms, close relatives. With criminality masked by invisibility, the criminal law was languid in recognising the wrongness (or even the fact) of husbands raping their wives. Witchcraft had no disguise. It was a fiction easily exposed by Enlightenment notions and once demonising witches was no longer perceived to be a mechanism for social cohesion its decriminalisation was readily achievable.

Yet it was not until 1991 in England and Wales (in *R v R*)[18] and across the whole of Australia (in *R v L*) that a stake was finally driven through the heart of the marital rape immunity. Statutory reversal in some cases preceded, and in others post-dated, these decisions by a handful of years in Canada,[19] the US and in the various states of Australia. This ended debate on marital rape immunity in these countries; and it seemed at the time, laid to rest an ugly piece of legal history. However, the *PGA* court needed to establish whether

also latecomers to ruling to reverse the immunity through its courts. See eg the Solomon Islands courts' reversal of the immunity in 2012: *R v Gua* [2012] SBHC 118 (8 October 2012).

[13] See G Geis, 'Revising Lord Hale, Misogyny, Witchcraft and Rape' (1986) 10 *Criminal Law Journal* 319, 320, citing M Hale, 'A Discourse Concerning the Great Meaning of God, in Preserving Us from the Power and Malice of Evil Angels' in *A Collection of Modern Relations of Matter of Fact Concerning Witches and Witchcraft* (1693).

[14] Men, often the husbands of witches, were accused of witchcraft but it was predominantly an accusation levelled against women who were typically unmarried, over 50 years old, and engaged in cooking, healing or midwifery: see A Garland, 'The Great Witch Hunt: The Persecution of Witches in England' (2003) 9 *Auckland University Law Review* 1152.

[15] (9 Geo II c 5), replaced by the Fraudulent Mediums Act 1951; and subsequently by consumer protection legislation.

[16] As JE Hasday, 'Contest and Consent: A Legal History of Marital Rape' (2000) 88 *California Law Review* 1373, 1500, notes: 'Modern courts, lawmakers, and commentators are never more anxious to expound upon the wonders of marital love, trust, intimacy, and respect than when a husband's freedom from prosecution for raping his wife is at stake.'

[17] *Two Steps Forward, One Step Back: Community Attitudes to Violence against Women: Progress and challenges in creating safe, respectful and healthy environments for Victorian women—A summary of findings of the Violence Against Women Community Attitudes Project* (Victorian Health Promotion Foundation, 2006) 61.

[18] *R v R* [1992] 1 AC 599, 610 (Lord Lane CJ, CA): 'It seems to us that where the common law rule no longer even remotely represents what is the true position of a wife in present day society, the duty of the court is to take steps to alter the rule if it can legitimately do so in the light of any relevant parliamentary enactment.' See also *SW and CR v UK* (1996) 21 EHRR 363, holding that there was no breach of the European Convention on Human Rights, Art 7.

[19] See M Randall, 'Sexual Assault in Spousal Relationships, "Continuous Consent", and the Law: Honest But Mistaken Judicial Beliefs' (2008) 32 *Manitoba Law Journal* 144; Randall, above n 2.

rape-in-marriage was an offence known to the law of South Australia in 1963. This created a challenge, because the alleged events pre-dated by over a quarter of a century the same court's 1991 proclamation that the immunity was no longer part of modern Australian jurisprudence. It also made the marital rape immunity a twenty-first-century issue.

1. A 1963 Claim of Marital Rape in 2010: *PGA v R*

The rape-in-marriage charges against Mr P came to light from evidence Mrs P gave to the Mullighan Inquiry[20] into the sexual abuse of children in state care. The prosecution depended on the existence of the immunity in what appeared to be a case-law void because the first South Australian rape-in-marriage criminal trial did not take place until 1978,[21] and even then its facts brought it within an immunity exception acknowledged by English precedent because the parties were subject to a court-ordered separation. No party in *PGA* could point to any single event directly defining legislative intent or the status of the marital immunity in South Australia in 1963. In terms of case law, the *PGA* court was limited to nineteenth-century cases asserting (typically by assumption) Hale's proposition, a clutch of English cases pre-dating 1963,[22] and a slightly larger group of English and Australian cases from the 1970s onwards.[23] These cases all acknowledged the immunity's continued existence, subject to a bit of clipping around the edges. The reason for the low incidence of prosecution is a matter of speculation, but it seems that potential charges were frozen out by a widespread belief that the immunity existed, doubtless reinforced by a raft of social factors combining to disempower and silence victims of intimate partner violence.[24]

---

[20] See *Children in State Care Commission of Inquiry: Allegations of sexual abuse and death from criminal conduct, presented to the South Australian Parliament by the Hon EP Mullighan QC*, Children in State Care Commission of Enquiry (Adelaide, 2008) (Mullighan Inquiry). Mr P was interviewed in 2007 and the prosecution commenced after lengthy consideration by the Director of Public Prosecution of the legal issues. This detail comes from W Larcombe and M Heath, 'Developing the Common Law and Rewriting the History of Rape in Marriage in Australia: *PGA v R*' (2012) 34 *Sydney Law Review* 785, 788. See also the critique of common law method and the absence of prosecutions by MJ Mossman, 'Feminism and Legal Method: the Difference it Makes' (1987) 3 *Wisconsin Women's Law Journal* 147.

[21] *R v Greenway* (1978), unreported, discussed in P Sallmann and D Chappell, *Rape Law Reform: A Study of the South Australian Experience*, Report to the Australian Criminology Research Council (Canberra, Australian Institute of Criminology, 1981) 46–51.

[22] *R v Clarke* [1949] 2 All ER 448; *R v Miller* [1954] 2 QB 282; *R v Chapman* [1959] 1 QB 10.

[23] *R v O'Brien* [1974] 3 All ER 663; *R v Steele* (1977) 65 Cr App R 22; *R v Roberts* [1986] Crim LR 188 ('The status of marriage involves that the woman has given her consent to her husband having intercourse with her during the subsistence of the marriage. She cannot unilaterally withdraw it.'); *R v Sharples* [1990] Crim LR 198. See also *R v Cogan* [1976] QB 217, 223; *R v Caswell* [1984] Crim LR 111; *R v Henry*, unreported, 14 March 1990 (Auld J); *R v J (rape: marital exemption)* [1991] 1 All ER 759, 762–63; *R v Shaw* [1991] Crim LR 301; *R v Kowalski* (1987) 86 Cr App R 339, 341; *R v Greenway* (1978), unreported.

[24] Of domestic violence, the Australian Medical Association says that it manifests 'the domination, coercion, intimidation and victimisation of one person by another by physical, sexual or emotional means within intimate relationships': quoted in *Two Steps Forward, One Step Back*, above n 17, 26. Fear of an aggressor's retaliation is a common consequence of chronic victimisation. These dynamics can traumatise victims of domestic violence, eroding their capacity and willingness to report crime and to support criminal prosecutions. These compounded features can persist for years beyond the ending of violence and threats of violence: see R Römkens and R Letschert, *Feasibility Study for a Convention Against Domestic Violence, European Committee On Crime Problems* (Strasbourg, European Committee on Crime Problems, 2007) 6. See also text to nn 104–110, below.

The *PGA* majority (French CJ, Gummow, Hayne, Crennan and Kiefel JJ) held that South Australian legislation in 1935 affirming the common law of rape marked a point where immunity from criminal liability for rape-in-marriage no longer existed.[25] By this time, if not earlier, the majority stated:

> [S]tatute law had removed any basis for continued acceptance of Hale's proposition as part of the English common law received in the Australian colonies. Thus, at all times relevant to this appeal, and contrary to Hale's proposition, at common law a husband could be guilty of rape committed by him upon his lawful wife. Lawful marriage to a complainant provided neither a defence to, nor an immunity from, a prosecution for rape.[26]

The majority decision is in stark contrast with the pervasive support courts and legislatures in Australia and in comparable jurisdictions gave to entrenching the immunity during the period in question. The judgment raises searching questions about the meaning, and hence the integrity of the decision, how it was reached and how it is expressed. The case raises the additional question of whether the decision takes more than it gives, especially (but not solely) for South Australian women who suffer, and may continue to suffer, the consequences of the immunity's legacy. To Mrs P and to all future complainants of historic (pre-1990s) marital rape, *PGA* clarifies that substantive law is no longer any obstacle to their allegations being tested in court. This notable gain—which it surely is—must also be seen for what it is. It is a green light to prosecute a procedurally and forensically complex delayed accusation. These elements create a situation that enlarges both the emotional toll upon the complainant and the uncertainty of a prosecution succeeding. However, for many potential complainants there can be no prosecution because law's tardiness may have meant that they or their husband are no longer alive. This indeed was the fate of the prosecution of Mr P. It ended with his death in late 2012. However, in return for the opportunity to see a prosecution proceed, these women are left with an official history of gender equality that airbrushes (to the point of concealment) the harm done to numerous women by the existence of the immunity.[27] This airbrush also masks the fear with which many married women lived when the criminal law failed to lift a finger.[28] The further implication of the judgment is its implicit (presumably unintended) message to later generations that, for married women from 1935, South Australian criminal law (and by implication, all common law states of Australia) acknowledged *all* women as equal and sought to protect them from rape, even in their homes. In truth it did not.

Australian law is no stranger to the practice of creating a legal fiction by airbrushing inconvenient facts. In Australia, the traditional owners of its land have intimate and piercing experience of this. Until *Mabo v Queensland (No 2)*[29] in 1992, the law treated the land that the British took over as 'practically unoccupied', *terra nullius*. Upon Federation, the Australian Commonwealth of Constitution Act contained 'without any dissent or, for that

---

[25] In 1935 (and continuing at least to 1963) Criminal Law Consolidation Act 1935 (SA), s 48 provided that, 'any person convicted of rape shall be guilty of felony, and liable to be imprisoned for life, and may be whipped'. This section reflected its English equivalent in the Offences Against the Person Act 1861, the legislation, though not the actual provision, relied upon in *R v Clarence* (1888) 22 QBD 23.

[26] *PGA v R* (2012) 245 CLR 355, [2012] HCA 21, [64].

[27] Or, at least, the widespread belief of its existence.

[28] See n 98, below.

[29] *Mabo v Queensland (No 2)* (1992) 175 CLR 1.

matter, any real discussion' the dismissive (and now removed) reference that 'in reckoning the numbers of the people of the Commonwealth, or of a State or other part of the Commonwealth, aboriginal natives shall not be counted'.[30] *Mabo* acknowledged these legal fictions. It recognised the fact of, lies about and the shocking consequences of this dispossession of Aboriginal and Torres Strait Islander (ATSI) people. We return to *Mabo* later in this chapter where the High Court judgments serve as analytical foils for further evaluating the majority judgment in *PGA* for its meaning and its methodology.

For the present, it is sufficient to foreshadow two themes that raise issues regarding how we evaluate the integrity of judicial decision-making. First, in *PGA* the majority's application of the traditional common law method allowed it to avoid confronting the intrinsic criminality of intimate partner rape—the violation, objectification, exploitation, subjugation, dehumanisation and betrayal of women that accompanies this crime; and secondly, by preferring law's own insular sources, its majority judgment (that is, law's official story) was infused with a sense of constancy and certainty so that it appeared an 'inevitable outcome of a triumphant historical process'.[31] These two elements combine to impede what one should expect of an apex court, namely, that it use its institutional space to give an authoritative, defensible and socially useful account of the law and its true impact. In this respect, instead of being notable as a radical judgment green-lighting the prosecution, *PGA* will be known as one in the long line of cases, chiefly from a bygone generation, where traditional substantive, procedural and evidentiary law shaped a disappointingly narrow information base to form a legal response to sexualised violence.[32] Could the majority in *PGA* have been better informed? Both *PGA* and *Mabo* bring to the fore consideration of the challenges courts and parties face in drawing upon evidence from the humanities to enlighten the law. In *PGA* this matter is writ large. The scant facts offered by the law (and also by the parties) challenged construction of a solid understanding of the complex relationship between the criminal law of rape and mid twentieth-century morality and mores. Instead, the dribble of criminal cases—for that is all it was—focused on defining and justifying marital rape, but on no account analysing its consequences in terms of the harm done to its victims.

The next section summarises how the *PGA* court undertook its task of rewinding the legal clock 50 years to determine whether the 1963 common law incorporated into South Australian law by section 48 of the Criminal Law Consolidation Act 1935 (SA) assimilated Hale's immunity. It should be kept in mind that the High Court was between a rock and a hard place. If it could not establish the early demise of the immunity, Mr P could raise another impediment to the marital rape prosecution, that of retrospective criminalisation. This would create the haunting spectre of the immunity being visited upon a twenty-first-century prosecution. Retrospective criminalisation is not a matter of easy resolution under Australian jurisprudence. In 1987 former Australian High Court justice, Deane J, had written that to ignore this limb of the rule of law is to treat 'the administration of the criminal

---

[30] Ibid [52] (Deane and Gaudron JJ).

[31] A Reilly, 'How *Mabo* helps us Forget' (2006) 6 *Macquarie Law Journal* 25, 30 quoting B Southgate, *History: What and Why Ancient, Modern and Post-Modern Perspectives* (London, Routledge, 2001) 119; in turn quoting H Butterfield, *The Whig Interpretation of History* (London, G Bell & Sons, 1963).

[32] See KL Scheppele, 'Just the Facts, Ma'am: Sexualized Violence, Evidentiary Habits, and the Revision of Truth' (1992) 37 *New York Law School Law Review* 123; R Kaspiew, 'Rape Lore: Legal Narrative and Sexual Violence' (1995) 20 *Melbourne University Law Review* 350.

law [as] … a macabre lottery by … flagrant violation of the "well-established judicial poli-cies of the criminal law in *favorem libertatis*, and against *ex post facto* punishment".[33] For Heydon and Bell JJ, dissenting in *PGA*, it was insurmountable.[34] However, a different view on retrospectivity with respect to crimes that are never excusable was expressed by Toohey J in the Australian war crimes case of *Polyukhovich*.[35] Rape *might* likewise be viewed as a crime that is a 'moral transgression [justifying] … the public interest in seeing the trans-gressors called to account [and outweighing] … the need of society to protect an individual from prosecution on the basis that a law did not exist at the time of the conduct'.[36] For our purposes, we leave this weighty question for others. The task for the next section is to understand law's retention (or not) of the marital rape immunity.

2. The Precocious Demise of the Marital Rape Immunity

(a) The Majority Judgment

The *PGA* majority expressly set its task as establishing whether society's view of married women at that time was in keeping with Hale's proposition. The majority Justices drew upon their own 1991 approach in *R v L*[37] to focus upon married women's civil status at law, rather than upon the intrinsic criminality of the husband's conduct. As discussed below, they expressly rejected submissions that relied upon a sociological analysis; and they ulti-mately found that they had no need to take judicial notice of 'social circumstances and attitudes which had occurred in this country by 1935'.[38]

In contrast to Lord Lane CJ's observation at the Court of Appeal level in *R v R* that Hale's proposition had been 'accepted as an enduring principle of the common law',[39] the *PGA* majority commenced with soft doubt of the validity of Hale's *proposition*,[40] and further infused it with weakness. The proposition, after all, was merely 'based on a statement in a text published in 1736, many years after the death of the author, without citation of prior authority and lacking subsequent exposition in cases'.[41] The majority pointed to the propo-sition's lack of foundational precedent,[42] its sparse detail, and dependence on transmission

---

[33] *PGA v R* (2012) 245 CLR 355, [2012] HCA 21, [245]–[247] (Bell J, quoting Dean J in *Zecevic v DPP (Vic)* (1987) 162 CLR 645, 677–68; in turn quoting J Stone, *Precedent and Law* (Sydney, Butterworths, 1985) 190).

[34] *PGA v R* (2012) 245 CLR 355, [2012] HCA 21, [160]. Of course the majority's approach pre-empted this issue.

[35] *Polyukhovich v The Commonwealth* (1991) 172 CLR 501.

[36] Ibid 689. See also K Toole, 'Marital Rape in South Australia: *R v P, GA*' (2011) 35 *Criminal Law Journal* 237, 244–48, 251.

[37] That is, they sought to establish that, before 1963, the immunity was 'a notion that [was] … so out of keeping with the view society … [took] of the relationship between the parties to a marriage': *R v L* (1991) 174 CLR 379, [1991] HCA 48 (Mason CJ, Deane and Toohey JJ). Cf *R v R* [1992] 1 AC 599.

[38] Or what they referred to as 'judicial perceptions' of these attitudes: see *PGA v R* (2012) 245 CLR 355, [65].

[39] *R v R* [1992] 1 AC 599. This was noted by Heydon J, but not by the majority.

[40] *PGA v R* (2012) 245 CLR 355, [2012] HCA 21, [40]–[43]. Note it was only a 'proposition' and never a rule of law.

[41] Ibid [22] (French CJ, Gummow, Hayne, Crennan and Kiefel JJ).

[42] Ibid [42]. Though this was in fact not atypical for Hale's time, see JH Baker, *The Oxford History of the Laws of England* (Oxford, Oxford University Press, 2003) vol 6, 486.

through extra-judicial treatises, including East, Chitty and Russell.[43] Always, the majority left the doubt hanging. The majority observed that nineteenth-century Canadian and Australian codes solidified the immunity by defining rape with the rider 'not his wife'.[44] It quoted Oliver Wendell Holmes to help diagnose how Hale's proposition had proceeded unchecked into the twentieth century:

> New cases will arise which will elude the most carefully constructed formula. The common law ... by a continual reconciliation of cases ... is prepared for this, and simply modifies the form of its rule. But what will the court do with a code? If the code is truly law, the court is confined to a verbal construction of the rule as expressed, and must decide the case wrong.

The inference the majority sought to make is clear. Treatise writers were not really part of the common law natural order, and the Australian codes assisted to create a climate that also kept the immunity alive. The majority considered the important 1888 English case of *R v Clarence*[45] which held that Clarence's wife's 'consent' was not vitiated by her husband's failure to disclose his venereal disease. Most of the judgments in *Clarence* implicitly assumed the validity of Hale's proposition and, through varying pathways, justified quashing the assault conviction. The *PGA* majority characterised *Clarence* as offering 'differing views', but the decision was in fact an overwhelming affirmation of Hale's proposition by the 13-man bench, notably including Stephen J,[46] Pollock B,[47] Huddleston B,[48] Coleridge CJ and Hawkins J.[49] These eminent jurists saw no flaw in the proposition's paternity; only four of them would have upheld Clarence's conviction.[50] Even then, two of these dissentients, Field and Hawkins JJ, in the words of Heydon J in *PGA* 'plainly thought that Hale's proposition was correct in some circumstances'.[51] Even Hawkins J, on the side of the angels in ruling to maintain the conviction, described the improbability of extending the reach of criminal justice protection to a marital rape by suggesting that:

> No jury would be found to convict a husband of rape on his wife except under very exceptional circumstances, any more than they would convict of larceny a servant who stealthily appropriated to her own use a pin from her mistress's pincushion.[52]

The *PGA* majority drew upon the 1959 Australian High Court decision of *Papadimitropoulos*,[53] where it was observed that the twentieth century saw the common law whittling away legalistic constraints with respect to force and penetration that had earlier defeated rape prosecutions. In all, as the *PGA* majority noted, the common law proceeded satisfactorily

---

[43] Ibid [4]. By the twentieth century there was hint of slight wobble in the immunity. For example, the 1929 annotation in TW Chitty, *Halsbury's Statutes of England* (London, Butterworth & Co (Publishers) Ltd, 1929), vol 4, 615 prefaced its summation of the marital immunity with 'it is said that'; and by 1931 the 28th edition of JF Archbold, *Archbold's Pleading, Evidence and Practice in Criminal Cases* (London, Sweet & Maxwell, 1931), 1043, described it as 'a general proposition', (quoted in majority judgment in *PGA* at [7]).

[44] Criminal Code 1892 (Canada), s 266; Criminal Code 1899 (Qld), s 347, with subsequent revised amendments to the latter, and to the Codes of Western Australia and Tasmania, in 1989, 1985 and 1987 respectively.

[45] (1888) 22 QBD 23, CCR.

[46] Stephen J gave the leading judgment and accepted the Hale proposition.

[47] Pollock B accepted the Hale proposition as good law.

[48] Coleridge CJ and Huddleston B concurred with Stephen J.

[49] Hawkins J accepted the proposition in principle, but upheld the conviction.

[50] Charles, Day, Hawkins and Field JJ.

[51] *PGA v R* (2012) 245 CLR 355, [96]. Day J concurred with Hawkins J; Charles J, with Field J.

[52] *R v Clarence* (1888) 22 QBD 23, 52.

[53] *Papadimitropoulos v R* (1957) 98 CLR 249, 255; [1957] HCA 74.

by 'reasoning from accepted notions about remedies and rights to the evolution of rules "to govern new or changed situations to which an ever developing social order gives rise"'.[54] We return to these themes later; but it is noteworthy that, while musing on the strength of the common law method, the *PGA* majority failed to mention that *Papadimitropoulos*[55]— which concerned rape allegations within a *faux* marriage—applied reasoning consistent with Hale's proposition.

Having ostensibly undermined the strength and reach of the immunity, the *PGA* majority then collected a cluster of what it deemed to be signals of gender equality in the law. These focused on South Australian marriage law, married women's property rights and women's right to vote. In these fields, the majority dwelt on the traditional focal points of precedent, anodyne points of law featuring a range of conceptual dichotomies:

— regarding a functionally-ended marriage and a robustly lawful one;[56]
— regarding husbands' conjugal rights,[57] the legal significance of restitution of conjugal rights, specific performance of the marriage contract, and the potential for a husband's action for damages in these contexts, and various considerations deemed relevant to non-consent, such as the fragility of a wife's health;
— regarding various manifestations of deception (pretending to be a husband, not revealing sexually transmitted disease and the like);[58] and
— between rape and differently performed non-consensual acts of sexual penetration or touching, collateral assault and the presence of violence.[59]

The following jurisprudential resources grounded the majority's conclusion that a precociously enlightened common law attitude to marital rape existed in South Australia by 1935:

(1) *Women's suffrage*: The majority noted South Australia's leadership globally in achieving women's suffrage (for non-ATSI citizens) in 1894.[60] In 1902 Australia became the first country in the world where most women had the right both to vote and to stand for the national parliament.[61]

(2) *Mutual matrimonial consent and divorce law*: Hale's description of the immunity was based on irrevocable mutual matrimonial consent. Perhaps, reasoned the majority,

---

[54] Quoting from *Commissioner for Railways (NSW) v Scott* (1959) 102 CLR 392, 399-400; [1959] HCA 29 (Dixon CJ).

[55] (1957) 98 CLR 249. The High Court overruled the trial judge and the Court of Appeal to hold that this fraud was not of the nature to remove consent because 'consent demands a perception as to what is about to take place, as to the identity of the man and the character of what he is doing ... [and as such] the inducing causes cannot destroy its reality and leave the man guilty of rape'. See eg *R v Flattery* (1877) 13 Cox CC 388 (CCR) (where the complainant believed she was submitting to a medical procedure).

[56] *R v O'Brien* (1974) 3 All ER 663; *R v Clarke* (1949) 33 Cr App R 216, (1949) 2 All ER 448; *R v Miller* (1954) 2 QB 282; *R v Steele* (1976) 65 Cr App R 22; *R v Roberts* [1986] Crim LR 188; *R v Sharples* [1990] Crim LR 198. In *Sharples* there was a family protection order in the wife's favour requiring Sharples to 'not use or threaten to use violence against the person of the applicant'. The judge held that obtaining an order permitted the inference that the wife had withdrawn her consent to sexual intercourse.

[57] But not the distinctly asymmetrical approach courts took to damages for loss of consortium.

[58] *Papadimitropoulos v R* (1957) 98 CLR 249, 255; [1957] HCA 74.

[59] *R v Caswell* [1984] Crim LR 111; *R v Kowalski* (1987) 86 Cr App R 339; and *R v H*, unreported, 5 October 1990.

[60] The UK granted universal suffrage in 1928.

[61] M Sawer, *Women and Government in Australia* (Canberra, Australian Bureau of Statistics, 1301.0—Year Book Australia, 2001).

Hale may have assumed that, as there was no divorce law in his time, the matrimonial vow was irrevocable and therefore so was implied consent to conjugal rights. By parity of logic, divorce legislation turned the tables on irrevocability. The first generation of divorce legislation emerged from 1857.[62]

(3)   *Married women's status and property rights*: The *PGA* majority noted, by reference to the High Court case of *Wright v Cedzich*,[63] that by 1930 Isaacs J was able to say that, 'women are admitted to the capacity of commercial and professional life in most of its branches ... they are received on equal terms with men as voters and legislators, that they act judicially, can hold property, may sue and be sued alone'. Notably (but not mentioned in the *PGA* judgment), Isaac J was in dissent. However, it is clear that by 1930 much *had* changed since Hale's time when only equity permitted property rights to a feme sole through the very limited mechanism of a trust. By 1882 in England,[64] and a little later in the Australian colonies,[65] married women's property legislation simplified and democratised equitable trust law's goal of allowing married women to acquire, hold and dispose as their own, real and personal property, including their own earnings. For the *PGA* majority this legislation revealed law's recognition that society viewed married women on equal terms to men and fuelled the likelihood that the common law (given the chance) would disown the marital rape immunity. That the presence of these civil rights[66] failed to impact upon the decision in *Clarence* is left unacknowledged.

(b) The Dissentients

PGA featured two strong dissenting opinions by Heydon and Bell JJ. Heydon J posed the rhetorical question:

> What would a bad man in South Australia have learned if he had asked for a prophecy as to what the South Australian courts, and this Court, would be likely to say in the years 1963 to 1965, for example, if he had been charged in April 1963 with raping his wife in March ... ?[67]

In response to his own question, Heydon J noted that Australian criminal cases from the mid 1970s to the early 1990s all affirmed Hale's proposition[68] and that the views in *Clarence*

---

[62] Matrimonial Causes Act 1857. The Australian colonies followed. Matrimonial Causes Act 1858 (SA); Matrimonial Causes Act 1860 (Tas); Matrimonial Causes Act 1861 (Vic); Matrimonial Causes Act 1863 (WA); Matrimonial Causes Act 1865 (Qld); Matrimonial Causes Act 1873 (NSW). Divorce was available more freely to husbands than wives. However, by the end of the nineteenth century a number of Australian states extended the bases for divorce on a wife's petition beyond those available in England.

[63] *PGA v R* (2012) 245 CLR 355, [2012] HCA 21, [63]. *Wright v Cedzich* (1930) 43 CLR 493, 505.

[64] *Married Women's Property Act* 1882.

[65] Married Women's Property Act 1883 (Tas); Married Women's Property Act 1883–84 (SA); Married Women's Property Act 1890 (Qld); Married Women's Property Act 1884 (Vic); Married Women's Property Act 1892 (WA); Married Women's Property Act 1893 (NSW).

[66] Note also that submissions by the appellant regarding the recency of anti-discrimination legislation (*PGA v R* [2011] HCATrans 267) were not discussed in the judgments.

[67] *PGA v R* (2012) 245 CLR 355, [2012] HCA 21 [139]; appropriating the 'bad man' perspective famously proposed by OW Holmes, 'The Path of the Law' (1897) 10 *Harvard Law Review* 457, 461.

[68] *R v Brown* (1975) 10 SASR 139, 141, 153; *R v Wozniak* (1977) 16 SASR 67, 71; *R v Sherrin (No 2)* (1979) 21 SASR 250, 252; *R v C* (1981) 3 A Crim R 146, 148–50; *Question of Law Reserved on Acquittal (No 1 of 1993)* (1993) 59 SASR 214, 230; *R v Bellchambers* (1982) 7 A Crim R 463, 466.

were persistently influential worldwide. Both Heydon and Bell JJ acknowledged that the first moves towards widespread rape law reform and the immunity's eventual statutory demise began in the 1970s. Legal commentary, some of which was cited by the dissentients, universally treated the immunity as representing the common law. For example, the respected Australian legal academics Morris and Turner wrote in 1954 that permitting a wife to refuse sex with her husband raised two problematic options: it might wreck the marriage, or it might create an 'intolerable' situation 'if he [the husband] were to be conditioned in his course of action by the threat of criminal proceedings for rape'.[69] For Justice Bell, it could not be 'sensibly suggested'[70] that in 1963 Mr P would have been prosecuted for rape-in-marriage. Heydon J dismissed the idea that the immunity was plausibly challengeable at this time as tantamount to believing 'that history can be rewritten in complete defiance of all contemporary evidence'.[71] Academic commentary and law reform in England[72] and the US[73] into the 1980s reinforced the view that married women's rights to personal autonomy were constrained and subservient to a family law framework.[74] An illustration of this logic was expressed in the 1976 South Australian Mitchell Committee Report[75] where it was noted that 'it is only in exceptional circumstances that the criminal law should invade the bedroom … [otherwise it] might put a dangerous weapon into the hands of the vindictive wife and an additional strain upon the matrimonial relationship'.[76]

3. Signs of Substantive Gender Inequality in Twentieth-Century Law

The *PGA* court sought to determine whether in 1963 the rape immunity was a notion that was out of keeping with society's view of the marital relationship. The majority, as we have seen, focused on formal indicators of women's civil rights to reach its conclusion. It

---

[69] N Morris and G Turner, 'Two Problems in the Law of Rape' (1954) 2 *University of Queensland Law Review* 247, 259, quoted by Bell J in PGA v R (2012) 245 CLR 355, [2012] HCA 21, [237].

[70] *PGA v R* (2012) 245 CLR 355, [2012] HCA 21, [164].

[71] Ibid [157]. Heydon J, discussing *Shaw v DPP* [1962] AC 220, 275; *DPP v Smith* [1961] AC 290, also explored the common law's antipathy to radical change and appraised the potential local judicial *dramatis personae* of 1963–1965 to consider the bad man's query and concluded that these judges were committed to the principle that the legislature alone could extend criminal responsibility.

[72] Criminal Law Revision Committee Report No 15, *Sexual Offences*, Cmnd 9213 (London, HMSO, 1984) 21 [2.69]: 'Some of us consider that the criminal law should keep out of marital relationships between cohabiting partners—especially the marriage bed—except where injury arises, when there are other offences which can be charged.'

[73] American Law Institute, *Model Penal Code and Commentaries (Official Draft and Revised Comments)* (1980), Pt 2, Art 213, 345 ('the law of rape, if applied to spouses, would thrust the prospect of criminal sanctions into the ongoing process of adjustment in the marital relationship').

[74] See also *PGA v R* (2012) 245 CLR 355, [2012] HCA 21, [240] (Bell J).

[75] The Criminal Law and Penal Methods Reform Committee of South Australia (Chair: Roma Mitchell), *Special Report on Rape and other Sexual Offences* (Adelaide, Government Printer, 1976) 46 (Mitchell Committee) recommended the retention of the immunity. See also Royal Commission on Human Relationships (Chair: Elizabeth Evatt), *Final Report*, vol 5 (Canberra, AGPS, 1977) 194.

[76] Mitchell Committee Report, above n 75, 14 [6.2], quoted by Bell J in PGA v R (2012) 245 CLR 355, [2012] HCA 21, [239].

is, however, fair to conclude that the court's inquiry into the existence of the marital rape immunity made evaluation of the social position of women and society's view of married women's power and sexual autonomy particularly apposite. South Australia in the 1970s provided highly pertinent food for thought on these topics.

(a) Married Women's Civil Rights

It is revealing to go beyond civil law's formal signs of gender equality to examine substantive rights for single and married women. The South Australian record on women's suffrage appears impressive, but formal equality belies women's actual gains. Despite possessing for decades formal rights to political candidature, no women were elected to the State parliament in South Australia until 1959. Even then, the winning candidate was (unsuccessfully) challenged in the courts on the basis that 'person' in the South Australian Constitution did not include a woman! Despite women's groups agitating throughout the twentieth century it was not until 1965 that South Australian women gained the right to sit on juries (albeit without equal pay).[77]

As was commonly the case in the first three quarters of the twentieth century, married women represented a small fraction of the workforce and were typically subordinated to their husband's career. A similar asymmetry existed with respect to education and training. Thus, the trend for women to remain economically disenfranchised continued despite married women's property legislation. Often this disenfranchisement was through asymmetrical employment opportunities leaving women's contributions to the family home in forms which the law did not readily translate into property rights. Courts were quick to disqualify providing domestic support and caring for children from conferring 'any equitable interest in her husband's property'.[78] These contributions were instead 'likely to be found in natural love and affection'.[79] Twentieth-century case law reveals a conceptual framework where the marital home was held in the husband's name as his 'property' (typically, though not invariably because he was or became the sole bread-winner) and subject to the wife seeking an equitable claim for a portion of it.[80] Sometimes the family home would be placed in a husband's name despite financial contributions from a wife.[81] Further, a wife's claims were determined within the apparently gender-neutral legal framework of parties' intentions, but in reality the probative hurdles for a woman were impossibly high because there was little evidence of negotiated arrangements regarding women's financial or non-financial contributions.

With respect to employment specific to married women, Australia legislated its own copy of the British civil service marriage bar that deemed women to retire upon marriage. Women's careers in the Commonwealth and state civil service were cut short,[82] single

---

[77] Juries Act Amendment Act 1965 (SA). See *Women & Politics in South Australia: Political Awareness* (Adelaide, State Library of South Australia, 2001).

[78] *Bryson v Bryant* (1992) 29 NSWLR 188, 225 (Samuels AJA).

[79] Ibid 220 (Sheller JA).

[80] JC Williams, 'Married Women and Property' (1994) 1 *Virginia Journal of Social Policy & the Law* 383, speaking of the US position but with equal force in Australia.

[81] See eg *Bryson v Bryant* (1992) 29 NSWLR 188, 191–92 (Kirby P).

[82] Sawer, above n 61.

women were denied training, married women occupied temporary staff positions, not supervisory ones, and without superannuation rights. As early as 1933 the conference of the Women Voters' Federation held in Adelaide, South Australia, carried a resolution endorsing the principle that 'married women are entitled to be regarded as responsible citizens with a right to choose for themselves whether they will continue in … work'.[83] The 1933 conference determined that its 'to-do' list of key 'issues to be fought for' included equal pay for women and creating gender-neutral language for all legislation and regulation 'dealing with public morals'.[84] But despite much criticism by women's groups the marriage bar remained embedded in legislation until 1966.[85] Australia was almost the last democratic country to remove it. Even by 1975 women represented only 24 per cent of permanent public service staff and over half of female employees were telephonists, typists, steno-secretaries or clerical assistants.[86] These structural inequalities have persisted beyond the twentieth century. Writing in 2010, Australian employment specialist, Glenda Strachan, pointedly observed:

> There are many more opportunities for women to enter the workforce … these opportunities decrease if women choose to move to managerial ranks. Most managers are men. Women may be constrained in their choices by hostile organisational cultures and lack of practices that assist with managing both paid work and family care. Are women still working for a man? Most probably.[87]

(b) Rape-in-Marriage Law and Social Attitudes

In 1976, flowing from the South Australian Mitchell Committee's report, the Attorney-General presented a Bill[88] expressly revoking the marital rape immunity. This immediately became a lightning rod for conservative legal and public criticism of the broad law reform package. Ultimately, the Act that passed through the South Australian legislature included only a compromised removal of the immunity.[89] Sallmann and Chappell writing in 1981 as contemporaries to the passage of this reform package describe the 'rape-in-marriage' issue as its cause célèbre.[90] The reforms finally located the immunity within the realm of criminal rather than family law,[91] and in 1976 the compromised immunity was viewed as a victory

---

[83] ELP Littlejohn, 'Equal Social Rights For Sexes', *Women's Weekly* (Australia), 10 June 1933, 1. Linda Littlejohn was an Australian feminist with an international profile, particularly during the 1930s.

[84] Women's employment after the First World War was additionally compromised by official policy articulating women's perceived intrinsic physiological weaknesses. This continued post-1945: Sawer, above n 61, citing the *Royal Commission on Public Service Administration Report* (1920) and the report by RS Parker, *Public Service Recruitment in Australia* (Carlton Vic, Melbourne University Press, 1942) 223.

[85] Public Service Act 1922 (Cth), 49. This was inherited at the time of Federation and replicated throughout Australia. Sheridan and Stretton observe that in the 1950s few married women had permanent professional jobs in the South Australian and Tasmanian public services; and only where men or single women were not available: T Sheridan and P Stretton, 'Mandarins, Ministers and the Bar on Married Women' (2004) 46 *Journal of Industrial Relations* 84.

[86] Sawer, above n 61.

[87] G Strachan, 'Still Working for the Man? Women's Employment Experiences in Australia Since 1950' (2010) 45 *Australian Journal of Social Issues* 117, 126.

[88] This Bill went further than the recommendations of the Mitchell Committee.

[89] That is, on proof of aggravated circumstances, see Criminal Law Consolidation Act Amendment Act (No 83 of 1976) inserting s 73 into the 1935 Act. See above n 8.

[90] Sallmann and Chappell, above n 21, 56.

[91] P Wilson, *The Other Side of Rape* (St Lucia Qld, University of Queensland Press, 1978) 105.

for women. It was first to ameliorate the marital rape immunity in the English-speaking world.[92] The reforms nevertheless provided an imperfect solution for a number of reasons. First, they did not include robust rape shield protection, nor did they address the treatment of sexual assault complainants in committal proceedings or the presence of anachronistic corroboration warnings. Trials might still include submissions from the defence regarding the prevalence of false complaints and no extra-judicial complaint evidence was admissible unless it was made in the accused's presence.[93] Secondly, a successful marital rape prosecution required the prosecution to show the sexual act was accompanied by violence or threats.[94] Thirdly, the reform posed a real danger of severe unintended consequences. As one lawyer interviewed at the time of these reforms observed:

> For every conviction you get there are going to be acquittals and that is going to leave the woman even more prone to violence. Where a woman alleges rape and the man is acquitted he is not going to worry about the fact that the standard of proof is beyond reasonable doubt. He has then got open sesame to thump her as much as he likes because she is never going to be believed again having been disbelieved once. It has got that sort of danger. I think the Mitchell Committee saw that danger. You never needed to bring the complicated features of the rape law into what are fundamentally crimes of violence.[95]

Wilson showed that spousal rape was drastically under-reported, observing himself that '[i]t may well be difficult to prove that rape has occurred within a marriage—particularly as it would take a very brave woman to test the [new South Australian] legislation'.[96] From a twenty-first century perspective the obligation to prove violence where rape was alleged to have occurred during marriage is mystifying.[97] One needs to understand 1960s and 1970s attitudes to what constituted authentic rape to appreciate that a distinction might conceivably be drawn between violent rape and non-violent rape. These attitudes explain why police, prosecutors and the community so often failed to take rape victims' allegations seriously.[98] Importantly, public opinion treated a prior relationship between victim and offender as confirmation of victim-initiated sex[99] and so, in effect, no commission of a crime—unless there was evidence of violence. In 1978 criminologist Paul Wilson described the prevailing assumption of authentic rape as a 'crime perpetrated by unmarried working class drunk young males'. With reference to Queensland in the early 1960s and 1970s, Wilson described

---

[92]   T Buddin, 'Revision of Sexual Offences Legislation: A Code for NSW?' (1977) 2 *University of New South Wales Law Journal* 117, 130, n 68.

[93]   Royal Commission on Human Relationships, above n 75, 194.

[94]   See J Scutt, 'Consent in Rape: The Problem of the Marriage Contract' (1977) 3 *Monash University Law Review* 255, 278.

[95]   Lawyer interview, Sallmann and Chappell, above n 21, 54.

[96]   Wilson, above n 91, 105. See also Australian Law Reform Commission Report 69, *Equality before the Law: Justice for Women*, Part 1 (Canberra, 1994) [2.30]–[2.39].

[97]   Notably, even this compromise scraped through on the speaker's casting vote: Sallmann and Chappell, above n 21, 35.

[98]   For example, the District Court judge in 2010 with respect to the *PGA* proceedings noted that 'it is notorious that domestic violence matters were not taken as seriously in those times as they should have been' when referring to Mrs P's other contemporaneous assault allegations reported to police regarding Mr P that police 'decided to take no action'. Transcript of Proceedings, *R v PGA* (District Court of South Australia, 1418/2009, Herriman J, 5 July 2010) 2, 38. See Larcombe and Heath, above n 20, 789).

[99]   Wilson, above n 91, 14–21. For example, if there is a 'prior acquaintanceship [it is] the victim [who] initiates the crime, and … severe damage to the victim is [therefore] a relatively infrequent event': ibid 21. See also Royal Commission on Human Relationships, above n 75, 159 (referring to the perception of women as 'chattels').

findings from his own study of attitudes and experiences of 70 victims of unreported rape, further fleshing out social attitudes quick to blame married rape complainants:

'My husband would hate me. He's big on faithfulness and he'd hate me';

'He'd never believe me. He'd think I'd brought it on myself';

'John would just go crazy. He'd go looking for the guy just to find out if I led him on'.[100]

In keeping with these women's responses, Australian attitudinal studies of the day supported the perception that those who claimed to be rape victims were in fact willing and cooperative.[101] As striking proof of the pervasiveness of these views in the 1960s, Wilson quoted an American sociologist and victim studies expert, Stephen Schafer,[102] expressing his own doubts about being able to 'forgive' his wife if she were raped.[103] If Australian views chimed with US public attitudes, this decidedly odd view of rape has internal logic. At these times the most common explanation for not reporting rape was the fear of negative police reactions. One in five of the victims in Wilson's study stated that they left the rape unreported because they wanted to forget it. This rationale for not reporting violent (or any other) crime, as Wilson observed, is almost unique to rape victims.

Gains made in Australian domestic sexual assault prosecutions and also in community attitudes since the 1970s, like those in comparable common law jurisdictions, have been immense, but they are only faltering steps in a long journey. Government domestic and sexual violence initiatives have in more recent times turned their focus onto policing and prosecution[104] (and to holding endless inquiries into domestic and sexual violence). Nevertheless, statistical evidence from Australia and comparable countries paints a depressing picture that, despite change, there still exists a crisis level of substantive inequality between men and women with respect to sexual violence, particularly in the home. As well as being five times more likely than men to be victims of sexual violence,[105] women are 25 times more likely than men to be victims of sexual violence by an intimate partner.[106]

---

[100] Wilson, above n 91, 61.

[101] Ibid 20, citing D Chappell and J James, 'Victim Selection and Apprehension from the Rapist's Perspective: A Preliminary Investigation', paper to the *Second International Symposium on Victimology* (Boston MA, 1976) 22. A 1977 US study found that rape offenders when interviewed considered 'asking for it' included accepting rides in a car, walking in a secluded area late at night, going out with a stranger, hanging around bars, dancing closely, dressing 'invitingly' or using body language to ask for sex.

[102] Wilson, above n 91, 61, discussing 'highly regarded' author S Schafer, *The Victim and his Criminal: A Study in Functional Responsibility* (New York, Random House, 1968).

[103] Wilson, above n 91, quoting from DK Shaw, 'Women Attack Rape Justice', *National Observer*, 9 October 1971, 3.

[104] See J Phillips and P Vandenbroek, Domestic, Family and Sexual Violence in Australia: An Overview of the Issues, Parliamentary Library Research Paper (Parliament of Australia, 2014) 15–17; SD Muldoon, SC Taylor and C Norma, 'Patterned Characteristics of Continued and Discontinued Sexual Assault Complaints in the Criminal Justice Process' (2013) 24 *Current Issues in Criminal Justice* 395; A Diduck and K O'Donovan (eds), *Feminist Perspectives on Family Law* (Abingdon, Routledge-Cavendish, 2007).

[105] Australian Bureau of Statistics, *4530.0—Crime Victimisation* (Australia, 2013–14).

[106] Australian Bureau of Statistics, *Experimental Family And Domestic Violence Statistics, 4510.0—Recorded Crime—Victims* (Australia, 2014) Table 2. For England and Wales, see Ministry of Justice, Home Office, Office for National Statistics, *An Overview of Sexual Offending in England and Wales: Statistics Bulletin* (London, 2013). A European study suggests that across countries, that figures on sexual violence differ widely, due to varied definitions of sexual violence and rape. The narrowest definitions of rape as a 'forced' sexual act elicit prevalence figures indicating that from 5% to 7% of all women have been raped by a partner or ex-partner at some point in their lives. Broader definitions produce prevalence rates of sexual violence of around 10%. For Europe, see

These experiences have a cascading impact should a woman seek to leave a violent partner, or having left, not return. Phillips and Vandenbroek note:

> Australian researchers found that some women had not been allowed to work while in a violent relationship and found it difficult to enter or re-enter the workforce post separation. … domestic violence not only acts as a barrier to education, training and employment but can also escalate when survivors seek or participate in such activities. In order to maintain control over their partners, abusers may interfere with women's efforts to become self-sufficient.[107]

Financial insecurity as a result of domestic violence impinges on victims' capacity to leave their abuser and to rebuild their lives if they do leave. Sources of strain with respect to women's financial security arise 'in key areas of life: debts, bills and banking, accommodation, legal issues, health, transport, migration, employment, social security and child support'.[108] Clearly we have not reached the position where law-makers can say 'job done'. Public understanding of the incidence and seriousness of domestic violence is a continuing challenge. For example, the 2013 report of the third Australian *National Community Attitudes Survey* (NCAS) found that nearly 80 per cent of respondents from a sample of 17,500 telephone interviewees had no understanding of why a woman might not leave a violent relationship; and more than half agreed that women *often* fabricate cases of domestic violence in family law cases.[109] Further, 21 per cent of respondents held the view that violence can sometimes be excused if the perpetrator 'truly regrets' what they have done.[110]

4. Integrity and Common Law Methodology

Ultimately, the decision in *PGA* is unsettling because it shows the common law method failing to acknowledge law's inadequacies with respect to a wrong that should be included in the shortlist of crimes 'everywhere in the civilized world' and the decriminalisation of which 'no reasonable person could advocate'.[111] Further, there is a very real danger that the judgment subliminally conveys that even today rape is not under-reported or hidden in police, prosecution and appeal practices. It seems patently clear that *PGA* reinforces the view that there *is* something about the law's approach to rape that sets rape apart from other crimes.

Römkens and Letschert, above n 24, 6. For the US, see J Langhinrichsen-Rohling and CM Monson, 'Marital Rape: Is the Crime Taken Seriously Without Co-occurring Physical Abuse?' (1998) 13 *Journal of Family Violence* 433. Prevalence studies indicate that between 10% and 14% of all married women in the US have been raped by their husbands. For Canada, see Randall (2008), above n 19, 149. See also, K Daly and B Bouhours, 'Rape and Attrition in the Legal Process: A Comparative Analysis of Five Countries' (2010) 39 *Crime And Justice: A Review of Research* 565.

[107] Phillips and Vandenbroek, above n 104, 20.
[108] Ibid (citations omitted).
[109] VicHealth, NCAS, 13.
[110] VicHealth, *Australians' Attitudes to Violence against Women: Findings from the 2013 National Community Attitudes towards Violence Against Women Survey* (Melbourne, Victorian Health Promotion Foundation, 2014) 13 (based on the 'general community sample'). 59% of the 'culturally and linguistically diverse sample' held this view: Phillips and Vandenbroek, above n 104, 14. See also Randall, above n 2, 413.
[111] Gardner and Shute, above n 1.

PGA exemplifies two troubling aspects of common law methodology. The first concerns the *type* of information thought pertinent to judicial reasoning and legal decision making. The second relates to the *language* of legal judgments.

(a) Informing the Common Law

The traditional common law method supposedly progresses through conceptual refinement and is fuelled by a methodology privileging continuity and incremental change. Yet as Brennan J expressed it in *Mabo*, such change is limited. It should not 'fracture a skeletal principle of our legal system'.[112] This preference for subtle change by small degrees rather than radical alteration or wholesale transformation is at the heart of the *PGA* majority determination. The *PGA* majority discusses different conceptions of the common law and judicial method extensively.[113] The majority explained its approach by indicating that it was determined to avoid 'sociological analysis'[114] or 'some sort of general social glow'.[115] It wished submissions by parties to respond to '[t]he question … whether the views of society have been expressed in particular changes to the law',[116] on the 'legal underpinning … of Sir Matthew Hale's reasoning'[117] and 'in terms of legal reasoning, not some empathy about social values'.[118] Once it reached its conclusions the majority found it unnecessary (leaving open whether it was possible) to resort to judicial perceptions of social circumstances and attitudes in 1935.[119] If it had travelled down that path it might have considered whether the views expressed in 1992 by a Justice of the South Australian Supreme Court reflected an attitude that might well have been more prevalent a generation earlier. Bollen J had directed a jury in a 1992 trial:

> There is, of course, nothing wrong with a husband, faced with his wife's initial refusal to engage in intercourse, in attempting, in an acceptable way to persuade her to change her mind, and that may involve *a measure of rougher than usual handling*. It may be in the end that handling and persuasion will persuade the wife to agree. *Sometimes it is a fine line between not agreeing, then changing the mind and consenting.* You will bear that in mind when considering the totality of the evidence about each act of intercourse.[120]

---

[112] *Mabo v Queensland (No 2)* (1992) 175 CLR 1, [29].

[113] Citing a conception that is based on non-statutory law, on the institutional setting of judge-made law, differentiating it from equity etc. See *PGA v R* (2012) 245 CLR 355, [2012] HCA 21, [19]–[32].

[114] *PGA v R* [2011] HCATrans 267 (Hayne J during submissions).

[115] Ibid (French CJ).

[116] Ibid.

[117] Ibid (Gummow J).

[118] Ibid.

[119] *PGA v R* (2012) 245 CLR 355, [2012] HCA 21, [65].

[120] *R v Johns*, unreported, Supreme Court of South Australia, 26 August 1992, 5–6, quoted in *Question of Law Reserved on Acquittal Pursuant to Section 351(1a) Criminal Law Consolidation Act (No 1 of 1993)* (1993) 59 SASR 214, 216, 226. On appeal held, by a 2:1 majority, to be wrong because it 'was apt to convey the impression that consent might be induced by force'. There was a public outcry following the reporting of this judicial direction. A Bill to require the training of judges was defeated. Similarly a judge was reported in 1994 to have said of victim impact statements, 'I never bother to read them, to me it—that is, the victim impact statement—is a political thing to appease the feminist lobby in rape cases': *Hansard*, South Australia, Legislative Council, Wednesday 24 August 1994, 181, per Hon Carolyn Pickles. See also the defeat of *Supreme and District Courts (Appointment of Judges) Amendment Bill*: Hansard, South Australia, Legislative Council, Wednesday 7 September 1994, 279; Hansard,

The *PGA* majority ultimately approached its task loyal to the common law preference for what Butterfield has described as 'a thin version of its past'.[121] That the majority wished to avoid 'sociological analysis' and 'some sort of general social glow' indicates that it considered the views of society could not be established adequately, or perhaps with sufficient legitimacy, through the testimony of social historians. Instead, the letter of the law would be revelatory of these communal views. Yet social historians may well have assisted the court in *PGA* to gauge more accurately South Australian social attitudes shaping gender equality and the common law of rape from 1935 in the same way that evidence from historians and social anthropologists revealed in *Mabo* that the removal of Aboriginal people from their lands was marked by a colonial history founded on violent dispossession. In *Mabo* the expertise of historians, anthropologists, linguists and archaeologists contributed significantly to that court's information base. Their evidence forced the Court to confront the lie underpinning *terra nullius* to reconcile how dispossession could have occurred within the law. The Court could not do so.[122] Deane and Gaudron JJ expressly stated that they had been assisted

> not only by the material placed before us by the parties but by the researches of the many scholars who have written in the areas into which this judgment has necessarily ventured. We acknowledge our indebtedness to their writings and the fact that our own research has been largely directed to sources which they had already identified.[123]

The picture painted by the *PGA* majority through married women's property law, women's suffrage and divorce law reform is in stark contrast to the information available through sources utilised by social and economic historians. These reveal the dark side of women's lives and society's views of women in the relevant parts of the twentieth century. They also show the law perpetuating women's social and economic disempowerment. Importantly, they reveal that to the extent that social attitudes might be reflected in law and that 1963 offered little cause for optimism for gender equality. By summarily placing off-limits information that would have challenged its assumptions,[124] the *PGA* majority narrative of twentieth-century women received a veneer of coherence and neutrality. However, there are reasons why these other sources were not relied upon in *PGA*.

In Australia, both at common law and under the uniform evidence legislation,[125] little opinion evidence from the humanities is brought forward to assist courts' finding and interpretation of fact outside native title contexts[126] (and to a lesser extent, in war

South Australia, Legislative Council, Tuesday 2 December 2008, 1111, per Sandra Kanck. For a discussion of a Canadian variation of judicial conduct treating consent in a marital relationship differently, see Randall (2008), above n 19.

[121] Reilly, above n 31, referring to Butterfield, above n 31, 34.

[122] Reilly, above n 31, 36.

[123] *Mabo v Queensland (No 2)* (1992) 175 CLR 1, [78].

[124] That is 'sociological analysis' and the like, see text to nn 114–15, above. See also S Bandes, 'Moral Imagination in Judging' (2011) 51 *Washburn Law Journal* 1, 23–24.

[125] South Australia applies common law principles to its reception of expert evidence. More broadly (and applying across the major Australian jurisdictions) uniform evidence legislation permits opinion evidence where it is given by an expert and within the confines of 'specialised knowledge based on training, study or experience'. See s 79(1), Uniform Evidence Acts: Evidence Act 1995 (Cth); Evidence Act 1995 (NSW); Evidence Act 2001 (Tas); Evidence Act 2004 (Norfolk Island); Evidence Act 2008 (Vic); Evidence Act 2011 (ACT); Evidence Act 2011 (NT); *Dasreef Pty Ltd v Hawcher* (2011) 243 CLR 588.

[126] A Connolly, 'Legal Facts and Humanist Stories: The Humanist as Expert Witness' in I McCalman and A McGrath (eds), *Proof and Truth: The Humanist as Expert* (Canberra, Australian Academy of the Humanities, 2003).

crime cases).[127] The reason for this limited reliance, at least with respect to social history, is linked to the common law's deeply embedded tendency to circumscribe expert opinion evidence. In contrast to a legal judgment, which is by its nature definitive of the events in question, social history is a discipline that recognises as intrinsic to its methodology that gaps exist in any information base and that they may be filled by others over time. Retelling the past is an unfinished story and 'complex messiness' and uncertainty of the past is elemental to the discipline. It is neither a threat nor a deficit[128] because these qualities ultimately enhance the integrity (*qua* historical fidelity) of contemporary accounts of the past. Further, the generality of the output of historians and social scientists typically sits uncomfortably with a court's mission—as does social scientists' reliance on information bases that are not widely accepted in law. For the historian, 'unlike judge or jury, must listen to every sort of gossip and second hand hearsay … sifting from them any light that they may throw upon the facts … checked only by his conscience'.[129] Further, unlike law's appellate structures that review the law (moderated of course by the occasional *stare decisis*-induced calcification of obsolete but undiscarded law), social science relies on the unstructured academic domain of robust (and public) peer critique to expose flaws.[130] As seen in other legal settings where disciplinary goals diverge,[131] a resolution of the clash of paradigms is not easily achieved. At the very least the disciplines need to understand each other's modus operandi and goals. Even then compromise may be unpalatable.[132] Courts' traditional scepticism further reduces experts' and courts' opportunity to learn to appreciate the other's disciplinary imperatives and to learn, on the one hand, optimal techniques for informing jurisprudence; and on the other hand, to acquire literacy in domains beyond the law.

When a case like *PGA* comes along it is hardly surprising that legal representatives do not turn to historians for expert guidance. Nevertheless, the broad pictures of society painted by history and the social sciences can guide courts' interpretations of the past.[133] This is the sense in which the research of social and economic historians would have assisted the courts in *PGA*. Of course, the question posed to the *PGA* court could not be answered solely by recourse to social historians. Nor could it be answered adequately solely by recourse to the law selected by the majority in *PGA*.

---

[127] For an English example featuring historians as expert witnesses, see *Irving v Penguin Books Ltd & Lipstadt*, QBD, 11 April 2000.

[128] 'So where the law seeks only positive proof from its sources, historians are equally interested in what cannot be proved. Historians are interested in the silence in documents, and are free to speculate about those silences': Reilly, above n 31, 33.

[129] D Thomson, *The Aims of History* (London, Thames & Hudson, 1969) 42, quoted by Reilly above n 31, 44. Regarding historical accounts of ATSI people Reilly urges historians to 'read between the lines, hear the silences, use other sources, and keep in mind that most of the blood spilt in the name of colonisation was not spilt in the archive'.

[130] For an example relating to the history of cohabitation, see C Lind, 'The Truth of Unmarried Cohabitation and the Significance of History' (2014) 77 *Modern Law Review* 641, reviewing R Probert, *The Changing Legal Regulation of Cohabitation: From Fornication to Family, 1600–2010*, (Cambridge, Cambridge University Press, 2012).

[131] JB Hunter, L Pearson and M San Roque, 'Mental Health Expertise in Refugee Status Decision-Making: Judging or Caring?' (2014) 18 *International Journal of Evidence and Proof* 310.

[132] With reference to 'juridical history' in the pejorative sense of over-simplification, see Reilly, above n 31, 43.

[133] A Glass, 'Making Facts Speak' in McCalman and McGrath, above n 126, 123.

(b) The Language of Law

A judgment with integrity is not merely determined by courts' information base. In *Mabo* Deane and Gaudron JJ observed that they expressed themselves in a manner that 'some may think to be unusually emotive for a judgment in this Court'.[134] An example is the description of an 1804 incident as 'the first stages of the conflagration of oppression and conflict which was, over the following century, to spread across the continent to dispossess, degrade and devastate the Aboriginal peoples and leave a national legacy of unutterable shame'.[135] Defending their use of 'unrestrained language', Deane and Gaudron JJ explain:

> [T]he full facts of that dispossession are of critical importance to the assessment of the legitimacy of the propositions that the continent was unoccupied for legal purposes and that the unqualified legal and beneficial ownership of all the lands of the continent vested in the Crown. *Long acceptance of legal propositions, particularly legal propositions relating to real property, can of itself impart legitimacy and preclude challenge.*[136]

In contrast, the *PGA* majority (in common with marital rape immunity precedents and the English and Australian apex courts' 1991 decisions that ended the immunity) made nary an emotive whimper of the terrible harm and degradation caused by the immunity (and how the law crafted legal devices to allow it to flourish). All this case law sat in a parallel universe in both tone and content to the academic commentary of the preceding quarter of a century detailing the indignities and horrors endured by women.[137]

This brings us to a most profound integrity concern in the methodology of the majority in *PGA*. It is that in 2012 Australia's apex court crafted its judgment by exhuming the shadow of a long dark stretch of history, a time when criminal law treated the marital bedroom as off-limits (for fear that 'the vindictive wife' might act out of turn).[138] In so doing, the majority put off-limits recognition of law's active maintenance of women's substantive inequality and the resulting hardship and harm this created through much of the twentieth century.

Conclusion–Integrity in Meaning

An authoritative legal story of what the applicable law means is joined to an authoritative legal story about what the relevant facts are in order to generate an authoritative legal story of the legal situation between the parties. The trial serves as an institutional space of authoritative and, arguably, socially useful story-telling.[139]

---

[134] *Mabo v Queensland (No 2)* (1992) 175 CLR 1, [78].

[135] Ibid [50].

[136] Ibid [78] (emphasis added).

[137] Cf W Larcombe and M Heath, '*PGA v R*' in H Douglas, F Bartlett, T Luker and R Hunter (eds), *Australian Feminist Judgments: Righting and Rewriting Law* (London, Bloomsbury, 2014) 271 (referring to the 'humiliation and harm' caused by the immunity). As the US commentator Jill Hasday, above n 16, observed in 2000, it is a good strategy for the 'historical record [to] make this harm [to victims of marital rape] concrete, revealing the ways in which it is buried by the contemporary defense of the marital rape exemption'.

[138] Mitchell Committee Report, above n 75, 14 [6.2], quoted by Bell J in *PGA v R* (2012) 245 CLR 355, [2012] HCA 21, [239].

[139] Connolly, above n 126, 135, 136–37. Notably in sexual assault, the reshaping of the legal story is particularly prominent in all stages of the process. See Scheppele, above n 32. For illustrations and a persuasive summation of

What is the authoritative story told by *PGA*? It is a story implying that for the major part of the twentieth century the common law perceived women as equal to men and that consequently the criminal law, in a formal sense at least, protected them from marital rape. This story affirms that this status quo was consistent with 'the views of society [that had] ... been expressed in particular changes to the law' by 1935 in South Australia.[140] By this time the common law supposedly acknowledged one of two states of affairs: either it recognised that Hale's proposition failed married women and was therefore obsolescent; or alternatively, that Hale's proposition was never a true reflection of the common law. It is implicit in this story that the common law reached this conclusion silently, without debate or discussion, without prosecutions or any tangible signs that the criminal law acted effectively against husbands who raped their wives. Nevertheless, the law supposedly recognised women's personal autonomy.

In assessing the social utility of this conclusion one needs to keep in mind that it is an enduring feature of the common law's attitude to women that since earliest times the criminal law and its processes have been quick to blame, not protect women.[141] Outside the *PGA* account is irrefutable evidence of a vista of centuries-long profound injustice, degradation and betrayal of raped wives who were disbelieved or ignored by police and prosecutors, by judges and jurors and by many sectors of the community. This vista stretched from legal time immemorial to *at least* the 1990s. It applied to married women who, like Mrs P, were told that the law was not interested in private matters, 'just see a doctor about those injuries'. For them, their homes were not 'castles' as they were for their husbands.[142] The flimsy integrity in *PGA*'s methodology and conclusion is writ large. Whether one focuses on substantive civil or criminal law's deficient protection of women, the weakness in the authoritative story remains. *PGA*'s focus on women's acquisition in the twentieth century of formal civil rights effectively masks legal and social reality. Any well-informed substantive examination of women's rights is revelatory of the South Australian (and broader Australian, English, Canadian, US etc) criminal law and practice of effectively maintaining the husband's immunity from wife-rape well into the late twentieth century. It was unforgiving, tenacious and aided by investigative and trial processes and by legalistic notions of consent.

Only by slow and small degrees did the discriminatory elements of rape law recede in England, Australia and comparable jurisdictions. Social attitudes meant that these laws were an iceberg's tip of rape complainants' low standing in society. They were an iceberg's tip also of criminal law's frozen attitude towards rape complainants. Procedural and evidentiary rules, now recognised as potentially re-traumatising victims of crime,[143] then treated rape victims as '"game" to be stalked and cornered, harried, bullied and hemmed

---

the academic commentary regarding the causes and impact of judges, lawyers, police and process shaping the rape narrative by distortions of complainants' own accounts, see Kaspiew, above n 32.

[140] *PGA v R* [2011] HCATrans 267 (Gummow J during submissions).

[141] For example, Bracton required proof of violence by the assailant and of the victim's virginity for a successful rape prosecution: WS Holdsworth, *A History of English Law*, 3rd edn (London, Methuen, 1923) vol 3, 316.

[142] For a parallel in the dispossession suffered by Aboriginal and Torres Strait Islanders arising from colonisation, see M Krygier, 'The Meaning of What We Have Done: Humanity, Invisibility and Law in the European Settlement of Australia' in C Cordner (ed), *Philosophy, Ethics and a Common Humanity: Essays in Honour of Raimond Gaita* (London, Routledge, 2011) 121.

[143] P van de Zandt, 'Heroines of Fortitude' in P Easteal (ed), *Balancing the Scales: Rape Law Reform and Australian Culture* (Australia, Federation Press, 1998) 125.

in, their credibility, integrity and morality attacked'.[144] For more than three quarters of the twentieth century the rules permitted, indeed they were premissed upon, degrading cross-examination: 'In the name of eliminating false complaints ... [complainants were] "sized up" [and treated by police as] "objects of curiosity, suspicion and humiliating investigative practices".[145]

What is lacking in this judgment is what Bandes describes as 'moral imagination'. That is, 'the ability to understand one's own limitations, the limitations of perspective [and] ... the range of values at stake ... to understand that things might be ordered differently, a way out of arid formalism and closed systems'.[146] Bandes adds, '[t]oo many trappings of the court's role encourage the belief in judicial omniscience'; and she concludes, 'without moral imagination our ability to articulate, debate, and achieve the goals of our system of justice is impoverished'.[147] The case of *Mabo* throws *PGA* into sharp relief. *Mabo* tells a socially useful story because it removed a legal fiction of applying the principle of *terra nullius* to Australia and in doing so acknowledged that it was and had always been unfounded. It had caused and continues to cause incalculably serious injustice, harm, degradation and betrayal. Further, the judgment used language befitting the terrible human consequences of the harm. This lent authenticity to its acknowledgment, elevating *Mabo* from a case about native title that reached the 'right' conclusion (though perhaps it should have gone further) to a case in which Australian law acknowledged 'the full humanity of Aborigines ... [who] had relations to the land that would make dispossession a terrible crime'.[148] *PGA*, however, is a case about marital rape law reaching a conclusion, the 'correct' conclusion in a critically limited sense. It permitted a rape prosecution to proceed to trial. But the majority decision does not tell a socially useful story. Unlike victims of the Australian *terra nullius* legacy, victims (both direct and indirect) of the marital rape immunity from 1935 remain unacknowledged.[149] In *PGA*, a legal fiction was invoked to define the workings of another legal fiction, but neither legal fiction is socially useful.

This is not the first—nor is it likely to be the last—essay on law's approach to rape to conclude, *plus ça change, plus c'est la même chose*.

---

[144] T Henning and JB Hunter, 'Finessing the Fair Trial for Complainants and the Accused: Mansions of Justice or Castles in the Air?' in P Roberts and JB Hunter (eds), *Criminal Evidence and Human Rights* (Oxford, Hart Publishing, 2012) 364–65 (adapting observations by Y Kamisar, 'Equal Justice in the Gatehouse and Mansions of American Civil Procedure' in A Howard (ed), *Criminal Justice in Our Time*, (Charlottesville, Virginia University Press, 1965) 19–20).

[145] Ibid.

[146] Bandes, above n 124, 24.

[147] Ibid. See also M Kirby, 'Deconstructing the Law's Hostility to Public Interest Litigation' (2011) 127 *Law Quarterly Review* 537.

[148] R Gaita, *A Common Humanity. Thinking about Love and Truth and Justice* (London, Routledge, 2000), 81, quoted by Krygier, above n 142.

[149] See also Larcombe and Heath, above n 20, 807. Cf K Lesses, '*PGA v The Queen*: Marital Rape in Australia: The Role of Repetition, Reputation and Fiction in the Common Law' (2014) 37 *Melbourne University Law Review* 786.

15

Against Innocence

CHARLES D WEISSELBERG[*]

Introduction

The original Innocence Project—that extraordinary organisation founded by Barry Scheck and Peter Neufeld at Cardozo School of Law—is now over two decades old.[1] The Innocence Project helped spawn the Innocence Network, whose member organisations in the US and several other countries are dedicated to freeing the innocent and addressing the causes of wrongful convictions.[2] By March 2016, the Project claimed 336 exonerations through DNA testing, including 20 former residents of death row.[3] These exonerations are truly compelling. They have taught legislators, policymakers, lawyers, judges and ordinary citizens that the criminal justice system is not error-free. High-profile exonerations have promoted greater scrutiny of the criminal process and fostered significant efforts at reform.

In addition to releasing individuals who have been wrongly convicted, we must identify systemic causes of miscarriages of justice and, if possible, correct them. Innocence 'commissions' and other organised efforts to study such convictions are making vital contributions to the process of criminal justice reform. Yet if one is concerned about misconduct of government officials, the relationship of citizens and police, discrimination, privacy, unreasonable searches and seizures, individual freedoms, and the overall integrity of the criminal justice system, our lens must be broader than issues that strictly relate to factual innocence: misconduct and mistakes producing convictions of the factually innocent cannot be our exclusive concern. Focusing primarily on the US,[4] this chapter explores whether the 'Innocence movement' has changed the terms of the reform debate to such a degree that we have devalued—or, at least, reduced our attention to—errors or societal concerns that do not bear directly on factual innocence. Bound up with this question is how we even think about 'wrongful convictions' and 'miscarriages of justice'. Do these familiar-sounding concepts encompass only claims of factual innocence of the underlying crime? Or are they much

---

[*] I am grateful to Samantha Buckingham, David Dixon, Carolyn Hoyle, Jill Hunter, Sang Won Lee, Sara Oh, Taek Rim Oh, Paul Roberts, Marcy Strauss and Simon NM Young for comments on previous drafts; and to Eugene Chao and Molly Smolen for skilful research assistance.

[1] See *Our Work*, www.innocenceproject.org/free-innocent (accessed 1 February 2016); B Scheck, P Neufeld and J Dwyer, *Actual Innocence* (New York, Doubleday, 2000) xiv.

[2] See *About the Innocence Network*, www.innocencenetwork.org/about/ (accessed 1 February 2016).

[3] See *Exonerating the Innocent*, www.innocenceproject.org/free-innocent/exonerating-the-innocent (accessed 21 March 2016).

[4] Parallel developments in the UK are discussed by Carolyn Hoyle in Chapter 16.

broader, including sentencing claims, constitutional violations committed by police, unfair treatment, and procedural errors? Does 'integrity' in the criminal justice system mean simply 'integrity in the *outcome*', or does it also encompass 'integrity in the *process*' leading to the final judgment?

The chapter begins by addressing the power inherent in proof of actual innocence, the reasons why exonerations can influence public opinion and policy, and competing conceptions of miscarriages of justice. Section 2 examines several reform efforts that the Innocence movement has directly spurred. Section 3 addresses one specific aspect of the criminal justice process—police interrogation—and asks how reform initiatives have been influenced by greater attention to actual innocence. The chapter concludes with some cautionary words about 'factual innocence' and its double-edged implications for the integrity of criminal proceedings.

1. The Power of Innocence

The release of an exonerated inmate can be an extraordinarily moving event. The doors of the penitentiary or courthouse swing open wide. Out walks a former prisoner, perhaps even a former death-row inmate, into the sun and the warm embrace of family members and supporters.[5] The story is about vindication, a fight against long odds, not losing hope, multiple system failures, grievous injustice and rebuilding lives. The images may seem made for television, and indeed they sometimes are.[6] Members of the legal team may be present, possibly to talk about how errors occur in even the most advanced legal systems. We might forgive defence counsel for using these public events to make larger points about failures in the criminal justice system, and to influence ordinary citizens' thinking about it. Law enforcement agencies in a number of jurisdictions have long used images of arrests in high-profile cases to promote their own interests. In New York City, the public 'perp walk' is a time-honoured tradition, with the press having a field day filming former Wall Street executives and other arrestees.[7] Media coverage of the release of exonerees—'reverse perp walks', perhaps—surely may include images that are just as powerful in shaping public opinion and motivating reform agendas.

In the US, the exoneration cases have had a substantial impact on judges, lawyers, and criminal justice professionals. One scholar writes: 'Just as Columbus's revelations exploded many assumptions about the shape of the world, DNA has exploded many of our assumptions about the reliability of certain forms of evidence and the accuracy of

---

[5] See M Raymond, 'The Problem With Innocence' (2001) 49 *Cleveland State Law Review* 449 ('we have repeatedly been moved and inspired by the vision of an individual, fully exonerated of the heinous crime of which he was wrongfully convicted, stepping out of the confines of unjust imprisonment and into the sunshine of freedom').

[6] See eg www.cbsnews.com/8301-505263_162-57404647/wrongly-convicted-man-freed-after-25-years/ (accessed 1 February 2016); www.worldstarhiphop.com/videos/video.php?v=wshhcBLpHodII1764k1p (accessed 1 February 2016).

[7] See R Hagglund, 'Constitutional Protections Against the Harms to Suspects in Custody Stemming From Perp Walks' (2012) 7 *Mississippi Law Journal* 1757, 1758–67 (describing the history of 'perp walks' in high-profile cases); *Lauro v Charles*, 219 F 3d 202, 203–04 (2d Cir 2000) (describing the 'perp walk' as 'a widespread police practice in New York City').

convictions.'[8] Scheck and Neufeld characterise DNA testing as 'a revelation machine';[9] they have been the foremost advocates for the formation of innocence commissions 'to investigate and monitor errors in the criminal justice system just as the [National Transportation Safety Board] investigates and monitors airplane and other major transportation accidents in the United States'.[10] As we shall see, numerous states have heeded that call.

But why has actual innocence emerged as the most significant lever for wide-scale criminal justice system reform? Surely other features of the American system affect enormous numbers of people, are well-documented, and cry out for attention. The US has the highest incarceration rate among major industrialised countries.[11] We imprison people of colour at a much higher rate than whites.[12] Police use of excessive force, and unreasonable searches and seizures, are far from rare events.[13] Indigent defence systems are severely underfunded.[14] The list of institutional shortcomings is both long and serious. The way in which 'factual innocence' has emerged in recent decades as an effective lever to gain traction on these system failures is exemplified by the impact of exonerations in capital cases.

Ever since the modern age of the death penalty was ushered in 40 years ago with *Gregg v Georgia*[15] and its companion cases, scholars have examined every aspect of the capital punishment system. Studies show that the death penalty is not race-neutral[16] and death judgments appear to be imposed arbitrarily.[17] In 2009, the American Law Institute voted to withdraw the capital punishment provision of the Model Penal Code 'in light of the current intractable institutional and structural obstacles to ensuring a minimally adequate system' for administering the death penalty.[18] Despite these well-recognised systemic

---

[8] LC Marshall, 'The Innocence Revolution and the Death Penalty' (2004) 1 *Ohio State Journal of Criminal Law* 573, 575.

[9] Scheck et al, above n 1, xv.

[10] BC Scheck and P Neufeld, 'Toward the Formation of "Innocence Commissions" in America' (2002) 86 *Judicature* 98, 99.

[11] See 'Prison Population', *OECD Factbook 2010* (Paris, OECD Publishing, 2010) 248–49.

[12] See LE Glaze, *Correctional Populations in the United States, 2010*, NCJ 236319 (US Department of Justice, December 2011) 8 (Appendix Table 3) (in 2010, black and Hispanic/Latino inmates in prisons and local jails were held at rates of 4,357 and 1,775 per 100,000 US residents, respectively, compared with 678 white inmates per 100,000 US residents): www.bjs.gov/content/pub/pdf/cpus10.pdf (accessed 1 February 2016). In the same year, whites comprised 72.4% of the US population, a much greater proportion than African Americans (12.6%) and residents of Hispanic or Latino origin (16.3%): KR Humes, NA Jones and RR Ramirez, *Overview of Race and Hispanic Origin: 2010*, Census Briefs C2010BR-02 (US Census Bureau, March 2011) 4, Table 1.

[13] In 2014 and 2015, deaths at the hands of police in Ferguson, Missouri; Staten Island, New York; and Baltimore, Maryland led to widespread protests: see eg H Bruinius, 'Amid Garner and Brown outrage, bill would reform federal grand juries', *Christian Science Monitor*, 12 December 2014, www.csmonitor.com/USA/Justice/2014/1212/Amid-Garner-and-Brown-outrage-bill-would-reform-federal-grand-juries (accessed 1 February 2016); 'State of Emergency', www.propublica.org/article/baltimore-freddie-gray-protest-photos (accessed 1 February 2016).

[14] See EH Holder Jr, 'Editorial: A Crisis for Public Defense', *Washington Post*, 23 August 2013, A17 (US Attorney General Holder calls the US indigent defence systems 'in financial crisis').

[15] 428 US 153 (1976).

[16] See DC Baldus and G Woodworth, 'Race Discrimination and the Death Penalty: An Empirical and Legal Overview' in JR Acker et al (eds), *America's Experience with Capital Punishment*, 2nd edn (Durham, Carolina Academic Press, 2003) 501, 511–26, 536–45.

[17] See BD Steiner, 'Still Arbitrary: Capital Sentencing in the Post-Furman Era' (1999) 10 *Criminal Justice Policy Review* 85; SF Shatz, 'The Eighth Amendment, The Death Penalty, and Ordinary Robbery-Burglary Murderers: A California Case Study' (2007) 59 *Florida Law Review* 719, 736–52, 768–70; DC Baldus et al, 'Arbitrariness and Discrimination on the Administration of the Death Penalty: A Challenge to State Supreme Courts' (1986) 15 *Stetson Law Review* 133, 146–56.

[18] American Law Institute, *86th Annual Meeting Proceedings* (ALI, 2009) 217–18.

failures, federal legal challenges to capital sentences have encountered difficulties. The US Supreme Court turned aside one discrimination-based challenge identifying statistical correlations between imposition of the death penalty and the victim's race.[19] Moreover, in maintaining the significant distinction between legal error and factual innocence, Supreme Court Justices have been willing only to *assume*—without actually determining—that 'a truly persuasive demonstration of "actual innocence" made after trial would render the execution of a defendant unconstitutional'.[20] Yet in the court of public opinion, if not in the courts of law, actual innocence is enormously salient. In 2003, Illinois Governor George Ryan commuted the sentences of 150 inmates on the state's death row.[21] Citing the exonerations of 17 capital defendants in Illinois alone, he declared that '[o]ur capital system is haunted by the demon of error—error in determining guilt, and error in determining who among the guilty deserves to die'.[22] Larry Marshall, a law professor who played a key role in the Illinois exonerations and commutations, has rightly observed that 'convincing the American people about the arbitrariness and unfairness of the death penalty was not enough: it is the issue of innocence that carries the real potential to transform American opinion on the use of capital punishment'.[23] A keen understanding of this point has launched death penalty abolitionists on a grisly search for their Holy Grail—incontrovertible proof that we have executed a defendant who is factually innocent of the crime.[24]

Several scholars and lawyers have offered explanations for the power of actual innocence to transform views on the death penalty and the criminal justice system in general. Brandon Garrett observes that, '[p]art of the gripping drama in these exonerees' stories is how DNA finally succeeded when all else had failed for so many years'.[25] District Attorney Joshua Marquis acknowledges the power of media and popular culture, though he flatly contests the characterisation of many exonerees as 'innocent'. Pointing to what he considers a misleading narrative of exoneration in movies, plays, television and literature, Marquis argues that 'popular culture ... has created an entire alternate universe that posits a legal system that regularly hurls doe-eyed innocents onto death row through the malevolent machinations of corrupt cops and district attorneys'.[26] Daniel Medwed, an innocence project

---

[19] *McClesky v Kemp*, 481 US 279 (1987).

[20] *Herrera v Collins*, 506 US 390, 417 (1993); see also *District Attorney's Office for the Third Judicial District v Osborne*, 557 US 52, 72 (2009) (assuming without deciding that there is a federal constitutional right to be released upon proof of actual innocence).

[21] The Governor also pardoned four inmates on grounds of actual innocence and barred 14 other inmates from receiving a death sentence at their re-sentencing hearings. See R Warden, 'Illinois Death Penalty Reform: How It Happened, What It Promises' (2005) 95 *Journal of Criminal Law and Criminology* 381, 382 n 6.

[22] J Wilgoren, 'Citing Issue of Fairness, Governor Clears Out Death Row in Illinois', *New York Times*, 12 January 2003, www.nytimes.com/2003/01/12/us/citing-issue-of-fairness-governor-clears-out-death-row-in-illinois.html (accessed 1 February 2016).

[23] Marshall, above n 8, 577. As Marshall observes, abolitionist arguments based on discrimination or arbitrary punishment could conceivably be answered by *extending* the death penalty to eliminate inconsistent 'leniency'.

[24] For a description of the strategic use of innocence, see CS Steiker and JM Steiker, 'The Seduction of Innocence: The Attraction and Limitations of the Focus on Innocence in Capital Punishment Law and Advocacy' (2005) 95 *Journal of Criminal Law and Criminology* 587, 607. See also LE Bowman, 'Lemonade Out of Lemons: Can Wrongful Convictions Lead to Criminal Justice Reform?' (2008) 98 *Journal of Criminal Law and Criminology* 1501, 1514–15 (describing O'Dell case); S Wiseman, 'Innocence After Death' (2010) 60 *Case Western Reserve Law Review* 687 (general description of posthumous exoneration efforts).

[25] BL Garrett, *Convicting the Innocent* (Cambridge MA, Harvard University Press, 2011) 244.

[26] J Marquis, 'The Myth of Innocence' (2005) 95 *Journal of Criminal Law and Criminology* 501, 509.

advocate and scholar who has written more broadly about exonerations in capital and non-capital cases, applauds the rise of the new 'innocentrism'—defined as 'the increasing centrality of issues relating to actual innocence in courtrooms, classrooms, and newsrooms'. According to Medwed, 'the effort to free the innocent has become the civil rights movement of the twenty-first century'.[27]

Looking beyond the role of the media, Carol and Jordan Steiker detect the influence of cognitive bias. They note that individuals tend to overestimate risks of harm that they may themselves face, while underestimating comparable risks to which (only) others might be exposed. The Steikers suggest that many Americans might imagine themselves becoming erroneously caught up in the justice system, and thus exaggerate the risk of a conviction of a factually innocent person relative to other errors and injustices.[28] Susan Bandes advances a somewhat different argument, positing that the Innocence movement has 'bridged the gaping empathetic divide' between the general public and even a death-row inmate, a divide entrenched in race and class, among other factors.[29] These cognitive and affective biases in the public understanding of miscarriages of justice might go some way to explain the media appeal of 'actual innocence'. Gripping stories of wrongful conviction of the factually innocent have undeniably become part of our popular culture, whatever one's view of the truth of the narratives. The characters in the stories are personally appealing, if not truly heroic—think Harrison Ford in *The Fugitive*, or *In the Name of the Father* featuring Daniel Day-Lewis. William Dillon, who was exonerated by a DNA test after serving over 27 years for a murder he did not commit, was invited to sing the national anthem at a professional baseball game.[30] Such honours are not afforded defendants found in possession of large quantities of narcotics, but freed on account of unlawful searches; or those whose convictions were quashed on grounds of procedural error.

Although empathy undoubtedly plays its part in particular proceedings,[31] I tend to think that sympathy plays a larger role than empathy in shaping public attitudes to broadly-based criminal justice reform.[32] I have no empirical basis for this judgment, but I am inclined to

---

[27] DS Medwed, 'Innocentrism' [2008] *University of Illinois Law Review* 1549, 1549–51.

[28] Steiker and Steiker, above n 24, 606.

[29] S Bandes, 'Framing Wrongful Convictions' [2008] *Utah Law Review* 5, 12–13.

[30] www.abcnews.go.com/US/wrongly-convicted-man-sings-national-anthem-rays-game/story?id=16804555#. UHn1W1GzknU (accessed 1 February 2016).

[31] In capital cases (especially those with random victims), jurors who empathise with victims are more likely to choose death: see SE Sundby, 'The Capital Jury and Empathy: The Problem of Worthy and Unworthy Victims' (2003) 88 *Cornell Law Review* 343, 359–64. Defence lawyers have long understood the importance of humanising their clients, and themselves, to engage juries' empathy: see eg CE Bennett and RB Hirschhorn, *Bennett's Guide to Jury Selection and Trial Dynamics in Civil and Criminal Litigation* (St Paul, West Publishing, 1993) 201–16 (building rapport with juries); American Bar Association, 'Guidelines for the Appointment and Performance of Defense Counsel in Death Penalty Cases' (2003) 31 *Hofstra Law Review* 913, 1062 (calling witnesses to humanise the client at the penalty phase of a capital case). Even judges—whom we prefer to construct as dispassionate legal actors—must work to recognise and regulate their own emotions: see TA Maroney, 'Emotional Regulation and Judicial Behavior' (2011) 99 *California Law Review* 1485; SR Anleu and K Mack, 'Magistrates' Everyday Work and Emotional Labour' (2005) 32 *Journal of Law and Society* 590, 601–11 (discussing Australian magistrates).

[32] Though definitions vary across disciplines, *sympathy* generally indicates our own feelings of sorrow or concern for others, whereas *empathy* may be defined as understanding others' mental or emotional states from their perspective and, perhaps, even feeling those emotions. See N Eisenberg, 'Empathy and Sympathy' in M Lewis and JM Haviland-Jones (eds), *Handbook of Emotions*, 2nd edn (New York, Guilford Press, 2000) 677–78; A Coplan, 'Understanding Empathy: Its Features and Effects' in A Coplan and P Goldie (eds), *Empathy: Philosophical and Psychological Perspectives* (Oxford, Oxford University Press, 2011).

believe that most citizens more readily feel sorrow for the disrupted lives of the exonerated than think of themselves as being at risk of wrongful conviction or experience the same emotions as exonerees. If sympathy is the predominant driving force, we can usefully turn to research on motivated cognition to shed light on its limitations. Psychological theories of motivated cognition explain 'how and why judgments ... might be motivated, without the decision maker's awareness, in morally loaded contexts'.[33] Researchers have shown that factual determinations, such as attributions of causal responsibility for outcomes, can be influenced by extraneous knowledge concerning, for example, a person's bad moral character.[34] In a provocative study, Kevin Carlsmith and Avani Mehta Sood tested whether research subjects would support harsher treatment during the interrogation of a person in possession of critical information needed to save lives if that person were guilty rather than innocent. Having found a strong correlation between preference for interrogative severity and guilt, these researchers concluded that their subjects' 'endorsement of harsh interrogation techniques may be fuelled, at least in part, by retributive motives'.[35]

If this study indicates a more general tendency for assessments of moral culpability to influence legal judgments, this may help to explain the limited appeal of procedural reforms that potentially benefit all defendants, innocent and guilty alike. It is not only that policymakers and the public lack sympathy for the guilty, but their assessments of procedural due process may themselves be coloured by retributive sentiments. And while some scholars maintain that wrongful convictions of the factually innocent 'arise in the context of broadly applied practices', which resist attempts to remove the causes of wrongful convictions 'surgically ... from the system',[36] some reformers may prefer to be seen as targeting their efforts entirely on the 'deserving' innocent and to tailor procedural reforms accordingly.

Contemporary debates about the role of 'actual innocence' in US criminal process reform hint at a more fundamental disconnect between popular discourse and legal concepts. While the public may be motivated by the belief that innocent people are wrongly convicted, and may straightforwardly equate such convictions to 'miscarriages of justice', the legal system has different concerns and a more comprehensive vision. Criminal adjudication functions through the introduction of evidence and application of standards of proof, and it must be concerned with the integrity of its own processes. Recognising these concerns, Clive Walker proposes an expansive conception of 'miscarriage of justice' that does not turn on factual innocence. His 'individualistic rights-based approach' would encompass (among other things) breaches of rights—such as arrest without due cause, treatment or punishment without factual justification (including conviction of the factually innocent), unfair processes or application of unjust laws—and disproportionate treatment

---

[33] AM Sood and JM Darley, 'The Plasticity of Harm in the Service of Criminalization Goals' (2012) 100 *California Law Review* 1313, 1320.

[34] See J Nadler and MH McDonnell, 'Moral Character, Motive, and the Psychology of Blame' (2012) 97 *Cornell Law Review* 255, 274–76 (experiment participants were more likely to find that a person caused the death of fire service pilots when the pilots died during an attempt to put out a fire from a methamphetamine laboratory explosion than a fire from an explosion of fertilizers that were used to care for orchids); MD Alicke, 'Culpable Causation' (1992) 63 *Journal of Personality and Social Psychology* 368, 369–70 (experiment subjects were more likely to find that a person driving a speeding vehicle was the cause of an accident when he was driving fast due to a socially undesirable reason (eg to hide a vial of cocaine) than for a socially acceptable reason (eg concealing a surprise anniversary gift)).

[35] KM Carlsmith and AM Sood, 'The Fine Line Between Interrogation and Retribution' (2009) 45 *Journal of Experimental Social Psychology* 191, 193, 195.

[36] Bowman, above n 24, 1509.

by the state.[37] Building on Walker's proposal, Sam Poyser and Becky Milne contend that any adequate definition of 'miscarriages of justice' must also encompass routine reversals of convictions, 'which can be just as damaging … to the individual … and to the integrity and legitimacy of the Criminal Justice System' as high-profile exonerations.[38]

For a public fixated on factual innocence, 'the challenge is to … make people angry at a broader spectrum of injustice', as Bandes puts it,[39] and to recognise the virtues of a broader conception of 'miscarriages of justice'. We need reforms that honour and advance the central values of the criminal justice system—such as honesty in the application of governmental processes, respect for people, non-discrimination, and protection for individual autonomy—whether or not individuals are factually innocent or their convictions are otherwise lawful or 'safe'. We need to continue to protect against unreasonable searches and seizures, regardless of the criminal culpability of those searched or seized. We need a broad, 'due process' conception of integrity in criminal proceedings, drawing moral force not just from the final judgment itself, but from how the judgment was reached and how members of society are treated. The remainder of this chapter assesses how well reform efforts further this broad conception of an 'integrity principle' in an age of innocence.

2. Commissions and Such

In the US, during the last decade, exonerations and the Innocence movement have spurred the most significant efforts at broad-based criminal justice system reform. As shown in Tables 1 and 2 in the Appendix, below, government-sponsored commissions or task forces have examined the problem of wrongful convictions in at least 11 states; in at least three states, bar associations or coalitions have formed their own such organisations. While several of these commissions review individual claims of factual innocence,[40] almost all are also charged with recommending systemic reforms.[41] To the extent that state-level law reform initiatives extend beyond innocence-based exonerations, two fairly narrow concerns have come to predominate, at least until now. Some states have established sentencing initiatives aimed at increasing public safety and reducing incarceration costs.[42] In addition, other states—and the federal government—have expended considerable energy on reforming

---

[37] C Walker, 'Miscarriages of Justice in Principle and Practice' in C Walker and K Starmer (eds), *Miscarriages of Justice: A Review of Justice in Error* (London, Blackstone Press, 1999) 33–38. See also S Poyser and B Milne, 'Miscarriages of Justice: A Call for Continued Research Focussing on Reforming the Investigative Process' (2011) 13 *British Journal of Forensic Practice* 61, 62; M Zalman, 'An Integrated Justice Model of Wrongful Convictions' (2011) 74 *Albany Law Review* 1465, 1470–71.

[38] Poyser and Milne, above n 37, 62.

[39] Bandes, above n 29, 14. See also J Simon's 'Foreword' to M Naughton, *Rethinking Miscarriages of Justice: Beyond the Tip of the Iceberg* (Basingstoke, Palgrave MacMillan, 2012) xii.

[40] See eg The North Carolina Innocence Inquiry Commission and the Connecticut Advisory Commission on Wrongful Convictions, Table 1, Appendix.

[41] See generally, Tables 1 and 2, ibid. The Louisiana State Law Institute has a more generalised law reform mandate, though it was recently charged with studying wrongful convictions. The (resonantly-named) Texas Criminal Justice Integrity Unit explores reforms in areas such as preservation of evidence, eyewitness identification, forensics, and reliability of confessions.

[42] See eg D Patrick, 'Governor's Budget FY2013, Criminal Justice Reforms', www.mass.gov/bb/h1/fy13h1/exec_13/hbudbrief8.htm (accessed 1 February 2016); South Dakota State News, 'Criminal Justice Reform Initiative', news.sd.gov/newsitem.aspx?id=13262 (accessed 1 February 2016).

drug laws and releasing non-violent drug offenders.[43] However, such initiatives tend to be eclipsed by policymakers' central preoccupation with innocence-based exonerations.

When factual innocence powers the engine for reform, significant practical consequences follow. First, reformers naturally confine their attentions to aspects of criminal proceedings associated with factually erroneous convictions. Having examined 250 exoneration cases, Garrett reports high levels of eyewitness misidentifications (76 per cent of defendants) and unreliable forensic science evidence (61 per cent of cases).[44] Innocence commissions routinely recommend improved procedures for handling eyewitness identifications and scientific evidence.[45] They have also devoted much attention to reforming interrogation practices to address the problem of false confessions—a topic explored in detail in the next section of this chapter. A second implication of focusing too narrowly on actual innocence may be a tendency to de-emphasise other rights and values in our criminal justice system.

The Innocence movement has also impacted US criminal justice scholarship, with the potential to shape reform efforts for years to come. A new cadre of academics has taken up the cause of wrongful convictions, firmly emphasising factual innocence.[46] Meanwhile,

---

[43] See eg New York State Division of Criminal Justice Services, 'Drug Law Changes', criminaljustice.state. ny.us/drug-law-reform/index.html (accessed 1 February 2016); The White House Office of National Drug Control Policy, 'Criminal Justice Reform: Breaking the Cycle of Drug Use and Crime', www.whitehouse.gov/ ondcp/criminal-justice-reform (accessed 1 February 2016); S Horwitz, 'Justice Department set to free 6,000 prisoners, largest one-time release', *Washington Post*, 6 October 2015, www.washingtonpost.com/world/national-security/justice-department-about-to-free-6000-prisoners-largest-one-time-release/2015/10/06/961f4c9a-6ba2-11e5-aa5b-f78a98956699_story.html (accessed 1 February 2016).

[44] See Garrett, above n 25, 9.

[45] See eg California Commission on the Fair Administration of Justice, *Report and Recommendations Regarding Eye Witness Identification Procedures* (2006); and *Report and Recommendations Regarding Forensic Scientific Evidence* (2007), www.ccfaj.org/reports.html (accessed 1 February 2016); State of Connecticut Advisory Commission on Wrongful Convictions, *Report of the Advisory Commission on Wrongful Convictions* (February 2009) 4 (Commission will monitor the use and effectiveness of new eyewitness identification protocols), www.jud. ct.gov/committees/wrongfulconviction/WrongfulConvictionComm_Report.pdf (accessed 1 February 2016); Florida Innocence Commission, *Final Report to the Supreme Court of Florida* (June 2012) (discussing eyewitness identification and forensic evidence), www.flcourts.org/core/fileparse.php/248/urlt/Innocence-Report-2012. pdf (accessed 1 February 2016); Illinois Capital Punishment Reform Study Commission, *Sixth and Final Report* (October 2010) 37–60, 142–50 (eyewitness identifications and forensic laboratories), www.chicagobar.org/AM/ NavigationMenu/Home/Files/IllinosCapitalPunishmentReformStudyCommitteeSixthAndFinalReport.pdf (accessed 1 February 2016); New York State Justice Task Force, *Recommendations for Improving Eyewitness Identifications* (February 2011) and *Recommendations Regarding Forensics and Expansion of the New York State DNA Databank* (February 2011), www.nyjusticetaskforce.com/recommendations.html (accessed 1 February 2016); Oklahoma Justice Commission, *Report to the Oklahoma Bar Association* (February 2013) 14–25, www.okbar. org/Portals/15/PDF/2013/Commission_Final_Report.pdf (accessed 1 February 2016); Joint State Government Commission, *Report of the Advisory Committee on Wrongful Convictions* (General Assembly of the Commonwealth of Pennsylvania, September 2011) 21–82, 157–66 (eyewitness identifications and forensic science), jsg.legis.state. pa.us/resources/documents/ftp/documents/9-15-11%20rpt%20-%20Wrongful%20Convictions.pdf (accessed 29 January 2016); Innocence Commission for Virginia, *A Vision for Justice: Report and Recommendations Regarding Wrongful Convictions in the Commonwealth of Virginia* (Arlington VA, March 2005) 25–42, 83–93 (eyewitness identifications and science), www.exonerate.org/ICVA/full_r.pdf (accessed 1 February 2016).

[46] See eg T Wells and R Leo, *The Wrong Guys: Murder, False Confessions, and the Norfolk Four* (New York, New Press, 2008); JB Gould and RA Leo, 'One Hundred Years Later: Wrongful Conviction After a Century of Research' (2010) 100 *Journal of Criminal Law and Criminology* 825; JB Gould, *The Innocence Commission: Preventing Wrongful Convictions and Restoring the Criminal Justice System* (New York, New York University Press, 2008); Scheck et al, above n 1; KA Findley, 'Defining Innocence' (2010–2011) 74 *Albany Law Review* 1157; KA Findley, 'Adversarial Inquisitions: Rethinking the Search for Truth' (2011–2012) 56 *New York Law School Law Review* 911; SR Gross

some established voices in the field have focused on innocence. Thus, Dan Simon's book on the psychology of the criminal justice process, while touching on broader themes, is framed by wrongful conviction of the factually innocent and erroneous acquittals of the guilty.[47] Likewise, the highly respected criminal procedure scholar, George Thomas, has argued that 'the prime directive of a criminal justice system is to protect the innocent, at a reasonable cost'.[48] Thomas proposes sweeping changes to the adversarial structure of the US system, drawing in part upon the French model of magisterial supervision of the investigative and pre-trial processes, as well as on the English tradition of an independent criminal Bar comprised of barristers who both prosecute and defend.[49] The January 2015 meeting of the Association of American Law Schools provided the occasion for a panel titled 'Reprioritizing Accuracy as the Primary Goal of the Criminal Justice Process', featuring Professors Simon and Thomas and other leading scholars.[50]

These views have not gone unchallenged within the academy. Susan Bandes has advanced a detailed critique of Thomas' proposals.[51] Abbe Smith decries the 'arrogance' of the Innocence movement and the characterisation of constitutional rights as mere 'technicalities'.[52] Margaret Raymond similarly worries about elevating factual innocence over other reasons for acquittal, and its effect on the criminal defence bar.[53] Exposing the perils of 'actual innocence' in capital cases, Carol and Jordan Steiker underscore the impact on defence lawyering and the significance of other questions besides actual innocence. They also offer a cautionary tale, describing how federal habeas corpus review has been severely constricted, with some *exceptions* to procedural bars being allowed for strong claims of actual innocence.[54] Without attempting here to resolve the debates between the 'innocentrists' and their critics, we can at least note that exonerations rooted in claims of actual innocence have plainly influenced recent US criminal justice scholarship, and seem likely to shape law reform efforts for years to come.

---

and B O'Brien, 'Frequency and Predictors of False Conviction: Why We Know So Little, and New Data on Capital Cases' (2008) 5 *Journal of Empirical Legal Studies* 927; Medwed, above n 27; Garrett, above n 25.

[47] See D Simon, *In Doubt: The Psychology of the Criminal Justice Process* 4 (Cambridge MA, Harvard University Press, 2012) ('Criminal cases can break down in two ways. A person who perpetrated a crime might escape punishment, or an innocent person might be convicted and punished for a crime he did not commit.')

[48] GC Thomas III, *The Supreme Court on Trial: How the American Justice System Sacrifices Innocent Defendants* (Ann Arbor, University of Michigan Press, 2008) 2.

[49] Ibid 184–214.

[50] See memberaccess.aals.org/eweb//DynamicPage.aspx?webcode=SesDetails&ses_key=15f8fedf-4af7-4cbd-859a-3700945163a2 (accessed 1 February 2016). To be fair, panel members acknowledged that by prioritising accuracy, they did not mean to diminish the respect accorded other goals and values of the criminal justice system. Professor Thomas also noted that his earlier proposals had not received much support.

[51] See generally, SA Bandes, 'Protecting the Innocent as the Primary Value of the Criminal Justice System' (2009) 7 *Ohio State Journal of Criminal Law* 413.

[52] See A Smith, 'In Praise of the Guilty Project: A Criminal Defense Lawyer's Growing Anxiety about Innocence Projects' (2010) 13 *University of Pennsylvania Journal of Law and Social Change* 315, 319–22.

[53] See Raymond, above n 5, 456–61.

[54] See Steiker and Steiker, above n 24, 606, 609–21. The US Supreme Court continues to wrestle with the impact of claims of innocence. In *McQuiggen v Perkins*, 133 S Ct 1924 (2013), the Court ruled 5:4 that 'actual innocence', if proved, can provide a gateway to federal habeas corpus review, even if the petitioner failed to file her petition within the one-year limitation period.

3. An Illustration: Police Interrogations and Actual Innocence

This section examines the influence of the Innocence movement on the law and practice of police interrogation and associated reform proposals, by way of a detailed case study of recent trends. It begins by briefly reviewing the current legal framework for regulating confessions and identifying the values it protects.

Although US states are free to grant their citizens greater rights than are guaranteed by the US Constitution, and to establish additional restrictions on policing, the Constitution—whose relevant provisions bind the states—affords the most significant protections to individuals subject to police investigation and interrogation.[55] The US Constitution and federal civil rights laws govern the way in which confessions are obtained, largely by regulating the admission of confession evidence in criminal trials (and sometimes through civil rights actions for constitutional violations).[56] Thus, the Due Process Clauses of the Fifth and Fourteenth Amendments prohibit police officers from overbearing a suspect's will through the application of physical force, psychological methods, and other factors that may make a statement 'involuntary'.[57] As the voluntariness doctrine has developed, it has targeted the *officers'* misconduct in eliciting a confession, rather than the suspect's subjective frame of mind or the reliability of the statement;[58] and a successful claim of coercion must satisfy a demanding standard of proof.[59] The Fifth Amendment privilege against self-incrimination prevents the government from compelling a suspect to speak, and also affords the legal basis for the much-heralded rule in *Miranda v Arizona*.[60] Under *Miranda*, a statement that police obtain from a suspect in custody is generally inadmissible unless preceded by warnings and waivers of the right to remain silent and the right to counsel. The Sixth Amendment right to counsel prohibits law enforcement from eliciting

---

[55] There are political and practical reasons why the US Constitution establishes the most significant protections. The Constitution provides a mandatory 'floor', and state and federal legislators are loath to craft laws that afford greater rights to criminal defendants. As Stephen Schulhofer has observed, in explaining why we have not had statutory replacements for the procedures required by *Miranda v Arizona*, 384 US 436 (1966), 'politically attractive alternatives to *Miranda* cannot pass constitutional muster, and constitutional alternatives cannot attract political support': SJ Schulhofer, '*Miranda, Dickerson*, and the Puzzling Persistence of Fifth Amendment Exceptionalism' (2001) 99 *Michigan Law Review* 941, 955. See also Y Kamisar, '*Miranda* Thirty-Five Years Later: A Close Look at the Majority and Dissenting Opinions in *Dickerson*' (2001) 33 *Arizona State Law Journal* 387, 425.

[56] See *Terry v Ohio*, 392 US 1, 13 (1968) ('in our system evidentiary rulings provide the context in which the judicial process of inclusion and exclusion approves some conduct as comporting with constitutional guarantees and disapproves other actions by state agents'); *Missouri v Seibert*, 542 US 600, 617 (2004) (plurality opinion) (condemning a police tactic designed to circumvent Constitutional protections, and excluding the resulting statement); *California Attorneys for Criminal Justice v Butts*, 195 F 3d 1039 (9th Cir 1999) (federal civil rights action challenging interrogation tactics and training).

[57] *Brown v Mississippi*, 297 US 278 (1936) (brutality and torture); *Spano v New York*, 360 US 315 (1959) (non-physical coercive circumstances).

[58] *Colorado v Connelly*, 479 US 157 (1986) (no violation where mentally ill suspect confessed to officers, who did not elicit the statement).

[59] See eg *Arizona v Fulminante*, 499 US 279 (1991) (coercion where statement obtained in exchange for protection from possible inmate violence); *Miller v Fenton*, 796 F 2d 598 (3d Cir 1986) (no coercion where officers appealed to mentally ill suspect's religious beliefs, and he collapsed at the end of the interrogation).

[60] 384 US 436 (1966).

an uncounselled statement from a suspect for whom the right has attached, unless the right is waived.[61] And the Equal Protection Clause of the Fourteenth Amendment (along with its Fifth Amendment counterpart) generally prohibits disparate treatment attributable to unfair discrimination.

These rights serve multiple overlapping interests and values. While they all inure to the benefit of the accused, at least to some degree, their rationales are discrete. The Due Process Clause protects against officials' brutality, force, and extreme misconduct in the criminal justice system. The principles of equal protection promote non-discrimination. The Fifth Amendment privilege has been said to be founded on 'a complex of values',[62] some systemic and institutional, others individualistic.[63] But as it finds expression in the *Miranda* rule, the primary role of the privilege against self-incrimination is to safeguard individual autonomy; that is, 'to ensure that the individual's right to choose between speech and silence remains unfettered throughout the interrogation process'.[64] The Sixth Amendment right to counsel likewise encapsulates a range of values, closely tied to preserving the adversarial nature of our trial process. Thus framed, all three major constitutional protections are vital to the integrity of the criminal justice system, at least in theory—they strive to keep law enforcement within lawful and ethical bounds, to enable suspects to make the critical decisions that are theirs alone to make, and to retain a form of a system that is predominately adversarial, not inquisitorial.[65]

One might think, naively, that false confessions would never occur with such fulsome protections in place. Yet we have seen a substantial number of defendants ultimately exonerated, even though they originally confessed to police. Richard Leo, Richard Ofshe, Steven Drizin, Gisli Gudjonsson and others have documented many false confessions in the US.[66] Garrett calculates that 16 per cent of the first 250 DNA exonerations involved

---

[61] See *Montejo v Louisiana*, 556 US 778, 786 (2009) (officers can seek a waiver of the right to counsel from a suspect for whom the Sixth Amendment right has attached); *Patterson v Illinois*, 487 US 285, 296–98 (1988) (*Miranda* warnings may also apprise a suspect of his Sixth Amendment rights and support a knowing and intelligent waiver of the Sixth Amendment right to counsel).

[62] *Miranda v Arizona*, 384 US 436, 460 (1966).

[63] *Murphy v Waterfront Commission*, 378 US 52, 55 (1964) (the values include 'our unwillingness to subject those suspected of crime to the cruel trilemma of self-accusation, perjury or contempt; our preference for an accusatorial, rather than an inquisitorial, system ...; our fear that self-incriminating statements will be elicited by inhumane treatment and abuses; ... our respect for the inviolability of the human personality...; [and] our distrust of self-deprecatory statements'). The history of the privilege and the values underlying it are much debated. One noted scholar observes that the history reveals 'the tyranny of slogans', as shorthand phrases 'have eclipsed the goals of the doctrines that they purported to describe': AW Alschuler, 'A Peculiar Privilege in Historical Perspective' in RH Helmholz, CM Gray, JH Langbein, E Moglen, HE Smith and AW Alschuler (eds), *The Privilege Against Self-Incrimination* (Chicago, University of Chicago Press, 1997) 181, 200–201.

[64] *Connecticut v Barrett*, 479 US 523, 528 (1987); quoting *Miranda*, 384 US 436, 469 (1966).

[65] Other common law jurisdictions have replaced the 'voluntariness' test with tailor-made statutory provisions. In England and Wales, s 76 of the Police and Criminal Evidence Act 1984 now governs the admission of confession evidence, which must not be obtained by oppression or in circumstances conducive to unreliability: see P Roberts and A Zuckerman, *Criminal Evidence*, 2nd edn (Oxford, Oxford University Press, 2010) ch 12. In Australia, s 84 of the uniform Evidence Acts renders a defendant's extrajudicial confession inadmissible 'unless the court is satisfied that the admission, and the making of the admission, were not influenced by ... violent, oppressive, inhuman or degrading conduct' or by any 'threat of conduct of that kind'; unreliable admissions may be excluded under s 85: see Australian Law Reform Commission, *Uniform Evidence Law*, ALRC Report 102 (Sydney, December 2005) 325.

[66] See eg RA Leo and RJ Ofshe, 'The Consequences of False Confessions: Deprivations of Liberty and Miscarriages of Justice in the Age of Psychological Interrogation' (1998) 88 *Journal of Criminal Law and Criminology* 429; R Leo, *Police Interrogation and American Justice* (Cambridge MA, Harvard University Press, 2008) 195–268;

a false confession.[67] In an earlier study, Leo and Drizin put that figure at closer to 25 per cent.[68] While we cannot know the true incidence of false or inaccurate statements during the many thousands of interrogations that take place each year, these cases are both troubling and revealing. Reformers have examined them closely, and addressing the problem of false confessions has been a central preoccupation of innocence commissions in California, Connecticut, Florida, Illinois, New York, Oklahoma, Pennsylvania, Texas and Virginia.[69]

With one exception, these commissions have recommended that some or all custodial interrogations be electronically recorded.[70] While other benefits are acknowledged,[71] reformers mainly emphasise that recording will allow judges and juries to identify false confessions and thereby decrease the incidence of wrongful convictions.[72] Avoiding wrongful convictions is their touchstone. Thus, the Florida Innocence Commission endorsed tape-recording, but did not support other reforms to the interrogation process—such as banning deceptive techniques or using special care with juveniles and suspects with disabilities—which are arguably related to voluntariness as well as reliability.[73] Having conducted an exhaustive review of the research literature relating to false confessions, *Miranda* warnings and interrogation practices, the Pennsylvania Commission recommended only that custodial interrogations be recorded and that a rule should be adopted to require defence counsel in capital cases to receive additional instruction regarding the incidence and causes of false confessions.[74] Virginia's non-governmental Commission issued some additional recommendations, also keyed to the issue of false confessions. It proposed that officers avoid using high-pressure tactics when questioning children and suspects with

---

SA Drizin and RA Leo, 'The Problem of False Confessions in the Post-DNA World' (2004) 82 *North Carolina Law Review* 891, 905; G Gudjonnson, 'The Making of a Serial False Confessor: The Confessions of Henry Lee Lucas' (1999) 10 *Journal of Forensic Psychiatry* 416. But cf PG Cassell, 'The Guilty and the "Innocent": An Examination of Alleged Cases of Wrongful Conviction from False Confessions' (1999) 22 *Harvard Journal of Law and Public Policy* 523.

[67] See Garrett, above n 25, 18.

[68] Drizin and Leo, above n 66, 905 (examining 140 cases).

[69] See California Commission on the Fair Administration of Justice, *Report and Recommendations Regarding False Confessions* (2006), www.ccfaj.org/documents/reports/false/official/falconfrep.pdf (accessed 1 February 2016); State of Connecticut Advisory Commission on Wrongful Convictions, above n 45, 4; Florida Innocence Commission, above n 45; Illinois Capital Punishment Reform Study Commission, *Sixth and Final Report*, above n 45, 26–35; New York State Justice Task Force, *Recommendations Regarding Electronic Recording of Custodial Interrogations* (January 2012), www.nyjusticetaskforce.com/ElectronicRecordingOfCustodialInterrogations.pdf (accessed 1 February 2016); Oklahoma Justice Commission, above n 45, 7–13; Joint State Government Commission, above n 45, 83–127, 167–72; Timothy Cole Advisory Panel on Wrongful Convictions, *Report to the Texas Task Force on Indigent Defense* (August 2010) 18–22, www.prisonlegalnews.org/media/publications/timothy_cole_advisory_panel_on_wrongful_convictions_report_to_tx_task_force_on_indigent_defense_2010.pdf (accessed 1 February 2016); Innocence Commission for Virginia, above n 45, 42–59.

[70] The Connecticut Commission, above n 45, did not make that recommendation, but set up a pilot programme to record interrogations.

[71] See eg New York State Justice Task Force, above n 45, 2 ('recording helps identify false confessions; provides an objective and reliable record of what occurred …; assists in determining a statement's voluntariness and reliability; prevents disputes about how an officer conducted himself or treated a suspect, and serves as a useful training tool to police officers').

[72] Ibid 3. See also California Commission on the Fair Administration of Justice, above n 69, 4–5; Joint State Government Commission, above n 45, 109; Innocence Commission for Virginia, above n 45, 54.

[73] Florida Innocence Commission, above n 45, §§VI(b) and (c).

[74] Joint State Government Commission, above n 45, 83–127.

developmental disabilities, and that the courts permit some expert testimony about factors that can contribute to false confessions.[75]

Electronic recording of police interviews would doubtless reinforce core values and legal principles of criminal adjudication. David Dixon recounts how the practice of tape-recording ended the corrosive practice of 'verballing' in New South Wales.[76] Tape-recording was introduced in England and Wales under the Police and Criminal Evidence Act (PACE) Codes of Practice in part to avoid accusations of that same practice.[77] Electronic recording enables a trier of fact to hear for itself whether *Miranda* warnings were properly given, whether suspects asserted or waived their rights, whether confessions were induced by promises or threats, and whether the accused really did provide full post-admission narratives. Sometimes a recording permits us to assess the mental and physical condition of suspects. Yet accepting these benefits as *by-products* of a recording requirement implemented for a different, innocence-related reason, means that we are less likely to give appropriate consideration to other pressing and difficult issues, divorced from factual innocence.

And there are many such issues to examine and normative questions to address. For instance, does the *Miranda* regime truly empower individuals to exercise autonomy during police interrogation, or is it essentially an empty ritual, which provides scant protection to suspects but a safe harbour for police (who know that a statement will be admissible so long as the magic words are spoken)?[78] To what extent do we truly value suspects' autonomy in the stationhouse? Are suspects sufficiently well informed about their situation to make meaningful choices to speak or remain silent? Should courts more carefully scrutinise the voluntariness of even truthful confessions, including the distorting effects of implied threats or promises as well as the vulnerabilities of particular suspects? Should deception and lies continue to be regarded as legitimate interrogation strategies, or does immoral conduct corrode the integrity of law enforcement, undermine public trust, and distort suspects' choices?[79] Do minimisation tactics, and suggestions of 'themes' to suspects—including 'themes' that blame the victim—actually hurt victims even if the techniques succeed in eliciting inculpatory statements.[80] Would providing counsel to suspects

---

[75] Innocence Commission for Virginia, above n 45, 58–59.

[76] D Dixon, *Interrogating Images* (Sydney, Sydney Institute of Criminology, 2007) 262. 'Verballing' refers to the provision of false evidence by police that a suspect had confessed or made inculpatory remarks: see Royal Commission into the New South Wales Police Service (The Hon Justice JRT Wood), *Final Report Volume 1: Corruption* (Sydney, Government of the State of New South Wales, 1997) xii, 51, 68–70, www.pic.nsw.gov.au/files/reports/RCPS%20Report%20Volume%201.pdf (accessed 1 February 2016).

[77] See J Baxter, P Rawlings and J Williams, 'PACE: Protecting the Suspect' (1986) 50 *Journal of Criminal Law* 68, 73; Royal Commission on Criminal Procedure (Sir Cyril Philips), *Report* Cmnd 8092 (London, HMSO, 1981) [4.2].

[78] See CD Weisselberg, 'Mourning *Miranda*' (2008) 96 *California Law Review* 1519, 1590–99.

[79] See C Slobogin, 'Deceit, Pretext, and Trickery: Investigative Lies By the Police' (1997) 76 *Oregon Law Review* 775, 799–800.

[80] See Dixon, Chapter 3 in this volume, for illustrations; and for further discussion, see C Weisselberg and S Bibas, 'Debate: The Right to Remain Silent' (2010) 159 *University of Pennsylvania Law Review PENNumbra* 69, 86–87, www.pennlawreview.com/online/159-U-Pa-L-Rev-PENNumbra-69.pdf (accessed 1 February 2016); F Inbau, JE Reid, JP Buckley and BC Jayne, *Criminal Interrogation and Confessions*, 4th edn (Gaithersburg, Aspen Publishers, 2001) 256–57.

under interrogation be more consistent with the basic values of the US adversary system?[81] As Dixon reminds us, audio-visual recording is 'no panacea' and we should not treat it as such. Recording 'can even be counterproductive if it instils a false confidence that all is well'.[82] For one thing, tapes are always 'subject to interpretation'[83] and they do not capture what occurs off camera.[84] For another, even if recordings were capable of establishing an incontrovertible historical record, they would not resolve the question of what *normative standards* to apply to the undisputed facts or how much protection we *should* afford to our system's central rights and values.

Beyond the commissions' reformist focus on electronic recording, the Innocence movement has shaped scholarship about interrogation law and practice in more varied and diffuse ways. Among the most influential interrogation scholars are psychologists and other social scientists who study false confessions, some of whom not infrequently serve as experts in cases involving alleged false confessions. In a policy paper adopted by the American Psychology-Law Society (a division of the American Psychological Association), six leading scholars exhaustively reviewed police practices and the law and psychology of interrogation. Their recommendations centre on reducing the risk of wrongful convictions arising from false confessions. Predictably, they advocate electronic recording.[85] However, they also raise concerns about the plasticity of the law's 'totality of the circumstances' test for judging voluntariness as a precondition to admissibility. The policy paper urges that 'the process of interrogation should be structured in theory and practice to produce outcomes that are accurate, as measured by the observed ratio of true to false confessions'.[86] The authors address a variety of possible reforms, including investigative interviewing, limiting custody and interrogation time, restricting false evidence ploys and minimisation tactics, and protecting vulnerable populations.[87] Their polestar is reducing false confessions. While their proposed reforms *may* cohere with our criminal justice system's long-held values and principles, such as protecting individual autonomy and resolving charges through an adversarial process, they do not *necessarily* do so.

The Innocence movement has influenced criminal procedure scholarship as well. George Thomas has advocated reducing the risk of wrongful convictions by, among other things, diminishing the entrenched perspectives of career prosecutors and defence lawyers by creating a pool of 'criminal law specialists', lawyers who would *both* prosecute and defend.[88]

---

[81] There is a fair argument that a custodial suspect's access to legal counsel is a requirement in all modern criminal justice systems, whether they are characterised as 'adversarial' or 'inquisitorial'. See *Salduz v Turkey* (2008) EHRR 421 [55] (ECHR Article 6 requires 'access to a lawyer ... from the first interrogation of a suspect' unless there are compelling reasons to restrict this right); D Giannoulopoulos, 'Custodial Legal Assistance and Notification of the Right to Silence in France: Legal Cosmopolitanism and Local Resistance' (2013) 24 *Criminal Law Forum* 291, 302–306 (surveying practices in 22 countries).

[82] Dixon, above n 76, 3.

[83] See Bandes, above n 29, 12.

[84] See M McConville, 'Videotaping Interrogations: Police Behaviour On and Off Camera' [1992] *Criminal Law Review* 532.

[85] See SM Kassin, SA Drizin, T Grisso, GJ Gudjonsson, RA Leo and A Redlich, 'Police-Induced Confessions: Risk Factors and Recommendations' (2010) 34 *Law and Human Behavior* 3, 25–27. These scholars are regularly cited by law reform commissions: see eg California Commission on the Fair Administration of Justice, above n 69, 1–3; Joint State Government Commission, above n 45, 84–107; Innocence Commission for Virginia, above n 45, 45–46.

[86] Kassin et al, above n 85, 27.

[87] Ibid 27–31.

[88] Thomas, above n 48, 190–92.

As well as introducing tape-recording, Thomas would prohibit certain types of police lies and deception, where such tactics are more likely to induce false confessions. Admissions should also be actively screened by magistrates for reliability, promoting more routine exclusion of false confessions.[89] Richard Leo and colleagues, who have long advocated such screening, have proposed specific reliability tests.[90] Advancing similar proposals based on his study of false confession cases, Garrett insists that '[a] new focus on accuracy can help to safeguard the reliability and legitimacy of confessions'.[91] While reliability-screening in circumstances involving governmental coercion is arguably already part of the Due Process Clause's voluntariness determination, exclusion of a statement purely on grounds of unreliability would require an explicit legal basis outside the US Constitution.[92]

False confessions have influenced the way that some scholars assess *Miranda* and the ability of suspects to assert their Fifth Amendment privilege in the police stations. Thomas would leave *Miranda* in place, but only by default: although any benefit to suspects 'is ephemeral, [*Miranda*] probably does little harm'.[93] Stephanos Bibas, by contrast, would jettison *Miranda* because it may prevent officers from obtaining some truthful confessions and '*Miranda*'s protections map poorly onto the kinds of compulsion that produce false confessions and the categories of people likely to confess falsely'. Consequently:

> We should not stand in the way of interrogation techniques that produce truthful confessions so long as they do not create an unacceptable risk of producing false ones ... If criminal justice is a search for the truth, then *Miranda* should be no obstacle.[94]

These snapshots of contemporary US interrogation scholarship and innocence commissions' law-reform agendas exemplify how exonerations are reshaping the policy debate. For some 'innocentrists', preventing wrongful convictions of the factually innocent should determine how we regulate police interrogation practices and admit confession evidence, perhaps even by realigning constitutional protections, although voices of moderation can also be heard from within the Innocence movement.[95] Some of those who may have intentionally harnessed the power inherent in exonerations to serve a larger reform agenda have started to wonder about the sustainability of this approach, especially if the pace of exonerations has already peaked—as the greater availability of pre-trial DNA testing in recent criminal proceedings might lead one to expect. Gould neatly states the problem:

> If justice reform has largely turned on innocence, what will happen to other worthy issues of reform in the criminal justice system if the number of DNA exonerations declines? ... The central question ... is not whether further reforms are needed apart from those necessary to protect the innocent from wrongful conviction. That is elementary. The more difficult, strategic question is how to pursue such an agenda even if innocence 'sells' but clear claims of innocence are likely to decline ...

---

[89] Ibid 194–96.

[90] See eg Leo, above n 66, 283–91.

[91] Garrett, above n 25, 248.

[92] See AE Taslitz, 'High Expectations and Some Wounded Hopes: The Policy and Politics of a Uniform Statute on Videotaping Custodial Interrogations' (2012) 7 *Northwestern Journal of Law and Social Policy* 400, 420–27.

[93] Thomas, above n 48, 195.

[94] Weisselberg and Bibas, above n 80, 77, 79.

[95] See eg D Givelber, 'The Adversary System and Historical Accuracy: Can We Do Better?' in S Westervelt and J Humphrey (eds), *Wrongly Convicted: Perspectives on Failed Justice* (New Brunswick NJ, Rutgers University Press, 2001) 253, 263 ('reform should not be undertaken solely in the name of assuring that we never convict the innocent').

Americans are reluctant to press for reforms that would largely benefit the guilty. Fundamentally, the public wants protection from crime, not necessarily assurance that the rights of defendants, and especially guilty ones at that, will be protected.[96]

Although we all rejoice when a factually innocent person is released from prison, my own cheer is in a slightly different register. Like Bandes, among other commentators, I am deeply concerned that the use of exonerations to spur reforms has diverted our attention from endemic problems in the administration of criminal justice, and has diminished our dedication to fundamental rights and core values. We see this loss of integrity, and more, in the context of custodial interrogations, where the Innocence movement even influences how we interpret basic constitutional protections.

Conclusion

For Zalman et al, '[a]ctual innocence is, in political science terms, a valence issue—one about which there can be no reasonable opposition'.[97] Nobody can seriously contest the goals of increasing the accuracy of criminal adjudication and reducing the likelihood of wrongly convicting the factually innocent. At the same time, however, pursuit of factual accuracy should not blind us to other core values and principles of criminal proceedings: there must be integrity in the process of enforcing criminal law, as well as in the final outcome.

This chapter provides a cautionary tale. While 'actual innocence' is an enormously effective lever for reforming criminal proceedings, it may also serve to erode or even undermine the 'integrity principle', broadly defined. Reformers and scholars alike should mind this risk. The Innocence movement has trained a powerful new spotlight on the wrongful convictions of the factually innocent. I worry that its beam is narrow, leaving other corners of our criminal justice system in still greater darkness.

---

[96] Gould, above n 46, 236–37.

[97] M Zalman, B Smith and A Kiger, 'Officials' Estimates of the Incidence of "Actual Innocence" Convictions' (2008) 25 *Justice Quarterly* 72, 74.

Appendix

Table 1: Government-Sponsored Commissions

State	Manner of Initiation	Start Date	End Date	Mission/Goals
California California Commission on the Fair Administration of Justice	Senate Resolution	2004	2008	(1) To determine the extent of wrongful executions or wrongful convictions of innocent persons in California; (2) To examine ways of providing safeguards and making improvements in the criminal justice system; (3) To make recommendations to ensure that the system is just, fair and accurate.
Connecticut Connecticut Advisory Commission on Wrongful Convictions	Statute	2003	Unknown (appears dormant: report issued in 2009; no meetings held since 2008)	To review any criminal or juvenile case involving a wrongful conviction and recommend reforms to lessen the likelihood of a similar wrongful conviction occurring in the future.
Florida Florida Innocence Commission	Florida Supreme Court Administrative Order	2010	2012	To conduct a comprehensive study of the causes of wrongful conviction and of measures to prevent such convictions; the Commission may propose statutory changes that are directly related to the wrongful conviction of the innocent.
Illinois Capital Punishment Reform Study Committee	Executive Order/Statute	2000	2010	To study the capital punishment process to determine why it has failed, resulting in sentencing innocent people to death, and to suggest improvements and safeguards; to study the impact of various reforms to the capital punishment system and report on them to the General Assembly.

(continued)

Table 1: *(Continued)*

State	Manner of Initiation	Start Date	End Date	Mission/Goals
Louisiana Louisiana State Law Institute	Statute/House Resolution	1933/2010	Ongoing, (but does not appear to be studying wrongful convictions)	Special study of wrongful convictions and recommendations for revising laws regarding procedure, preservation of forensic evidence, confessions, and other issues regarding the finality and accuracy of convictions.
Maryland Maryland Commission on Capital Punishment	Statute	2008	2008	To address racial, social, and jurisdictional disparities in the capital punishment process, and to address the risk of innocent people being executed
New York New York State Justice Task Force	Chief Judge of State of New York	2009	Ongoing	(1) To eradicate the systemic and individual harms caused by wrongful convictions; (2) To promote public safety by examining the causes of wrongful convictions; (3) To recommend reforms to safeguard against wrongful convictions in the future.
New York Conviction Integrity Program	District Attorney of New York County	2010	Ongoing	Created to address claims of actual innocence and seeks to prevent wrongful convictions from occurring.
North Carolina North Carolina Innocence Inquiry Commission	Statute	2006	Ongoing	To investigate and determine claims of factual innocence.
North Carolina North Carolina Actual Innocence Commission	Chief Justice of State of North Carolina	2002/2005	Unknown (appears dormant)	To make recommendations which reduce or eliminate wrongful convictions. Led to formation of the North Carolina Innocence Inquiry Commission.

(continued)

Table 1: *(Continued)*

State	Manner of Initiation	Start Date	End Date	Mission/Goals
Pennsylvania Pennsylvania's Advisory Committee on Wrongful Convictions	Senate Resolution	2006	Unknown (last report issued 2011; appears dormant)	To explore the causes of wrongful convictions and make recommendations to reduce the possibility of future convictions of innocent persons.
Texas Texas Criminal Justice Integrity Unit	Texas Court of Criminal Appeals	2008	Ongoing	To bring about meaningful criminal justice reforms in areas including: (1) improving quality of defence counsel for indigent defendants; (2) improving eyewitness identification procedures; (3) eliminating improper interrogations and protecting against false confessions; (4) reforming standard for collection; preservation, and storage of evidence; (5) improving attorney practices; and (6) adequately compensating the wrongfully convicted.
Texas The Timothy Cole Advisory Panel on Wrongful Convictions	Statute	2009	2010	To study: (1) the causes of wrongful convictions; (2) procedures and programmes to prevent future wrongful convictions; and (3) the effects on wrongful convictions of laws regarding eyewitness identifications, recording of interrogations, post-conviction DNA testing, and habeas corpus.

(continued)

Table 1: *(Continued)*

State	Manner of Initiation	Start Date	End Date	Mission/Goals
Wisconsin Avery Task Force	Wisconsin Judiciary Committee	2003	2005	(1) To examine causes of wrongful convictions; (2) To investigate other ways the criminal justice system can be reformed so that only the guilty are convicted.
Wisconsin Wisconsin Criminal Justice Study Commission	Law Schools, State Bar, Wisconsin Department of Justice	2005	2008	To identify and correct problems in the criminal justice system, and produce the best possible system, which 'justly convicts the guilty and not the innocent.'

Table 2: Non-Government-Sponsored Commissions

State	Manner of Initiation	Start Date	End Date	Missions/Goals
New York New York State Bar Association's Task Force on Wrongful Convictions	New York State Bar Association	2008	2009/ 2010	(1) To identify and attempt to eliminate the causes of wrongful convictions; (2) To propose solutions in the form of procedural changes and legislation; (3) To educate the legal profession and the public on the causes of wrongful convictions, to reduce the risk of convicting the innocent and increase the likelihood of convicting the guilty.
Oklahoma Oklahoma Justice Commission	Oklahoma Bar Association	2010	2013	(1) To research the causes of conviction of the innocent; (2) To recommend remedial strategies to reduce the possibility of convicting the innocent.
Virginia Innocence Commission for Virginia	Mid-Atlantic Innocence Project and two Universities	2003	2005	To chronicle the common errors in wrongful conviction cases, propose policy reforms and offer a series of best practices to improve the investigation and prosecution of serious criminal cases.

Notes on Sources for Missions and Goals in Tables 1 and 2[98]

California: Senate Resolution 44 (24 August 2004) (establishing Commission); Senate Resolution 10 (28 June 2007) (extending Commission to 2008).

Connecticut: Connecticut General Statutes §54-102pp (establishing Commission). The Commission's website lists nine specific objectives of the Commission, which also make clear that the focus is on the wrongful conviction of people who are factually innocent. See Advisory Commission on Wrongful Convictions, 'Objectives', www.jud.ct.gov/committees/wrongfulconviction.]

Florida: Administrative Order, *In re: Florida Innocence Commission*, No. AOSC10-39 (2 July 2010), www.floridasupremecourt.org/clerk/adminorders/2010/AOSC10-39.pdf (establishing Commission); www.flcourts.org/gen_public/innocence.shtml (containing the Commission's Interim and Final Reports). The Florida Commission expired in 2012. See www.huffingtonpost.com/2012/06/06/rick-scott-defunds-florid_n_1574259.html (noting that it was set to expire, and so continuing funds were not requested from the Florida legislature).

Illinois: The Commission was initially established by Executive Order, but was reauthorised by statute. For a history of the Commission, see Illinois Capital Punishment Reform Study Committee, *Sixth and Final Report* (October 2010) 1–8, www.chicagobar.org/AM/NavigationMenu/Home/Files/IllinosCapitalPunishmentReformStudyCommitteeSixthAndFinalReport.pdf.

Louisiana: The Institute, a permanent institution, was established 'to secure the better administration of justice and to carry on scholarly legal research and scientific legal work.' Louisiana Revised Statutes §§ 24:201, 204 (establishing Institute, listing purposes). In 2010, the Louisiana Legislature directed the Institute to study wrongful convictions and report back to the Legislature by 1 January 2013. See House Committee Report 9 (Regular Session 2010).

Maryland: Senate Bill 614/House Bill 111 (2008) (establishing the Maryland Commission on Capital Punishment). Also see 'Capital Punishment in Maryland—Timeline', www.goccp.maryland.gov/capital-punishment/hearings.php. The Commission's Final Report is available at www.goccp.maryland.gov/capital-punishment/documents/death-penalty-commission-final-report.pdf.

New York (State Justice Task Force): 'Mission Statement', www.nyjusticetaskforce.com/mission.html.

New York (Conviction Integrity Program): Description available at www.manhattanda.org/wrongful-conviction.

New York (State Bar Association): New York State Bar Association Task Force on Wrongful Convictions, 'Final Report' 5, www.nysba.org/WorkArea/DownloadAsset.aspx?id=26663.

---

[98] All URLs accessed 1 February 2016.

North Carolina (Innocence Inquiry Commission): North Carolina General Statutes §§15A-1460, *et seq.* For the most recent activities of the Commission, see The North Carolina Innocence Inquiry Commission, *Annual Report to the 2015–16 Regular Session of the General Assembly of North Carolina and The State Judicial Council*, www.innocence-commission-nc.gov/Forms/pdf/gar/2014%20Annual%20Report%20%28sent%20to%20General%20Assembly%20in%202015%29.pdf. See also www.innocencecommission-nc.gov/about.html (describing Commission and archiving reports).

North Carolina (Actual Innocence Commission): The Commission originated in 2002 under the supervisory authority of the Chief Justice of the Supreme Court of North Carolina, and was then more formally established by an order of the full Court in 2005. It had a broad mission to study and address the causes of convictions of the innocent: www.innocenceproject.org/news-events-exonerations/criminal-justice-reform-commissions-case-studies#nc. The Commission is described, ibid, as 'dormant since 2007', and its abolition has been debated: see 'Bill would eliminate Actual Innocence Commission', www.indyweek.com/indyweek/bill-would-eliminate-actual-innocence-commission/Content?oid=4171282.

Oklahoma: The Oklahoma Bar Association Resolution Establishing the Oklahoma Justice Commission is available at Oklahoma Justice Commission, *Report to the Oklahoma Bar Association* (February 2013) 40, www.okbar.org/Portals/15/PDF/2013/Commission_Final_Report.pdf.

Pennsylvania: Pennsylvania Senate Resolution 381 (2006). The Committee's full report, which issued in September 2011, is available at jsg.legis.state.pa.us/resources/documents/ftp/documents/9-15-11%20rpt%20-%20Wrongful%20Convictions.pdf

Texas (Criminal Justice Integrity Unit): 'Welcome to the Texas Criminal Justice Integrity Unit (TCJIU)', www.txcourts.gov/cca/texas-criminal-justice-integrity-unit.aspx. For the issues addressed by the Unit, see Texas Criminal Justice Integrity Unit, *2008 Annual Report of Activities* 4, www.txcourts.gov/media/253234/tcjiu-2008-report.pdf.

Texas (Timothy Cole Panel): Texas House Bill 498, §1(d), 81st Legislature (Regular Session 2009).

Virginia: Innocence Commission for Virginia, 'Mission Statement,' in Gould, above n 46, at 64. The Commission's March 2005 report is available at www.exonerate.org/ICVA/full_r.pdf.

Wisconsin (Avery Task Force): 'Avery Task Force examines wrongful convictions, new study commission to examine criminal justice system' (2005) 78 *Wisconsin Lawyer* (July), www.wisbar.org/newspublications/wisconsinlawyer/pages/article.aspx?volume=78&issue=7&articleid=823.

Wisconsin (Criminal Justice Study Commission): 'Charter Statement' 3, available at law.wisc.edu/fjr/clinicals/ip/wcjsc/index.html. The Commission last met in 2008: see law.wisc.edu/fjr/clinicals/ip/wcjsc/meetings.html.

16

Compensating Injustice: The Perils of the Innocence Discourse

CAROLYN HOYLE[*]

Introduction

In January 2007, the English Court of Appeal quashed Andrew Adams' conviction for murder, having found it to be 'unsafe'.[1] Adams, the son of a wealthy aircraft engineer, had been only 21 when he was arrested 14 years earlier. The crime for which Adams was convicted and sentenced to life was a horrifying, gangster-style execution, in which a teacher, Jack Royal, was blasted at point-blank range with a sawn-off shotgun when he went to answer his front door. But according to the Court of Appeal, Adams' trial defence lawyers failed to make use of 'unused material' collected during the police investigation which would have assisted his case. This material included details of a 'deal' between the police and the main prosecution witness, Kevin Thompson, who avoided a long prison sentence for various armed robberies in return for giving evidence against Adams, and evidence which pointed towards another suspect who had already been tried for and acquitted of the same murder. It was, in other words, an investigation and prosecution which, like too many others, lacked integrity.

The Court of Appeal based its conclusion on the cumulative effect of several, discrete 'criticisms and failures' in the handling of the original case, none of which, taken on their own, would have been enough to quash the conviction. Moreover, although they did not order a re-trial, so allowing Adams' immediate release, they added an important caveat: 'We are not to be taken as finding that if there had been no such failures the appellant would inevitably have been acquitted.' This, in other words, was certainly not a case in which the

[*] I wish to thank the University of Oxford John Fell Fund for its generous funding of this research, the Criminal Cases Review Commission (CCRC) for granting me permission to conduct research, the individual Commissioners and Case Review Managers I have interviewed, and interviewees outside the CCRC including Alex Bailin QC, Henry Blaxland QC, Daniel Machover, Paul May, John Merry and Ben Rose. Thanks are also due to the miscarriages of justice team at the Ministry of Justice for conducting research and providing me with data on compensation claims and awards. Mary Bosworth, David Rose and Lucia Zedner provided helpful comments on an earlier version of the paper, and Paul Roberts was a ferocious though effective editor.
[1] *R v Adams* [2007] 1 Cr App R 34, [2007] EWCA Crim 1.

court proclaimed the defendant's factual innocence.[2] Indeed, for the reasons explored in this chapter, the Court rarely does so.

Adams did not find his renewed freedom easy. He was virtually penniless, he had spent the best years of his youth in high security prisons and had no profession or qualifications. During his incarceration, his mother had died and his father had developed severe Alzheimer's disease. Although Adams began seeing the woman he had been living with at the time of his arrest, she had meanwhile had three children with another man, and the relationship with Adams soon broke down. Within a year of his appeal, he was depressed, unemployed and homeless, sleeping alternately in hostels or on friends' floors.[3]

Those most closely associated with the case, including his legal team, disagreed with the somewhat grudging tone of the appeal court's ruling. The investigative journalists John Merry and David Rose, who had written extensively about the case for the British newspaper *The Observer* within a few months of Adams' conviction, were convinced he was factually innocent.[4] Ben Rose, the solicitor who had spent many months drawing up a meticulous application to the Criminal Cases Review Commission (CCRC) after Adams lost his first appeal in 1998, took the same view. However, when he applied to the Ministry of Justice for compensation under the Criminal Justice Act 1988 for his lost 14 years, he was refused. Adams' legal challenge to this decision reached the UK Supreme Court in May 2011. In a judgment which effectively sets new rules for all future applicants in his position, the panel of nine justices determined that henceforth, compensation would be payable to applicants like Adams only when a 'new fact' not considered at trial had so undermined the Crown's case that no conviction could possibly be based upon it—that no jury, properly directed, could convict.[5]

This essay will consider the background, origins and consequences of this ruling. It will argue that its moral and legal bases lack integrity, and that it marks a significant step towards the creation of a highly problematic two-tier system for quashed convictions. Under English law, the legal principle governing criminal appeals is supposed to be the safety or otherwise of the conviction: no more, and no less.[6] This, it will be argued, reflects the reality that appellate tribunals hear only a portion of a case's significant facts, precluding any appeal panel from making an informed assessment of an appellant's factual innocence or guilt. Such a determination, in the absence of a truly exhaustive inquiry, is bound to be flawed, especially when, as often happens, a conviction is quashed without the court even needing to consider some of the grounds of appeal. Moreover, in seeking to downgrade quashed convictions based on mere 'technicalities' in relation to other, supposedly more worthy appellants, the Supreme Court in *Adams* was thought by some to have reversed the burden of proof: to have imposed on those people whose cases had been judged to be unsafe by the Court of Appeal an obligation to prove themselves innocent.[7] Nevertheless,

---

[2] For the purposes of this chapter, I have preferred the term 'factual' as opposed to 'actual' innocence, though the two are largely interchangeable for most purposes.

[3] For a persuasive account of the harms of wrongful conviction, see A Grounds, 'Psychological Consequences of Wrongful Conviction and Imprisonment' (2004) 46 *Canadian Journal of Criminology and Criminal Justice* 165.

[4] D Rose, 'Who Really Killed Jack Royal?' *The Observer*, 26 February 2006.

[5] *R (Adams) v Secretary of State for Justice* [2012] 1 AC 48, [2011] UKSC 18.

[6] Criminal Appeal Act 1968, s 2 (as amended).

[7] Interview with Alex Bailin QC.

an 'innocence discourse' is increasingly being espoused by campaigners on behalf of the wrongly-convicted. This development, which might influence judicial responses to appeals, I contend, is fraught with peril.

1. Miscarriages of Justice and the CCRC

The first system of regular appeals against criminal conviction was introduced in England and Wales by the Criminal Appeal Act 1907, which created the Court of Criminal Appeal— the forerunner of today's Court of Appeal (Criminal Division). Since 1908, the only further recourse for people convicted of criminal offences, who had been refused leave to appeal or whose appeals had been dismissed, was to apply to the Home Secretary for executive intervention. A small unit, known as the Criminal Case Unit of the C3 (Criminal Policy) Division of the Home Office, was established within central government to review applications. C3 had the power to order investigations of alleged miscarriages of justice and refer appropriate cases back to the Court of Appeal for reconsideration. In 1994 there were 12 case workers and two and a half senior staffing posts committed to working full time on these cases.[8] In almost half of its cases, C3 would ask for further inquiries to be made by the police, the very organisation responsible for many if not most of the wrongful convictions under consideration.[9] In the final years of C3's existence, the Home Secretary received between 700 and 800 representations of wrongful convictions a year—some for more trivial summary convictions, some for sentencing only, but most were appeals against convictions of serious offences in the Crown Court that had resulted in long prison sentences. There had been a sharp upturn in 1989 to 1990, possibly as a result of the exposure of high-profile miscarriages of justice connected with Irish terrorism,[10] but the rising trend could be traced back to the early 1980s when the number of representations received was lower than 500. In this era, subsequent appeals by referral were rare.[11] The English criminal justice system, unlike its US counterparts with their labyrinthine tiers of state and federal review, valued the notion of finality. Over the years that C3 operated, successive Secretaries of State showed themselves extremely reluctant to disturb jury verdicts.

The implicit complacency about the general reliability of police investigations and the safety of convictions was shaken to the core by the series of high-profile miscarriages of justice which began to come to light with the 1989 release of the 'Guildford Four' after 15 years' wrongful imprisonment for terrorist bombings.[12] As he heard their second

---

[8] R Pattenden, *English Criminal Appeals 1844–1994* (Oxford, Oxford University Press, 1996) 348–53.

[9] Criminal Appeal Act 1968, s 17. The Home Office had no formal powers to direct the police but it was rare for a force to be uncooperative: Pattenden, above n 8, 350.

[10] Particularly the cases of the 'Birmingham Six' and the 'Guildford Four': see C Mullin, *Error of Judgement: The Truth About the Birmingham Bombings* (Dublin, Poolbeg Press, 1990); R Kee, *Trial and Error: The Maguires, the Guildford Pub Bombings and British Justice* (London, Penguin Books, 1989); D Rose, *In the Name of the Law: Collapse of Criminal Justice* (London, Vintage Press, 1996).

[11] C3 contributed to an annual average of five cases being quashed by the Court of Appeal between 1980 and 1992 and before the 1980s references were even fewer: Pattenden, above n 8, 363.

[12] The Guildford Four were convicted in 1975 of bombings carried out in public houses in Guildford, Surrey, by the Provisional Irish Republican Army (IRA).

appeal, and the Crown's presentation of new evidence demonstrating that their confessions had been fabricated by detectives, Lord Chief Lane commented: 'The officers must have lied'.[13] While formerly he may have believed that individual officers might lie under oath, it was clear from his comment that he had never imagined that systematic, orchestrated group perjury was possible in the British justice system. Indeed, Lord Lane, along with his fellow judges, had adamantly resisted the idea that miscarriages of justice could be anything other than wholly exceptional. With those epochal words, and the widespread upheaval which followed them, came a general acceptance that the criminal process lacked integrity and that a fairer and more easily accessible method for remedying alleged miscarriages of justice was essential. The result, following a recommendation by the Royal Commission on Criminal Justice (RCCJ),[14] was the CCRC, established by the Criminal Appeal Act 1995.[15]

The CCRC was set up to review possible miscarriages of justice in England, Wales and Northern Ireland (Scotland has its own Commission) in cases in which applicants have exhausted other avenues of appeal. To decide on referral to the Court of Appeal, it draws on its own resources: approximately 37 Case Review Managers, one legal and one investigations advisor, nine Commissioners, and administrative/executive support. To date, the CCRC has received nearly 20,000 applications and has referred about 600 cases to the Court of Appeal. Each year, it typically refers about 30 cases, as a result of which about two-thirds of these convictions will be quashed.[16] Its referral decisions are governed, pursuant to section 13 of the Criminal Appeal Act 1995, by a 'real possibility' test (RPT). The Commission must be satisfied there is a 'real possibility' that the Court of Appeal will quash the trial verdict as legally 'unsafe' due to fresh arguments or evidence not yet considered by the courts. While constrained by the requirement to find something 'new' that has not previously been put before the trial court or the Court of Appeal, the CCRC's investigatory process is open-ended, and can include investigation of the police or prosecution case; the commission of new forensic tests and expert reports; and instigation of fresh police enquiries, where necessary by an outside police force. Even absent a prior appeal, the CCRC can also refer a case on the grounds of 'exceptional circumstances', so long as it determines that it meets the RPT.

The contrast between the work of the CCRC and the Innocence Projects, which have led to the reversal of some 200 capital convictions in America, mainly through the use of DNA testing, is marked. US campaigning focuses on evidence of innocence, while proof of actual innocence is not required by the RPT, or by the Court of Appeal in determining whether a conviction is 'safe'. Accordingly, the CCRC is able to examine a wide range of legal issues and fresh evidence.

---

[13] D Rose, *A Climate of Fear* (London, Bloomsbury Publishing, 1992) 1.

[14] The Royal Commission on Criminal Justice, under the chairmanship of Lord Runciman, reviewed the criminal process, and had at its heart the reform of the mechanism for reviewing possible miscarriages of justice: *The Royal Commission on Criminal Justice: Report* Cm 2263 (London, HMSO, 1993), www.official-documents.gov. uk/document/cm22/2263/2263.pdf (accessed 1 February 2016).

[15] The only other jurisdictions with CCRCs are Scotland and Norway, where the Commissions operate along similar lines, albeit with smaller caseloads.

[16] See www.ccrc.gov.uk/case-statistics (accessed 1 February 2016); CCRC, *Annual Report and Accounts 2014/15*, HC 2310 (CCRC, 2015).

(a) How does the Court of Appeal Determine Whether a Conviction is Unsafe?

According to its statutory framework, the CCRC's main role is to identify and refer convictions that raise a 'real possibility' that they would be quashed if referred for appeal. In other words, it considers whether there is a real possibility that the Court of Appeal will find a conviction unsafe. Section 2 of the Criminal Appeal Act 1968 (as amended by the Criminal Appeal Act 1995) states that an appeal against conviction will be allowed if the Court thinks that the conviction is unsafe and that in any other case, the appeal shall be dismissed. The most clear-cut case of an unsafe conviction is one where there is new evidence available to show that the convicted person did not commit the offence of which he or she was convicted, or at least to raise significant doubt as to guilt. These are known as 'fresh evidence' cases. However, the CCRC often deals with cases that turn on fresh legal argument rather than fresh evidence and, less often, where the safety of the conviction has been undermined by significant procedural irregularities.[17] Clearly, the test of unsafety is more widely protective than a test of innocence. Equally, it has the potential to 'police' the rules of due process, and so to ensure the integrity of trials, much more effectively than a system requiring proof of factual innocence before a conviction can be quashed. Serious procedural irregularities, such as the non-disclosure of significant exculpatory evidence to the defence before a trial, are much more likely to lead to a conviction being reversed in England than they would be in many states in the USA. The unsafety test therefore conforms much more closely to the due process model described many years ago by the American legal scholar, Herbert Packer.[18]

The Court of Appeal's focus on the safety of the conviction, as opposed to innocence, and indeed due process, was summed up in *Hickey*, with explicit reference to 'the integrity of the criminal process':

> This court is not concerned with [the] guilt or innocence of the appellants; but only with the safety of their convictions ... [T]he integrity of the criminal process is the most important consideration for courts which have to hear appeals against conviction. Both the innocent and the guilty are entitled to fair trials. If the trial process is not fair; if it is distorted by deceit or by material breaches of the rules of evidence or procedure, then the liberties of all are threatened.[19]

However, as Lord Bingham CJ stressed in the subsequent case of *R v Criminal Cases Review Commission, ex parte Pearson*, 'lurking doubt' over a defendant's guilt was in itself enough to render a conviction 'unsafe' and therefore unsustainable:

> If on the consideration of all the facts and circumstances of the case before it, the court entertains real doubts about whether the appellant was guilty of the offence of which he has been convicted, the court will consider the conviction unsafe.[20]

---

[17] L Elks, *Righting Miscarriages of Justice: Ten Years of the Criminal Cases Review Commission* (London, JUSTICE, 2008) 31.

[18] H Packer, *The Limits of the Criminal Sanction* (Palo Alto, Stanford University Press, 1968). For an illustration of gross procedural irregularities failing to reverse a verdict in an American capital case, see D Rose, *Violation: Justice, Race and Serial Murder in the Deep South* (London, Harper Press, 2007).

[19] *R v Hickey, Robinson and Molloy*, CA No 96/5131/51, 30 July 1997; quoted in *R v Davis, Rowe and Johnson* [2001] 1 Cr App R 8, [53].

[20] *R v Criminal Cases Review Commission, ex parte Pearson* [2000] 1 Cr App R 141, 146; [1999] 3 All ER 498, 503 (DC).

The contrast with American jurisprudence—under which the US Supreme Court has stated explicitly that factual innocence does not render even a capital conviction and sentence unconstitutional[21]—is marked. According to its narrow, 'black letter' definition of due process, an innocent person may be put to death as long as legal standards have been met.

The English position has been summarised by Stephanie Roberts. The Court of Appeal's use of the term 'unsafe' has two distinct, if often overlapping, meanings: either that a factually innocent person has been wrongly convicted; or that the pre-trial and/or trial process has been irregular, and hence unfair. In the second scenario, the Court of Appeal may quash a conviction following significant procedural irregularity irrespective of factual guilt or innocence.[22] However, some critics have argued that the Court of Appeal is, in practice, reluctant to quash convictions on factual grounds, such as fresh evidence or lurking doubt,[23] and that both the Court and the CCRC care more about procedural irregularities than innocence. This, it is argued, puts those who are factually innocent but received fair process at a grave disadvantage, because the Court is reluctant to revisit the substantive facts of the case which go to the issue of guilt or innocence. This, critics add, is because the Court remains too deferential to the jury's verdict, unduly reverent to the principle of finality, and afraid that there may be a deluge of appeals. These factors are said to 'contribut[e] to the current inadequacy of appellate measures for innocent applicants'.[24] Concerns about the Court of Appeal's deference to jury verdicts were also raised by the RCCJ (whose report ultimately led to the creation of the CCRC),[25] which, having considered pertinent empirical research, concluded that the Court should more readily intervene to set aside factually dubious verdicts.[26]

(b) Appeals and the Innocent

Whatever English Court of Appeal judges may have felt about the guilt or otherwise of the defendants whose convictions they have quashed, they have traditionally kept their opinions to themselves. The Court did not even express regret at the years of wrongful imprisonment endured by the appellants in the Guildford Four case, nor the Birmingham Six and Maguire Seven cases which soon followed in its wake. However, at the end of the Court's 1991 judgment in the second appeals of 'the Tottenham Three', who were wrongly convicted

---

[21] *Herrera v Collins*, 506 US 390 (1993).

[22] S Roberts, 'Unsafe Convictions: Defining and Compensating Miscarriages of Justice' (2003) 66 *Modern Law Review* 441.

[23] Pattenden, above n 8, 77; S Roberts, 'The Royal Commission on Criminal Justice and Factual Innocence: Remedying Wrongful Convictions in the Court of Appeal' (2004) 1 *Justice Journal* 86; K Malleson, *Review of the Appeal Process*, RCCJ Research Study No 17 (London, HMSO, 1993); JUSTICE, *Miscarriages of Justice* (London, JUSTICE, 1989) [4.21]; JR Spencer, 'Criminal Law and Criminal Appeals: The Tail That Wags The Dog' [1982] *Criminal Law Review* 260.

[24] S Roberts and L Weathered, 'Assisting the Factually Innocent: The Contradictions and Compatibility of Innocence Projects and the Criminal Cases Review Commission' (2009) 29 *Oxford Journal of Legal Studies* 43, 55.

[25] RCCJ, above n 14.

[26] See K Malleson, *Review of the Appeal Process*, RCCJ Research Study No 17 (London, HMSO, 1993).

of murdering PC Keith Blakelock during the 1987 riot at Broadwater Farm housing estate in London, Lord Justice Farquharson intimated a shift in attitude:

> In allowing these appeals we wish to express a profound regret that they have suffered as a result of the shortcomings of the criminal process. No system of trials is proof against perjury, but this will be of little comfort to its victims.[27]

However, unequivocal judicial statements that an appellant was factually innocent remain exceedingly rare. Having examined the CCRC's database of Court of Appeal judgments following referrals, I have found only one clear declaration of innocence—relating to Peter Fell, who was convicted in 1984, largely on the basis of his confession, of murdering two women two years earlier.

Fell's second appeal in 2001 followed a lengthy campaign on his behalf, and the broadcast of an investigative TV programme, *Trial and Error*. His conviction was referred by the CCRC on several, relatively technical grounds, including new medical evidence of mental ill-health, particularly indicating Fell's potential suggestibility under interrogation, and material non-disclosure of reasons to doubt the testimony of several key prosecution witnesses. The Court accepted the argument in emphatic terms:

> If the evidence we have heard had been before the jury, would the only reasonable and proper verdict of the jury have been one of guilty? We are clear that the answer to that question must be in the negative, and indeed, the longer we listened to the medical evidence and the longer we reviewed the interviews, the clearer we became that the appellant was entitled to more than a conclusion simply that this verdict is unsafe ... [S]ince our reading of the interviews and the evidence we have heard leads us to the conclusion that the confession was a false one, that can only mean that we believe *he was innocent of these terrible murders*, and he should be entitled to have us say so.[28]

Such candour stands in notable contrast to the terms of the Court's 2009 judgment quashing the conviction of Sean Hodgson for a rape and murder for which he had spent 27 years in prison. On this occasion, the word 'innocence' did not figure. Perhaps it was thought unnecessary, because Hodgson—who like so many, had confessed to crimes he did not commit—had been exonerated by a DNA test conveying an aura of infallibility. The Court of Appeal stated:

> The conviction will be quashed for the simple reason that advances in the science of DNA, long after the end of the trial, have proved a fact which, if it had been known at the time, would, notwithstanding the remaining evidence in the case, have resulted in a quite different investigation and a completely different trial ... The Crown's case at trial was that the man who raped the dead girl was also responsible for killing her. The new DNA evidence has therefore demolished the case for the prosecution.[29]

Perhaps not surprisingly, given widespread confidence in DNA evidence, even without a declaration of innocence, the Secretary of State awarded compensation to Hodgson. Unfortunately, although just under £1 million was awarded in March 2009, it was not paid

---

[27] *R v Silcott, Braithwaite and Raghip*, *The Times*, 9 December 1991. See also D Rose, *A Climate of Fear: Blakelock Murder and the Tottenham Three* (London, Bloomsbury, 1992) 220.

[28] *R v Fell* [2001] EWCA Crim 696 (emphasis added).

[29] *R v Hodgson* [2009] EWCA Crim 490

to Hodgson until July 2011 and he died in October 2012, having suffered from poor emotional and physical health during his time in prison and following his release.

At the opposite end of the spectrum to *Fell* are cases in which serious procedural irregularities, completely irrespective of factual innocence, have prompted the Court of Appeal to quash an 'unsafe' conviction. *R v Mullen*[30] provides a striking illustration. In 1999, Nicholas Mullen, a member of the Provisional IRA, won his appeal against his conviction for conspiracy to cause explosions, for which he had been sentenced to 30 years' imprisonment. Eight years after his trial, the Court of Appeal heard that newly disclosed material showed that the police, MI6, the Security Service, and officials from the Foreign Office and the Home Office had colluded with the authorities in Zimbabwe to procure Mullen's deportation in circumstances which were contrary to both Zimbabwean and international law. This, the Court stated, represented 'a blatant and extremely serious failure to adhere to the rule of law' amounting to a clear abuse of process.[31] The claimant's conviction was accordingly to be regarded as 'unsafe', notwithstanding the fact that there was 'no challenge to the propriety of the outcome of the trial itself'. In this case, what amounted to the illegal abduction of a suspect from abroad was sufficient to quash the conviction of a man who was legally proven guilty as charged.

2. Compensating Injustice: A Brief History of the Present

When the last Labour government came to power in 1997 two separate schemes by which victims of miscarriages of justice might obtain compensation were operating simultaneously. The first was a broad, discretionary and flexible *ex gratia*[32] system available for innocent people who had been imprisoned pending trial or after conviction, and in the latter case, irrespective of the circumstances in which the conviction was later set aside. Indeed, the only criterion for a claim was that someone had suffered hardship.[33] This scheme was modelled on Article 14(6) of the International Covenant on Civil and Political Rights (ICCPR) 1966, which provides:

> When a person has by a final decision been convicted of a criminal offence and when subsequently his conviction has been reversed or he has been pardoned on the ground that a new or newly discovered fact shows conclusively that there has been a miscarriage of justice, the person who has suffered punishment as a result of such conviction shall be compensated according to law, unless it is proved that the non-disclosure of the unknown fact in time is wholly or partly attributable to him.

Just before the ICCPR was ratified by the UK and entered into force in 1976, Home Secretary Roy Jenkins set out the procedure to be adopted for making *ex gratia* payments in recognition of the hardship caused by what he referred to as a 'wrongful conviction'.[34] The original scheme

---

[30] *R v Mullen* [2000] QB 520 (CA).
[31] Ibid 535.
[32] That is, without any admission of legal liability to pay.
[33] For authoritative discussion, see JR Spencer, 'Compensation for Wrongful Conviction' [2010] *Criminal Law Review* 803.
[34] HC Deb, 29 July 1976, cols 328–30.

was put onto a more formal basis in November 1985.[35] The then Home Secretary, Douglas Hurd, announced that compensation would normally be paid on application to anyone who had a spent time in custody and who met one of several triggering criteria. An applicant might have received a Royal Pardon, or had his conviction quashed by the Court of Appeal or the House of Lords following a reference for a subsequent appeal under the Criminal Appeal Act 1968. Alternatively, the applicant would have to show that his period in custody followed a wrongful conviction or charge that resulted from serious irregularities by the police or some other public authority, or that his case was exceptional, in that facts had emerged at trial or on appeal within time that completely exonerated him. In relation to this last criterion, the Home Secretary stressed that he would not pay compensation 'simply because … the prosecution was unable to sustain the burden of proof beyond a reasonable doubt in relation to the specific charge that was brought'—in other words, because the court had merely found the defendant was not guilty.[36]

In April 2006, the government abolished the *ex gratia* scheme, on the grounds that its continued existence was 'confusing and anomalous' given that there was a statutory route in place.[37] This decision was influenced by the cost of the scheme (over £2 million a year) in light of the minimal benefits accruing to just five to ten applicants annually.[38] The scheme was dismantled without notice or consultation, attracting considerable criticism from appeal lawyers and legal academics.[39] Its abolition was challenged in a judicial review by three people who had been in the process of preparing compensation applications. The Divisional Court ruled that the Home Secretary had not acted unfairly or in breach of applicants' legitimate expectations,[40] a decision upheld by the Court of Appeal.[41]

The second scheme, a statutory programme established under the Criminal Justice Act 1988, was also designed to meet the UK's obligations under Article 14(6), as is clear from section 133(1) of the 1988 Act which gives the Secretary of State the discretion to pay compensation to a wrongly convicted person when

> his conviction has been reversed or he has been pardoned on the ground that a new or newly discovered fact *shows beyond reasonable doubt* that there has been a miscarriage of justice … unless the non-disclosure of the unknown fact was wholly or partly attributable to the person convicted. (emphasis added)

Those whose convictions have been quashed on an out-of-time appeal or who have been granted a pardon may apply to the Ministry of Justice (formerly the Home Office), which will consider their claim in light of the evidence contained in the Court of Appeal judgment, the perfected grounds of appeal, and the form submitted by the appellant in applying for leave to appeal. Ordinarily, applicants must apply within two years of their conviction being

---

[35] HC Deb, 29 November 1985, cols 689–90.

[36] HC Deb, 29 November 1985, cols 691–92.

[37] S Lipscombe and J Beard, *Miscarriages of Justice: Compensation Schemes*, SN/HA/2131 (House of Commons Library, 20 June 2014) 3.

[38] Ibid.

[39] Campbell Malone, who specialises in representing the wrongfully convicted described the consequences for many of his clients as 'not just damaging but fatal', while Professor John Spencer QC of Cambridge University, called the abolition of the ex gratia scheme 'monstrous'. See J Robins, 'Righting New Labour's Wrong to Victims of Miscarriages of Justice', *The Guardian*, 8 July 2011.

[40] *R v Home Secretary, ex parte Niazi* [2007] EWHC 1495 (Admin).

[41] *R v Home Secretary, ex parte Niazi* [2008] EWCA Civ 755.

quashed or pardon granted. An applicant *may* qualify if his conviction has been quashed by the Court even if a retrial is ordered, as long as the appellant is acquitted of all offences at the retrial.[42] The decision as to whether to award compensation is made by the Secretary of State, although such ministerial determinations (like any other administrative act) are open to challenge by way of judicial review.

If the Secretary of State decides to award compensation, the quantum is determined by an independent assessor, currently Dame Janet Smith, a former Lady Justice of Appeal.[43] Section 133A of the 1988 Act sets out the steps the assessor must follow. She must have regard in particular to the seriousness of the offence concerned and the severity of the punishment imposed as a result of the conviction, and the conduct of the investigation and prosecution. Reductions in the size of the award can be made for any conduct of the applicant that contributed to the conviction, for his criminal record and, most controversially, pursuant to a 2007 House of Lords ruling, for 'saved living expenses' that the applicant would have incurred had he not been incarcerated—what the news media have described as 'deductions for board and lodgings'.[44]

The scheme is supposed to compensate only those who can prove that they have suffered a miscarriage of justice and that the system failed to protect them. In other words, if the system corrects an initial trial error in a timely fashion, the wrongly convicted defendant will not be eligible for compensation. This rules out those who win their first, 'in time' appeal; in contrast to the position in some other European jurisdictions,[45] including Germany, Greece, Italy and the Netherlands.[46] It is also the case that the previous non-disclosure of the new fact or evidence that leads to the quashing of the conviction must not have been attributable to the convicted person, since that would pre-empt the inference of *systemic* failure. The total amount of compensation payable will not exceed £1 million, a sum payable only in cases where the applicant had been imprisoned for at least ten years when the conviction was reversed. For those given shorter sentences, the maximum is £500,000.

(a) Compensation Awards Before and After Abolition of the *Ex Gratia* Scheme

The Ministry of Justice holds data on compensation claims and their outcomes for all CCRC referrals of convictions for serious offences[47] quashed by the Court of Appeal since 2000.

---

[42] Experienced lawyers, such as Alex Bailin QC, believe that the Phillips test will make it much less likely that compensation will be awarded following a retrial, as in the case of *Barry George*, discussed below. See text to n 67.

[43] Her two predecessors were Sir David Calcutt QC and Lord Brennan of Bibury QC.

[44] *R (O'Brien) v Independent Assessor* [2007] 2 AC 312, [2007] UKHL 10, [23].

[45] The old discretionary scheme was capable of covering cases where the applicant's conviction was quashed on an appeal brought within time. This is still the case in France and Germany: see Spencer, above n 33.

[46] For detailed information on compensation schemes across Europe, see Fair Trials International, Pre-Trial Detention Comparative Research, Appendix 2, ec.europa.eu/justice/newsroom/criminal/opinion/files/110510/appendix_2_-_comparative_research_en.pdf (accessed 1 February 2016).

[47] Defined to include murder, sexual offences, robbery, offences of violence more serious than assault occasioning actual bodily harm, kidnap and conspiracy to murder, but excluding other conspiracy offences and drug offences.

This excluded a few anonymised cases,[48] cases where the appeal outcome was unknown, and the Northern Ireland cases, which are dealt with by the Northern Ireland Court of Appeal. Out of a total of 111 cases in this sample, 68 involved compensation claims but 43 did not. Forty of the 68 claims were lodged prior to April 2006, when the *ex gratia* scheme was withdrawn. Their success rate was high: there were only five refusals. Of these 35 successful applications, just two were paid under the *ex gratia* provisions, whilst the remaining 33 were statutory awards under the 1988 Act. Although it is therefore evident that *ex gratia* payments were already comparatively rare, it became significantly more difficult to obtain compensation under the 1988 Act after the *ex gratia* scheme was abolished. Of the 28 applicants who applied for compensation after April 2006, 22 were refused—a refusal rate of 79 per cent, compared to just 13 per cent prior to this watershed.[49]

It is not immediately apparent why awards under the 1988 Act became so much harder to obtain after the abolition of the parallel but separate *ex gratia* scheme. One explanation may be straightforwardly political: that it was part-and-parcel of the government's broader policy programme of 'getting tough' with offenders, even those whose convictions had been deemed unsafe, and an expression of Prime Minister Tony Blair's oft-stated desire to 'rebalance' the criminal justice system in ways that gave less weight to defendants' rights.[50] Another driver might have been the imperative of paring back public sector spending over the past few years of fiscal crisis. However, a further significant influence might well have been an evolving strand of jurisprudence, developed in the cases of *Mullen* and *Allen (née Harris)*, which redefined the meaning of 'miscarriage of justice' in English law. Indeed, abolition of the *ex gratia* scheme in 2006 was sufficiently contemporaneous with the decision in *Allen* in 2008 to imply a direct impact on compensation policy. It is to this evolving jurisprudence that we now turn.

(b) Two-Tier Exoneration: Compensation and the UK Supreme Court

As we have seen, the Court of Appeal's traditional reluctance to express a view as to whether a defendant might be factually guilty or innocent at the point of quashing his conviction has begun to soften somewhat in recent years. A similar process has been at work when the courts have reviewed decisions by the Home Secretary not to award compensation to people whose convictions have been quashed.

Difficult cases always test the law, and there have been few compensation cases more challenging than that of Nicholas Mullen, the former IRA man previously mentioned, whose conviction for conspiracy to cause explosions was quashed after evidence emerged that he had been unlawfully abducted from Zimbabwe. Following his release, Mullen applied for

---

[48] A handful of cases were anonymised to protect the identity of the victims if, for example, the perpetrator had the same name.

[49] The awards of the six who were granted compensation after April 2006 ranged from £170,000 to £1.2 million. Their mean average was £610,000. Awards prior to the abolition of the *ex gratia* scheme ranged from £1,562,501 to £1,939,951.16, with a mean average of £484,000.

[50] Home Office, *Justice for All*, Cm 5563 (London, TSO, 2002) [0.3]; J Jackson 'Justice for All: Putting Victims at the Heart of the Criminal Justice System?' (2003) 30 *Journal of Law and Society* 309.

compensation under the 1988 Act. When this was refused, he applied for judicial review of that decision.

The Divisional Court found against him, saying that the Home Secretary's decision had been right because the term 'miscarriage of justice' ought to be interpreted as applying only to those who could prove themselves innocent.[51] Mullen appealed, and this time won, the Court of Appeal holding that proof of innocence is not after all a precondition of entitlement to compensation. In the words of Lord Justice Schiemann: 'Our criminal law system does not provide for proof of innocence.'[52] However, this victory was temporary and short-lived. The House of Lords reversed the Court of Appeal decision because, although Mullen's prosecution had been unlawful, the trial itself had not exhibited any defects and, their Lordships pointed out, Mullen had not contested his factual guilt on appeal.[53]

The Lords were divided in their analysis. Lord Steyn wanted to confine compensation payable under the 1988 Act to cases of provable innocence, while Lord Bingham preferred a much wider interpretation, which would have allowed compensation to anyone who 'guilty or not, should certainly not have been convicted'.[54] In making subsequent decisions about compensation, the Secretary of State followed Lord Bingham, granting eligibility on a reasonably generous definition, until the next case in the sequence changed the law again in 2008.

Lorraine Allen (née Harris) was convicted in 2000 of the manslaughter of her four-month-old son, Patrick. She continued to protest her innocence and a high-profile campaign for her release ensued, culminating in a referral back to the Court Appeal (which was heard in 2005 after Allen had already served her three-year prison sentence). This was one of a batch of CCRC referrals involving contested expert evidence of 'shaken baby syndrome'. Allen's conviction was quashed in the light of new evidence,[55] but she was still denied compensation because medical experts gave conflicting opinions on the possible causes of her son's injuries. She sought judicial review of that decision, but was unsuccessful before the High Court.[56] On further appeal against that refusal, the Court of Appeal identified the following three issues for decision:

(i)   the proper meaning of s 133 of the Criminal Justice Act 1988 and of the expression 'miscarriage of justice' contained in it; in particular which of the two interpretations advanced respectively by Lord Bingham of Cornhill and Lord Steyn in *Mullen* … is correct;

(ii)   whether, if Lord Bingham's construction be correct, this appellant was treated by the [Court of Appeal] as someone against whom there was, on the evidence as now understood, no basis on which a jury could properly convict, and should for that reason be considered to be a person who has suffered a miscarriage of justice;

(iii) whether, even if this is not so, the presumption of innocence, enshrined in Art 6(2) of the European Convention on Human Rights (ECHR) has the effect that the appellant, having had her conviction quashed, is entitled to be treated as having had her innocence established and therefore *ipso facto* to have suffered a miscarriage of justice.[57]

---

[51] *R (Mullen) v Secretary of State for the Home Department* [2002] 1 WLR 1857, [2002] EWHC 230 (Admin).
[52] *R (Mullen) v Secretary of State for the Home Department* [2003] QB 993, [2002] EWCA Civ 1882, [28].
[53] *R (Mullen) v Secretary of State for the Home Department* [2005] 1 AC 1, [2004] UKHL 18.
[54] Ibid [9].
[55] *R v Harris; R v Rock; R v Cherry; R v Faulder* [2006] 1 Cr App R 5, [2005] EWCA Crim 1980.
[56] *R (Harris) v Secretary of State for the Home Department* [2007] EWHC 3218 (Admin).
[57] *R (Allen, formerly Harris) v Secretary of State for Justice* [2009] 1 Cr App R 2, [2008] EWCA Civ 808, [1].

The Court of Appeal unanimously rejected Allen's claim to have suffered a miscarriage of justice within the meaning of section 133, and proclaimed Lord Steyn's definition in *Mullen* to be definitive. The Article 6(2) presumption of innocence argument was likewise rebuffed. Subsequent to this decision, the Secretary of State for Justice (to whom responsibility for compensation awards passed in 2010) adopted Lord Steyn's definition for the purpose of determining compensation claims, which appears to have choked off the flow of successful applicants.

It was whilst Lord Steyn's definition of 'miscarriage of justice' was in the ascendency that Andrew Adams' compensation claim was denied. Adams' appeal against this refusal was pursued all the way up to the recently established UK Supreme Court, which in 2009 superseded the House of Lords as the UK's final court of appeal in most legal matters (including all criminal appeals arising from England, Wales and Northern Ireland, and Scottish appeals with a human rights dimension). The Supreme Court handed down judgment in the cases of Adams, Eamonn MacDermott and Raymond McCartney in 2011.[58] All three had originally been convicted of involvement in three murders and, in the latter two cases, membership of a proscribed organisation, the IRA. The Secretary of State had rejected their compensation claims on the basis that these applicants had failed to satisfy the 1988 Act's requirement of proving, beyond a reasonable doubt, that they were victims of a miscarriage of justice.

The nine-judge panel reviewed various sources and precedents, including the House of Lords' judgment in *Mullen* and parliamentary statements during the passage of section 133. None of them, however, was considered decisive. In developing a new approach, Lord Phillips PSC revisited the four categories of potential miscarriage of justice outlined by Dyson LJ at the Court of Appeal level in *Adams*, which Lord Phillips regarded as 'a useful framework for discussion':

(1) Where the fresh evidence shows clearly that the defendant is innocent of the crime of which he has been convicted.
(2) Where the fresh evidence is such that, had it been available at the time of the trial, no reasonable jury could properly have convicted the defendant.
(3) Where the fresh evidence renders the conviction unsafe in that, had it been available at the time of the trial, a reasonable jury might or might not have convicted the defendant.
(4) Where something has gone seriously wrong in the investigation of the offence or the conduct of the trial, resulting in the conviction of someone who should not have been convicted.[59]

Section 133 evidently had two complementary objectives: on the one hand, to provide compensation to those convicted and punished for crimes they did not commit; whilst on the other, still denying compensation to those who have been convicted and punished for a crime they *did* commit. The issue now, the Supreme Court Justices agreed, was how to interpret section 133 in a way that balanced those two objectives, and how that balance should in practice be achieved.[60]

A minority of four Justices supported the most restrictive of Dyson LJ's four categories, maintaining that compensation should be awarded only to those who could prove their

---

[58] *R (Adams) v Secretary of State for Justice* [2012] 1 AC 48, [2011] UKSC 18.
[59] Ibid [9].
[60] Ibid [37].

factual innocence. Had they been joined by a single swing-voter, had just one other Justice defected from the majority, compensation would henceforth have been available only for a tiny minority of applicants, presumably those who could provide compelling DNA evidence or something equally decisive. However, the five-member majority decided that limiting compensation claims to category 1 would be too restrictive. Clear evidence of innocence was not necessary to compensate those whose convictions had been overturned. As Lord Phillips observed, limiting the scope of section 133 to category 1 cases would, '[d]eprive some defendants who are in fact innocent and who succeed in having their convictions quashed on the grounds of fresh evidence from obtaining compensation'. It would 'exclude from entitlement to compensation those who no longer seem likely to be guilty, but whose innocence is not established beyond reasonable doubt'. His Lordship thought this 'a heavy price to pay for ensuring that no guilty person is ever the recipient of compensation'.[61] But by the same token, categories 3 and 4 were regarded as too broad, in potentially compensating factually guilty people who had not been denied fair and lawful process—those who, as the news media sometimes put it, 'got off on a technicality'.

Rather than simply opting for category 2 by process of elimination, the majority in *Adams* formulated its own, 'more robust' test to demarcate eligibility for compensation under section 133:

> A new fact will show that a miscarriage of justice has occurred when it so undermines the evidence against the defendant that no conviction could possibly be based upon it.[62]

Lord Phillips acknowledged that this test would not guarantee that all those who are entitled to compensation are in fact innocent. However, it would, in his view, ensure that innocent defendants convicted on evidence that was subsequently discredited would not be precluded from obtaining compensation because they could not prove their innocence beyond reasonable doubt.

If the *Allen* judgment partly explains why approvals onto the compensation scheme suddenly became more restrictive, the UK Supreme Court's judgment in *Adams* now supersedes *Allen* in establishing the legal framework for determining compensation claims. Lord Phillips' test is less restrictive than Dyson LJ's category 1, but does not extend much beyond Lord Steyn's position in *Mullen*. In practice, the Phillips test is likely to restrict successful compensation claims to those cases in which convictions are quashed on the basis of truly compelling new evidence of innocence, such as exculpatory DNA profiling evidence, a reliable third-party confession to the crime, or plausible admissions of perjury by key prosecution witnesses. Yet conventional wisdom amongst experienced criminal lawyers suggests that, 'it's random in which cases you would be able to establish your innocence'.[63] As to whether the Court of Appeal has the power to pronounce someone innocent, the Supreme Court judges were divided. Lord Phillips maintained that it did not, but Lord Judge disagreed.

---

[61] Ibid [50].
[62] Ibid [55]. Lord Brown, dissenting [281], regretted that the Court had not settled on category 1: 'Naturally I recognise that the application of the innocence test will exclude from compensation a few who are in fact innocent. ... That, however, seems to me preferable to compensating a considerable number ... who are guilty. ... Why should the state not have a scheme which compensates only the comparatively few who plainly can demonstrate their innocence ... rather than a larger number who may or may not be innocent?'
[63] Interview with Alex Bailin QC.

Turning to the instant applications, all nine judges were agreed that Adams fell within category 3, and that his appeal must therefore be dismissed. MacDermott and McCartney, on the other hand, were found, by a 5:4 majority, to fall within the scope of section 133. Moreover, the prosecution case had been so damaged by further revelations during the appeal proceedings that there was no prospect of a re-trial. In their cases, at least, failings of integrity in the pre-trial process were such that the court sought to make good the harms done by a wrongful conviction.

The appellants' lawyers were not surprised by this outcome on the facts on the individual appeals. The more enduring issue, however, is whether the bar was set at the right height. According to Adams' solicitor, Daniel Machover, the Phillips test is, 'an attack on the presumption of innocence'. Evidence that a person was probably factually innocent, he argues, would be considered strong enough to permit compensation to be paid only in a very few cases. Most successful appellants, whose convictions were merely deemed, as the law requires, 'unsafe', would belong in a second-class, lower tier which was undeserving of compensation.[64] Lord Phillips had stated that he did not think the Court of Appeal should pronounce on factual guilt or innocence as it had done, for example, in *Fell*. But the inevitable consequence of his own judgment in *Adams* was that, from then on, this is exactly what would happen in judicial reviews of compensation decisions by the Secretary of State.

In the wake of the *Adams* precedent, lower courts were bound by the Phillips test. In October 2012, the High Court in judicial review proceedings reconsidered five refusals of compensation, dismissing all but one of the appeals.[65] The unsuccessful applicants included Barry George, whose conviction for murdering the television presenter Jill Dando was overturned after he had spent eight years in prison, mainly because the Court of Appeal decided that potentially misleading expert evidence of a single microscopic particle of gunpowder residue had been presented to the jury at trial.[66] A retrial was ordered, at which the jury unanimously acquitted. However, the very fact that the Court of Appeal had decided that there remained sufficient prosecution evidence for a retrial was fatal to George's application for compensation under the Phillips test. The High Court's rulings were subsequently affirmed by the Court of Appeal (Civil Division),[67] though the Court of Appeal decried any attempt to gloss the Phillips test propounded by the *Adams* majority.

Meanwhile, in November 2012, Lorraine Allen challenged her refusal of compensation before the European Court of Human Rights (ECtHR) in Strasbourg. It was common ground that Allen's case fell within Dyson LJ's category 3. Issue was joined on the scope of compensation. Allen's legal team argued that category 3 cases should be awarded compensation by implication of ECHR Article 6(2)'s presumption of innocence—an argument previously considered, and rejected, by the UK Supreme Court in *Adams*.[68] Her solicitor nicely summed up the central contention: 'It was unclear why or how Patrick died.

---

[64] Interview with Daniel Machover of Hickman & Rose solicitors.
[65] *R (Ali) v Secretary of State for Justice* [2013] 1 WLR 3536, [2013] EWHC 72 (Admin).
[66] *R v George (Barry)* [2007] EWCA Crim 2722.
[67] *R (Ali) v Secretary of State for Justice* [2014] 1 WLR 3202, [2014] EWCA Civ 194.
[68] Alex Bailin QC informed me that there are various other 'presumption of innocence' cases wending their way through the ECHR process.

A question mark always remained over her innocence ... [Q]uashing the conviction meant she shouldn't have to prove it.'[69]

The ECtHR ruled that Article 6(2) does not guarantee to anyone acquitted of a criminal offence 'a right to compensation for miscarriage of justice'.[70] Disappointed, Allen's legal team called on the UK government to reinstate the old discretionary scheme, representing a 'moral approach to compensation'. The government responded 'that the European Court of Human Rights agreed with the judgment of domestic courts'.[71] However, even if the ECtHR judgment had been different, recent governments are clearly disinclined to be more generous with compensation. The Anti-Social Behaviour, Crime and Policing Act 2014 amended section 133 of the 1988 Act so that, after 13 March 2014, applicants for compensation for miscarriage of justice must demonstrate that a 'new or newly discovered fact shows beyond reasonable doubt that the person did not commit the offence'.[72]

The clear implication is that even those wrongly convicted as a consequence of gross police or prosecutorial misconduct will not be paid a penny unless they can also show themselves 'clearly innocent'. In many cases, this will be factually or evidentially impossible. Many years, even decades, will have elapsed since the crime, witnesses may be dead, and records destroyed. There are numerous cases where factual innocence simply cannot be proven, even though every aspect of the case made at trial by the prosecution has collapsed. It is difficult to see how the reformed section 133 is compatible with the UK's legal obligations under the ICCPR.

(c) The Growing Scope and Insidious Character of Two-Tier Exoneration

Although the UK Supreme Court's decision in *Adams* ostensibly addressed the scope of compensation, the de facto implication of the Phillips test was the creation of a two-tier system of acquittals following successful appeals against conviction. An early indication of this was the case of Sam Hallam, whose seven-year-old conviction for murder was quashed by the Court of Appeal after a CCRC referral in May 2012.[73]

There were sound reasons for believing that Hallam was factually innocent. There was no forensic or CCTV evidence that linked him to the street gang killing of which he had been convicted, and even at trial, the evidence of the two eye-witnesses who identified him as having been at the scene was deeply flawed. One witness had been given Hallam's name by the other, and she in turn admitted under cross-examination that she had been 'looking for someone to blame' for the victim's death when she and a friend happened to come across Hallam in the street. Her earliest statements claimed that the young man who dealt the fatal blow was black; Hallam is white. At another interview this witness spoke of the assailant as having blond hair, whereas Hallam's hair is brown.

---

[69] S Mesure, 'Jailed for a crime you didn't commit: Landmark case could be costly for UK' *The Independent*, 11 November 2012.

[70] *Allen v United Kingdom*, App No 25424/09, Grand Chamber Judgment, 12 July 2013; *The Times*, 30 July 2013.

[71] *BBC News*, 12 July 2013, www.bbc.co.uk/news/uk-england-derbyshire-23282695 (accessed 1 February 2016).

[72] Anti-social Behaviour, Crime and Policing Act 2014, s 175, inserting s 133(1ZA).

[73] *R v Hallam* [2012] EWCA Crim 1158.

This conviction's manifest lack of safety became clearer after a meticulous investigation carried out by Thames Valley police at the behest of the CCRC. Officers exposed failures by the Metropolitan police and Crown Prosecution Service to disclose significant exculpatory evidence, including the identify of an alternative, arguably more plausible, suspect who had been arrested in possession of what may have been the murder weapon; a mobile phone belonging to Hallam with timed and dated photographs in its memory which lent support to his alibi, which the Crown had claimed was false and therefore evidence of guilt; messages to the police incident room identifying an entirely different person called Sam as the killer; and major discrepancies between the evidence of the main identification witness and other, easily verifiable facts.

In presenting Hallam's appeal, his barrister, Henry Blaxland QC, had at least one eye on a future compensation claim. Counsel specifically had in mind Lord Judge's observations in *Adams*, that the Court of Appeal is entitled to state its opinion that an appellant is innocent and that the Secretary of State should thereafter pay the closest possible attention to the terms of the judgment.[74] Hence, far from confining itself to addressing whether the conviction was unsafe, Blaxland's skeleton argument stated:

> There is a body of evidence to lead to the firm conclusion that, as the appellant said from the moment that he was first arrested, he was not present at the scene of the crime and is innocent of the offences of which he was convicted.[75]

There was, of course, no need to make such a submission in order to succeed with an appeal against conviction. There were ample evidential grounds to enable the Court of Appeal to conclude that Hallam's conviction was unsafe and must be quashed. However, believing in his client's innocence and perturbed by the failure of the lower courts to recognise this at his trial and first appeal, Henry Blaxland QC wanted the Court not only to quash the conviction, but also to make it plain where the trial judge and the original Court of Appeal had gone wrong. He was inviting the Court to go as far as it could towards making a declaration of innocence.[76]

On this occasion, the Court of Appeal declined to be drawn. Rather crossly, as it seemed to those present (including me), Hallett LJ interrupted Blaxland during his oral argument, interjecting: 'This is not a court of compensation.'[77] Her ladyship also opened the way to a possible rejection of Hallam's eventual claim, by suggesting that Hallam's trial defence had been at fault for not conducting their own examination of his mobile phone, and advising him not to comment during his police interviews. Four years on, in the autumn of 2014, this rejection came. Hallam, it was decided, was not to be granted compensation for his time in prison and for the significant impact of his wrongful conviction on him and his family.[78] This decision came just weeks after Victor Nealon's request for compensation was

---

[74] Lord Judge stated: 'There are … occasions when a new or newly discovered fact may well demonstrate the factual innocence of the appellant. And if it does, the judgment of the court may say so … Although the conviction is quashed not on the ground that the defendant is "innocent", but because his conviction is "unsafe", the terms of the judgment should conscientiously reflect the true reasons for its decision that the conviction should indeed be quashed as "unsafe"': *R (Adams) v Secretary of State for Justice* [2012] 1 AC 48, [2011] UKSC 18, [251]–[252].

[75] *R v Hallam*, Court of Appeal, 2011 04293-C5, perfected grounds of appeal and skeleton argument.

[76] Interview with Henry Blaxland QC.

[77] Lady Hallett appeared unaware of *Adams*. Blaxland subsequently provided the Court with a reference, but her judgment suggests that Lady Hallett remained unpersuaded.

[78] Interview with Paul May, Campaigner on the Hallam legal team.

refused. Nealon had served 17 years in prison for attempted rape when his conviction was quashed by the Court of Appeal in December 2013, following a referral by the CCRC.[79] Both applicants then sought judicial review of the Secretary of State's refusal in conjoined proceedings,[80] but the High Court was unimpressed.[81] In *Nealon*, DNA evidence pointed to another man as the perpetrator, leading the Court of Appeal to conclude that 'it was a real possibility that the "unknown male"—and not the appellant—was the attacker'.[82] However, without proof of innocence 'beyond reasonable doubt', *Nealon*, as with most cases now,[83] falls under the category of second-class acquittals.

3. The Institutional Epistemology of Factual Innocence

Consideration of the *Hallam* and *Nealon* cases leads directly to a broader question of profound significance for the integrity of criminal proceedings: irrespective of its desirability or legal permissibility, is the Court of Appeal *capable* of reliably pronouncing on an appellant's factual innocence? In short, can either the Phillips test or the amended section 133 actually work in practice? Is the Court's new innocence discourse, with its implicit shift away from an unvarnished concept of 'safety' as the determining legal concept, reasonable and just? Or does it pose a fundamental challenge to the integrity of the appeals process?

The professionals who deal with alleged miscarriages of justice on a daily basis—the staff of the CCRC—are not convinced. Case reviewers are not mind-readers: they cannot 'tell' by some mysterious, psychological process whether a convict who protests his innocence is being truthful or not. They have also learnt from experience that, in almost all forensic settings, evidence will be partial and incomplete. It might sometimes be possible to make a confident determination of factual innocence or guilt. But much more commonly, in the words of one CCRC investigator, 'it's not about innocence or guilt, it's about safety'. This interviewee added: '[In] the cases that we refer ... the spectrum could be technicality to genuine innocence, and we'll never know whether anyone is genuinely innocent'. Another CCRC employee stated:

> It's not very often that I think, 'I feel this person is innocent', because I don't really believe in this. You hear it a lot from the campaign groups, this kind of 'look' em in the eye test', and it has no place for the Commission in my view. Because how can we possibly know whether this person's innocent or not? You have to go on the evidence and what you have, and it'll be a sad day when we start to do that kind of more campaign group type test.[84]

---

[79] *R v Nealon* [2014] EWCA Crim 574.

[80] J Robins, 'Victor Nealon: MoJ to be challenged over refusal to pay compensation for 17 years in jail', *The Justice Gap*, thejusticegap.com/2014/09/victor-nealon-moj-challenged-refusal-pay-compensation-17-years-jail/ (accessed 1 February 2016).

[81] *R (Nealon); R (Hallam) v Secretary of State for Justice* [2015] EWHC 1565 (Admin) (further appeal pending).

[82] *R v Nealon* [2014] EWCA Crim 574, [35].

[83] Also see *R (Clark) v Secretary of State for Justice* [2015] EWHC 2383 (Admin); *R (Ali) v Secretary of State for Justice* [2014] 1 WLR 3202, [2014] EWCA Civ 194.

[84] Interviews with CCRC staff.

Peter Duff, who served on the Scottish Commission for eight years, is similarly sceptical of his own ability to know, with certainty, just who is innocent:

> In practice, I cannot remember the Commission referring a case where I was absolutely certain that the applicant was factually innocent; quite simply, it was never possible to be sure about precisely what had happened ... In all such cases, however, I was convinced there had been a 'miscarriage of justice' in legal terms.[85]

It should be stressed that, in almost all cases—Sam Hallam's, as a conspicuous example— these appropriately cautious CCRC staffers will have a far broader knowledge of a case's full details and context than the Court of Appeal. Unlike appellate judges, CCRC case workers will have dealt with an application over the course of many months, or even years. From the outset, they will have read and examined in meticulous detail all the documents pertaining to the original investigation, trial and first appeal, and considered any subsequent developments. Potential problems with the application will have been explored thoroughly. The Case Review Managers in both *Hallam* and *Adams* were not only trained lawyers, but also tenacious and scrupulous investigators who invested years in these two cases. Furthermore, the statutory RPT means that, in practice, the CCRC is unlikely to refer a case on the basis of relatively minor difficulties with the trial evidence, if the file also includes overwhelming evidence of guilt. A so-called 'technicality', such as the non-disclosure of a significant piece of exculpatory evidence, could render a conviction unsafe in the judgement of the Court of Appeal. But although such 'technicalities' may demonstrate official negligence or even deliberate suppression of evidence, it is often impossible to tell whether they also imply factual innocence.

Yet there is a still more fundamental problem with the courts' emerging tendency to endorse Lord Phillips' two-tier approach. CCRC referrals, the formal 'Statement of Reasons' by which referrals are justified, and eventual Court of Appeal decisions themselves, are all pre-eminent examples of the socio-legal process known as 'case construction'—the selection of facts and arguments from among many possibilities in order to advance a particular factual narrative.[86] By definition, they are not a complete statement of every known fact. One construction may point strongly towards factual innocence. Another, though still sufficient to render a case unsafe, may suggest the appellant only meets the standard set down in Dyson LJ's category 3. Which version the Court of Appeal is asked to consider may ultimately depend on nothing more than the suspicion of an individual lawyer that certain facts are more likely than others to persuade the Court. One barrister may decide to stress an important procedural irregularity; another, new exculpatory evidence.

For it needs to be appreciated that the Court is not likely to deliberate on the entire case construction presented by the CCRC. Although it will receive and read ahead of the hearing the CCRC's Statement of Reasons, the appellant's perfected grounds of appeal and the Crown's grounds of opposition, the appeal hearing itself, during or after which the Court decides the fate of the appellant, will not consider all of that evidence and argument

---

[85] P Duff, 'Straddling Two Worlds: Reflections of a Retired Criminal Cases Review Commissioner' (2009) 72 *Modern Law Review* 721.

[86] On the concept and processes of case construction, see M McConville, A Sanders and R Leng, *The Case for the Prosecution* (London, Routledge, 1991). Also see Dixon's discussion of confession evidence in Chapter 3 of this volume.

in detail, and some not at all. The appellant's barrister acts as a filter, and while a Statement of Reasons may advance numerous probative points, when it comes to the actual
appeal, counsel will advance only those which she or he thinks carry the strongest chance
of success—what judges often term the appellant's 'best points'. Moreover, the Court may
well indicate after hearing just one or two of the grounds which counsel does argue that it
has now heard enough to determine that the conviction is unsafe. Those points that remain
unargued may have been very powerful, but will get little attention in court.

In *Hallam*, this 'editing' of possible grounds took place at every stage. It was exacerbated
by the Crown's decision to concede the appeal part-heard. At this point, what mattered
most to Sam Hallam—freedom—became inevitable. Given this turn of events, Hallet LJ
and her judicial colleagues would not have been inclined to examine further grounds of
appeal too closely; even though these aspects of the case might well have persuaded them
of Hallam's factual innocence.

In light of these current arrangements, any attempt by the Court of Appeal or courts
in compensation proceedings to assess factual innocence must be irredeemably flawed.
Analysis of the *Adams* case supports this proposition. To the Supreme Court, his appeal
fitted the definition of Dyson's category 3: one where the fresh evidence might or might
not have led the trial jury to reach a different verdict. However, there was other, persuasive
evidence available at the time of his second appeal, which had been carefully examined
by investigative journalists, by the solicitor who assisted Adams in his application to the
CCRC, and then by the CCRC Case Review Manager and his investigations advisor who
were responsible for investigating the case, all of whom made visits to the scene of the
crime and explored carefully the sustainability of the prosecution's case. The evidence they
gathered and their observations at the scene suggested Adams might well have been factually innocent. They found, for example, that it would have been physically impossible
for him to have driven to the scene of the murder from a place some miles distant where,
earlier on the night in question, he had been stopped by police for a motoring offence. In
order to reach the house where the victim was murdered, an event which could, like the
police stop, be timed precisely, he would have had to have driven at an average speed of
almost 100 miles per hour through a dense urban district. There happened to be several
road works en route at the time. This and other matters were never even raised before the
Court of Appeal, and apparently did not influence its judgment. Had the full case circumstances been considered, the outcome of Adams' compensation claim might have been
different.

(a) The CCRC's Critics

The rising tide of interest in factual guilt or innocence is not confined to the judiciary.
Unfortunately, the so-called 'innocence movement', itself an import from the very different legal environment obtaining in the US (described by Weisselberg in Chapter 15),
is also now fostering innocence-talk, in the academy, through the media, and even, perhaps, in the courts. In an effort to champion the cause of defendants who are factually innocent, but who have found it impossible to obtain redress through the existing
appeals system, proponents of this view have sponsored an unfortunate and unhelpful division of wrongful convictions into cases of 'actual' and 'legal' innocence. Critics
regard the RPT as excessively restrictive and the CCRC, as presently constituted, 'not fit

for purpose'.[87] As a result of these failings, they assert, large numbers of innocent people are languishing in prison without hope. In their view, the way to remedy the plight of the wrongly convicted is to privilege factual innocence above all else when miscarriages of justice are reviewed, even in cases where no new evidence is available.[88] Yet this discourse is fraught with peril.

Some campaigners and academic commentators argue that Britain should emulate the approach taken by America's innocence projects. The CCRC has failed, in their eyes, because it has not exonerated people campaigners believe to be innocent,[89] including Jeremy Bamber, serving a whole life tariff for murdering five members of his family in 1988, and Susan May, released on licence for killing her aunt in 2005 but whose conviction for murder still stood when she died in 2013.[90] In fact, the CCRC investigated both of these cases and referred them back to the Court of Appeal, but the Court upheld their convictions. Yet according to the journalist, Bob Woffinden, in these and other 'meritorious cases … the injustice remains unaddressed'.[91]

It is further argued that the CCRC, constrained as it is by the RPT, fails to refer cases of the potentially innocent if they are believed to conflict with the interests of the legal system. Because it refers cases only on the basis of so-called 'legal innocence', which to its critics is a debased category, it is accused of not caring about factual innocence.[92] Innocence Projects UK (INUK), a voluntary, non-statutory body that was until September 2014 an umbrella organisation for all the University Innocence Projects in the UK,[93] claims that INUK meets the 1994 Royal Commission's recommendation for a new body to review miscarriages of justice more faithfully than the CCRC because INUK's exclusive concern is with claims of factual innocence, as opposed to allegations of 'technical' miscarriages of justice. But this position traduces three crucial facts. First, 'unsafe' convictions represent a much broader category than convictions of the provably factually innocent. Secondly, unsafe convictions inevitably include convictions of the factually innocent: it is not as if such persons are somehow prevented from winning their appeals by the criteria of 'legal innocence' or 'unsafe conviction'. Finally, factual innocence is remarkably difficult to prove. If followed to its logical, legal conclusion and enshrined in a new appeals regime, these arguments would inevitably lead to a drastic reduction in the number of successful appeals, as well as a system of first- and second-class referrals.

These points are not new. They were made forcefully during the debates which led to the establishment of the CCRC. Then, the idea that the Commission should be required to consider factual innocence whenever it made a referral was, for just and powerful reasons, emphatically rejected.[94] Clearly the two-tier system encouraged by the innocence discourse

---

[87] www.innocencenetwork.org.uk/news-2 (accessed 1 February 2016).

[88] See eg the various contributions to M Naughton (ed), *The Criminal Cases Review Commission* (Basingstoke, Palgrave Macmillan, 2010).

[89] B Woffinden, 'The Criminal Cases Review Commission has Failed', *The Guardian*, 30 November 2010, www.guardian.co.uk/commentisfree/libertycentral/2010/nov/30/criminal-cases-review-commission-failed (accessed 1 February 2016).

[90] E Allison, 'Susan May Obituary', *The Guardian*, 13 November 2013.

[91] Woffinden, above n 89.

[92] Naughton, above n 88, 2.

[93] It has now reverted back to its original independent form at the University of Bristol, with other University Projects become independent; see www.innocencenetwork.org.uk/ (accessed 1 February 2016).

[94] As recalled by Michael Zander in a presentation to the Annual CCRC Stakeholders' Conference, 28 November 2012.

is dangerous and to be avoided. The integrity of the pre-trial and trial criminal process cannot be protected if the appeals process, which monitors and reviews them, itself lacks integrity.

(b) What's Wrong with the Innocence Movement?

There is no doubt that, in the US at least, the achievements made by Innocence Projects are impressive. However, the limitations of these endeavours, which are clearly flagged on the current Illinois Innocence Project website under the heading 'Cases we Take', need to be appreciated:

> The Illinois Innocence Project (IIP) provides investigative and legal research services to attorneys representing inmates who both the attorneys and the Project have good reason to believe did not commit the crimes for which they were convicted ... The inmate must be seeking to establish his or her *actual innocence* of the crime(s) for which he or she is incarcerated. More specifically, we take those cases in which there appears to be a significant chance that substantial evidence can be found to prove one innocent. Further, once we have agreed to work on a case, we reserve the right to withdraw for any reason, including an inability to prove a claim of actual innocence.[95]

This fastidious focus on innocence means that, for example, the North Carolina Innocence Project, which has a strong reputation, has referred back to the courts only a handful of cases of the many hundreds of applications it receives each year. The highly restrictive 'case filter' used by the US innocence projects—evidently very different to the criteria applied by the CCRC—owes it origins to the equally restrictive approach taken by US courts to quashing convictions, especially in death penalty cases. On paper, the multiple levels of review which usually take place, from direct appeal to successive state and federal habeas corpus petitions, appear rigorous in eliminating errors. In practice, and especially following the enactment of the federal Antiterrorism and Effective Death Penalty Act of 1996, absent truly compelling fresh evidence of innocence, each successive tier will tend to rubberstamp the decisions of the courts below. The overall message, echoed by US Supreme Court decisions,[96] in sharp contrast to the British approach, is that a high degree of apparent unfairness and procedural irregularity will be tolerated.[97] So much for the role of appeals courts in preserving the integrity of criminal proceedings.

Understandable as its origins therefore are, legal scholars in the US have begun to express concerns about the Innocence movement and the premium it places on factual innocence. According to Margaret Raymond, it has created a 'super category of innocence, elevating factual innocence over the other categories ... which may have unintended consequences for the criminal justice system'.[98] By privileging cases where DNA may be the 'silver bullet', the movement tends to marginalise convictions where profiling evidence is unavailable. Rosen argues:

> [F]or every defendant who is exonerated because of DNA evidence, there have been certainly hundreds, maybe thousands, who have been convicted of crimes on virtually identical evidence.

---

[95] www.uis.edu/innocenceproject/cases/index.html (accessed 1 February 2016) (emphasis added).
[96] *Strickland v Washington*, 466 US 668 (1984).
[97] For detailed discussion of these issues, see R Hood and C Hoyle, *The Death Penalty*, 4th edn (Oxford, Oxford University Press, 2008).
[98] M Raymond, 'The Problem with Innocence' (2001) 49 *Cleveland St Louis Law Review* 449, 456, 457.

For these thousands of defendants, though, there was no opportunity to scientifically test their guilt, because there was no physical evidence that could have been subjected to scientific scrutiny.[99]

Carol and Jordan Steiker contend that the emphasis on factual innocence may actually weaken public concern about the criminal justice system's deeper shortcomings: 'Americans can empathize with the harms that they fear could happen to themselves, rather than those that happen only to "bad people" … [L]urking behind innocence's appeal … might be indifference if not hostility to other types of injustice'.[100] Meanwhile, many US academics have also focused their empirical endeavours on factual innocence. Leading scholars on miscarriages of justice in the US, such as Richard Leo,[101] recommend that criminologists collaborate with innocence commissions to build databases of rightful acquittals and wrongful convictions. Sam Gross' 2005 prevalence study explicitly focused on factual innocence cases, excluding those who were likely involved in the crimes they were convicted of but whose convictions were nonetheless overturned. He commented: 'It is possible that a few of the hundreds of exonerated defendants we have studied were involved in the crimes for which they were convicted, despite our efforts to exclude such cases.'[102] A further study by Brandon Garrett of those found innocent through DNA testing also excludes others whose cases were overturned without this apparently foolproof evidence of factual innocence.[103] Many American academics who research miscarriages of justice now appear to see wrongful convictions only in terms of provable factual innocence.[104] Hughes rightly urges us to reclaim an understanding of innocence unmodified by qualifiers such as 'factual' or 'legal', in order to safeguard fundamental constitutional rights that protect us all.[105] This seems an unlikely prospect in the US, and the principled approach is now also under attack in the UK.

Conclusion: The Meaning of 'Miscarriage of Justice' in English Law

Like its counterparts in Illinois and other US states, INUK clearly advertises its lack of interest in 'legal innocence': its website invites applications only from 'prisoners with a declaration of factual innocence, as opposed to claims of a procedural miscarriage of justice'.[106]

---

[99] RA Rosen, 'Innocence and Death' (2003) 82 *North Carolina Law Review* 61, 73.

[100] CS Steiker and JM Steiker, 'The Seduction of Innocence: The Attraction and Limitations of the Focus on Innocence in Capital Punishment Law and Advocacy' (2005) 95 *Journal of Criminal Law and Criminology* 587, 610–11.

[101] R Leo, 'Rethinking the Study of Miscarriages of Justice: Developing a Criminology of Wrongful Conviction' (2005) 21 *Journal of Contemporary Criminal Justice* 201.

[102] SR Gross, K Jacoby, DJ Matheson and N Montgomery, 'Exonerations in the United States 1989 through 2003' (2005) 95 *Journal of Criminal Law and Criminology* 523, 527.

[103] BL Garrett, 'Judging Innocence' (2008) 108 *Columbia Law Review* 55.

[104] M Zalman, 'Criminal Justice System Reform and Wrongful Conviction: A Research Agenda' (2006) 14 *Criminal Justice Policy Review* 468; R Huff, 'What Can We Learn from Other Nations about the Problem of Wrongful Conviction?' (2002) 86 *Judicature* 91; JB Gould and RA Leo, 'One Hundred Years Later: Wrongful Convictions after a Century of Research' (2010) 100 *Journal of Criminal Law and Criminology* 825.

[105] E Hughes, 'Innocence Unmodified' (2011) 89 *North Carolina Law Review* 1083.

[106] www.innocencenetwork.org.uk/.

The implication is unmistakable. If the Supreme Court's decision in *Adams* has already tilted UK jurisprudence towards the restrictive, US model when it comes to determining compensation—not forgetting that the four justices in the minority would have gone further in this direction—the UK innocence movement seems determined to follow its American predecessors when investigating wrongful convictions. Of course, these voluntary organisations are free to take whatever approach they choose and this argument is in no way a criticism of their dedicated and professional approach to that mission. However, the innocence-centred approach has simultaneously subjected existing legal institutions to sustained attack. It is therefore essential to recognise the perils this may create. In the UK, we have in the CCRC, a state-funded commission with both powers and resources to investigate thoroughly and effectively, and an appeals process that deems a conviction unsafe if there is evidence that due process protections were significantly breached. These are priceless assets.

Innocence projects undoubtedly have merit. Promoting closer working relationships with the CCRCs is sensible,[107] provided that they operate effectively and efficiently and do not hang onto cases that would proceed more rapidly under the CCRC's jurisdiction, with its substantial powers to insist on the disclosure of all relevant evidence from the police or other public bodies.[108] Indeed, the CCRC recognises the benefits of a cooperative relationship, and has invited innocence projects to various stakeholder events. It has sought to develop mutual trust and a clearly defined working relationship. Furthermore, there is enormous potential for the UK's first non-profit criminal legal service provider, the recently established Centre for Criminal Appeals,[109] also to work cooperatively with the CCRC. Its mission is to provide investigation and legal advocacy on criminal appeal cases and would therefore be of assistance to those applying to the CCRC to review their case. It remains essential, however, that these non-statutory organisations do not detract from the CCRC's and CA's respective mandates, which are predicated on the assumption that an 'unsafe' conviction may be overturned without proof of factual innocence.

As Hannah Quirk has pointed out,[110] while the concept of innocence can be valuable as a campaigning tool, importing a 'campaigning discourse' of innocence into the legal arena would be a risky strategy. The proposition that the appeal courts and CCRC should address issues of factual innocence is ill-founded, out-dated and potentially counter-productive. In a reasonably regulated and relatively well-funded criminal justice system, which does not see the routine, egregious abuse of suspects, the debate has to progress beyond the simplistic dichotomy of guilt and innocence, not just because it is simplistic but because it misses the larger problem of procedural improprieties.

Instead, as before, the focus here should be on identifying and responding to 'unsafe convictions', and to ensuring that due process protections apply to all those accused of crimes—not on erecting ultimately spurious systems which seek to identify the factually innocent. As Lord Simon observed in *Shannon*, 'The law in action is not concerned with

---

[107] S Roberts and L Weathered, 'Assisting the Factually Innocent: The Contradictions and Compatibility of Innocence Projects and the Criminal Cases Review Commission' (2009) 29 *Oxford Journal of Legal Studies* 43, 49.

[108] Concerns raised by H Quirk, 'Identifying Miscarriages of Justice: Why Innocence Is Not The Answer' (2007) 70 *Modern Law Review* 759.

[109] www.criminalappeals.org.uk (accessed 1 February 2016).

[110] Quirk, above n 108.

absolute truth, but with proof before a fallible human tribunal to a requisite standard of probability in accordance with formal rules of evidence.'[111] A system that seeks to uphold and preserve due process values will, by definition, also safeguard innocence, but that outcome must not become its primary goal.

It is impossible and unnecessary to identify all the manifold reasons why a defendant may be convicted when he should not have been. It may be because the evidence against him was fabricated or perjured. It may be because flawed expert evidence was relied on. It may be because evidence helpful to the defence was concealed or withheld. It may be because the jury was the subject of malicious interference. It may be because of judicial unfairness or misdirection. In cases of this kind, it may, or more often may not, be possible to say that a defendant is innocent, but it is possible to say that he has been wrongly convicted. The common factor in such cases is that something has gone seriously wrong in the investigation of the offence or the conduct of the trial, resulting in the conviction of someone who should not have been convicted. All of the high profile 'innocence' cases that led to the Royal Commission and the establishment of the CCRC were, first and foremost, 'unsafe' convictions. The defendants were convicted after a flawed criminal process. That they were in fact innocent may make their imprisonment more tragic, but the fact that their convictions were based on police malpractice or legal incompetence, and that their initial appeals were rejected by an appeals process that was highly deferential to the lower courts, even when the evidence suggested systemic flaws in the criminal process, imply that their cases deserved to be overturned even if it had not been possible to 'prove' that they were 'factually innocent'.

The Court of Appeal's reluctance to acknowledge innocence might dismay appellants and their supporters. But the line should be held: the Court's judgment in *Fell* was, and should remain, an aberration. As Nobles and Schiff state, 'innocence is not something that exists, out there, to be touched, felt, or measured, any more than guilt'.[112] Reform should run in the opposite direction, towards a restatement of the idea that once a conviction has been quashed, a person's presumption of innocence—reinforced by ECHR Article 6(2)—should be restored, and with it, his or her right to compensation. The courts' attempts to distinguish between deserving and underserving appellants—between those who could prove themselves innocent and those that could not, as sanctified in *Adams* and enforced in *Allen*—are odious and flawed. It is disappointing that the ECtHR has not declared them to be incompatible with the European Convention.

Any appellate regime under which only the convictions of the provably innocent were quashed would be far more restrictive than one in which the test to be applied is safety. The history of English compensation cases recounted in this chapter illustrates this critically important point. The two-tier system instituted by *Adams* has already left those who cannot prove factual innocence with a cloud of suspicion hanging over their heads, and deprived them of compensation for the harms inflicted by the state. Meanwhile, a movement which prioritises actual innocence threatens to divert attention from the safeguards that protect each and every one of us, and which preserve the integrity of the system. The supporters of the new innocence discourse need to be very careful what they wish for.

---

[111] *DPP v Shannon* [1975] AC 717, 763 (HL).

[112] R Nobles and D Schiff, 'Guilt and Innocence in the Criminal Justice System: A Comment on *R (Mullen) v Secretary of State for the Home Department*' (2006) 69 *Modern Law Review* 80, 91.

INDEX